Chris Amaris, MCITP, CISSP
Rand Morimoto, Ph.D., MCITP
Pete Handley, MCITP
David E. Ross, MCITP
Technical Edit by Guy Yardeni

Microsoft® System Center 2012

UNLEASHED

D1501558

SAMS | 800 East 96th Street, Indianapolis, Indiana 46240 USA

Microsoft® System Center 2012 Unleashed

Copyright © 2012 by Pearson Education, Inc.

ISBN-13: 978-0672-33612-6
ISBN-10: 0-672-33612-X

Library of Congress Cataloging-in-Publication Data is on file.

Printed in the United States of America

Second Printing August 2012

Trademarks

Warning and Disclaimer

Bulk Sales

Sams Publishing offers excellent discounts on this book when ordered in quantity for bulk purchases or special sales. For more information, please contact

U.S. Corporate and Government Sales
1-800-382-3419
corpsales@pearsontechgroup.com

For sales outside of the U.S., please contact

International Sales
international@pearson.com

Editor-in-Chief
Greg Wiegand

Executive Editor
Neil Rowe

Development Editor
Mark Renfrow

Managing Editor
Kristy Hart

Project Editor
Andy Beaster

Copy Editor
Karen Annett

Indexer
Erika Millen

Proofreader
Jess DeGabriele

Technical Editor
Guy Yardeni

Publishing Coordinator
Cindy Teeters

Book Designer
Gary Adair

Compositor
Gloria Schurick

Contributing Writers
Alec Minty
John Rodriguez
Tyson Kopczynski

Contributing Editors
Ed Crowley
Aman Ayaz

Contents at a Glance

Introduction 1

1 Overview of the System Center Suite 5

2 Configuration Manager 2012 Design and Planning 55

3 Configuration Manager 2012 Implementation and Administration 115

4 Using Configuration Manager 2012 to Distribute Applications,
Updates, and Operating Systems 181

5 Using Configuration Manager 2012 for Asset Management and
Reporting 245

6 Operations Manager 2012 Design and Planning 289

7 Operations Manager 2012 Implementation and Administration 355

8 Using Operations Manager 2012 for Monitoring and Alerting 421

9 Using Operations Manager 2012 for Operations and Security
Reporting 511

10 Data Protection Manager 2012 Design, Planning, Implementation,
and Administration 567

11 Using Data Protection Manager 2012 to Protect File Systems,
Exchange, SQL, and SharePoint 619

12 Virtual Machine Manager 2012 Design, Planning,
and Implementation 663

13 Managing a Hyper-V Environment with Virtual Machine
Manager 2012 703

14 Service Manager 2012 Design, Planning, and Implementation 761

15 Using Service Manager 2012 for Incident Tracking and
Help Desk Support 819

16 Using Service Manager 2012 for Service Offerings and Change
Control Management 871

17 System Center Orchestrator 2012 Design, Planning,
and Implementation 921

Index 969

Table of Contents

Introduction   **1**

1   **Overview of the System Center Suite**   **5**

What Is System Center? 6
Understanding System Center Configuration Manager 9
Understanding System Center Operations Manager 18
Understanding System Center Data Protection Manager 26
Understanding System Center Virtual Machine Manager 34
Understanding System Center Service Manager 40
Understanding System Center 2012 Orchestrator 45
Understanding System Center Licensing 50
Summary 51
Best Practices 52

2   **Configuration Manager 2012 Design and Planning**   **55**

What's New in ConfigMgr 2012 56
Explaining How Configuration Manager Works 60
Understanding Content Distribution 66
Understanding Asset Management 70
Reporting from Configuration Manager 74
Configuration Manager Architecture Components 75
Securing Configuration Manager 88
Understanding Component Requirements 92
Configuration Manager Design Considerations 94
Understanding Client Schedules 105
Planning for Internet-Based Client Management 106
Putting It All Together in a Design 110
Summary 112
Best Practices 112

3   **Configuration Manager 2012 Implementation and Administration**   **115**

Sample Organization 115
Configuring Installation Prerequisites 118
Implementing the Central Administration Site 124
Deploying the Primary Sites 129
Deploying the Secondary Sites 134
Configuring the Hierarchy 138

Configuring Sites..148
Configuring Client Settings..156
Implementing Internet-Based Client Management......................163
Summary..177
Best Practices..178

**4   Using Configuration Manager 2012 to Distribute Applications,
     Updates, and Operating Systems   181**

Understanding Content Distribution..181
Defining Collections..185
Understanding Application Management..189
Managing Deployments..203
Understanding Software Updates..215
Deploying Software Updates..219
Understanding Operating System Deployment....................................225
Deploying Operating Systems..234
Extending with Microsoft Deployment Toolkit....................................238
Summary..243
Best Practices..243

**5   Using Configuration Manager 2012 for Asset Management and
     Reporting   245**

Understanding Asset Data..246
Configuring Client Settings for Inventory Collection..........................248
Understanding Reporting..249
Customizing Hardware Inventory..261
Understanding Asset Intelligence..269
Understanding Software Metering..277
Understanding Compliance Settings..278
Monitoring the Baselines and Compliance..283
Summary..285
Best Practices..285

6   Operations Manager 2012 Design and Planning   289

What's New With Operations Manager 2012..290
Understanding How OpsMgr Works..291
OpsMgr Architecture Components..296
Securing OpsMgr..311
Fault Tolerance and Disaster Recovery..317
Understanding OpsMgr Component Requirements..............................323
OpsMgr Design Considerations..328

Putting It All Together in a Design 335
Planning an Operations Manager Deployment 345
Summary 353
Best Practices 354

7 Operations Manager 2012 Implementation and Administration   355

Installing Operations Manager 2012 356
Deploying OpsMgr Agents 373
Monitoring DMZ Servers with Certificates 385
Configuring Operations Manager 2012 393
Administering Operations Manager 2012 403
Backing Up OpsMgr 2012 411
Summary 418
Best Practices 418

8 Using Operations Manager 2012 for Monitoring and Alerting   421

Using OpsMgr Consoles 422
Working with Management Packs 425
Exploring the Operations Manager Management Pack 432
Exploring the Windows Management Pack 440
Exploring the Active Directory Management Pack 451
Exploring the Exchange 2010 Management Pack 466
Exploring the SQL Server Management Pack 478
Exploring the Cross Platform Management Packs 487
Management Pack Templates 491
Custom Management Packs 503
Summary 508
Best Practices 508

9 Using Operations Manager 2012 for Operations and Security Reporting 511

Reporting from OpsMgr 512
Generating and Scheduling Reports 514
OpsMgr 2012 Maintenance Reports 532
Audit Collection Services Reporting 541
Service Level Tracking 548
OpsMgr 2012 Dashboards 554
Publishing Dashboards into SharePoint 2010 561
Summary 565
Best Practices 566

10   Data Protection Manager 2012 Design, Planning, Implementation, and Administration   567

What Is System Center Data Protection Manager?...............568

Data Protection Manager Background.................572

Data Protection Manager Prerequisites................578

Planning a Data Protection Manager Deployment.............580

Deploying Data Protection Manager.................587

Completing Required Configuration Tasks................591

Creating Protection Groups....................601

Administrating Data Protection Manager...............606

Summary..........................616

Best Practices........................617

11   Using Data Protection Manager 2012 to Protect File Systems, Exchange, SQL, and SharePoint   619

Protecting File Servers.....................620

Protecting System State....................622

Protecting Exchange Servers..................624

Protecting SQL Servers....................635

Protecting SharePoint Farms..................643

Protecting Virtualized Environments................654

Summary..........................660

Best Practices........................661

12   Virtual Machine Manager 2012 Design, Planning, and Implementation   663

Understanding Virtual Machine Manager...............663

Virtual Machine Manager Background................673

What's New in System Center Virtual Machine Manager 2012.........677

Virtual Machine Manager Prerequisites...............678

Planning a Virtual Machine Manager Deployment............682

Deploying Virtual Machine Manager................687

Summary..........................700

Best Practices........................701

13   Managing a Hyper-V Environment with Virtual Machine Manager 2012   703

Understanding the VMM Private Cloud...............704

Using the VMM Management Interfaces...............707

Understanding Virtual Machine Conversions.............716

Managing VMM User Roles...................729

Deploying Virtual Machines...................740

Migrating Virtual Machines...................747

Understanding and Implementing Server App-V 753
Summary 758
Best Practices 759

14   Service Manager 2012 Design, Planning, and Implementation   761

What's New in Service Manager 2012 762
Explaining How Service Manager Works 763
Service Manager Design Parameters 769
Putting It All Together in a Service Manager Design 775
Planning a Service Manager Deployment 783
Deploying Service Manager 791
Deploying Service Manager Connectors 805
Backing Up Service Manager 2012 814
Summary 817
Best Practices 817

**15   Using Service Manager 2012 for Incident Tracking and
      Help Desk Support   819**

Incidents and Problems 819
Configuring Incident Settings 821
Service Manager Notifications 830
Creating New Incidents 836
Working with Incidents 846
Configuring Problem Settings 856
Working with Problems 859
Incident and Problem Reports 863
Summary 869
Best Practices 870

**16   Using Service Manager 2012 for Service Offerings and Change
      Control Management   871**

Service Manager 2012 and the Infrastructure Optimization Model 871
Service Offerings and Request Offerings in SM 2012 872
Release Management in SM 2012 882
Change Requests and Activities 885
Configuring Change Settings 887
Change Management Templates and Workflows 889
Initiating Change Requests 892
Working with and Approving Change Requests 896
Implementing Change Requests 903
Managing Configuration Items 910

Working with Change, Activity, and Configuration Management
  Reports 914
Summary 919
Best Practices 920

**17 System Center Orchestrator 2012 Design, Planning,
    and Implementation   921**
Overview of System Center Orchestrator 921
History of System Center Orchestrator 924
System Center Orchestrator 2012 Installation Prerequisites 924
Orchestrator Security Planning 926
Installing System Center Orchestrator 2012 on a Single Server ... 928
Installing System Center Orchestrator 2012 on Separate Systems ... 933
Additional Tasks Following Orchestrator Installation 939
Getting Familiar with the Orchestrator 2012 Management Consoles 942
Installing Integration Packs 949
Designing and Using Runbooks 952
Runbook Permissions 967
Summary 967
Best Practices 968

Index   969

About the Authors

Chris Amaris, MCITP, MCTS, CISSP/ISSAP, CHS III, is the chief technology officer and cofounder of Convergent Computing. He has more than 20 years experience consulting for Fortune 500 companies, leading companies in the technology selection, design, planning, and implementation of complex information technology projects. Chris has worked with Microsoft System Center products, such as Operations Manager and Configuration Manager, since their original releases in 2000 and 1994. He specializes in messaging, security, performance tuning, systems management, and migration. Receiving his first Microsoft technologies certification in 1993, Chris is a current Microsoft Certified IT Professional (MCITP) with multiple Microsoft Certified Technology Specialist designations (MCTS) in System Center technologies, a Certified Information Systems Security Professional (CISSP) with an Information System Security Architecture Professional (ISSAP) concentration, Certified Homeland Security (CHS III), a Novell CNE, a Banyan CBE, and a Certified Project Manager. Chris is also an author, writer, and technical editor for a number of IT books, including *Network Security for Government and Corporate Executives*, *Exchange 2010 Unleashed*, and *Microsoft Windows Server 2008 R2 Unleashed*.

Rand Morimoto, Ph.D., MVP, MCITP, CISSP, has been in the computer industry for over 30 years and has authored, coauthored, or been a contributing writer for dozens of books on Windows, Security, Exchange, BizTalk, and Remote and Mobile Computing. Rand is the president of Convergent Computing, an IT-consulting firm in the San Francisco Bay area that has been one of the key early adopter program partners with Microsoft, implementing the latest Microsoft technologies, including Microsoft Windows Server 2008 R2, System Center 2012, Windows 7, Exchange Server 2010, Windows Server 2012, and SharePoint 2010 in production environments over 18 months before the initial product releases.

Pete Handley, MCITP, CISSP, has more than 15 years of experience in IT, including extensive knowledge of Active Directory, Microsoft Exchange, Windows Server 2008, and the System Center suite of products. He has been a contributing author for the Sams books *Microsoft Exchange 2003 Unleashed* and *Windows PowerShell Unleashed*. Pete specializes in Visual Basic and PowerShell scripting and is a subject matter expert on the integration and migration of Novell technologies to Microsoft technologies. Pete holds the Microsoft Certified Systems Engineer 2003 (MCSE) certification, the Microsoft Certified Information Technology Professional (MCITP) certification, the Novell Certified Directory Engineer (CDE) certification, and the Certified Information Systems Security Professional (CISSP) certification.

David E. Ross, MCITP, VCP, CCEA, CCSP, has over 13 years of experience in IT consulting, the majority of which have been spent playing the lead architect role on network design and implementation projects throughout the San Francisco Bay area. David is currently acting as a principal engineer for Convergent Computing, and is frequently involved in creating hybrid solutions involving multiple vendor technologies for organizations of all sizes. Specialties for David include Active Directory, Exchange, System Center, Lync, Citrix XenApp and XenDesktop design, virtualization solutions using VMware vSphere and Microsoft Hyper-V, and Cisco routing, switching, and security technologies.

Dedication

I dedicate this book to my wife Sophia, light of my life. And to my children, Michelle, Megan, Zoe, Zachary, and Ian, who give meaning to my life and work.

—**Chris Amaris, MCITP, MCTS, CISSP/ISSAP, CHS III**

I dedicate this book to Ana, looking forward to continuing a wonderful life together!

—**Rand Morimoto, Ph.D., MVP, MCITP, CISSP**

I dedicate this book to my parents Hal and Denise, who encouraged my early love of reading and gave me my first computer. You have each made it possible for me to learn and grow in so many ways, but the greatest lessons that I have learned have been by your examples. And to my wonderful and irrepressible wife Melissa, you are the joy at the center of my life and never far from my thoughts.

—**Pete Handley, MCITP, CISSP**

I dedicate this book to my wife Lisette, who serves as an inspiration to everyone around her, and encourages everyone to reach their full potential. Thanks for your loving support during this project, and for the sacrifices you made to help me reach my potential. Also to my fun-loving boys Caden and Cole, who keep me on my toes and provide the best distraction from long hours of book writing. Thanks for being a great family worth working hard for!

—**David E. Ross, MCITP**

I dedicate this book to everyone at Convergent Computing. Credit for the book should be spread throughout the entire organization for an effort that would be largely impossible without the contribution of the whole team.

—**Guy Yardeni, MCSE, MCITP, CISSP**

Acknowledgments

Chris Amaris, MCSE, MVP, CISSP
I want to thank Rand for providing the leadership and direction as we have transitioned from a server centric focus, to enterprise data center centric focus, to now a cloud centric focus. Your vision on the IT industry needs, trends, and technologies has allowed you to keep a steady hand on the tiller, ensuring that we are always ahead of the latest technology wave. The breadth and depth of knowledge of the Convergent Computing organization in the System Center technologies that allow us to support our clients and provide the basis for this book are all thanks to your vision and leadership.

And many, many thanks to my family! Sophia, thank you for keeping everything together while I disappeared at the drop of a hat into my office to finish another lab or chapter. Michelle, Megan, Zoe, Zachary, and Ian, thank you for keeping focused on your academics and seeing that through hard work anything is possible.

Rand Morimoto, Ph.D., MVP, MCITP, CISSP
Congratulations Chris for getting this System Center 2012 title out the door! And a big thanks to Pete and Dave who jumped in to the middle of this book, GREAT job in rounding out the authoring team on this one! And a huge thanks to Guy for doing the edits and making sure this book was prime time!

I want to thank the team at Sams Publishing for continuing to support our writing efforts and turning this book around and out to print in record time! Thank you Neil, Mark, Andy, and all the folks behind the scenes in making this happen! And my thanks to Karen Annett, who continues to be my favorite copy editor!!!

I also wanted to thank the consultants at Convergent Computing and our early adopter clients who fiddle with these new technologies really early on and then take the leap of faith in putting the products into production to experience (and at times feel the pain) as we work through best practices. The early adopter experiences give us the knowledge and experience we need to share with all who use this book as their guide in their production environments based on the lessons learned.

To Kelly, Noble, and Chip, yeah, one down, three more books to go before the year is up. You know where to find me in the wee hours of the night, downstairs at the kitchen table writing. Remember to work hard at everything you do, as you've found so far, you can accomplish a lot when you put your mind to things!

Pete Handley, MCITP, CISSP
I want to thank Rand for the opportunity to contribute to this book, and to Chris for your thorough and patient approach to learning. Thanks to Guy for your meticulous tech editing, and to Karen and the SAMS team for always sweating the details!

David E. Ross, MCITP

Thanks to my family for the sacrifices they made without complaint while I was getting oriented with the whole book-authoring process. Big thanks also to Rand not only for providing me the opportunity to work on this project, but for providing excellent guidance on the whole process. You made it very easy to come up to speed and learn the ropes very quickly; I appreciate it!

We Want to Hear from You!

As the reader of this book, *you* are our most important critic and commentator. We value your opinion and want to know what we're doing right, what we could do better, what areas you'd like to see us publish in, and any other words of wisdom you're willing to pass our way.

You can email or write me directly to let me know what you did or didn't like about this book—as well as what we can do to make our books stronger.

Please note that I cannot help you with technical problems related to the topic of this book, and that due to the high volume of mail I receive, I might not be able to reply to every message.

When you write, please be sure to include this book's title and author as well as your name and phone or email address. I will carefully review your comments and share them with the author and editors who worked on the book.

E-mail: feedback@samspublishing.com

Mail: Neil Rowe
Executive Editor
Sams Publishing
800 East 96th Street
Indianapolis, IN 46240 USA

Reader Services

Visit our website and register this book at informit.com/register for convenient access to any updates, downloads, or errata that might be available for this book.

Introduction

The release of System Center 2012 is a major shift in the System Center family of products of going from a product line that was previously sold and viewed as a series of individual products, to System Center 2012 being sold as a single product with tight integration between the various components. In addition, this shift is not just from the perspective of a sales or marketing focus of a single product, but also from the engineering integration of System Center 2012 where the components work better and tighter together.

Additionally, with System Center 2012, Microsoft has expanded beyond the traditional "only Microsoft" solution support to one that broadly embraces other platforms, such as the support for VMware, Citrix, storage area network products from various vendors, non-Microsoft mobile devices and operating systems, and the like. From a data center perspective where the data center has more than just Windows servers and Microsoft applications, this multivendor support is critical in Microsoft's ability to be a true data center management solution provider.

And as the industry evolves to support traditional on-premise servers and applications and now cloud-based products and technologies, System Center's ability to support applications and services in the cloud is a critical inclusion in the System Center 2012 product.

This book covers real-world experiences with System Center 2012, not like a "product guide" simply with step-by-step installation and feature configurations, but with real-world notes, tips, tricks, best practices, and lessons learned in the design, planning, implementation, migration, administration, management, and support of the System Center technologies based on years of early adopter and enterprise production deployments.

The 17 chapters of this book are written to highlight the most important aspects of the technologies that make up the System Center family of components. To combine the components into groups of technologies, this book covers the following:

- ▶ **Introduction**—The first chapter of this book provides an introduction to the System Center 2012 family of components, what they are, what they do, and what business and IT challenges they solve. The introduction paints the picture of what the rest of the book covers and how you as the reader can jump to those sections of the book most important to you in your day-to-day IT management tasks.

- ▶ **System Center 2012 Configuration Manager**—The first component covered in this book is the System Center 2012 Configuration Manager (SCCM) component, which is a toolset that has come a long way in the past decade. The earlier releases of Configuration Manager went by the name SMS, or Systems Management Server, which was known to take full-time personnel to manage the management system. However, now easily four or five generations later, SCCM 2012 has really helped organizations with the patching, updating, imaging, reporting, and compliance management of their systems, both Microsoft and non-Microsoft endpoint clients and servers. The four chapters in this book that cover SCCM address the planning and design process of implementing SCCM in an enterprise, the implementation of the component, and, more important, how administrators use SCCM to image, update, manage, and support the servers and client systems in their environments.

▶ **System Center 2012 Operations Manager**—The second component covered in this book is the System Center 2012 Operations Manager (SCOM) component, which provides monitoring and alerting on servers and client systems as well as internet-working devices (routers/switches/firewalls) and cloud-based services. Rather than waiting for users to alert the help desk that a server is down, SCOM proactively monitors systems and networks and provides alerts before failures impact opera-tions, plus it logs error events and system issues to help organizations address system problems—usually before they occur. The chapters dedicated to SCOM cover the planning and design of SCOM, the rollout and implementation of servers and monitoring agents, and the best practices on how to understand errors and alerts that allow IT administrators to be more proactive in managing their servers and the systems in their environments.

▶ **System Center 2012 Data Protection Manager**—System Center 2012 Data Protection Manager (DPM) is a relatively new addition to the Microsoft manage-ment family of components. As traditional tape backups have been replaced by digital snapshots and digital data backups of information, DPM provides organiza-tions the ability to have backup copies of their data. DPM incrementally backs up information from servers so that instead of backing up information once a night, DPM makes backups all day long for faster backup times and more granular recovery windows. This book covers the planning, design, implementation, and general recovery process of file systems, Microsoft Exchange, SharePoint Server, SQL, Hyper-V hosts and guests, and Windows client systems using DPM 2012.

▶ **System Center 2012 Virtual Machine Manager**—In the past three to four years, virtualization has gone from something that was only done in test labs to data centers that are now fully virtualized—enabling organizations to have more than one server session running on a physical server system, and sometimes upward of 10 or 20 server sessions running on a single system. With the huge growth in virtu-alization in the data center, Microsoft released four major updates to the System Center Virtual Machine Manager (VMM) component in three years to address the needs of the enterprise. The two chapters dedicated to VMM go beyond the installa-tion and setup of VMM 2012, and get into core components of the component that help organizations manage virtual guest sessions running on Microsoft Hyper-V, VMware, and Citrix XenServer, and also how to convert physical servers to virtual servers (P2V), delegate the ability to administer and manage guest sessions, manage the "fabric" of a network (storage and internetworking), and the ability to share virtual host resources with users and administrators in the enterprise.

▶ **System Center 2012 Service Manager**—After an initial five years in development and over two years in production deployments, Microsoft now has a help desk/incident management/asset life-cycle management/change management component called System Center 2012 Service Manager (SCSM) that organizations are finding extremely valuable in their enterprises. Being involved with the development of SCSM from its inception, the authors of this book have shared years of experience, tips, best practices, and lessons learned in the deployment, information tracking, reporting, and support of the SCSM component. SCSM brings together the information gathering, reporting, alerting, and knowledge-base information in the other System Center components into a single component that will help organizations better manage their IT infrastructures.

▶ **System Center 2012 Orchestrator**—System Center Orchestrator is a newcomer to the System Center family and has been instrumental in real-world implementations of System Center in helping to make process and runbook automated tasks that simplify IT processes. For tasks that IT professionals have manually done day in and day out in the past that takes hours or days to complete, Orchestrator scripts run through the processes methodically in minutes and seconds. The consistency with Orchestrator scripts helps organizations maintain standards and consistency in processes and achieve end goals more efficiently and effectively than in the past.

It is our hope that the real-world experience we have had in working with the entire System Center family of components and our commitment to relaying to you information that will be valuable in your planning, implementation, operation, and administration of System Center in your enterprise will help you more quickly gain and receive benefits from these management tools from Microsoft!

CHAPTER 1

Overview of the System Center Suite

IN THIS CHAPTER

▶ What Is System Center?

▶ Understanding System Center Configuration Manager

▶ Understanding System Center Operations Manager

▶ Understanding System Center Data Protection Manager

▶ Understanding System Center Virtual Machine Manager

▶ Understanding System Center Service Manager

▶ Understanding System Center 2012 Orchestrator

▶ Understanding System Center Licensing

▶ Best Practices

System Center, which is licensed as a bundled suite of multiple separate components, is a series of tools that help administrators manage their servers, client systems, and applications (whether on-premise or in the cloud) to be more proactive in responding to the needs of an organization's IT operations. In fact, the name "System Center" actually didn't come about until just a few years ago; prior to that, the products were all sold separately.

Like with many families or suites of products, the first rendition of the suite was nothing more than a bunch of disparate products bundled together under a common brand name, but really had no integration in working together. System Center was no different—with the first couple of years of the product line being nothing more than a name and branding.

Today, however—several years and three to four versions later—System Center is more than just common product branding. All of the products fully work better together and an IT organization that has one component of System Center can leverage that tool with other System Center components, making the management of an environment easier and for a common benefit.

This chapter introduces the System Center family of products, what the components are, and how the balance of the chapters in this book provide tips, tricks, best practices, and guidance on how to best leverage System Center in the enterprise.

What Is System Center?

As mentioned at the start of this chapter, System Center is a family or suite of management tools from Microsoft. With the System Center 2012 release, you can no longer buy individual System Center components separately. When you buy System Center 2012, you now buy a license for the entire System Center suite. An organization can still install just a single component like System Center 2012 Configuration Manager for patching and updating systems, or just install a single component like System Center 2012 Operations Manager for monitoring. The organization just owns all of the components, so at any time, the organization can install the other components to expand manageability to include backup, virtual system management, help desk, and more without having to buy additional licenses. Additional details on the software licensing of the System Center products can be found in the section "Understanding System Center Licensing" later in this chapter.

Systems Management in the Enterprise

For years, IT departments have struggled with managing their servers and client systems, and hundreds of companies had arisen to provide tools for patching computer systems, imaging workstations, pushing out new software, monitoring servers and network devices, and backing up systems. However, over the years, organizations have found that each individual product would require a separate server, a separate set of policies or rules set up, a separate agent to be installed on the computer system, and a separate set of tasks to inventory the systems all doing similar things. With several different products installed on a system and no real sharing of information between the management agents and tools, enterprise systems management had become quite a clumsy process.

As an example, an organization would inventory its systems for asset tracking with one product to keep track of corporate assets. With a separate product, the organization would put an image onto its system. Yet another product would be used to patch and update the system. Another product would monitor the system and alert the administrators of a problem; this monitoring program would typically have to inventory the system to know what hardware and software it was monitoring and managing. The organization would have yet a completely different product to track help desk calls and problem tickets, in some cases capturing asset information from one of the other two tools mentioned earlier in this paragraph, but frequently the help desk tool would have its own management components to remotely control and support the user and system. Finally, the organization would have a separate product to back up data on the system, plus yet another separate product to provide security management of the system for security policies and controls.

With all this going on for just a single network environment, there's no wonder why systems management has been a dirty word in the computer industry. Everyone knows they need to do something about it, but when you try to do something about it by going out and getting the best-of-breed product from each vendor in the industry, they end up with 5 or 10 different products all vying to do some type of management of the system. Naturally, with that many different products doing different but similar things, changes made by one of the 5 or 10 products frequently would cause problems with one of the other components—setting the organization's systems management efforts back a step at a time.

Five to eight years ago, Microsoft provided tools for systems to do patching, monitoring, asset inventory, backup, and the like, but no better than the 5 to 10 separate vendor products, Microsoft tools were all separately installed, configured, and managed. Microsoft Systems Management Server (SMS) has a bad name in the industry for old-timers who tried to use the system years ago because even within this tool itself, it installed several separate agents on a computer to try to "help" the system monitor and manage updates, software installation, inventory tracking, and remote control, with the SMS components themselves frequently conflicting and causing system problems.

Roll forward several years, and Microsoft has combined all of their products under a single brand called System Center and has spent the past decade getting the products to work together. Four or five generations later under the System Center brand, Microsoft now has tools that work together so an organization that buys a suite license isn't just buying a bundle of separate products, but a family of products that work together.

Timing couldn't have been better for Microsoft on this strategy as economic and budget pressures are forcing organizations to be more efficient and effective at what they do. IT administrators and executives are realizing that having 5 or 10 tools that don't work together is costly in terms of the integration and management of that many tools, but also costly in terms of managing multiple overlapping licensing agreements. Most enterprises already have a Microsoft Enterprise licensing Agreement (EA) and own a number of System Center licenses, so to standardize on System Center (now that it all works together) is not only a good technical integration decision, but a huge financial cost-benefit decision.

Instead of just saying the System Center components work better together, organizations that have begun their evaluation or implementation of System Center 2012 are finding that the tools indeed do provide significant cross-integration benefits. Organizations have truly begun eliminating point solutions for monitoring, systems management, remote support, help desk, and security and simplifying their environment with System Center 2012.

The whole premise of this book is how organizations can deploy the separate System Center components and then ultimately tie them together so that there is a coordinated effort from cradle to grave on a system that can be imaged, deployed, patched, updated, maintained, supported, and retired under a common management process. It's the full life cycle for both server and client systems, as well as a holistic approach of managing systems that are on-premise, mobile, and in the cloud that is addressed in this book.

System Center Family of Products

In looking at the cradle-to-grave life cycle, how the System Center products fit in, and how the various chapters in this book cover the topics, the family of products are as follows:

▶ **System Center Configuration Manager**—System Center Configuration Manager (SCCM) starts with the ability of imaging or laying down the base operating system on a server or client system based on specific organizational guidelines for configurations. Once the operating system has been installed, SCCM continually patches and updates the system as well as provides the ability to push out new software to the system, also based on specific templates and guideline configurations. SCCM keeps track of system inventory, provides remote-control capabilities, and provides IT administrators the ability to ensure the system configuration is maintained in a common configuration.

▶ **System Center Operations Manager**—Once an organization lays down the base configuration of its systems and keeps them patched and updated, System Center Operations Manager (SCOM) monitors the ongoing health of the systems as well as the applications installed on the systems. Specific rules are created that track the normal operations of the systems, and any time the systems fall out of the standards, the organization's IT personnel are notified of the changes.

▶ **System Center Data Protection Manager**—Although SCCM and SCOM deploy and monitor system operations, there are times when data is corrupted or lost or systems fail and having a backup of the data is crucial. This is where Data Protection Manager (DPM) fits in as it backs up client systems, server file systems, Exchange databases, SharePoint data, SQL databases, Hyper-V guest sessions, and Windows 7 workstations on a continuous basis, providing an organization the ability to recover a single lost or corrupted file all the way through restoring a completely dead system.

▶ **System Center Virtual Machine Manager**—As the industry has shifted from one made up of primarily physical server systems to one where servers are now virtualized in the data center, the Virtual Machine Manager (VMM) product from Microsoft helps organizations manage their virtual systems. In the fully managed scenario, in the event that SCOM identifies a physical or virtual system is about to fail, it can automatically create a new guest session using SCCM to a Hyper-V or VMware virtual host, build out a brand-new system, and use DPM to automatically restore the latest backup of information all as a scripted disaster recovery process. VMM can also transfer fully running physical servers and transfer the operating system, application, and data to a virtual server in an automated physical-to-virtual (P2V) conversion process.

▶ **System Center Service Manager**—Although all of the previous tools chug along doing IT-related tasks, such as imaging, patching, monitoring, and backing up, organizations also have a need to manage processes and change control. The System Center Service Manager (SCSM) product is an incident management and change-control system that tightly integrates with SCOM, SCCM, and VMM to take alerts, automatically log the problems, take inventory information, and track system configurations so that help desk personnel and support individuals have at their fingertips information they need to support users and application owners in the enterprise. SCSM brings together management policies and processes as the umbrella under which the other System Center tools facilitate day-to-day tasks and procedures.

▶ **System Center Orchestrator**—System Center 2012 Orchestrator is a runbook automation tool that effectively provides a graphical and text-based scripting environment that helps organizations do things in enterprise management that might not be directly supported in any of the System Center products in the box. This might be special processes an organization needs to do, such as launch a script, process a report, move data from one system to another, or the like. Orchestrator takes mundane tasks and standardizes the tasks that can be automatically triggered and run to ensure auditable consistency in operational processes. System Center Orchestrator used to be called Opalis and is now an integral piece of the System Center suite in providing automation that helps organizations make mundane processes more efficient, effective, trackable, and verifiable in the enterprise.

Each of the products have had variations over the years (for example, 2003, 2007, 2008, 2010, SP1, SP2, R2) with each successive version adding more functionality and capabilities than the version before it. The balance of this chapter details each of the System Center products and provides a snapshot of what to expect throughout the chapters of this book.

> **NOTE**
>
> For those who purchased the previous edition of this book, *Microsoft System Center Enterprise Suite Unleashed*, based predominantly on the System Center 2007 line of products, in this edition of the book, we have dropped System Center Capacity Planner, System Center Mobile Device Manager, and System Center Essentials, and have added System Center Orchestrator. System Center Capacity Planner has shifted into a series of tools Microsoft now provides for free called Microsoft Solution Accelerators (http://technet.microsoft.com/solutionaccelerators). System Center Mobile Device Manager has been merged and integrated into System Center 2012 Configuration Manager. And System Center Essentials has never been part of the System Center Enterprise Suite, but rather a tool for small businesses, and as such we removed it from this edition of the book. The addition by Microsoft of System Center Opalis to the licensing suite of System Center 2010, and the subsequent upgrade of the product to System Center 2012 Orchestrator made it a logical addition to this edition of the book.

Understanding System Center Configuration Manager

The first product covered in this chapter is the System Center Configuration Manager (SCCM) product shown in Figure 1.1; the current rendition is System Center 2012 Configuration Manager. SCCM is the start of the life cycle that deploys a system's operating system as well as installs the applications onto a server or client system, and then it keeps the system patched and updated all based on common templates the IT department creates to ensure standardization from system to system.

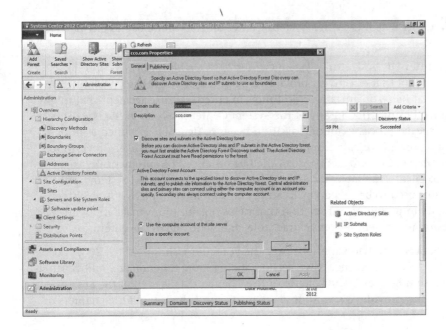

FIGURE 1.1   The System Center Configuration Manager Console.

Business Solutions Addressed by System Center Configuration Manager

System Center 2012 Configuration Manager helps maintain consistency in system configuration and management. Rather than having each and every workstation, laptop, and server built from scratch in an ad hoc manner with configuration settings based on the individual desires of the IT professional building the system, SCCM uses templates in the build process.

The templates are created by the IT personnel to meet specific business, security, and functional application needs of the organization. Once a template is created, all systems of similar function can use the exact same template to build and configure the system with only the unique server name or other identifier being different from system to system. With the template-based installation, the organization can depend on consistency in build configuration for like servers, like desktops, and like laptops throughout the enterprise.

In fact, SCCM has additional components (called Compliance Settings) that ensure that the systems, once deployed, maintain the consistency by preventing users from updating systems using unsupported or unique update parameters. Rather, policies are established to update all systems of a similar functional role to be upgraded or updated the same. If a patch or update goes out to one system of a configuration type, then all systems of that configuration type are updated at the same (or relatively same) time. This concept, formerly known as Desired Configuration Management (DCM) but now called Compliance Settings, can be audited and reports can be generated to show security officers and compliance auditors that standards are enforced throughout the data center and throughout workstation systems across an entire organization.

Major Features of System Center Configuration Manager

System Center 2012 Configuration Manager has hundreds of features and functions that IT administrators can leverage as part of their system configuration and management practices; some of the major features in the product are as follows:

▶ **Operating system deployment**—At the start of the system's life cycle is the installation of the core operating system. SCCM provides all the tools an organization needs to deploy an operating system, either as an imaged installation (formerly, organizations used Norton Ghost, but no longer need to because SCCM includes image creation and deployment tools) or as a scripted method of installation.

▶ **Patching and updating**—Once the operating system has been deployed, SCCM includes the mechanism to patch and update systems. Although many organizations use the Windows Server Update Services (WSUS), a free tool for patching and updating systems, SCCM leverages everything WSUS does but also provides IT administrators with a more active patching and updating addition to WSUS. The Software Updates portion of the SCCM Console, shown in Figure 1.2, is an example of the detail of the update information. The active update system enforces updates, forcing systems to be patched, updated, and rebooted based on policies that the IT department publishes and ensuring consistency in the update cycle of systems.

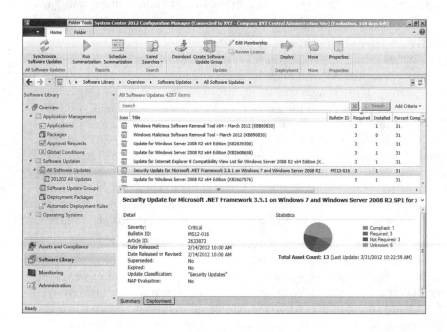

FIGURE 1.2   Details in the SCCM Console relative to patching and updating systems.

▶ **Asset tracking**—As part of the operating system deployment and patching and updating process, the management tool needs to know what type of hardware, software, and applications make up the system so the system can be properly updated. SCCM includes the tools necessary to track the hardware and software assets of the systems it is managing.

▶ **Remote control**—In the event that a user working on a system needs help, or that a system needs to be serviced, SCCM has a remote-control process that allows the IT administrator or a help desk individual to remotely control and support a user or manage a system, whether the system is on the network or remote of the network.

▶ **Software deployment**—Although the operating system deployment will install the base operating system on a server or client system, applications need to be installed and managed as well. SCCM provides the tools to push out software applications, whether it is something as simple as a plug-in or utility or as complex as a complete suite or server-based application, including unique application configuration and customization.

▶ **Compliance management**—Beyond just having an operating system and applications installed on a system, keeping a system configured in a standard setup is crucial in consistency controls. SCCM provides a configuration option called Compliance Settings that has policies established for system configurations so that a system cannot be changed or modified beyond the configuration standards set by policy for the system. This ensures all systems have the same software, drivers, updates, and configuration settings meeting stringent audit and controls standards consistent with regulatory compliance rules.

▶ **HTTP and HTTPS client connections**—A very significant component in SCCM is its ability to allow client connections for management to connect to Configuration Manager either through HTTP or HTTPS. In many systems management tools, for a system to be managed, the system had to be directly connected to the network, meaning the system has to be on the network or VPN'd remote to the network to have patches and updates applied or for the IT department to inventory or remotely control the system. With the flexibility of connectivity by HTTP or HTTPS connections, a remote or mobile system merely needs to be connected to the Internet anywhere in the world, and the SCCM client will automatically connect back to the corporate SCCM server through a secured HTTPS tunnel to allow SCCM to inventory, patch, apply policies, and update the system. The remote system does not need to VPN into the network nor do anything other than simply establish connectivity to the Internet.

▶ **Reporting**—SCCM integrates into the product a report generation tool, shown in Figure 1.3, that comes with a full set of out-of-the-box reports, including the ability for IT personnel to create customized reports on everything from asset inventory reports to standard configuration reports to reports on the patch and update level of each laptop and desktop in the entire enterprise. Reports can also be customized in the report tool querying any data sets of information collected by SCCM and producing reports specific to the needs of the organization.

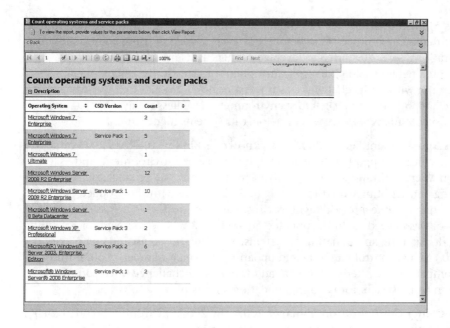

FIGURE 1.3   Reports tool built in to SCCM.

Background on System Center Configuration Manager

System Center 2012 Configuration Manager is easily a dozen or more generations into the life cycle of the product. From its early roots as Systems Management Server, or SMS, that had a bad reputation for being a management product that took more to manage the management system than managing workstations and servers themselves, SCCM has come a long way.

Some of the major revisions and history of the product are as follows:

▶ **Systems Management Server v1.x**—Systems Management Server (SMS) v1.x had a few versions, 1.0, 1.1, and 1.2, all available in the mid-1990s to support systems typically in a Windows NT environment. Because Windows NT domains were clusters of systems but not really a highly managed hierarchy of systems, SMS 1.x had its own site structure for identifying and managing systems. With most organizations at the time using Ghost to deploy system images, and patching and updating not really a common practice, SMS pretty much just provided the packaging of software programs and upgrades of software programs for systems. An expert who knew how to bundle up Microsoft Office or Adobe Acrobat into an MSI installation script had a full-time job as the process of packaging applications during these early days was neither easy nor intuitive. Smaller organizations found it was easier to just take a CD-ROM and walk from computer to computer to install software than try to create a "package" and hope that the package would deploy properly over the network.

▶ **Systems Management Server v2.0**—SMS 2.0 came out in 1999 and provided similar software-deployment processes as before; however, instead of using ad hoc site configurations, SMS 2.0 started to leverage subnets as its method of identifying systems on a network. SMS 2.0 also transitioned into the Active Directory era, although not without its challenges as it was a non-AD product that was somewhat set up to support an Active Directory environment. Needless to say, SMS 2.0 was about as successful as SMS 1.x was in helping in systems management.

▶ **Systems Management Server 2003 (also known as SMS v3.0)**—SMS 2003 came out to specifically support systems in an Active Directory environment, and although Microsoft now supported Active Directory sites, the product still required a packaging and scripting expert to be able to do anything with the product. Patching and updating became a requirement as viruses and worms spread across the Internet and a tool was needed to do the updates. So SMS 2003 was best known for its ability to provide patching and updating of systems; however, the setup and complexity of SMS 2003 to just control patching and updating allowed a number of other third-party companies like Alteris, Marimba, and LanDesk to challenge Microsoft in having an easier system for patching, updating, and deploying software.

▶ **System Center Configuration Manager 2007**—By 2007, Microsoft rebranded their management products under the System Center designation and finally broke away from the old legacy "site" concept of the Windows NT-based SMS product and fully redesigned the product for Active Directory, calling it System Center Configuration Manager 2007. With significantly better packaging, patching, and inventory tools along with a much better server role structure, SCCM 2007 finally "worked." Organizations were now able to create software packages in minutes instead of days. Patching and updating leveraged the highly successful WSUS patching tool with enhancements added into the SCCM update for patching and updating to enforce updates, force system reboots, and better manage the mobile workforce.

▶ **System Center Configuration Manager 2007 SP1, SP2, R2, R3**—SCCM 2007 evolved with various service pack (SP) and interim releases (R2, R3) that added support for managing Windows Vista and Windows 7 systems as well as support for remote-management components that Intel built in to their chipset called vPro technologies. With systems with vPro built in, an SCCM administrator can wake up a powered-off system, boot the system to a remote-management guest operating system, and perform management tasks, including flashing the system BIOS without ever touching the actual system. Updates also added automatic computer provisioning and multicast support for operating system deployments and also added App-V support in addition to ForeFront integration into subsequent updates to the product.

▶ **System Center 2012 Configuration Manager**—Most recently, the release of SCCM 2012 added the support of dozens of features, functions, and tools that support the imaging, management, and tighter integration with other System Center components. Most notably are improvements in central administration, inclusion of more sophisticated endpoint management functionality, better application management, and support for managing systems, devices, and applications both on-premise as well as in the cloud.

What's New in System Center 2012 Configuration Manager

System Center 2012 Configuration Manager adds a number of new features and functions to the product. For the IT professional who is familiar with SCCM 2007, the overall look and feel of SCCM has not changed, so for the most part an administrator can consider the update to SCCM 2012 as being more like a feature pack upgrade of new functionality. The focus of the additions to SCCM helps to improve SCCM's ability to support a more distributed environment, one where data centers or even on-premise/cloud configurations exist. Microsoft also put a focus on mobile devices as part of the rollout of SCCM 2012. Some of the top new functions in SCCM 2012 that are covered in this book include the following:

▶ **New setup options**—One of the first comments from IT pros who have worked with SMS and SCCM in the past is that the installation process is different for SCCM 2012. The IT pro is now given the option of installing additional site system roles, such as Management Points and Distribution Points, during the setup process. The roles can be configured as local or remote site system servers with the option of using the local computer account for the site server in a remote site system configuration. Additionally, the Site Repair Wizard familiar in previous version of SCCM is now integrated in the SCCM 2012 setup wizard for the repair and recovery of SCCM 2012 sites, site server roles, and servers. Administrators will also find that secondary sites are no longer installed from the setup wizard, but instead are created from the SCCM 2012 Console after the installation of the primary site.

▶ **Addition of a Central Administration Site**—SCCM 2012 has added a new configuration option of setting up Central Administration Site at the root of the SCCM 2012 hierarchy. Instead of having the Central Site also being the Primary Site for all SCCM roles, the SCCM 2012 Central Administration Site is used for reporting and to facilitate communications between primary sites, thus adding the option of an additional layer for administration. This is key for organizations that want to have a central reporting site, yet have Primary Sites in their on-premise private cloud and a separate Primary Site in a managed colocation data center or hosted cloud environment. This is an option in the hierarchy configuration of SCCM 2012 for organizations looking for better management, control, and distribution of systems management.

▶ **Behind-the-scenes changes**—SCCM 2012 made changes behind the scenes that most administrators normally are unaware of. One of the changes in SCCM 2012 is its use of database replication to transfer data and update changes of site database content with other sites in the environment. SCCM 2012 has removed the need to configure Network Load Balancing (NLB) Management Points; instead, when more than one Management Point is added to a site, load balancing is automatically configured.

▶ **Elimination of Native mode versus Mixed mode sites**—SCCM 2012 no longer distinguishes Native mode versus Mixed mode for sites, where previous versions required either one or the other configuration. In SCCM 2012, Management Points can be configured to provide either HTTPS or HTTP, potentially allowing organizations to communicate with internal Management Points over HTTP, while at the same time require external Management Points to communicate over HTTPS. This provides better flexibility in the configuration of SCCM to suit the security needs (and complexity) of configurations.

▶ **Elimination of site roles**—SCCM 2012 no longer has system roles for reporting points, PXE service points, server locator points, or Branch Distribution Points. These site roles are rolled up into other roles to eliminate redundancy. Specifically, the reporting point rolls up to the reporting services point, the PXE service point is now included in the Distribution Point, the server location point is now part of the Management Point, and the Branch Distribution Point is now part of the BranchCache setting in Windows 2008 R2. With the elimination of site roles, there's also no longer a need to specify a default Management Point. With SCCM 2012, multiple Management Points can be configured in the same site and the endpoint client will automatically connect to one based on the network or site location and whether the connection should be HTTP or HTTPS for the device. Additionally, sites are no longer administrative boundaries, providing the ability for organizations to manage sites with more granularity, whether that is multiple administration groups for a single site or combining multiple sites into a single administrative group.

▶ **Addition of role-based administration**—Previous versions of SCCM provided security and administration through class and instance settings. With SCCM 2012, security and administrative roles are created, providing the organization the ability to manage and administer endpoints across the entire enterprise with settings that can apply to all sites without having to individually specify sites or objects for management.

▶ **Improvements in the use of certificates**—SCCM 2012 takes better advantage of certificates for authentication, signing, and encryption of communications for SCCM servers and endpoint devices. SCCM 2012 adds a site system server certificate for authentication of other site systems in the same site, and a certificate for the site system role to identify site servers in the environment.

▶ **Introduction of user collections and device collections**—SCCM 2012 now includes two new nodes, one for user collections and one for device collections. Users and devices are no longer combined into a single collection. This helps organizations separate users and devices for better mobility and manageability of objects in the organization's environment.

▶ **Desired Configuration Management is now Compliance Settings**—SCCM 2007's Desired Configuration Management (DCM) that helped organizations set and enforce default policies and settings is now simply a security role called Compliance Settings Manager. As a security role, it is now easier to create configuration baselines and apply them as any other endpoint policy, simplifying the task of policy management.

▶ **Improvements in software deployment**—SCCM 2012 now uses software upgrade groups instead of update lists, maintaining the consistency of updates and software deployment rules. Additions in software update monitoring to better understand the state of key software updates, detailed state messages for deployments, and more specific error codes help the SCCM administrator better manage users and devices in the environment.

▶ **Mobile Device Management**—Lastly, a long-anticipated addition to SCCM 2012 is its inclusion of what used to be called System Center Mobile Device Manager into SCCM for the management of mobile devices. This includes the ability to enroll mobile devices for the purpose of applying device settings, configuring mobile device policies, and remotely managing mobile devices. Mobile devices require a certificate for better encryption, authentication, and device identification as part of SCCM 2012.

What to Expect in the System Center Configuration Manager Chapters

In this book, four chapters are dedicated to the System Center Configuration Manager product. These chapters are as follows:

▶ **Chapter 2, "Configuration Manager 2012 Design and Planning"**—This chapter covers the architectural design, server placement, role placement, and planning of the deployment of System Center 2012 Configuration Manager in the enterprise. The chapter addresses where to place site servers, discusses how to distribute images and large update files, introduces the various server roles and how the server roles can be placed all on a single server in a small environment or distributed to multiple servers, and covers the best practices that have been found in combining certain roles and the logic behind combining roles even in the largest of enterprises.

▶ **Chapter 3, "Configuration Manager 2012 Implementation, Migration, and Administration"**—Chapter 3 dives into the installation process of SCCM along with routine administrative tasks commonly used in managing an SCCM environment. This includes the familiarization of the SCCM management console features and how an administrator would use the management console to perform ongoing tasks.

▶ **Chapter 4, "Using Configuration Manager 2012 to Distribute Software, Updates, and Operating Systems"**—Chapter 4 gets into the meat of SCCM, focusing on core capabilities like distributing software, patching and updating, and creating and deploying operating systems. Any organization with SCCM implemented tends to use these features and functions at a minimum. The whole value in SCCM is to deploy operating systems (either imaged or scripted), patch and update systems, and deploy new software programs. This chapter covers the process as well as digs into tips, tricks, and lessons learned in sharing best practices when deploying these features in the enterprise.

▶ **Chapter 5, "Using Configuration Manager 2012 for Asset Management and Reporting"**—The final chapter on SCCM in this book covers other components, such as the asset management feature and the reporting capabilities built in to SCCM. Some organizations only use the asset feature in SCCM as the prerequisite to patch and update the system, whereas other organizations greatly utilize the asset management function for regulatory and compliance purposes. It's the same with reporting: Some organizations never generate a report out of SCCM, just using SCCM for operating system deployment, updates, and software pushes. However, other organizations heavily depend on the reporting capabilities in SCCM to generate reports for Sarbanes-Oxley (SOX) auditors or security compliance officers to prove the operational status of the systems.

System Center 2012 Configuration Manager is a very powerful tool that is the start of the life cycle of a networked environment, providing templates and standard configurations for systems all the way through updates, management, and reporting. Jump to Chapters 2 through 5 of this book for specific information and deployment and configuration guidance on how SCCM can be best leveraged in your enterprise.

Understanding System Center Operations Manager

System Center Operations Manager (SCOM) 2012 is the second product being addressed in this chapter. SCOM is used to monitor and alert network administrators when something (a server, workstation, network device, application, and so forth) is not working as expected, such as being offline, in a failed state, or even not running as fast as normal. The SCOM management console, shown in Figure 1.4, provides details about the events and errors of the systems being monitored and managed by SCOM.

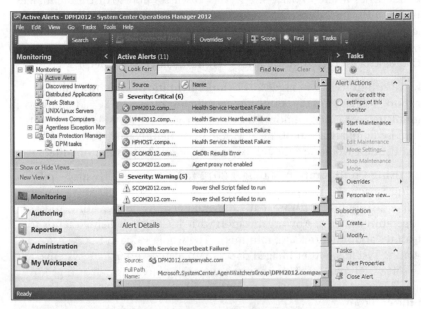

FIGURE 1.4   The System Center Operations Manager Console.

In the past, system monitoring was simply monitoring and alerting when something was "down"; however, with SCOM, the monitoring is proactive and alerts are triggered before problems cause a system to fail. SCOM proactively checks the operation of systems and devices, and when the devices are performing differently than normal—which many times is a precursor to a pending system failure—SCOM begins the alert and notification process.

SCOM also has the ability to monitor applications as if a user is accessing the application and not just based on whether a system is operational or not. A system can appear to be fully operational, yet when users try to log on to the system, they could get logon errors or terrible access performance. SCOM has the ability to utilize automation by having a client system log on to a web server or an application server with stored credentials and validate that systems throughout the enterprise are more than operational and are serving users as expected.

Business Solutions Addressed by System Center Operations Manager

System Center Operations Manager helps an organization be proactive about system operations rather than waiting for a server or application to fail, incur operational downtime, and recover from the failure. SCOM helps IT personnel ensure systems are running as expected. SCOM monitors the normal operation of servers, workstations, and applications to create a known baseline on how the systems are operating. When the systems fall out of the norm of the baseline, meaning that something is wrong, and while downtime has not occurred, the systems or applications are not running as they always do and IT personnel are then notified to review the situation and take corrective action.

SCOM also helps the IT department identify systems that should be replaced before others due to reliability issues. SCOM can keep track of system uptime and downtime and generate a report that ranks the reliability of systems based on their ongoing performance. If all things were equal in terms of age or depreciation schedule of systems, yet an organization will be replacing a portion of the systems, the reports can be used to identify which systems should be replaced first.

SCOM monitors not only the state of the server and application, but also the state of virtual host servers. With a vast focus on virtualization, rather than looking at just individual systems, SCOM can monitor a physical host server that is running several virtualized guest sessions at the same time. This broader view of system performance can identify a potential physical host problem that is impacting the performance of several guest sessions rather than being alerted by a dozen guest sessions of performance problems that all roll up and relate to a single physical host problem.

SCOM also has a client-facing focus to not just see performance and system problems from the perspective of the host server, but to also measure performance from a client system. As IT professionals know, a server could be running at 5% or 10% utilization and "appear" to be running just fine, but users complain of a slowdown or sluggishness in access to an application. By having SCOM monitor performance from the endpoint, the end-to-end experience that includes performance of the user's location application, LAN or WAN connection impact, and server-based responsiveness can be assessed. This can help the management professional to determine whether a performance slowdown is potentially caused by a slow endpoint system or network connectivity of that remote user rather than simply looking at the back-end server(s).

SCOM can also be used to produce reports that help auditors and regulators validate that the organization's IT operations meet regulatory compliance requirements. Automated report generation for information such as password attempt violations, service-level agreement details, encrypted data access validation, and the like makes SCOM more than just a monitoring tool, but an information compliance reporting tool.

The bottom line is that SCOM helps IT personnel identify problems that need to be fixed before the problems create downtime that impacts the operations of the business. This is critical in keeping employees productive at managing their internal servers, and helps an organization maintain business continuity when their servers host applications that help the organization generate revenues. A properly designed, implemented, and configured monitoring tool like SCOM can mean the difference of an organization focused on productivity and continuity versus an organization that is constantly recovering from system failures.

Major Features of System Center Operations Manager

System Center 2012 Operations Manager has hundreds of features and functions that IT administrators can leverage as part of their system monitoring and proactive management practices; some of the major features in the product are as follows:

▶ **Server and client system monitoring**—Key to SCOM is its ability to monitor servers and client systems. Using an agent that installs on the system (or agentless if the administrator desires), information about the system(s) is reported back to the SCOM monitoring server with operational data tracked and logged on a continuous basis.

▶ **Event correlation**—SCOM is smart enough to know that when a WAN connection is down, the status of all of the servers and devices on the other side of the WAN connection becomes unknown. Rather than sending hundreds of alerts that SCOM has lost contact with every device on the other side of a WAN, SCOM instead sends a single alert that the WAN connection is down and that the status of devices on the other side of the WAN are in an unknown state.

▶ **Event log collection**—Key to regulatory compliance reporting is to note system changes as well as potential security violations. SCOM has the ability to collect event logs and syslogs from systems, consolidate the data, and provide reports on the aggregate of information such as failed password attempts against all monitored servers in the environment.

▶ **System monitoring**—Monitoring in SCOM is more than just noting that a system is up or down, but also the general response time of the system and applications running on the system. Specific applications can be monitored using SCOM, such as monitoring SharePoint servers, SQL servers, or Exchange servers, as shown in Figure 1.5.

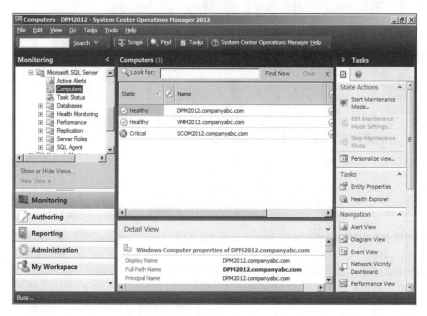

FIGURE 1.5   System monitoring and alerting in SCOM of specific servers in an environment.

▶ **Client system monitoring**—Added in recent updates to SCOM is the ability to monitor and report on not just servers, but also client workstations in a network. Client system monitoring is commonly used to monitor and help manage and support critical client systems. A critical client system might be a laptop that belongs to a key executive, or it could be a workstation that serves as a print server or data collection device. Whatever the case, SCOM has the ability to monitor servers as well as client systems in the enterprise.

▶ **Application monitoring**—SCOM has the ability to monitor specific application and website URLs, not just to see if the servers are running or if the website is responding, but to actually confirm that the site is responding in a timely manner. This deep level of monitoring, shown in Figure 1.6, confirms response time and can even have test-user accounts log on to session states to validate that a site or protected site is responding as expected.

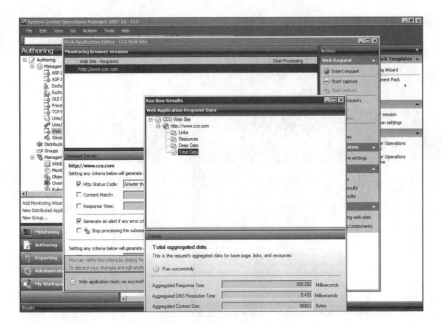

FIGURE 1.6   Monitoring applications and web URLs in SCOM.

▶ **Service-oriented management**—Traditional system monitoring treated all systems the same, so whether a single (only) system of its type in a network or a system that has multiple redundant nodes, any system failure would result in a page or alert. SCOM is service oriented, meaning that if multiple servers exist for redundancy, the administrator will not be urgently paged or alerted if one of many systems is down. As long as the service (such as email routing, web hosting, or domain authentication) continues to operate, a different level of response (such as an email notification instead of an urgent page) is triggered.

▶ **Integrated solutions databases**—For administrators debugging a problem, the process usually involves grabbing event errors out of the log files, going to Microsoft TechNet to research the information, finding the solution, and then going back to the server to try the solution. With SCOM, it has Microsoft's TechNet information integrated into the system so that when an event occurs and shows up on the SCOM Console, right there with the event error is the symptom information and recommended solution that an administrator would normally find in TechNet online. Additionally, SCOM not only has the information of what an administrator should do (like start and stop a service), but SCOM also presents a Restart Service option on the SCOM Console screen for the administrator to simply click the option to restart the service. If that solution solves the problem, SCOM allows the administrator to choose to have that solution (like restarting the service) automatically run the next time the event occurs on *any* server in the environment. This self-healing process allows an organization to set processes that automatically trigger and resolve problems without having an administrator manually identify and perform a simple task.

▶ **Service-level agreement (SLA) tracking and reporting**—Many organizations have, publish, and manage to a specific service-level agreement metric, so if a network service is offline or degraded, the service-level quality is triggered and the overall service-level agreement is measured. SCOM has reports as well as a Dashboard view component that provide administrators the ability to know the status of system operations in the network.

▶ **Reporting**—With previous versions of SCOM, reporting was an external add-on. Effectively, if an administrator wanted a report on the status of systems, a separate report tool was run. With the latest releases of SCOM, the reports are available right within the SCOM Console. From a common console, an administrator can monitor systems as well as generate reports on every managed system in the environment.

Background on System Center Operations Manager

System Center 2012 Operations Manager has over a decade of history at Microsoft and many years before that before Microsoft acquired the technology back in 1999. From its early roots as Operations Manager 2000 to what is now System Center 2012 Operations Manager, SCOM has come a long way.

Some of the major revisions and history of the product are as follows:

▶ **NetIQ Enterprise Event Manager**—System Center Operations Manager has its roots from a 1999 product acquisition Microsoft made from NetIQ. The product, NetIQ Enterprise Event Manager, was already a well-established tool for monitoring network environments and formed the basis of Microsoft's operations management offering.

▶ **Microsoft Operations Manager (MOM) 2000**—In 2000, Microsoft took the NetIQ product and rebranded it as Microsoft Operations Manager 2000, doing a little to include support for monitoring and managing the newly released Active Directory 2000 and Windows 2000 Server; however, for the most part, MOM 2000 was the NetIQ product with a new name. For the next five years, Microsoft released service packs and management packs to update the product to support all of the new Active Directory–supported products Microsoft was releasing like Exchange 2000 Server, Exchange Server 2003, SharePoint Portal Server 2001, SQL Server 2000, and the like.

▶ **Microsoft Operations Manager (MOM) 2005**—With the release of MOM 2005, Microsoft now had its first fully revised Microsoft monitoring and management product. Most organizations would consider this the Microsoft v2.0 of the product where core components such as event monitoring, event correlation, proactive monitoring, integration with TechNet support data, and the like made MOM 2005 a good Microsoft-focused monitoring and alerting product.

▶ **System Center Operations Manager 2007, SP1, R2**—SCOM 2007 was a major improvement from Microsoft and one where the product was truly revised to meet the needs of enterprises. SCOM 2007 was fully integrated with Active Directory so that servers and server roles (such as all Exchange front-end servers or all domain controllers) could be identified as a group. Role-based security was added so that there was better granular control over views and tasks that an administrator was able to perform. Also, the addition of an audit log collection system that auditors and regulators were looking for consolidated log information in which SCOM 2007 was able to extract log information and make that available for reporting. Service Pack 1 (SP1) and the R2 to SCOM included a rollup of all hotfixes for SCOM 207, support for Windows 2008 and 2008 R2 as the base operating system that SCOM could run on, and a significant update to the Asset Intelligence component of SCOM for organizations that need better asset tracking and awareness.

▶ **System Center 2012 Operations Manager**—For those who have been using SCOM for a long time, the release of SCOM 2012 was seen as a huge turning point of making SCOM a truly enterprise monitoring and management solution. SCOM 2012 provides support for not only Windows-based servers and applications, but also now has fully integrated support for non-Windows-based systems like UNIX and Linux system monitoring. SCOM 2012 also has the ability of granularly defining Service Level Objectives (SLOs), such as monitoring and assessing the response time of a specific logon procedure or web page view rather than simply pinging the system to see if it is up. In addition, significant improvements in scalability as well as the ability to monitor cloud-based applications and services are great enhancements in the latest SCOM release. Monitoring of workloads can now be measured in the thousands of events per agent, allowing SCOM to reach into the largest data centers and cloud environments to manage Windows and non-Windows servers, network appliances and devices, and client systems throughout an enterprise.

What's New in System Center 2012 Operations Manager

System Center 2012 Operations Manager adds a number of new features and functions to the product. For the IT professional who is familiar with SCOM 2007, just like with SCCM 2012, the overall look and feel of SCOM has not changed, so for the most part an administrator can consider the update to SCOM 2012 as being more like a feature pack upgrade of new functionality. The focus of the additions to SCOM helps to improve SCOM's ability to support a more distributed environment, one where data centers or even on-premise/cloud configurations exist. Some of the top new functions in SCOM 2012 that are covered in this book include the following:

▶ **Removal of the Root Management Server**—With System Center 2012 Operations Manager, Microsoft replaced the long-standing concept of a Root Management Server and instead made all SCOM servers peer servers of one another. Management workload is split across all management servers in a management group, which provides high availability without the need for clustering or other hierarchical replication functionality.

▶ **Addition of a resource pool**—SCOM 2012 adds the concept of a resource pool that provides a method of associating workload performance across multiple management servers, including high availability, network device monitoring, health rollup monitoring, and group calculation.

▶ **Operations Console and Web console changes**—The consoles for SCOM 2012 have been updated to allow for easier navigation and task management in terms of the Operations Console and the ability to view all SCOM views within the Web console.

▶ **Enhancements in application and network monitoring**—SCOM 2012 improves web application monitoring that includes the ability to view server-side and client-side operations of applications in terms of performance and availability with controls to monitor event collection, measure performance goals, and pinpoint specific applications on specific servers to monitor. For network monitoring, SCOM 2012 improves everything from the discovery process of routers and switches to monitoring of network interfaces and ports, including virtual local area networks (VLANs) to the deletion of discovered network devices.

▶ **Improvements in dashboards**—Dashboard views in SCOM 2012 now provide a multipanel but single screen view of monitoring information along with the ability to create custom layouts and nested Dashboard views. Additionally, a SharePoint web part can be added to SharePoint 2010 sites for viewing of information from a SharePoint environment.

▶ **Expanded support for UNIX- and Linux-based systems**—SCOM 2012 expands on the support for UNIX and Linux systems by adding the ability to configure sudo elevation in a RunAs account to be able to perform administrative tasks on target systems. Additionally, SCOM 2012 adds Windows PowerShell cmdlets to allow for scripting and background operation tasks against UNIX- and Linux-based systems.

What to Expect in the System Center Operations Manager Chapters

In this book, four chapters are dedicated to the System Center Operations Manager product. These chapters are as follows:

▶ **Chapter 6, "Operations Manager 2012 Design and Planning"**—This chapter covers the architectural design, server placement, role placement, and planning of the deployment of System Center 2012 Operations Manager in the enterprise. The chapter addresses where to place management servers and where management packs fit in to SCOM for providing better data collection and reporting. This chapter also introduces the various server roles and how the server roles can be placed on a single server in a small environment or distributed to multiple servers, including best practices that have been found in combining certain roles and the logic behind combining roles even in the largest of enterprises.

▶ **Chapter 7, "Operations Manager 2012 Implementation and Administration"**—Chapter 7 dives into the installation process of SCOM along with routine administrative tasks commonly used in managing a SCOM environment. This includes the familiarization of the SCOM management console features and how an administrator would use the management console to perform ongoing tasks.

▶ **Chapter 8, "Using Operations Manager 2012 for Monitoring and Alerting"**—Chapter 8 gets into the meat of SCOM, focusing on core capabilities, such as monitoring individual servers and events and monitoring a collection of servers and creating event correlation to associate a series of servers, network devices, and applications for a better monitored view of key applications and network resources. Many organizations tend to just turn on the basic monitoring that SCOM has, which is good, but that's not where the value is in SCOM. The value is in creating automation tasks so that when an event occurs, SCOM can automatically assess the problem, correlate the problem to other events, and send the IT administrator a specific notification or alert that will help the administrator better manage the environment as a whole. This chapter covers the process as well as digs into tips, tricks, and lessons learned in sharing best practices of monitoring and alerting in the enterprise.

▶ **Chapter 9, "Using Operations Manager 2012 for Operations and Security Reporting"**—The final chapter on SCOM in this book covers the reporting capabilities built in to SCOM. In earlier versions of the Operations Manager product, Crystal Reports was used as an external reporting tool that reached into the MOM databases to generate reports, which was cumbersome and really more of an afterthought for reporting. With SCOM 2012, reporting is done through SQL Reporting Services and integrated right into the main SCOM Console. Rather than seeing reporting as something some people use occasionally, SCOM's reporting takes management reports seriously as compliance officers, auditors, and executives want and need meaningful reports on the operations and management of their systems. SCOM 2012 reporting provides out-of-the-box reports to track the most common business information reports needed out of the monitoring and security alerting system, with the ability to customize reports specific to the needs of the organization. This chapter covers the out-of-the-box reports as well as how an administrator can customize reports specific to his or her needs.

System Center 2012 Operations Manager is a very powerful tool that helps network administrators be proactive in the monitoring of their servers and network devices, both Microsoft and non-Microsoft, and have the ability to address problems before downtime occurs. Jump to Chapters 6 through 9 of this book for specific information and deployment and configuration guidance on how SCOM can be best leveraged in your enterprise.

Understanding System Center Data Protection Manager

System Center Data Protection Manager (DPM) 2012 is the recent update to the DPM product that has been out for years. DPM 2012 backs up Windows-based servers in the environment, including domain controllers, Exchange servers, SharePoint servers, file servers, SQL servers, Windows workstations, and Hyper-V host servers. Unlike traditional backup systems that used to kick off in the middle of the night to "stream" the entire content of a server to tape, DPM backs up servers incrementally all day long and, in fact, does incremental backups of critical servers like Exchange or SharePoint every 15 minutes. Because the data backups are now done incrementally throughout the day, the load on the servers is minimal and the data is no more than a few minutes behind.

At any time, the administrator can reach into a backup from just a few minutes ago and initiate a restore of the data. Additionally, components within DPM 2012 allow the end user to restore information themselves in what is called self-service recovery. As an example, if a user is working off a file share in Windows (XP SP2 or higher) and accidentally deletes or overwrites a file, that user can simply right-click the file share, choose Previous Versions, and see previous versions of the file that was deleted or overwritten and choose to self-recover the file immediately.

Also, because DPM does not use tape as the primary medium but rather hard disk storage, the recovery of data, whether it is 15 minutes old, 15 days old, or even 15 weeks old, is done in seconds. Digital data backups as a primary method of backup and recovery provide faster backup and restore times, and DPM data can secondarily be written to tape or replicated across a WAN or the Internet to be stored offsite. Third-party providers can provide DPM secondary storage "in the cloud" so that an organization can bypass tape altogether and just push critical backups to an external third-party provider for safe recovery over the Internet in the event of a local site failure.

System Center 2012 Data Protection Manager provides the ability for protection groups to be created, as shown in Figure 1.7, where file servers, Exchange servers, SharePoint servers, SQL servers, or the like have varying backup schedules to ensure the successful backup of the application in a manner specific to the application.

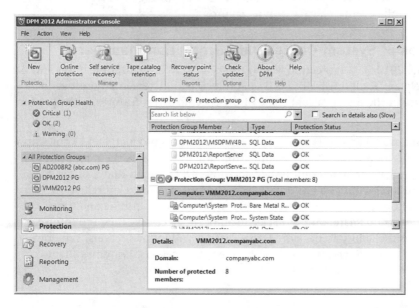

FIGURE 1.7   The System Center 2012 Data Protection Manager Console.

Business Solutions Addressed by System Center Data Protection Manager

For most organizations, *backup* has traditionally been something that is done every night as a "set-it-and-forget-it" process as insurance that if a server catastrophically fails, the administrator can go back to a tape and perform a recovery. Unfortunately, because *backup* has been seen as a necessity to take tapes offsite, but not a serious method of actual recovery, most organizations who have had to go back to tape have found that the data on the tape was either not accessible (due to tape corruption) or not complete (the organization was only backing up one component of a server, not all data components). DPM provides a "set-it-and-forget-it" medium for backup that is more reliable than the traditional method in that the medium is digital hard disk data, not flimsy electromagnetic tape. In addition, DPM has the intelligence of backing up not only "the server," but also backing up databases and logs together, or System State and databases together that are necessary for a successful recovery.

However, for organizations that want more than just data backed up, DPM is a component of a disaster recovery and actual business continuity strategy. By incrementally backing up data to DPM and then replicating the DPM data to other sites in real time, an organization has effectively created a process for full data recovery in a separate site. The same backup process in DPM that provides full recovery in the once-every-30-year type of scenario can be used from day to day by users themselves to self-recover deleted documents or email messages.

DPM takes an age-old process of full backups and provides day-to-day value to users to perform a simple recovery task of their own data all the way through the recovery of an entire data center in the event of a catastrophic failure.

Major Features of System Center Data Protection Manager

The System Center 2012 Data Protection Manager product has a wealth of features and functions that help an IT administrator back up, protect, and incrementally recover data on servers throughout the organization; some of the specific major features in the product are as follows:

▶ **Back up Microsoft-based servers**—As a Microsoft backup product, DPM knows how to back up Microsoft products in a manner that Microsoft wants their applications like Exchange, SQL, or SharePoint to be backed up. DPM knows that a successful SharePoint restoral requires a clean backup of the System State, Configuration Database, and Content Database at a specific snapshot point in time and, thus, when DPM backs up SharePoint, it backs up all of the necessary files and information. DPM has the ability to back up Active Directory, Windows servers, Windows file systems, Exchange servers, SharePoint servers, SQL servers, Windows client systems, and Hyper-V host servers.

The biggest complaint about DPM is that although it does back up Microsoft products really, really well, it has no facility to back up non-Microsoft products today. For organizations that want to back up their Oracle databases, their Linux servers, or the like, the organization needs another backup product at this time. Choosing DPM as a backup product for an organization that is exclusively Microsoft-based is an easy decision. For mixed environments, many organizations still choose DPM to back up their Microsoft products as it is the best-of-breed solution in backing up (and, more important, recovering) Microsoft servers and applications.

▶ **Back up file server data with self-service user recovery**—DPM has the ability to back up file servers, including file permissions on the files on the system. With DPM file backup implemented, end users can self-service recover files that have been accidentally deleted or even overwritten with versions of files that have been backed up and are stored on the DPM 2012 server. This self-service function leverages the "previous versions" capability in Windows, as shown in Figure 1.8.

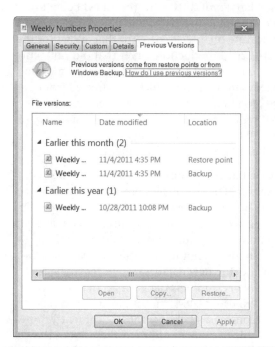

FIGURE 1.8   Self-service recovery of files leveraging DPM.

▶ **Back up Microsoft Exchange databases**—DPM also has built-in intelligence to back up Exchange servers, including Exchange Server 2007 and Exchange Server 2010, and not just the databases but also the log files and associated information necessary to allow for a successful recovery of a single Exchange database or an entire Exchange server. Additionally, DPM can back up a passive node of an Exchange cluster, or in Exchange 2010, DPM can back up a replica copy of the Exchange data (not the primary active database), thus allowing a backup to proceed in the middle of the day with absolutely no impact on users. The recovery process of Exchange leverages the recovery storage group/recovery database concept in Exchange, where the data can automatically be recovered to a live running Exchange server that then allows the administrator to mount the database and selectively recover a single mailbox or even a single mail message directly into a user's mailbox.

▶ **Back up SharePoint data, including recovery straight to the source data location**—DPM is intelligent enough to know to back up all components of a SharePoint environment for the ability to successfully restore the SharePoint server. DPM can back up SharePoint 2007 and SharePoint 2010 with the added benefit of SharePoint 2010 backups that it can do a restoral directly to a live working SharePoint 2010 server. This is more a feature of SharePoint 2010 that allows for the recovery straight to a running SharePoint 2010 production server that did not exist in SharePoint 2007. SharePoint 2007 required data to be restored to a replica of the SharePoint 2007 production environment and then the data was extracted from that replica farm and inserted into the production SharePoint 2007 environment. SharePoint 2010 can have data restored right into a production document library or list, or even the full recovery of a site. DPM 2012 has the ability of facilitating the successful recovery process into a live SharePoint 2010 environment.

▶ **Back up SQL data, including automatic backup of databases added to the SQL server**—DPM 2012 can back up and recover SQL servers in a production environment. DPM 2012 backups of SQL servers not only allow for the backup of a specific targeted server, but an option can be triggered so that when additional databases or instances are added to a server, DPM automatically adds those additions to the backup group. In the past, if an administrator did not update the tape backup software to specifically back up a new database, the new database would never be backed up. DPM can be set to dynamically back up new databases added to a server. Additionally, once data has been backed up using DPM, the administrator can go into the Recovery tab of the DPM 2012 Console and choose files, documents, databases, or entire servers from any specific backup and initiate a restoral of the information. The information from the recovery page of the console is shown in Figure 1.9.

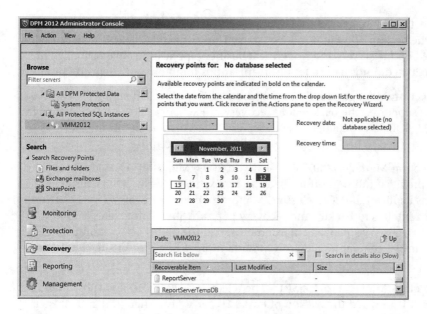

FIGURE 1.9   Recovery page from the DPM 2012 Console.

▶ **Backup of Hyper-V physical servers, including direct VHD recovery**—DPM 2012 has the ability to back up Hyper-V host servers, including the ability to selectively recover a specific Hyper-V guest session from that server-based backup. This provides an administrator the ability to target a server or series of Hyper-V host servers and then selectively choose to recover specific guest session instances.

▶ **Long-term storage of data to tape**—Although DPM provides the initial backup of information digitally to hard disk media, data on the DPM server can then secondarily be written to tape for long-term storage. Data written to tape can be used to recover a single backup instance or can be used to recover an entire DPM server itself.

▶ **Long-term storage of data pushed to the cloud**—Lastly, DPM 2012 data can be replicated offsite, whether that is replicating data to another DPM server in another organization-owned or managed data center, or replicating the DPM data to a third-party hosted storage provider. By replicating DPM data offsite over a WAN or Internet connection, an organization might not even need to ever have tapes or manage tapes again.

Background on System Center Data Protection Manager

System Center 2012 Data Protection Manager has gone through several revisions in just the past three to four years at Microsoft. Microsoft has done a good job updating the product to support more and more of what organizations want in a backup and recovery product. Each successive update of DPM has brought along major feature improvements; some of the major revisions and history of the product are as follows:

▶ **Data Protection Manager 2006**—DPM was released in 2005 as DPM 2006 and provided the backup of basic Windows Active Directory and file servers. Because it only backed up file servers and not critical business applications like Exchange or SQL, DPM 2006 did not have a lot of organizations jump on and adopt the product.

▶ **Data Protection Manager 2007**—At the end of 2007, Microsoft shipped DPM 2007 that finally supported the backup and recovery of Exchange Server 2003, Exchange Server 2007, SQL Server 2000, and SQL Server 2005. This was significant as DPM could now be used to back up real applications in the enterprise.

▶ **Data Protection Manager 2007 SP1**—Early in 2009, Microsoft released SP1 of DPM 2007 that provided full support for backing up Exchange Server 2007 Cluster Continuous Replication (CCR) clusters, Microsoft Office SharePoint Server 2007 servers with intelligent backup and recovery of entire SharePoint states, support for backing up Hyper-V virtualized environments, and the ability to back up to the cloud with initial companies like Iron Mountain providing host-offsite cloud services.

▶ **Data Protection Manager 2010, SP1**—The release of DPM 2010 and subsequently DPM 2010 SP1 provided the backup of entire Hyper-V Live Migration and Cluster Shared Volume (CSV) backups and recoveries, backup of Windows client systems, and the ability to back up the latest Exchange Server 2010 and Microsoft SharePoint 2010 environments.

▶ **Data Protection Manager 2012**—With the release of DPM 2012, organizations now have further enhancements in backup, including the ability to do SQL Filestream backups, do SharePoint item-level recovery without restoring the Content DB, and back up non-AD joined machines, including file servers, SQL servers, Hyper-V servers, and clustered data source. Microsoft continues to fine-tune DPM to make it a more effective tool for providing backup and recovery of key data sources in the enterprise.

What's New in System Center 2012 Data Protection Manager

System Center 2012 Data Protection Manager adds a number of new features and functions to the product. Just like in SCCM 2012 and SCOM 2012, for the IT professional who is familiar with earlier versions of DPM like DPM 2007 or DPM 2010, the overall look and feel of DPM has not changed. The focus of the additions to DPM helps to improve DPM's ability to back up more diverse systems and configurations with better granularity for both backup or information and the restoral of information. Some of the top new functions in DPM 2012 that are covered in this book include the following:

▶ **Centralized management**—New to DPM 2012 is its ability to centrally monitor and provide remote administration and recovery capabilities for administrators. With earlier releases of DPM, each DPM server had its own console for administration of servers backed up by the specific DPM system. With DPM 2012, an administrator can install the Central Console on a system and monitor multiple DPM 2012 (and

DPM 2010) servers, conduct remote administration of the local and remote DPM servers, and initiate the recovery of guest sessions and data from the Central Console.

▶ **Role-based access**—DPM 2012 also provides the ability to designate and delegate administration tasks to other individuals. This includes the ability to have other administrators (like an Exchange administrator or SharePoint administrator) receive alerts and notifications from System Center Operations Manager on the status of DPM backups and restores, and the ability to distribute administrator tasks to other individuals.

▶ **Restoring item-level content of SharePoint 2010 data**—While DPM 2010 SP1 provided the ability for an administrator to back up SharePoint data and recover it directly to an existing SharePoint 2010 server (eliminating the need to set up a separate recovery lab server to perform the restoral), the restoral process of DPM 2010 SP1 was a full content database recovery. With DPM 2012, content can now be restored at the item level (document library, list, or even a specific file) straight back to a running SharePoint 2010 server.

▶ **SQL Filestream support**—DPM 2012 provides SQL Filestream support. SQL Filestream is a data storage mechanism included in SQL 2008 that provides the ability to store data files (like documents, images, and audio/video content) to a file server, yet have SQL manage the content. SharePoint 2010 took advantage of SQL Filestream in its implementation of SharePoint Remote Blob Storage (RBS), where SharePoint data is stored outside of the SQL database. SharePoint RBS solved a long-standing problem in SharePoint where organizations storing massive amounts of image files, large computer-aided design (CAD) files, video files, or the like caused the SharePoint SQL servers to be unmanageably large. But with SharePoint RBS, the data can be redirected to write directly to a server or SAN's file storage system. DPM 2012 now has the ability of backing up and recovering this SQL Filestream data in a managed and organized manner that maintains the integrity of the stored information.

▶ **Certificate-based protection of non–Active Directory machines**—DPM 2012 provides the ability to back up non–Active Directory joined systems using certificates. In early releases of DPM, the target system had to be an AD-joined system, which prevented organizations from being able to back up kiosks, servers in the organization's demilitarized zone (DMZ), standalone Hyper-V hosts, and the like. DPM 2010 SP1 added the ability to back up Windows "workgroup" members by preinstalling an agent on the remote system and target it for backup. DPM 2012 now allows the ability to target a system for backup based on a certificate issued to the system, providing better flexibility and better security of identifying specific systems by certificates.

▶ **Support for multiple DPM servers to share a single SQL instance**—DPM 2012 now provides the ability to allow DPM servers to share a single SQL instance for DPM management. With previous versions of DPM, each DPM server had to have its own SQL instance, frequently installed on the DPM server itself because DPM did not support more than one DPM server using the same SQL instance. With DPM

2012, the target SQL server can support multiple DPM host server configurations; as such, multiple DPM servers can be added to an environment without the need of setting up (and buying) multiple copies of SQL.

What to Expect in the System Center Data Protection Manager Chapters

In this book, two chapters are dedicated to the System Center Data Protection Manager product. These chapters are as follows:

> ▶ **Chapter 10, "Data Protection Manager 2012 Design, Planning, and Implementation"**—This chapter covers the architectural design, server sizing, server placement, and planning of the deployment of System Center 2012 Data Protection Manager in the enterprise. The chapter provides modeling information on how much hard disk storage is needed to back up servers as well as best practices on the retention period of data (whether data should be backed up every 15 minutes, every hour, or every day and whether data should be stored for three days, a week, a month, or a year).

> ▶ **Chapter 11, "Using Data Protection Manager 2012 to Protect File Systems, Exchange, SQL, and SharePoint"**—This chapter provides information on how an administrator would use DPM 2012 to specifically protect and recover key applications and workloads such as file systems, Exchange, SQL, and SharePoint.

System Center 2012 Data Protection Manager with its support for doing 15-minute incremental backups of key business applications along with the ability to have self-service of information by end users themselves has vaulted DPM as a valuable tool for an organization to have in its business continuity and data recovery strategy. Jump to Chapters 10 and 11 of this book for specific information and deployment and configuration guidance on how DPM can be best leveraged in your enterprise.

Understanding System Center Virtual Machine Manager

In the past few years, server virtualization has shifted from something that organizations used to do in their test and development environments to something where organizations have 50% or more of their production servers virtualized. Microsoft's System Center Virtual Machine Manager (VMM) 2012 provides a number of very valuable tools for an organization with both Microsoft Hyper-V virtual servers as well as VMware virtual servers to better manage and support their virtualized environment.

VMM, like DPM, is a relative newcomer to the Microsoft management suite of products; however, just like how VMware dominated the virtualization marketplace in 2007 as the de facto standard, in just a few short years, Microsoft released five significant products and updates that now Hyper-V has thrust into being one of the major players in virtualization. The key to the growth of virtualization came from the release of x64-bit systems along with vendor support for virtualization.

With 32-bit systems and a limitation of 4GB of RAM in a server, there weren't many ways you could split 4GB of RAM and host production server workloads. At most, maybe an organization could get two to three small applications to run on a single virtual host system. However with 16GB, 32GB, even 64GB being common in 64-bit servers with 8-core or 16-core CPUs in a single host server, a single system can easily be split 5 ways, 10 ways, or even 15 ways, providing a significant density of virtual guest sessions in a single hosted server system.

With that many guest sessions running on a single server, organizations need a way to best manage the environment. VMM 2012 provides the tools to migrate physical servers into a Hyper-V guest session, and from a single console view, shown in Figure 1.10, administrators can view and manage all of the virtual host servers and guest sessions.

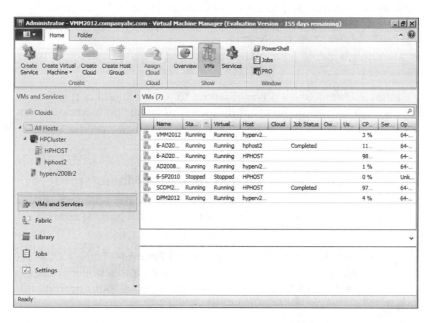

FIGURE 1.10   System Center Virtual Machine Manager Console.

Business Solutions Addressed by System Center Virtual Machine Manager

The business value that VMM 2012 provides is the ability for the IT administrator to centrally manage the host servers and guest session, regardless of whether the systems are Microsoft Hyper-V or VMware ESX hosts from a single console. With the proliferation of virtual hosts, VMM provides the needed tool to manage the guest sessions with standard builds, allocate the proper amount of memory and processing capacity, balance the work-load of guest sessions across host servers, and ultimately maintain uptime of host servers in an environment.

With VMM 2012, Microsoft has focused heavily on the addition of managing servers not only on-premise, but also in the cloud. Instead of a focus on a single or handful of physi-cal servers connected by typical switched networks, VMM 2012 adds the support for the "fabric" that makes up an enterprise. A back-end fabric may include physical servers stretched across multiple data centers over virtual local area networks (VLANs), storage systems that provide high availability and redundancy across multiple sites, and systems management that span not just a handful of host servers, but potentially dozens, hundreds, or thousands of host servers running tens of thousands of guest sessions and applications.

As organizations take advantage of server consolidation by getting rid of physical servers and creating significantly fewer virtual host systems, the need to migrate physical work-loads into virtualized workloads quickly and easily becomes an important task. VMM 2012 can capture physical systems and migrate them to virtual guest sessions as well as migrate other virtualized guest sessions (running on previous versions of Microsoft Virtual Machine Manager, Microsoft Hyper-V, or on VMware ESX) and migrate them to the latest Hyper-V host environment.

Organizations have migrated hundreds of physical servers to just a handful of physical host servers, saving the organization hundreds of thousands of dollars on hardware main-tenance contracts, electrical power, physical server rack space, and physical host server support costs.

Major Features of System Center Virtual Machine Manager

System Center Virtual Machine Manager has a whole list of features and functions that help an IT administrator manage virtual host servers as well as virtual guest sessions; some of the major features in the product are as follows:

▶ **Single view of all virtual host systems (Hyper-V and VMware)**—At the root of the Virtual Machine Manager product is its ability to consolidate into a single console view all Microsoft Hyper-V and VMware host servers and guest sessions running in the environment.

▶ **Ability to perform physical-to-virtual (P2V) conversions**—Once the centralized monitoring console is available, servers can be easily migrated from physical systems to virtual systems in what is called a P2V migration process.

▶ **Ability to perform virtual-to-virtual (V2V) conversions**—For systems that are already running on a different, possibly older virtualization platform like Microsoft Virtual Machine Manager 2008 or VMware, the virtual-to-virtual (V2V) feature in VMM 2012 converts the virtual guest sessions into the latest Microsoft Hyper-V virtual guest session standard.

▶ **Ability to delegate the administration and management of virtual guest sessions to other administrators**—For larger enterprises where certain administrators are in charge of all of their servers, instead of having, for example, 10 physical servers in a rack that an Exchange or SQL administrator would be in charge of, the administrator might find his or her servers spread across several shared Hyper-V physical host servers. Rather than giving an administrator access to all of the guest sessions running on all of the host servers, VMM 2012 provides an administrator the ability to group together servers and delegate the administration of those virtual guest server sessions to other administrators. Therefore, an Exchange administrator will be able to see, administer, and manage the Exchange servers regardless of which physical host server the guest sessions are running on. And likely, the SQL administrator and the SharePoint administrator will be able to see their servers in a centralized view without having access to servers that they should not have access to.

▶ **Self-service creation of guest sessions from templates**—As much as the administration of guest sessions can be delegated to various administrators, when those administrators (or others in the organization) need to create a new guest session, the ability to delegate the creation of guest sessions is a core component of the VMM 2012 product. An administrator can delegate guest session creation to other users, nonadministrators, using the self-service portal Web console, shown in Figure 1.11, that is part of the Virtual Machine Manager 2012 product. A self-service user is given a set amount of resources like 8GB of RAM and four core processors to use as he or she wants. The user can create a single guest session using all 8GB and four cores, or the user can create four guest sessions running 2GB and a single core each, or any variation of resource allocation. This provides administrators the ability to share Hyper-V host resources without having to give a user full access to create as many guest sessions as he or she wants and impact the overall performance of the host servers in the environment.

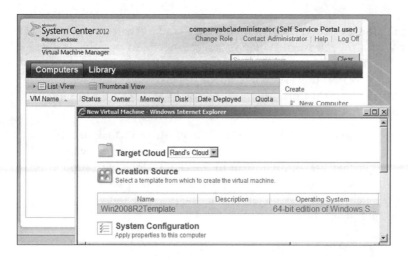

FIGURE 1.11   Self-service creation of guest sessions in VMM.

▶ **Manage both Hyper-V and VMware guest sessions**—Finally, as mentioned previously, VMM 2012 can connect to a VMware vSphere environment as well as directly manage VMware ESX servers, and as such can help an administrator in a mixed environment to manage and support virtual servers from both Microsoft and from VMware from a single console.

Background on System Center Virtual Machine Manager

System Center Virtual Machine Manager is a relative newcomer to the System Center family of products. From the first version of Virtual Server that came out in 2005 to the current version of Virtual Machine Manager 2012, Microsoft has made significant headway in advancing the virtualization support and features and functions of the product.

Some of the major revisions and history of the product are as follows:

▶ **Virtual Machine Manager 2007 (VMM 2007)**—Virtual Server 2005 entered the market to support virtual guest sessions running on Microsoft Virtual Server 2005. All of the current technologies like P2V, V2V, and delegated administration existed in the VMM 2007 product; however, because Virtual Server 2005 only supported 32-bit guest sessions and not 64-bit guest sessions, very few organizations adopted Virtual Server 2005 and, thus, VMM 2007 did not have a significant following.

▶ **Virtual Machine Manager 2008 (VMM 2008)**—With the release of Hyper-V in Windows Server 2008 along with the support for 64-bit hosts and guest sessions, now organizations had the ability of getting 5, 10, or 15 guest sessions on a single host server, and the ability to manage that many guest sessions suggested that a management tool was necessary. VMM 2008 was updated to support Hyper-V and as organizations started to deploy Hyper-V, more organizations started to install and use VMM 2008.

▶ **Virtual Machine Manager 2008 R2 (VMM 2008 R2)**—In less than a year, Microsoft updated Hyper-V with the release of Windows Server 2008 R2 so that Hyper-V R2 supported "live migration" failover between host servers. Hyper-V R2 was seen as enterprise ready and organizations started to adopt Hyper-V R2 as their server virtualization platform. At the same time, Microsoft released VMM 2008 R2 to support the added capabilities found in Hyper-V R2.

▶ **Virtual Machine Manager 2012 (VMM 2012)**—The release of Virtual Machine Manager 2012 provides a huge advancement in terms of supporting virtualized guest sessions whether they are on-premise or in the cloud, along with support for private cloud environments. Instead of looking just at a physical server, VMM 2012 can view the storage fabric, networking fabric, and the physical and virtual servers connected to the enterprise fabric.

What's New in System Center 2012 Virtual Machine Manager

Out of all of the System Center 2012 updates, System Center 2012 Virtual Machine Manager has had the most radical changes in terms of look and feel to the IT professional. VMM 2012 was completely rewritten with a focus on the cloud and fabric as the overall look and structure of the tool. VMM 2012 starts off with the premise that in order to build and deploy virtual images, the organization needs to have the appropriate storage subsystems and networking fabric in place. As such, the changes and additions to VMM 2012 over previous versions are pretty extensive. Some of the top new functions in VMM 2012 that are covered in this book include the following:

▶ **Inclusion of fabric management**—With the focus on being able to manage virtual machines and a mixed private and public cloud infrastructure, VMM 2012 starts with the configuration and management of fabric resources. VMM 2012 allows for the ability to create and manage Hyper-V clusters, use Citrix XenServers as target virtual hosts, and discover physical host systems and automatically make the host into a Hyper-V managed host server. VMM also allows for the configuration of network and storage resources, including creating logical networks, IP address pools, load balancing, storage logical units, and storage pools.

▶ **Support for private cloud configurations**—VMM 2012 allows for the creation of private clouds, including combining hosts, networks, storage subsystems, and resource libraries to identify a private cloud environment. Application profiles can then be created to automatically install server application virtualization (Server App-V), Web-deployed applications, Microsoft SQL data-tier applications (DACs), and creation of virtual guest sessions from virtual machine templates. A service template designer has been included to improve the template build process combined with automated deployment of templates to build private cloud infrastructure as required by the organization.

▶ **Administration improvements**—VMM 2012 adds administration improvements, including a new functionality in the Delegated Administrator and Self-Service User roles along with a Read-Only Administrator user role for better role-based access and management. Additionally, the ability to create and use RunAs accounts allows an organization to delegate administration and management tasks without having to directly give each role administrator critical credential access information.

▶ **Improvements in scalability and high availability**—Additions in VMM 2012 provide improvements for scalability by providing the ability to add additional virtual machines to a deployed service as well as update a service within a private cloud for dynamic growth as required by the application or needs of an organization. Additionally, VMM 2012 provides the ability to install a highly available VMM management server so that the management of VMM services can keep up with the demands and needs for reliability in an enterprise environment.

What to Expect in the System Center Virtual Machine Manager Chapters

In this book, two chapters are dedicated to the System Center Virtual Machine Manager product. These chapters are as follows:

▶ **Chapter 12, "Virtual Machine Manager 2012 Design, Planning, and Implementation"**—This chapter covers the architectural design, planning, and rollout of VMM 2012 in the enterprise. Concepts such as console servers, self-service portal servers, and management servers are defined with best practices shared on how to properly set up, configure, and tune VMM 2012.

▶ **Chapter 13, "Managing a Hyper-V Environment with Virtual Machine Manager 2012"**—This chapter covers the management and administration tasks in VMM. Performing tasks like delegated administration and self-service portals is covered and addressed in this chapter.

System Center 2012 Virtual Machine Manager, even just for the P2V and V2V capabilities, is of great value to organizations—let alone the ability for administrators to see all virtual servers in their environments along with the ability to delegate administration to others in their organizations. Jump to Chapters 12 and 13 of this book for specific information and deployment and configuration guidance on how VMM can be best leveraged in your enterprise.

Understanding System Center Service Manager

System Center Service Manager (SCSM) 2012 is an update to System Center Service Manager 2010 that Microsoft added to the System Center suite in 2010. SCSM 2010 took over five years to develop—something Microsoft built as an entire tool and released as a beta only to be pulled back, completely redone, and rereleased as a completely new and improved product. SCSM 2012 adds to what Microsoft released in the 2010 edition in its help desk and change-control management tool that rolls up information collected in other System Center products. SCSM 2012 provides IT staff the ability to track, manage, and report on information from all of the various System Center components. The System Center 2012 Service Manager Console, shown in Figure 1.12, is the focal point of the key management capabilities built in to SCSM.

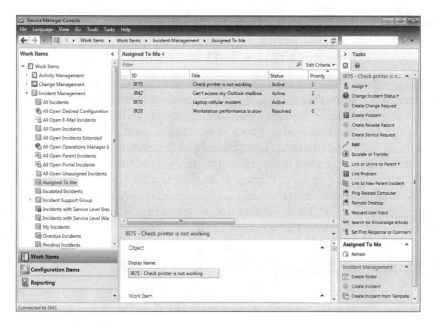

FIGURE 1.12   System Center Service Manager Console.

Business Solutions Addressed by System Center Service Manager

System Center 2012 Service Manager consolidates reports from client, server, physical, and virtual environments into a single reporting repository. SCSM allows an organization to leverage its investment in one System Center product into other System Center products. With the need to have formalized structure in change management, incident management, and reporting, SCSM leverages ITIL practices and procedures for an organization. Even being ITIL based, organizations that don't have a formal management practice can begin developing one based on the built-in processes in SCSM 2012.

Also important to organizations is managing and maintaining change-control processes so that network administrators don't patch or update systems in the middle of the day and accidentally bring down servers in the process. Or, as updates are needed on servers, rather than doing them one at a time, a maintenance window can be created where all updates are applied to a system at the same time. This managed change-control and maintenance process is something that SCSM 2012 helps to maintain and manage.

SCSM 2012 improves the integration between existing investments in System Center products, including inventory information, error reports, reporting details, and the like rolled up to SCSM for centralized information access and report generation.

Major Features of System Center Service Manager

System Center Service Manager is a very extensive product covering information report-ing and management; some of the major features in the product are as follows:

▶ **Incident management**—Incident management is probably better known as a "help desk"; however, beyond just taking in problem reports and processing the problem reports from users, SCSM ties into the System Center Operations Manager product so that errors and events coming off servers and workstations automatically trigger incident events in SCSM. Additionally, users can submit problem tickets or incidents, whether through a console screen or by submitting the request via email or even text message that enters the incident management system where help desk or IT staff can provide support and assistance. The incident management system in SCSM, as shown in Figure 1.13, provides the ability to have problems or incidents easily submitted to the organization's IT support personnel.

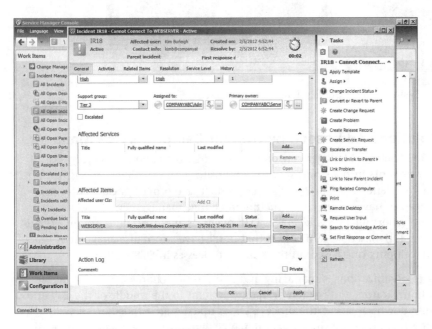

FIGURE 1.13   Incident management within SCSM.

▶ **Change control**—Built in to SCSM 2012 is a change-control monitoring and management system. Change control leverages a workflow process where a change request is submitted, and a workflow routes the change request to key personnel who need to review and approve the change to be performed. Beyond just a work-flow approval process, SCSM 2012 tracks that change control, logs the change, monitors and manages the change, and keeps a running record of the change so that if problems occur in the future on the system, the information about all histori-cal updates and changes is tracked and available for the administrators to see.

▶ **Consolidated reporting**—SCSM 2012 collects information from other Microsoft System Center products as well as creates connectors and links to the databases in other System Center products for consolidated reporting. Rather than having each individual database store isolated information, data from multiple sources can be viewed and analyzed to help make decisions about the operation, maintenance, and support of the environment.

▶ **Self-service access**—Rather than simply a help desk submission system, the self-service access feature in SCSM 2012 allows a user to search the knowledge base to see if anyone else in the organization has had the same problem and, if so, what the fix was to the problem. Many users would rather fix a problem themselves if the fix is known and works, and as such, SCSM tracks the problem tickets and solutions of previous fixes on systems and databases. The problems and solutions can be queried by the IT staff or by end users to share the knowledge and experiences of previous service requests.

Background on System Center Service Manager

System Center 2012 Service Manager is the second public release of the SCSM product line. As previously noted, Microsoft actually had a version 1.0 release several years ago as a SharePoint-based tool, which was called System Center Service Desk at the time that Microsoft released it in beta to a limited number of organizations. Although the feedback was very positive on the feature sets, because it was based on SharePoint (2003 at the time), the product did not fit into the mold of other System Center products, such as the robust management consoles found in System Center Configuration Manager or Operations Manager.

Microsoft went back to the drawing board and released a new version of System Center Service Manager, this time with the same management interface found in other System Center products. This release, probably dubbed v2.0 of the product, was limited to just help desk–type incident management and reporting at a time when all other management tools in the industry had evolved to support more than just trouble tickets, but to really address fully formed ITIL-based change-control and incident management systems.

Not ready yet for release, Microsoft spent another couple of years adding more functions to the Service Manager product to get it at par with what other service management tools on the marketplace included. With the release of System Center Service Manager 2010, the product is probably like a v3.0 or v4.0 of the product, with years of development, redevelopment, and updates before its formal debut.

Since that release of SCSM 2010, Microsoft has updated the forms, workflows, and integration with other System Center components and has really worked to improve the overall product. This leads to the System Center 2012 Service Manager product covered in this book.

What's New in System Center 2012 Service Manager

System Center 2012 Service Manager adds a number of new features and functions to the product over its predecessor, SCSM 2010 that released just a couple of years earlier. For the IT professional who has worked with SCSM 2010, the overall look and feel of SCSM has not changed, so for the most part an administrator can consider the update to SCSM 2012 as being more like a feature pack upgrade of new functionality. The focus of the additions to SCSM was to integrate SCSM into more System Center, Microsoft application, and non-Microsoft services and applications so that the integration and management from SCSM is better achieved. Some of the top new functions in SCSM 2012 that are covered in this book include the following:

▶ **Improved portal support**—System Center 2012 Service Manager provides a new self-service portal that provides extensive functionality for creating service requests and incident requests, the ability to browse the service catalog, functionality to search for knowledge-base articles, and the ability to approve and mark tasks and activities as completed. Administrators can create custom views to help simplify finding information on subsequent return visits to the portal, and a customizable web part provides the organization the ability to create views in SCSM 2012 with information specific to the needs of the organization or even to the needs of a specific administrator.

▶ **Enhancements in service catalog and service request functionality**—Improvements have been made to make the service catalog and service request tasks easier and more logical to use and execute tasks. Service offerings and request tasks can be more easily created, edited, and published, improving the efficiency in using SCSM 2012. Service requests can be reduced to templates that can then be duplicated to quickly enter or log pertinent information as efficiently as possible.

▶ **Ability to perform service-level management**—SCSM 2012 allows for the creation and editing of calendars along with the creation of service-level objects that can be monitored and measured so that reports can be generated to validate incident-level and service-level request performance. Alerts can be created to notify key personnel when there is a warning or a breach in targeted service-level agreement performance.

▶ **Tight integration with System Center 2012 Orchestrator and Virtual Machine Manager 2012**—SCSM 2012 includes connectors to tightly communicate with Orchestrator 2012 and VMM 2012, including the ability to create runbook templates in Orchestrator and automate service requests using the Orchestrator runbook activity functionality. And VMM 2012 data can be easily imported through the Operations Manager connector.

▶ **Authoring tool for customization**—SCSM 2012 includes an authoring tool that provides for great flexibility in customizing Service Manager in terms of views, templates, reports, tasks management, workflow, and operations specific to the needs of an enterprise.

▶ **Enhanced reporting and data warehouse support**—SCSM 2012 now aggregates data from Operations Manager and Configuration Manager to build custom reports. Reports can be stored for long-term analysis that includes the ability to view lists of cubes and the ability to access information from Microsoft Excel for easier portability of data for analysis purposes.

What to Expect in the System Center Service Manager Chapters

In this book, three chapters are dedicated to the System Center 2012 Service Manager product. These chapters are as follows:

▶ **Chapter 14, "Service Manager 2012 Design, Planning, and Implementation"**— This chapter covers the architectural design, server placement, and planning of the deployment of System Center 2012 Service Manager in the enterprise. The chapter addresses where to place management console servers as well as self-service portals for users to access, submit, and get responses back from the SCSM system. This chapter also covers the integration of SCSM 2012 into other System Center products as well as the integration of SCSM into Active Directory.

▶ **Chapter 15, "Using Service Manager 2012 for Incident Tracking and Help Desk Support"**—Chapter 15 drills down into incident tracking and help desk support features in SCSM 2012 on how to configure the tracking system as well as how IT personnel and users interact with the tracking and incident management system. This chapter also covers the self-service features and capabilities built in to System Center 2012 Service Manager.

▶ **Chapter 16, "Using Service Manager 2012 for Service Offerings and Change-Control Management"**—Chapter 16 details the change management control process where information comes in from System Center Operations Manager as well as from users and administrators to be managed and processed. This includes the workflow process, the integration of the workflow into day-to-day systems management, and the scheduled maintenance and update process key to a managed change-control system.

System Center 2012 Service Manager brings together the various System Center products into a single tool that helps IT organizations manage problems or incidents in their environments. Jump to Chapters 14 through 16 of this book for specific information and deployment and configuration guidance on how SCSM can be best leveraged in your enterprise.

Understanding System Center 2012 Orchestrator

System Center 2012 Orchestrator is one of the newest products added to the System Center line of products. Orchestrator 2012 was originally called Opalis, which Microsoft acquired in 2009/2010 and slipped into the System Center enterprise licensing suite in 2010. Orchestrator 2012 is a "runbook automation tool," which in plain English is simply a scripting tool that helps organizations build common processes and practices and allows those processes to be launched and run repeatedly with consistency.

Although scripting has been available and used in systems management processes for years, most of the scripts have been created from a variety of scripting languages (for example, Visual Basic, Visual C, Java, Windows Management Instrumentation [WMI])— with no auditing, no tracking, and no centralized management of the scripts. In environments that need to have, show, and prove regulated and managed processes, having a tool like System Center 2012 Orchestrator helps the organization have very clearly tracked and managed routines executed to complete key operational tasks.

The System Center 2012 Orchestrator main screen, shown in Figure 1.14, provides the main console for launching capacity assessments.

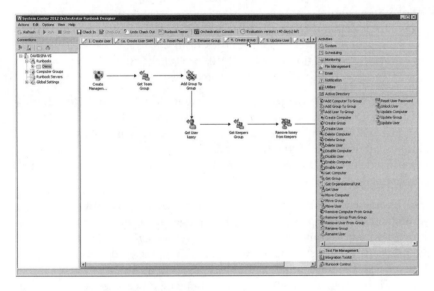

FIGURE 1.14   System Center Orchestrator main screen.

Business Solutions Addressed by System Center 2012 Orchestrator

In addressing automated runbook tasks, System Center 2012 Orchestrator is used to help organizations complete processes including generating consistent and timely reports, scanning and monitoring key systems, processing and auditing logs, transferring key data sets between systems, and the like. Orchestrator 2012 is a platform that runs processes, so it is up to the organization to determine what key processes it needs to have done, when the organization wants those processes done, and who should get updated that the processes have been completed.

Orchestrator 2012 is a key tool in facilitating business solutions for organizations. The key for organizations to determine is what the organization is required to track or manage, what step-by-step procedures need to be followed, and what audit trails need to tracked. The programmer working with Orchestrator 2012 will just take the processes and put them into code that will be entered into the Orchestrator authoring console to be tested and then ultimately implemented.

Flawed process will result in flawed end results. Failure to track key auditing tasks or required output components will result in the lack of key information being processed or generated. So the important part of Orchestrator 2012 is to sit down and write out all of the tasks that need to occur to meet the desired end goal. When properly documented on the front end, an organization will be able to see the results and outcome on the back end.

Major Features of System Center 2012 Orchestrator

The end goal in leveraging System Center 2012 Orchestrator is the ability to create, execute, and repeat processes that are well auditable and well documented that help the organization maintain standards within the enterprise. Key features in Orchestrator 2012 include the following:

▶ **Runbook creation**—The first step in Orchestrator 2012 is to create runbooks from known processes that include monitoring tasks and executing operational tasks from internal and external triggers. Commonly called a workflow process, organizations can take manual processes and put them into a runbook that is similarly designed and executed.

▶ **Runbook tester**—After a runbook has been created in System Center Orchestrator, it can be tested to validate that the script is working properly. The runbook tester runs through the process, as shown in Figure 1.15.

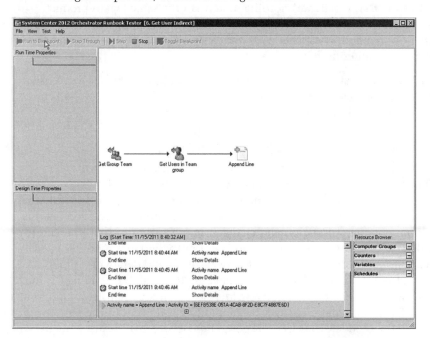

FIGURE 1.15   System Center 2012 Orchestrator Runbook Tester.

▶ **Process validation**—Once a runbook has been tested, the results need to be reviewed and confirmed that what was initiated resulted in the expected outcome. This process validation will ensure that the automation of a task results in a predictable outcome.

▶ **Reporting and documentation**—Orchestrator 2012 provides for reporting and ultimate documentation of the runbook task so that hard-copy or electronic copies of runbook processes properly document systems and operations.

▶ **Auditing review**—Orchestrator 2012 allows for the auditing of processes to ensure that appropriate individuals can test, validate, and confirm that the runbook process not only resulted in the proper end result, but also that the entire end-to-end process meets the needs, expectations, and operational requirements of the organization.

Background on System Center Orchestrator

System Center Orchestrator was acquired by Microsoft as a product called Opalis in 2009/2010. Opalis was around for more than five years prior to Microsoft's acquisition. Although Opalis did what it did very well, it was limited in its integration with other products, even its support in 2010 was for Microsoft's 2003 and 2005 products, not even the 2007 and 2010 line of Microsoft products. As such, the acquisition by Microsoft and the investment—Microsoft has the ability to invest in terms of product integration—has been key to the increased value of the product.

Throughout 2010 and 2011, Opalis was nothing more than the same Opalis product Microsoft had acquired with periodic enhancements released, including integration packs for System Center Configuration Manager 2007 and System Center Operations Manager 2007 among many other interim improvements.

System Center 2012 Orchestrator is more than just the rebranding of Opalis to a System Center named product, but also provides added consistency in integration support for other products in both Microsoft as well as non-Microsoft technologies.

What's New in System Center 2012 Orchestrator

System Center 2012 Orchestrator changes not only the name (from Opalis to Orchestrator), but also adds some new functionality. For the most part, though, Orchestrator is still based on the same back-end server platform engine and structure that the product Microsoft acquired a couple of years earlier (good and bad). The good part is that the product has not gone through major changes, so organizations that have already set up Opalis will be able to continue their development of the product. Another good part is that Microsoft has drastically improved the installation and deployment tools used to deploy Orchestrator 2012 to actually make it a *lot* easier to install. The bad part is that Orchestrator 2012 will eventually need to be rewritten to fit a more mainstream Microsoft product–line model, meaning major changes to the product will occur in the next two or three generations of the product. However, for now, Orchestrator 2012 is just a major cleanup and extension of Opalis that provides support for more Integration Packs (IPs) hooking Orchestrator into more applications for better support. Some of the top new functions in Orchestrator 2012 that are covered in this book include the following:

▶ **Simplification through standards and templates**—Orchestrator 2012 provides better standards, templates, and runbook controls that help administrators more easily create runbooks. Instead of requiring an administrator to manually build common sequences and tasks, Orchestrator 2012 provides more out-of-the-box functionality, making runbook creation easier than in the past.

▶ **Better integration with Microsoft and non-Microsoft technologies**—The key to runbook automation is to be able to support the common applications and operating environments common in an enterprise. And not just Microsoft technologies, but also key non-Microsoft technologies, as a common enterprise has a mix of solutions and technologies. Orchestrator 2012 includes support through Integration Packs for all of the 2012 System Center technologies like Configuration Manager 2012, Operations Manager 2012, Data Protection Manager 2012, Virtual Machine Manager 2012, and Service Manager 2012. And for non-Microsoft technologies, in addition to updated support for Integration Packs available in the earlier Opalis version of the product, Microsoft added support for runbook automation for VMware vSphere as well as IBM Netcool/OMNIbus support.

▶ **Extensibility for custom integration**—Orchestrator 2012 includes an extensible integration toolkit that provides for the ability to create customer integrations that allows Orchestrator 2012 to connect to other environments where existing Integration Packs do not exist. Runbook tasks can be triggered both manually at the request of an administrator, or automatically through a trigger or launch of another runbook or application task to ensure that Orchestrator 2012 provides key management operations for an enterprise.

What to Expect in the System Center Orchestrator Chapter

In this book, a single chapter is dedicated to the System Center Orchestrator product. Chapter 17, "Orchestrator 2012 Implementation and Automation," covers the base installation of Orchestrator through common automation tasks created and used by organizations on a day-to-day basis.

System Center 2012 Orchestrator is not a common Microsoft operating system/application installation product, so the installation is a little more unique. The original Opalis product is built on using Java Virtual Machine (JVM), and even with Orchestrator 2012, Microsoft has retained the JVM runtime as the core operating environment of the product. However, unlike the original Opalis versions that required the implementer to go find and download various JVM components from all over the Internet, Microsoft has simplified the installation process so that everything needed is packed in the Orchestrator 2012 installer, and the basic configuration is executed like any other Microsoft product.

Once installed, Chapter 17 walks through a number of common Orchestrator 2012 runtime automation scripts to familiarize you with what Orchestrator can do. From basic automated Active Directory tasks to more complicated application-specific scripts, the chapter provides a solid background to get you, an Orchestrator developer, headed down the right path to get the best use out of the Orchestrator 2012 product.

Understanding System Center Licensing

System Center is sold and licensed only as a suite with all of the System Center components bundled together. It is always best to visit the Microsoft website (http://www.microsoft.com/systemcenter/en/us/pricing-licensing.aspx) to best understand the current licensing scheme as the licensing model changes, or better yet, contact a licensing specialist who can provide information on special discounts that apply based on your organization's purchasing and licensing contract.

However, in general, the core System Center products, including System Center Configuration Manager, System Center Operations Manager, System Center Data Protection Manager, System Center Virtual Machine Manager, System Center Service Manager, and System Center Orchestrator are all sold as a server license suite along with a client access or endpoint system license.

The server license is typically the main license for the application itself. As an example, SCCM and SCOM require a server to host the software, and, thus, the server itself needs to have a System Center 2012 license. Likewise, SCCM and SCOM also have client systems associated with the servers that are managed; in the case of SCCM, which patches, updates, and manages workstations, an SCCM client license is required for each client system under management. For SCOM, because frequently it is a server that is being monitored and managed, the SCOM managed endpoint needs to have a System Center 2012 endpoint license.

Core Client Access Licenses

For products that have client access licenses like SCCM, Microsoft bundles licenses within their client license platform. As an example, organizations that have a core client access license, or CoreCAL, that provides them rights to use Windows, standard Exchange features, and standard SharePoint features, the CoreCAL also includes a license for SCCM. Pretty much every mid- and large-sized enterprise has an enterprise agreement with the CoreCAL and, as such, these organizations already own the client license for SCCM. All the organization needs to do is purchase a server license for System Center to be able to set up a full SCCM-managed environment.

Server Management Suite Volume Licensing

For products where Microsoft licenses the products based on servers, an organization can purchase a System Center 2012 Datacenter license or a System Center 2012 Standard license. More details on Microsoft licensing are available at http://www.microsoft.com/licensing/licensing-options/enrollments.aspx.

But, in general, a System Center 2012 Datacenter license provides an organization the ability to run an unlimited number of copies of System Center 2012 components on an unlimited number of virtual guest sessions running on the host server with up to two physical processors. The System Center 2012 Standard license provides the ability for an organization to run any/all of the System Center 2012 components on up to two instances per server, whether that is running just a single instance of the System Center 2012 component on a single physical server, or running a host and a guest instance of System Center 2012 on a virtualized server with a single guest session.

Additionally, Microsoft has simplified the SQL Server licensing requirements for System Center, now allowing an organization to run the included SQL Server 2008 Standard Edition server without having to purchase SQL Server or any SQL client licenses. The version of SQL Server that comes with System Center 2012 is the same SQL Server Standard Edition that can be installed on any system, just from a licensing perspective, no separate licenses are required for SQL Server.

Microsoft has several discount levels on licensing and it is best to discuss the licensing requirements as well as specific license pricing with an organization that can assess the licensing pricing level of your organization.

Summary

This first chapter of the book was intended to provide you, the reader, with a background of the various System Center products available, how the products fit into the management scheme of an organization, and what to expect in the subsequent chapters in this book.

Overall, the life cycle in an enterprise has a system operating system deployed on a system using System Center Configuration Manager that also patches and updates the system and keeps the system in a standardized configuration. The System Center Operations Manager product then monitors the system, whether a server or a client system, and proactively alerts administrators of any pending problems.

The System Center Data Protection Manager backs up server and application data and provides the ability for the administrator or even an end user to recover information based on as little as 15-minute increments of time. In addition, the System Center Virtual Machine Manager product helps to manage physical and virtual server systems, including the conversion of physical systems to virtual guest sessions as well as intelligently placing guest sessions on physical servers with the most available capacity.

The overall tool that helps an organization manage its environment is the System Center Service Manager that provides incident management, change control, and consolidated reporting for servers and client systems within the environment.

Enterprises that need to have consistency in runtime processes can leverage System Center Orchestrator to build scripts and processes that can be automated for real-time or scheduled tasks.

All of these tools are purchased in a bundled suite to simplify licensing and purchasing of System Center 2012. The focus of this book is to help you, the reader, better understand not only what the products are, but how the products tie together so that you can develop an overall strategy for managing and administering your servers and client systems throughout your enterprise.

Best Practices

The following are best practices from this chapter:

▶ Utilize the capabilities built in to System Center Configuration Manager to deploy the base operating system for both servers and client systems in your enterprise.

▶ Use templates and standard configurations so that all system images and all applications deployed use the same settings and parameters for organizational consistency.

▶ Leverage the System Center Configuration Manager product's Compliance Settings if you want to enforce policy-based system standards.

▶ Implement System Center Configuration Manager to support HTTPS for remote and mobile systems that need to be managed, but rarely or never VPN or directly connect to the network backbone.

▶ Use System Center Operations Manager to proactively monitor systems and alert IT of any pending problems.

▶ Utilize the event-correlation capabilities of SCOM to more easily isolate system problems and errors to root causes of the problems.

▶ Implement the application-monitoring capabilities of SCOM to monitor specific application sessions critical to the safe operations of an application server.

▶ Back up servers and applications with System Center Data Protection Manager using incremental timed backups for more flexibility on recovery of information.

▶ Choose to back up secondary systems in an environment (such as the second node of a cluster) so as to not impact the performance of the primary server during a backup.

▶ Consider pushing DPM backup data to a cloud service provider and eliminate tapes altogether in an enterprise by having short-term backups reside on the DPM server and long-term backups reside in the cloud.

▶ Use the System Center Virtual Machine Manager product to manage physical host servers of both Microsoft Hyper-V and VMware host systems for centralized virtual host management.

▶ Use the physical-to-virtual (P2V) tool in VMM to convert physical servers into virtual guest sessions.

▶ Use the virtual-to-virtual (V2V) tool in VMM to convert virtual guest sessions (either Hyper-V or VMware) into Hyper-V virtual guest sessions.

▶ For organizations that delegate administration to multiple levels of administrators, use the administration delegation feature in VMM to distribute rights to multiple administrators.

▶ To allocate virtual host resources to users to create guest sessions as they require, use the Self-Service Portal feature in VMM to assign usable templates and configuration options for users.

▶ Implement the System Center Service Manager product to centralize incident management in the organization and provide help desk controls for IT personnel throughout the organization.

▶ Leverage the change-control capabilities in SCSM to ensure and to enforce the organization's change-control policies in the enterprise.

▶ Provide self-service capabilities to users so they can submit problems and incidents themselves and can check to see if there are known fixes to the problems where they can fix the problem quickly and easily themselves.

▶ Use System Center Orchestrator to automate mundane tasks to ensure the process is run consistently each and every time.

▶ Leverage System Center Orchestrator to create and execute processes that require auditing and reporting so that the tasks in the script are clearly documented and the outcome can be reviewed by auditors to ensure successful compliance completion.

CHAPTER 2

Configuration Manager 2012 Design and Planning

IN THIS CHAPTER

▶ What's New in ConfigMgr 2012

▶ Explaining How Configuration Manager Works

▶ Understanding Content Distribution

▶ Understanding Asset Management

▶ Reporting from Configuration Manager

▶ Configuration Manager Architecture Components

▶ Securing Configuration Manager

▶ Understanding Component Requirements

▶ Configuration Manager Design Considerations

▶ Understanding Client Schedules

▶ Planning for Internet-Based Client Management

▶ Putting It All Together in a Design

▶ Best Practices

System Center Configuration Manager (SCCM) 2012 provides the comprehensive end-to-end management of Windows systems. This includes current Windows-based servers, workstations, laptops, and mobile devices. Configuration Manager helps administrators simplify and automate enterprise management while providing greater administrative control and insight into the infrastructure.

With Configuration Manager 2012, also known as ConfigMgr, an organization can achieve a greater level of environmental automation and life-cycle management of assets. With Configuration Manager, an administrator can efficiently deploy Windows-based servers and user operating systems to a bare-metal hardware or as a migration from a previous operating system. Newly deployed and existing operating systems can be easily managed internally with a highly scalable, distributed infrastructure, and over the Internet through Configuration Manager's secure web-based services. Software can be published for on-demand installation and provisioned automatically to managed endpoints. Patch compliance can be easily monitored and updates systematically deployed based on preset conditions, such as collection-based recurring windows designated for maintenance. Settings and the configuration of objects on managed endpoints can be closely monitored through an extensible management engine. Reports can be easily developed and subscriptions created through a highly scalable reporting infrastructure based on SQL Server Reporting Services.

For Configuration Manager to accomplish all this effectively, the infrastructure must be designed and implemented properly. This ensures that the systems have the resources and capacity to handle the anticipated data flows and storage requirements. To be able to create an effective design, a good understanding of the Configuration Manager components, requirements, and constraints is important.

What's New in ConfigMgr 2012

Configuration Manager 2012 includes a large number of long-awaited upgrades and enhancements to the existing product. From a complete redesign of the legacy console, to changes to the site roles of hierarchy, to role-based administration, to numerous improvements in the operations, the new Configuration Manager 2012 is a much improved and mature product.

Redesigned Console

The console in Configuration Manager 2012 has been redesigned to be more in line with the other System Center products, featuring a workspace model with a context-sensitive ribbon that displays only the appropriate tasks and options for the current selection.

The various operations that need to be performed in Configuration Manager are logically grouped into workspaces. These workspaces are as follows:

▶ Assets and Compliance

▶ Software Library

▶ Monitoring

▶ Administration

When using the console, the administrator only sees the workspaces and nodes within the workspaces that have been assigned to that administrator by role-based administration.

In addition, an extensive search capability has been built in to the console to allow administrators to quickly find objects and data.

Although existing Configuration Manager 2007 administrators might find the console confusing and have difficulty locating familiar settings, they will likely find that the console is far more efficient once they are familiar with it.

Hierarchy Changes

A number of hierarchy changes in Configuration Manager 2012 improve, simplify, or add new functionality.

Site architecture changes include the following:

▶ **Central Administration Site**—The new central administration site formalizes the central site concept, eliminating its ability to support clients directly.

▶ **Primary Site**—In Configuration Manager 2012, primary sites support more clients. Primary sites cannot have child primary sites, which flattens the hierarchy. Primary sites are no longer boundaries of security or agent settings, allowing more flexible agent settings and security settings based on requirements rather than architecture. Taken together, these changes allow primary sites to support enterprise organizations much more effectively.

▶ **Secondary Site**—Secondary sites now require SQL Server, which can be SQL Server Express. The local database replicates configuration information from the parent primary site, allowing for more efficient and effective data transfers. Secondary sites now automatically include a Distribution Point and a Management Point as well.

General site changes include the following:

▶ **Database replication**—Database replication is used to copy and merge data between sites servers in the hierarchy. This reduces the replication requirements and allows a multimaster model, ensuring that all sites share the same information.

▶ **Native mode removed**—The Native Mode option has been removed in favor of a role selectable option. This allows much greater flexibility over the all-or-nothing Native mode.

▶ **HTTPS selectable by roles**—The option for secure communications with certificates (HTTPS) is now selectable by role, eliminating the need for Native mode.

▶ **Fallback site**—If the client cannot locate a site automatically, there is now an option to designate a site as a fallback site. Thus, clients will always be assigned to a site, rather than being unmanaged.

▶ **Exchange Server Connector**—This connector allows SCCM to find and manage mobile devices that are connected to Exchange via the ActiveSync protocol. This allows mobile devices to be managed by SCCM when the SCCM agent cannot be installed on the mobile device.

▶ **Endpoint Protection**—System Center 2012 Endpoint Protection is now integrated into SCCM 2012. The Endpoint Protection server is now a Site System role and the Endpoint Protection client is now a setting in the SCCM client.

▶ **Content library**—The new content library in SCCM 2012 stores all content. This includes content files for software updates, applications, operating system deployment, and any other content. The content library is a single instance store, ensuring that content files are not unnecessarily duplicated.

The hierarchy and site changes provide a host of new features and improvements over the previous version of SCCM.

Site System Role Changes

Configuration Manager 2012 includes a number of Site System role changes that simplify and improve operations. These include new Site System roles, enhancements to existing Site System roles, and elimination of unnecessary Site System roles.

New Site System roles include the following:

▶ **Application Catalog Website Point and Web Services Point**—The Application Catalog Website Point is a new role that provides users with a list of available software. The Application Catalog Web Services Point provides software information to the Website Point from the new software library.

▶ **Enrollment Point**—The Enrollment Point uses certificates to complete the mobile device enrollment.

▶ **Endpoint Protection Point**—The Endpoint Protection Point implements the anti-malware features of SCCM 2012, using the System Center 2012 Endpoint Protection.

Enhancements to Site System roles include the following:

▶ **Management Points include automatic load balancing**—Management Points now include automatic load balancing within the primary site and don't use Network Load Balancing (NLB). This simplifies installation and allows for greater scalability.

▶ **Multiple Internet-based Management Points**—Sites can now be configured with multiple Internet-based Management Points. This allows clients to locate their closest Internet-based Management Point when on the Internet, allowing for greater fault tolerance and scalability.

▶ **Management Points include server locator functionality**—Including this functionality in the Management Points simplifies installation and administrative complexity, and now all Management Points include those capabilities.

▶ **Distribution Points include PXE functionality**—Distribution Points now incorporate the PXE Point functionality, which simplifies installation and administrative complexity.

▶ **Distribution Points supported on servers and workstations**—Installation of Distribution Points is now supported on both servers and workstations, eliminating the need for the Branch Distribution Point.

Site system roles that have been removed are as follows:

▶ **Reporting Point**—The legacy ASP-based Reporting Point has now been completely replaced by the Reporting Services Point.

▶ **PXE Service Point**—The PXE Service Point functionality has been rolled into the Distribution Point and the role has been eliminated.

▶ **Server Locator Point**—The Server Locator Point functionality has been rolled into the Management Point and the role has been eliminated.

▶ **Branch Distribution Point**—The standard Distribution Point now supports workstations and prestaged content, so the Branch Distribution Point role has been eliminated.

Operations Changes

A number of operations changes have been made in SCCM 2012 that address long-
standing issues within the previous version of the product.

A few of the major operations changes include the following:

▶ **State-based alerting**—SCCM 2012 now includes alerting in the console. These alerts
provide status information on conditions within the SCCM infrastructure. This
allows administrators to understand the current state of their environment and to
receive e-mails in the event of any alerts.

> **NOTE**
>
> These alerts are not designed to replace those found in Operations Manager 2012,
> but rather to supplement those alerts.

▶ **Remote control Control+Alt+Delete**—The SCCM 2012 agent remote control functionality now includes the ability for an administrator to press Control+Alt+Delete
on remote computers. This allows the ability to unlock computers or log on to
computers, a feature sorely missed in SCCM 2007.

▶ **Automatic client push to all systems**—This includes pushing agents not only to
discovered systems, but also to the systems that don't have agents. This ensures
better coverage of agent deployments.

▶ **Automatic upgrade for clients below threshold**—Automatic agent upgrades can be
configured for agents whose client version falls below a certain revision.

▶ **64-bit client**—SCCM 2012 now includes a native 64-bit agent, rather than a 32-bit
agent that works on 64-bit computers.

▶ **Custom hardware inventory replaces `sms_def.mof` editing**—Rather than the error-
fraught editing of the `sms_def.mof`, there is now a graphical user interface for
extending hardware inventory.

▶ **Application management**—SCCM 2012 now includes applications. These are
enhancements to the standard software deployment functionality, including different methods of deployment, device affinity, monitoring, and client self-service.

▶ **Task sequence deployment via IBCM**—Task sequences can now be deployed to
Internet-based clients, though operating systems cannot be deployed via IBCM. This
allows flexible multistep deployments with conditions.

▶ **Compliance Settings support remediation**—Compliance Settings in SCCM 2012, formerly Desired Configuration Management (DCM), now allow for remediation of detected compliance issues.

These changes address operational functionality issues that administrators had on their wish lists for a long time.

Administration Changes

Configuration Manager 2012 includes a number of administration changes that make it easier for administrators to manage the infrastructure. This includes security administration, recovery, installation changes, and the reduction of repetitive tasks.

Some of the major administration changes include the following:

▶ **Role-based administration**—SCCM 2012 moves from a site-based instance permissions model, to a role-based hierarchy model. Roles are configured at the hierarchy level, with the appropriate scopes and permissions. This allows much greater flexibility in assigning rights, while at the same time reducing administrative effort.

▶ **Automatic Active Directory site and subnet detection for boundaries**—SCCM 2012 will automatically detect Active Directory sites and subnets from the configuration container. In large, complex environments with frequent changes, this can save a tremendous amount of time and ensure that SCCM effectively covers the environment.

▶ **Prerequisite checker**—The standalone prerequisite checker provides accurate information on the requirements when installing Site Systems, both from installation media and when pushing secondary sites from the console. This allows administrators to remediate potential issues in advance of installation.

▶ **Improved recovery options**—Recovery options are now integrated into the SCCM Setup Wizard. Additional recovery options include recovering the entire Site Server or recovering the Site Server database. In addition, recovery uses data replication to get the latest objects from other Site Servers in the hierarchy.

Combined with the improved console, the administration changes to Configuration Manager 2012 have the potential to dramatically improve the effort-to-value ratio for administrators.

Explaining How Configuration Manager Works

Configuration Manager is a sophisticated system that effectively allows for large-scale management of Microsoft Windows-based systems. Organizations with an investment in Microsoft technologies will find that Configuration Manager allows for an unprecedented ability to keep on top of any size environment. In its simplest form, Configuration

Manager provides enterprise management of active Windows client and server assets. The data collected from managed systems can be used directly for IT life-cycle management along with security, configuration, and compliance management.

> **NOTE**
>
> For organizations with existing configuration management database (CMDB) implementations, use Configuration Manager to supply data for Windows-based managed assets. This can be accomplished several different ways, including through the predefined SQL views and the Windows Management Instrumentation (WMI) provider.

Configuration Manager implements the concept of sites. A Configuration Manager site has a designated set of boundaries, to which the site provides management functionality. In a small enterprise, this might be a single server responsible for managing all systems across the entire network. In a large enterprise, this typically consists of several different Configuration Manager sites.

Sites can be linked together to form a hierarchy; each site in the hierarchy is assigned one or more boundaries to which the site provides management functionality. Configuration Manager boundaries are defined within the Configuration Manager console and can be based on Active Directory sites, IP subnets, IP ranges, IPv6 prefixes, or a combination of several different boundary types.

Within each Configuration Manager site, separate roles can be established. A Configuration Manager role provides a specific type of functionality. For example, the Distribution Point role stores content and provides a way for managed systems to efficiently download that content.

> **NOTE**
>
> The Distribution Point is one of the key roles in Configuration Manager. It is very important to place Distribution Points in the correct locations to make effective use of available bandwidth.

Another key role is the Management Point. This role facilitates the majority of client communication. For example, when a managed system has been told to install a software update, it asks the Management Point for a list of local Distribution Points. The Management Point provides appropriate Distribution Points for the client to choose among, based on where the client is located within the Configuration Manager hierarchy. During the process of installing the software update, the client sends state messages back to the Management Point. These state messages provide details and insight as to what the client is doing, such as "Downloading content" or "Installing updates." The Management Point delivers the state messages to the Site Server. An administrator can use the Configuration Manager reports to monitor the status of software update deployments based on these state messages. The Management Point is also used when the client submits various reports, such as the Hardware Inventory report or the Compliance report.

Managed systems are assigned to a single site within the hierarchy. A managed system can be a server, workstation, laptop, mobile device, or any number of Windows-based systems. Managed systems are referred to as clients of Configuration Manager. Each client is assigned to a single site within the hierarchy, which is referred to as the client's *assigned* site. The client almost always communicates with the Management Point in its assigned site to retrieve policies and submit data, such as the Hardware Inventory report.

When Active Directory schema extensions have been implemented, a client can use the information published in Active Directory to locate and communicate with a Management Point in a different site. This is called roaming, and allows a client to travel to a different site and ask the local Management Point for a list of local Distribution Points.

> **NOTE**
>
> Roaming is only used for locating local Distribution Points for content. The client still communicates with its assigned site for policy updates and to submit data.

Configuration Manager clients are told what to do through policies. A policy is dynamically created based on configuration done by an administrator in the Configuration Manager Console. For example, from within the Configuration Manager Administration Console, a software package can be assigned to one or more clients by an administrator. When the clients to which the software package has been assigned query the Management Point, they'll receive the policy that tells the client what software has been assigned, how to execute the software, when to install the software, how long the software should take to install, along with all the other details that allow the software package to be installed correctly. Policies also include configuration settings, such as how often to check with the Management Point for new policies and how often to run a hardware and software inventory scan.

Understanding the Hierarchy

The Site Server is the core component in the Configuration Manager hierarchy. The Site Server role manages the other roles that facilitate the different areas of client systems management, such as content provisioning and asset management. Site Servers can be configured in a hierarchical model. This parent/child relationship can be grown both horizontally and vertically for a high degree of scalability.

A multilevel Configuration Manager hierarchy is shown in Figure 2.1.

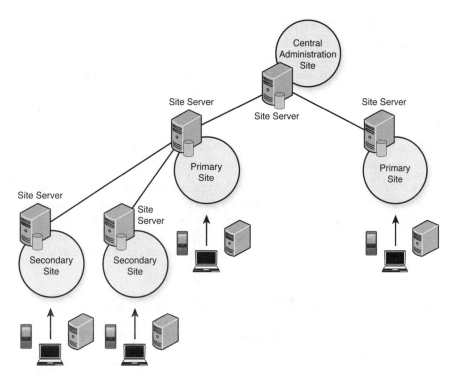

FIGURE 2.1   Configuration Manager 2012 hierarchy.

Each site in the hierarchy must be configured with a three-character site code. Site codes must be unique and shouldn't be reused to avoid potential replication issues. Valid site codes contain letters and numbers, and cannot be Windows-reserved AUX, CON, NUL, or PRN names.

In a multisite hierarchy, Configuration Manager can be managed from any primary site. It is important to note that the Configuration Manager hierarchy is typically managed from the central site as this provides access to the entire infrastructure and all managed systems. Opening a Configuration Manager Administration Console on a lower-level primary child site only provides access to clients assigned to that site and child sites below that site.

Site Servers in a parent/child relationship communicate with each other through Site Senders and Addresses, as well as database replication. The Site Sender controls how many processing threads can be active at any given time and how often to retry the delivery if a problem occurs. Site Addresses can be used to control the bandwidth utilization between sites. Addresses provide both a schedule and data rate limits to throttle communication between Site Servers.

Understanding Secondary Sites and Management Points

In addition to primary sites, Configuration Manager provides an infrastructure component referred to as a secondary site. Secondary sites control content distribution for clients in locations with limited bandwidth, typically across the wide area network (WAN) link.

When a client is located within the network boundaries supported by a secondary site and a Management Point, the client communicates with the Management Point to receive policies and send inventory data and state messages. The secondary site communicates with the primary sites based on Site Senders and Addresses, as well as database replication.

If the secondary site doesn't have a Management Point configured, the site is only used to manage bandwidth. For example, if an administrator at a primary site assigns a package to a Distribution Point that belongs to a secondary site, the content first travels from the primary site to the secondary site, and then the secondary site is responsible for placing the content on the Distribution Point. The bandwidth between the primary site and the secondary site can be managed with Site Addresses.

> **NOTE**
>
> By default, the contents of a package are pushed to Distribution Points from the Site Server that created the package. Enable the *Send Package from the Nearest Site in the Hierarchy* option to make effective use of Senders and Addresses.

The secondary site along with the Management Point doesn't provide a significant savings in network bandwidth. Deploying a secondary site does, however, provide the ability to manage bandwidth with Site Senders and Addresses. Instead of using a secondary site with a Management Point, consider using a Distribution Point to manage bandwidth.

> **NOTE**
>
> In SCCM 2012, secondary sites by default are installed with both Management Points and Distribution Points. This ensures that secondary sites are achieving their maximal benefit.

Understanding AD Schema Extensions and Client Roaming

The Active Directory (AD) schema should be extended to support dynamic client assignment during Configuration Manager agent deployment and to assist clients with the location of the local Configuration Manager server infrastructure after deployment. When the Active Directory schema is extended, clients can use the values provided through Active Directory to locate Configuration Manager infrastructure servers and automatically choose the correct site assignment during installation.

CAUTION

Take the appropriate safety measures when extending the Active Directory schema. Changes to the schema cannot be easily reversed; plan to test the schema extensions in a preproduction environment before implementing them in your production environment.

The Configuration Manager infrastructure, along with Active Directory integration, provides clients with the ability to roam the entire Configuration Manager infrastructure and find the closest Distribution Point (DP) to receive content. A client will attempt to get content from a local Distribution Point before a remote Distribution Point.

NOTE

Global roaming can only be achieved when the Active Directory schema has been extended. If the schema hasn't been extended, only regional roaming is available. Regional roaming only allows client roaming to child sites below the client's assigned site.

When a client is started or changes networks, a local discovery is triggered to identify the closest Management Point. If the client has a policy that requires the installation of content, such as software updates, the client queries the closest Management Point for local Distribution Points. This Management Point is referred to as the resident or local Management Point. If a local Management Point is not available, the client defaults back to its assigned Management Point.

The resident Management Point provides the client with a list of Distribution Points that currently have the correct content. The agent evaluates the list of DPs and chooses the most appropriate DP to obtain content based on several factors. For example, the client will choose BITS-enabled Distribution Points over non-BITS Distribution Points. Client roaming between peer sites is shown in Figure 2.2. When the client assigned to the site CA1 roams to the site FN1, the client queries the Management Point in the site FN1 for a list of Distribution Points when it needs to obtain content such as software and software updates.

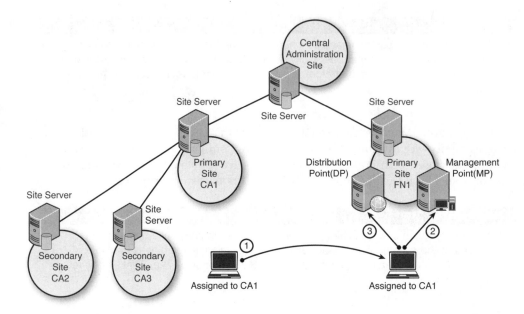

FIGURE 2.2   Client roaming.

To receive new policies and submit data, such as inventory reports and state messages, the managed system still must communicate with its assigned Management Point—the Management Point in the site the client was assigned. This is because the Management Point queries the Configuration Manager Site Database to acquire client-specific policies and only the assigned Site Database has this information. Other Site Servers are not aware of clients from different sites in the hierarchy, and cannot provide policy updates or provide a way for the client to submit inventory data.

Understanding Content Distribution

Configuration Manager provides a highly scalable content distribution, execution, and reporting system. Several of Configuration Manager's key roles have been designed specifically to facilitate the provisioning of software, software updates, and operating systems.

Application Management

Application management provides a way to publish and distribute software to user targets and managed system targets. The application management features provide a reliable method to deploy and update software while maintaining control over the different aspects of delivery. From who gets licensed software to how much bandwidth is available in remote locations can all be defined through the Configuration Manager Administration Console.

There are two forms of application management, the traditional Packages and the new Applications.

Packages

Packages provide the same functionality, albeit with some name changes, as the SCCM 2007 R2 Software Distribution. You should become familiar with the following software distribution terminology:

▶ **Package**—The package consists of the software name, version number, and manufacturer. The package installation files' source location and distribution settings are also defined within the package. Each package container holds the Access Account, Distribution Points, and Programs subcontainers.

▶ **Program**—The program is a component of the package and defines how the content is executed on the target. This includes settings, such as the command line, maximum runtime, disk space requirements, and execution environment. A package can contain several programs, each with a unique configuration.

▶ **Deployment**—The deployment, formerly known as an advertisement, makes a package/program combination available on target systems. The deployment controls when and where the content is executed. This includes the target collection, execution schedule, and how to obtain content from Distribution Points.

Software can be published for a set of users or computers. When software is published, the user has the ability to execute the software when it's convenient for them. This is often beneficial for more savvy technical users, such as IT staff; however, nontechnical users can quickly get the hang of self-service software distribution with a little training.

Software can also be installed automatically based on a predefined schedule. This is a convenient way to systematically update computers when the user is not using the system, during nonpeak hours, or when the installation simply must occur.

A Configuration Manager administrator creates advertisements for a package/program combination. For example, a package can be created called Microsoft Office 2010. This package would tell Configuration Manager the name and versions of the software, where to locate the installation files, and the priority for replicating the information to other sites in the hierarchy.

One or more programs can be created for the package. Each program defines a command line to execute the software, how much disk space is needed, if the user can interact with the installation, and many other elements. Being able to create multiple programs for each package is beneficial, as different command lines can perform different types of installations, removals, and updates. For example, silently installing Microsoft Office 2010 on a new system requires a different command line than performing an update to an existing installation.

Applications

Applications in Configuration Manager 2012 are fundamentally usercentric, allowing users to be associated with devices and then targeting applications at users. This allows software to follow users, no matter which device they're using.

Applications support a wider array of constraints and options than packages, including detection of the installation, requirements such as processor or language for installation, and other application dependencies. This allows the administrator to control exactly what systems are allowed to install the application.

The application terminology is similar to the package terminology:

▶ **Application**—The application consists of the software name, version number, and manufacturer. The application distribution settings are defined within the package, including additional information, such as references and supersedence.

▶ **Deployment type**—The deployment type is a component of the applications and defines how the content is executed on the target. This includes settings such as content location, download behavior, the command line to run the install, maximum runtime, disk space requirements, and execution environment. It also includes the detection methods to identify if the application is installed—for enforcement purposes. An application can contain several deployment types, each with a unique configuration.

▶ **Deployment**—The deployment, formerly known as an advertisement, makes a package/program combination available on target systems. The deployment controls when and where the content is executed. This includes the target collection, execution schedule, user experience options, and console alert options.

The new applications method of deploying software provides a wealth of new options geared toward usercentric deployments, which is something that has been requested by administrators for many years.

Software Update Distribution

Patch management features provide insight into all the Microsoft security vulnerabilities throughout the Windows infrastructure. Compliance statistics for the infrastructure can be published through reports and email subscriptions, and updates can be easily deployed to managed systems.

You should become familiar with the following software update distribution terminology:

▶ **All Software Updates**—The All Software Updates container shows all the metadata synchronized from Microsoft Update through the Windows Server Update Services (WSUS) component integration. The updates listed here are broken down by category for relatively simple navigation.

▶ **Software Update Groups**—A software update group, formerly update list, is a list of updates and a way to report on the compliance for the updates. Individual updates are added from the All Software Updates container to the update list or automatically via an automatic deployment rule. If updates are added to an update group, these new updates are automatically deployed.

> ▶ **Automatic Deployment Rules**—An automatic deployment rule, formerly deployment template, is settings for deploying updates to a collection. The automatic deployment rule contains information such as the name of the collection, if updates should restart the target system, custom notification options, update deadlines, and if the system should be restarted outside of the predefined maintenance windows. The automatic deployment rule also contains criteria for automatically selecting updates to be deployed and an evaluation schedule, hence automating the deployment.

At a high level, the software update process consists of two parts. This is similar to a package/advertisement configuration of a standard software distribution. The first part of the deployment contains a list of updates and is primarily used to get the update files to Distribution Points. The second part of the deployment is responsible for advertising the software updates on managed systems and controls the deadline to install updates. The All Software Updates, Software Update Group, and Automatic Deployment Rule are used to assist with the creation of the two software update parts. For additional information, see Chapter 4, "Using Configuration Manager 2012 to Distribute Software, Updates, and Operating Systems."

Like the software distribution features, an administrator establishes the contents of the deployment and the installation options. However, with software updates, additional features are available beyond standard software distribution. The polling cycle for software updates is independent, so clients can become aware of new software update assignments quickly. Software updates can be configured with the ability to rescan and redeploy missing updates during subsequent deployment if previously approved patches have been removed.

Operating System Deployment

With operating system deployment functionality, the IT department can commoditize the provisioning of all Windows workstation and server systems. This is achieved through modular image-based and full-file deployment of operating systems to both new and existing hardware platforms. After the operating system is deployed, the IT department can leverage the extensive reporting and asset management functionality to improve and assist with the infrastructure decision-making process. For example, having accurate reports on the hardware of workstations makes the assessment of the requirements to deploy newer operating systems significantly easier.

Common OS deployment technologies are as follows:

> ▶ **WinPE**—The Windows Preinstallation Environment runs a small version of Windows used to initiate the OS deployment. The WinPE environment is typically initiated over the network with the PXE Service Point.

> ▶ **Operating system source**—This is the location of the OS files. The OS media images are typically downloaded from Microsoft. The files are extracted and placed in the Operating System Source folder on the network.

▶ **Operating system install package**—This is the operating system package inside the Configuration Manager console that points to the Operating System Source folder on the network.

▶ **Task sequence**—This set of tasks is used to execute the complete deployment. This includes everything from configuring the hardware, to installing the OS, to deploying the correct software packages.

▶ **Drivers**—These are the drivers that have been uploaded to the Configuration Manager driver repository. These drivers can be installed dynamically during the deployment process.

▶ **Driver packages**—Specific drivers are grouped together for easier management. For example, all the drivers for a specific make and model of a server can be grouped together in a Driver package.

The deployment of server operating systems to enterprise server hardware can be greatly simplified by leveraging vendor-specific Configuration Manager add-ons. HP, Dell, and IBM have all made add-ons and whitepapers for Configuration Manager 2012 available at no additional cost. These publications contain detailed guidance for deploying server operating systems to their hardware and include things like configuring the RAID controller and performing hardware firmware updates from within the WinPE environment.

For operating system deployment, each component can be managed independently. For example, standard Software Distribution packages are created and maintained separately from the actual OS image. In addition, drivers are also maintained and stored separately from the OS image. Drivers can be updated without needing to change any existing images. During deployment, drivers along with Software Distribution packages are dynamically added to the image. This modular approach significantly reduces overhead by eliminating the need for many different images due to driver and software differences.

NOTE

Use the Microsoft Deployment Toolkit (MDT) 2012 for additional OS deployment functionality, including full-file scripted-based installation without needing to capture an image. MDT integrates directly into the Configuration Manager console and can be downloaded from http://technet.microsoft.com/en-us/solutionaccelerators/dd407791.aspx.

Understanding Asset Management

Asset management features help manage the environment by collecting granular details about the hardware and software running in the environment. The data is stored in a SQL database and can be easily queried to assist management and IT with infrastructure-based decisions.

Configuration Manager provides exceptional functionality for managing and reporting on Microsoft Windows assets. The asset management functionality includes things like hardware inventory, software inventory, software metering, software and license management through Asset Intelligence, and Desired Configuration Management.

Hardware and Software Inventory

All of the data collected from managed systems is located in the Configuration Manager database, and can be reported on through the built-in reporting features. This data can also be accessed with external applications and programmatically through a variety of methods, including WMI and with the predefined database views.

Inventory collection is the process of scanning for hardware configuration and file data on the managed system and reporting the results back to Configuration Manager. Both the Hardware and Software Inventory Client Agents use WMI to perform the actual scan of the managed system. The Configuration Manager client is told what to include in the inventory with rules sent to the client as policies.

The results of the inventory are temporarily stored in an XML file on the managed system before being sent to the Management Point. Both the hardware inventory and the software inventory process can be customized and extended. The hardware inventory is particularly useful when custom, business-specific attributes need to be collected from managed systems. For example, information such as server owner and contract information can be stored on the system as it is provisioned. This information can be inventoried and reported on from within Configuration Manager.

The Configuration Manager Resource Explorer is shown in Figure 2.3.

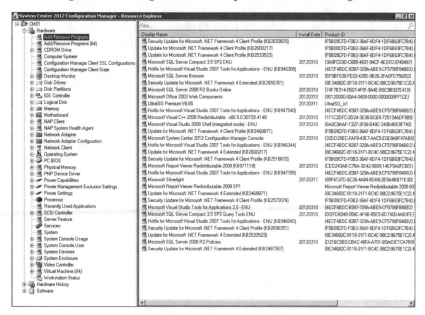

FIGURE 2.3   The Configuration Manager 2012 Resource Explorer.

Asset Intelligence

The Asset Intelligence (AI) functionality in Configuration Manager is used to identify and report software licensing and licensing compliance information for both Microsoft and non-Microsoft software. In addition to managing active licenses, several features provide information on software that isn't being used and should be targeted for removal.

The Asset Intelligence components have dependencies on the hardware inventory process. Specialized Asset Intelligence classes added to the hardware inventory are used to facilitate the identification of software and usage. Several of the Asset Intelligence reports in the "software" category also have dependencies on the Software Metering component.

CAUTION

Don't use Configuration Manager as an authoritative source for making licensing purchases. The actual counts of licenses should be tracked as systems are provisioned and deprovisioned throughout the enterprise. Configuration Manager should be used to validate those numbers. For example, each SQL component is tracked separately. This artificially increases the count of some of the license reports.

The AI components in Configuration Manager receive updates from Microsoft System Center Online Services. These updates are used to organize software that has been inventoried throughout the enterprise. Metadata from software that has not been categorized can be submitted to Microsoft. The System Center Online team will research and add the software information to subsequent catalog updates.

Asset Intelligence provides the ability to upload license information and compare the numbers from actual installed software. This is available for both Microsoft and non-Microsoft software. The Software 08A – Recently Used Executable Programs By the Count of Users report is shown in Figure 2.4 and is a good example of the detailed information that can be gleaned from Asset Intelligence.

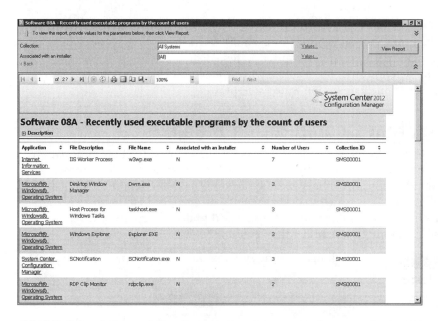

FIGURE 2.4   Software 08A – Recently Used Executable Programs By the Count of Users report.

Software Metering

The software metering functionality provided with Configuration Manager simply tracks software usage on managed systems. The creation of software metering rules can assist in identifying how often software is used. This is beneficial when tracking licensed software and targeting the removal of software that isn't used.

Compliance Management

The Compliance Management component, formerly Desired Configuration Management, is now a powerful feature. Compliance Management allows an administrator to create configuration baselines to validate the settings of managed systems. The validation of customizable settings determines the overall compliance of the target system. Compliance Management provides many options for monitoring the state of both objects and settings on managed systems. Compliance Management can monitor several types of objects, including Registry keys, files, and managed code assemblies. Compliance Management can also be configured to validate settings. Settings data can be obtained through Active Directory, IIS, Registry, VBScript, JScript, PowerShell, SQL, WQL, and XML-based queries.

Individual items monitored by Compliance Management are grouped together to create a baseline, which is then applied to a collection of systems. The results are reported back to the Configuration Manager hierarchy. Systems that failed to meet the requirements are flagged as being noncompliant. Several reports are available to monitor the compliance of different baselines created.

New to Configuration Manager 2012 is the ability to remediate noncompliant settings. Where a compliant rule is deterministic, for example when the setting clause is an "equal" clause, then the UI presents an option to remediate noncompliant systems. When compliance is nondeterministic, for example when the setting clause is "one of" or "contains," then the remediate option is not present.

Reporting from Configuration Manager

Configuration Manager includes a variety of preconfigured reports to show information about managed systems and the Configuration Manager infrastructure. These reports are run in the powerful Reporting Services Point, based on SQL Server Reporting Services. Report subscriptions can be created to deliver reports via email or to a file share on a regular basis, reducing the administrative effort needed to deliver reports. The reports can be found in the Monitoring space under the Reporting folder.

A Reporting Services report detailing operating systems and service packs is shown in Figure 2.5.

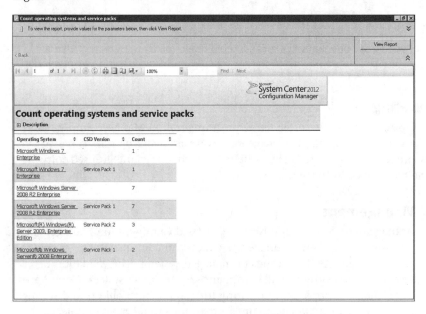

FIGURE 2.5   The Count Operating Systems and Service Packs report.

Reports are important as they provide insight into the different functionality of Configuration Manager, including the health of the infrastructure and managed systems. For example, reports show client installation problems, the status of software distribution, the compliance of software updates, and many other things.

> **NOTE**
>
> Don't modify existing reports. Always make a copy of the report and make changes to the copy. During Configuration Manager service pack upgrades, the original reports can be updated by Microsoft; if they're customized, your changes will be lost.

Configuration Manager Architecture Components

Configuration Manager is composed of several basic roles: the Site Database, Site Server, SMS Provider, Management Point, Distribution Point, Clients, and Administration Console. These components make up a very basic deployment scenario.

The following list describes each Configuration Manager role. Each role can be installed on a separate server for a very high degree of scalability or collocated on the same server for smaller environments.

The following list describes the different Configuration Manager components:

- ▶ Clients
- ▶ Site Servers
- ▶ Site Database Servers
- ▶ Client Health Components
- ▶ Asset Intelligence Synchronization Point
- ▶ Distribution Point
- ▶ Fallback Status Point
- ▶ Health Validator Point
- ▶ Management Point
- ▶ Out-of-Band Service Point
- ▶ Reporting Service Point
- ▶ Software Update Point
- ▶ State Migration Point
- ▶ Remote Tools
- ▶ Wake On LAN
- ▶ Mobile Device Management

Configuration Manager was specifically designed to be scalable and can subsequently be configured to meet the needs of any size company. This flexibility stems from the fact that almost all roles can either reside on one server or can be distributed across multiple servers.

Each of these various roles provides specific Configuration Manager functionality. Configuration Manager design scenarios often involve the separation of roles onto multiple servers. For example, the database components can be delegated to a dedicated server, and the Management Point can reside on a second server.

The Configuration Manager 2012 architecture is shown in Figure 2.6, with all the major components and their data paths.

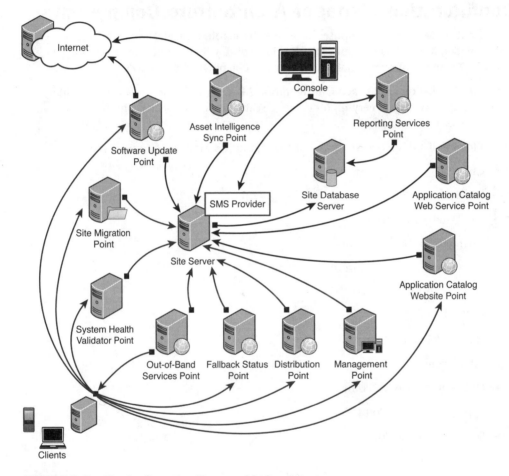

FIGURE 2.6   The Configuration Manager 2012 architecture.

In the next sections, each of the components is discussed.

Clients

Clients are installed on each managed system to provide efficient management of the environment. Almost all communication is initiated from the client with the exception of the actual installation and specific out-of-band tasks run from the Administration Console. A client must be installed to be managed by Configuration Manager.

The Windows client natively supports both 32-bit and 64-bit operating systems. The Windows client supports the following minimum operating systems:

- ▶ Windows Server 2003 Web SP2

- ▶ Windows Server 2003 SP2, Standard, Enterprise, and Datacenter Editions

- ▶ Windows Server 2003 R2 SP2, Standard, Enterprise, Datacenter, and Storage Editions

- ▶ Windows Server 2008 SP2, Standard, Enterprise, and Datacenter Editions

- ▶ Windows Server 2008 R2, Standard, Enterprise, and Datacenter Editions

- ▶ Windows Server 2008 for Itanium-based Systems

- ▶ Windows XP Professional SP3 and above

- ▶ Windows XP Tablet PC SP3

- ▶ Windows XP Embedded SP3

- ▶ Windows Embedded Standard 2009

- ▶ Windows Embedded Point of Sales 1.1 SP3

- ▶ Windows Embedded POSReady 2009

- ▶ Windows Fundamentals for Legacy PCs

- ▶ Windows Vista SP2 Business, Enterprise, or Ultimate Editions

- ▶ Windows 7 Professional, Enterprise, or Ultimate Edition

The Configuration Manager client relies heavily on WMI. Any type of WMI corruption can cause issues with the client, such as missing hardware inventory or not executing software.

The minimum requirements are traditionally set extremely low and modern equipment should be used when appropriate. At a minimum, 5GB hard drive space should be available for cached content. This includes space for software and software update distribution.

Clients can be installed through a push from the Configuration Manager Site Server, through Group Policy software deployment, through WSUS, through a logon script, manually, or as part of an image. Running the `client.msi` file directly is not supported; always install the client with the `CCMSetup.exe` utility.

Central Administration Site Servers

The Central Administration Site Server is an optional parent site to all primary sites in the hierarchy. This server has the ability to manage all clients throughout the hierarchy. The Central Site Server provides replication coordination and central administration of configuration for the enterprise. The central site does not, however, manage clients directly and does not support all Site System roles.

The maximum supported number of clients in a single hierarchy is 400,000, assuming the default SCCM 2012 setting and SQL Server Enterprise Edition. If SQL Server Standard Edition is used, then database partitioning limitations reduce the maximum supported clients to 50,000 per hierarchy. However, the actual number of supported clients highly depends on configured options.

> **NOTE**
>
> If a central Site Server was originally installed with SQL Server Standard Edition, then later upgrading to Enterprise Edition will not increase the maximum supported clients. The central Site Server database must be created on a SQL Server Enterprise Edition for the partitioning to be set up for higher scalability.

Primary Site Servers

A primary site server provides core functionality for Configuration Manager. This server manages Site Component Servers, provides an interface to manage systems, and manages data in the Site Database.

A Site Server must be part of an Active Directory domain. The maximum supported number of clients in a single site is 100,000. If the SQL Server is installed on the same server as the Site Server, then the maximum supported clients is 50,000. Each primary site supports a maximum of 250 secondary sites.

SMS Provider

The SMS Provider is a WMI provider that facilitates accessing and manipulating the Configuration Manager Site Database. All communication from the Site Server and the Configuration Manager Administration Console goes through the SMS Provider.

> **NOTE**
>
> The Windows Automated Installation Kit (WAIK) is installed with the SMS Provider to facilitate OS deployment–related functionality.

This component can be installed in several different locations. It is typically installed on the Site Server along with the Site Database in small- and medium-sized deployments, as the resources needed by the SMS Provider can be managed within the Site Server hardware.

For improved performance, this component can be moved to a second server with the SQL server, thus splitting the workload between the database server and other site roles and transferring the provider load from the Site Server to the SQL server. To support very large environments, the SMS Provider can be installed on a third, standalone server, eliminating resource utilization on both the SQL and Site Server hardware.

NOTE

The SMS Provider cannot be installed on a SQL cluster node.

The SMS Provider provides a WMI namespace to facilitate the automation of the Configuration Manager infrastructure. This feature can play an important part in the Total System Automation objectives that are desirable when managing large, dynamic environments. For example, through custom integration with System Center Operations Manager, workloads can be monitored; in the event of a problem, the workload can be removed from service and redeployed to a new system automatically. With the correct workflow automation, a very high level of efficiency can be achieved using both Configuration Manager and Operations Manager.

Site Server Database

Each site requires a separate database. This database holds configuration settings and management data, such as hardware inventory for managed systems. Several site maintenance tasks are available to remove data after a predefined retention period.

The following list shows Site Maintenance tasks that affect the retention of information in the database along with additional maintenance tasks that assist with the overall health of the database:

- ▶ Backup Site Server: Daily (enabled)

- ▶ Check Application Title with Inventory Information (enabled)

- ▶ Clear Install Flag: 21 days (disabled)

- ▶ Delete Aged Application Request Data (enabled)

- ▶ Delete Client Operations (enabled)

- ▶ Delete Aged Collected Files: 90 days (enabled)

- ▶ Delete Aged Computer Association Data: 30 days (enabled)

- ▶ Delete Aged Delete Detection Data: 30 days (enabled)

- ▶ Delete Aged Device Wipe Record: (enabled)

- ▶ Delete Aged Devices Managed By The Exchange Connector: (enabled)

- ▶ Delete Aged Discovery Data: 90 days (enabled)

- ▶ Delete Aged Endpoint Protection Health Status History Data: (enabled)

- ▶ Delete Aged Enrolled Devices: (enabled)

- ▶ Delete Aged Inventory History: 90 days (enabled)

- ▶ Delete Aged Log Data: (enabled)

- ▶ Delete Aged Replication Tracking Data: (enabled)

- ▶ Delete Aged Software Metering Data: 5 days (enabled)

- ▶ Delete Aged Software Metering Summary Data: 270 days (enabled)

- ▶ Delete Aged Status Messages: (enabled)

- ▶ Delete Aged Threat Data: (enabled)

- ▶ Delete Inactive Client Discovery Data: 90 days (disabled)

- ▶ Delete Obsolete Alerts: (enabled)

- ▶ Delete Obsolete Client Discovery Data: 7 days (disabled)

- ▶ Delete Obsolete Forest Discovery Sites and Subnets: (enabled)

- ▶ Delete Unused Application Revisions (enabled)

- ▶ Evaluate Collection Members (enabled)

- ▶ Evaluate Provisioned AMT Computer Certificates: 42 days (enabled)

- ▶ Monitor Keys: (enabled)

- ▶ Rebuild Indexes: (enabled)

- ▶ Summarize Installed Software Data (enabled)

- ▶ Summarize Software Metering File Usage Data: (enabled)

- ▶ Summarize Software Metering Monthly Usage Data: (enabled)

- ▶ Update Application Catalog Tables: (enabled)

The Configuration Manager database is a Microsoft SQL Server (or SQL Server Express) database that contains all of the data needed to manage the infrastructure. Each Site Server has a database and it is very important to ensure that it is sized appropriately, especially on primary sites. The most critical resource used by the Configuration Manager database is the I/O subsystem, but the CPU and RAM are also important.

Configuration Manager operates through a hierarchical collection of data and management of assets. All of the data collected by Configuration Manager secondary sites is replicated up the hierarchy to a parent primary site. If installed, data from all primary sites is replicated up the hierarchy to the Central Administration Site. As a result, the database server at the top of the hierarchy holds all of the asset data from lower-level sites. The Site Database at lower-level sites only contains asset data from clients directly assigned to the site. This is an important aspect to consider when managing assets.

> **NOTE**
>
> The Site Server database cannot be backed up by database jobs or agents while the SMS Executive service is running. Backing up the database while the SMS Executive service is running might result in inconsistencies between information in the database and the Configuration Manager site control file, which will prevent the site from being successfully restored in a disaster recovery scenario. Use the backup tasks from within the Configuration Manager Administration Console to schedule backups.

In small- and medium-sized deployments, the database is typically installed on the Site Server. This provides good performance as the communication between the SMS Provider and the Site Database doesn't need to travel over the network.

The SQL server needs three unique service accounts to support the Configuration Manager Site Database and Reporting Services Point functionality. It is currently recommended to use a limited domain user account for SQL service accounts.

Wake On LAN

The Wake On LAN (WOL) functionality provides a method to wake up client systems for deployments. This ultimately improves the success of different types of deployments while still allowing systems to hibernate to save power. The Wake On LAN is a site-specific option; once it is enabled, the advertisement for mandatory software, software updates, and OS deployment task sequences can be configured to leverage WOL functionality to start systems or resume systems from hibernation prior to deployment.

Configuration Manager can use a unicast transmission or a subnet-directed broadcast to send the wake-up packet. A unicast transition targets the system's IP address while a subnet-directed broadcast simply performs a broadcast on the subnet with the client. In both cases, the MAC address is used to ensure the correct system receives the wake-up signal.

> **NOTE**
>
> The local NIC, infrastructure routers, and switches all need to support Wake On LAN for this feature to work correctly between separate client and server subnets.

The Site Server uses the Configuration Manager hardware inventory to identify the correct IP address, subnet, and MAC address for the client. Clients that move around and change IPs or subnets are not good candidates for WOL. To improve the likelihood that Configuration Manager knows about the correct client settings, increase the hardware inventory reporting cycle. The WOL packet is originated from the primary site server.

Asset Intelligence Synchronization Point

The Asset Intelligence Synchronization Point communicates with System Center Online Services to retrieve updates to the asset catalog. This catalog contains software families and categories, along with hardware requirements for hundreds of thousands of pieces of software.

> **NOTE**
>
> Microsoft does *not* use the Asset Intelligence Synchronization Point to audit your licenses or validate compliance.

The Asset Intelligence Synchronization Point can also be used to submit metadata from unclassified software packages to Microsoft. The System Center Online team will research and classify the software. Newly classified software will be made available in subsequent catalog updates.

> **NOTE**
>
> Software information that is uploaded and eventually categorized by Microsoft is made available to all Microsoft customers through System Center Online Services. Avoid uploading private software information that could be used to identify your business to other customers.

Distribution Point

The Distribution Point site role hosts content for clients in a specific location. Content includes software, updates, and images used for OS deployment. Strategically placed Distribution Points are important for effectively deploying content. Distribution Points can be deployed on servers and on clients, with the exact same functionality.

> **NOTE**
>
> As a safety measure, when content is downloaded from a DP, a hash value is calculated. The hash is compared with the hash on the Site Server. If the hash doesn't match, the content is discarded.

When a client is started or changes networks, a local discovery is triggered to identify the closest Management Point. The closest Management Point then provides the client with a list of Distribution Points for content. The agent evaluates the list of DPs and chooses the most appropriate DP to obtain content based on several factors. For example, the client will choose BITS-enabled Distribution Points over non-BITS Distribution Points.

If the Distribution Point chosen by the client is not available, the client attempts to download content from that Distribution Point for 8 hours. After 8 hours, the client system attempts to locate the content on a different Distribution Point and begin the download process. It is important to monitor the health of Distribution Points and make sure they are available. If necessary, remove the Distribution Point role from unhealthy servers to prevent clients from selecting the server for content.

The Distribution Point role is available in two different configurations, both the standard and BITS-enabled Distribution Points.

In addition, Distribution Points now provide PXE services. The PXE-enabled DP provides network boot capabilities for managed systems during an OS deployment or refresh. Using the PXE functionality is one of the most effective methods to deploy operating systems throughout the environment. This is essential to achieving a greater level of total systems automation. The PXE network boot can be initiated by assigning an OS deployment task sequence to an existing managed system. In this case, the current operating system runs the prerequisite tasks, such as capturing the user state and data, and then reboots. During the reboot, the system automatically initiates the network boot process. The PXE network boot process can also be initiated on a bare-metal or unmanaged system during the POST. This is usually done by pressing the F12 key when prompted after the network ROMs are loaded.

When a system attempts to boot using PXE, it broadcasts that it's a PXE-enabled client, and receives an IP address along with the location of the network boot OS that is needed to allow the PXE process to work. The PXE service is similar to DHCP as both services listen for these client broadcasts and respond accordingly. The PXE-enabled Distribution Point, which uses the Windows Deployment Services Windows role, provides the Trivial File Transfer Protocol (TFTP) location where the WinPE image is located. The client downloads the WinPE image into memory and starts the operating system. From within WinPE, the preconfigured scripts contact the Configuration Manager hierarchy for the sequence of OS deployment tasks.

The location of the PXE-enabled DP is important. Because the client uses broadcasts during the boot process, the DP along with the DHCP server needs to be able to receive these broadcasts. This requires the DP to be located on the same network as the client system or the appropriate PXE/IP helper addresses need to be configured to forward the broadcast to the correct servers.

Up to 250 Distribution Points can be installed in each site, both primary sites and secondary sites. A primary site can support a combined total of 5,000 Distribution Points. Each Distribution Point can support up to 4,000 clients. However, this largely depends on how much content is being provisioned simultaneously.

Understanding Standard (SMB) Distribution Points

The standard Distribution Point for Configuration Manager essentially provides clients with the ability to either run content from the server or download content to the local cache. A SMB-based Distribution Point is typically used when running content over the network from the Distribution Point. However, because it is recommended to download content locally to ensure the software can successfully install even if disconnected from the network, avoid using SMB-only Distribution Points.

Understanding BITS-Enabled Distribution Points

The BITS-enabled Distribution Point is one of the most common methods to deploy software and updates. This type of Distribution Point provides a web service where content is downloaded to the client through HTTP or HTTPS. The bandwidth usage can be controlled by configuring BITS communication settings from within the Configuration Manager Administration Console or from an Active Directory Group Policy Object.

BITS-enabled Distribution Points also allow Configuration Manager clients to resume downloading content if the download is interrupted. This is very important; this technology allows the staging of large software packages on the client through a gradual download instead of trying to run the software over the network.

A BITS-enabled Distribution Point requires IIS and WebDAV to be installed. Also, both mobile clients and Internet-based clients require a BITS-enabled Distribution Point and cannot use SMB-based DPs.

Understanding BranchCache Features

Both Windows Server 2008 R2 and Windows 7 support a feature called BranchCache. When this option is enabled in Distributed mode, a client that initially downloads content from a BITS-enabled Distribution Point will make this content available for other clients on the local subnet. The BITS 4.0 client is required to support this configuration. Microsoft recommends a maximum of 50 clients when configured for BranchCache Distributed mode.

Understanding Protected Distribution Points

All Distribution Points can be protected. The protection is configured based on the available boundaries established for the site. This prevents clients that are outside the protected boundary from obtaining content from the protected Distribution Point and prevents clients from within the protected boundary from getting content from outside the protected boundary. For example, suppose the Configuration Manager site provides service for two different boundaries. Distribution Points for the site can be protected for either of the boundaries in that site, or both of the boundaries depending on business requirements.

The protected boundary limitations can be overridden from within a software deployment package. This allows important content to be downloaded without regard for boundaries, if necessary. This is typically used for emergency or very small deployments.

> **NOTE**
>
> To override protected boundary behavior, enable the *Allow Clients to Fall Back to Unprotected Distribution Points When the Content Is Not Available on the Protected Distribution Point* option on the package advertisement.

Fallback Status Point

The Fallback Status Point (FSP) provides a safety net for clients. A client system can send status messages to a Fallback Status Point when initial communication has been established, such as when a new agent is installed, or when communication has failed and the client is orphaned or otherwise unable to establish normal communication with the site.

The FSP can support up to 100,000 clients. Only a single FSP can be installed in each site. During deployment, clients send state messages to the FSP. During a large deployment, the throttling thresholds should be adjusted to accommodate the expected load. The default FSP settings are configured to process 10,000 messages per hour.

Health Validator Point

The Health Validator Point must be installed on a Windows server with the Network Access Protection (NAP) component installed. The Health Validator simply tells NAP what software updates are required before the client can pass validation and communicate with the network. NAP essentially validates the configuration of a client; if the validation passes, the client is allowed to communicate with the network.

NAP can be configured for IP Security (IPSec) enforcement, 802.1X enforcement, Virtual Private Network (VPN) enforcement, Dynamic Host Configuration Protocol (DHCP) enforcement, Remote Desktop Services Gateway enforcement, and integration with Cisco Network Access Control (NAC) for hardware-based network enforcement. The Health Validator Point works with the existing NAP infrastructure. For additional planning, review the Network Access Protection (NAP) guide on TechNet at http://technet.microsoft.com/en-us/network/bb545879.aspx.

Management Point

All managed clients communicate with the Management Point (MP) web service. This communication is established by the client to receive management policies, send state messages, and send data such as inventory reports. The Management Point provides policies based on information in the Site Database and delivers client data and status messages to the primary site server for processing.

Factors that impact the Management Point include the following:

- Number of managed systems
- Client Agent polling cycles
- Size and frequency of inventory reports

The Management Point role is one of the first roles to move off the Site Server to improve performance. The Management Point can support 25,000 clients on a single server and as many as 100,000 clients total when additional Management Points are added. A primary site can support up to 10 Management Points. Additional Management Points beyond 4 will not increase the maximum clients supported, but rather provide for increased fault tolerance.

In SCCM 2012, the Management Point also provides Server Locator Point functionality. The Server Locator Point (SLP) functionality provides a way for managed systems to find Site Systems. This is typically used when managing non–domain clients or when Active Directory schema has not been extended. Internal clients use the MP to locate the correct Management Point if Active Directory and DNS cannot be used. Active Directory cannot be used to locate a Management Point if either the schema is not extended or if the client is not a member of the Active Directory Forest. DNS cannot be used to locate a

Management Point if the service location resource record for the Management Point has not been created.

When a client on the intranet attempts to locate the resident Management Point, it first attempts to use Active Directory and then DNS; only if both of those options fail, the Server Locator Point (SLP) functionality of the MP is used. If heavy SLP usage is expected (such as when AD and DNS don't have Management Point information), the MP should be moved off the Site Server and onto dedicated hardware.

Out-of-Band Service Point

Out-of-band management refers to the management of a system while the system has been turned off, or is otherwise not responding, such as when an operating system error has occurred. To support out-of-band management, the Intel vPRO chipset along with a supported version of the Active Management Technology (AMT) is required.

State Migration Point

The State Migration Point (SMP) provides a secure location to store the user state from a client system during the OS deployment process. Before the deployment of a new operating system to a target system, the user state can be captured, encrypted, and stored on the State Migration Point. The existing operating system can be wiped and a new operating system deployed. After the new operating system is deployed, the OS deployment can apply the existing user state to the new system, thus preserving the user's configuration and local data.

Similar to the PXE-enabled DP, the State Migration Point should be deployed in each area that OS deployments will take place. This is typically implemented on the local network with the PXE-enabled DP role. The DP and State Migration Point can exist on the same hardware.

During implementation of the State Migration Point, the storage location of the captured user state needs to be specified. The maximum number of supported clients and the server minimum amount of free space safety configuration also need to be set.

Factors that impact the State Migration Point include the following:

- ▶ Number of OS deployments
- ▶ Size of the user state
- ▶ Length of time to retain user state data

During the state migration phase of an OS deployment, the client chooses the closest SMP based on several conditions. SMPs in the same subnet will be chosen before SMPs from a different subnet, and finally a remote site.

Reporting Services Point

The Reporting Services Point (RSP) provides an extensible reporting infrastructure based on SQL Reporting Services. This provides a powerful way to access data in the Site Database and includes the ability to schedule reports through subscriptions.

Software Update Point

The Software Update Point (SUP) communicates with the WSUS 3.0 components to receive data from Microsoft Update about patches and updates available for clients.

Each primary site server that will leverage Software Update Deployment of Configuration Manager needs to have the WSUS 3.0 components installed along with the Software Update Point. The Software Update Point manages the Software Update Client Agent on systems that are managed by Configuration Manager. The Software Update Client Agent is installed with the Configuration Manager client.

Only the Software Update Point at the top of the Configuration Manager hierarchy (the Central Administration Site in a multisite hierarchy) will actively download software update metadata from the Microsoft Update site. This Software Update Point is called the "Active" SUP. An additional SUP can also be deployed to support Internet-based client management (IBCM) communication. In this scenario, the SUP would be accessible from the Internet over TCP port 443.

Factors that impact the Software Update Point include the following:

- ▶ Number of managed clients
- ▶ Frequency of software update detection

The SUP can support 25,000 clients when hosted on the same server as the Site Server. When the SUP is located on a separate server, as many as 100,000 clients can be supported. To support more than 25,000 clients, the SUP needs to be part of a Network Load Balancing (NLB) cluster.

NOTE

Use a Network Load Balancing cluster to improve scalability of the Software Update Point and to reduce the impact during a server failure.

Mobile Device Management

The Mobile Device Management features in Configuration Manager allow the management of mobile assets with the Configuration Manager infrastructure. Configuration Manager allows both software and hardware inventory collection, file collection, and the distribution of mobile software. Configuration Manager also provides the ability to configure settings on mobile devices.

Configuration Manager natively supports the following Mobile Device operating systems:

▶ Windows Mobile 6 Standard, 6 Professional, 6 Classic, 6.1 or 6.5

▶ Windows CE 5.0 (ARM and x86 processors), 6.0 (ARM and x86 processors) or 7.0 (ARM and x86 processors)

▶ Nokia Symbian Belle

To support Mobile Device Management, a Management Point role and a Distribution Point role must be configured to allow access by mobile devices. In addition, the correct certificates need to be placed on the mobile device when the Configuration Manager environment is operating in Native mode.

Mobile devices that are currently managed by an existing infrastructure management environment, such as SCCM 2007, can be updated over the air. New clients are installed through Active Sync or Mobile Device Center on the system where the mobile device is attached. Configuration Manager can be used to identify clients that currently use mobile devices. A custom package can then be created to target these systems for the mobile device agent installation. During subsequent synchronization of the mobile device, the client will be installed and will be managed by Configuration Manager.

Securing Configuration Manager

Security has evolved into a primary concern that can no longer be taken for granted. The inherent security in any IT system is only as good as the services that have access to it; therefore, it is wise to perform a security audit of all systems that access information from servers. This concept holds true for management systems as well because they collect sensitive information from every system in an enterprise. This includes potentially sensitive data that could be used to compromise a system. Consequently, securing the Configuration Manager infrastructure should not be taken lightly.

Securing Server Communication

The HTTPS option available for several site roles is only used to secure client communications. To secure server communications, several options exist. First, enable the option to require secure key exchange between sites. This is a default setting for new Configuration Manager implementations and is significantly simplified when the Active Directory schema has been extended. When the Configuration Manager schema extensions have been implemented, the secure key exchange between Site Server happens automatically with the help of Active Directory. The Site Server key allows data, such as the site control files, to be signed.

IPSec can be implemented to encrypt server-to-server communication. This offers a very high degree of security and can be used if the back-end infrastructure is located in nonsecure locations.

Securing the Management Console

Configuration Manager 2012 introduces true role-based administration, allowing users and groups to be assigned roles in SCCM.

Components of the role-based administration include the following:

▶ **Security Roles**—These are groups of security permissions that can be assigned to users to allow them to perform their administrative tasks. The security permissions define tasks that an administrator can perform and rights to particular object types.

▶ **Collections**—These specify the users and devices that an administrator can view or manage. These collections can be based on geographic parameters, organizational parameters, or functional parameters. This allows very flexible division and organization of the resources to which administrators have access.

▶ **Security Scopes**—These provide administrative users with access-specific securable object instances, such as specific applications, configuration items, sites, and other objects.

The difference between security roles and security scopes can sometimes be difficult to distinguish. The bottom line is that security roles assigned rights to object types, such as all applications. Security scopes, on the other hand, assigned rights to specific object instances.

Role-based administration in SCCM 2012 simplifies providing the correct least privilege access to administrators of SCCM.

Understanding Port Requirements

Site Servers communicate with each other using RPC ports. This includes the RPC Endpoint mapper (TCP 135) and SMB (TCP 445). RPC communication also uses dynamic ports above 49152 (1024 on Server 2003) for communication. Server communication can be secured with IPSec. This includes Site Server to Site Server, and server to SQL server. Client communication can also be secured using IPSec.

Client communication ports are listed in Table 2.1. In Native mode, almost all client communication occurs over Secure Sockets Layer (SSL; TCP Port 443) with few exceptions. Both the Fallback Status Point and the Server Locator Point roles communicate using HTTP.

TABLE 2.1   Client Communication

Role	Port
Distribution Point	443/445
Fallback Status Point	80
Management Point	443
Reporting Point	443
Reporting Services Point	443
Server Locator Point	80
Software Update Point	443
State Migration Point	443

The client communication ports are shown in Figure 2.7, with all the major components and their data paths.

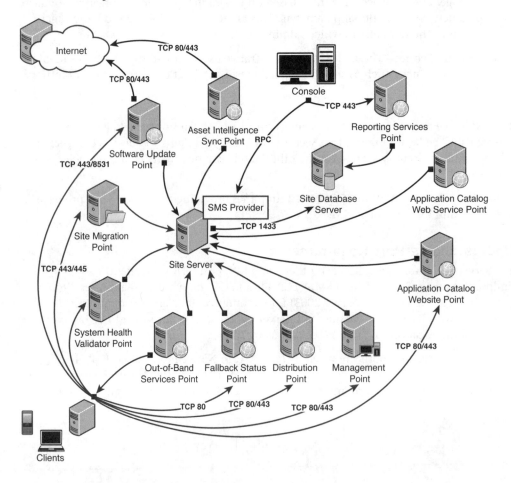

FIGURE 2.7   The Configuration Manager 2012 client communication paths and ports.

Understanding Service Account Security

The Configuration Manager servers use the Local System account for the majority of network authentication, moving the security boundary out to the operating system. When the Local System account is used, unauthorized users should not be allowed on the server. The Local System account has several benefits because the password is managed automatically with Active Directory membership.

When deploying Configuration Manager, several permissions groups should be established. These permissions groups should hold Site Servers and Component Servers and should be given rights to objects as needed.

CAUTION

When a computer object is added to a group, the change will not take effect until the next refresh of the computer's Kerberos ticket. Because this can take up to seven days, instead, restart the computer to refresh the Kerberos ticket.

Configuration Manager provides many different areas where an access account can be configured. This includes providing service accounts for several roles when they need to access the Site Database. Typically, use the Local Service account when possible. At a minimum, the following service accounts are needed to support basic deployments:

▶ **Domain Join**—This account is used during OS deployments to join the system to the domain. This should be a limited user account with the right to add new computers to a specific OU in which this account has been delegated the correct permissions.

▶ **Network Access**—This account is used by non–domain members to access content and infrastructure components. This scenario is common during OS deployment and when managing demilitarized zone (DMZ) systems. This account should be a limited user account.

▶ **Client Push Installation**—This account is used by the Site Server to connect to a remote system, copy required client files, and initiate the installation under the Local Service account. This account requires administrative rights on managed systems to install the client.

▶ **OS Capture Account**—This account provides access to the OS capture share. This is the network share where OS images are copied during the OS capture process. The captured image can be imported into Configuration Manager for delivery to client systems. This account should be a limited user with only permissions on the OS capture location.

Understanding Component Requirements

Configuration Manager's simple installation and relative ease of use often belie the potential complexity of its underlying components. This complexity can be managed with the right amount of knowledge of some of the advanced concepts of Configuration Manager design and implementation.

Each Configuration Manager component has specific design requirements and a good knowledge of these factors is required before beginning the design of Configuration Manager. Hardware and software requirements must be taken into account as well as factors involving specific Configuration Manager components, such as the Site Server, Management Point, Distribution Points, Native mode authentication, and backup requirements.

Exploring Hardware Requirements

Having the proper hardware for Configuration Manager to operate on is a critical component of Configuration Manager functionality, reliability, and overall performance. Nothing is worse than overloading a brand-new server only a few short months after its implementation. The industry standard generally holds that any production servers deployed should remain relevant for three to four years following deployment. Stretching beyond this time frame might be possible, but the ugly truth is that hardware investments are typically short term and need to be replaced often to ensure relevance. Buying a less-expensive server might save money in the short term but could potentially increase costs associated with downtime, troubleshooting, and administration. The following are the suggested minimums for any server running a Configuration Manager 2012 server component:

- ▶ 4 cores (Intel Xeon E5504 or better)
- ▶ 64-bit Windows 2008 R2 operating system
- ▶ 64-bit SQL Server 2008 R2 SP1 with Cumulative Update 4
- ▶ 300GB of free disk space
- ▶ 16GB of RAM

These recommendations apply only to the smallest Configuration Manager deployments and should be seen as minimum levels for Configuration Manager hardware. More realistic deployments would have the following minimums:

- ▶ 8 cores (Intel Xeon E5504 or better)
- ▶ 64-bit Windows 2008 R2 operating system
- ▶ 64-bit SQL Server 2008 R2 SP1 with Cumulative Update 4
- ▶ 600GB of free disk space on RAID 1+0 for performance
- ▶ 32GB of RAM (8GB of RAM if the SQL server is remote from the Site Server)

Configuration Manager 2012 can be resource intensive in a large enterprise, so generous processor, disk, and memory are important for optimal performance. Future expansion and relevance of hardware should be taken into account when sizing servers for Configuration Manager deployment to ensure that the system has room to grow as agents are added and the databases grow.

Determining Software Requirements

A Configuration Manager 2012 primary site requires Windows 2008 64-bit SP2 or Windows Server 2008 R2. Standard, Enterprise, and Datacenter Editions are supported.

The Configuration Manager Site Server must be installed on a member server in a Windows Active Directory domain. It is commonly recommended to keep the installation of Configuration Manager on a separate server or set of dedicated member servers that do not run any other applications that could interfere with normal operations.

A few other requirements critical to the success of Configuration Manager implementations are as follows:

▶ .NET Framework 3.51 SP1

▶ .NET Framework 4.0

▶ Remote Differential Compression feature

▶ Background Intelligent Transfer Service (BITS) feature

The configuration of the Primary Site Server will automatically enable the appropriate Windows roles and features depending on the Site System roles selected.

Sizing the Databases

Depending on several factors, such as the type of inventory data collected, the length of time that collected data will be kept, or the amount of database grooming that is scheduled, the size of the Configuration Manager database will grow or shrink accordingly. It is important to monitor the size of the database to ensure that it does not increase well beyond the bounds of acceptable size.

> **NOTE**
>
> Use Operations Manager to monitor the database size along with other components in the Configuration Manager hierarchy.

It is common to expect to store about 5MB of data for each managed client. The size of the database can be estimated through the following formula:

```
Number of agents x 5MB = estimated database size
```

Configuration Manager Design Considerations

To be able to design a Configuration Manager 2012 architecture, it is necessary to have a working understanding of not just the components of the architecture, but also important design constraints. This includes how Configuration Manager handles data, how to connect Configuration Manager sites, and how Configuration Manager behaves over the WAN. One of the most critical design points is ensuring that the Site Database, Site Server, and Management Point components can handle the volume of data, which is constrained by the disk subsystem and the version of SQL deployed.

Designing Collections

Collections provide a way to organize resources within the Configuration Manager console. A system can be part of many different collections. For example, a computer can be part of a location-specific collection and one or more functional collections.

Each collection updates membership based on a predefined schedule. By default, this is every 24 hours, based on the time the collection was created. The update schedule can be changed as necessary; however, be sure to monitor load to ensure the system is performing adequately. Even in large environments, a small set of collections that update quickly to address specific needs is acceptable. If workflow automation scripts are built, consider programmatically triggering the collection update only when needed.

> **NOTE**
>
> Avoid customizing the default collections; they can be changed and reverted back to the defaults during subsequent service pack upgrades.

Collections also provide several management settings. For example, how often the client system polls the Management Point for new policies can be configured. This is typically used for critical clients to increase the polling cycle, allowing them to become aware of new advertisements quickly. Maintenance windows can be set on collections. The maintenance window prevents systems within the collection from installing packages and restarting unless specifically allowed or overridden from within an advertisement.

Collections also provide a security boundary for administration. Groups of users can be blocked from managing systems in a specific collection or only allowed to do specific actions like run Remote Support Tools.

Discovering and Deploying Clients

Potential client systems can be discovered through scheduled tasks available within the Configuration Manager console. The Active Directory system discovery is primarily used to locate systems. The groups to which a computer system belongs can also be discovered with the Active Directory System Group Discovery method. The groups each system is a member of are added to the computer objects as a searchable attribute.

> **NOTE**
>
> Use the Active Directory Group Discovery from the client's assigned site. The group discovery works by enumerating the list of managed systems then querying Active Directory for the list of groups of which the system is currently a member.

Potential client system can also be discovered through the Network Discovery method. This discovery method provides the ability to query the Address Resolution Protocol (ARP) cache on a router, through Simple Network Management Protocol (SNMP), and through a Microsoft DHCP query.

Configuration Manager can be set to automatically install the client on target systems. This is done by copying a small amount of code to the \\computername\Admin$\ccmsetup folder on the system and then creating a service called ccmsetup. This service attempts to download the full client through BITS, for a more bandwidth-friendly installation. This service also manages the installation; if the installation fails or the computer reboots while the installation is being done, the service repairs and reinstalls the client correctly. This service is automatically removed once the installation has completed successfully.

> **NOTE**
>
> Use the Network Access Account to allow network access from clients who are not in the same forest or workgroup. Normally, communication is done with the computer$ account; if the computer$ account fails, communication with the Network Access Account is attempted.

Provisioning Content to Users and Groups

Additional discovery methods are available to locate users and user groups within Active Directory. The Active Directory user discovery allows searches and creates Data Discovery Records (DDRs) for users. Within the discovery, the groups of which the user is a member can be identified and added to the user as a searchable attribute. In addition, the Active Directory Security Group discovery locates groups within the domain. This allows collections of groups to be created for user-targeted provisioning.

Considerations for a Multisite Configuration Manager Hierarchy

There are a few common considerations for deploying multiple Configuration Manager sites. This includes creating security and political boundaries to address demarcation points, managing and controlling bandwidth across WAN links, managing different settings for different clients, and addressing scalability along with reducing impact due to single points of failure.

In Configuration Manager 2012, the site hierarchy has been simplified to a stratified three-tier site architecture. In a multisite SCCM 2012 architecture, there is a Central Administration Site at the top of the hierarchy. It cannot have clients report to it and does not support the Management Point role or the Distribution Point role. The next level of the hierarchy consists of the primary sites, which support agents and all system roles. All primary site are child sites off of the Central Administration Site. The third level of the hierarchy is secondary sites, which support a limited number of roles. All secondary sites are child sites of primary sites.

> **NOTE**
>
> It is highly recommended to implement the fewest number of Site Servers possible to support the requirements of the organization. This substantially reduces administrative overhead and directly improves the return on investment.

Deploying additional sites is commonly used to distribute load across multiple systems. This effectively reduces resources needed on server hardware in addition to reducing network cost and directly improving scalability. For example, an organization with multiple data center locations can host a Configuration Manager primary site server in each data center rather than having all client communication travel to a single data center.

In addition to improving scalability, having multiple sites reduces the impact of having a single site disaster stop all Configuration Manager functionality. If one of the data centers has a communication issue, only part of the infrastructure is affected, whereas clients that are assigned to other sites can continue to be managed. Only clients in the affected site will experience the impact.

Deploying Sites to Control Bandwidth

Another consideration for deploying different sites is to control bandwidth. Servers in a parent/child relationship communicate with each other through Site Senders and Addresses. The Site Sender (found in the properties of the Site object under the Sender tab) controls how many processing threads can be active at any given time and how often to retry the delivery if a problem occurs. Site Addresses can be used to control the bandwidth utilization between sites. Addresses provide both a schedule and rate limits to effectively throttle communication between Site Servers.

As an alternative to deploying different sites to control bandwidth, an effective Distribution Point strategy can be used. Using correctly placed Background Intelligent Transfer Service (BITS) Distribution Points can effectively address many different bandwidth scenarios. A Distribution Point provides a lower cost of maintenance compared with a Site Server, and the BITS technology allows the throttling of content downloads.

By default, the contents of a package are pushed to Distribution Points from the Site Server that created the package. This behavior can be changed by enabling the *Send Package from the Nearest Site in the Hierarchy* option, located on the Distribution Point tab of the Software Distribution component configuration properties.

Placement of PXE-Enabled Distribution Points and State Migration Points

An important aspect in the design is the placement of the PXE-enabled Distribution Points and State Migration Points. A PXE-enabled Distribution Point is similar to DHCP where it responds to specific broadcast requests. Because this is a broadcast, the placement and configuration of a PXE-enabled Distribution Point is important. For the PXE service to receive the request, it needs to be located within the same broadcast network as the client or an IP helper needs to be configured on the router. Similar to the IP helper for DHCP, this simply forwards the broadcast traffic directly to the PXE server located on a different network.

When the PXE service receives the request, it provides the client with details for where it can locate the WinPE network boot image. Although the IP helper address can forward the broadcast message to any PXE server, this should be avoided across WAN links. Because the WinPE boot image is downloaded dynamically, a considerable amount of bandwidth is needed to make this process work efficiently. For additional information on the PXE protocol, see the Microsoft knowledge-base article at http://support.microsoft.com/kb/244036.

Like a Distribution Point, the client will locate a SMP on the local subnet before choosing a remote SMP. Although the SMP can be located anywhere, depending on how much data needs to be captured from the client system, this is typically not appropriate for spanning a WAN link.

For branch sites, the PXE-enabled Distribution Point and State Migration Point can be collocated on the same hardware. For large sites, these roles should be separated to improve scalability.

Establishing Boundaries

Establishing site boundaries is one of the most important aspects of Configuration Manager. Boundaries let managed systems receive content and communicate status to the closest server in the Configuration Manager hierarchy.

> **NOTE**
>
> If a client is not within a defined boundary, it is considered to be in a slow boundary. Package execution is controlled by the slow boundary options.

Site boundaries can be created based on IP subnet, IPv6 prefix, IP address range, and Active Directory sites. Typically in an Active Directory environment, the Configuration Manager is based on Active Directory site boundaries. Because the Active Directory site infrastructure should already map directly to the network topology, many of the same principles that apply to an Active Directory site topology also apply to the Configuration Manager topology. For example, instead of taking all the subnets in a specific network location and adding them as a site boundary, it is much easier to add the already configured Active Directory site boundary.

New in SCCM 2012 is the ability to automatically discover sites and subnets from Active Directory. This feature dramatically reduces the administrator's level of effort to maintain boundaries in SCCM. In most large organizations, SCCM administrators are not informed when network subnets are added or removed. This can result in erratic SCCM client behavior, as the clients might or might not fall within boundaries. Figure 2.8 shows the configuration of the sites and subnets discovery.

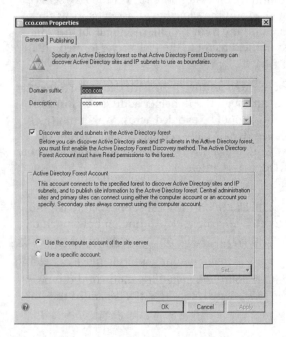

FIGURE 2.8   Site and subnet discovery.

That said, in many different scenarios and environments, using an Active Directory site boundary simply isn't possible or practical for technical or even political justification. Configuration Manager allows a mixture of all the different boundaries. It is possible to configure different combinations of site boundaries in the console to address these scenarios.

CAUTION

Never configure overlapping boundaries. This can cause managed systems to use the wrong Site Server or Distribution Management Point. This often happens when using a combination of IP and Active Directory boundaries.

When a site boundary is configured, the Network Connection type needs to be selected. The Network Connection types are limited to "Slow or Unreliable" and "Fast (LAN)" and are somewhat misleading. The true purpose of the network types is during the creation of an advertisement. When you want to deploy software, such as an application or patches, to a system, a deployment is needed. When configuring the deployment, several different distribution options are available. The deployment content options for an application deployment type are shown in Figure 2.9.

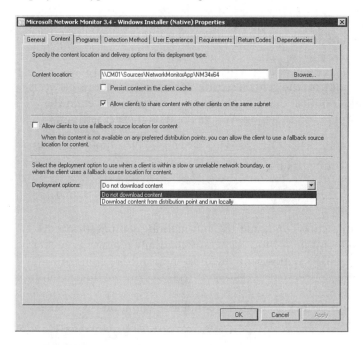

FIGURE 2.9   Application Deployment type content options.

The deployment content options allow the administration to specify distribution characteristics depending on the configuration of the site boundaries. For example, if you configure a site boundary as "slow or unreliable" and then configure the application to "Do not download content" when the client is connected to a slow or unreliable network boundary, the software will not run on any system that identifies itself as being within this boundary.

Planning Configuration Manager Client Settings

The Configuration Manager client that is installed on managed systems is made up of several subcomponents, called *agents*. Agents are configured using the Client Agents container under the Site Settings container. Computer Client Agent is always enabled; this agent provides core functionality.

In Configuration Manager 2012, the ability to create custom client settings was introduced. This allows different client settings to be targeted at different systems via deployments targeted at collections. These custom client settings override the Default Client Settings object. The custom client settings are created for either users or devices, whereas the Default Client Settings object targets both users and devices.

The client settings are organized by topic.

Background Intelligent Transfer

The Background Intelligent Transfer section controls bandwidth and throttling for BITS.

Client Policy

The Client Policy section controls core Configuration Manager client functionality. This includes how often the client checks for new policies.

Computer Agent

The Computer Agent section controls the general settings for communications between server and client. This includes notifications, the organization name displayed in the Software Center, the default Application Catalog Website Point, and other settings.

Computer Restart

The Computer Restart section configures the default Computer Restart notification windows.

Endpoint Protection

The Endpoint Protection Point section configures the anti-malware settings for clients. This includes enabling the endpoint protection client, automatically removing previously installed versions, and allowing users to postpone restarts.

Compliance Settings

The Compliance Settings section defines how often baseline configuration is validated against target systems by default.

Hardware Inventory

The Hardware Inventory section provides access to enable or disable the ability to collect hardware inventory on managed systems. From within the agent, the inventory schedule can be configured and the IDMIF and NOIDMIF file collection can be enabled if necessary. The hardware information collected by this agent can be extended through this section. To customize the hardware inventory, select the Set Classes button and add the custom hardware inventory classes.

Mobile Device

The Mobile Device section controls all mobile device functionality. This includes the polling interval and user settings.

Network Access Protection (NAP)

The Network Access Protection section enables the NAP client and configures how often the client health evaluation occurs. If the client does not pass the health test, communication might be blocked based on the NAP enforcement policy.

Remote Tools

The Remote Tools section provides the ability to configure the different aspects of remote tools in the site. This includes the level of access and the user notifications that can be provided or suppressed based on the business requirements. This agent also has the ability to configure the local Remote Desktop and Remote Assistance settings on the managed system.

Software Deployment
The Software Deployment section specifies how often deployments are reevaluated.

Software Inventory
The Software Inventory section provides access to enable or disable the ability to collect file properties on managed systems. From within the agent, the inventory schedule can be configured and the file extensions to search managed systems can be modified.

Software Metering
The Software Metering section provides access to enable or disable the ability to collect software metering data on managed systems. From within the agent, the inventory schedule can be configured, which controls how often data is sent to the Configuration Manager hierarchy.

Software Update
The Software Update Client Agent is responsible for the core functionality of the Software Updates Client Agent component on the client system. The default scan schedule and the deployment reevaluation schedule can be changed from within the Software Updates Client Agent. These settings control how often the local scans occur. The software updates scan defines how often the client reports compliance information to the Management Point. The scan done by the deployment reevaluation initiates a reinstallation of the patches that were previously installed but are now missing.

> **NOTE**
>
> The deployment reevaluation simply reruns existing Software Update deployment against the client. If the deployment doesn't have a deadline, or if the deadline for the updates hasn't passed, the client can schedule the installation of the previously removed updates.

Understanding the Data Flow
The site settings for each site in the hierarchy can be managed independently. This includes settings to configure the client, such as how often an inventory is run, how clients are discovered, the networks to which the site provides management functionality, Configuration Manager component roles such as Distribution Points and Management Points, and all of the other configuration options found within the Site Management node in the Configuration Manager Administration Console.

Conversely, all of the computer management settings are replicated to child primary sites in the hierarchy. This includes objects such as collections, software distribution packages, software update packages, and all of the other configuration options found within the Computer Management node of the Configuration Manager Administration Console.

NOTE

When opening a Configuration Manager Administration Console on a lower-level child site, a small padlock icon is shown on some objects. This indicates the object was created on a parent site and cannot be modified from the lower-level site.

Only the data, such as hardware and software inventory along with client state and component status messages, is replicated up from lower-level sites to the parent site. Status messages provide information about the Configuration Manager components. State messages come from managed systems and provide insight as to what the client is doing, such as downloading content or installing updates.

Disk Subsystem Performance

The disk performance is a critical factor in the Configuration Manager overall performance. Because of the volume of data that flows from the components into the various databases, data must make it into the databases quickly. However, for usability, console performance is the single most important factor. The console places a significant load on the server, primarily reading the data from the Configuration Manager database. If this read access is slow, console performance will be impacted and users will be dissatisfied with Configuration Manager.

Choosing Between SAN and DAS

One of the common points of contention is what storage systems to use when deploying Configuration Manager. The two main contenders are a storage area network (SAN) disk subsystem and a direct attached storage (DAS) disk subsystem. The SAN is typically a switched-based, fiber-channel fabric and a large array of disks, which is managed by a dedicated storage team. The SAN provides high reliability and high performance, but also high cost. The DAS is a RAID subsystem of disks that are directly attached to the servers. Depending on the RAID configuration, this can have high reliability and high performance, but costs less than a SAN.

Choosing between SAN and DAS can be tough, as there are competing claims as to which subsystem actually performs better. Consider the following three important performance measures when deciding on a disk subsystem:

▶ **I/Os Per Second (IOPS)**—This indicates how many I/O requests can be handled in a second. This measure is impacted by the size of the requests, with larger requests reducing the number of requests that the system can handle in a second.

▶ **I/O Latency (Latency)**—This indicates how long it takes to handle a given request. This measure is also impacted by the size of the requests, with larger requests increasing the latency.

▶ **Megabytes Per Second (MBps)**—This indicates how many megabytes of data can be handled in a second. This measure is also impacted by the size of the requests, but larger requests actually increase the amount of data that can be handled (which is a good thing).

For small data transfers, the IOPS and Latency are the critical measures. For large data transfers, the MBps is the critical measure. The Site Database accesses are all large data transfers usually put into the database in batches through the SMS Provider, so the MBps measurement is the critical measure for the performance and scalability of the system. SQL uses 8KB pages, leading to random and sequential 8KB I/O on the disks that host the databases, which are relatively large data requests.

In general, a SAN provides better performance than a DAS. This is especially true for large, block-level data transfers, which is what the SQL database will be doing. The SAN provides a faster data transfer due to the higher MBps.

In general, most Configuration Manager database servers operate appropriately with DAS disk subsystems.

> **NOTE**
>
> The configuration of the SAN and the DAS can dramatically affect the performance of the two disk subsystems. For example, a DAS subsystem with six controllers, RAID 1+0, and a separate channel and disks for each set of databases and logs outperforms a standard SAN.
>
> However, for most implementations, the SAN is going to be the better bet for performance.

If using DAS, the design of the DAS is critical to ensuring the performance of the disk subsystem. Choose the RAID appropriately, as not all RAIDs are created equal in terms of performance. The following list compares the common RAID choices and their performance:

- ▶ **RAID 1**—This is a pair of drives that are mirrored. RAID 1 provides no performance benefit, as the read/write performance is that of a single drive. The second drive in the RAID array is used simply for fault tolerance.

- ▶ **RAID 5**—This is a set of drives with the data striped across them and with one drive providing parity for fault tolerance. RAID 5 provides mostly read performance benefit, as the parity drive is a write bottleneck in the RAID array.

- ▶ **RAID 10**—The data is mirrored across drives and then striped to the other half of the drives in the array. There is both read and write performance benefit, which is a multiple of the number of disks in the RAID array divided by two.

Given the read and write performance benefits, RAID 10 is always the preferred method. An important benefit of RAID 10 is that the size of the array can be increased by adding spindles (that is, disks) and this also increases the performance of the array. As the Configuration Manager servers are scaled up and better performance is needed, the disk subsystem needs to be scaled to increase performance. This allows target performance (that is, IOps) to be reached.

A 10K RPM SCSI disk will be able to sustain approximately 125 IOps of random read/writes. Using this as a base, a target rate of IOps can be computed in terms of number of disks needed (because RAID-10 performance scales with the number of disks). The computation for the number of disks needed in the RAID-10 array is as follows:

```
Target IOps / (125 IOps per disk / 2) = Number of Disk is RAID 10 Array
```

For example, if a target of 500 IOps is needed, the computation is simply:

```
500 IOps / (125 IOps per disk / 2) = 8 disks
```

A RAID-10 array of eight disks would be sufficient to meet the 500 IOps goal.

This allows designers to compute the sizing of RAID-10 arrays needed to achieve the desired performance in terms of IOps. For RAID 1 and RAID 5, the write performance is limited to that of a single drive, that is, 125 IOps.

Choosing SQL Versions

Another issue is the edition of SQL to use. For Configuration Manager, which leverages the power of SQL heavily, there can be serious performance impacts in choosing the wrong edition of SQL. SQL Server Enterprise Edition is designed to scale to the largest of hardware platforms and handle large workloads, but has an associated high cost. SQL Server Standard Edition has built-in technology scalability limitations, but a much lower cost.

SQL Server Enterprise Edition supports more parallel operations, allowing multiple data-bases to coexist. Both Enterprise and Standard Editions support parallel queries, but only Enterprise Edition supports parallel index and consistency check operations. Enterprise Edition has a host of other performance benefits, such as indexed views, table and index partitioning, dynamic memory management, and enhanced read-ahead and scanning. These enhancements allow Enterprise Edition to handle much larger Configuration Manager implementations and to handle multiple components on the same SQL server.

SQL Server Standard Edition has a four-CPU limit, whereas SQL Server Enterprise Edition is only limited by the operating system. In other words, SQL Server Standard Edition limits parallel processing of queries to a maximum of four CPUs. This is a good example of when the difference between CPUs (that is, sockets on the motherboard) and cores is important. SQL Server Standard Edition counts the physical CPUs toward the limitation.

> **NOTE**
>
> The SQL license that is included in the Configuration Manager Server 2012 with SQL Server Technology is a SQL Server 2008 Standard Edition license.

SQL licensing costs can be a complicated topic. In general, SQL can be licensed in three ways from a Configuration Manager perspective, as shown in Table 2.2.

TABLE 2.2   SQL Licensing Costs

SQL Server 2008 R2 License	Standard Edition Edition	Enterprise
Server Plus CAL	$1,849 with 5 CALs	$13,969 with 25 CALs
Per Processor	$5,999 x CPUs	$24,999 x CPUs
Configuration Manager Server 2007 R2 with SQL Server Technology	$1,321 x management servers	N/A

The Server Plus CAL option is licensed per SQL server and includes a certain number of CALs, but the number of processors is unlimited. The Per Processor option is licensed by the number of CPU sockets (not cores), but the number of CALs is unlimited.

For Configuration Manager implementations, the best option is the Server Plus CAL licensing. Configuration Manager has very low CAL requirements, as the agents do not require CALs. Purchasing Per Processor licensing is not recommended, as a typical Configuration Manager database server will have a lot of CPUs and would not benefit from unlimited CALs.

In general, the best-practice guidance is to use SQL Server Enterprise Edition when

- Multiple Configuration Manager Site Databases will coexist on the same database server, as SQL Server Enterprise Edition handles parallel processing more effectively and can take advantage of additional resources in a scaled-up server.

- More than four CPU sockets will be used, as SQL Server Enterprise Edition can use the additional resources.

- Clustering more than two SQL nodes is a requirement.

Given the cost differential, sometimes it is necessary to deploy SQL Server Standard Edition. Best-practice guidance when using SQL Server Standard Edition is to

- Keep each Site Server database component on a separate SQL server.

- Deploy 64-bit versions.

- Create a small two-node active-passive cluster.

- Use extra memory in database servers to compensate.

Understanding Client Schedules

Several client actions, such as hardware and software inventory, provide the ability to define a simple schedule or a custom schedule. The simple schedule typically improves the overall scalability of the Configuration Manager infrastructure by distributing the load placed on the network, Management Points, and Site Servers.

> **NOTE**
>
> Use the simple schedule and a throttled agent deployment to distribute load and improve scalability of the infrastructure.

The simple schedule works by configuring the client to execute and schedule the inventory schedule dynamically. The first iteration of the schedule is set as the time of the client installation. Throttling the deployment of the Configuration Manager client keeps a relatively consistent load on the environment.

The custom schedule instructs all clients to report inventory at a set time and recurrence pattern. If this configuration is desirable, ensure adequate resources are available for the expected load on the network and Configuration Manager hierarchy.

Clients that are not members of the domain can also be supported. For example, if bastion hosts located in the DMZ need to be inventoried and managed, a Configuration Manager agent can be installed. In addition to the client software, the correct certificate configuration is imperative for secure mode communication.

The Configuration Manager client can be installed many different ways, including manually on the target system, through Group Policy Objects (GPOs), through a logon script, as part of an OS image, through an existing WSUS infrastructure, and automatically through any of the Configuration Manager discovery methods. The Active Directory discovery method is commonly used to find and install clients.

When a discovery method runs, a DDR file is generated and placed in a specific location on the Site Server. The Site Server monitors this folder and kicks off an installation. It's possible to programmatically create DDR files based on a custom discovery and place them in this folder.

Planning for Internet-Based Client Management

Internet-based client management (IBCM) requires a Public Key Infrastructure (PKI). With the correct certificates and infrastructure components in place, clients can be managed over the Internet. This includes receiving policies; downloading content; and uploading inventory reports, state messages, and compliance results.

A Public Key Infrastructure is an important aspect of the Configuration Manager 2012 implementation. If the client doesn't authenticate, either because it doesn't have a client authentication certificate or the current client authentication has been revoked or is otherwise invalid, the client cannot communicate with the Configuration Manager infrastructure.

If the client cannot identify itself with a certificate, or the certificate has been expired or revoked, subsequent communication to the Configuration Manager infrastructure will fail.

In Configuration Manager 2012, Site System components such as the Distribution Point and Management Point can be configured for either HTTP or HTTPS communications. In addition, agents will try HTTPS first and then fall back to HTTP if needed.

Understanding Requirements and Limitations

With IBCM, several limitations are presented and should be understood. The following features are not supported for Internet-based clients:

- ▶ Automatic site assignment
- ▶ Client deployment
- ▶ Network Access Protection
- ▶ OS deployment
- ▶ Out-of-band management
- ▶ Remote tools
- ▶ User-based software distribution
- ▶ Wake On LAN

The primary functionality for IBCM is to be able to deliver software updates, deliver software, and collect inventory data and compliance data without requiring the client to establish a VPN tunnel to the corporate infrastructure.

An Internet client is also required to communicate with an Internet-enabled Management Point. This Management Point must reside in the client's assigned site. This is a very good reason to deploy as few Configuration Manager sites as possible.

A protected Site System cannot be used for Internet-based client management.

Planning Site System Placement

The Management Point, Distribution Point, Fallback Status Point, and Software Update Point can all support Internet clients. Existing roles within the organization can be enabled to support Internet clients or new roles can be established, dedicated to Internet clients. How infrastructure servers are deployed largely centers on the security requirements of the organization.

> **TIP**
>
> Use a wild card certificate or a certificate with Subject Alternate Name configured to allow the Site Server to support both intranet and Internet clients with two unique fully qualified domain names (FQDNs).

For example, if servers in the DMZ cannot directly communicate with servers on the intranet, additional work must be done to create a SQL replica in the DMZ and configure the Management Point so it doesn't talk directly to the Site Server. Instead, the Site Server reaches out and gets information from the Management Point in the DMZ.

The Internet-based roles can be deployed as non–domain members. In this case, when the role is installed on the remote server, a specific Windows account must be specified to complete the installation. In addition, the Site Server can be configured to only allow Site Server–initiated data transfers. This configuration is provided to allow internal Site Servers to communicate into the DMZ, but prevent DMZ servers from communicating directly with the internal network.

Understanding Client Site Assignment

Clients are typically assigned an Internet Management Point and Internet Fallback Status Point during installation. However, these settings can be configured after the client has already been deployed. When a client is deployed, both for mobile and standard clients, the options to enable Internet only and intranet only are available. Standard clients can also support both intranet and Internet management. This allows the client to roam between both management types.

During installation, the client must be configured with the name of the Management Point and the Fallback Status Point. Although an FSP is not required, it is a good idea to enable this role to monitor the communication health of Internet clients.

Understanding Certificate Requirements

When a certificate is issued, its usage is governed by an Object Identifier (OID). A certificate can have more than one OID, essentially allowing the certificate to be used for more than one purpose.

A certificate with the Client Authentication OID is required on all managed clients, including mobile devices, to communicate with a secure Configuration Manager site role. Client Authentication certificates are easily deployed through Group Policy Auto-enrollment. This method of enrollment is important, especially when managing a large number of clients.

A certificate with the Server Authentication OID is required on all Configuration Manager 2012 Site Systems, including Site Servers, Management Points, Distribution Points, Software Update Points, and State Migration Points. The Server Authentication certificate is used on each Site Server to encrypt communication between the managed systems and the Configuration Manager component. These certificates can be created through the Certificate Enrollment website or with the certreq.exe command-line utility.

A certificate is also needed for operating system deployment. This is a Client Authentication (CA) certificate that is uploaded to the Site Server when the PXE Service Point role is deployed. This certificate is used to allow communication to the Configuration Manager infrastructure during all stages of the deployment process. The root certificate for the CA must also be uploaded into each site in the hierarchy to support OS deployment.

A certificate with the Subject Alternate Name (SAN) of each Configuration Manager component should match each component's fully qualified domain name (FQDN).

Planning the Public Key Infrastructure

Care should be taken to ensure the Public Key Infrastructure is well maintained. The security for the PKI is critical. If the PKI environment is compromised, the integrity of the Configuration Manager environment can also be compromised.

> **CAUTION**
>
> The Windows Server 2008 Enterprise certificate template option is not compatible with System Center Configuration Manager 2012. Choosing the Windows Server 2008 Enterprise option results in a version 3 template. To create a version 2 template, select the Windows Server 2003 Enterprise template version.

You should become familiar with the following PKI terminology:

- ▶ **Enterprise root CA**—This is a Certificate Authority that is integrated with Active Directory. The root certificate is automatically distributed to domain members through Active Directory. All domain members trust an enterprise root CA by default.

- ▶ **Client certificate**—This is a unique certificate that is installed in the computer's personal certificate store on each managed system. The Configuration Manager agent uses this certificate to identify the computer when communicating with Site Component Servers.

- ▶ **Server certificate**—This certificate is used by the different Configuration Manager components to encrypt the communication between the Configuration Manager server and the managed client.

Using Certificate Templates

Leveraging Active Directory certificate templates, an enterprise CA, along with automatic enrollment, greatly reduces the amount of overhead associated with Native mode site security.

An enterprise CA that integrates with Active Directory provides a way to automatically provision certificates to systems. This can be used for both Client Authentication certificates and Server Authentication certificates. When the server or client is started, it can be configured to automatically request the correct certificate needed to communicate with Configuration Manager over HTTPS.

> **NOTE**
>
> The Enterprise version of Windows is required to support custom certificate templates used with SCCM 2012.

The certificate for mobile devices must be in Distinguished Encoding Rules (DER) encoded binary X.509 format. The Mobile Device certificate must also be placed in the personal store. All other certificates must be placed in the personal store for the computer account, with the exception of the OS Deployment certificate. The OSD certificate is uploaded to the Configuration Manager console when the PXE-enabled Management Point is created.

Putting It All Together in a Design

The primary components that directly affect scalability are the Site Server, Site Database, Management Point, and Distribution Point. It is also important to note that the configuration of various settings within the environment also affect performance. For example, configuring 1,000 clients to poll the Management Point every 1 minute and submit hardware and software inventory data based on a hard-coded hourly schedule will consume a lot of resources and will require very large, expensive servers.

> **CAUTION**
>
> The preceding guidance should be validated with the desired Configuration Manager settings, before implementing a production infrastructure.

These high-level design scenarios cover a range of organizations from small to medium to large. The profile of the three enterprises is given in the following list:

▸ **Small enterprise**—A total of 30 servers and 500 workstations, in 3 locations, a main office with a shared T1 to the branch offices, and 25% bandwidth availability.

▸ **Medium enterprise**—A total of 500 servers and 2,000 workstations, in 10 locations, a main office with a shared 11Mbps Fractional T3 to the branch offices, and 25% bandwidth availability.

▸ **Large enterprise**—A total of 2,000 servers and 10,000 workstations, in 50 locations, a main office with a shared 45Mbps T3 to the branch offices, and 25% bandwidth availability.

Small and Medium Enterprise

In a small-sized implementation of Configuration Manager, all major components can be hosted on the same server. For best performance, consider separating the following components onto separate physical drives:

▸ Operating system

▸ Configuration Manager installation

▸ Site Database

▸ Distribution Point content

For very small environments, the OS and Configuration Manager installation can potentially reside on the same set of disks. However, the database should almost always be separated from the Configuration Manager installation files. The Distribution Point content should also be moved to a different set of disks, but this is dependent on how much content will be provisioned to target systems. For medium-sized deployments, the Distribution Point and Management Point should be moved to separate hardware if the load on the Site Server becomes heavy. Leverage Perfmon and Operations Manager to monitor load on the disk subsystem, memory usage, and CPU usage.

A Distribution Point should be placed in each remote office to allow the efficient provisioning of large software packages. Smaller deployments can be timed during off-peak hours and are capable of going across the WAN from the main office, assuming BITS downloading will be used. If Distribution Points are not applicable, such as when the remote office consists of laptop users who travel, consider using the BITS throttling to manage bandwidth. In this scenario, large packages can be trickled down to clients to prepare for a deployment.

Large Enterprise

In a large-sized implementation of Configuration Manager, the Site Database and the Site Server component can likely be hosted on the same server but can be moved to a separate SQL server to improve performance or to meet business requirements. For best performance, consider separating the following components onto separate physical drives:

▶ Operating system

▶ Configuration Manager installation

▶ Backup location

▶ VSS temporary location

▶ Site Database

▶ Site Database transaction log

▶ SQL Temp DB

▶ Distribution Point content

NOTE

Use the `VSSAdmin` command-line tool to change the VSS storage backup association. For example, to set a 15GB maximum size on the E: drive for the VSS backup association for the D: drive, run the following command: `vssadmin Add ShadowStorage /For=D: /On=E: /MaxSize=51360MB`.

In this type of environment, it is important to move the Management Point role to a separate server. Also, if the environment has multiple data centers, consider establishing a site in each data center. This spreads the load across data centers and reduces the impact if a single site experiences a problem, so that systems in the other site can still be managed. Don't go overboard with the definition of *data center*; the closet that holds the file and print server in half of the larger remote locations doesn't count.

Performance in a large environment can be improved by implementing a Central Administration Site. In this scenario, all boundaries would be placed in one to two child primary sites. The Central Administration Site wouldn't have any boundaries and would only be used to manage the environment and run reports. The Central Administration Site would not have a Management Point on separate hardware because it won't be actively managing clients.

Remote offices with existing server infrastructure can leverage that hardware for a standard BITS-enabled Distribution Point. A standard Distribution Point is recommended when a remote site has more than 100 active workstations.

One or more Distribution Points should be placed in each remote office that supports between 50 and 100 workstations and doesn't have existing server infrastructure. Distribution Points can also be installed on server operating systems, but will only support clients with the SMB protocol, which is not as efficient as BITS.

Smaller deployments can be timed during off-peak hours and are capable of going across the WAN from the main office, assuming BITS downloading is used.

Summary

Configuration Manager 2012 supports a large array of functionality. From deploying and managing new operating systems to provisioning content to intranet and Internet-based clients, Configuration Manager provides end-to-end management. Before starting a Configuration Manager project, it is important to understand the goals and objectives of the business and plan the implementation accordingly. By understanding how the components and roles work, a successful implementation can be achieved.

Best Practices

The following are best practices from this chapter:

▶ For organizations with existing configuration management database (CMDB) implementations, use Configuration Manager to supply data for Windows-based managed assets. This can be accomplished several different ways, including through the predefined SQL views and the WMI provider.

▶ Manage the Configuration Manager hierarchy from the Central Administration Site, as this provides access to the entire infrastructure and all managed systems. Opening a Configuration Manager Administration Console on a primary site only provides access to clients assigned to that site and child sites below that site.

▶ By default, the contents of a package are pushed to Distribution Points from the Site Server that created the package. Enable the *Send Package from the Nearest Site in the Hierarchy* option to make effective use of Senders and Addresses.

▶ To achieve global roaming, the Active Directory schema has to be extended. If the schema hasn't been extended, only regional roaming is available. Regional roaming only allows client roaming to child sites below the client's assigned site.

▶ Use software publishing to provide users with the ability to execute the software when it's convenient for them. This is often beneficial for more savvy technical users, such as IT staff.

▶ Use the Microsoft Deployment Toolkit (MDT) 2012 for additional OS deployment functionality, including full-file scripted-based installation without needing to capture an image. MDT integrates directly into the Configuration Manager console and can be downloaded from http://technet.microsoft.com/en-us/solutionaccelerators/dd407791.aspx.

▶ Don't use Configuration Manager as an authoritative source for making licensing purchases. The actual counts of licenses should be tracked as systems are provisioned and deprovisioned throughout the enterprise. Configuration Manager should be used to validate those numbers. For example, each SQL component is tracked separately. This artificially increases the count of some of the license reports.

▶ Don't modify existing reports. Always make a copy of the report and make changes to the copy. During Configuration Manager service pack upgrades, the original reports can be updated by Microsoft; if the reports are customized, your changes will be lost.

▶ The Site Server database cannot be backed up while the SMS Executive service is running. Backing up the database while the SMS Executive service is running might result in inconsistencies between information in the database and the Configuration Manager site control file, which will prevent the site from being successfully restored in a disaster recovery scenario. Use the backup tasks from within the Configuration Manager Administration Console to schedule backups.

▶ Software information that is uploaded and eventually categorized by Microsoft is made available to all Microsoft customers through System Center Online Services. Avoid uploading private software information that could be used to identify your business to other customers.

▶ To override protected boundary behavior, enable the *Allow Clients to Fall Back to Unprotected Distribution Points when the Content Is Not Available on the Protected Distribution Point* option on the package advertisement.

▶ Avoid customizing the default collections; they can be changed and reverted back to default during subsequent service pack upgrades.

▶ Use the Network Access Account to allow network access from clients who are not in the same forest or workgroup. Normally, communication is done with the computer$ account; if the computer$ account fails, communication with the Network Access Account is attempted.

▶ Never configure overlapping boundaries. This can cause managed systems to use the wrong Site Server or Distribution Management Point. This often happens when using a combination of IP and Active Directory boundaries.

▶ The Windows Server 2008 Enterprise certificate template option is not compatible with System Center Configuration Manager 2012 with Service Pack 2. Choosing the Windows Server 2008 Enterprise option results in a version 3 template. To create a version 2 template, select the Windows Server 2003 Enterprise template version.

▶ The certificate enrollment website provides a convenient way to generate the OS Deployment certificates. As an alternative to using the web enrollment site, certificates can be requested with the `Certreq.exe` command-line tool. For more information, visit the Certreq TechNet site at http://technet.microsoft.com/en-us/library/cc725793(WS.10).aspx.

▶ Use the simple schedule and a throttled agent deployment to distribute load and improve scalability of the infrastructure.

▶ Use a certificate with Subject Alternate Name (SAN) configured to allow the Site Server to support both intranet and Internet clients with two unique FQDNs.

CHAPTER 3

Configuration Manager 2012 Implementation and Administration

IN THIS CHAPTER

▶ Sample Organization

▶ Configuring Installation Prerequisites

▶ Implementing the Central Administration Site

▶ Deploying the Primary Sites

▶ Deploying the Secondary Sites

▶ Configuring the Hierarchy

▶ Configuring Sites

▶ Configuring Client Settings

▶ Implementing Internet-Based Client Management

▶ Best Practices

System Center Configuration Manager (ConfigMgr) 2012 helps reduce the cost of managing the Windows infrastructure by providing scalable, secure, end-to-end administration and reporting functionality for the enterprise. It is important to fully understand the architectural design before Configuration Manager 2012 infrastructure servers and roles are deployed.

This chapter walks through the steps necessary to deploy, configure, and administer key Configuration Manager 2012 functionality. This functionality includes deploying and administering the roles and features needed to enable operating system deployment, systems configuration management, patch management, software provisioning, asset management, and reporting.

Sample Organization

To illustrate the implementation and administration of Configuration Manager 2012, a multilocation sample organization named Company XYZ will be used. This will provide a backdrop of reality against which the Configuration Manager 2012 design can be developed.

Existing Environment

Company XYZ is headquartered in San Francisco with offices in Paris, London, Tokyo, and New York City. The company has over 3,000 employees distributed primarily between San Francisco and Paris. London and Tokyo are medium-sized branch offices. Finally, the New York office is a very small office with only a handful of employees.

There is a network connection between the San Francisco and Paris offices. London and Tokyo connect to the Paris office. New York is connected to the separate San Francisco office. Figure 3.1 shows the corporate wide area network (WAN) topology.

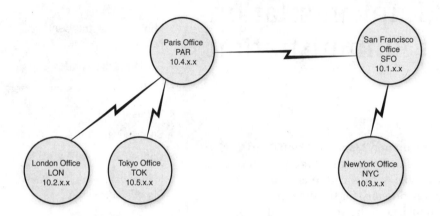

FIGURE 3.1   Company XYZ WAN topology.

The company has a single Active Directory forest and domain. The domain name is companyxyz.com and has a domain controller DC1. Each office has its own Active Directory site in the Active Directory site topology. Table 3.1 summaries the location information.

TABLE 3.1   Company XYZ Location Information

Location	AD Site	Network	Users
San Francisco	SFO	10.1.x.x	2,000
Paris	PAR	10.4.x.x	1,000
London	LON	10.2.x.x	100
Tokyo	TOK	10.5.x.x	100
New York	NYC	10.3.x.x	5

The San Francisco office has the central IT organization that covers the entire Company XYZ organization, but the Paris office also has a smaller IT organization that covers the Paris, London, and Tokyo locations. The Paris office has significant autonomy and needs administrative control over its infrastructure due to regulatory concerns.

This information will be used to inform the Configuration Manager 2012 design.

Developing a Configuration Manager 2012 Design

Based on the Company XYZ existing environment, the recommendation would be to have a Primary Site Server in San Francisco and a Primary Site Server in Paris based on the local IT presence and the requirement for local administrative control. The recommendation would be to place Secondary Site Servers in London and Tokyo based on the size of the offices. Given the small size of the New York office with only five users, no servers will be placed there.

Table 3.2 summarizes the locations, server roles, and server names needed for the infrastructure.

TABLE 3.2   Company XYZ Configuration Manager 2012 Design

Location	SCCM Site	Site Code	Server Name
San Francisco	Central Administration Site	XYZ	CM1
	Primary Site	SFO	CM2
Paris	Primary Site	PAR	CM3
London	Secondary Site	LON	CM4
Tokyo	Secondary Site	TOK	CM5
New York		NYC	

Figure 3.2 shows a diagram of the recommended Configuration Manager 2012 infrastructure.

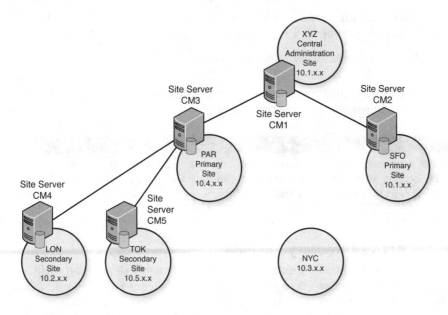

FIGURE 3.2   The Company XYZ ConfigMgr 2012 design.

The balance of this chapter implements and configures the Configuration Manager 2012 design for Company XYZ.

Configuring Installation Prerequisites

Before implementing SCCM 2012, several prerequisite steps need to be taken to prepare Active Directory and the Site Servers. These steps ensure that the SCCM implementation goes smoothly.

The required SCCM prerequisites are as follows:

▶ Extending the Active Directory schema

▶ Configuring the System Management container in Active Directory

▶ Adding Windows roles and features on Site Servers

These prerequisites prepare the environment for Configuration Manager 2012.

These installation prerequisites are in addition to the hardware and software requirements covered in Chapter 2, "Configuration Manager 2012 Design and Planning." The software requirements include the following:

▶ Windows Server 2008 64-bit SP2 or Windows Server 2008 R2 operating system

▶ Windows Active Directory domain

▶ .NET Framework 3.51 SP1

▶ .NET Framework 4.0

▶ SQL Server 2008 SP2 with Cumulative Update 7 or SQL Server 2008 R2 SP1 with Cumulative Update 4 (can be on a separate server)

▶ Opened TCP port 1433 and 4022 for SQL replication

The hardware and software requirements for all prospective Site Servers must be met before the installation prerequisites can be configured.

> **NOTE**
>
> If you install IIS after installing .NET Framework 4.0, then open a command prompt, browse to the location `%windir%\Microsoft.NET\Framework64\v4.0.30319`, and execute `aspnet_regiis.exe —i —enable`.

Extending the Active Directory Schema

The Active Directory schema should be extended to support dynamic client assignment during Configuration Manager agent deployment and to assist clients with the location of Configuration Manager server infrastructure. When the Active Directory schema is extended, clients can use the values provided through Active Directory to locate regional Site Servers and Distribution Points for package and content delivery.

> **NOTE**
>
> The Active Directory schema extensions for SCCM 2012 are identical to the Active Directory schema extensions for SCCM 2007. If the schema was already extended for SCCM 2007, the schema does not need to be extended again for SCCM 2012.

> **CAUTION**
>
> Take the appropriate safety measures when extending the Active Directory schema. Changes to the schema cannot be easily reversed; plan to test the schema extensions in a development environment before implementing them in your production environment.

To extend the Active Directory schema, execute the following steps:

1. Log on to a domain controller with an administrative account that is a member of the Schema Admins group.

2. Copy the `EXTADSCH.exe` from `\SMSSETUP\BIN\x64\` on the Configuration Manager installation media to a local folder on the Active Directory domain controller with the schema master FSMO role.

3. Open a command window as an administrator and execute the `EXTADSCH.exe` command with a Schema Admin account.

The command should report, "Successfully extended the Active Directory schema" when complete (as shown in Figure 3.3).

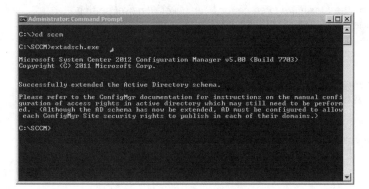

FIGURE 3.3   Successful Active Directory schema extension.

Review the `ExtADSch.log` file for any errors. This log file is located in the root of drive C on the server used to execute the schema extensions. The log file should show 14 attributes and four classes have been defined.

> **TIP**
>
> Sometimes, the attribute extensions will succeed, but the class extensions will fail. This is typically due to replication latency, especially in large distributed environments. The EXTADSCH.exe command can be run multiple times with no ill effect. Wait for replication to complete and then run the schema extension command again.
>
> After replication is completed, the class extensions should be successful.

Configuring the System Management Container

When the Active Directory schema has been extended, Configuration Manager Site Servers store information about the hierarchy in special Active Directory objects. These objects are kept in a specific folder in the System container of the domain partition. The location for these objects doesn't exist by default, and must be manually created and configured.

In a distributed Configuration Manager hierarchy, it is considered best practice to place the Configuration Manager Site Servers in a custom security group, and delegate this security group's permissions to the System Management container in Active Directory. The following tasks assume the Configuration Manager Site Servers (CM1, CM2, CM3, CM4, and CM5) are members of the "SCCM Site Servers" universal security group. If this group doesn't exist, create it before continuing.

> **CAUTION**
>
> When a computer object is added to a group, it can take a long time for the setting to take effect. This is because the Kerberos ticket takes seven days to renew. The renewal time is governed by the *Maximum Lifetime for User Ticket Renewal* setting located in the Default Domain Policy GPO. It is not recommended to change this setting. Instead, restart the computer to refresh the Kerberos ticket.

The System Management container holds the Configuration Manager objects in Active Directory. This container can be created with the ADSI Edit console on the DC1 domain controller.

To create the System Management container with ADSI Edit, complete the following steps:

1. Run ADSI Edit from DC1.

2. Right-click the ADSI Edit node and select Connect To.

3. Type **Domain** in the Name field.

4. Select Default Naming Context from the list of well-known naming contexts.

5. Click OK.

6. Expand Default Naming Context.

7. Expand DC=companyxyz,DC=com.

8. Select the CN=System container.

9. Right-click CN=System, click New, and then click Object.

10. Select Container from the list and click Next.

11. Enter **System Management** for the CN attribute value, and then click Next.

12. Click Finish to complete the change.

The permissions for the System Management container need to be configured before the first Site Server is implemented.

To set the System Management container permission with ADSI Edit, complete the following steps:

1. Right-click the System Management container and select Properties.

2. Select the Security tab.

3. Click Advanced.

4. Click Add.

5. Type **SCCM Site Servers** and click OK.

6. Continue with the default selection of This Object and All Descendant Objects from Apply To.

7. Choose Allow in front of Full Control in the Permissions field and then click OK.

8. Click OK two times to commit all the changes and then close ADSI Edit.

As Configuration Manager Site Servers are added to the hierarchy, be sure to add them to the custom Site Servers security group (SCCM Servers). This ensures they can create the required Active Directory objects.

Adding Windows Roles and Features on Site Servers

The majority of client communications is over HTTP or HTTPS, which is serviced by the Windows IIS web server. IIS is a key component of many Configuration Manager Site Systems roles. This includes the Site Server itself in the following optional roles:

▶ Application Catalog Web Service Point

▶ Application Catalog Website Point

▶ Distribution Point

▶ Enrollment Point

▶ Enrollment Proxy Point

▶ Fallback Status Point

▶ Management Point

▶ Software Update Point

> **NOTE**
>
> Some Configuration Manager 2012 Site System roles will require additional installation of Windows roles or features, such as for the software update point, which requires the Windows Server Update Services (WSUS) role, or Distribution Point, which requires IIS request filtering to be configured. These additional configurations will be done as part of configuring those Site System roles.

It is important to make sure that IIS is installed correctly on each of the Site Systems; otherwise, SCCM will not operate correctly.

To implement IIS on the Site Server and Component Servers on a Windows Server 2008 R2–based system, complete the following steps:

1. Open Server Manager on the Site/Component Server.

2. Select the Features node.

3. Click the Add Features action.

4. Enable Background Intelligent Transfer Service (BITS).

5. When prompted, click Add Required Role Services.

> **NOTE**
>
> Clicking the Add Required Role Services button automatically enables IIS and common related features required to host the Configuration Manager service. This includes Web Server components, Management Tools, and Remote Server Administration Tools.

6. Enable the Remote Differential Compression feature and click Next.

7. On the Web Server Overview page, click Next.

8. Enable the ASP.NET role service, and click Add Required Role Services.

9. Enable the ASP role service.

10. Enable the Windows Authentication role service.

11. Enable the IIS 6 WMI Compatibility role service and the IIS 6 Metabase Compatibility if they are not already, and then click Next.

12. Review the components selected and click Install.

13. Close the wizard when the installation completes.

During this process, a number of roles, role services, and features get enabled automatically. If the preparation is being done on a system with some of these enabled or disabled, it can be confusing to know which ones need to be added.

To install using the command line, open Windows PowerShell as an administrator and enter the following commands:

```
Import-Module ServerManager
Add-WindowsFeature Net-Framework,BITS,RDC,Web-ASP-Net,Web-ASP,Web-Windows-Auth,
Web-WMI,Web-Metabase
```

When the preparation process is completed, at minimum the Web Server (IIS) role should be installed with the following list of role services:

- Static Content
- Default Document
- Directory Browsing
- HTTP Errors
- HTTP Redirection
- ASP.NET
- .NET Extensibility
- ISAPI Extensions
- ISAPI Filters
- HTTP Logging
- Logging Tools
- Request Monitor
- Tracing
- Windows Authentication
- Request Filtering
- Static Content Compression
- Dynamic Content Compression
- IIS Management Console
- IIS 6 Metabase Compatibility
- IIS 6 WMI compatibility

In addition, the following Windows features should be installed:

▶ Background Intelligent Transfer Service (BITS)

▶ Remote Differential Compression

▶ Web Server (IIS) Tools

▶ BITS Server Extensions Tools

In preinstalled systems, ensure that the preceding role services and features are installed.

Implementing the Central Administration Site

The Configuration Manager Central Administration Site is the primary site located at the very top of the Configuration Manager hierarchy. This site is needed if there will be more than one primary site in the hierarchy.

There is a very important implementation difference between the Configuration Manager 2012 Central Administration Site and the central site in previous versions. In previous versions, Primary Site Servers can be installed and later connected to the central site. This is no longer possible in Configuration Manager 2012 and Primary Site Servers must be connected to their Central Administration Site during installation. This means that the Central Administration Site must be installed before any primary sites in the hierarchy.

The net result of these changes is that the Central Administration Site is required and must be the first site implemented if there will be more than one Primary Site Server in the hierarchy, as is the case in the sample Company XYZ architecture.

Verify that all of the hardware and software requirements have been met and that the installation configuration prerequisites have been completed.

Installing the Central Administration Site Server

Before running the Configuration Manager setup, run the prerequisite checker to verify the required components have been successfully installed. The prerequisite checker can be launched from a link on the `splash.hta` page. The `splash.hta` page can be found in the root of the Configuration Manager media.

TIP

Make sure the Configuration Manager Site Server Computer Account is in the local administrators group on all component servers and other Site Servers—this includes the Site Database server. The computer account of the Site Server is used to access and manage the remote server by default. One way to accomplish this is by creating a group named SCCM Site Servers with the computer accounts of all SCCM Site Servers as members and then adding that group to the Local Administrator group on all Site Servers.

Before starting the installation process, create a folder on the C: drive called "SCCMUpdates" and share this folder. This folder will store the latest prerequisite components downloaded during the installation process. This folder can be reused during subsequent Site Server installations.

To install the XYZ Central Administration Site Server on the CM1 server and establish the Company XYZ hierarchy, complete the following steps:

1. Launch splash.hta from the Configuration Manager 2012 media.

2. To run the Prerequisite Checker tool, click on the Assess Server Readiness link in the Tools and Standalone Components section.

> **NOTE**
>
> The Prerequisite Checker tool has been much enhanced in SCCM 2012. It runs a wider range of checks and is a standalone executable (prereqchk.exe) that can be run unattended via a command line or script. This allows the prerequisite checking process to be automated for large organizations.

3. Remediate any issues the Prerequisite Checker tool finds and click OK to close the window.

4. After ensuring all the prerequisites have been met, click the Install link in the splash screen.

5. At the Before You Begin screen, click Next.

6. Select the Install Configuration Manager Central Administration Site option and click Next.

7. Enter a 25-character product key and click Next.

8. Accept the license terms and click Next.

9. Accept the license terms for the software that will be downloaded and installed automatically on Site Systems pushed through the hierarchy and click Next.

> **NOTE**
>
> This automates the prerequisite installations of Microsoft SQL Server 2008 R2 and Microsoft Silverlight for secondary site servers in SCCM 2012. This reduces the amount of preparation needed on a secondary site server and eases the administrative burden of deploying additional servers in the hierarchy.

10. Enter the location to download prerequisites and updates, in this example the previously created share \\CM1\SCCMUpdates, and click Next.

11. In the Server Language Selection, leave the default English and click Next.

12. In the Client Language Selection, leave the default English and click Next.

13. In the Site and Installation Settings, enter a site code and site name. In this example, the site code is **XYZ** and the site name is **Company XYZ Central Administration Site**.

14. Leave the default installation folder and click Next.

15. In the Database Information, specify the database server name and instance. Click Next.

16. In the SMS Provider Settings, leave the default of CM1 and click Next.

17. In the Customer Experience Improvement Program Configuration, choose the appropriate option and click Next.

18. In the Settings Summary (shown in Figure 3.4), review the settings and click Next.

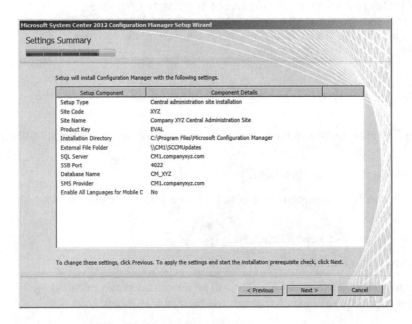

FIGURE 3.4   The central site installation Settings Summary.

19. The Prerequisite Checker executes a last-minute check. Verify that all prerequisites have been met or remediate any errors, and then click Begin Install.

20. The installation completes and should have green status symbols next to each component installation.

21. Click Close to exit the setup wizard.

Installation is now complete for the Central Administration Site and the console can be launched.

Validating the Installation of the Central Administration Site

To validate the installation, check the contents of the System Management container in Active Directory. The System Management container can be seen by launching Active Directory Users and Computers, selecting the View menu, choosing Advanced Features, and expanding the System folders or with ADSI Edit. The Site Server object should exist in this container for the Central Administration Site. In this example, the XYZ Central Administration Site should create an object in the System Management container named SMS-Site-XYZ of type mSSMSSite. As additional Site Servers in Site System roles are deployed, additional objects are created automatically.

It is important to validate the installation after each role is deployed; this ensures everything is functioning correctly before moving to the next step. It is also important to monitor site status on a continuous basis to ensure the health of the environment. For additional information on automatically monitoring the Configuration Manager hierarchy with Operations Manager, review Chapter 8, "Using Operations Manager 2012 for Monitoring and Alerting."

In addition, open the Configuration Manager console and review the Site Status component in the System Status container. This console is called Configuration Manager console and is located under the Microsoft System Center 2012\Configuration Manager folder in the Start menu on the Site Server.

To view the Component Status in the ConfigMgr console, do the following:

1. Launch the Configuration Manager console.

2. Choose the Monitoring space.

3. Expand the System Status node.

4. Select the Site Status node and confirm that all statuses show as OK with green icons.

5. Select Component Status and confirm that all statuses show as OK with green icons.

The Site Status page shows a high-level summary of the Site System roles and the status. This is useful for seeing an overview of the Site Systems and ensuring that they are healthy. If a role is marked with a red error or a yellow warning icon, the component has received status messages indicating a problem with the component. Right-click the component, select Show Messages - All from the menu and select a viewing period for the messages.

The Component Status page shows all of the components that make up the Configuration Manager infrastructure for this site. The component status is based on status messages that are received from the component. Because the component has to send the Site Server status, and the Site Server has to process the status message, the condition of components can be delayed. This is especially true when looking at the status of child sites within the Central Site console because status messages are sent to parent sites based on the Site Sender configuration.

If a component is marked with a red error or a yellow warning icon, the component has received status messages indicating a problem with the component. Right-click the component, select Show Messages - All from the menu and select a viewing period for the messages.

TIP

The status summarizer for the different components is not automatically changed from red or yellow to green if the component that experienced the problem is fixed. The component summarizer simply counts the number of warning and error status messages that have been received.

To reset the status of a component, right-click the component and select Reset Counts - All from the menu. The count of status messages is reset and the icon will change back to green in a few minutes.

The delay in status messages is often a source of frustration for administrators starting out with Configuration Manager. For a better, real-time view into site components, check the log files with cmtrace.exe, a Configuration Manager 2012 utility. You can identify the log file for a specific component by right-clicking the component and selecting Start, ConfigMgr Service Manager from the menu. Navigate to the component within the Service Manager, right-click the component from the Actions pane, and then select Logging.

NOTE

The cmtrace.exe log viewing utility replaces the previous trace32.exe utility from the Configuration Manager toolkit. The cmtrace.exe is included with the SCCM 2012 server and installs with the default setup.

The site component Logging option is shown in Figure 3.5. The SMS Executive logging option has been chosen and shows the name and location of the log file, which is c:\Program Files\Microsoft Configuration Manager\Logs\smsexec.log. The size of the log file, 2 MB, is also shown and can even be adjusted here.

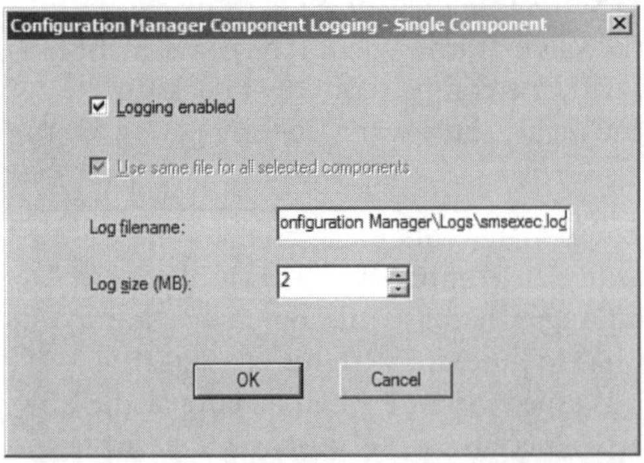

FIGURE 3.5   The component log location.

Now that the top-level Central Administration Site has been deployed successfully, the primary sites and other sites can be deployed in the Configuration Manager 2012 hierarchy.

Deploying the Primary Sites

Deploying primary sites follows a similar process as deploying the Central Administration Site Server. In the case of the Company XYZ Configuration Manager 2012 hierarchy, there are two primary sites. These are San Francisco (SFO) with the CM2 server and Paris (PAR) with the CM3 server.

Verify that all the hardware and software requirements have been met and the installation configuration prerequisites have been completed.

Installing a Primary Site Server

Before running the Configuration Manager setup, run the prerequisite checker to verify the required components have been successfully installed. The prerequisite checker can be launched from a link on the `splash.hta` page. The `splash.hta` page can be found in the root of the Configuration Manager media.

> **TIP**
>
> Make sure the Configuration Manager Site Server Computer Account is in the local administrators group on all component servers and other Site Servers; this includes the Site Database server. The computer account of the Site Server is used to access and manage the remote server by default. One way to accomplish this is by creating a group named **SCCM Site Servers** with the computer accounts of all SCCM Site Servers, then adding the local administrator groups on all Site Servers.

To install the SFO Primary Site Server on the CM2 server in the Company XYZ hierarchy, complete the following steps:

1. Launch `splash.hta` from the Configuration Manager 2012 media.

2. To run the Prerequisite Checker, click on the Assess Server Readiness link in the Tools and Standalone Components section.

3. Remediate any issues the prerequisite checker tool finds and click OK to close the window.

> **NOTE**
>
> It is normal to get a `WSUS SDK on site server` issue during the prerequisite check on a new Primary Site Server. If this server is intended to host the Site Server Software Update role, then the Windows WSUS role will be installed at that time.

4. After ensuring all the prerequisites have been met, click the Install link in the splash screen.

5. At the Before You Begin screen, click Next.

6. Select the Install Configuration Manager Primary Site option and click Next.

7. Enter a 25-character product key and click Next.

8. Accept the license terms and click Next.

9. Accept the license terms for the software that will be downloaded and installed automatically on Site Systems pushed through the hierarchy and click Next.

NOTE

This automates the prerequisites installations of Microsoft SQL Server 2008 R2 and Microsoft Silverlight for secondary site servers in SCCM 2012. This reduces the amount of preparation needed on a secondary site server and eases the administrative burden of deploying additional servers in the hierarchy.

---

10. Because the prerequisites were downloaded previously, choose the Use Previously Downloaded Files option and enter the location of the downloaded prerequisites and updates, in this example the previously created share \\CM1\SCCMUpdates, and click Next.

11. In the Server Language Selection, leave the default English and click Next.

12. In the Client Language Selection, leave the default English and click Next.

13. In the Site and Installation Settings, enter a site code and site name. In this example, the site code is SFO and the site name is Company XYZ San Francisco Site.

14. Leave the default installation folder and click Next.

15. Enter the name of the Central Administration Site Server to join the existing hierarchy, in this case cm1.companyxyz.com and click Next.

16. In the Database Information, specify the database server name and instance. Click Next.

17. In the SMS Provider Settings, leave the default of CM2 and click Next.

18. In the Client Computer Communication Settings, choose the Configure the Communication Method on Each Site System Role option and click Next.

19. In the Site Systems Roles, leave the options to install a Management Point and a Distribution Point checked and click Next.

20. In the Customer Experience Improvement Program Configuration, choose the appropriate option and click Next.

21. In the Settings Summary (shown in Figure 3.6), review the settings and click Next to begin the installation.

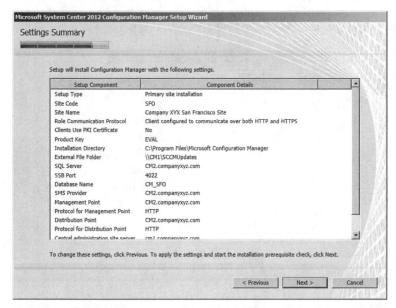

Microsoft System Center 2012 Configuration Manager Setup Wizard

Settings Summary

Setup will install Configuration Manager with the following settings.

Setup Component	Component Details
Setup Type	Primary site installation
Site Code	SFO
Site Name	Company XYX San Francisco Site
Role Communication Protocol	Client configured to communicate over both HTTP and HTTPS
Clients Use PKI Certificate	No
Product Key	EVAL
Installation Directory	C:\Program Files\Microsoft Configuration Manager
External File Folder	\\CM1\SCCMUpdates
SQL Server	CM2.companyxyz.com
SSB Port	4022
Database Name	CM_SFO
SMS Provider	CM2.companyxyz.com
Management Point	CM2.companyxyz.com
Protocol for Management Point	HTTP
Distribution Point	CM2.companyxyz.com
Protocol for Distribution Point	HTTP
Central administration site server	cm1.companyxyz.com

To change these settings, click Previous. To apply the settings and start the installation prerequisite check, click Next.

[< Previous] [Next >] [Cancel]

FIGURE 3.6   The primary Site installation Settings Summary.

22. The Prerequisite Checker executes to do a last-minute check. Verify that all prerequisites have been met or remediate any errors, and then click Begin Install.

23. Installation completes and should have green status symbols next to each component installation.

24. Click Close to exit the setup wizard.

Installation is now complete for the Primary Site and the console can be launched.

Repeat the preceding steps for Company XYZ Paris Site, the PAR Primary Site Server on the CM3 server.

Validating the Installation of the Primary Site

To validate the installation, check the contents of the System Management container in Active Directory. The System Management container can be seen with the Advanced view of Active Directory Users and Computers, or with ADSI Edit. In this example, the Site Server object should exist in this container for the Central Administration Site of type mSSMSSite. The SFO primary site should create a record in the System Management container named SMS-Site-SFO of type mSSMSSite. There should also be an object for the Management Point, named SMS-MP-SFO-CM2.COMPANYXYZ.COM of type mSSMSManagementPoint. Similarly, the PAR primary site should create an object in the

System Management container named SMS-Site-PAR of type mSSMSSite. There should also be an object for the Management Point, named SMS-MP-PAR-CM3.COMPANYXYZ.COM of type mSSMSManagementPoint. Figure 3.7 shows the Active Directory records for the sites created.

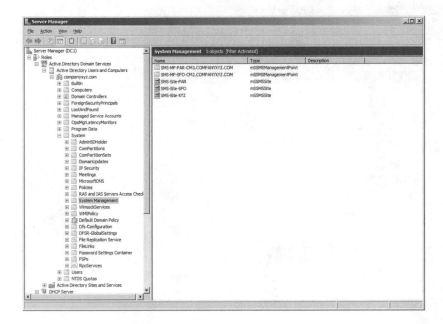

FIGURE 3.7   The Active Directory SCCM records for Primary Sites.

It is important to validate the installation after each role is deployed; this ensures everything is functioning correctly before moving to the next step. It is also important to monitor site status on a continuous basis to ensure the health of the environment. For additional information on automatically monitoring the Configuration Manager hierarchy with Operations Manager, review Chapter 8.

In addition, open the Configuration Manager console located under the Microsoft System Center 2012\Configuration Manager folder in the Start menu on the Site Server, expand the Monitoring option, and review the Site Status component in the System Status container.

To view the component status in the Configuration Manager console, do the following:

1. Launch the Configuration Manager console.

2. Choose the Monitoring space.

3. Expand the System Status node.

4. Select the Site Status node and confirm that all statuses show as OK with green icons.

5. Select Component Status and confirm that all statuses show as OK with green icons.

The Site Status page shows a high-level summary of the Site System roles and the status. This is useful for seeing an overview of the Site Systems and ensuring that they are healthy. If a role is marked with a red error or a yellow warning icon, the component has received status messages indicating a problem with the component. Right-click the component, select Show Messages - All from the menu and select a viewing period for the messages.

The Component Status page shows all of the components that make up the Configuration Manager infrastructure for this site. The component status is based on status messages that are received from the component. Because the component has to send the Site Server status, and the Site Server has to process the status message, the condition of components can be delayed. This is especially true when looking at the status of child sites within the Central Site console because status messages are sent to parent sites based on the Site Sender configuration.

If a component is marked with a red error or a yellow warning icon, the component has received status messages indicating a problem with the component. Right-click the component, select Show Messages - All from the menu, and select a viewing period for the messages.

TIP

The status summarizer for the different components is not automatically changed from red or yellow to green if the component that experienced the problem is fixed. The component summarizer simply counts the number of warning and error status messages that have been received.

To reset the status of a component, right-click the component and select Reset Counts - All from the menu. The count of status messages is reset and the icon will change back to green in a few minutes.

The delay in status messages is often a source of frustration for administrators starting out with Configuration Manager. For a better, real-time view into site components, check the log files with cmtrace.exe, a Configuration Manager 2012 utility. You can identify the log file for a specific component by right-clicking the component and selecting Start, ConfigMgr Service Manager from the menu. Navigate to the component within the Service Manager, right-click the component from the Actions pane, and then select Logging.

NOTE

The cmtrace.exe log viewing utility replaces the previous trace32.exe utility from the Configuration Manager toolkit. The cmtrace.exe is included with the SCCM 2012 server and installs with the default setup.

Now that the primary sites have been deployed successfully, the secondary sites can be deployed in the Configuration Manager 2012 hierarchy.

Deploying the Secondary Sites

Configuration Manager 2012 secondary sites are deployed through the console, via a push from a Primary Site Server. All the prerequisites, such as SQL Server 2008 and .NET Framework 4.0, are pushed out with the role remotely. However, this requires two features to be installed to work correctly. Those features are as follows:

- Remote Differential Compression

- .NET Framework 3.5

To install these prerequisites using the command line, run PowerShell as an administrator and enter the following commands:

```
Import-Module ServerManager
Add-WindowsFeature Net-Framework,RDC
```

In addition, the Primary Site Server Active Directory account (for example, CM3$) is the account performing the remote installation, so it must have local administrator rights to the target secondary site server.

If the Windows Firewall is in use, open ports 1433 and 4022 for SQL Server access.

> **TIP**
>
> The computer account of the Site Server is used to access and manage the remote secondary site server by default. One way to accomplish this is by creating a group named SCCM Site Servers with the computer accounts of all SCCM Site Servers, then adding the local administrator groups on all Site Servers.

To deploy a secondary site from a primary site, execute the following steps:

1. Launch the Configuration Manager console.

> **NOTE**
>
> The Configuration Manager console can be launched from the Central Administration Site Server or the Primary Site Server. Even if the installation is initiated with the Configuration Manager console on the Central Administration Site, the actual installation is performed from the Primary Site Server. This is a great example of the improved centralized administration capabilities of Configuration Manager 2012.

2. Choose the Administration space, expand Site Configuration, and select Sites.

3. Select the primary site from which to deploy the secondary site, in this example the PAR site.

4. Right-click on the Primary Site Server (the CM3 server in this example) and select Create Secondary Site.

5. At the Before You Begin screen, click Next.

6. In the Site and Installation Settings, enter a site code, Site Server, and site name. In this example, the site code is **LON**, the server is **CM4.companyxyz.com**, and the site name is **Company XYZ London Site**.

7. Leave the default installation folder and click Next.

8. Leave the default to copy the installation source files from the parent Site Server (in this case cm3.companyxyz.com) and click Next.

9. Leave the default to install SQL Server Express on the secondary site server and click Next.

10. Make sure to check the Install and Configure IIS option, as shown in Figure 3.8, and click Next.

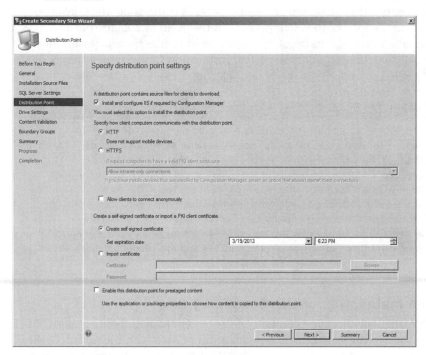

FIGURE 3.8   Specify Distribution Point Settings.

Later in the chapter, when configuring Internet-based client management (IBCM), the protocol setting will be changed from HTTP to HTTPS.

11. Leave the default drive settings and click Next.

12. Leave the default Content Validation settings and click Next.

13. Leave the Boundary Groups settings empty and click Next. These will be configured later.

14. Review the summary and click Next.

15. Click Close to exit the wizard.

The setup begins from the Primary Site Server. A new Site Server appears in the list of sites with a status of Pending. To see the summary status, right-click on the secondary server and select Show Install Status. This shows the summary status message for the secondary site server install.

Because installation is being done remotely, it can be difficult to ascertain what could've gone wrong with the installation. However, the Show Install Status messages are very informative and specific. They show the prerequisite checks being done, the download progress, and the installation progress step-by-step. In the event of a failure of the secondary site installation, these messages can be reviewed for the specific reason for the failure. Once remediated, the secondary site server installation can be retried simply by right-clicking the failed secondary site server and selecting Retry Secondary Site.

TIP

The status of the secondary site server install can also be monitored in detail from the source Primary Site Server and the target secondary site server. In the root of the system drive of the Primary Site Server doing the push installation, the log file ConfigMgrSetup.log will show the status of the install in detail. Once the installation commences, there will be a corresponding ConfigMgrSetup.log in the root of the system drive of the secondary site server, which shows where the installation picks up locally. Review the log on the source Primary Site Server to troubleshoot remote access and file transfer issues. Review the log on the target secondary site server to troubleshoot issues with the installation of prerequisites and the secondary site role.

Validating the Installation of the Secondary Site

To validate the installation, check the contents of the System Management container in Active Directory. The System Management container can be seen with the Advanced view of Active Directory Users and Computers, or with ADSI Edit. The Site Server object should exist in this container for the Secondary Sites. In this example, the LON secondary site should create an object in the System Management container named SMS-Site-LON of type mSSMSSite. There should also be an object for the Management Point, named SMS-MP-LON-CM4.COMPANYXYZ.COM of type mSSMSManagementPoint. Similarly, the TOK secondary site should create an object in the System Management container named SMS-Site-TOK of type mSSMSSite. There should also be an object for the Management Point, named SMS-MP-TOK-CM5.COMPANYXYZ.COM of type mSSMSManagementPoint. Figure 3.9 shows the Active Directory objects for the sites created.

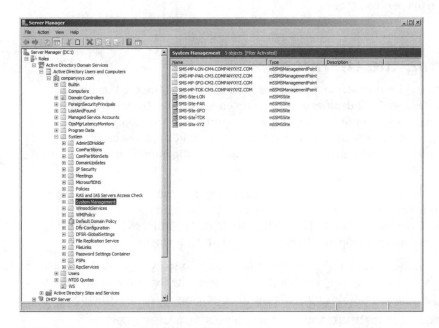

FIGURE 3.9   The Active Directory SCCM records for Secondary Sites.

To view the component status for the secondary site servers in the Configuration Manager console, do the following:

1. Launch the Configuration Manager console.

2. Choose the Monitoring space.

3. Expand the System Status node.

4. Select the Site Status node and confirm that all statuses show as OK with green icons.

5. Select Component Status and confirm that all statuses show as OK with green icons.

If a component is marked with a red error or a yellow warning icon, the component has received status messages indicating a problem with the component. Right-click the component, select Show Messages - All from the menu and select a viewing period for the messages.

> **TIP**
>
> Sometime, the secondary site server installation process will not correctly install the prerequisite Background Intelligent Transfer Service (BITS) Windows feature. If this is the case, there'll be Message ID 4957 error messages in the `SMS_MP_CONTROL_MANAGER` component for the secondary site server. Add the BITS feature manually on the secondary site server if this occurs. The errors should resolve themselves in the next hourly cycle.

Configuring the Hierarchy

With the SCCM 2012 servers deployed, the next task is to configure the hierarchy. Configuration Manager 2012 deploys a more complete set of roles by default than the previous versions, but there still remain roles to be configured. The Configuration Manager 2012 console is divided into four spaces: Assets and Compliance, Software Library, Monitoring, and Administration. The hierarchy configuration takes place within the Administration space.

The Site Settings container within the Site Management node can be used to configure the different components and functionality provided by Configuration Manager. Prior to managing clients, the appropriate functionality should be implemented and configured to ensure clients are managed properly following the agent deployment.

The Configuration Manager console with the Administration space expanded is shown in Figure 3.10. This view also has the sites selected and shows the five servers that have been deployed (CM1, CM2, CM3, CM4, and CM5) in the Company XYZ infrastructure.

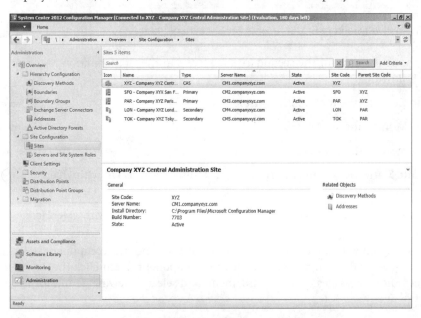

FIGURE 3.10   The Configuration Manager console Administration space.

Establishing Boundaries and Boundary Groups

Establishing site boundaries and boundary groups is one of the most important aspects of Configuration Manager. Boundaries let managed systems receive content and communicate status to the closest server in the Configuration Manager hierarchy.

The boundaries, in effect, map physical locations, based on IP address, to systems such as workstations. Boundary groups allow administrators to logically group boundaries together and then assign resources such as Distribution Points for them to use.

Boundaries can be created based on IP subnet, IPv6 prefix, IP address range, and Active Directory sites. Typically in an Active Directory environment, the Configuration Manager is based on Active Directory site boundaries. Because the Active Directory site infrastructure should already map directly to the network topology, many of the same principles that apply to an Active Directory site topology also apply to the Configuration Manager topology. For example, instead of taking all the subnets in a specific network location and adding them as a site boundary, it is much easier to add the already configured Active Directory site boundary.

That said, there are still many different scenarios and environments where using an Active Directory site boundary simply isn't possible or practical for technical or even political justification. Configuration Manager allows a mixture of all the different boundaries. It is possible to configure different combinations of site boundaries in the console to address these scenarios.

> **CAUTION**
>
> Never configure overlapping boundaries. This can cause managed systems to use the wrong Site Server or Distribution Management Point. This often happens when using a combination of IP and Active Directory boundaries.

New to Configuration Manager 2012 is the ability to have the Active Directory sites be discovered automatically in the forest. This saves a tremendous amount of time. The Active Directory forest discovery operates very similarly to the Active Directory system discovery or group discovery.

To configure Active Directory forest discovery, do the following:

> **NOTE**
>
> Launching the console on the Central Administration Site provides complete administrative access to the entire Configuration Manager 2012 hierarchy.

1. Launch the Configuration Manager console on the Central Administration Server.
2. Choose the Administration space.
3. Expand the Hierarchy Configuration and select Discovery Methods.

4. Right-click on Active Directory Forest Discovery and select Properties.

5. Check Enable Active Directory Forest Discovery and the check box to automatically create site boundaries.

6. Change the Schedule option to run every day.

7. Click OK to save changes and Yes to run the full discoveries as possible.

Once the Active Directory forest discovery is completed, the Active Directory site boundaries will be created. Figure 3.11 shows the Active Directory site boundaries created for the Company XYZ organization.

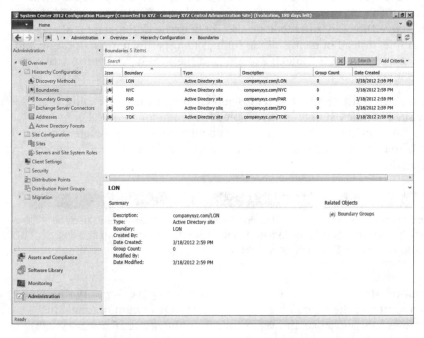

FIGURE 3.11   Discovered Active Directory boundaries.

Boundary groups are not discovered automatically, but rather are configured by the administrator. Boundary groups logically group the agents (through the boundaries) with resources such as Management Points and Distribution Points. This allows administrators to control where agents download their content from, thus controlling bandwidth utilization. For example, the Company XYZ organization has five locations: San Francisco, Paris, London, Tokyo, and New York. New York is the only office without a Configuration Manager 2012 Site Server. Boundary groups will be created for each location with the Site Server, so that local clients will download content from the local Site Servers. However, the New York boundary will be added to the SFO boundary group to ensure that the New York agents download content from the San Francisco Site Server. These boundary groups are shown in Figure 3.12.

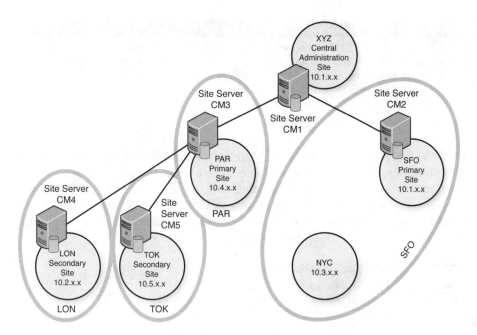

FIGURE 3.12   Company XYZ boundary groups.

To create a boundary group (in this example the Company XYZ SFO boundary group), execute the following steps:

1. Make sure that your Active Directory sites and subnets are configured correctly and include all subnets and physical sites in the environment.

2. Launch the Configuration Manager console on the Central Administration Site Server.

3. Choose the Administration space.

4. Expand the Hierarchy Configuration and select the Boundary Groups node.

5. Right-click on the boundary group node and select Create Boundary Group.

6. In the general tab, enter the name of the boundary group (in this case, **SF0**).

7. Click the Add button to add boundaries to the boundary group.

8. Check the SFO boundary, and then click OK.

9. Choose the Reference tab.

10. In the Site Assignment section, check the Use This Boundary Group for Site Assignment check box and select the SFO site in the drop-down.

11. In the Content Location section, click the Add button.

12. Select the SFO Site Server and click OK.

NOTE

The connection defaults to "Fast." This can be changed to "Slow" by clicking on the Change Connection button. This can be used to control how content is downloaded or if content is downloaded. This is useful for having backup content locations.

13. Click OK to create the boundary group.

When a server is configured within a boundary group, the server connection type defaults to Fast. The connection types are limited to Fast or Slow and are somewhat misleading. The true purpose of the connection types is during the creation of a deployment. When you want to deploy software, such as an application or patches, to a system, a deployment is needed. When configuring the deployment, several different distribution options are available. The deployment distribution options are shown in Figure 3.13.

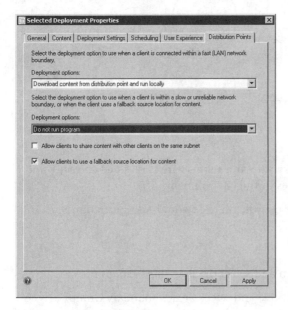

FIGURE 3.13   Distribution options.

The deployment allows the administrator to specify distribution characteristics depending on the configuration of the boundary groups. For example, if you configure a server connection in the boundary group as Slow and then configure the deployment to not run when the client is connected to a slow or unreliable network boundary, the software will not run on any system that identifies itself as being within this boundary.

NOTE

The topic of deployments is covered in Chapter 4 "Using Configuration Manager 2012 to Distribute Applications, Updates, and Operating Systems."

The remaining boundary groups for Paris, London, and Tokyo can be created following the previous procedure. Now clients in the boundaries will automatically assign themselves to the appropriate site and download content from the appropriate location.

Configuring Discovery Methods

The Active Directory System Discovery option is the most common method used to find potential systems to manage. The main advantage to the AD System Discovery option is its efficiency in a well-maintained domain. Ensure that computer accounts that are no longer used have been disabled or removed from the Active Directory domain.

> **NOTE**
>
> Discovery of systems, groups, and users can be configured on each primary site in the SCCM 2012 hierarchy. However, discovery information is shared with all sites in the hierarchy. Rather than have duplicate discoveries, the best practice is to designate a single primary site in the hierarchy to do the discovery.

To enable the Active Directory System Discovery method, do the following:

1. From the ConfigMgr console, select the Administration space and expand the Hierarchy Configuration folder.

2. Select the Discovery Methods node.

3. Right-click and open the properties of the Active Directory System Discovery method for the SFO site. The SFO site will be the Company XYZ designated discovery site.

4. Enable Active Directory System Discovery.

5. Click the "*" button to add an AD container.

6. Click the Browse button and then click OK to select the entire companyxyz.com domain.

7. Accept the default options and click OK.

8. Select the Polling Schedule tab and click the Schedule button.

9. Change the recurrence to 1 hour and click OK.

10. Click OK to save the changes.

11. Click Yes at the pop-up to run the full discovery as soon as possible.

The status of the AD system discovery can be viewed in the `adsysdis.log` file.

To review the results of the discovery, do the following:

1. From the ConfigMgr console, expand Asset and Compliance.

2. Expand Overview, expand Devices, and right-click on the All Systems collection.

3. Click Update Membership.

4. Click Yes when prompted.

5. Click the Refresh action.

The collection should show all of the clients in the domain.

To enable the Active Directory Group Discovery method, do the following:

1. From the ConfigMgr console, select the Administration space and expand the Hierarchy Configuration folder.

2. Select the Discovery Methods node.

3. Open the properties of the Active Directory Group Discovery method for the SFO site. The SFO site will be the Company XYZ designated discovery site.

4. Enable Active Directory Group Discovery.

5. Click the Add button and select a location. Enter `Company XYZ Domain` for the Name.

NOTE

Active Directory Group Discovery supports the discovery of single groups for all groups with the location, such as a domain.

---

6. Click the Browse button and then click OK to select the entire companyxyz.com domain.

7. Accept the default options and click OK.

8. Select the Polling Schedule tab and click the Schedule button.

9. Change the recurrence to 1 hour and click OK.

10. Click OK to save the changes.

11. Click Yes at the pop-up to run the full discovery as soon as possible.

The previous steps should be repeated for the Active Directory User Discovery for SFO.

The Active Directory discoveries can be triggered manually by right-clicking on the discovery method and selecting Run Full Discovery Now. The detailed results of the discovery can be seen in the log files on the discovery server. The log files for each of the discoveries are as follows:

▶ Active Directory System Discovery (adsysdis.log)

▶ Active Directory Group Discovery (adsgdis.log)

▶ Active Directory User Discovery (adusrdis.log)

Any discovery errors or access errors will be shown in these detailed logs.

Configuring Hierarchy and Geographic Views

Configuration Manager infrastructures can be complex and hard to monitor. A very common request for administrators is to be able to view the hierarchy in a dynamic way. Another very common request is for administrators to be able to see their hierarchy map out geographically, with components in the correct place on a map. Configuration Manager 2012 delivers on both these requests.

The Configuration Manager 2012 hierarchy diagram shows the hierarchy in a graphical, dynamic, and active view. Each site is displayed in the diagram, with links and status. As sites are added and states change, the hierarchy diagram will update automatically.

Figure 3.14 shows the hierarchy diagram for Company XYZ. The diagram shows each of the five Configuration Manager 2012 Site Servers with a different icon for each site type. The overall alert status for each site is indicated as well, as can be seen in the warning state for the PAR site. Right-clicking on any component gives you detailed status, as is shown for the SFO site. The detailed status also allows you to link to key information such as site status messages and site properties.

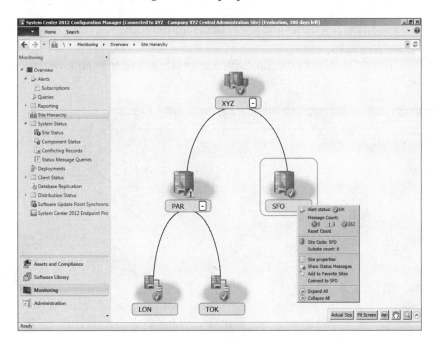

FIGURE 3.14   Company XYZ hierarchy diagram.

To access the hierarchy diagram, do the following:

1. Launch the Configuration Manager console.

2. Select the Administration space.

3. Select the Site Hierarchy folder.

In addition to the hierarchy diagram, there is also a geographical view. This view shows all the Site Servers on a Bing map. However, physical location information needs to be specified to enable the display of Site Servers on the map.

To specify the location information and display the geographical view, execute the following steps:

1. Launch the Configuration Manager console.

2. Select the Monitoring space.

3. Select the Site Hierarchy folder.

4. Right-click the Site Hierarchy folder and select Configure View Settings.

5. Select the Site Location tab.

6. For each site, enter a location. The location can be general, such as the city, or specific, such as the address.

7. Click OK to save the changes.

8. Right-click the Site Hierarchy folder and select Geographical View.

The view now shows a world map with the Site Servers correctly placed in their locations, as shown in Figure 3.15.

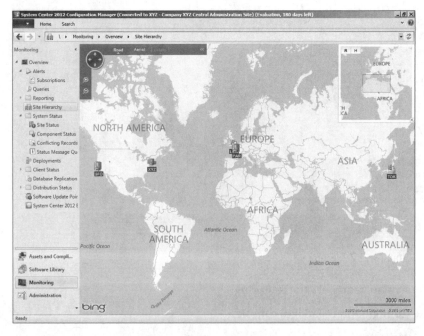

FIGURE 3.15   Company XYZ geographical view.

Like the hierarchy view, when the geographical view is active, hovering over a site with a mouse gives a high-level alert status and subsite count. The basis for the underlying map is the Bing Map engine. The map can be viewed either as a road map or an aerial satellite view. The map can also be zoomed into, to get detailed street information. In addition, selecting a site shows site links to neighboring sites. Figure 3.16 shows a zoom into the Company XYZ European region, with expanded map detail. The Paris site has been selected, which then shows the site links, including the site link to London.

> **NOTE**
>
> If it displays some instructions instead of the Bing Map, it may be because of the server's Internet Explorer settings; follow the instructions to solve the issue.

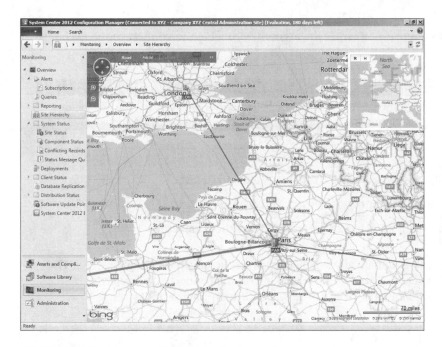

FIGURE 3.16   Company XYZ detailed geographical view.

Either view can be printed to capture the key information.

The hierarchy diagram and the geographical view provide exciting new and dynamic ways to view the Configuration Manager 2012 infrastructure.

Configuring Exchange Connectors

The Configuration Manager 2012 Exchange connector allows administrators to manage mobile devices that do not or cannot have agents installed on them, such as Apple iPhone, Apple iPad, or Google Android devices. Essentially any device that supports ActiveSync and is connected to Exchange Server can be managed through the connector.

To configure the Exchange connector, do the following steps:

1. Launch the Configuration Manager console.

2. Choose the Administration space.

3. Expand the Hierarchy Configuration folder.

4. Right-click on the Exchange Server Connectors node and select Add Exchange Server.

5. In the Server Address (URL) field, enter the address of the Exchange Client Access Server. The format of the URL is http://excas.companyxyz.com/powershell.

6. Select the Configuration Manager site to run the Exchange Server connector.

7. Click Next.

8. In the Account section, enter the account with which to connect to the Exchange server and click Next.

> **NOTE**
>
> The Account page very helpfully lists the Exchange Server cmdlets that the connector will need to be able to run the function correctly. The specified account should have the appropriate rights to run those cmdlets.

9. In the Discovery page, leave the defaults and click Next.

10. Adjust the policy settings as needed, and then click Next.

11. Review the summary and click Next to create the connector.

The connector will automatically synchronize with the targeted Exchange server. The synchronization can be forced by right-clicking on the connector and selecting Synchronize Now. Mobile devices will appear shortly in the list of devices.

Configuring Sites

Configuration Manager 2012 deploys certain Site System roles such as Management Points and Distribution Points, but does not deploy other roles nor completely configure those that it does deploy by default. Site configuration entails completing the configuration of the deployed roles and deploying of the required roles.

When deploying Site System roles to either the Site Server or a remote server, it is important to note the component installation wizard doesn't actually do the installation—it simply queues the installation for the Site Component Manager service. Even through the wizard always completes with a successful message, it is important to review the corresponding log files and the System Status container to ensure the component was actually installed correctly.

The log files for component installation are typically located on the server the component is being installed on, in a folder called `\Program Files\Microsoft Configuration Manager\Logs`. Additional status messages can be viewed in the `sitecomp.log` file on the Primary Site Server.

Deploying the Fallback Status Point Role

The Fallback Status Point (FSP) is very important. It provides a safety net for clients. The Configuration Manager agent should always be able to communicate status messages to the FSP, even if other communication has failed or is being blocked due to certificate or other issues.

To install FSP, complete the following steps:

1. From within the Administration space, expand Site Configuration and select Servers and Site Systems Roles.
2. Right-click CM2 and select Add Site System Roles.
3. On the General page, click Next.
4. Enable the Fallback Status Point role and click Next.
5. Accept the default configuration and click Next.

> **TIP**
>
> When a client is deployed, it sends several status messages to the FSP, even when the deployment is successful. If a large client rollout is planned, increase the number of messages allowed to prevent a backlog.

6. Review the summary and click Next.
7. Wait for the installation to complete, and then close the wizard.

Review the `fspMSI.log` and the `SMSFSPSetup.log` files for installation status. During normal operation, problems can be identified with the `fspmgr.log` file and using reports such as the Client Deployment Status Details or the Client Deployment Failure report.

Deploying the Reporting Service Point Role

The Reporting Service Point (RSP) provides reporting of Configuration Manager data through SQL Reporting Services (SRS). SRS is a significantly more powerful platform for developing and delivering reports.

The Reporting Service Point component is installed in three steps. Initially, the role is added to the correct server from the Site Management\Site Systems node. Then the Reporting Point needs to be configured with a data source; this is necessary to establish communication with the database holding the Configuration Manager data. Finally, reports need to be migrated from the legacy Reporting Point to the Reporting Service Point.

To install RSP on the Central Administration Site (CM1), complete the following steps:

1. From within the Administration space, select Servers and the Site System Roles folder.

2. Right-click CM1 and select Add Site System Roles.

3. On the General page, click Next.

4. Enable the Reporting Services Point role and click Next.

5. The Site Database Connection Settings will be discovered automatically. Click the Verify button to verify the settings.

6. In the Reporting Services Point Account, click the Set button and choose New Account.

7. Enter the appropriate credentials, and then click OK.

8. Click Next.

9. Review the summary and click Next.

10. Wait for the installation to complete, and then close the wizard.

This process should be completed not only for the Central Administration Site, but also for each primary site as well. This allows each of the sites to generate reports covering their specific information. For example, reports generated from the Central Administration Site in San Francisco will include information from the entire Company XYZ hierarchy. Reports generated from either the SFO or PAR primary sites will only include information from their portion of the hierarchy.

Review the SRSRPSetup.log and the srsrp.log files. These log files are located on the server hosting the Reporting Service Point in the Configuration Manager log folder (often c:\Program Files\Microsoft Configuration Manager\Logs). To check the status of the Reporting Services Point, go to the Monitoring space in the console, expand the Reporting folder, and select the Reports node. Reports will be listed there once the role is completed deploying.

Deploying Software Updates Point Role

For Site Servers that will be supporting the Software Updates role, there are two parts to the role setup. The first is to set up Windows Server Update Services (WSUS) and the second is to set up the Software Update Point role. In a Configuration Manager 2012 hierarchy that includes a Central Administration Site, the Software Update Point role will be installed on the Central Administration Site Server.

The Windows Server Update Services (WSUS) 3.0 SP2 components are required by Configuration Manager to support synchronization of patch data from Microsoft Update. WSUS is not used to deliver patches to managed systems; instead, the Configuration Manager hierarchy is used to effectively create an enterprise patch delivery and installation system.

To install WSUS 3.0 SP2, do the following on the Central Site Server (CM1 in the Company XYZ hierarchy):

1. Launch Windows Server Manager.

2. Right-click on the Roles folder and select Add Roles.

3. Click Next to skip the Welcome page.

4. Check the Windows Server Update Services role.

5. Click the Add Required Role Services if it pops up.

6. Click Next.

7. Click Next and Next past the Web Server (IIS) options.

8. At the WSUS welcome screen, click Next.

9. At the Confirmation screen, click Install.

NOTE

The WSUS installer downloads the latest version from the Internet and launches, continuing the installation.

10. Once the Windows Server Update Services 3.0 SP2 Setup Wizard launches, at the Welcome screen click Next.

11. Accept the terms of the license agreement and click Next.

12. Store the updates on c:\WSUS and click Next.

13. Select Using an Existing Database Server on This Computer.

14. Click Next.

15. If the connection is successful, click Next.

16. Leave the default website preference and then click Next.

17. Review the installation configuration and click Next.

18. Close the wizard when the installation is complete.

19. In the Before You Begin page of the Windows Server Update Services Configuration Wizard, click Cancel.

NOTE

There is no need to bother with the WSUS Configuration Wizard. All configuration of WSUS will be administered and managed using the Configuration Manager console.

Once the Windows WSUS role has been installed, the next step is to deploy the Software Update Point role. To do this, complete the following steps:

1. On the Central Administration Site Server (CM1 in the Company XYZ hierarchy), launch the Configuration Manager console.

2. In the Administration space, expand the Site Configuration folder and select the Servers and Site System Roles node.

3. Right-click the Central Administration Site Server, in this case CM1, and choose Add Site System Roles.

4. Click Next.

5. Check the Software Update Point role and click Next.

6. At the Software Update Point screen, leave the defaults and click Next.

7. At the Active Settings screen, check the Use This Server as the Active Software Update Point check box and click Next.

8. At the Synchronization Source screen, leave the defaults and click Next.

9. At the Synchronization Schedule screen, check the Enable Synchronization on a Schedule check box.

10. Change the schedule to run every 1 Days and click Next.

11. At the Supersedence Rules screen, leave the default and click Next.

12. At the Classifications screen, check All Classifications and click Next.

13. At the Products screen, check the required products and click Next.

14. At the Languages screen, check the appropriate languages and click Next.

15. Review the summary screen and then click Next.

16. Close the wizard when completed.

The Central Administration Site will now perform update synchronization for the entire Configuration Manager 2012 hierarchy.

Deploying Endpoint Protection Point Role

In Configuration Manager 2012, the System Center 2012 Endpoint Protection is integrated into the product rather than a separate install. There is now a Site Server role called Endpoint Protection Point, which provides endpoint protection services.

In a Configuration Manager 2012 hierarchy that includes a Central Administration Site, the Endpoint Protection Point role will be installed on the Central Administration Site Server.

To deploy the Endpoint Protection Point role, complete the following steps:

1. On the Central Administration Site Server (CM1 in the Company XYZ hierarchy), launch the Configuration Manager console.

2. In the Administration space, expand the Site Configuration folder and select the Servers and Site System Roles node.

3. Right-click the Central Administration Site Server, in this case CM1, and choose Add Site System Roles.

4. Click Next.

5. Check the Endpoint Protection Point role.

6. There will be a pop-up warning that software updates require special configuration or endpoint protection needs to use a different source. Click OK.

7. Click Next.

8. At the Endpoint Protection screen, accept the license terms and click Next.

9. Choose the appropriate Microsoft Active Protections Service (MAPS) membership type and click Next.

10. Review the summary screen and then click Next.

11. Close the wizard when completed.

The Central Administration Site will now perform endpoint protection for the entire Configuration Manager 2012 hierarchy.

Deploying Asset Intelligence Synchronization Point Role

An additional component called the Asset Intelligence Synchronization Point is also available. This component provides integration between Configuration Manager and Microsoft System Center Online services provided by Microsoft.

In a Configuration Manager 2012 hierarchy that includes a Central Administration Site, the Asset Intelligence Synchronization Point role will be installed on the Central Administration Site Server.

To deploy the Asset Intelligence Synchronization Point role, follow these steps:

1. On the Central Administration Site Server (CM1 in the Company XYZ hierarchy), launch the Configuration Manager console.

2. In the Administration space, expand the Site Configuration folder and select the Servers and Site System Roles node.

3. Right-click the Central Administration Site Server, in this case CM1, and choose Add Site System Roles.

4. Click Next.

5. Check the Asset Intelligence Synchronization Point role and click Next.

6. At the Asset Intelligence Synchronization Point Settings screen, leave the defaults and click Next.

> **NOTE**
>
> A certificate is not required. This was a legacy requirement back when Microsoft controlled what organizations could do asset intelligence synchronization, limiting it to organizations with Software Assurance contracts. After a time, Microsoft relaxed the requirement and now allows all organizations to perform asset intelligence synchronization without the certificate requirement.

7. At the Proxy Server Settings screen, leave the defaults and click Next.

8. At the Synchronization Schedule screen, leave the Enable Synchronization on a Schedule check box checked.

9. Change the schedule to run every one days and click Next.

10. Review the summary screen and then click Next.

11. Close the wizard when completed.

The Central Administration Site will now perform asset intelligence synchronization for the entire Configuration Manager 2012 hierarchy.

Preparing for OS Deployment

To support OS deployment user state migration and using network boot, the State Migration Point and PXE-enabled Distribution Point are required. To also support a complete operating system refresh with the ability to capture the users' existing settings, store them securely on the network, then reapply them to the new operating system; the State Migration Point is required.

The PXE functionality requires the WDS transport feature. This is available by default on Windows Server 2008, and can be installed automatically during the PXE configuration.

To enable CM2 to support PXE for OS deployment, complete the following steps:

1. Launch the Configuration Manager console.

2. In the Administration space, expand the Site Configuration folder and select the Servers and Site System Roles node.

3. Select the Primary Site Server, in this case CM2, and choose the Distribution Point role from the details window below.

4. Right-click the Distribution Point role and select Properties.

5. Select the PXE tab.

6. Enable PXE support for clients.

7. Click Yes after reviewing the ports information pop-up.

8. Check the Allow This Distribution Point to Respond to Incoming PXE Requests check box.

9. Check the Enable Unknown Computer Support check box and click OK to the warning pop-up.

10. Uncheck the Require a Password when Computers Use PXE check box.

11. Click OK to save changes to the Distribution Point.

The next step is to install the State Migration Point. This allows systems that are undergoing operating system deployment to upload the captured user state and then download the captured user state once the operating system is upgraded.

To deploy the State Migration Point role, follow these steps:

1. Launch the Configuration Manager console.

2. In the Administration space, expand the Site Configuration folder and select the Servers and Site System Roles node.

3. Right-click the Primary Site Server, in this case CM2, and choose Add Site System Roles.

4. Click Next.

5. Select the State Migration Point and click Next.

6. Click the orange "*" to specify a new folder to store state.

7. Enter a folder to use, such as `c:\StateMigration` and click OK.

8. Click Next.

9. Leave the default boundary groups and click Next.

10. Review the summary screen and then click Next.

11. Close the wizard when completed.

The preceding steps to configure PXE functionality and state migration functionality need to be completed on each Distribution Point and Site Server where Operating System Deployment (OSD) functionality is needed. Typically, this is all Primary Site Servers and all secondary site servers in the Configuration Manager 2012 hierarchy, as well as locations with just Distribution Points.

Configuring Client Settings

Client settings control 18 different areas of client configuration, ranging from BITS configuration through User and Device Affinity. In the past, these settings were monolithic and applied to the entire site. There was no granularity within the site nor any way to transfer settings across the hierarchy. In Configuration Manager 2012, the client settings are configured at a hierarchy level, meaning that the settings apply to the site and all child sites. In addition, custom settings can be created and deployed to collections. These custom settings and flexible targeting mechanism allow settings to be adjusted in a very fine-grained manner.

In the next sections, each of the settings are covered along with recommended settings. To review and edit any of the settings, select the Administration space.

Background Intelligent Transfer

The Background Intelligent Transfer settings allow administrators to control the download behavior of clients via the BITS protocol. By default, these settings are disabled, but if enabled, these settings allow the client to be throttled within a specified window with maximum transfer rates.

For most organizations, it is recommended that this be left disabled.

Client Policy

The client policy settings control how often the client checks in for policy updates, by default every 60 minutes. This essentially establishes a heartbeat for the policy refresh. If new policies are deployed, this polling interval limits how quickly that policy can be deployed.

This was a classic example where different settings were needed for different types of devices. Many organizations were comfortable with a one-hour polling interval for workstations, but wanted a much shorter polling interval for servers along the lines of 15 minutes. This was difficult to do in previous versions of SCCM, but in SCCM 2012 is easy to do with the custom client settings targeted at servers.

In addition, user policy polling can be disabled or enabled. This controls whether users will see user policy. Machine policies are always applied.

Is recommended that the default polling interval of 60 minutes be left in place unless there are specific reasons to adjust it.

Compliance Settings

The Compliance Settings section controls whether compliance is enabled or disabled. This setting is enabled by default. The schedule for compliance evaluation is also set in this section, with the default of every seven days.

It is recommended that compliance evaluation be left enabled and that schedule be adjusted to run every one day.

Computer Agent

The Computer Agent section contains a smorgasbord of settings related to notifications, the Application Catalog, and installation permissions. A few these have very useful applications.

The Install Permissions setting allows administrators to control which users can initiate installation of software and software updates in task sequences. The options are as follows:

- ▶ All Users
- ▶ Only Administrators
- ▶ Only Administrators and Primary Users
- ▶ No Users

This setting, in combination with custom settings targeted at collections, allows administrators to control who is allowed to manually install software advertised by SCCM.

The PowerShell Execution Policy allows administrators to control whether unsigned PowerShell scripts are allowed or not. The default Restricted setting prevents unsigned scripts from executing, whereas the Bypass setting allows unsigned scripts to execute.

The Deployment Deadline options control how often users will see pop-ups of impending deployment deadlines over 24 hours out, less than 24 hours out, and less than an hour away. This set of options combined with custom settings targeted at collections allows administrators flexibility in notifying users.

Computer Restart

The Computer Restart section controls the notifications that users receive before pending restart. The temporary notification, by default 90 minutes, is the advance warning the user gets before restart. The countdown notification, by default 15 minutes, is the countdown window that the user gets before restart.

Endpoint Protection

The Endpoint Protection section covers the settings related to the Microsoft anti-malware features of Configuration Manager 2012. It is disabled by default, but is highly recommended that it be enabled.

Most of the settings in this section control agent installation behavior, such as to install the agent (default is True), remove previously installed agents (default is True), and suppress restarts after installation (default is True).

Interestingly, the default remove previously installed agents will remove both Microsoft and non-Microsoft antivirus agents. The list of antivirus agents that will be removed includes the following:

▶ All current Microsoft anti-malware products except for Windows InTune and Microsoft Security Essentials

▶ Symantec AntiVirus Corporate Edition version 10

▶ Symantec Endpoint Protection version 11

▶ Symantec Endpoint Protection Small Business Edition version 12

▶ Mcafee VirusScan Enterprise version 8

▶ Trend Micro OfficeScan

Given the ease with which SCCM 2012 endpoint protection deploys, it may come as a surprise when it uninstalls other antivirus agents. To prevent this, it is recommended to use custom client settings with this option disabled.

The one setting that needs to be changed, after enabling the agent, is the Disable Alternate Sources option. This is enabled by default, which prevents the Endpoint Protection agent from using other sources such as Microsoft Windows Update to get definition updates. This option should be set to False, to allow the agent to get definition updates from Windows Update.

Hardware Inventory

The Hardware Inventory section, enabled by default, primarily controls the interval on which hardware inventory is collected. The default of seven days is usually too long and it is recommended to change the schedule to once per day.

In addition, in this section additional hardware inventory classes can be configured to be collected. This includes Registry values for other important information, which previously required modifying text files directly. Embedding a graphical user interface (GUI) to do this in Configuration Manager 2012 is a very welcome enhancement.

Remote Tools

The Remote Tools section controls the remote tools if enabled on agents and the behavior of the remote tools if it is enabled. Remote tools are by default disabled.

A new feature of the remote tools settings is the ability to set the Windows Firewall as part of enabling the tool. As shown in Figure 3.17, the remote control feature is enabled in the check box to configure the remote control port and program exception for just the domain firewall. This ensures that while computers are connected to the domain, remote control will be allowed through the firewall. When not connected to the domain, those ports will be closed and not present a security risk.

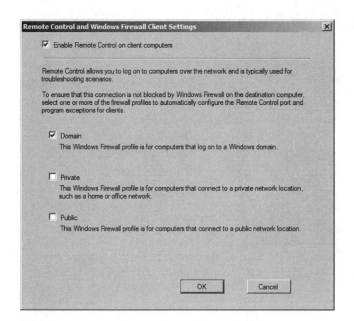

FIGURE 3.17   Enabling remote control with domain firewall exception.

Another welcome enhancement to Configuration Manager 2012 is the Allow Remote Control of an Unattended Computer option. This feature was completely absent from the previous version of SCCM, meaning that the user always had to be present when using remote tools. With SCCM 2012, administrators can now press Ctrl+Alt+Delete on a remote agent. However, this is explicitly allowed (the default) or disallowed in the remote tools client settings.

Software Deployment

In the Software Deployment section, the only setting is for the deployment reevaluation schedule. This defaults to seven days and can be left at the default.

Software Inventory

The Software Inventory section of client settings controls how software inventory is collected. It is enabled by default with the schedule of every seven days.

It is recommended that the schedule be changed to every one days, to ensure that software reporting is as current as possible.

Unfortunately, in SCCM 2012 the inventory file types is blank. This means that no files will be inventoried by default. In previous versions of SCCM, all EXE files were inventoried out of the box. It is recommended that organizations inventory at a minimum all EXE (*.exe), all DLL (*.dll), and all PST (*.pst) files. Figure 3.18 shows the recommended file inventory types.

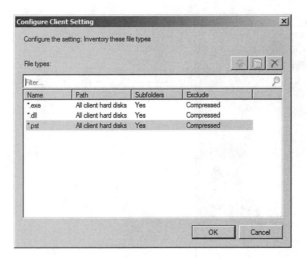

FIGURE 3.18   The recommended file inventory types.

Software Metering

In the Software Metering section, the only settings are to enable software metering and for the deployment reevaluation schedule. This defaults to seven days and should be adjusted to every one day, if the feature is enabled.

Software Updates

The Software Update section of client settings controls updates behavior. It is enabled by default, but there are several schedule options within the section that should be adjusted.

The software update scan schedule defaults to every seven days, but should be adjusted to every one days. This allows much more timely information to be collected, such as what updates have been applied. This is reflected in reports, which will be current as of the previous day.

The scheduled deployment reevaluation schedule defaults to every seven days and should be left as is. The schedule determines how often the agent checks to see if it is still in compliance with previous deployments, which might result in updates being deployed.

The next setting controls what the agent does when a particular software update deployment deadline is reached, should the agent also opportunistically install any other pending software update deployments. And it allows how far in advance to look for pending software update deployments. Because update deployments frequently result in reboots, it makes sense to deploy future updates at the same time.

The setting defaults to False, so it is recommended to change that to True and the next setting to seven days. This ensures that any updates with mandatory deadlines scheduled up to a week in advance will be deployed at the same time.

State Messaging

The State Messaging section of client settings controls a little-known, but key aspect of the Configuration Manager agent. As the agent is executing policy, deployments, and tasks, it generates status messages and delivers them to the server to be stored in the database.

The State Messaging section controls the frequency with which those messages get uploaded. The default is every 15 minutes, but can be adjusted depending on conditions.

User and Device Affinity

The User and Device Affinity section of client settings controls a much requested feature that Configuration Manager 2012 delivers. Device affinity allows devices such as desktops and laptops to be associated with their users. In SCCM 2012, this can be done automatically.

In the User and Device Affinity section, administrators can specify how much time a user needs to spend with the device for it to be automatically associated with the user account.

There are two threshold settings that create the automatic association. The first is the User Device Affinity Usage Threshold (min) setting, which sets how much time a user needs to spend using the machine for it to be considered associated with that user. The second is the User Device Affinity Usage Threshold (days) setting, which sets the span of time over which usage is measured.

To enable User und Device Affinity, the Automatically Configure User Device Affinity from Usage Data setting needs to be set to True.

In addition, the Allow Users to Define Their Primary Devices setting allows users to actually specify their primary device (that is, set the affinity). It is recommended that this be set to True to give users control.

Figure 3.19 shows the recommended User and Device Affinity settings.

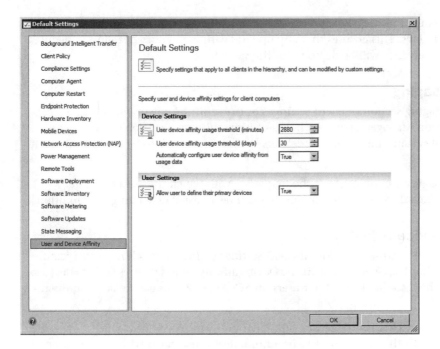

FIGURE 3.19   The User and Device Affinity settings.

Configuring the Client Installation Settings

In Configuration Manager 2012, the client push installation settings are associated with each primary or secondary site in the hierarchy. The Client Installation Settings menu for each site holds the two installation options: Client Push Installation and Software Update-Based Client Installation. The Client Push Installation option is typically used to perform client deployments. The settings within the Client Push Installation configure the command-line options used when the client is pushed, the account used to access the remote computer, and if one of the Configuration Manager discovery methods triggers an installation of the client on remote systems.

A client can be pushed manually from the Configuration Manager console or executed automatically when a Discovery Method is executed. It is important to disable the Automatic Push Installation option until the client is tested and the correct options are set.

To configure the Client Installation account, complete the following steps:

1. Open the console, browse to Administration, expand Site Configuration, expand Sites, and select SFO Site.

2. Right-click on SFO Site and select Client Installation Settings, Client Push Installation.

3. Check the Enable Automatic Site Wide Client Push Installation check box.

4. Select the Accounts tab, click "*", and then click New Account.

5. Add an account with local administrative rights to the systems.

6. Select the Installation Properties tab. The current installation property is SMSSITE-CODE=SFO.

7. Add FSP=CM2 to the Installation properties. This specifies the fallback status point for clients. Separate the properties with a space.

8. Apply the changes.

This account will be used to push the Configuration Manager agent to client systems. The SMSSITECODE=SFO command is configured by default to set the agent's assigned site. If the agent is being pushed from a primary site, but will be managed by a different primary site or secondary site, this value should be changed to SMSSITECODE=AUTO, allowing the client to choose the correct site code based off of the configured boundaries.

Repeat the previous steps for each primary site and secondary site that will be pushing out agents.

Implementing Internet-Based Client Management

Internet-based client management in Configuration Manager 2012 is really just configuring key roles to support the secure HTTPS protocol rather than the insecure HTTP protocol. That said, considerable preparation work needs to be done to implement the Public Key Infrastructure and certificates to support this change efficiently and effectively.

Creating a Public Key Infrastructure

A Public Key Infrastructure (PKI) is an important aspect of the Configuration Manager 2012 implementation. When a certificate is issued, its usage is governed by an Object Identifier (OID). A certificate can have more than one OID, essentially allowing the certificate to be used for more than one purpose.

A certificate with the Client Authentication OID is required on all managed clients, including mobile devices, to communicate with a Configuration Manager site via HTTPS.

A certificate with the Server Authentication OID (1.3.6.1.5.5.7.3.1) and Client Authentication OID (1.3.6.1.5.5.7.3.2) is required on all Configuration Manager 2012 Site Systems, including Site Servers, Management Points, Distribution Points, Software Update Points, and State Migration Points. The Server Authentication certificate is used on each Site Server to encrypt communication between the managed systems and the Configuration Manager component.

Deploying an Active Directory Enterprise Root CA

This example details the steps required to deploy an Enterprise Root CA in the Company ABC domain. When an Enterprise Root CA is configured, all clients in the domain automatically trust certificates issued from this CA.

All Configuration Manager Site Servers and managed clients must trust the Certificate Authority. Any Configuration Manager Site Servers or managed clients that don't trust this Certificate Authority will not communicate with the infrastructure and might become orphaned. This typically happens when non–domain member servers, such as bastion hosts in the demilitarized zone (DMZ), are not part of the domain but have a Configuration Manager agent installed. To correct this problem, install the CA certificate into the local computer's Trusted Root Certificate Authorities certificates store.

> **NOTE**
>
> Status messages will still be sent to the Fallback Status Point, even if the client system has become orphaned due to certificate configuration issues. It is important to deploy the Fallback Status Point before deploying clients.

To deploy an Enterprise Root CA, complete the following steps:

1. Open the Server Manager console on CERT, the intended CA server.

2. Select the Roles node.

3. Click the Add Roles action.

4. Click Next to skip the Roles Overview page.

5. Enable the Active Directory Certificate Services role, and then click Next.

6. Click Next to skip the AD CS overview page.

7. Enable the Certification Authority role service.

8. Enable the Certification Authority Web Enrollment role service.

9. Click Add Required Role Services when prompted, and then click Next.

10. Select Enterprise and click Next.

11. Select Root CA and click Next.

12. Select Create a New Private Key and click Next.

13. Accept the default Cryptography settings and click Next.

14. Accept the default CA Name settings and click Next.

15. Accept the default Validity Period settings and click Next.

16. Accept the default Certificate Database Location settings and click Next.

17. Click Next to skip the IIS Overview page.

18. Accept the default IIS Role Services and click Next.

19. Confirm the installation selections and click Install.

20. Wait for the installation to complete and click Close.

After implementing the CA, the CRL Distribution Point (CDP) settings need to be configured to allow HTTP access to the CRL files. For security reasons, this typically wouldn't be done on the issuing CA; the CRL would be published on a system designated for that role. However, for demonstration purposes, the CRL will be published on the server CERT, allowing Internet-based clients to check the CRL.

To publish the CRL, complete the following steps:

1. Open the Server Manager console on CERT.

2. Expand the Roles node.

3. Expand the Active Directory Certificate Services node.

4. Right-click companyxyz-CERT-CA and click Properties.

5. Select the Extensions tab.

6. Select http://<ServerDNSName>/CertEnroll/<CaName>… from the list of CDPs.

7. Enable Include in CRLs. Clients use this to find Delta CRL locations.

8. Enable Include in the CDP Extension of Issued Certificates.

9. Apply the changes, click Yes when you are prompted to restart the Active Directory Certificate Services, and then click OK to close the window.

Validating the Enterprise Root CA

The newly installed Enterprise Root CA should be validated before certificates are issued to clients. To validate the CA, check the local application event log on the server CERT. This can be accessed through the Diagnostics node of Server Manager.

If the application event log is clean and doesn't contain any error or warning messages about Certificate Services or related components, the server should be ready to issue certificates to clients. It is always a good practice to restart the certificate server to ensure the Certificate Services can start and stop without logging any issues. It is also important to resolve all problems before moving to the next section and deploying certificates to managed clients and Site Servers.

Deploying Certificates

An enterprise Certificate Authority simplifies management of certificates by providing a secure, scalable certificate provisioning process through Active Directory. This task assumes all of the Configuration Manager servers and the Enterprise Root CA server have been moved to an organizational unit (OU) called Servers, and all of the workstations have been moved to an OU called Workstations.

The Servers and Workstations OUs are child objects of an OU called Managed. The Managed OU is located in the root of the domain.

> **CAUTION**
>
> Do not move domain controllers from the default OU. Moving domain controllers out of the default Domain Controllers OU is not supported.
>
> When an Enterprise Root CA is deployed, all domain controllers automatically receive a "Domain Controller" certificate. This certificate can be used for both client and server authentication.

Configuring the Auto-Enrollment Group Policy Object

A Group Policy Object (GPO) called Certificate Auto-Enrollment will be created and linked to the Servers OU and the Workstations OU. This group policy will be used to enable the certificate auto-enrollment function for all managed systems.

To create the Certificate Auto-Enrollment GPO, complete the following steps:

1. Open the Group Policy Management Console on DC1.

2. Expand Forest: companyabc.com.

3. Expand Domains.

4. Expand companyabc.com.

5. Select the Group Policy Objects container.

6. Right-click the Group Policy Objects container and select New.

7. Enter **Certificate Auto-Enrollment** in the Name field and click OK.

Once the GPO has been created, the setting that allows Certificate Auto-Enrollment can be enabled.

To enable the Certificate Auto-Enrollment setting in the GPO, complete the following steps:

1. Right-click the Certificate Auto-Enrollment GPO and select Edit.

2. The Group Policy Management Editor opens.

3. Expand Computer Configuration.

4. Expand Policies.

5. Expand Windows Settings.

6. Expand Security Settings.

7. Select the Public Key Policies container.

8. Double-click Certificate Services Client - Auto-Enrollment.

    The Certificate Services Client - Auto-Enrollment location is shown in Figure 3.20.

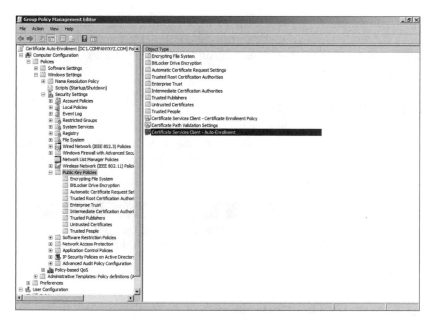

FIGURE 3.20   Certificate Services Client - Auto-Enrollment.

9.   Select Enabled as the Configuration Model.

10.   Enable the option to Renew Expired Certificates.

11.   Enable the option to Update Certificates That Use Certificate Templates.

12.   **Click OK to** save changes and close the Group Policy Management Editor.

Once the Auto-Enrollment setting within the GPO has been configured to allow automatic certificate enrollment, the GPO can be linked to the correct OUs.

To link the Certificate Auto-Enrollment GPO to the correct OUs, complete the following steps:

1.   Open the Group Policy Management Console.

2.   Expand the Managed OU and select the Servers OU.

3.   Right-click the Servers OU and select Link an Existing GPO.

4.   Select Certificate Auto-Enrollment from the list of GPOs and click OK.

5.   Right-click the Workstations OU and select Link an Existing GPO.

6.   Select Certificate Auto-Enrollment from the list of GPOs and click OK.

When this is complete, any domain member server or workstation placed in the corresponding OUs will be configured for automatic certificate enrollment. To complete the process, a certificate template with the correct settings and permissions needs to be created and then published.

Configuring Certificate Templates

The next step is to create certificate templates with the appropriate settings and permissions. The permissions on the certificate template govern the clients' ability to request the certificate. This is important because only the required certificates should be deployed to the system.

> **CAUTION**
>
> Provisioning certificates with unnecessary OIDs is not recommended. Only provision the minimum requirements needed by the client to communicate with Configuration Manager.

Creating the Client Authentication Certificate Template

Security permissions on the certificate template for Client Authentication will be configured to allow the domain computers security group to automatically request and receive this certificate through Active Directory. All systems in the Workstations and Servers OUs will receive this certificate.

To create Client Authentication templates for auto-enrollment, complete the following steps:

1. Open the Server Manager console on CERT.

2. Expand the Roles node.

3. Expand the Active Directory Certificate Services node.

4. Select the Certificate Templates container.

   The Certificate Templates container is shown in Figure 3.21.

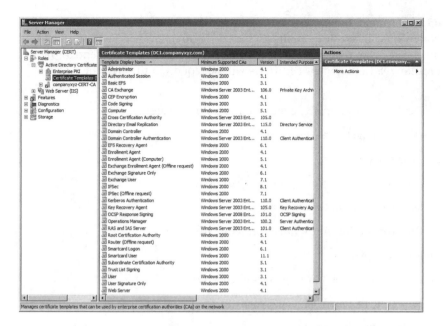

FIGURE 3.21   The Certificate Templates container.

5. Right-click the Workstation Authentication template.

6. Select Duplicate Template.

7. Choose Windows Server 2003 Enterprise and click OK.

CAUTION

The Windows Server 2008 Enterprise certificate option is not compatible with System Center Configuration Manager 2012. Choosing Windows Server 2008 Enterprise will result in a version 3 template. To create a version 2 template, select Windows Server 2003 Enterprise.

---

8. Type **Client Certificate Auto-Enrollment** in the Template Display Name field.

9. Select the Security tab.

10. Enable the Autoenroll permission for domain computers.

11. Select the Extensions tab.

12. Select the Application Policies item.

13. Verify the description states Client Authentication.

14. Click Apply and then click OK to close the window.

Creating the OS Deployment Template

Security permissions on the certificate template for OS Deployment will be configured to only allow manual certificate requests. Before PXE Service Points are implemented, the Client Authentication OS Deployment certificate will be requested through the web enrollment page.

To create the OS Deployment template, complete the following steps:

1. Open the Server Manager console on CERT.

2. Expand the Roles node.

3. Expand the Active Directory Certificate Services node.

4. Select the Certificate Templates container.

5. Right-click the Workstation Authentication template.

6. Select Duplicate Template.

7. Choose Windows Server 2003 Enterprise and click OK.

8. Type `Configuration Manager OS Deployment` in the Display Name field.

9. Select the Issuance Requirements tab.

10. Enable CA Certificate Manager Approval.

11. Select the Request Handling tab.

12. Enable the Allow Private Key to Be Exported option.

13. Select the Subject Name tab.

14. Enable the Supply in the Request option.

15. Select the Security tab and remove Domain Computers from the list.

16. Click Apply and then click OK to close the window.

Creating the Server Authentication Certificate Template

Security permissions on the certificate template for Server Authentication will be configured to only allow a custom security group to automatically request this certificate through Active Directory. Ultimately, all systems that will host web services will receive this certificate.

Before executing the next task, create a universal security group called SCCM Site Servers in the domain. Add the Configuration Manager servers and the Certificate Authority server to this group.

CAUTION

When a computer object is added to a group, it can take a long time for the setting to take effect. This is because the Kerberos ticket takes seven days to renew. The renewal time is governed by the *Maximum Lifetime for User Ticket Renewal* setting located in the Default Domain Policy GPO. It is not recommended to change this setting. Instead, restart the computer to refresh the Kerberos ticket.

To create Server Authentication template for auto-enrollment of the SCCM Site Servers, complete the following steps:

1. Open Server Manager and expand Roles, expand Active Directory Certificate Services, and select the Certificate Templates container.

2. Right-click the Workstation Authentication template.

3. Select Duplicate Template.

4. Choose Windows Server 2003 Enterprise and click OK.

5. Type **Server Certificate Auto-Enrollment** in the Display Name field.

6. Select the Security tab.

7. Remove the Domain Computers security group.

8. Click Add, type the group **SCCM Site Servers**, and then click OK.

9. Highlight SCCM Site Server.

10. Uncheck the Read permission.

11. Check the Enroll and Autoenroll permissions.

    The permission for this certificate is shown in Figure 3.22.

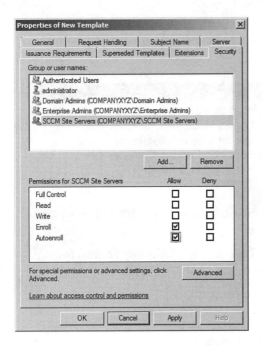

FIGURE 3.22   Permissions for the Server Authentication template.

12. Select the Extensions tab.

13. Select the Application Policies extension item and click Edit.

14. Highlight the Client Authentication Policy and click Remove.

15. Click Add, choose Server Authentication from the list, and then click OK.

16. Click OK, click Apply to apply the settings, and close the window.

All servers that are added to the Servers OU and are members of the SCCM Site Servers security group will receive a certificate that can be used for server authentication.

Publishing the Certificate Templates

Now that the Client and Server Authentication certificates have been created, they can be published. This tells the Certificate Authority the template is available for client consumption.

To publish the authentication templates for auto-enrollment, complete the following steps:

1. Open Server Manager on CERT.

2. Expand Roles.

3. Expand Active Directory Certificate Services.

4. Expand companyxyz-CERT-CA.

5. Select the Certificate Templates container.

   The CA Certificate Templates container is shown in Figure 3.23.

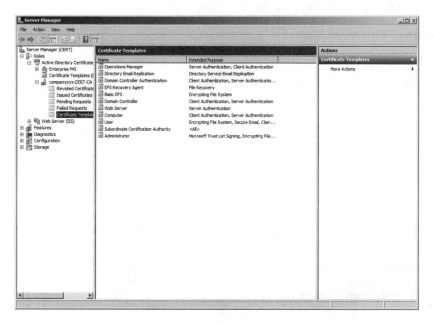

FIGURE 3.23   The CA Certificate Templates container.

6. Right-click Certificate Templates.

7. Click New and then click Certificate Template to Issue.

8. Select the Client Certificate Auto-Enrollment template from the list.

9. Hold down the Ctrl key.

10. Select the Server Certificate Auto-Enrollment template from the list.

11. Select the Configuration Manager OS Deployment template from the list.

12. Click OK to complete the process.

The three certificates should be listed in the Certificates Template container for the CA. These certificates are ready for consumption by Configuration Manager Site Servers and managed clients.

Configuring the Certificate Services Website for SSL

Certificates cannot be issued with the Certificate Services Enrollment web server unless it is configured to use SSL. This section describes the steps needed to secure the website with a server certificate. This also validates the ability for the certificate server to issue certificates.

To configure the Certificate Services website for SSL, complete the following tasks:

1. Open the command prompt on CERT.

2. Type **gpupdate /force** to refresh the group policies.

3. After the group policy is refreshed, open Server Manager.

4. Expand Roles.

5. Expand Active Directory Certificate Services.

6. Expand companyxyz-CERT-CA.

7. Select the Issued Certificates container.

The two new certificates should be listed in the container.

The CA Issued Certificates container is shown in Figure 3.24.

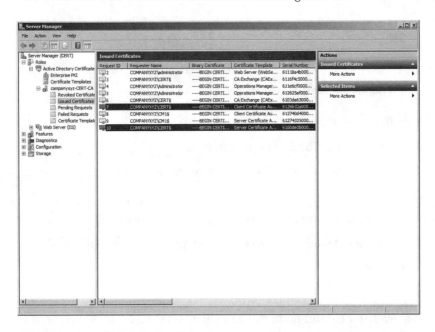

FIGURE 3.24   The CA Issued Certificates container.

The server CERT has received both the client and server signing certificate. The server signing certificate can be used to secure the Certificate Services website.

To secure the Certificate Services website, complete the following steps:

1. Open the Server Manager on CERT.

2. Expand Roles.

3. Expand Web Server (IIS).

4. Select Internet Information Services.

5. Expand the CERT web server.

6. Expand Sites.

7. Select Default Web Site.

8. Select Bindings from the Actions pane.

9. Click Add.

10. Select HTTPS for the binding type.

11. Select the correct certificate from the SSL certificate menu.

12. Click View to verify the correct certificate has been selected and then click OK.

13. Click OK and then click Close.

To test the newly installed certificate, open Internet Explorer and browse to the URL https://cert.companyxyz.com/certsrv. The Certificate Enrollment web page should open. Click the small lock icon beside the address bar, which shows the status of the certificate and that the Certificate Authority companyxyz-CERT-CA has identified this computer as cert.companyabc.com.

Configuring the WSUS Website for SSL

Because the WSUS component was installed on the CM1 server, the same certificate that was used to secure the Default Site can be used to secure the WSUS Administration site from within IIS.

> **CAUTION**
>
> Do *not* enable all virtual directories within the WSUS Administration site to use SSL. Only the APIRemoting30, ClientWebService, DSSAuthWebService, ServerSyncWebService, and SimpleAuthWebService should require SSL.

To configure WSUS for SSL communication, complete the following steps:

1. Open Internet Information Services Manager.

2. Expand Sites, and select the WSUS administration site, which is often the Default Web Site.

3. Click the Bindings action.

4. Click Add, select HTTPS, and click Edit.

5. Choose the certificate from the list.

6. Click View to verify the correct certificate was selected, click OK, and then click Close.

7. Select the APIRemoting30 virtual directory.

8. Double-click the SSL Settings option.

9. Enable the Require SSL option and click Apply.

10. Repeat for the ClientWebService, DSSAuthWebService, ServerSyncWebService, and SimpleAuthWebService virtual directories.

When the WSUS virtual directories are correctly configured, run the following command on the WSUS server to finalize the configuration needed to support SSL:

```
WSUSUtil.exe configuressl cm1.companyxyz.com
```

This utility is located in the Tools folder located within the WSUS installation folder. By default, this is folder is `c:\Program Files\Update Services\Tools`.

Requesting the OS Deployment Certificate

The OS Deployment client certificate is used by all systems during the OS deployment. This is essentially a shared certificate that is imported when the PXE Service Point is established.

The same procedure used to request the Document Signing certificate can be used to request the OS Deployment certificate. The main differences are instead of selecting the Configuration Manager Document Signing template from the template list, the Configuration Manager OS Deployment template must be selected. In the Name field, enter `osd01.companyxyz.com`.

> **NOTE**
>
> This certificate does *not* need to be added to the Local Computer certificate store. The Personal Information Exchange (PFX) file created will be imported during the deployment of the PXE Service Point detailed later.

Remember to approve the certificate osd1.companyxyz.com from within the Pending Requests container. When exporting the certificate, enter `c:\Temp\OSD01.pfx` as the file.

Enabling Internet-Based Client Management

In Configuration Manager 2012, the Site Servers roles have to be explicitly configured to enable Internet-based client management (IBCM). Each Management Point and Distribution Point that are to be enabled for IBCM will need to be configured to communicate over

HTTPS rather than HTTP. This is typically done on one or more systems dedicated to handling Internet traffic, but the actual configuration can depend on specific business and security requirements.

When a client communicates over the Internet, it needs to communicate with the following:

- Management Point
- Distribution Point
- Software Update Point
- Fallback Status Point
- Enrollment Proxy Point
- Application Catalog Website Point

All communication is done over HTTPS, with the exception of the Fallback Status Point, which communicates over HTTP. The first step in the process is to enable IBCM on the Site Server.

The FSP and SUP do not require additional configuration and are automatically enabled with the Site Server. Finally, to support IBCM, the following ports need to be open from the Internet:

- CRL Web Site: TCP 80
- Fallback Status Point: TCP 80
- Management Point: TCP 443
- Distribution Point: TCP 443
- Software Update Point: TCP 443

It is not recommended to connect any internal system directly to the Internet; for production deployments, consider using a reverse proxy, such as the Microsoft Threat Management Gateway (TMG).

Summary

System Center Configuration Manager 2012 provides a scalable, secure, end-to-end administration and reporting functionality. The deployment can be scaled out over many servers to support hundreds of thousands of managed clients, or installed on a single server for small enterprise deployments. In both cases, it is important to understand how each of the Configuration Manager roles work and the required dependencies for each role so the implementation is successful.

Best Practices

The following are best practices from this chapter:

▶ It is important to fully understand the architectural design before Configuration Manager 2012 server infrastructure servers and roles are deployed.

▶ If communication issues are a problem, make sure the settings on the local firewall have been configured correctly. For troubleshooting purposes, disable the local firewall temporarily.

▶ Status messages will still be sent to the Fallback Status Point, even if the client system has become orphaned due to certificate configuration issues. It is important to deploy the Fallback Status Point before deploying clients.

▶ Do not move domain controllers from the default OU. Moving domain controllers out of the default Domain Controllers OU is not supported. When an Enterprise Root CA is deployed, all domain controllers automatically receive a Domain Controller certificate. This certificate can be used for both client and server authentication.

▶ Provisioning certificates with unnecessary OIDs is not recommended. Only provision the minimum requirements needed by the client to communicate with Configuration Manager.

▶ The Windows Server 2008 Enterprise certificate option is not compatible with System Center Configuration Manager 2012. Choosing Windows Server 2008 Enterprise results in a version 3 template. To create a version 2 template, select Windows Server 2003 Enterprise.

▶ When a computer object is added to a group, it can take a long time for the setting to take effect. This is because the Kerberos ticket takes seven days to renew. The renewal time is governed by the Maximum Lifetime for User Ticket Renewal setting located in the Default Domain Policy GPO. It is not recommended to change this setting. Instead, restart the computer to refresh the Kerberos ticket.

▶ Make sure the subject name of the Site Servers' Document Signing certificate is set to: The site code of this Site Server is <SITE CODE>. The <SITE CODE> represents the site code that will be entered during the Configuration Manager implementation.

▶ Review the ExtADSch.log file for any errors after the AD schema has been extended. This log file is located in the root of drive C on the server used to execute the schema extensions. The log file should show 14 attributes and four classes have been defined.

▶ Do not bother with the WSUS Configuration Wizard. When the wizard opens after WSUS is successfully installed, click the Cancel button. The Configuration Manager console provides the interface to configure synchronization with Microsoft.

▶ Make sure the Configuration Manager Site Server Computer Account is in the local administrators group on all component servers and other Site Servers; this includes the Site Database server. The computer account of the Site Server is used to access and manage the remote server by default.

▶ The status summarizer for the different components is not automatically changed from red or yellow to green if the component that experienced the problem is fixed. The component summarizer simply counts the number of warning and error status messages that have been received. Manually reset the counts of status messages to clear the error or warning status.

▶ The `cmtrace.exe` log viewer provides a real-time view of the Configuration Manager status logs. This tool is invaluable when troubleshooting problems and understanding the environment.

▶ When deploying Site System roles to either the Site Server or a remote server, it is important to note the component installation wizard doesn't actually do the installation. Check the Site Status container from within the console along with the local installation logs for details on role installation.

▶ Increase the number of messages allowed per hour by the FSP to support large client deployments. This prevents a backlog of status messages from occurring.

▶ Never configure overlapping boundaries. This can cause managed systems to use the wrong Site Server or Distribution Point. This often happens when using a combination of IP and Active Directory boundaries.

▶ Define the Network Access Account on the Computer Client Agent when managing non–domain members. This account is provided as a way for non–domain members to authenticate to Configuration Manager. This account should be a Domain User without additional permissions.

▶ The default list of "Products" supported by the Software Update Point is refreshed and updated during the synchronization process. This adds things like Windows 7 and Windows Server 2008 R2 to the Windows section. Because the entire Windows product was selected, new operating systems will automatically be enabled as they are made available on the Windows Update site and through WSUS.

▶ Configuring Client Agents with a "simple" schedule allows the distribution of load placed on the system. Unless the server and environment have been sized to receive and process data from all clients simultaneously, care should be taken to distribute the load over a longer period.

Using Configuration Manager 2012 to Distribute Applications, Updates, and Operating Systems

IN THIS CHAPTER

▶ Understanding Content Distribution

▶ Defining Collections

▶ Understanding Application Management

▶ Managing Deployments

▶ Understanding Software Updates

▶ Deploying Software Updates

▶ Understanding Operating System Deployment

▶ Deploying Operating Systems

▶ Extending with Microsoft Deployment Toolkit

▶ Best Practices

System Center Configuration Manager (ConfigMgr) 2012 provides a highly scalable, bandwidth-aware distribution and execution system. Several Configuration Manager key roles have been designed specifically to facilitate the provisioning of applications, updates, and operating systems across a variety of devices, such as workstations, servers, and mobile devices.

This chapter helps the administrator understand how each role within the System Center Configuration Manager (SCCM) hierarchy is used and how to create an effective way for managed systems to locate and receive content. This includes how to provision content based on an array of complex business deployment scenarios. In addition, this chapter explains how to monitor distribution of content to ensure accuracy and compliance.

Understanding Content Distribution

A big part of distributing software, updates, and operating systems is getting the bits and bytes of the code to the user's devices. This accounts for the vast majority of the bandwidth utilization and, thus, the staging requirements. Before the deployment can occur, those bits and bytes need to be locally accessible to the user or device. SCCM 2012 uses a sophisticated content distribution mechanism to ensure that the code is available when needed in the most efficient manner possible.

Understanding How Clients Locate Content

The Configuration Manager infrastructure along with Active Directory (AD) integration provides clients with the ability to roam the entire Configuration Manager infrastructure and find the closest Distribution Point (DP) to receive content. A client will attempt to get content from a Resident Distribution Point before a remote Distribution Point.

> **NOTE**
>
> Global roaming can be achieved when the Active Directory schema has been extended. If the schema hasn't been extended, then only regional roaming is available. Regional roaming only allows client roaming to sites lower in the hierarchy. If the client roams to a peer site, or a parent site, content cannot be downloaded from Resident Distribution Points.

When a client is started, or changes networks, a local discovery is triggered to identify the closest Management Point. The closest Management Point then provides the client with a list of Distribution Points for content. The agent evaluates the list of DPs and chooses the most appropriate DP to obtain content based on several factors. For example, the client will choose a BITS-enabled Distribution Point over a non-BITS Distribution Point.

An agent locates content in the following way:

1. The client queries Active Directory to identify the closest Management Point in the hierarchy. The client will choose the Management Point based on the network boundaries in which the client currently resides.

2. If a Resident Management Point is unavailable, the client will default to the Management Point in the site the client was originally assigned. The client communicates with the selected Management Point to locate content. The Management Point provides the list of Distribution Points that contain the appropriate content. Only applicable DPs are provided.

3. If the client is within the boundaries of a fast site, the Management Point only provides a list of preferred DPs for the fast site, even if a slow Distribution Point with the content is available.

> **NOTE**
>
> To override preferred Distribution Point behavior, enable the Deployment Options selection *Download Content from Distribution Point and Run Locally* option on the Deployment Type of the application or package.

If the preferred Distribution Point chosen by the client is not available, the client will attempt to download content from that Distribution Point for 8 hours. If after 8 hours the client's default Distribution Point is unavailable, the client system will locate the content on a different Distribution Point and begin the download process. It is important to monitor the health of Distribution Points and make sure they are available. If necessary, remove the Distribution Point role from unhealthy servers to prevent clients from selecting the server for content.

How a client locates content is shown in Figure 4.1. The figure shows two laptops from the Tokyo location (TOK), WS1 and WS2. The WS1 laptop is at the Tokyo location. The WS1 agent first checks with the domain controller to locate its Resident Management Point (step 1), contacts the Resident Management Point to locate its closest Distribution Point (step 2), and finally begins to download content from its local Distribution Point in TOK (step 3). The WS2 laptop is traveling and happens to be in the San Francisco location (SFO). The WS2 agent first checks with the domain controller to locate its assigned Management Point (step 1), contacts the assigned Management Point in Paris (PAR) to locate its closest Distribution Point (step 2), and finally begins to download content from its local Distribution Point in SFO (step 3).

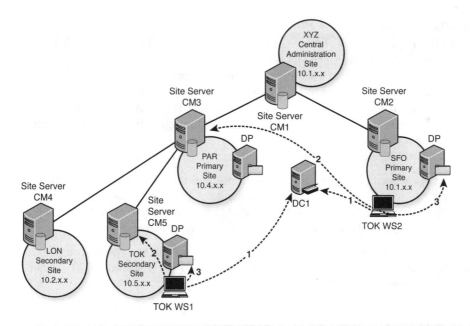

FIGURE 4.1   How clients locate content.

This process ensures that clients download their content from the closest Distribution Point with the required content.

Understanding How Internet Clients Locate Content

A client configured for Internet-based client management is configured with the fully qualified domain name (FQDN) of a Management Point accessible from the Internet. This is typically done with specific command-line options during installation, but can also be done after the agent is installed.

NOTE

It is important to only assign an Internet Management Point from the client's assigned site. Assigning an Internet Management Point from a different site than the client's assigned site is not supported.

If multiple Configuration Manager sites have been implemented and they support clients on the Internet, multiple Internet-facing Management Points are needed. When a client on the Internet contacts the assigned Internet Management Point, the Management Point provides the list of Distribution Points that are also accessible from the Internet. The client chooses from one of these Distribution Points to locate content.

Understanding Distribution Points Selection

Client computers request policies from Management Points. When the client receives a policy for content, the content for the target can be executed interactively or automatically. In either scenario, the client asks the Management Point for a list of potential Distribution Points, and the Management Point returns a list of Distribution Points based on the current location of the client. This includes Resident Distribution Points when the client roams throughout the hierarchy and Internet Distribution Points when the client roams outside the hierarchy. It is imperative that Distribution Points are strategically placed and assigned the correct protected boundaries to ensure cost-effective deployment.

When content is assigned to a standard Distribution Point, it's pushed to the Distribution Point from the Site Server. This push takes place using the Server Message Block (SMB) protocol, essentially a file copy. The Site Server must have administrative access to the Distribution Point server to be able to remotely copy the content files.

After the Management Point provides the list of available Distribution Points to the client, the client chooses the best-suited Distribution Point to receive content. The order in which they are chosen is as follows:

1. Distribution Points with the content that are located in a boundary group that contains a client's boundary with fast connectivity

2. Distribution Points with the content that are located in a boundary group that contains a client's boundary with slow connectivity

3. Distribution Points with the content that have the Allow Fallback option enabled

It is important to note that no matter what, Distribution Points that do not contain the content are not returned by the Management Point and, thus, are not available for selection by the client. For additional information on Distribution Point design, review Chapter 2, "Configuration Manager 2012 Design and Planning."

Defining Collections

Collections are an important aspect of successfully delivering content and are even more widely used in Configuration Manager 2012 than in previous versions. A collection defines a group of systems or users based on many different attributes. For example, all of the systems in a specific area can be part of a site-specific collection, or all the systems that share a common piece of software can be part of a software-specific collection. A system can be part of more than one collection. It is important to define collections based on your requirements. Collections can be used for the following:

- ▶ Targeting deployments

- ▶ Targeting client settings

- ▶ Targeting anti-malware settings

- ▶ Targeting firewall settings

- ▶ Power management settings

- ▶ Targeting content Distribution Points

- ▶ Reporting

- ▶ Administrative security scopes

A collection can be based on any of many different attributes, essentially anything that can be queried in the database. For example, it is common to create collections for each location, which allow region-specific content provisioning and reporting. Even if content is provisioned to the entire organization, region-specific collections can be used to report compliance and status for each area.

Collections can be created with static, manually added members. However, this type of management is not very scalable and should only be used when other means are not feasible. Designing collections based on queries is recommended for a much more scalable infrastructure. The query that defines a collection can be based on any hardware or software inventory data, along with information collected during the client discovery cycles. Essentially any data in the Site Database is available in the queries.

> **NOTE**
>
> The collection query language is based on WMI Query Language (WQL), which is a subset of SQL. For example, the % character is used for wildcard matching. For additional information, see the following Microsoft TechNet site:
>
> http://msdn.microsoft.com/en-us/library/aa394552.aspx

To create this custom collection that only contains workstations from the SFO Active Directory site, complete the following steps:

1. Select the Assets and Compliance space and select the Device Collections node.

2. Right-click Device Collections and select the Create Device Collection action.

3. Type **SFO-Workstations** as the name.

4. In the Limiting Collection section, click the Browse button.

5. Choose the All Desktop and Server Clients collection and click OK.

6. Click Next.

7. In the Add Rule pull-down, choose Query Rule.

8. Enter **SFO-Workstations** as the name, and then click Edit Query Statement.

9. Select the Criteria tab and click the * button.

10. Click the Select button and then choose the System Resource attribute class.

11. Choose the Active Directory Site Name attribute, and click OK.

12. Click the Value button, select SFO from the list, and then click OK twice.

13. Click the "*" button again.

14. Click the Select button, and then choose the System Resource attribute class.

15. Choose the Operating System Name and Version attribute, and then click OK.

16. Choose the Is Like operator, and then type **%Workstation%** in the Value field.

17. Click OK, and then click OK again to save the query statement.

18. Click OK again to save the query.

19. Click the Schedule button.

NOTE

The default schedule in SCCM 2012 is to update the collection every seven days, which is a change from previous versions where the default schedule was every one day. This means that changes in the environment that would result in changes to the collection membership will not be reflected for up to a week by default. This is something that is frequently changed when creating new collections.

20. Change the schedule to recur every one day and click OK.

21. Check the Use Incremental Updates for This Collection check box. This ensures that new objects that match the query for the collection will get added immediately, rather than wait for the schedule.

22. Click Next to review the summary.

23. Click Next to create the collection.

24. Click Close to exit the wizard.

Repeat this process for each of the other Active Directory sites (PAR, LON, TOK, and NYC). The software distribution and update distribution tasks will use these new collections for software deployments.

NOTE

Because the scope of a collection is limited based on another collection, be sure to set the appropriate collection update schedule. The source collection should update before the target collection, or the results of the collection could be almost a complete update cycle behind. By default, a new collection is updated every seven days, starting from when it was created. However, the built-in collections update every day.

Maintenance windows on collections (select the Collection Properties and then the Maintenance Windows tab to see defined maintenance windows) control when a system can run a deployment. This is important because it can affect how content is provisioned. For example, if the sum of the package program Run Time and the countdown delay time are greater than the maintenance window, the scheduled advertisement won't run.

NOTE

It is important to understand how maintenance windows work. When more than one maintenance window affects a system, the maintenance windows are effectively combined.

A maintenance window on the SFO-Servers collection is shown in Figure 4.2.

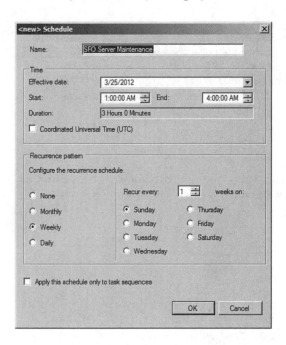

FIGURE 4.2   Maintenance window for a collection.

When working with operating system deployment, a sequence of tasks is assigned to a collection. This task sequence tells the system to reboot and install a new operating system. It is not recommended to assign a task sequence to a collection of systems that are currently being used; the systems in the collection might automatically deploy a new operating system, which typically includes formatting the system drive and other potentially harmful operations. Instead, create a staging collection to hold systems temporarily during operating system deployment.

To create the staging collection, select the Device Collections container from within the Configuration Manager console. Click the Create Device Collection action and type **Workstation-Prerelease** in the Name field and select the All Systems collection for the Limiting Collection. Complete the New Collection Wizard, but don't add any query rules. This collection will be used in the subsequent operating system deployment tasks.

Understanding Application Management

Application management leverages the Configuration Manager infrastructure to provision content for both interactive and automatic installations. Two main types of application management are available in Configuration Manager 2012:

- ▶ Applications
- ▶ Packages

The type of deployment is typically based on the business and technical requirements of the organization.

Application management requires several steps to ensure success. This includes the following:

1. Preparing the software source

2. Creating the package or application

3. Defining deployments within the package

4. Staging the content on Distribution Points

5. Deploying the software to target systems

6. Reporting on the status of the software deployment

These general steps are required whether using the new application model or the legacy packages model. The first three steps vary depending on how the application is installed, which is different for Windows Installer (MSI) packages, executable (EXE) packages, or complex applications like Microsoft Office. The latter three steps are generally the same for all applications. In this section, examples of each package type are covered.

> **NOTE**
>
> The Windows Installer package uses the extension MSI, which can be confusing. Originally, Microsoft developed the technology and called it the Microsoft Installer, hence the extension MSI for MS Installer. They later renamed the technology Windows Installer, but the MSI extension remained.

Applications

New in Configuration Manager 2012, applications allow a user-focused deployment model, which was not easily achieved previously. Applications can be targeted at users or devices, but the user targeting allows the application to follow the users no matter what device they're using.

The components of applications include the following:

▶ **Application**—The application consists of the software name, version number, and manufacturer. The distribution settings, Application Catalog information, and supersedence settings are also defined within the package.

▶ **Deployment type**—The deployment type is a component of the application, specifying content location, configuring user experience during installation, and defining how the content is installed and uninstalled on the target. This includes requirements such as the user's primary device, operating system, memory, disk space, and environment such as AD site or organizational unit (OU). There is also a detection method to know if the application is installed, which can include MSI product code, files, or Registry settings. An application can contain several deployment types, each with a unique configuration.

▶ **Software Center**—This new user interface is available wherever the agent is installed. This allows end users to manage software that is installed on their devices.

▶ **Application Catalog**—This is a new self-service web portal that allows users to browse catalogs of applications and install them without requiring administrative assistance.

▶ **Deployment**—The deployment makes an application/deployment type combination available on target collections. The deployment controls when and where the application is deployed. This includes the target collection, execution schedule, and how to obtain content from Distribution Points. This also includes if the application is required or just available. Alerts for the deployment can also be configured to notify when too many deployments fail or not enough deployments are completed by a specific deadline.

Applications in Configuration Manager 2012 give administrators new functionality and features to help control application deployment.

Packages

Packages are the traditional Configuration Manager method of deploying applications. This has been available since the first version of the product and has evolved into the mature offering available in Configuration Manager 2012 today. Packages are fundamentally targeted at devices such as workstations and servers.

Some packages terminology you should become familiar with is as follows:

▶ **Package**—The package consists of the software name, version number, and manufacturer. The package source location and distribution settings are also defined within the package. Each package also defines the Access Accounts.

▶ **Program**—The program is a component of the package and defines how the content is executed on the target. This includes settings such as the command line, maximum runtime, disk space requirements, and execution environment. A package can contain several programs, each with a unique configuration.

▶ **Deployment**—The advertisement makes a package/program combination available on target systems. The advertisement controls when and where the content is executed. This includes the target collection, execution schedule, and how to obtain content from Distribution Points.

Interactive installation only requires publishing the software to clients. The software installation can be automated or user driven, and can be run with elevated privileges or user privileges, depending on business requirements.

Configuring a Windows Installer Package (MSI) Application

MSI packages are the easiest to configure. They typically include default deployment types or programs as well as have all the program, version, language, and other information already integrated into the package.

By way of example, the Microsoft XML Notepad will be configured. This is a handy utility for viewing and editing XML files. It is deployed using a Windows Installer package and its MSI is downloadable from the following link: http://www.microsoft.com/download/en/details.aspx?displaylang=en&id=7973.

To configure Microsoft XML Notepad as a Configuration Manager 2012 application, execute the following steps:

1. On server CM1, create the directory `c:\Sources` and share it with the same name, granting Everyone read right.

2. Create the directory `c:\Sources\XMLEditor`.

3. Download and copy the source file, `XmlNotepad.msi`, to `\\CM1\Sources\` folder `XMLEditor`.

4. Launch the Configuration Manager 2012 console.

5. Choose the Software Library space, expand Application Management, and select the Applications node.

6. Right-click on the Applications node and select Create Application.

7. Leave the default Type as Windows Installer (Native).

8. Click the Browse button to select the source location.

9. Navigate to `\\CM1\Sources\XMLEditor`, select `XmlNotepad.msi` and click Open.

10. Click Next.

11. Click Summary to see a summary of the import.

12. Click Next to confirm the setting for the application.

13. Click Close to close the wizard.

The configuration of the Windows Installer package automatically populates the deployment type (shown in Figure 4.3), including unattended installation, detection, and uninstallation options. It also required no real analysis in advance, just simply import the MSI.

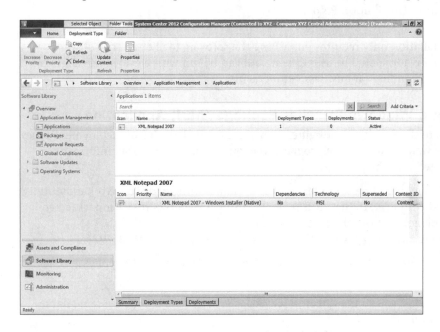

FIGURE 4.3   MSI package with default deployment type.

Additional deployment types and customizations can be done, but it really doesn't get any simpler than this. If an MSI package is available for the software, this is almost always the best way to go.

Configuring an EXE Application

In many cases, the software setup will be packaged as an executable with an EXE extension. These cases will require some analysis to determine how to deploy them in an unattended fashion. This also makes it more difficult to do automatic detection of the installation state and uninstallation.

For purposes of illustration, the Microsoft Network Monitor 3.4 will be used. This is a full-featured protocol analyzer, which allows administrators to sniff network traffic and analyze protocol traces. It is deployed using an EXE and is available for download at the following link: http://www.microsoft.com/download/en/details.aspx?id=4865.

When analyzing Network Monitor in preparation for creating the SCCM 2012 application, it is important to note that the application installer is different for different processor architectures (NM34_x86 and NM34_x64). When launching the appropriate installer, it launches into an interactive wizard. This needs to be automated to allow unattended installations via SCCM.

To determine the unattended installation parameters, the installation executable was launched with the /? parameter to get the command-line options, as shown in Figure 4.4. In reviewing the command-line options, the /Q option will install in Quiet mode. Manually install Network Monitor 3.4, and then review the Registry for changes. The application creates a Registry key HKLM\SOFTWARE\Microsoft\Netmon3 with a number of values including a string value NetmonVersion with the value 3.4.2350.0.

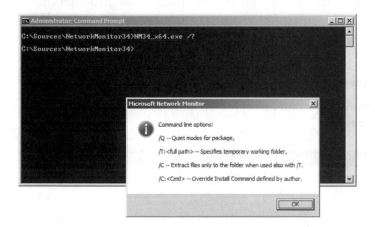

FIGURE 4.4   Getting the EXE command-line options for unattended installs.

The results of the analysis are that there will be separate deployment types for the different processor architectures and that the setup programs need to run with the /Q command-line option for silent installations. And the Registry value can be used to detect the presence of the software.

To configure Microsoft Network Monitor as a Configuration Manager 2012 application, execute the following steps:

1. Create the directory \\CM1\Sources\NetworkMonitor34.

2. Download and copy the source files, NM34_x64.exe and NM34_x86.exe, to folder \\CM1\Sources\NetworkMonitor34.

3. Launch the Configuration Manager 2012 console.

4. Choose the Software Library space, expand Application Management, and select the Applications node.

5. Right-click on the Applications node and then select Create Application.

6. Select the Manually Specify the Application Information option button and click Next.

7. Enter **Network Monitor** for the Name.

8. Enter **Microsoft** for the Manufacturer.

9. Enter **3.4** for the Software Version.

10. Click Next.

11. In the Application Catalog section, leave the defaults and click Next.

12. In Deployment Types, click the Add button to add a new deployment type.

13. Select the Manually Specify the Deployment Type Information option button and click Next.

14. Enter **Install x64** for the Name and click Next.

15. In the Content Location section, enter the location of the source code. In this case, it is **\\CM1\Sources\NetworkMonitor34**.

16. In the Specify the Command Used to Install the Content section, enter the command **NM34_x64.exe /Q**.

NOTE

Because there was no uninstall command-line option, the deployment type will not be able to automatically uninstall the application.

---

17. Click Next.

18. In the Detection Method section, click the Add Clause button.

19. Change the Setting Type to Registry.

20. For Hive, select HKEY_LOCAL_MACHINE.

21. For Key, enter **SOFTWARE\Microsoft\Netmon3**.

22. For Value, enter **NetmonVersion**.

23. For Data Type, select String.

24. Select the This Registry Setting Must Satisfy the Following Rule to Indicate the Presence of This Application option button.

25. For Operator, select Equals.

26. For Value, enter **3.4.2350.0**. The results are shown in Figure 4.5.

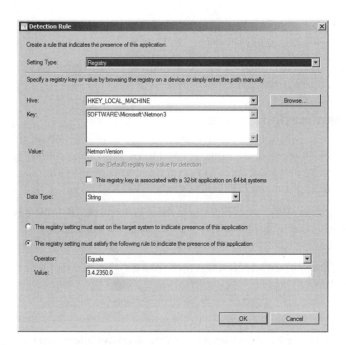

FIGURE 4.5   Registry detection settings.

27. Click OK to save the detection rule.

28. Click Next.

29. For Installation Behavior, select Install for System.

30. For Logon Requirement, select Whether or Not a User Is Logged On and click Next.

31. In Requirements settings, click Add. Select Operating System as the Condition and select all the 64-bit operating systems. Then click OK to save and Next to continue.

32. Click Next to leave the default Dependencies settings.

33. Review the Summary and then click Next.

34. Click Close to close the Create Deployment Type Wizard.

35. Repeat steps 12 through 34 to add a second deployment type for x86 systems, but use **Install x86** for the Name, **NM34_x86.exe /Q** for the command, and 32-bit operating systems for the Requirements.

36. Click Next to continue.

37. Review the Summary and click Next to create the application.

38. Click Close to close the wizard.

There is now an application for Network Monitor that includes two deployment types, one for 64-bit and one for 32-bit processor architectures.

For non-Windows Installer packages, there's clearly a lot more manual effort required to analyze, test, and configure applications for SCCM 2012 deployment.

Configuring a Complex Application Source

Configuring complex applications requires special configuration of the source, installation automation, and deployment types. In some cases, updates need to be slipstreamed into the source or software keys need to be provided. The next several sections go over the deployment of a common complex application, Microsoft Office 2010.

The subsequent sections describe the creation of a Microsoft Office Enterprise 2010 software deployment. The first step when setting up a software deployment is establishing the software source directory. This is typically a share on a file server.

First, copy the contents of the Office 2010 media to the source folder. For the subsequent example, create the following share:

```
\\CM1\sources\Office2010x86
```

Next, extract each of the Microsoft Office 2010 service packs to the Updates folder located within the Microsoft Office Enterprise 2010 folder. This is a great addition to Microsoft Office 2010; updates and service packs that are placed in the Updates folder are automatically installed during setup. Download the Office 2010 Service Pack 1 file from Microsoft. The download is located within the following Microsoft Knowledge Base article: http://www.microsoft.com/download/en/details.aspx?id=26622.

> **NOTE**
>
> Only MSP files can be placed in the Office Updates folder. Copying the downloaded Microsoft Office 2010 EXEs to the Updates folder directly is not supported. The EXE needs to be extracted first, and the extracted MSP files need to be placed in the Updates folder within the source directory.

When the service pack download is complete, run the following commands to extract the MSP files. When prompted, accept the Microsoft software license terms and click Continue.

```
officesuite2010sp1-kb2460049-x86-fullfile-en-us.exe
/extract:\\CM1\Sources\Office2010x86\Updates
```

This ensures that each time Microsoft Office is installed, the latest service pack is applied automatically as part of the setup process.

Automating a Complex Application Installation

The automation mechanism for a complex application is often unique and supplied by the vendor. For the Office 2010 suite, Microsoft provides the Office Customization Tool, which generates an MSP file. The MSP file holds the customization information, and is specified on the command line when setup is launched to customize the installation.

To launch the Office Customization Wizard, complete the following steps:

1. Download the Office Customization Tool from http://www.microsoft.com/download/en/details.aspx?id=18968.

2. Run the downloaded file and when prompted, extract the files into the `c:\Sources\Office2010x86` folder.

3. Map a drive to the software source directory.

4. Navigate to the Microsoft Office Enterprise 2010 folder.

5. Run the command `setup.exe /admin`.

6. Select Microsoft Office Enterprise 2010 from the product list, and then click OK.

The first step is to customize the actual installation of Office. This includes providing the product key and telling the installation to suppress any notifications. The User mode is set to Basic, which provides a progress bar for users. This allows the software to be used for both interactive provisioning by the user and fully automated deployment.

To customize the Office Enterprise 2010 setup, complete the following steps:

1. Select Install Location and Organization Name.

2. Enter **Company XYZ** in the Organization Name field.

3. Select Licensing and User Interface.

4. Enter the product key in the field provided.

5. Set the display level to Basic.

6. Enable the Suppress Modal option.

7. Enable the No Cancel option.

8. Accept the terms in the license agreement.

The features selected can be customized as necessary based on business requirements. The usage profile for Microsoft Office users should be understood before removing components.

To set the Office Enterprise 2010 installation features, complete the following steps:

1. Select Set Feature Installation States.

2. Select Microsoft Office from the top of the tree.

3. Choose Run All from My Computer from the menu.

4. Select File, Save As and save the file as `msoffice2010.msp` to the folder
   `c:\Sources\MS2010x86`, the same location as `setup.exe`.

The Additional Content section provides the ability to customize files and Registry entries
and configure the default shortcuts. The Outlook section provides a way to customize the
email configuration during installation.

> **NOTE**
>
> Do not include Microsoft Office 2010 service packs or hotfixes in the Additional
> Content section of the Office Customization Tool. Updates need to be placed in the
> Updates folder; adding them as part of the installation is not supported.

After the `msoffice2010.msp` file has been created, close the Office Customization Tool.
The same process can be repeated to create an MSP file for other Office Enterprise products, such as Microsoft Office Visio 2010 and Microsoft Office Project 2010.

> **NOTE**
>
> The Office Customization Tool is only available for Enterprise Editions of Microsoft
> Office 2010. If you have a different edition, then the `setup.exe /admin` command will
> generate a setup error indicating that it is missing files and a qualifying product needs
> to be used. Other editions, such as Professional Plus, can be automated by editing the
> `ProPlusr.WW\config.xml` and adding the two lines:
>
> ```
> <Display Level="none" CompletionNotice="no" SuppressModal="yes" AcceptEula="yes" />
> <PIDKEY Value="AAAAABBBBBCCCCCDDDDDEEEEE" />
> ```
>
> Where the `PIDKEY` value is the product key.
>
> This allows the Office 2010 Professional Plus installation to run silently.

Creating a Complex Application

To configure Microsoft Office 2010 as a Configuration Manager 2012 application, execute
the following steps:

1. Launch the Configuration Manager 2012 console.

2. Choose the Software Library space, expand Application Management, and select the
   Applications node.

3. Right-click on the Applications node and select Create Application.

4. Select the Manually Specify the Application Information option button and click
   Next.

5. Enter **Office 2010** for the Name.

6. Enter **Microsoft** for the Manufacturer.

7. Enter **14.0.4763.1000** for the Software Version.

8. Click Next.

9. In the Application Catalog section, leave the defaults and click Next.

10. In Deployment Types, click the Add button to add a new deployment type.

11. Select the Manually Specify the Deployment Type Information option button and click Next.

12. Enter **Install Self-Service** for the Name and click Next.

13. In the Content Location section, enter the location of the source code. In this case, it is **\\CM1\Sources\Office2010x86**.

14. In the Specify the Command Used to Install the Content section, enter the command **setup.exe /adminfile "msoffice2010.msp" /config .\Enterprise.WW\config.xml**.

> **NOTE**
>
> For the Professional Plus Edition, the command is setup.exe /config .\ProPlusr.WW\config.xml.

15. In the Uninstall Program section, enter the command **setup.exe /uninstall ProPlus /config   .\ Enterprise.WW \SilentUninstallConfig.xml**. Then click Next.

> **NOTE**
>
> For the Professional Plus Edition, the command is setup.exe /uninstall ProPlus /config .\ProPlusr.WW\SilentUninstallConfig.xml.

16. In the Detection Method section, click the Add Clause button.

17. Change the Setting Type to Windows Installer.

18. Click Browse to locate an MSI file.

19. Navigate to \\CM1\Sources\Office2010x86\Enterprise.WW, select EnterpriseWW.msi, and click Open.

> **NOTE**
>
> For the Professional Plus edition, the directory is \\CM1\Sources\Office2010x86\ProPlusr.WW, and then select ProPlusrWW.msi.

20. The product code will automatically populate from the MSI.

21. Click OK to save the detection rule.

22. Click Next.

23. For Installation Behavior, select Install for User.

24. Click Next.

25. In Requirements settings, click Next to continue.

26. Click Next to leave the default Dependencies settings.

27. Review the Summary and then click Next.

28. Click Close to close the Create Deployment Type Wizard.

29. Click Next.

30. Review the Summary and click Next to create the application.

31. Click Close to close the wizard.

There is now an application for Office that will install, uninstall, and detect the installation state.

A new feature of Configuration Manager 2012 is the ability to limit deployments to a user's primary system. The primary system is the one that they designate as their main computer or it can be detected automatically based on usage. Deployment types can be created that restrict the installation to the primary system.

To create the deployment type that is targeted at the primary system of a user, execute the following steps:

1. Launch the Configuration Manager 2012 console.

2. Choose the Software Library space, expand Application Management, and select the Applications node.

3. Right-click on the Office 2010 application and select Create Deployment Type.

4. Select the Manually Specify the Deployment Type Information option button and click Next.

5. Enter **Install on Primary System** for the Name and click Next.

6. In the Content Location section, enter the location of the source code. In this case, it is **\\CM1\Sources\Office2010x86**.

7. In the Specify the Command Used to Install the Content section, enter the command **setup.exe /adminfile "msoffice2010.msp" /config .\Enterprise.WW\config.xml**.

> **NOTE**
>
> For the Professional Plus Edition, the command is `setup.exe /config .\ProPlusr.WW\config.xml`.

8. In the Uninstall Program section, enter the command **setup.exe /uninstall ProPlus /config .\ Enterprise.WW \SilentUninstallConfig.xml**. Then click Next.

> **NOTE**
>
> For the Professional Plus Edition, the command is `setup.exe /uninstall ProPlus /config .\ProPlusr.WW\SilentUninstallConfig.xml`.

9. In the Detection Method section, click the Add Clause button.

10. Change the Setting Type to Windows Installer.

11. Click Browse to locate an MSI file.

12. Navigate to `\\CM1\Sources\Office2010x86\Enterprise.WW`, select `EnterpriseWW.msi`, and click Open.

> **NOTE**
>
> For the Professional Plus Edition, the directory is `\\CM1\Sources\Office2010x86\ProPlusr.WW`, and then select `ProPlusrWW.msi`.

13. The product code will automatically populate from the MSI.

14. Click OK to save the detection rule.

15. Click Next.

16. For Installation Behavior, select Install for System.

17. For Logon Requirement, select Whether or Not a User Is Logged On and click Next.

18. In Requirements settings, click Add.

19. In the Category drop-down, select User.

20. The condition automatically populates with the value Primary Device Equals True. This requirement will restrict deployments to only the user's primary system. Click OK to save the requirement.

21. Click Next.

22. Click Next to leave the default Dependencies settings.

23. Review the Summary and then click Next.

24. Click Close to close the Create Deployment Type Wizard.

There is now a deployment type for Office that will install, uninstall, and detect the installation state, but only on a user's primary system.

Getting Content to Distribution Points

For each of the content types (Windows Installer, executable, and complex), the preparation of the source, automation of the installation, and the packaging differed from one content type to the other. To get content to Distribution Points, each of the content types is treated the same.

The next step is to select the Distribution Points for the application. To support the most effective global roaming and reduce bandwidth utilization, it is important to get the content on as many Distribution Points as possible. It is almost as important to monitor the progress of content as it's placed on Distribution Points throughout the hierarchy.

To assign an application, for example Office 2010, to Distribution Points, do the following:

1. Right-click on the application, Office 2010, in the Application Management folder, Applications subfolder and choose the Distribute Content action.

> **NOTE**
>
> New to Configuration Manager 2012, multiple applications can be selected at once, using the Shift and Control keys, to distribute content for more than one application at a time.

2. Click Next to skip the General page.

3. At the Content page, click Next.

4. At the Content Destination page, click the Add button and select Distribution Point.

5. Select the appropriate Distribution Points and click OK.

6. Click Next.

7. Review the Summary and click Next to begin distribution.

8. Close the wizard when it is finished.

The Site Server pushes the content to standard Distribution Points. To monitor the progress of the content distribution, select the application and review the content status information in the Summary tab. This information can also be found in the Monitoring space, in the Distribution Status folder under the Content Status node. Figure 4.6 shows the content status for the Office 2010 application. From the figure, it can be seen that one Distribution Point has received the content successfully, one is waiting for the content, and two are starting to process the content.

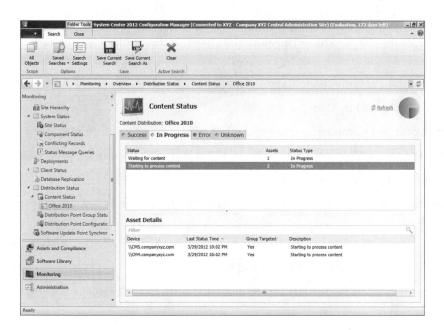

FIGURE 4.6   Content status.

Within a few minutes, depending on bandwidth, all Distribution Points should successfully receive the contents of the entire package. For additional information and real-time
diagnostics, review the Distmgr.log file on the Site Server.

Managing Deployments

Now that the application source has been prepared, deployment types configured, and
the content distributed, deployments can be done. The process of managing deployments
includes targeting users and devices, configuring self-service and automatic deployments,
and monitoring those deployments.

Targeting Users

A key feature of Configuration Manager 2012 is the ability to target users. Previous
versions had difficulty targeting the users or their associated systems, so the targeting was
mostly at systems independent of what user was assigned the system. Configuration
Manager 2012 introduces Applications and User Affinity to address this gap.

For example, the Company XYZ organization has Senior Directors and Directors that need
to be targeted with different software. The Senior Directors group includes user Greg Ogle
and the Directors group includes user Steve Upp. The administrator needs to target both
groups for Office 2010, but Office 2012 needs to be automatically installed on the Senior
Directors group's primary computer.

Applications and deployment types allow for more effective targeting of users based on collections. To target the sample Senior Directors and Directors, two collections will be created.

To create the collections, execute the following steps:

1. Launch the Configuration Manager console.

2. Go to the Assets and Compliance space and select the User Collections node.

3. Right-click the User Collections node and select Create User Collection.

4. In the Name field, enter **Senior Directors**.

5. In the Limiting Collection section, click Browse, select All Users and User Groups, and click OK.

6. Click Next.

7. In Membership Rules, click the Add Rule and select Query Rule.

8. In the Name field, enter **Senior Directors** and click Edit Query Statement.

9. Select the Criteria tab.

10. Click the Add Criterion button (the orange *).

11. Click the Select button.

12. Select User Resource as the Attribute Class and User Group Name as the Attribute, and then click OK.

13. Click the Value button to show available groups and select the appropriate group, in this case the Senior Directors group, and click OK.

14. Click OK to save the criterion.

15. Click OK to save the query.

16. Click OK to save the query rule.

17. Change the Schedule to recur every one days.

18. Check the Use Incremental Updates for This Collection option.

19. Click Next.

20. Review the Summary and click Next to create the collection.

21. Click Close to exit the wizard.

There will now be collection for the Senior Directors. Repeat the preceding steps for the Directors collection and for an All Directors collection (shown in Figure 4.7). These two new collections, the Senior Directors collection and the Directors collection, can be used to target application deployments at the Directors and Senior Directors.

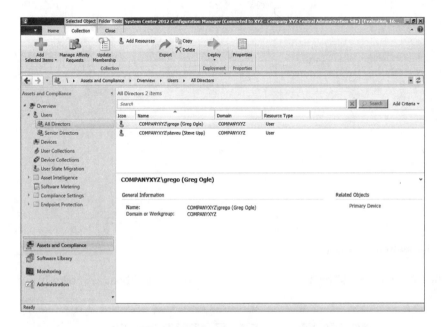

FIGURE 4.7   The All Directors collection.

The other new Configuration Manager 2012 feature that enhances user targeting is User Affinity. This allows administrators and users to designate which computer is their primary computer, allowing applications and application deployments to be targeted differently at the user's primary computer. This might include only deploying to the user's primary computer or deploying a full installation of the user's primary computer and virtual applications to all other computers that the user logs on to.

The users can designate which computer is their primary computer. In the preceding example, the administrator wants to target an automatic deployment to the Senior Director Greg Ogle's primary computer. To facilitate this, Greg would need to designate this primary computer using the new SCCM Software Center. To do this, the Greg would execute the following steps:

1. Log on to the primary computer (WS3 in Greg's case), select Start, All Programs, Microsoft System Center 2012, and Software Center (shown in Figure 4.8).

2. Click the Find Additional Applications from the Application Catalog link, underneath the Search field in the upper-right corner.

3. Click on the My Devices link in the large menu bar.

FIGURE 4.8   The Software Center.

4. Check the I Regularly Use This Computer to Do My Work check box, as shown in Figure 4.9.

FIGURE 4.9   Setting the primary computer or User Affinity.

5. Close the Application Catalog page.

6. Close the Software Center application.

Now the WS3 computer that Greg was logged on to is now designated as his primary computer.

The User Affinity process can also be automated in Client Settings. In the Client Settings, User Affinity can be set automatically based on a usage threshold. This defaults to 2880 minutes over the course of 30 days. The default Client Settings are shown in Figure 4.10.

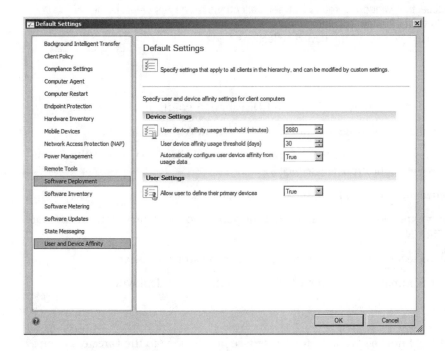

FIGURE 4.10   Automatic User Affinity.

The User and Device Affinity client settings ensure that the user's primary device is automatically set, even if the user does not take the initiative to set it.

The next step is to use collections and User Affinity to deploy applications to users.

Deploying Software Self-Service

When the Distribution Points have received the content, the software can be deployed to users as self-service applications. When software is deployed self-service, the user has the ability to execute the software when it's convenient for him or her. To deploy the software, a deployment needs to be created.

To create the Office 2010 self-service deployment for the Directors group, complete the following steps:

1. Select the Software Library space in the console.

2. Expand the Application Management folder and select the Applications container.

3. Right-click the Office 2010 application and select Deploy.

4. In the Collection section, click Browse.

5. From the list of collections, select the Directors collection and click OK.

> **NOTE**
>
> The Select Collection window defaults to User Collections in the upper-left corner of the screen. To target Device Collections instead, change the User Collections to Device Collections to display a list of the device collections.

6. Click Next.

7. In the Content section, leave the default Distribution Points and click Next.

8. In the Deployment Settings section, leave the default Action as Install.

9. In the Purpose setting, leave the default Available and click Next. This is the setting that makes the application self-service.

10. In the Scheduling section, leave the defaults and click Next.

11. In the User Experience section, note that the application will display in the Software Center. Click Next.

12. In the Alerts section, leave the default of no alerting and click Next.

13. Review the Summary, and then click Next to configure the deployment.

14. Click Close to exit the wizard.

The Office 2010 will now be available for self-service installations to the Directors group. Users can use the Software Center to install the application themselves.

> **NOTE**
>
> This deployment will use the Install Self-Service deployment type created previously.

For example, if the Company XYZ Director Steve Upp wants to install the software, then he would execute the following steps:

1. Log on to the primary computer (WS4 in Steve's case), select Start, All Programs, Microsoft System Center 2012, and Software Center (shown in Figure 4.7).

2. Click the Find Additional Applications from the Application Catalog link, underneath the Search field in the upper-right corner.

3. The Office 2010 installation shows as available in the Application Catalog, as shown in Figure 4.11.

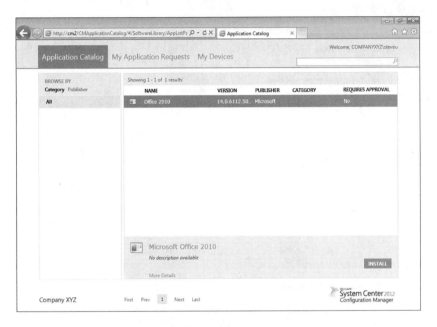

FIGURE 4.11   Self-service application install.

4. Click the Install button to begin the installation.

5. An Application Installation pop-up appears asking if you want to continue with the installation. Click Yes to continue.

6. The pop-up changes, indicating that the application installation is being prepared.

NOTE

The Application Installation pop-up will close automatically. Do not close the pop-up manually; this might interfere with the installation.

7. The Application Catalog shows that the application installation has started and a system tray pop-up indicates that the software is downloading (shown in Figure 4.12).

8. Close the Application Catalog web page.

9. The Software Center screen now shows the installation status for Office 2010, in this case the status is Installing (shown in Figure 4.13).

10. The Software Center tool can be closed while the software is installed.

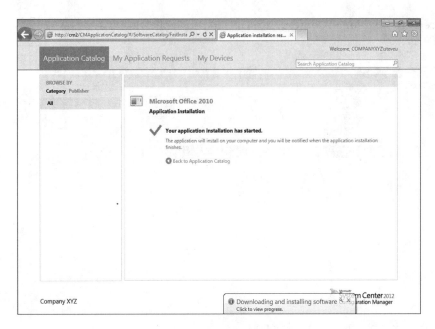

FIGURE 4.12   Self-service application install initiated.

FIGURE 4.13   Self-service application installing in Software Center.

The self-service application model provides a lot of flexibility for both end users and administrators. It allows end users to install the software they need when they need it and administrators are released from the burden of scheduling and coordinating mandatory installations.

Deploying Software Automatically

Software can be installed automatically based on a required deadline. This is a convenient way to systematically update computers when the user is not using the system or during nonpeak hours.

> **NOTE**
>
> A large software package deployment can negatively impact performance of the target system. A user might restart the system to address the perception of sluggish performance, possibly causing a corrupt installation. Establish an effective change-control and communication process prior to silently deploying software and making changes to systems in the environment.

To create the Office 2010 required deployment for the Senior Directors group, complete the following steps:

1. Select the Software Library space in the console.

2. Expand the Application Management folder and select the Applications container.

3. Right-click the Office 2010 application and select Deploy.

4. In the Collection section, click Browse.

5. From the list of collections, select the Senior Directors collection and click OK.

> **NOTE**
>
> The Select Collection window defaults to User Collections in the upper-left corner of the screen. To target Device Collections instead, change the User Collections to Device Collections to display a list of the device collections.

6. Click Next.

7. In the Content section, leave the default Distribution Points and click Next.

8. In the Deployment Settings section, leave the default Action as Install.

9. In the Purpose setting, select Required and click Next. This is the setting that makes the application automatically install.

10. In the Scheduling section, leave the defaults and click Next. This setting forces the software to install as soon as possible. If a future date is needed, then change the Installation Deadline as appropriate.

11. In the User Experience section, note that the application will display in the Software Center. Click Next.

NOTE

The Display in Software Center options allow users to install before the mandatory deadline. The Hide in Software Center option prevents users from manually installing before the deadline.

---

12. In the Alerts section, leave the default of no alerting and click Next.

13. Review the Summary, and then click Next to configure the deployment.

14. Click Close to exit the wizard.

Office 2010 will now be available for self-service installations to the Senior Directors group with an automatic installation deadline. Users can use the Software Center to install the application themselves or wait to have the application installed automatically.

NOTE

This deployment uses the Install Self-Service deployment type if the user elects to use the Application Catalog, but uses the Install on Primary System deployment type if it executes automatically.

The software package is downloaded and executed on the target system based on the time specified. If the default date and time is selected, the client system deploys the software after the next policy refresh cycle.

If the software has not been run by the time of the assigned schedule, the installation occurs automatically (shown in Figure 4.14). This can simplify the software deployment process, reduce the load of the environment, and reduce deployment complexity.

FIGURE 4.14   Automatic application downloading and installing.

Monitoring Software Deployment

Monitoring the deployment of the software package is key to ensuring the environment is secure and maintained. Standardized software helps reduce the overhead of maintaining and managing the environment.

There are several ways to monitor the deployment of software. From within the Configuration Manager console, an administrator can review the overall status of application deployment from the Deployments folder. The Deployments folder is located in the Monitoring space.

> **NOTE**
>
> Select the Run Summarization link to refresh the information in this folder. This can take some time to complete, depending on the size of the hierarchy.

Within the Deployments folder, each of the deployments can be viewed; this includes application deployments. The statistics and graphs on the detailed view of the deployment provides a visual representation of the deployment status, including successful and failed deployments, content status, and update states for the deployment. Select a deployment to see this detailed view, as shown in Figure 4.15. The figure shows the status of the Network Monitor deployment, which shows three successes and one in-progress deployment.

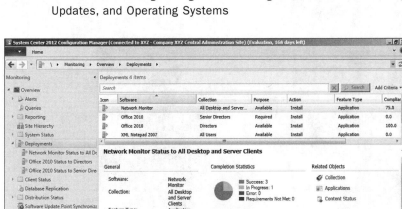

FIGURE 4.15   Application deployment Summary view.

For more detail, the administrator can right-click on an application and select View Status. This creates a temporary view for the application deployment with separate tabs for each completion state. Within each of those completion states, the administrator can see the specific deployment type that was attempted. This is useful for troubleshooting issues where the incorrect deployment type is selected by the deployment.

Figure 4.16 shows the detailed deployment status view for the Network Monitor deployment. The three successful systems are shown in the Success tab and it shows that the deployment type was "Install x64."

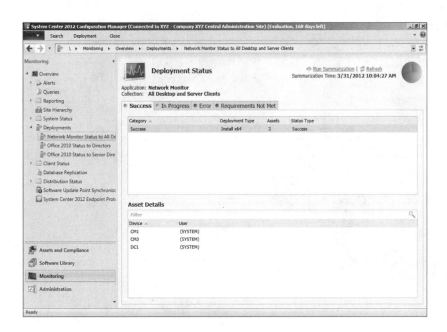

FIGURE 4.16   Application status Detail view.

For even more detailed information on deployment status, see the reports sections in Chapter 5, "Using Configuration Manager 2012 for Asset Management and Reporting."

Understanding Software Updates

Configuration Manager 2012 provides access to a large amount of Windows Update data. It is important to understand how to organize the data to establish an effective patch-management system. This includes creating a simple repeatable process to ensure the environment is kept up to date. The subsequent tasks show how to use the different Configuration Manager features and functionality to deploy patches to collections.

Viewing the Update Repository

The Software Updates home page shows all of the software updates. Additional columns can be added to the view by right-clicking on the columns and selecting desired columns from the context menu. The Date Released column, along with the Update Classification column, can be used to quickly view the compliance for the entire infrastructure. When update is selected, the additional information about the update is presented in the details window, including the compliance graph showing compliance for the organization.

The All Software Updates folder is shown in Figure 4.17. The selected MS12-016 security update shows that one system is compliant, three require the update, three do not require the update, and six systems have an unknown status.

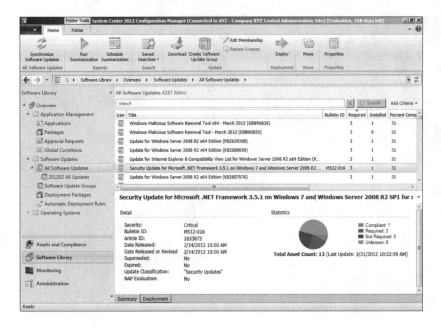

FIGURE 4.17   All Software Updates.

The Update Repository container located under the Software Updates container shows all the metadata synchronized from Microsoft Update through the WSUS component integration. The updates listed here are broken down by category for relatively simple navigation.

The All Software Updates view can be filtered by either searching or selecting Add Criteria link. The Add Criteria link allows the repository to be filtered by any field, including product, Update classification, release date, bulletin ID, article ID, and many other fields. This is very useful for narrowing down the exact updates needed.

Identifying Updates and Creating Software Update Groups

The appropriate updates for the environment need to be identified and added to the software update group. The software update group provides a simple method to add patches to a new or existing software update deployment and a way to report on the compliance for the patches on the software update group.

> **NOTE**
>
> Software update groups were known as update lists in previous versions of Configuration Manager.

It is common to create as many software update groups as necessary to meet the deployment and reporting requirements for the organization. For example, an administrator might create a new software update group each month to assist with the deployment and reporting for a specific group of patches. An update group can be as broad or granular as necessary. For example, all patches for all workstations can be added to a software update group, or individual software update groups can be created for each workstation operating system for more granular deployment and reporting.

Static software update groups can be created to list all patches, with new patches added each month. A static update group is a good candidate to schedule the Overall Compliance report through email delivery. This shows the ongoing compliance for specific collections.

The updates are identified with a search, which includes the Security Updates, Critical Updates, and Updates classifications for Windows 7 workstations.

To create the Windows 7 – All Updates search, complete the following steps:

1. Select All Software Updates in the Software Library space.

2. Click the Add Criteria link next to the Search button.

3. In the Criteria pull-down, check the Product option and the Update Classification option, and then click Add. This adds the two criteria to the search.

4. Click on the AND Product search term link and select Windows 7.

5. The AND Update Classification will have defaulted to Critical Updates. However, the other classifications need to be added to the search terms.

6. Click the Add Criteria link next to the Search button.

7. In the Criteria pull-down, check the Update Classification option, and then click Add. This adds a second Update Classification criterion to the search.

8. Click on the new OR Update Classification search term link and select Security Updates.

9. Click the Add Criteria link next to the Search button.

10. In the Criteria pull-down, check the Update Classification option, and then click Add. This adds a second Update Classification criterion to the search.

11. Click on the new OR Update Classification search term link and select Updates.

12. Click the Search button to execute the search (shown in Figure 4.18).

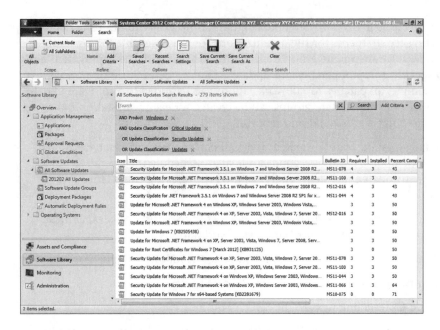

FIGURE 4.18   The Windows 7 - All Updates search results.

13. After confirming the results, click on Save Current Search and enter `Windows 7 - All Updates` as the name, and then click OK.

To see the results of the search again, click the Saved Searches, select the Manage Searches for Current Node, select the Windows 7 - All Updates search, and then click OK. All of the Windows 7 updates will be listed. This is a combined list from the Security Updates, Critical Updates, and Updates classifications. From this search, all of the missing patches for Windows 7 can be identified and added to a Windows 7 - All Updates group.

NOTE

Establish baseline software update groups and update deployments to get the environment current.

To create the Windows 7 - All Updates group, complete the following steps:

1. Select the Windows 7 - Updates search.

2. Sort the list by the required column.

3. Hold Ctrl and select each requested update, click the Home tab at the top of the page, and then click the Create Software Update Group action.

4. Enter `Windows 7 - All Updates` in the Name field, and then click Create.

The new software update group is created in the Software Update Groups folder. Selecting the software update group shows summary compliance information for the group (shown in Figure 4.19). To review the updates and detailed compliance in a software update group, right-click on the software update group and select Show Members.

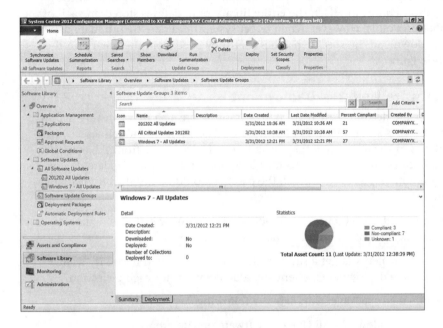

FIGURE 4.19   Windows 7 Updates compliance.

When new Windows 7 updates are released by Microsoft, they can be added to the Windows 7 - All Updates group for overall compliance reporting and a new software update group for controlled deployment. To add a single update to an existing software update group, right-click on the update and select Edit Membership. Check the boxes next to each software update group to which the update should belong.

Deploying Software Updates

The deployment is a combination of the patch list and the deployment parameters such as the target machines and the schedule of when to deploy the updates.

Creating Deployment Packages

To be deployed, updates must be downloaded from Microsoft. The updates can be downloaded in advance individually, from the software update group, or when configuring the deployment. Whenever the updates are downloaded, they are stored in deployment packages. Deployment packages serve as libraries of updates, allowing devices to search and download only those updates that they need. Deployment packages are stored on Distribution Points, much like application content. Each update is only downloaded once and stored in one deployment package, ensuring that content is not duplicated throughout the infrastructure.

The wizard downloads the requested updates from Microsoft Update and places them in the package folder on the network. The updates are automatically distributed to the selected Distribution Points. In effect, the entire library of updates is stored on each of the selected Distribution Points. However, when target systems evaluate their update deployment, they only download the specific patches that they need from the library on their local Distribution Point.

Creating Software Updates Deployment

When software update deadlines are used, it's common to create a new software deployment each time patches are released. The Software Update deployment defines the deadline for the patches in the deployment; by default, this is two weeks from the date the deployment was created. If patches were added to an existing Software Update deployment and the deadline has already expired, the patches would be installed immediately and the system restarted.

If deadlines are not used, the patches can be added to an existing software update deployment without causing the patches to be installed immediately.

Software update deployments target a single collection, so it is often necessary to have several software update deployments, essentially a deployment for each collection.

To create the deployment package, complete the following steps:

1. Right-click the Windows 7 - All Updates software update group.

2. Click the Deploy action.

3. Type **Windows 7 - Baseline** in the Name field.

4. In the Collection field, click Browse.

5. Select the SFO-Workstations collection and click OK.

6. Click Next.

7. In the Deployment Settings section, leave the default of Required and click Next.

8. In the Scheduling section, confirm the Client Local Time is set. This ensures that whatever schedule is set will be based on the client local time rather than universal time.

NOTE

In previous versions, this setting defaulted to universal time (UTC) and created many issues due to time zone differences. For example, if an administrator scheduled server updates for 8:00 p.m. in the local PST time zone, the UTC setting would actually launch those updates at 12:00 p.m. This would cause server reboots in the middle of the day rather than the evening.

---

9. Select the Installation Deadline needed for the updates. This defaults to one week from the current time. Then click Next.

10. In the User Experience settings, leave the default User Notification set to Display in Software Center and Show All Notifications. This allows users to install the updates in advance of the deadline if they choose. Click Next.

> **NOTE**
>
> Choosing Display in Software Center allows users to install the updates in advance of the deadline if they choose. Choosing Hide in Software Center causes the updates to deploy silently at the deadline.

11. In the Alerts section, leave the defaults and click Next.

12. In the Download Settings section, ensure that both option buttons are set to their respective Download options and then click Next.

13. Because there is no preexisting deployment package, select Create a New Deployment Package.

14. Enter **Updates Library** for the Name, enter **\\CM1\UpdatesLibrary** in the Package Source field, and then click Next.

15. Click Add, select Distribution Point, select the Distribution Point server check boxes, click OK, and then click Next.

16. In the Download Location settings, leave the default to download from the Internet and click Next.

17. In the Language Selection, leave the default languages for the site and click Next.

18. At the top of the Summary, click the Save As Template button.

> **NOTE**
>
> Deployment templates are a convenient time-saver, allowing the administrator to save settings for software update deployment. This reduces the likelihood of mistakes being made in the creation of new deployments, as in the template those are predefined. To use a saved deployment template, use the Select Deployment Template button in the opening screen of the Deploy Software Updates Wizard.

19. Enter **Windows 7 - Baseline Template** for the Name.

20. Review the Setting to save and click Save.

21. Review the Summary and then click Next.

> **NOTE**
>
> Updates will be downloaded from the Internet at this point into the package, so this step may take some time depending on the number of updates.

22. Click Close to exit the wizard.

If the software updates require a reboot, the user will be given 90 minutes by default to restart after which the system will be restarted automatically. The Restart Requirement notification reminder is shown in Figure 4.20.

FIGURE 4.20   The software update installation notification.

Automatic Deployment Rules

New to Configuration Manager 2012, automatic deployment rules allow administrators to automate the task of identifying monthly updates and adding them to deployments. If the organization has a standard methodology for deploying updates, then automatic deployment rules can completely automate the process. Examples of this could be an organization that has a security policy requiring that all critical updates, security updates, and updates be deployed within one week of release.

To create an automatic deployment rule to enforce the preceding sample policy on workstations, execute the following steps:

1. In the Configuration Manager console, select the Software Library space, expand Software Updates, and select the Automatic Deployment Rules folder.

2. Right-click on the Automatic Deployment Rules folder and select Create Automatic Deployment Rule.

3. In the Name field, enter **All Critical Updates to Workstations a Week After Release**.

4. In the Collection section, click the Browse button.

5. Select the All Windows 7 Systems collection and click OK.

6. Leave the default Add to an Existing Software Update Group option and click Next.

7. In the Deployment Settings section, leave the defaults and click Next.

8. In the Software Update section, check the Product and the Update Classification check boxes.

9. In the Search Criteria, click Items to Find and select Windows 7 for the Product. Select Critical Updates, Security Updates, and Updates for the Update Classification.

NOTE

These settings mirror the search criteria that was used to set up the Windows 7 - All Updates software update group. This means that the automatic deployment rule will keep the software update group up to date.

10. Click Next.

11. In the Evaluation Schedule section, leave the default of every seven days and click Next.

12. In the Deployment Schedule section, leave the default of a one week installation deadline and click Next.

13. In the User Experience section, select the Display in Software Center and Show All Notifications option and click Next.

14. In the Alerts section, leave the default and click Next.

15. In the Download Settings section, ensure that both option buttons are set to their respective Download options and click Next.

16. Click Browse and select the Update Library for the Deployment Package, click OK, and then click Next.

17. In the Download Location settings, leave the default to download from the Internet and click Next.

18. In the Language Selection, leave the default languages for the site and click Next.

19. Review the Summary and then click Next.

20. Click Close to exit the wizard.

Now, seven days after the release of updates, they will be evaluated and added to the automatic deployment if they match the criteria. Clients will then have one week to deploy the updates or they will be deployed automatically.

Monitoring Software Update Deployment

Monitoring the software update deployment is exactly the same as monitoring software deployments.

There are several ways to monitor the deployment of software updates. From within the Configuration Manager console, an administrator can review the overall status of software update deployment from the Deployments folder. The Deployments folder is located in the Monitoring space.

> **NOTE**
>
> Select the Run Summarization link to refresh the information in this folder. This can take some time to complete, depending on the size of the hierarchy.

Within the Deployments folder, each of the deployments can be viewed; this includes software update deployments. The statistics and graphs on the detailed view of the deployment provide a visual representation of the deployment status, including successful and failed deployments, content status, and update states for the deployment. Select a deployment to see this detailed view, as shown in Figure 4.21. The figure shows the status of the Windows 7 - All Updates software update deployment, which shows one success and two in progress.

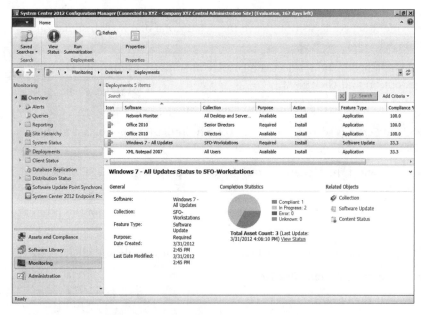

FIGURE 4.21   The software updates deployment Summary view.

For more detail, the administrator can right-click on a software update deployment and select View Status. This creates a temporary view for the software update deployment with separate tabs for each completion state. Within each of those completion states, the administrator can see the specific deployment type that was attempted. This is useful for troubleshooting issues where the incorrect deployment type is selected by the deployment.

For even more detailed information on software update deployment status, see the reports sections in Chapter 5. The chapter includes detailed software update reports on compliance, deployments, scans, and troubleshooting.

Understanding Operating System Deployment

The OS deployment functionality in Configuration Manager is highly modular. Each component is layered together to create a simple, effective system for distributing Windows operating systems.

For example, the drivers, updates, and software are all managed independently outside of the base OS image. Each component is dynamically installed during the deployment process. Software applications and Software Update deployments can be maintained as necessary without having to change the base OS image. New operating systems automatically get the latest software and updates during deployment.

Device drivers are managed the same way; during the OS deployment, the PnP IDs are enumerated and the best drivers are automatically selected from the list of available drivers. The list of available drivers is maintained within the Configuration Manager console. Updating the drivers can be done at any time; subsequent OS deployments automatically install the latest driver.

Common OS deployment technologies are as follows:

▶ **WinPE**—The Windows Preinstallation Environment runs a small version of Windows used to initiate the OS deployment. The WinPE environment is typically initiated over the network with the PXE-enabled Distribution Point.

▶ **Operating System Source**—This is the location of the OS files. The OS media images are typically downloaded from Microsoft. The files are extracted and placed in the Operating System Source folder on the network.

▶ **Operating system installer**—This is the operating system package inside the Configuration Manager console that points to the Operating System Source folder on the network. This allows operating systems to be created from scratch, as if booting to the original media. Typically this takes more time than applying an image.

▶ **Operating system image**—This is the capture of a prebuilt operating system into a Windows Imaging Format (WIM) file. This allows an operating system to be built, applications to be installed, and configurations to be applied before capturing the image. When the operating system is built starting from an operating system image, it saves a lot of time and ensures that the resulting systems are exactly the same.

▶ **Task sequence**—This set of tasks is used to execute the complete deployment. This includes everything from configuring the hardware, installing the OS, and deploying the correct software packages. Task sequences can also be used independent of operating system deployments to simply execute a series of steps, which is very useful for complex installations.

▶ **Drivers**—These are the drivers that have been uploaded to the Configuration Manager driver repository. These drivers can be installed dynamically during the deployment process.

▶ **Driver packages**—Specific drivers are grouped together for easier management. For example, all the drivers for a specific make and model of a server can be grouped together in a Driver package.

The operating system deployment functionality is powerful and provides the ability to fully automate all or part of the OS provisioning throughout the Windows environment. Common OS deployment scenarios are as follows:

▶ **OS deployment**—When a new system is procured, Configuration Manager is used to deploy a fully functional operating system either through a scripted installation or an image-based installation to a system that doesn't have an operating system. This is commonly used for both client and server systems.

▶ **OS refresh**—A new operating system or an updated version of the existing operating system is deployed to an existing system. Existing profile and user data can be saved to an encrypted network location and applied to the new OS. The workstation is fully patched with all required software when the deployment is complete. This is typically scheduled by an administrator to run automatically, or can be initiated by the end user. This is generally only done for workstations and not servers.

▶ **Hardware migration**—When a new system is procured for an end user, existing profile and user data can be copied from the original system to an encrypted network location and then applied to the new OS on the new system. The new system is fully patched with all required software when the deployment is complete. This is typically scheduled by an administrator to run automatically or can be initiated by the end user. This is generally only done for user systems.

Each scenario can be initiated several different ways. The most effective way to achieve an automated deployment is with the PXE Service Point and DHCP. If these protocols have not been made available on the network, deployments can be done with removable media, but this always requires additional administrative effort and should be avoided when possible.

The deployment of server operating systems to enterprise server hardware can be greatly simplified by leveraging vendor-specific Configuration Manager add-ons. HP, Dell, and IBM have all published add-ons and whitepapers for Configuration Manager 2012— available at no additional cost. These publications contain detailed guidance for deploying server operating systems to their hardware and include things like configuring the

RAID controller and performing hardware firmware updates from within the WinPE environment.

IMPORTANT

Make sure to configure the Network Access Account for all Primary Site Servers. This is the account that WinPE system uses to access content. If this account is not set, the operating system deployment will fail. To set the Network Access Account, go to the Administration space, Site configuration, Sites folder. Right-click the Primary Site Server, select Configure Site Components, then Software Distribution. Click the Network Access Account tab, select Specify the Account That Accesses Network Locations, and click the Set button to choose an existing ConfigMgr account or an account from Active Directory.

Preparing Applications and Deployment Types

Application and deployment types can be installed as part of the OS deployment on a target system. To prepare for OS deployment, an additional deployment type should be added to the existing package or an existing program can be modified with the correct settings to support OS deployment.

The OS Deployment Wizard does not allow selection of applications unless these options are configured correctly. Earlier in this chapter, an application was created for Microsoft Office 2010. The package contains a deployment type called Install for Primary Systems. To support deploying Microsoft Office 2010 during an OS deployment, create another deployment type called "Install Unattended" by copying the Install for Primary System deployment type. Then configure the copy with the correct program settings.

In the General tab of the application properties, check the Allow This Application to Be Installed from the Install Application Task Sequence Action Instead of Deploying It Manually check box. This allows the application to be used in the OS deployment.

NOTE

The command line used to install the package during OS deployment should never initiate a reboot. Instead, the return code 3010 should be used to tell the Configuration Manager client to restart the system and continue the deployment after the reboot. With Microsoft Installer (MSI)–based packages, reboots can be suppressed with the REBOOT=ReallySuppress command.

Creating the User State Migration Package

If the user state needs to be captured, a package that contains the User State Migration Tool is also required. The User State Migration Tool needed for Windows 7 deployments is already installed on the Configuration Manager Site Server as part of the Windows Automated Installation Kit (AIK) setup. The source files are located in the Windows AIK\Tools\USMT folder found within the Program Files folder.

To create the USMT package, complete the following steps:

1. In the Software Library space, expand the Application Management container.

2. Select Packages.

3. Click the Create Package action.

4. Type **User State Migration Tool** in the Name field.

5. Type **Microsoft** in the Manufacturer field.

6. Type **4.0** in the Version field.

7. Check the This Package Contains Source Files check box, set the source to c:\Program Files\Windows AIK\Tools\USMT, and then click OK.

8. Click Next.

9. Select Do Not Create a Program and click Next.

10. Review the Summary and click Next.

11. Click Close to exit the wizard.

Add the required Distribution Points to the package. All areas for which OS deployment will be used need access to this content from a Distribution Point.

> **NOTE**
>
> A user state can only be captured from within a full operating system, before the new operating system is deployed. The user state cannot be captured from the WinPE environment.

Managing Operating System Installers

Operating system installers are the code needed to install an operating system from scratch. This is essentially a copy of the installation CD, which can be used to install a fresh operating system. Operating system installers are managed the same way applications are managed for software distribution. It is important to establish a clean source on the network to host the operating system media.

The next tasks assume the operating system media for Windows 7 is located in the share called \\CM1\sources\Win7\.

The Windows 7 folder contains a copy of the files and folders on the Windows 7 SP1 DVD media.

To add the Windows 7 OS installer, complete the following steps:

1. In the Configuration Manager console, select the Software Library space.

2. Expand the Operating Systems folder.

3. Select the Operating System Installers container.

4. Click the Add Operating System Installer action.

5. Type the UNC of the Windows 7 folder in the field and click Next.

6. Type **Windows 7 with SP1** in the Name field and click Next.

7. Complete and close the wizard.

Right-click the newly added operating system installer and select the Distribute Content action to launch the Distribute Content Wizard. Use the wizard to distribute the operating system installer to the appropriate Distribution Points, as was done for applications.

Managing Operating System Images

Operating system images are preinstalled captures of an existing system in a WIM file, with all the settings and software configured. Typically, a base operating system image is used to jump-start the operating system deployment process, saving time during installation. Applications such as Office 2010 can be preinstalled in this image.

Operating system images are managed the same way operating system installers and applications are managed for software distribution.

The next tasks assume the operating system media for Windows 7 is located in the share called \\CM1\sources\Win7\Sources. The Windows 7 folder contains a copy of the Windows 7 SP1 DVD media, which contains a basic operating system image named the Windows 7 STARTER.

To add the Windows 7 OS installer, complete the following steps:

1. In the Configuration Manager console, select the Software Library space.

2. Expand the Operating Systems folder.

3. Select the Operating System Images container.

4. Click the Add Operating System Image action.

5. Type the UNC of Windows 7 folder in the field (**CM1****sources****Win7****Sources**) and click Browse.

6. Select the install.wim file and click Open.

7. Click Next.

8. Leave the automatically populated Windows 7 Edition in the Name field and click Next.

9. Click Next to complete and then close the wizard.

Right-click the newly added operating system image and select the Distribute Content action to launch the Distribute Content Wizard. Use the wizard to distribute the operating system image to the appropriate Distribution Points, as was done for applications.

Managing Drivers

The required drivers can be downloaded from vendor websites and extracted to a network source location, similar to the source location for the software distribution and OS images. It is important to categorize the drivers by manufacturer, name, and version to ensure the correct drivers are imported into the console.

When a driver is downloaded, it is often compressed inside an EXE file. The contents of the EXE need to be extracted. When drivers are imported, the INF, SYS, and CAT files are identified by Configuration Manager.

Drivers can be imported by selecting the Drivers container and clicking the Import action. During the import process, the drivers are identified and can be added to a Driver package. The task sequence for a specific installation can be configured to look for all matching drivers or only drivers in a specific Driver package. It is common for all the drivers of a specific make and model to be grouped within a Driver package.

To import the drivers for a Dell XPS 13 laptop, copy the drivers from the Dell driver CD or directory to a sources directory, such as \\CM1\Sources\XPS13. Then execute the following steps:

1. In the Configuration Manager console, select the Software Library space.

2. Expand the Operating Systems folder and select the Drivers folder.

3. Right-click on the Drivers folder and select Import Driver.

4. In the Locate Driver section, click the Browse button and navigate to the driver source directory, in this case \\CM1\Sources\XPS13.

> **NOTE**
>
> The entire driver directory can be specified in this process, as Configuration Manager will crawl through the entire directory to locate all the drivers.

5. Click Next to scan the Drivers folder.

6. In the Driver Details section, all of the drivers that were discovered will be listed.

7. Click the Categories button and click Create to add a new category.

8. Enter **Dell XPS 13** in the Name field and click OK.

9. Click OK to select the drivers and save.

10. Click Next.

11. In the Add Driver to Packages section, click on New Package to create a dedicated package for the set of drivers.

12. Type **Dell XPS 13** for the Name and specify a path for the Driver package, in this case **CM1\DriverPackages\XPS13**\, and click OK.

13. Click Next.

14. Click Next to skip adding drivers to the boot image.

15. Review the Summary and click Next.

16. Click Close to exit the wizard.

Right-click the newly added Driver package and select the Distribute Content action to launch the Distribute Content Wizard. Use the wizard to distribute the Driver package to the appropriate Distribution Points, as was done for applications.

If the driver being imported provides network or storage functionality, it is important to include the driver in the boot images. This ensures the WinPE environment can access the network and storage devices during deployment. During the import process, the drivers can be automatically added to the appropriate boot images. Make sure to update the Distribution Points after the boot images have been updated.

Managing Boot Images

Before deploying an operating system, make sure the boot images have been distributed to the correct Distribution Points. This can be done from the Boot Images node in the Configuration Manager console.

Right-click the boot image and select the Distribute Content action to launch the Distribute Content Wizard. Use the wizard to distribute the boot images to the appropriate Distribution Points, as was done for applications.

Creating Operating System Install Task Sequences

A task sequence is responsible for initiating the set of tasks on the target system. This can include capturing the user state; deploying the operating system, drivers, and software packages; and then reapplying the user state. If the deployment is to a server, the user state capture and reapplication process is not typically used.

> **NOTE**
>
> Capturing an existing user state is only necessary when performing a user migration. It is not required for new deployments or when the existing profile configuration and data is not required, for example, when roaming profiles are used.

To create the Windows 7 deployment task sequence, complete the following steps:

1. In the Configuration Manager console, select the Software Library space.

2. Expand the Operating Systems folder.

3. Select the Task Sequences container and click the Create Task Sequence action.

4. Select Install an Existing Image Package and click Next.

5. Type **Windows 7** in the Name field.

6. Click Browse, select the Boot Image (x86) boot image, click OK, and then click Next.

7. In the Install Windows section, click Browse, select the Windows 7 Edition operating system image, and then click OK.

8. Select the appropriate operating system from the image list.

9. Enter a product key and then click Next.

CAUTION

Be aware that not entering the product key might stop the Windows 7 installation during deployment, and an administrator needs to click Next to continue when prompted for a Windows 7 product key.

---

10. Select Join a Domain.

11. Click the Browse Domain button, choose companyabc.com, and then click OK.

12. Click the Browse Domain OU button, choose the appropriate OU, and then click OK.

13. Click the Set button, enter the domain join account, and then click Next.

NOTE

As a best practice, use a limited user account that has been delegated the ability to join systems to the domain as the domain join account for OS deployments.

---

14. Browse and locate the Microsoft Configuration Manager Client 2012 package.

15. Accept the default installation properties and click Next.

16. In the State Migration section, uncheck all of the options and click Next.

17. Choose All Software Updates and click Next.

18. Add the Network Monitor application and click Next.

19. At the Summary screen, click Next to create the task sequence.

20. Complete and close the wizard.

The deployment task sequence installs the Windows 7 operating system; the computer joins the domain and installs the Network Monitor tool and all applicable updates. The task sequence has nine steps in two groups. The list of steps in order is as follows:

- ▶ Restart in Windows PE

- ▶ Partition Disk 0

- ▶ Apply Operating System

- ▶ Apply Windows Settings

- ▶ Apply Network Settings

- ▶ Apply Device Drivers

- ▶ Setup Windows and Configuration Manager

- ▶ Install Updates

- ▶ Install Applications

The task sequence steps can be reviewed and edited by locating the task sequence in the Software Library space in the Task Sequences container. Right-click on the task sequence and select Edit to edit the task sequence. The task sequence for the Windows 7 operating system deployment is shown in Figure 4.22. The Apply Network Settings task is selected in the figure, which shows the domain join information.

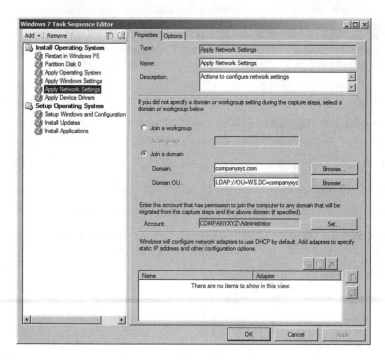

FIGURE 4.22   Editing the task sequence steps.

The basic Configuration Manager 2012 operating system deployment task sequence can be customized as much as is needed by the organization. Steps can be added, scripts can be run, reboots can be initiated, steps can be grouped, conditions can be added to both groups and steps, and variables can be used to preserve state between steps and reboots. The task sequence infrastructure is very flexible and easy to use.

Deploying Operating Systems

With the supporting images and packages configured, the operating system task sequences can now be targeted at a computer. In most organizations, these will be bare-metal deployments onto brand-new computers. These systems need to be prestaged by importing them into SCCM or enabling unknown computer support. Finally, the task sequence needs to be deployed targeting a collection.

Importing an Unknown Computer

Importing the computer is not necessary in Configuration Manager 2012 with the introduction of the Enable Unknown Computer Support option on the PXE-enabled Distribution Point role. This option allows a PXE-booted system to deploy an operating system without having to be imported into the console first.

> **NOTE**
>
> If the Enable Unknown Computer Support option is used for OS deployments, make sure to advertise the OS deployment task sequence to the All Unknown Computers collection.

However, for additional control around which systems can PXE boot and deploy an operating system, use the traditional method to import the computer information first.

To import computer information, complete the following steps:

1. Launch the Configuration Manager console.

2. Select the Assets and Compliance space and then select the Devices container.

3. Right-click the Devices container and click the Import Computer Information action.

4. Select Import a Single Computer and click Next.

5. Enter **WS5** as the Computer Name.

6. Enter the MAC or SMSBIOS GUID number and click Next.

7. Review the data and click Next.

8. Choose Add Computer to the Following Collection.

9. Click Browse, select the Workstation-Prerelease collection, and click Next.

10. Click Next to import the computer.

11. Click Close to exit the wizard.

Select the Workstation-Prerelease collection. Choose the Update Membership action, and then refresh the collection. The new computer WS5 should be listed.

Creating the Task Sequence Deployment

After importing images, drivers, software, boot images, and all the other objects needed to support operating system deployment, the infrastructure is now ready to actually deploy an operating system.

To assign the task sequence, complete the following steps:

1. In the Assets and Compliance space, select the Device Collections container.

2. Select the Workstation-Prerelease collection.

3. Right-click the Workstation-Prerelease collection, select Deploy, and click the Task Sequence action.

4. Click Browse, select the Windows 7 task sequence, click OK, and then click Next.

5. From the Purpose drop-down, select Required.

6. Enable the Make This Task Sequence Available to Boot Media and PXE option, and then click Next.

7. Click New and select Assign Immediately After This Event, leave the default As Soon As Possible, and then click OK.

8. Accept the default schedule and click Next.

9. In the User Experience section, check the Allow Users to Run the Program Independently of Assignments, and click Next.

10. In the Alerts section, leave the defaults and click Next.

11. Click Next to accept the default Distribution Point options.

12. Review the Summary, click Next to create the task sequence, and then close the wizard.

Once the task sequence deployment is created, the target computer can be booted via PXE. The PXE boot will download the WinPE image with the SCCM client, who will boot to the WinPE image, and begin communicating with the SCCM infrastructure. It will automatically detect that it is targeted by a task sequence and will begin executing it.

If, after a network (PXE) boot, the computer doesn't boot into WinPE and deploy the operating system, check the MAC address or SMSBIOS GUID. The PXE-enabled Distribution Point only responds to computers that exist in the Configuration Manager console unless the option to enable unknown computers has been configured.

The task sequence starting on a target system is shown in Figure 4.23.

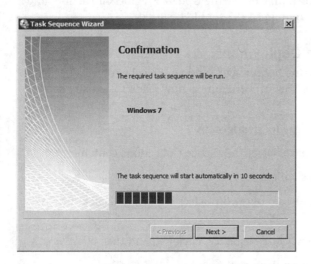

FIGURE 4.23   The task sequence starting from within WinPE.

A task sequence with a mandatory assignment will run automatically when the new system is PXE booted. A task sequence that does not have a mandatory assignment requires user interaction, specifically to press the F12 key to boot into the WinPE environment and to manually select the desired task sequence from the list of available task sequences.

Alternatively, the administrator can boot the target computer to a task sequence boot media ISO image or USB image. These are generated from the Configuration Manager console by right-clicking on the Task Sequences container and selecting Create Task Sequence Media. Choose the Bootable Media option to create either an ISO or USB boot stick that will launch Task Sequence deployments.

Monitoring the Operating System Deployment Process

Monitoring the operating system deployment is exactly the same as monitoring software deployments and updates deployments.

There are several ways to monitor the deployment of operating systems and task sequences. From within the Configuration Manager console, an administrator can review the overall status of operating system deployment from the Deployments folder. The Deployments folder is located in the Monitoring space.

Within the Deployments folder, each of the deployments can be viewed; this includes operating system task sequence deployments. The statistics and graphs on the detailed view of the deployment provides a visual representation of the deployment status, including successful and failed deployments, content status, and update states for the deployment. Select a deployment to see this detailed view, as shown in Figure 4.24. The figure shows the status of the Windows 7 operating system deployment, which shows one success.

FIGURE 4.24   The operating system deployment Summary view.

For more detail, the administrator can right-click on an operating system package and select View Status. This creates a temporary view for the operating system deployment with separate tabs for each completion state. Within each of those completion states, the administrator can see the specific deployment type that was attempted. This is useful for troubleshooting issues where the incorrect deployment type is selected by the deployment.

For even more detailed information on operating system deployment status, see the reports sections in Chapter 5. The distribution of operating systems can be monitored with the different reports provided with Configuration Manager. All reports are located in the Task Sequence folder on the Reporting Services Point. There are four main classifications of reports; each classification provides details on a different aspect of the OS deployment. It is important to understand each report.

For example, the Status Summary of a Specific Task Sequence Advertised for a Specific Computer report shows if any task sequences are running and provides drill-down functionality to subreports used to identify what step of the task sequence the computer is currently performing.

Extending with Microsoft Deployment Toolkit

The Microsoft Deployment Toolkit (MDT) 2012 is a comprehensive set of tools and guidance to facilitate and automate Windows 7 desktop and Windows Server 2008 server deployments. It is a standalone product that can deploy operating systems in its own right. However, it also integrates with Configuration Manager 2012 to provide a compelling "better together" solution. MDT with ConfigMgr include the following benefits:

- ▶ Unified tools and processes for desktop and server deployment

- ▶ Reduced deployment time and standardized desktop and server images

- ▶ Fully automated zero-touch installation deployments

- ▶ Detailed help and guidance for crafting sophisticated deployments

Configuration Manager 2012 and MDT 2012 together allow fully automated zero-touch bare-metal deployments and in-place upgrades of existing systems with complete state migration.

Installing MDT

MDT 2012 is a freely available Microsoft Solution Accelerator, available for download from the Microsoft Solution Accelerators website (http://technet.microsoft.com/en-us/solutionaccelerators/bb545941).

To install the MDT 2012, execute the following steps:

1. Copy the 64-bit version of the installer (`MicrosoftDeploymentToolkit2012_x64.msi`) to a local directory on the Central Site Server (CM1).

2. Double-click on the installer (`MicrosoftDeploymentToolkit2012_x64.msi`) to launch the installation.

3. At the Welcome screen, click Next.

4. Accept the license terms and click Next.

5. Adjust the installation location if needed and then click Next.

6. Click Install to start the installation.

7. Click Finish to close the Wizard.

MDT is now installed and ready to be integrated with Configuration Manager 2012.

Integrating MDT with Configuration Manager

The integration of MDT 2012 with Configuration Manager 2012 allows the administrator to use all the MDT functionality directly within the Configuration Manager console. The integration is seamless and the new MDT options appear in the menus alongside the standard Configuration Manager menu options.

To integrate MDT 2012 with Configuration Manager, execute the following steps:

1. On the Central Site Server where MDT was installed (CM1), click Start, All Programs, Microsoft Deployment Toolkit, and select Configure ConfigMgr Integration.

2. In the Options screen, the tool should have automatically detected the appropriate settings for the site, as shown in Figure 4.25.

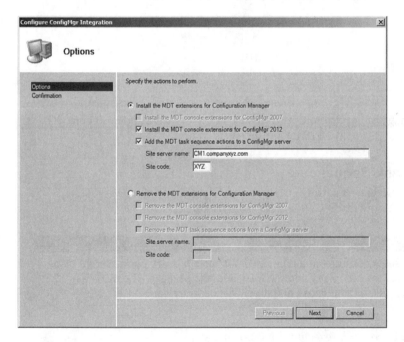

FIGURE 4.25   Automatically detected MDT options.

3. Click Next.

4. Click Finish to close the wizard.

The MDT tools will now be integrated into the Configuration Manager console and can be accessed from there.

To support the creation of MDT task sequences, an additional configuration step needs to be done. The MDT task sequences use an MDT version of the boot image, rather than the default Configuration Manager boot images. This boot image needs to be created and distributed.

To create the MDT boot image, execute the following steps:

1. Launch the Configuration Manager console and select the Software Library space.

2. In the Operating Systems folder, select the Boot Images container.

3. Select the Create Boot Image Using MDT action.

4. In the Package Source section, enter a location to store the boot image and click Next. In this case, the folder \\CM1\Sources\MDTBootImage is used.

5. In the General Settings section, enter MDT Boot Image for the Name and click Next.

6. In the Options section, leave the defaults and click Next.

7. In the Components section, leave the defaults and click Next.

8. In the Customization section, leave the defaults and click Next.

9. Review the Summary and click Next.

10. Close the Wizard when complete.

The new MDT boot image needs to be distributed to the appropriate Distribution Points, as with any other image or application. Also, if special drivers were added to default boot images, they must be added to the MDT boot image as well.

Creating MDT Task Sequences

With MDT installed, integrated with Configuration Manager, and the boot image prepared, the system is now ready to create MDT task sequences.

> **NOTE**
>
> The first time task sequences are created in MDT, a couple of extra packages are also created. This includes the MDT Files and the MDT Settings package. The MDT Task Sequence wizard will guide the process and it only needs to be done once.

To create an MDT task sequence, execute the following steps:

1. Launch the Configuration Manager console and select the Software Library space.

2. In the Operating Systems folder, select the Task Sequences container.

3. Right-click the Task Sequences container and select Create MDT Task Sequence.

4. In the Choose Template section, there are six different templates to choose from depending on the deployment scenario. Leave the default Client Task Sequence template selected and click Next.

5. In the General section, enter Windows 7 MDT for the Task Sequence Name and click Next.

6. In the Details section, enter the domain join information, organization name, and the product key. Then click Next.

7. In the Capture Settings section, leave the default and click Next.

8. In the Boot Image section, click Browse to select the previously created MDT Boot Image and click Next.

9. In the MDT Package section, select Create a New Microsoft Deployment Toolkit Files Package. Enter `\\CM1\Sources\MDTFiles` for the Package Source and click Next.

10. In the MDT Details section, enter `MDT files` for the Name and click Next.

11. In the OS Image section, click Browse to locate the Windows 7 STARTER image created earlier and then click Next.

12. In the OS Image Index section, choose the Windows 7 ULTIMATE image and click Next.

13. In the Client Package section, click Browse to locate the Microsoft Corporation Configuration Manager Client Package and click Next.

14. In the USMT Package section, click Browse to locate the Microsoft User State Migration Tool 4.0 Package and then click Next.

15. In the Settings Package section, select Create a New Settings Package. Enter `\\CM1\Sources\MDTSettings` for the Package Source and click Next.

16. In the MDT Details section, enter `MDT Settings` for the Name and click Next.

17. In the Sysprep Package section, leave the default of No Sysprep Packages Required selected and then click Next.

18. Review the Summary and click Next to create the task sequence.

19. Click Finish to exit the wizard.

The new packages that were created will need to be distributed to the appropriate Distribution Points, as with any other image or application. This includes the MDT Files and the MDT Settings packages.

The MDT operating system deployment task sequence installs the Windows 7 operating system in a much more sophisticated manner than the basic SCCM task sequence. The MDT task sequence has over 50 steps in multiple groups with a variety of conditions to automate the workflow, as compared with the simplistic nine steps of the default operating system deployment task sequence. Some of the features included in the task sequence are as follows:

▶ Prerequisite checking

▶ Replace vs. upgrade logic

▶ Hardware inventory gathering

- ▶ State capture and restore

- ▶ Tattoo of build information into Registry

- ▶ Backup of existing computer prior to upgrade

- ▶ Error checking and reporting

The MDT task sequence steps can be reviewed and edited by locating the task sequence in the Software Library space in the Task Sequences container. Right-click on the task sequence and select Edit to edit the task sequence. The task sequence for the Windows 7 MDT operating system deployment is shown in Figure 4.26. The Gather task is selected in the figure, which is the task that runs a custom script to gather hardware information model (manufacturer and model) and form factor (desktop, laptop, or server) to be used for more extensive customization.

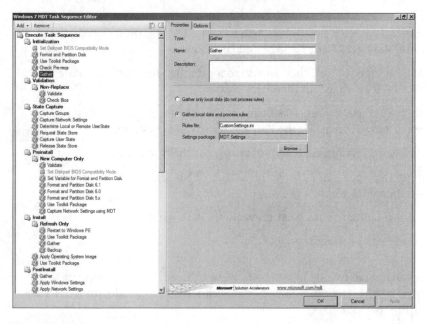

FIGURE 4.26   Editing the task sequence steps.

The level of complexity in the MDT 2012 operating system deployment task sequence can be daunting at first glance. For assistance in understanding the details of the process, task sequence steps, scripts, and variables, refer to the Microsoft Deployment Toolkit Documentation Library. This is a detailed reference to MDT 2012 and can be accessed by going to Start, All Programs, Microsoft Deployment Toolkit, and selecting the Microsoft Deployment Toolkit Documentation Library CHM file.

The MDT 2012 task sequence is far more sophisticated and reflects real-world requirements for desktop and server deployments. This makes a great starting point for developing an organization's operating system deployment or upgrade.

Summary

Configuration Manager 2012 provides an incredible array of technology to distribute content to users and managed systems, as well as manage the end-to-end system configuration and life cycle. From the initial operating system deployment to software deployment and software update deployment, Configuration Manager facilitates management of any size infrastructure.

Best Practices

The following are best practices from this chapter:

▶ Extend the Active Directory schema to support global roaming. Global roaming can be achieved when the Active Directory schema has been extended. If the schema hasn't been extended, only regional roaming is available. Regional roaming only allows client roaming to sites lower in the hierarchy. If the client roams to a peer site or parent site, content cannot be downloaded from Resident Distribution Points.

▶ To override protected boundary behavior, enable the Allow Clients to Fall Back to Unprotected Distribution Points when the Content Is Not Available on the Protected Distribution Point on the Package Advertisement option.

▶ Be cautious if lowering the default polling cycle for either policies or state messages because this directly increases the load on the Management Point and the underlying network infrastructure.

▶ If the scope of a collection is limited based on another collection, be sure to set the appropriate collection update schedule. The source collection should update before the target collection, or the results of the collection could be a complete update cycle behind. By default, a collection is updated every 24 hours, starting from when it was created.

▶ Only MSP files can be placed in the Office Updates folder. Copying the downloaded Microsoft Office 2010 EXEs to the Updates folder directly is not supported. The EXE needs to be extracted first, and then the extracted MSP files need to be placed in the Updates folder within the source directory.

▶ Do not include Microsoft Office 2010 service packs or hotfixes in the Additional Content section of the Office Customization Tool. Updates need to be placed in the Updates folder; adding them as part of the installation is not supported.

▶ It is recommended to set the estimated disk space requirements for the program high enough to ensure enough space for both the installation and continued normal operation after the software package has been deployed.

▶ A large software package deployment can negatively impact performance of the target system. A user might restart the system to address the perception of sluggish performance, possibly causing a corrupt installation. Establish an effective change-control and communication process prior to silently deploying software and making changes to systems in the environment.

▶ Keeping the source folder name and the software update deployment package name the same makes it easier to identify and clean up old patches and reclaim space on the file server.

▶ Establish baseline software update groups and update deployments to get the environment current.

▶ The deployment of server operating systems to enterprise server hardware can be greatly simplified by leveraging vendor-specific Configuration Manager add-ons. HP, Dell, and IBM have all published add-ons and whitepapers for Configuration Manager 2012 available at no additional cost. These publications contain detailed guidance for deploying server operating systems to their hardware and include things like configuring the RAID controller and performing hardware firmware updates from within the WinPE environment.

▶ The command line used to install the package during OS deployment should never initiate a reboot. Instead, the return code 3010 should be used to tell the Configuration Manager client to restart the system and continue the deployment after the reboot. With Microsoft Installer (MSI)–based packages, reboots can be suppressed with the REBOOT=ReallySuppress command.

▶ As a best practice, use a limited user account that has been delegated the ability to join systems to the domain as the domain join account for OS deployments.

▶ If the Enable Unknown Computer Support option is used for OS deployments, make sure to advertise the OS deployment task sequence to the All Unknown Computers collection.

▶ When possible, it is highly recommended to establish a task sequence installation to automatically create the base image. This allows new base images to be created very quickly through a controlled and reproducible method. This is key to eliminating human error when manually installing and configuring the operating system and software.

▶ For sophisticated operating system deployments, leverage the Microsoft Deployment Toolkit (MDT) 2012 by integrating it with Configuration Manager 2012. Configuration Manager and MDT provide a "better together" solution that supports complex real-world enterprise operating system deployments.

CHAPTER 5

Using Configuration Manager 2012 for Asset Management and Reporting

IN THIS CHAPTER

▶ Understanding Asset Data

▶ Configuring Client Settings for Inventory Collection

▶ Understanding Reporting

▶ Customizing Hardware Inventory

▶ Understanding Asset Intelligence

▶ Understanding Software Metering

▶ Understanding Compliance Settings

▶ Monitoring the Baselines and Compliance

▶ Best Practices

System Center Configuration Manager (ConfigMgr) 2012 provides exceptional functionality for managing and reporting on Microsoft Windows assets. The asset management functionality includes things like hardware inventory, software inventory, software metering, software and license management through Asset Intelligence, and Compliance Settings. All of the data collected is located in the Configuration Manager database, and can be reported on through the built-in reporting features. This data can also be accessed with external applications and programmatically through a variety of methods, including Windows Management Instrumentation (WMI) and with the predefined database views.

This chapter helps the administrator understand how each role within the Configuration Manager hierarchy is used to support the management and reporting of assets. This includes how to customize the hardware and software inventory, implement and manage software metering and Asset Intelligence features, monitor and remediate configuration through Compliance Settings, and edit reports to present the data from both an administrative and management viewpoint.

Understanding Asset Data

Configuration Manager 2012 collects detailed asset information from the clients and stores this in the database. However, only the Central Administration Site database contains the aggregate data from all clients in the hierarchy. Primary Site Server databases contain data for the agents that they support. It is important to understand where data is stored and how it is collected to be sure that the correct data is presented.

Understanding the Database

Configuration Manager data primarily flows up the hierarchy, which means the database server at the top of the hierarchy holds all of the asset data from lower-level sites. The Site Database at lower-level sites only contains asset data from clients directly assigned to the site. This is an important aspect to consider when managing assets.

> **NOTE**
>
> Create and run reports from the central site to ensure data from the entire infrastructure can be seen. Site-specific reports can be created by filtering out data that isn't needed.

Understanding Inventory Collection

Inventory collection is the process of scanning for hardware configuration and file data on the managed system and reporting the results back to Configuration Manager. Both the Hardware and Software Inventory Client Agents use WMI to perform the actual scan of the managed system. The Configuration Manager client is told what to include in the inventory with rules sent to the client as signed, encrypted policies.

The results of the inventory are temporarily stored in an XML file on the managed system before being sent to the Management Point. The inventory process can be monitored on the client system with the InventoryAgent.log file, which is located in the Logs folder within the Configuration Manager client installation folder.

The inventory collection process is shown for Company XYZ in Figure 5.1. The clients upload data to their local Management Point (MP), the Management Point forwards the data to the Site Server, and finally the Primary Site Server forwards the data to the Central Site Server. The data aggregates locally at the Primary Site Servers and hierarchy-wide at the Central Site Server.

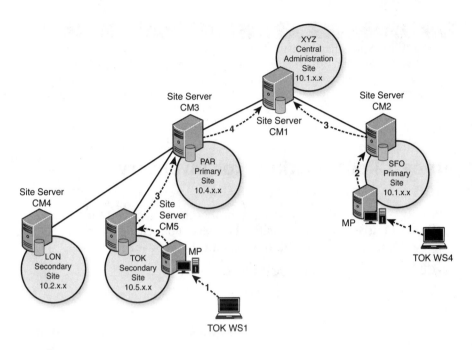

FIGURE 5.1   The inventory collection process.

The Management Point converts the files from XML to Management Information Format (MIF) and places the file in the `\inboxes\auth\dataldr.box` folder on the Site Server, which is located in the Configuration Manager installation folder. This process can be monitored through the `MP_Hinv.log` located in the Logs folder on the Management Point.

After the MIF file is copied to the correct folder on the Site Server, it's parsed, and the data is uploaded into the Site Database. This process can be monitored with the `Dataldr.log` file on the Site Server. If new hardware has been inventoried, the database is dynamically extended with custom tables, views, and other database objects necessary to allow Configuration Manager to manage and report the data.

Using IDMIF and NOIDMIF Files

Configuration Manager can also collect hardware inventory through custom MIF files. Both IDMIF and NOIDMIF files can be programmatically created and placed on the client. During inventory collection cycles, NOIDMIF files are parsed by the client and added to the hardware inventory report before being sent to the Management Point. Conversely, IDMIF files are sent to the Management Point, parsed by the Site Server, and added to the database as a separate record, not directly related to the actual managed system. IDMIF files would typically be used to identify and manage assets that cannot support a traditional client, such as a non-Windows system. For additional information on MIF files, review the Configuration Manager 2012 software development kit (SDK).

CAUTION

Avoid using IDMIF or NOIDMIF files to extend the hardware inventory. These files reside on the client computer and can dynamically modify the Configuration Manager database with custom data during the hardware inventory cycle. If this type of collection is necessary, ensure the risks are fully understood and the appropriate security has been implemented.

Configuring Client Settings for Inventory Collection

To enable inventory collection, the Hardware Inventory Client Agent and the Software Inventory Client Agent need to be configured and enabled. Both client agents can be accessed from the Client Agents node within the Configuration Manager console.

To access the Client Agents node, complete the following steps:

1. Open the Configuration Manager console and select the Administration space.

2. Expand Site Configuration.

3. Select Client Settings.

4. Right-click the Default Client Settings and select Properties.

Both the Hardware Inventory Client Agent and the Software Inventory Client Agent provide the ability to define a simple schedule or a custom schedule. The simple schedule typically improves the overall scalability of the Configuration Manager infrastructure by distributing the load placed on the network, Management Points, and Site Servers.

NOTE

Client settings can be customized for different collections of users or devices. Custom client settings can be created for either users or devices, configured with the appropriate values, and then targeted at collections via deployments. This allows a very fine-grained control over what settings are applied to specific users or devices.

The simple schedule works by configuring the client to execute and schedule the inventory schedule dynamically. The first iteration of the schedule is set as the time of the client installation. Throttling the deployment of the Configuration Manager client keeps a relatively consistent load on the environment.

The custom schedule instructs all clients to report inventory at a set time and recurrence pattern. If this configuration is desirable, ensure adequate resources are available for the expected load on the network and Configuration Manager hierarchy.

Configuring the Software Inventory Client Agent

The Software Inventory Client Agent provides access to enable or disable the ability to collect file properties on managed systems. From within the agent configuration, the inventory schedule can be configured and the file extensions to search on managed systems can be modified.

The software inventory cycle uses WMI queries to scan for files. If the agent is enabled, the default configuration searches all local drives for files with the EXE extension. Depending on the number of files, the software inventory cycle can take several hours. The inventory scan process has a timeout value assigned to each unique query; the default timeout is 14,400 seconds (4 hours).

> **NOTE**
>
> Similar queries are grouped together to improve performance. This is important to avoid searching the entire system multiple times when scanning for files. For example, searching all hard drives for EXEs and DLLs using the same options for the path, subdirectories, and exclusions results in a single query to find both types. If any of the options are different, multiple queries are used, which can significantly increase the time needed to complete the inventory.

To exclude a drive or folders from being inventoried, create a hidden file called `skpswi.dat`. This file can be placed in any folder to prevent that folder from being inventoried, or at the root of a drive to prevent the entire drive from being inventoried. Use Compliance Settings to locate rogue `skpswi.dat` files that could be used to hide file data.

Configuring the Hardware Inventory Client Agent

The Hardware Inventory Client Agent provides access to enable or disable the ability to collect hardware inventory on managed systems. From within the agent, the inventory schedule can be configured, and the IDMIF and NOIDMIF file collection can be enabled if necessary. To customize the hardware inventory, it is recommended to make changes to the `configuration.mof` and client settings. An example of this is detailed in the section "Customizing Hardware Inventory."

The complete hardware inventory cycle typically completes in a few minutes, with the actual scanning process typically placing a light load on managed systems. The initial inventory for hardware is relatively small, normally less than 1MB, and subsequent inventories are substantially smaller, as only changes are collected.

Understanding Reporting

The reporting functionality in Configuration Manager exposes the data collected from the different components in the hierarchy. Configuration Manager has more than 400 reports predefined, including several for each of the Configuration Manager computer management areas. All reports can be accessed through the Reports node in the Monitoring space of the Configuration Manager console.

Generating Reports

Configuration Manager 2012 reports are extensive and flexible. Reports are easy to generate and include parameters to allow different views of the collected asset information. Reports for almost any information are available, as long as you can locate the report. Fortunately, the reports are automatically organized into folders by category for ease of access.

For example, if an administrator is interested in tracking down a count of the operating systems in the environment, then the Configuration Manager reports are an excellent way to get that information.

To get a report of the count of operating systems, execute the following steps:

1. Launch the Configuration Manager console and select the Monitoring space.

2. Expand the Reporting folder and then expand the Reports folder. A number of automatically generated category folders are shown.

3. Select the Operating System folder to see the list of Operating System category reports. There should be nine reports listed.

4. Select the Count Operating Systems and Service Packs report.

5. Right-click on the report and select Run.

6. Because the report has no parameters, it generates automatically, as shown in Figure 5.2.

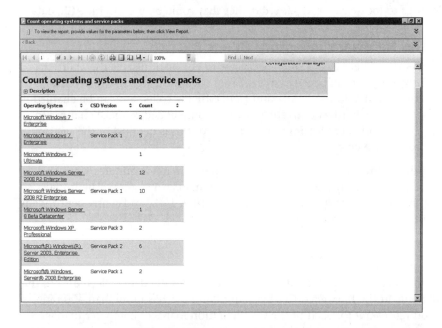

FIGURE 5.2   The Count Operating System and Service Packs report.

After being generated, the report can be printed by clicking on the icon or saved to any one of the following formats:

▶ XML file with report data

▶ CSV (comma delimited)

▶ PDF

▶ MHTML (web archive)

▶ Excel

▶ TIFF file

▶ Word

This allows great flexibility in saving the report and reusing it as data.

Another report that an administrator might look for is systems where memory is below a certain threshold—that is, systems that might need to be replaced before an operating system upgrade.

To get a report of the list of systems with low memory, execute the following steps:

1. Launch the Configuration Manager console and select the Monitoring space.

2. Expand the Reporting folder and then expand the Reports folder. A number of automatically generated category folders are shown.

3. Select the Hardware - Memory folder to see the list of the category reports. There should be five reports listed.

4. Select the Computers with Low Memory (Less Than or Equal to Specified MB) report.

5. Right-click on the report and select Run.

6. In the MB of Memory parameter, enter **2048** and click View Report.

7. The report generates, as shown in Figure 5.3, with seven systems showing low memory.

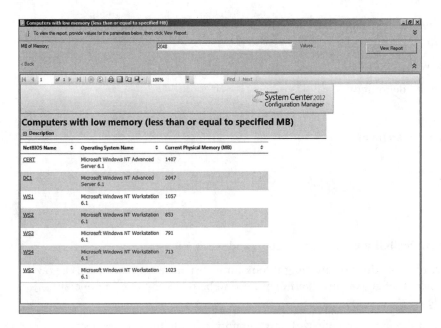

FIGURE 5.3   The Computers with Low Memory (Less Than or Equal to Specified MB) report.

Reports are easy to generate ad hoc as well as print or save as needed. However, what is even better is to have them delivered automatically via email or saved to a SharePoint folder. In the next section, scheduling reports is shown.

Short List of Reports

Given the multitude of reports available in Configuration Manager 2012, it's helpful to administrators to get some pointers on what reports to go to first. The following list represents a sampling of the more useful reports for each of the features in Configuration Manager 2012. This list is not intended to be comprehensive, but rather to kick-start the process of exploring the reports.

For inventory, the short list of reports to look at is as follows:

▶ **Count Operating Systems and Service Packs report**—Displays the number of computers inventoried by operating system and service pack combinations.

▶ **Software 04B - Computers with Specific Software Configured to Automatically Run report**—Displays all computers with specific software configured to automatically run.

▶ **Software 06A - Search for Installed Software report**—Provides a summary of installed software ordered by the number of instances based on search criteria for the product name, publisher, or version.

▶ **User Device Affinity Associations per Collection report**—Shows all User Device Associations for the selected collection, and groups the results by collection type (for example, user or device).

▶ **Software Registered in Add Remove Programs on a Specific Computer report—**Displays a summary of the software installed on a specific computer that is registered in Add Remove Programs.

▶ **Computers with a Specific File report—**Displays a list of the computers where a specified filename appears in the software inventory as well as information about inventoried files. A computer may appear more than once in the list if it contains more than one copy of the file.

For software updates, the short list of reports to look at is as follows:

▶ **Compliance 1 - Overall Compliance report—**Returns the overall compliance data for a software update group.

▶ **Compliance 2 - Update Group report—**Returns the compliance data for software updates defined in a software update group.

▶ **States 1 - Enforcement States for a Deployment report—**Returns the enforcement states for a specific software update deployment, which is typically the second phase of a deployment assessment.

▶ **States 2 - Evaluation States for a Deployment report—**Returns the evaluation state for a specific software update deployment, which is typically the first phase of a deployment assessment.

▶ **Management 2 - Updates Required but Not Deployed report—**Returns all vendor-specific software updates that have been detected as required on clients but that have not been deployed to a specific collection. To limit the amount of information returned, you can specify the software update class.

▶ **Scan 1 - Last Scan States by Collection report—**Returns the count of computers for a specific collection in each compliance scan state returned by clients during the last compliance scan.

▶ **Troubleshooting 1 - Scan Errors report—**Returns the scan errors at the site and a count of computers that are experiencing each error.

For application deployment, the short list of reports to look at is as follows:

▶ **All Application Deployments (Basic) report—**Displays summary information for all application deployments.

▶ **Application Compliance report—**Shows compliance information for the selected application within the selected collection. This is an application-level report and might not reflect certain kinds of deployment-specific errors, such as deployment conflicts. Total here represents the total number of machines and users where the SCCM system tried to detect the presence of the application and this value may be greater than the sum of the Success, Requirements Not Met, and Error.

For task sequence deployment, the short list of reports to look at is as follows:

▶ **All Task Sequence Deployments report**—Displays details of all task sequence deployments initiated from this site

▶ **Progress of All Task Sequences report**—Displays the progress of all task sequences

▶ **Status Summary of a Specific Task Sequence Deployment report**—Shows the status summary of all resources that have been targeted by a deployment

▶ **Deployment Status of All Task Sequence Deployments report**—Displays the overall progress of all task sequence deployments

For software metering, the short list of reports to look at is as follows:

▶ **Concurrent Usage for All Metered Software Programs report**—Displays the maximum number of users who concurrently ran each metered software program during the specified month and year

▶ **Total Usage for All Metered Software Programs report**—Displays the number of users who ran programs matching each software metering rule locally or using Terminal Services within the specified month and year

For Configuration Manager health, the short list of reports to look at is as follows:

▶ **Client Status Summary report**—Shows the client check results of active clients for a given collection.

▶ **Client Status History report**—Provides a historical view of the overall client status in the environment.

▶ **Client Push Installation Status Summary report**—Provides a summary view of the client push installation process for all sites.

▶ **Client Push Installation Status Details report**—Provides a detailed status of the client push installation process for all sites.

▶ **Clients That Have Not Reported Recently (in a Specified Number of Days) report**—Displays a list of clients that have not reported discovery data, hardware inventory, or software inventory in a specified number of days. An empty column indicates that a client has not reported any data of that type. A column with a * means that the client has reported data of that type within the specified time period.

For auditing, the short list of reports to look at is as follows:

▶ **All Audit Messages for a Specific User report**—Displays a summary of all audit status messages for a single user. Audit messages describe actions taken in the Configuration Manager console that add, modify, or delete objects in ConfigMgr. *Note*: Clicking the Values button to select a username might take a long time to return a list of values. If you know the name of the user, type it in using the "domain name\username" format.

▶ **Remote Control - All Computers Remote Controlled by a Specific User report**— Displays a summary of status messages indicating remote control of client computers by a single specified user.

These lists will help get administrators started using the Configuration Manager 2012 reports.

Scheduling Reports

From within the Configuration Manager console, subscriptions to reports can be established. A subscription will run the report automatically and deliver the report to a file share or an email address.

To configure email subscriptions for reports, complete the following steps:

1. To configure email report delivery, you must have a Simple Mail Transfer Protocol (SMTP) server the email can be sent through. It is common to use an existing email infrastructure for this purpose, such as an Exchange Hub Transport or Edge server.

2. Reporting Services must be configured with the SMTP server. This can be done with the Reporting Services Configuration Manager console on the server SQL1. Open the console and connect to the Reporting Services instance. Select the E-mail Settings page, and type the sender email address and the fully qualified domain name (FQDN) of the SMTP server.

3. The SQL Agent service for the SQL instance must be configured to automatically start. This can be done through the SQL Server Configuration Manager on the SQL1 server. Open the SQL Server Configuration Manager and select the SQL Server Service node. Right-click the SQL Server Agent service and select Properties. Select the Service tab, and set the Start mode to Automatic. Apply the settings, select the Log On tab, and click the Start button.

These are basic SQL Server 2008 R2 prerequisites and these would have been completed during the installation of the SQL Server.

For example, if the administrator wants the count of operating systems to be delivered into his Inbox every day, then he can use a report subscription to achieve that.

To schedule a report, execute the following steps:

1. Launch the Configuration Manager console and select the Monitoring space.

2. Expand the Reporting folder and then expand the Reports folder. A number of automatically generated category folders are shown.

3. Select the Operating System folder to see the list of Operating System category reports. There should be nine reports listed.

4. Select the Count Operating Systems and Service Packs report.

5. Right-click on the report and select Create Subscription.

6. In the Report Delivered By drop-down, select E-mail.

> **NOTE**
>
> The fields automatically change based on the delivery method selected.

7. In the To field, enter the email address to deliver the report to. If the report should be delivered to multiple recipients, use a semicolon to separate the email addresses.

8. In the Subject field, enter the name of the report (**Count of Operating Systems and Service Packs**).

9. Check the Include Report check box; otherwise, there will be no report in the email.

10. Select MHTML (web archive) as the Render Format. This shows the report in the body of the email.

11. Click Next.

12. In the Subscription Schedule section, select the Daily option button.

13. Check the check boxes for Mon through Fri.

14. Change the Start Time to the time the report should generate, for example 6:00 a.m.

15. Click Next.

16. Review the Summary and click Next.

17. Click Close to exit the wizard.

The report will now generate every weekday at 6:00 a.m. and be delivered via email.

> **NOTE**
>
> Although the report was created and configured in the Configuration Manager console, it is generated by the SQL Server 2008 R2 Reporting Services every morning directly from the database. Once scheduled, none of the Configuration Manager components are involved in the generation of the report.

The subscription for the report can be viewed, modified, and deleted in the Subscriptions container. The Subscriptions container is located in the Reporting folder in the Monitoring space.

Editing Reports

Although an extensive array of reports are available in Configuration Manager 2012, sometimes they are not quite what administrators or end users are looking for. Fortunately, it is relatively straightforward to edit Configuration Manager 2012 reports.

It is not a task for end users, as it requires significant understanding of the Configuration Manager database and schema. It also requires familiarity with the transact SQL (TSQL) language used to create SQL database queries.

> **NOTE**
>
> Don't modify existing reports. Always make a copy of the report and make changes to the copy. During Configuration Manager service pack upgrades, the original reports can be updated by Microsoft, and if they're customized, the changes are lost.

For example, in previous examples the administrator was using the Count Operating Systems and Service Packs report. This report summarizes the operating system and service pack information, but does not provide a list of the individual systems with their operating system and service packs. A quick review of the Configuration Manager 2012 reports shows that this specific report does not exist in the library of reports. Fortunately, the report can be edited and saved as a new report that shows the information the administrator is looking for.

To edit the report, execute the following steps:

1. Launch the Configuration Manager console and select the Monitoring space.

2. Expand the Reporting folder and then expand the Reports folder. A number of automatically generated category folders are shown.

3. Select the Operating System folder to see the list of Operating System category reports. There should be nine reports listed.

4. Select the Count Operating Systems and Service Packs report.

5. Right-click on the report and select Edit. If this is the first time the report has been edited, then Report Builder will download and install automatically.

> **NOTE**
>
> If the SCCM 2012 is using SQL Server 2008 R2, then a cryptic ClickOnce error is generated when trying to edit or create new reports. This is because SCCM 2012 defaults to Report Builder 2.0 and SQL Server 2008 R2 uses Report Builder 3.0. To have the Configuration Manager console use Report Builder 3.0, edit the `ReportBuilderApplicationManifestName` value in the `HKLM/SOFTWARE/Wow6432Node/Microsoft/ConfigMgr10/AdminUI/Reporting` key. Change the value from `ReportBuilder_2_0_0_0.application` to `ReportBuilder_3_0_0_0.application`. Now the console will launch the correct version of Report Builder.

6. Report Builder, the editor for reports, launches with the report loaded. The original report is shown in Figure 5.4.

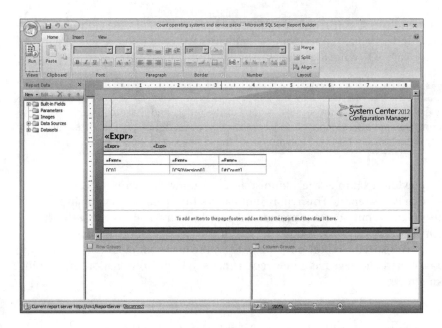

FIGURE 5.4   The Report Builder report.

7. The first thing to do is to save the report as a different name, to avoid overwriting the existing report. Click on the circle above the Run icon and select Save As.

8. For the Name, enter **List Computers with Operating Systems and Service Packs** and click Save. The new name is listed at the top of the Report Builder console.

9. To test that the report still functions, click the Run icon. The report should display. Click the Design icon to go back to designing the report.

> **NOTE**
>
> This is a great way to make sure that the report is looking like you want it to while editing the report.

10. Expand the Datasets and select DataSet0. This is what contains the database query to modify.

11. Right-click DataSet0 and select Dataset Properties to edit the data set.

12. In the Query section, there is a Query field with the TSQL query that gets the data from the database. Listing 5.1 shows the original query.

LISTING 5.1   Query for Count Operating Systems and Service Packs Report

```
SELECT OPSYS.Caption0 as C054, OPSYS.CSDVersion0, COUNT(*) AS 'Count'
FROM v_GS_OPERATING_SYSTEM OPSYS
inner join v_R_System sys on OPSYS.ResourceID=sys.ResourceID
GROUP BY OPSYS.Caption0, OPSYS.CSDVersion0
ORDER BY OPSYS.Caption0, OPSYS.CSDVersion0
```

13. The query needs to be modified to not count the operating systems, but instead list the systems' names. The modified query is shown in Listing 5.2.

LISTING 5.2   Query for Listing Systems with Operating Systems and Service Packs Report

```
SELECT sys.Name0, OPSYS.Caption0 as C054, OPSYS.CSDVersion0
FROM v_GS_OPERATING_SYSTEM OPSYS
inner join v_R_System sys on OPSYS.ResourceID=sys.ResourceID
GROUP BY sys.Name0, OPSYS.Caption0, OPSYS.CSDVersion0
ORDER BY sys.Name0, OPSYS.Caption0, OPSYS.CSDVersion0
```

14. Click OK to save the modified data set; you will be asked to provide the authenticated credentials. The syntax of the query will be checked automatically and the fields will be validated, so correct any issues if needed.

15. Now that the query has been modified, the report presentation area has an invalid Count column and is missing the system Name0 column.

16. Select the Count column, right-click the column, and select Delete Columns. The column is removed.

17. In the Report Data window, the DataSet0 has three fields below it. Drag and drop the Name0 field to the Presentation view to the left of the remaining two columns.

18. The columns in the report are a bit narrow for the data, so it's a good time to widen those columns to show the data better. Select each column and adjust its width. Figure 5.5 shows the modified report. Note the adjusted column widths and the modified data set fields.

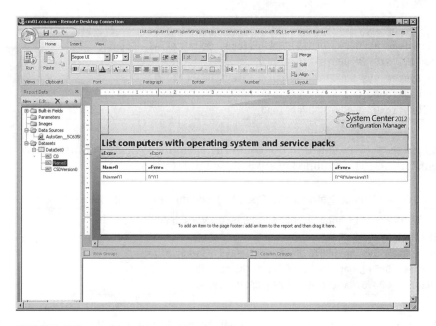

FIGURE 5.5   The Modified Report Builder report.

19. Click on the Run icon to generate the report and confirm that it looks as expected (shown in Figure 5.6).

20. Save the report and exit Report Builder.

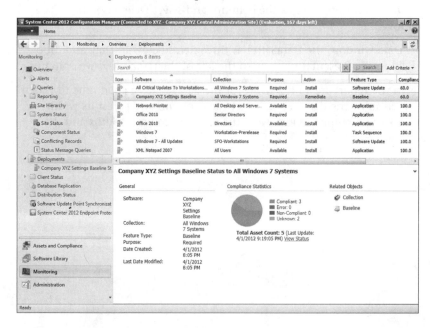

FIGURE 5.6   The Generated report.

The modified report is now available for ad hoc generation and subscriptions.

Understanding where the data is located is critical to editing reports and modifying the TSQL queries. Microsoft has created an extensive set of documentation detailing the Configuration Manager views needed to create custom reports. This can be obtained from the following URL: http://www.microsoft.com/downloads/details.aspx?FamilyId=87BBE64E-5439-4FC8-BECC-DEB372A40F4A&displaylang=en. The information was created for the Configuration Manager 2007 database, but the SQL views they reference have not fundamentally changed in Configuration Manager 2012 other than the addition of new views.

The `CreatingCustomReportsByUsingSQLViews.msi` download contains a Microsoft Compiled HTML Help (CHM) file, an Excel spreadsheet, and a Visio diagram detailing the extensive number of views available to create reports and provides numerous samples to help get started.

Customizing Hardware Inventory

The hardware inventory collection process can be customized by modifying the `configuration.mof` and the hardware inventory classes in the client settings. The `configuration.mof` file is automatically sent to the client and the information within the file is added to the local WMI repository. This file essentially shows the client how to collect the correct data. The hardware inventory classes in client settings defines the policy that tells the client what WMI classes to report during the inventory cycle.

> **NOTE**
>
> When editing the Configuration Manager MOF file, a backup is automatically created in the `\data\hinvarchive` folder located in the Configuration Manager installation directory. However, it's still recommended to make a copy of the MOF file before performing manual edits. Also, test hardware inventory extensions in a development environment before making changes to the production environment.

It is common to add additional custom data in the hardware inventory as this allows unique management of assets based on custom attributes, such as the hardware warranty and contract information for an asset.

Creating Registry Keys on the Client

The Registry on the local system contains a significant amount of information and is commonly used to hold custom data for the organization. For example, during the deployment of servers, the department responsible for the server along with extended functionality, such as warranty data, can be added to the Registry automatically with a custom OS deployment package.

5

For testing, the Registry can be manually populated on a test system with the appropriate data. In this example, several string values located in a custom Registry key are added to the hardware inventory.

To create the Registry entries on the client, do the following:

1. Open `regedit.exe` on a test Configuration Manager client system (WS2).

2. Expand HKEY_LOCAL_MACHINE, and then select the SOFTWARE key.

3. Right-click SOFTWARE, select New, and then click Key.

4. Type **CompanyXYZ** as the key name.

5. Right-click the CompanyXYZ key, select New, and then click String Value.

6. Type **Contract** as the string value name.

7. Repeat steps 6 and 7 to add the remaining attributes from Table 5.1.

TABLE 5.1   Sample List of CompanyXYZ Attributes

Name	Description	Sample Value
Contract	Warranty contract terms	24×7×365 4-hour Response
Expiration	Warranty end date	6/5/2012
Owner	Server owner	IT Operations

Organization-specific data is commonly stored in one or more locations external to Configuration Manager. It is common to query for information during the deployment of the operating system and dynamically add it to the Registry of the local system. For example, a custom package can match key values, such as the MAC address from the local system, to the external database to retrieve organization-specific values. These values can be used to dynamically update the Registry of the local system.

The Company XYZ Registry customizations are shown in Figure 5.7.

This information can be leveraged by Configuration Manager and other systems such as Operations Manager to dynamically group, report, and automate the management of assets.

FIGURE 5.7   Hardware Warranty information.

Editing the `configuration.mof` File

The `configuration.mof` file defines classes in the local WMI repository of the client. The WMI class has the information necessary to locate the hardware-related data for the inventory report. The `configuration.mof` file is sent to the managed systems during the policy polling cycle and is automatically compiled.

> **NOTE**
>
> Use the `mofcomp.exe` utility to compile and test custom hardware inventory classes before adding the information to the `configuration.mof` file. The following command adds the classes in the `test.mof` file to the correct location in the WMI repository: `mofcomp.exe -N:root/cimv2 test.mof`.

To edit the `configuration.mof` file, complete the following steps:

1. Navigate to the location `%Program Files% Microsoft Configuration Manager inboxes\clifiles.src\hinv` folder on the Central Administration Site Server (CM1).

2. Open the `configuration.mof` file with Notepad.

3. Scroll to the bottom of the file.

4. Enter the code in Listing 5.3 between the "Added extensions start" and "Added extensions end" sections at the bottom of the `configuration.mof` file.

LISTING 5.3   Customizing the `configuration.mof` File

```
//Company XYZ Custom Inventory Begin
#pragma namespace ("\\\\.\\root\\cimv2")
#pragma deleteclass("CompanyXYZ_Warranty",NOFAIL)

[DYNPROPS]
Class CompanyXYZ_Warranty
{
[key] string KeyName;
String Contract;
String Expiration;
String Owner;
};
[DYNPROPS]
Instance of CompanyXYZ_Warranty
{
KeyName="Company XYZ Warranty";
[PropertyContext("Local¦HKEY_LOCAL_MACHINE\\SOFTWARE\\CompanyXYZ¦Contract"),
Dynamic,Provider("RegPropProv")] Contract;
[PropertyContext("Local¦HKEY_LOCAL_MACHINE\\SOFTWARE\\CompanyXYZ¦Expiration"),
Dynamic,Provider("RegPropProv")] Expiration;
[PropertyContext("Local¦HKEY_LOCAL_MACHINE\\SOFTWARE\\CompanyXYZ¦Owner"),
Dynamic,Provider("RegPropProv")] Owner;
};

//Company XYZ Custom Inventory End
```

The `configuration.mof` after editing should look like that shown in Figure 5.8.

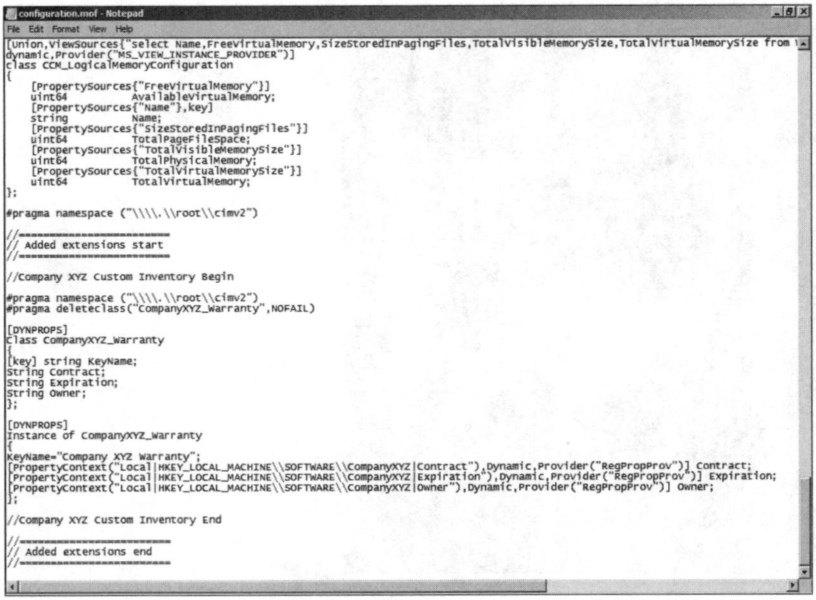

FIGURE 5.8   The edited configuration.mof file.

The preceding code creates a WMI class called CompanyXYZ_Warranty, which is configured to uses the RegProv provider. This provider allows Registry information to be dynamically queried during the hardware inventory cycle.

Manually Compiling configuration.mof on Test Client

To have Configuration Manager 2012 inventory the information, the class has to be instantiated into an existing WMI repository. This will be done on a test client.

On a test Configuration Manager client system (WS3), copy the configuration.mof to a test directory such as c:\test. Then execute the following two commands:

▶ mofcomp.exe   check configuration.mof

▶ mofcomp.exe configuration.mof

The first command will check the syntax of the configuration.mof file and the second command will compile the configuration.mof into the WMI repository of the local system. Figure 5.9 shows the results of the commands.

FIGURE 5.9   Check and compile the `configuration.mof` on a test client.

With the new `CompanyXYZ_Warranty` class now instantiated in the WMI repository of the
test client, the class can now be added to the Configuration Manager hardware inventory
collection.

Adding the Hardware Class in Client Settings

After compiling the `configuration.mof` on the test client (WS3), the next step is to add
the custom hardware information into the SCCM hardware inventory collection.

1. Launch the Configuration Manager console and select the Administration space.

2. Select the Client Settings container.

3. Select the properties of the Default Client Settings.

4. Select the Hardware Inventory section.

5. Click the Set Classes button. This shows all the classes that are collected by the
   hardware inventory.

6. Click the Add button.

7. Click the Connect button.

8. In the Computer Name field, enter the name of the computer where the
   `configuration.mof` file was compiled, in this case **WS3**, and click Connect.

9. In the class names returned, check the box next to the `CompanyXYZ_Warranty` class
   (as shown in Figure 5.10).

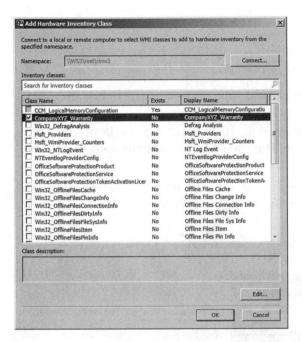

FIGURE 5.10   Adding the CompanyXYZ_Warranty class.

10. Click OK to save the new inventory class.

11. Click OK to close the Set Classes.

12. Click OK to save the Client Settings.

The Registry key and values will now be collected as part of the regular Configuration Manager 2012 hardware inventory cycle. The Registry information will not be collected until each client has done a machine policy refresh (approximately every 60 minutes) and the hardware inventory cycle. The client InventoryAgent.log file will show a line with the values and the class name when the information is collected during the hardware inventory cycle.

The newly collected inventory can be reviewed in the Resource Explorer, in the Hardware section.

Validating Custom Inventory Data

The CompanyXYZ_Warranty class on the managed system can be verified with the wbemtest.exe utility. This utility is installed by default on Windows computers and provides useful insight into the local WMI repository.

To verify the CompanyXYZ_Warranty WMI class on the client, complete the following steps:

1. Open wbemtest.exe on a managed test system.

2. Click the Connect button.

3. Accept the default namespace and click Connect.

4. Click the Enum Classes button.

5. Choose the Recursive option and click OK.

6. Wait for the enumeration to complete and scroll to the CompanyXYZ_Warranty class.

If the CompanyXYZ_Warranty class is not listed, the client hasn't successfully downloaded and compiled the configuration.mof file. This should happen automatically during the next policy update cycle.

Double-click the CompanyXYZ_Warranty class, and then click the Instances button to show the Registry keys. The Hardware instance should be listed; double-click this instance to see the value of each property.

The Hardware instance of the custom class is shown in Figure 5.11.

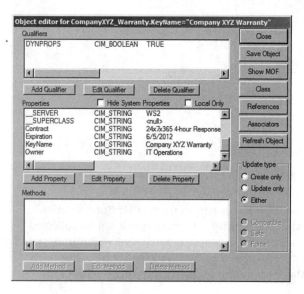

FIGURE 5.11   Hardware instance of the CompanyXYZ_Warranty class.

Viewing Custom Inventory Data

All inventoried hardware, custom hardware extensions, hardware inventory history, and software file data can be viewed from within the Configuration Manager console.

To view inventory data from the ConfigMgr console, do the following:

1. From within the ConfigMgr console, select the Assets and Compliance space.

2. Expand Overview and select Device Collection.

3. Select the collection that contains the test computer (WS2).

4. Select the test computer, and then select the Start, Resource Explorer action.

5. Use the Resource Explorer tool to view hardware and software inventory.

The Resource Explorer can also be used to see historical hardware inventory by selecting the Hardware History node. By default, Configuration Manager keeps 90 days of historical data. This can be configured by changing the Delete Aged Inventory History task located in the Site Maintenance node of the Site Settings.

Understanding Asset Intelligence

The Asset Intelligence (AI) functionality in Configuration Manager 2012 is used to identify and report software and licensing information for both Microsoft and non-Microsoft software.

The Asset Intelligence components have dependencies on the hardware inventory process. Custom Asset Intelligence classes added to the hardware inventory are used to facilitate the identification of software and usage. Several of the Asset Intelligence reports in the Software category also have dependencies on the Software Metering component.

CAUTION

Don't use Configuration Manager as an authoritative source for making licensing purchases. The actual counts of licenses should be tracked as systems are provisioned and deprovisioned throughout the enterprise. Configuration Manager should be used to validate those numbers. For example, each SQL component is tracked separately. This artificially increases the count of some of the license reports.

Enabling and Synchronizing the AI Catalog

To enable Asset Intelligence, the Asset Intelligence Synchronization Point needs to be deployed. Only one Synchronization Point can be deployed in the Configuration Manager hierarchy; this is done at the Central Administration Site. The Asset Intelligence Synchronization Point role can be installed on the server CM1 from the Sites node in the Administration space in the ConfigMgr console.

NOTE

The Asset Intelligence Synchronization Point does not need a certificate to be specified during installation of the role. The certificate is automatically downloaded from Microsoft System Center Online Services during synchronization.

The Asset Intelligence Synchronization Point provides the ability to enable or disable the synchronization functionality and to configure the synchronization schedule. The synchronization process essentially contacts the Microsoft System Center Online Services and downloads the latest updates to the Asset Intelligence catalog.

The initial synchronization process can take a long time. To monitor status, view the
`AIUpdateSvc.log` log file on the server hosting the Asset Intelligence Synchronization
Point role. The synchronization can only be performed a maximum of once every 12
hours and defaults to once every seven days.

Enabling the Asset Intelligence Reporting Classes

The Asset Intelligence reporting classes are modifications to hardware inventory collection. These modifications tell the client to report AI data during the hardware inventory
collection cycle.

To enable the Asset Intelligence reporting classes, do the following:

1. From within the ConfigMgr console, select the Assets and Compliance space.

2. Select the Asset Intelligence node.

3. Right-click the Asset Intelligence node and select Edit Inventory Classes.

4. Enable each of the desired reporting classes and click OK.

Each of the different Asset Intelligence reporting classes affects a different set of reports.
For additional information, click the Help button. The Help file details each of the listed
reporting classes and reporting dependencies, as shown in the following list:

▶ Hardware 01A - Summary of Computers in a Specific Collection

  ▶ SMS_SystemConsoleUsage

  ▶ SMS_Processor

▶ Hardware 02A - Estimated Computer Age by Ranges Within a Collection

  ▶ SMS_Processor

▶ Hardware 02B - Computers Within an Age Range Within a Collection

  ▶ SMS_SystemConsoleUsage

  ▶ SMS_Processor

▶ Hardware 03A - Primary Computer Users

  ▶ SMS_SystemConsoleUsage

  ▶ SMS_SystemConsoleUser

▶ Hardware 03B - Computers for a Specific Primary Console User

  ▶ SMS_SystemConsoleUsage

  ▶ SMS_SystemConsoleUser

- ▶ Hardware 04A - Shared (Multi-User) Computers
  - ▶ SMS_SystemConsoleUsage
  - ▶ SMS_SystemConsoleUser

- ▶ Hardware 05A - Console Users on a Specific Computer
  - ▶ SMS_SystemConsoleUsage
  - ▶ SMS_SystemConsoleUser

- ▶ Hardware 06A - Computers for Which Console Users Could Not Be Determined
  - ▶ SMS_SystemConsoleUsage

- ▶ Hardware 07A - USB Devices by Manufacturer
  - ▶ Win32_USBDevice

- ▶ Hardware 07B - USB Devices by Manufacturer and Description
  - ▶ Win32_USBDevice

- ▶ Hardware 07C - Computers with a Specific USB Device
  - ▶ SMS_SystemConsoleUsage
  - ▶ Win32_USBDevice

- ▶ Hardware 07D - USB Devices on a Specific Computer
  - ▶ Win32_USBDevice

- ▶ Hardware 08A - Hardware That Is Not Ready for a Software Upgrade
  - ▶ SMS_SystemConsoleUsage
  - ▶ SMS_Processor

- ▶ Hardware 09A - Search for Computers
  - ▶ SMS_SystemConsoleUsage
  - ▶ SMS_Processor

- ▶ License 01A - Microsoft License Ledger for Microsoft License Statements
  - ▶ SMS_InstalledSoftwareMS

▶ License 01B - Microsoft License Ledger Item by Sales Channel

   ▶ SMS_InstalledSoftwareMS

▶ License 01C - Computers with a Specific Microsoft License Ledger Item and Sales Channel

   ▶ SMS_InstalledSoftware

   ▶ SMS_InstalledSoftwareMS

   ▶ SMS_SystemConsoleUsage

▶ License 01D - Microsoft License Ledger Products on a Specific Computer

   ▶ SMS_InstalledSoftwareMS

▶ License 02A - Count of Licenses Nearing Expiration by Time Ranges

   ▶ SoftwareLicensingProduct

▶ License 02B - Computers with Licenses Nearing Expiration

   ▶ SMS_SystemConsoleUsage

   ▶ SoftwareLicensingProduct

▶ License 02C - License Information on a Specific Computer

   ▶ SoftwareLicensingService

   ▶ SoftwareLicensingProduct

▶ License 03A - Count of Licenses by License Status

   ▶ SoftwareLicensingProduct

▶ License 03B - Computers with a Specific License Status

   ▶ SMS_SystemConsoleUsage

   ▶ SoftwareLicensingProduct

▶ License 04A - Count of Products Managed by Software Licensing

   ▶ SoftwareLicensingProduct

- ▶ License 04B - Computers with a Specific Product Managed by Software Licensing Service
    - ▶ SMS_SystemConsoleUsage
    - ▶ SoftwareLicensingProduct

- ▶ License 05A - Computers Providing Key Management Service
    - ▶ SoftwareLicensingService

- ▶ Software 01A - Summary of Installed Software in a Specific Collection
    - ▶ SMS_InstalledSoftware

- ▶ Software 02A - Software Families
    - ▶ SMS_InstalledSoftware

- ▶ Software 02B - Software Categories with a Family
    - ▶ SMS_InstalledSoftware

- ▶ Software 02C - Software by Category and Family
    - ▶ SMS_InstalledSoftware

- ▶ Software 02D - Computers with a Specific Software Product
    - ▶ SMS_InstalledSoftware
    - ▶ SMS_SystemConsoleUsage

- ▶ Software 02E - Installed Software on a Specific Computer
    - ▶ SMS_InstalledSoftware

- ▶ Software 03A - Uncategorized Software
    - ▶ SMS_InstalledSoftware

- ▶ Software 04A - Auto-Start Software
    - ▶ SMS_AutoStartSoftware

- ▶ Software 04B - Computers with a Specific Auto-Start Software
    - ▶ SMS_SystemConsoleUsage
    - ▶ SMS_AutoStartSoftware

- ▶ Software 04C - Auto-Start Software on a Specific Computer
  - ▶ SMS_AutoStartSoftware

- ▶ Software 05A - Browser Helper Objects
  - ▶ SMS_BrowserHelperObject

- ▶ Software 05B - Computers with a Specific Browser Helper Object
  - ▶ SMS_SystemConsoleUsage
  - ▶ SMS_BrowserHelperObject

- ▶ Software 05C - Browser Helper Objects on a Specific Computer
  - ▶ SMS_BrowserHelperObject

- ▶ Software 06A - Search for Installed Software
  - ▶ SMS_InstalledSoftware

The Asset Intelligence reporting class configuration is shown in Figure 5.12.

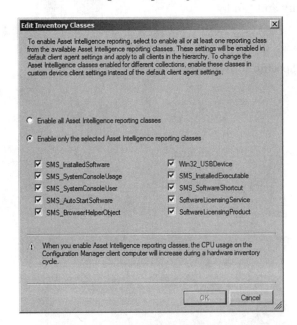

FIGURE 5.12   The Asset Intelligence reporting classes.

Importing Software License Data

The Microsoft Software Licensing spreadsheet can be obtained from your Microsoft rep. Once the spreadsheet has been acquired, it can be converted to an XML Spreadsheet 2003 formatted file and imported into Configuration Manager. After the licensing data has been imported, run the License 14A - Microsoft Volume Licensing Reconciliation report to view license data.

NOTE

Each time licensing data is uploaded, the previous license data is overwritten. To avoid accuracy problems, make sure the complete list of licensing information is uploaded every time.

The same process can be used to track non-Microsoft software by manually creating a CSV file with the correct information. The license fields for non-Microsoft software are shown in Table 5.2.

TABLE 5.2   License Fields for Non-Microsoft Software

Column	Data	Required	Sample
Name	255 characters	Yes	TextPad 5
Publisher	255 characters	Yes	Helios
Version	255 characters	Yes	5.3.1
Language	255 characters	Yes	1033
EffectiveQuantity	Number	Yes	1
PONumber	255 characters	No	
ResellerName	255 characters	No	
DateOfPurchase	MM/DD/YYYY	No	
SupportPurchased	0 or 1	No	
SupportExpirationDate	M/D/YYYY	No	
Comments	255 characters	No	

NOTE

Use the Installed Software node within the Hardware section of Resource Explorer to identify the correct values for the non-Microsoft software licensing CSV file.

In the following tasks, the CSV file created will be hosted on the following network share: \\CM1\Sources\Licensing.

To create the non-Microsoft license CSV file, do the following:

1. Open Microsoft Excel 2010 and enter the column names in the first row.

2. Enter the sample data for licensed software in the appropriate columns.

3. Save the file as a CSV (comma-delimited) file.

4. Copy the file to the network share.

Each time license data is updated or changed, the CSV file should be updated and imported into Configuration Manager.

To upload the non-Microsoft license CSV file, complete the following steps:

1. From within the ConfigMgr console, select the Asset Intelligence node.

2. Right-click the Asset Intelligence node and select the Import Software License action.

3. Click Next to skip the Welcome page.

4. Type \\CM1\Sources\Licensing in the path, and then click Browse.

5. Select the previously created CSV file, and then click Open.

6. Select the General License Statement (*.csv) option button.

7. Click Next, import the file, and close the wizard.

The resulting License 15A - General License Reconciliation report is shown in Figure 5.13.

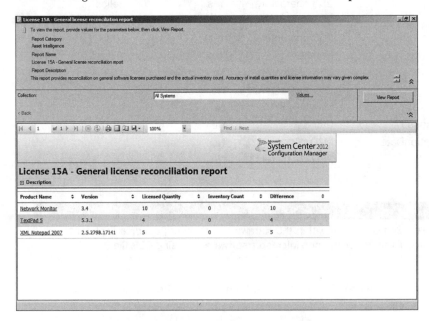

FIGURE 5.13   The General License Reconciliation report.

After the license information has been uploaded, the report License 15A - General License Reconciliation report and License 15B - General License Reconciliation Report by Machine can be used to reconcile license data.

Understanding Asset Intelligence Reporting

Asset Intelligence reports are available from the Reports node in the Configuration Manager console. The reports are all in the Asset Intelligence category folder. Reports are broken down into three categories:

- ▶ **Hardware**—This category contains hardware-related reports. For example, the Hardware 03A - Primary Computer Users report is useful to identify who uses a managed computer by analyzing data collected from the security event logs.

- ▶ **License**—This category contains all of the licensing-related reports. For example, this category contains many CAL license reports that can be used to track CAL usages and reconcile licenses.

- ▶ **Software**—This category contains reports that assist with the management of software throughout the organization. For example, several reports are available to find software installed on the computer and to determine how often the software is used.

It is highly recommended to take time to become conversant with the different reports as this will improve the ability to manage the environment.

Understanding Software Metering

The software metering functionality provided with Configuration Manager simply tracks software usage on managed systems. The creation of software metering rules can be automated through the properties of the Software Metering node.

To enable autocreation of software metering rules, do the following:

1. From within the ConfigMgr console, select the Assets and Compliance space.

2. Select the Software Metering container, and click the Software Metering Properties action.

3. The autocreation of software metering rules can be enabled or disabled.

Automatically creating the software metering rules simplifies management by determining what is actually being used in the environment and creating a disabledrule to automatically meter this software. To enable one of the automatically created rules, select the rule, and then click the Enable action. The software metering rules must be enabled before any of the metering reports will show data.

The software metering process can be monitored on the client system with the Mtrmgr.log and the SWMTRReportGen.log log files.

Configuring the Software Metering Client Agent

The Software Metering section of the Client Settings provides access to enable or disable the ability to collect software metering data on managed systems. From within the agent, the inventory schedule can be configured to control how often data is sent to the Configuration Manager hierarchy.

Reporting on Software Metering Data

All of the software metering reports are located in the Software Metering folder in the Reports folder. To effectively use software metering, familiarity with the reports is necessary.

As data is collected and summarized, the reports become more effective. For example, the Concurrent Usage Trend Analysis of a Specific Metered Software Program report shows the maximum and average number of users who concurrently ran the software each month for the previous year. This report requires a year's worth of metering summary data to be effective.

Another useful report is called Computers That Have a Metered Program Installed but Have Not Run the Program Since a Specified Date. This report can be used to target systems to uninstall the unused software, which can free up licenses for other users.

Understanding Compliance Settings

The Compliance Settings component in Configuration Manager is a powerful feature. Compliance Settings allows an administrator to create configuration baselines to validate the settings of managed systems and remediate those settings if appropriate.

In addition to creating custom configurations to monitor systems, Microsoft provides configuration packs for various Microsoft products, such as Windows Server 2008, Active Directory, Exchange, SQL, and IIS.

Desired Configuration Management Client Agent

The Compliance Settings section in Client Settings provides access to enable and disable the ability to evaluate systems in the site. In addition, the evaluation schedule can be configured.

Similar to the Hardware and Software Inventory settings, the simple schedule will begin the evaluation cycle based on the time the Configuration Manager client was installed. However, unlike the Hardware and Software Inventory settings, if a custom schedule is selected, the actual time the compliance agent triggers the evaluation is delayed by up to 2 hours to improve scalability.

Defining Configuration Items to Monitor

The configuration settings that will eventually constitute a baseline need to be defined. Compliance Settings provides many options for monitoring the state of both objects and settings on the managed system. Compliance Settings can monitor a variety of objects, including Registry keys, files, and managed code assemblies. Compliance Settings can also be configured to validate settings. Setting data can be obtained through AD-, IIS-, Registry-, Script-, SQL-, WQL-, and XML-based queries.

New to Configuration Manager 2012 is the ability to remediate settings if they are out of compliance. For example, if Compliance Settings is monitoring a Registry value and the value is changed or deleted, Compliance Settings can automatically remediate the value and replace it with the correct value. They can even create the Registry key and value if it is deleted.

Based on the Customizing Hardware Inventory section, several Registry keys were added to the Registry of managed systems. These settings contained a string value showing when the warranty of a specific system would expire. The Compliance Settings configuration item in the following tasks verifies the hardware warranty key is present on the system and checks the expiration value to determine if the warranty has expired.

The PowerShell script in Listing 5.4 can be used to query the string value, convert the string to a date, and then check if the date is older than the current date. If the date stored in the Registry has already passed, the script doesn't return anything. Conversely, if the warranty expiration date is in the future, the script returns the text "ok."

LISTING 5.4   PowerShell Script to Check the Hardware Warranty Status

```
$string = get-ItemProperty "hklm:\SOFTWARE\CompanyXYZ\"

if ((Get-Date) -lt [datetime]::ParseExact($string.Expiration, "M/d/yyyy", $null))
{
    "ok"
}
```

NOTE

Digitally sign PowerShell scripts. This allows the PowerShell execution policy to be configured for AllSigned. The AllSigned policy ensures that only authorized, signed scripts can be run in the environment. For additional information on script signing, type **get-help about_signing** in a PowerShell console.

By default, the PowerShell execution policy is set to Restricted. This essentially prevents scripts from being executed. The execution policy should be set to AllSigned if the script can be digitally signed, or RemoteSigned if PowerShell scripts will not be signed. This can be done with the command Set-ExecutionPolicy RemoteSigned.

If PowerShell is not an applicable option, the VBScript in Listing 5.5 does essentially the same thing.

LISTING 5.5   VBScript Script to Check the Hardware Warranty Status

```
option explicit
dim oShell, sValue, sKey
sKey = "HKEY_LOCAL_MACHINE\SOFTWARE\CompanyXYZ\Expiration"
set oShell = CreateObject("WScript.Shell")
sValue = oShell.RegRead(sKey)

if (Now() < CDate(sValue)) then
 wscript.echo "ok"
end If
```

To create a Configuration Item to monitor, follow these steps:

1. From within the ConfigMgr console, select the Assets and Compliance space.

2. Expand the Compliance Settings node.

3. Select the Configuration Items node.

4. Select the Configuration Items.

5. Right-click on Configuration Items and select Create Configuration Item.

6. Type **Check Warranty** in the Name field, and click Next.

7. At the Supported Platforms section, check only Windows 7 and click Next.

8. In the Specify Settings section, leave the default blank and click Next.

9. In the Compliance Rules section, click the New button.

10. In the Name, enter **Warranty Date Valid** and click Browse.

11. Click New Setting.

12. In the Name of the Setting, type **Warranty Check**.

13. In the Setting Type, select Script.

14. Select String for the Data Type.

15. Click the Add Script button.

16. Select VBScript as the language and type the VBScript from Listing 5.5.

17. Click OK to save the script.

NOTE

There is a section for an optional remediation script, which allows a script to run when noncompliant. This will not be used for the warranty check.

18. Click OK to save the setting.

19. Select the Warranty Check setting from the Available Settings window and click the Select button.

20. Change the Noncompliance Severity to Critical with Event.

21. In the Setting Must Comply with the Following Rule section, leave the default Equals and enter **ok** for the value.

> **NOTE**
>
> Note that the **ok** is lowercase to match the script output.

22. Click Next.

23. Review the Summary and click Next.

24. Click Close to exit the wizard.

The script runs during the compliance check and compares the warranty date in the Registry to the current date, returning **ok** if the warranty date is still valid. If the script doesn't return the text **ok**, the system is considered noncompliant and an error is generated.

In addition to checking the warranty, the administrator also wants to ensure that the Registry value Owners in the HKLM\SOFTWARE\CompanyXYZ key is set to IT Operations. If it is not, the value needs to be remediated to IT Owners.

To create a configuration item to do this, execute the following steps:

1. From within the ConfigMgr console, select the Assets and Compliance space.

2. Expand the Compliance Settings node.

3. Select the Configuration Items node.

4. Right-click the Configuration Items node and select Create Configuration Item.

5. Type **Remediate Owner Setting** in the Name field, and click Next.

6. At the Supported Platforms section, check only Windows 7 and click Next.

7. In the Settings section, leave the default blank and click Next.

8. In the Compliance Rules section, click the New button.

9. Enter **Remediate Owner Setting** for the Name and click Browse.

10. Click New Setting.

11. Type **Remediate Owner Setting** for the Name.

12. Select the Setting Type as Registry Value and the Data Type as String.

13. Select HKEY_LOCAL_MACHINE for the Hive, "SOFTWARE\CompanyXYZ" for the
Key, and Owner for the Value.

14. Click OK to create the setting.

15. In the Available Settings window, select the newly created setting and click Select.

16. In the Setting Must Comply with the Following Rule section, leave the default
Equals and enter **IT Operations** for the value.

17. Check the Remediate Noncompliant Rules When Aupported check box.

> **NOTE**
>
> This setting will force the creation of the Owner Registry value if it does not exist and
> set it to "IT Operations" automatically.

18. Change the Noncompliance Severity to Critical with Event and click OK.

19. Click Next.

20. Review the Summary and click Next.

21. Click Close to exit the wizard.

The new Remediate Owner Setting configuration item will check for the proper setting of
the Owner Registry value and remediate it to the correct value if it is not set properly.

With the two configuration items, a baseline can be created to apply this to systems.

Defining a Configuration Baseline

After the configuration items have been established, and the appropriate rules to monitor
them have been created, the baseline can be set up.

To create a configuration baseline, do the following:

1. From within the ConfigMgr console, select the Assets and Compliance space.

2. Expand the Compliance Settings node.

3. Right-click the Compliance Settings node and select the Configuration Baselines
node.

4. Click the Create Configuration Baseline option.

5. Enter **Company XYZ Settings Baseline** in the Name field.

6. Click Add Configuration Items, and add the Check Warranty and the Remediate
Owner Setting to the baseline.

7. Click OK to save.

8. Click OK to save the configuration baseline.

Many different configuration items can be added to a baseline. How the baselines are used depends on how the configuration items are related. For example, if one of the configuration items in a baseline is not compliant, then the system is not compliant for this baseline.

Applying a Baseline to a Collection

The baseline configuration is applied to a collection. This can be done from within the Desired Configuration Management node or the Collections node.

To add the baseline to a collection, complete the following steps:

1. From within the ConfigMgr console, select the Assets and Compliance space.

2. Expand the Compliance Settings node.

3. Select the Configuration Baselines node.

4. Select the Company XYZ Settings Baseline.

5. Right-click the configuration baseline and select Deploy Action.

6. Check the Remediate Noncompliant Rules When Supported and Allow Remediation Outside the Maintenance Window check boxes.

7. Check the Generate an Alert check box and leave the default threshold of 90%.

8. Click Browse to select a collection.

9. Change the collection type to Device Collections, select the All Windows 7 Systems collection, and then click OK.

10. Leave the Simple Schedule of every 1 hours.

11. Click OK to save and apply the configuration baseline.

The systems will now have the Company XYZ Settings Baseline applied to them.

Monitoring the Baselines and Compliance

The Deployments container in the Monitoring space provides a summary of the different baselines and other deployments. Select each baseline to view how many systems are compliant, how many systems are not compliant, and if any systems reported errors. Figure 5.14 shows the deployment status. One system is compliant and four systems have errors (that is, are noncompliant).

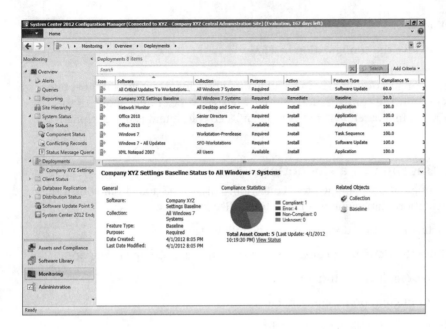

FIGURE 5.14   The compliance baseline deployment status.

When testing and troubleshooting issues, the configuration baselines results can be
viewed from the client.

To view the baseline report from a managed system, do the following:

1. Log on to a managed system.

2. Open Control Panel.

3. Open the Configuration Manager control panel applet.

4. Select the Configurations tab.

5. Select a baseline, and then click the View Report button.

The Agent Compliance report from WS2 is shown in Figure 5.15.

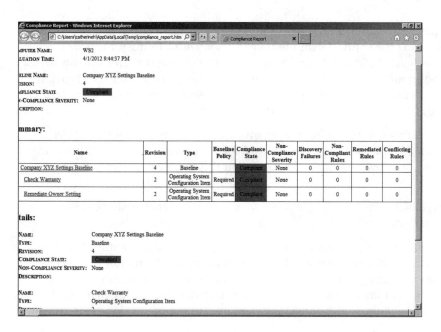

FIGURE 5.15   The Local Agent Compliance report.

Summary

System Center Configuration Manager 2012 provides a powerful set of features to facilitate end-to-end asset management. From the moment the system is born onto the network, it can be managed, tracked, and audited to ensure the hardware and software is monitored and managed correctly and effectively. With the highly customizable reporting infrastructure, both Configuration Manager administrators and IT managers can stay informed about assets and the overall compliance of the infrastructure.

Best Practices

The following are best practices from this chapter:

▶ Create and run reports from the Central Administration Site to ensure data from the entire infrastructure can be seen. Site-specific reports can be created by filtering out data that isn't needed.

▶ Avoid using IDMIF or NOIDMIF files to extend the hardware inventory. These files reside on the client computer and can dynamically modify the Configuration Manager database with custom data during the hardware inventory cycle. If this type of collection is necessary, ensure the risks are fully understood and the appropriate security has been implemented.

▶ Similar queries are grouped together to improve performance. This is important to avoid searching the entire system multiple times when scanning for files. For example, searching all hard drives for EXEs and DLLs using the same options for the path, subdirectories, and exclusions results in a single query to find both types. If any of the options are different, multiple queries are used, which can significantly increase the time needed to complete the inventory.

▶ To exclude a drive or folders from being inventoried, create a hidden file called `skpswi.dat`. This file can be placed in any folder to prevent that folder from being inventoried, or at the root of a drive to prevent the entire drive from being inventoried.

▶ Use Compliance Settings to locate rogue `skpswi.dat` files that could be used to conceal file data.

▶ When editing the Configuration Manager MOF files, a backup is automatically created in the \data\hinvarchive folder located in the Configuration Manager installation directory. However, it's still recommended to make a copy of the MOF file before performing manual edits. Also, test hardware inventory extensions in a development environment before making changes to the production environment.

▶ Use the `mofcomp.exe` utility to compile and test custom hardware inventory classes before adding the information to the `configuration.mof` file.

▶ Don't modify existing reports. Always make a copy of the report and make changes to the copy. During Configuration Manager service pack upgrades, the original reports can be updated by Microsoft, and if they're customized, the changes are lost.

▶ Microsoft has created an extensive set of documentation detailing the Configuration Manager views needed to create custom reports. Use this information when creating custom reports.

▶ Use the v_R_System_Valid view when obsolete and decommissioned systems need to be excluded from the report. This view contains a subset of information that can be obtained from the v_R_System view.

▶ Make sure the correct view is queried for hardware data. Most current hardware inventory data can be accessed with the v_GS_ views. Historical hardware inventory data can be accessed with the v_HS_ views.

▶ Don't use Configuration Manager as an authoritative source for making licensing purchases. The actual counts of licenses should be tracked as systems are provisioned and deprovisioned throughout the enterprise. Configuration Manager should be used to validate those numbers.

▶ Each time licensing data is uploaded, the previous license data is overwritten. To avoid accuracy problems, make sure the complete list of licensing information is uploaded every time.

▶ Use the Installed Software node within the Hardware section of Resource Explorer to identify the correct values for the non-Microsoft software licensing CSV file.

▶ Software information that is uploaded and eventually categorized by Microsoft is made available to all Microsoft customers through System Center Online Services. Avoid uploading private software information that could be used to identify your business to other customers.

CHAPTER 6

Operations Manager 2012 Design and Planning

IN THIS CHAPTER

▶ What's New With Operations Manager 2012

▶ Understanding How OpsMgr Works

▶ OpsMgr Architecture Components

▶ Securing OpsMgr

▶ Fault Tolerance and Disaster Recovery

▶ Understanding OpsMgr Component Requirements

▶ OpsMgr Design Considerations

▶ Putting It All Together in a Design

▶ Planning an Operations Manager Deployment

▶ Best Practices

System Center Operations Manager (OpsMgr) 2012 provides the best-of-breed approach to end-to-end monitoring and managing IT services. This includes servers, applications, and devices. OpsMgr helps to identify specific environmental conditions before they evolve into problems through the use of monitoring and alerting components.

OpsMgr provides a timely view of important server and application conditions and intelligently links problems to knowledge provided within the monitoring rules. Critical events and known issues are identified and matched to technical reference articles in the Microsoft Knowledge Base for troubleshooting and quick problem resolution.

For Operations Manager to accomplish all this effectively, the infrastructure must be designed and implemented properly. This ensures that the systems have the resources and capacity to handle the anticipated data flows and storage requirements. To be able to create an effective design, a good understanding of the Operations Manager components, requirements, and constraints is important.

This chapter provides specific analysis of the way OpsMgr operates, presents OpsMgr design best practices, and presents three sample designs. In addition, planning is discussed.

What's New With Operations Manager 2012

The new version of Operations Manager, OpsMgr 2012, includes a number of new features and incremental improvements. These improvements include the following:

▶ **Enhanced network monitoring**—Operations Manager 2012 now includes enhanced network monitoring. It can discover and monitor network switches and routers, discovering interfaces and ports on those devices. It will even discover virtual Local Area Network (LAN) information.

▶ **Application monitoring**—Application monitoring is now included in the OpsMgr 2012 product. This is based on the AVIcode product and allows the monitoring of Internet Infromation Server (IIS) hosted .NET applications. This is implemented as an easy-to-use monitoring template named .NET Application Performance Monitoring, similar to the Web Application Transaction Monitoring template.

▶ **Resource pools**—Resource pools are another new feature of Operations Manager 2012. Resource pools take the place of clustering, allowing the administrator to group Operations Manager objects such as management servers into fault-tolerant pools. This eliminates the need for a Root Management server (RMS) server and, more important, an RMS cluster. RMS clusters were notoriously difficult to maintain, so this is a very useful enhancement. Resource pools allow for easy fault tolerance to be created within the management group.

▶ **Enhanced Dashboard views**—Dashboard views have been enhanced in Operations Manager 2012. They allow for greater customization and flexibility. Rather than being based on other console views, the new dashboards are based on widgets. There are three types of widgets: the state widgets, performance widget, and alert widget.

▶ **SharePoint web part**—OpsMgr 2012 leverages dashboards even further by providing the SharePoint web part to integrate into SharePoint 2010. With this web part, any dashboard you create can be included in a SharePoint website. This allows operations data to be included within other SharePoint portals, providing both detailed and summary information.

▶ **Orchestrator replaces connectors**—Orchestrator 2012 now replaces connectors. In OpsMgr 2007, connectors provided the integration with other consoles and trouble ticket systems. However, they had limited programmability and customizable features via the notification process. In OpsMgr 2012, Orchestrator 2012 will allow for sophisticated customizations and complex workflows when forwarding alerts and creating trouble tickets.

▶ **New PowerShell 2.0 cmdlets**—OpsMgr 2012 provides a number of new PowerShell 2.0 cmdlets for working with agents, alerts, and management packs. Many of these new cmdlets required scripting before, but now can be executed with a single built-in command. All the cmdlets have been renamed and now include a System Center Operations Manager (SCOM) prefix, for example, `Get-SCOMAgent` rather than `Get-Agent`. There are also a whole new set of cmdlets for Linux and UNIX systems.

▶ **Improved UNIX and Linux monitoring**—OpsMgr 2012 can use unprivileged accounts with the sudo feature rather than require the root password to UNIX and Linux systems. The UNIX and Linux systems now participate fully in the resource pools, allowing them to failover to other management servers should their primary fail.

In addition to the above improvements, there have been subtle changes to the console and performance improvements throughout. OpsMgr 2012 now supports an in-place upgrade path when migrating from OpsMgr 2007, which is not supported previously.

Understanding How OpsMgr Works

OpsMgr is a sophisticated monitoring system that effectively allows for large-scale management of mission-critical servers. Organizations with a medium to large investment in Microsoft technologies will find that OpsMgr allows for an unprecedented ability to keep on top of the tens of thousands of event log messages that occur on a daily basis. In its simplest form, OpsMgr performs two functions: processing monitored data and issuing alerts and automatic responses based on that data.

The monitoring is accomplished using standard operating system components such as Windows Management Instrumentation (WMI) and WS-Management, Windows and UNIX event logs, and Windows and UNIX performance counters, along with application programming interface (API) calls and scripts. OpsMgr-specific components are also designed to perform synthetic transactions and track the health and availability of network services. In addition, OpsMgr provides a reporting feature that allows administrators to track problems and trends occurring on the network. Reports can be generated automatically, providing network administrators, managers, and decision makers with a current and long-term historical view of environmental trends. These reports can be delivered via email or stored on file shares for archiving or to power web pages.

The model-based architecture of OpsMgr presents a fundamental shift in the way a network is monitored. The entire environment can be monitored as groups of hierarchical services with interdependent components. Microsoft, in addition to third-party vendors and a large development community, can leverage the functionality of OpsMgr components through customizable monitoring rules.

OpsMgr provides for several major pieces of functionality, as follows:

▶ **Management packs**—Application-specific monitoring rules are provided within individual files called management packs. For example, Microsoft provides management packs for Windows Server systems, Exchange Server, SQL Server, SharePoint, DNS, and DHCP, along with many other Microsoft technologies. Management packs are loaded with the intelligence and information necessary to properly troubleshoot and identify problems. The rules are dynamically applied to agents based on a custom discovery process provided within the management pack. Only applicable rules are applied to each managed server.

▶ **Monitors**—Management packs contain monitors, which allow for advanced state-based monitoring and aggregated health rollup of services. There are monitors for events, performance, logs, services, and even processes. Monitors also provide self-tuning performance threshold monitoring based on a two- or three-state configuration.

▶ **Rules**—Management pack rules can monitor for specific event log data, collect performance data, or even run scripts on a timed basis. This is one of the key methods of responding to conditions within the environment. Management pack rules can monitor for specific performance counters. This data is used for alerting based on thresholds or archived for trending and capacity planning. A performance graph shown in Figure 6.1 shows DC Response Time data for the DC1 domain controller. Latency is normally above 2 seconds, but occasionally drops to less than 0.5. This would bear investigation, as something seems to be slowing response times.

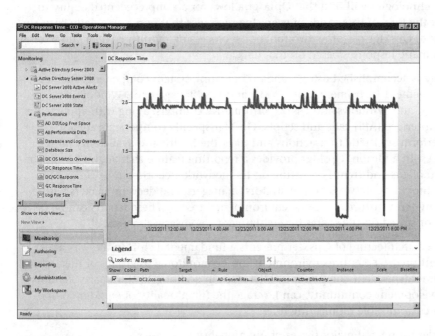

FIGURE 6.1   Operations Manager 2012 performance charts.

▶ **Alerting and notification**—OpsMgr provides advanced alerting functionality such as alert notifications via email, paging, Short Message Service (SMS), and instant messaging (IM). Alerts are highly customizable, with the ability to define alert rules for all monitored components.

▶ **End-to-end service monitoring**—OpsMgr provides service-oriented monitoring based on System Definition Model (SDM) technologies. This includes advanced object discovery and hierarchical monitoring of systems, as well as synthetic transactions that confirm the health of the system from a client perspective. This includes URLs, ports, Active Directory, LDAP, database access, and Exchange services.

Operations Manager 2012 can present the collected information in a variety of ways. The OpsMgr monitoring environment can be accessed through three sets of consoles: an Operations Console, a Web console, and a command shell. The Operations Console provides full monitoring of agent systems and administration of the OpsMgr environment, whereas the Web console provides access only to the monitoring functionality. The command shell provides command-line access to administer the OpsMgr environment.

Major OpsMgr components are as follows:

▶ **Consoles**—The main method for presenting information is the Operations Console and the Web console. The Operations Console is the full console and presents alert, event, and performance data in a highly scalable fashion. This allows an operator to drill into the information needed very quickly and effectively.

▶ **Notifications**—Notifications are generated from alerts and can be sent as email, SMS, or IM messages. There is also a generic command notification, which allows any command line or script to execute.

▶ **Reports**—Monitoring rules can be configured to send monitored data to both the operations database for alerting and the reporting database for archiving.

▶ **Dashboards**—Sophisticated dashboards can be configured to display alerts, performance, and state, both in the consoles and in SharePoint.

▶ **Service Level Dashboards**—The Service Level Dashboards Solution Accelerator leverages the Service Level Tracking feature of OpsMgr 2012 and the ubiquitous SharePoint to present a flexible view of how objects and applications are meeting defined Service Level Objectives (SLOs) such as 99.9% uptime or other metrics.

NOTE

Service Level Dashboards are a Solution Accelerator and require Microsoft SharePoint. This is an add-on developed by Microsoft to leverage the functionality of Operations Manager, but is not really a part of the product.

Interestingly, the Service Level Tracking (SLT) feature of Operations Manager was developed expressly to enable Service Level Dashboards, though SLTs can be used completely independently using the Operations Manager reporting feature.

These consoles, management packs, monitors, and rules are covered in detail in Chapter 8, "Using Operations Manager 2012 for Monitoring and Alerting." Reports are covered in Chapter 9, "Using Operations Manager 2012 for Operations and Security Reporting."

Processing Operational Data

OpsMgr manages Windows Server 2008 R2 infrastructures through monitoring rules used for object discovery, Windows event log monitoring, performance data gathering, and application-specific synthetic transactions. OpsMgr 2012 monitors UNIX and Linux infrastructures very similarly to Windows infrastructures, monitoring processes, resources, agents, performance, and availability.

Monitoring rules define how OpsMgr collects, handles, and responds to the information gathered. OpsMgr monitoring rules handle incoming event data and allow OpsMgr to react automatically, either to respond to a predetermined problem scenario, such as a failed hard drive, with predefined corrective and diagnostics actions (for example, trigger an alert or execute a command or script), or to provide the operator with additional details based on what was happening at the time the condition occurred.

Another key feature of OpsMgr is the capability to monitor and track service-level performance. OpsMgr can be configured to monitor key performance thresholds through rules that are set to collect predefined performance data, such as memory and CPU usage over time. Rules can be configured to trigger alerts and actions when specified performance thresholds have been met or exceeded, allowing network administrators to act on potential performance issues. Performance data can be viewed from the OpsMgr Operations Console.

In addition, performance monitors can establish baselines for the environment and then alert the administrator when the counter subsequently falls outside the defined baseline envelope.

Generating Alerts and Responses

OpsMgr monitoring rules can generate alerts based on critical events, synthetic transactions, or performance thresholds and variances found through self-tuning performance trending. An alert can be generated by a single event or by a combination of events or performance thresholds. Alerts can also be configured to trigger responses such as email, pages, Simple Network Management Protocol (SNMP) traps, and scripts to notify you of potential problems. In brief, OpsMgr is completely customizable in this respect and can be modified to fit most alert requirements. A sample alert is shown in Figure 6.2. The selected alert shows that the database server could not allocate space for an object. Note that the description is clear and specific. Notice also that the figure shows the alert knowledge and suggested resolutions as well—in this case, to free disk space.

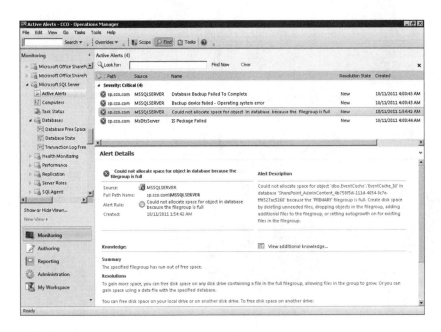

FIGURE 6.2   Operations Manager 2012 alert.

Reporting from OpsMgr

OpsMgr management packs commonly include a variety of preconfigured reports to show information about the operating system or the specific application they were designed to work with. These reports are run in SQL Reporting Services. The reports provide an effective view of systems and services on the network over a custom period, such as weekly, monthly, or quarterly. They can also help you monitor your networks based on performance data, which can include critical pattern analysis, trend analysis, capacity planning, and security auditing. Reports also provide availability statistics for distributed applications, servers, and specific components within a server.

Availability reports are particularly useful for executives, managers, and application owners. These reports can show the availability of any object within OpsMgr, including a server (shown in Figure 6.3), a database, or even a service such as Windows Server 2008 R2 that includes a multitude of servers and components. The Availability report shown in Figure 6.3 indicates that the CM server was down the week of 12/16/11 pretty much every day of the week for up to 6.63% or 1.5 hours. The worst day was 12/22/11. The rest of the time it had been up.

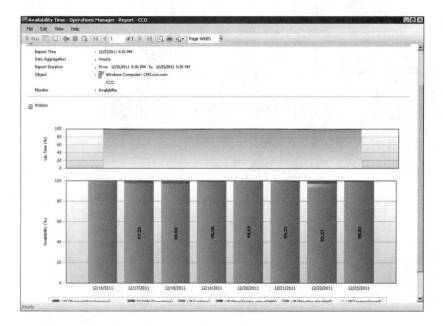

FIGURE 6.3   Availability report.

The reports can be run on demand or at scheduled times and delivered via email. OpsMgr can also generate HTML-based reports that can be published to a web server and viewed from any web browser. Vendors can also create additional reports as part of their management packs.

OpsMgr Architecture Components

OpsMgr is primarily composed of five basic components: the operations database, reporting database, management server, management agents, and Operations Console. These components make up a basic deployment scenario. Several optional components are also described in the following bulleted list; these components provide functionality for advanced deployment scenarios.

The following list describes the different OpsMgr components:

- ▶ Agents

- ▶ Management server

- ▶ Operations Manager database

- ▶ Reporting data warehouse

- ▶ Reporting Server

- ▶ Operations Console

- ▶ Web console

▶ Command shell

▶ Gateway

▶ Audit forwarder

▶ Audit collector

▶ Audit collection database

▶ Audit Collection Services reporting

OpsMgr was specifically designed to be scalable and can subsequently be configured to meet the needs of any size company. This flexibility stems from the fact that all OpsMgr components can either reside on one server or can be distributed across multiple servers.

Each of these various components provides specific OpsMgr functionality. OpsMgr design scenarios often involve the separation of parts of these components onto multiple servers. For example, the database components can be delegated to a dedicated server, and the management server can reside on a second server.

The Operations Manager 2012 architecture is shown in Figure 6.4, with all the major components and their data paths.

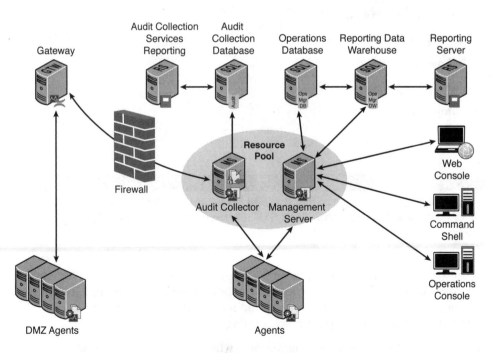

FIGURE 6.4   Operations Manager 2012 architecture.

The components are organized by two major architectural structures, the management group and resource pools. All of the components are contained within a management group, which can contain only a single operations database and a single reporting database. The management group can contain multiple management servers and other components. For fault tolerance, management servers can be organized into resource pools. These resource pools provide fault tolerance for notifications, for UNIX and Linux servers, and for network devices. Management servers inherently provide fault tolerance for Windows servers, although they are also organized into a default resource pool.

In the next sections, each of the components is discussed in detail.

Agents

Agents are installed on each managed system to provide efficient monitoring of local components. Almost all communication is initiated from the agent with the exception of the actual agent installation and specific tasks run from the Operations Console. Agentless monitoring is also available with a reduction of functionality and environmental scalability.

The Windows agent natively supports both 32-bit and 64-bit operating systems (x86, x64, IA64). The Windows agent supports the following operating systems:

▶ Windows Server 2003 SP2

▶ Windows Server 2008 SP2

▶ Windows Server 2008 R2

▶ Windows Server 2008 R2 SP1

▶ Windows XP Professional x64 SP2

▶ Windows XP Professional SP3

▶ Windows Vista SP2

▶ Windows 7

> **NOTE**
>
> Windows Server 2008 released at the SP1 level, so all versions are SP1 or higher. In other words, the Windows Server 2008 RTM release was really Windows Server 2008 SP1.

Agents can report to more than one management group at the same time by using multi-homing, allowing for different administration and bifurcation of operations. For example, an agent might report to one management group for operations monitoring and to another management group for security monitoring.

OpsMgr 2012 includes cross-platform monitoring, which is the ability to monitor UNIX/Linux computers using a native UNIX agent. This agent can be pushed out to the supported UNIX/Linux client using the Discovery Wizard, just like with Windows agents. The operating systems supported by the UNIX/Linux agent are as follows:

▶ IBM AIX 5.3, 6.1 (Power), and AIX 7.1 (POWER)

▶ HP-UX 11i v2 and v3 (PA-RISC and IA64)

▶ Red Hat Enterprise Server 4, 5, and 6 (x64 and x86)

▶ Oracle Solaris 9 (SPARC) and 10 (SPARC and x86)

▶ Novell SUSE Linux Enterprise Server 9 (x86), 10 SP1 (x86 and x64), and 11 (x86 and x64)

The cross-platform agents place somewhat of a greater load on the management server than do the Windows agents.

Windows computers can also be monitored as agentless, in which case the management server will perform the monitoring. No agent is deployed, but rather the management server makes Remote Procedure Call (RPC) connections to the managed computer to poll the event and performance data. This places a tremendous load on the management server and the network, so agentless monitoring is not recommended.

> **NOTE**
>
> When virtual components are discovered, such as the virtual cluster machines, they are shown as separate monitored objects and are listed in the Administrative space in the Agentless node. The agents are deployed to the physical nodes, but not to the virtual node. These virtual systems are monitored by their physical nodes and not by the management server, thus there is no undue load placed on the management servers. These agentless virtual objects should not be confused with agentless managed computers.

Factors that impact the agent include the following:

▶ Number of management packs deployed

▶ Type of management packs deployed

The maximum supported number of agents in a management group is 10,000 agents; however, due to the impact of the consoles, that is with a maximum of 25 open consoles. If 50 consoles will be open (the maximum per management group), then only 6,000 agents are supported. The maximum number of agentless managed computers per management group is 60.

The software requirement for the agent component is as follows:

▶ %SYSTEMDRIVE% must be formatted with the NTFS file system.

▶ Windows Installer version: at least Windows Installer 3.1.

▶ Microsoft Core XML Services (MSXML) 6.0.

Management Server

Optionally, additional management servers can be added for redundancy and scalability. Agents communicate with the management server to deliver operational data and pull down new monitoring rules.

The management server in 2012 is similar to the Microsoft Operations Manager 2007 management server. It manages communication with managed agents and forwards events and performance data to the operations database. The management server also supports agentless monitoring of managed systems, and it provides support for audit collection. Management servers now write directly to the operations database and data warehouse, which eliminates the need to transfer data from one database to another. This arrangement enables near-real-time data for reporting.

Each management server runs the software development kit (SDK) and Configuration service and is responsible for handling console communication, calculating the health of the environment, and determining what rules should be applied to each agent.

Compared with Microsoft Operations Manager 2007, management server fault tolerance, performance, and scalability is generally improved. In OpsMgr 2007, all operational data passed through the Root Management Server (RMS) and it was also responsible for rollups and notifications. Thus, the RMS was a single point of failure unless clustered. Operations Manager 2012 eliminates the single point of failure by grouping management servers into resource pools in which all management servers share in the duties. The most important resource on a management server is the CPU; however, management servers do not typically require high-end hardware.

Factors that impact the management server include the following:

▶ Number of agents

▶ Configuration changes to agents

▶ Number of consoles

The maximum number of open consoles supported by a management group is 50, due to the load that the console places on the RMS SDK service and the database. Operations Manager can support a maximum of 3,000 Windows agents or 500 UNIX/Linux agents per management server. The maximum number of agentless managed computers per management server is 10.

NOTE

The value of 10 for the maximum number of agentless monitored computers per management server is not a typo. Agentless managed computers place a huge load on the management server, which must gather and process all the workload of the rules, monitors, and other elements. This takes place over RPC, which has a heavy performance penalty on the network and the processor of the management server.

Due to the heavy load and abysmal scalability, agentless managed computers are not recommended.

OpsMgr does not have a hard-coded limit of management servers per management group. However, it is recommended to keep the environment to 10 or less management servers per management group.

The minimum supported hardware configuration for the management server component is as follows:

▶ 2.8GHz or faster x64 processor

▶ 2GB of RAM or more

▶ 20GB of available hard disk space (a minimum of 1GB on the OS drive)

The software requirements for the management server component are as follows:

▶ Windows Server 2008 R2 SP1

▶ .NET Framework 3.5 SP1

▶ .NET Framework 4.0

▶ Microsoft Core XML Services (MSXML) 6.0

▶ Windows PowerShell version 2.0.

Operations Manager Database

The operations database (OperationsManager) stores the monitoring rules and the active data collected from monitored systems. This database has a seven-day default retention period.

The Operations Manager database is a Microsoft SQL Server 2008 database that contains all of the data needed by Operations Manager for day-to-day monitoring. Because you can only have a single Operations Manager database, it is very important to ensure that it is sized appropriately. The most critical resource used by the Operations Manager database is the I/O subsystem, but the CPU and RAM are also important.

OpsMgr operates through a principle of centralized, rather than distributed, collection of data. All event logs, performance counters, and alerts are sent to a single, centralized database, and there can subsequently be only a single operations database per management group. Considering the use of a backup and high-availability strategy for the OpsMgr database is, therefore, highly recommended to protect it from outage.

Factors that impact the Operations Manager database include the following:

▶ Volume of data collection

▶ Configuration changes to agents

▶ Number of consoles open simultaneously

There is only one Operations Manager database per management group. The maximum number of open consoles supported by a management group is 50, due to the load that the consoles place on the Operations Manager database and the RMS SDK service.

It is recommended to keep this database with a 50GB limit to improve efficiency and reduce alert latency.

The minimum supported hardware configuration for the Operations Manager database component is as follows:

▶ 2.8GHz or faster x64 processor

▶ 4GB of RAM or more

▶ 50GB of available hard disk space

The software requirements for the Operations Manager database component consist of the following:

▶ Windows Server 2008 SP2 64 bit or Windows Server 2008 R2 SP1

▶ SQL Server 2008 SP1 or higher

▶ SQL Server 2008 R2 or higher

▶ .NET Framework 3.5 SP1

▶ .NET Framework 4.0

▶ SQL Collation—SQL_Latin1_General_CP1_CI_AS

▶ %SYSTEMDRIVE% formatted with the NTFS file system

▶ SQL Server Full Text Search

Reporting Data Warehouse

The reporting database (OperationsManagerDW) stores archived data for reporting purposes. This database has a 400-day default retention period.

Operations Manager 2012 uses Microsoft SQL Server Reporting Services 2008 (SRS 2008) for its reporting engine. SRS provides many enhancements to previous reporting solutions, including easier authoring and publishing. Operations Manager 2012 includes an easy-to-use graphical report designer as part of the Operations Manager 2012 console. Several new controls are also included to allow sophisticated reports and dashboards to be created. Most common reports are shipped as part of the management packs, so very little customization is needed to start working with best-practice reports.

Because Operations Manager 2012 inserts data into the Reporting data warehouse in near-real time, it is important to have sufficient capacity on this computer that supports writing all data being collected to the Reporting data warehouse. As with the Operations Manager database, the most critical resource on the Reporting data warehouse is the I/O subsystem. On most systems, loads on the Reporting data warehouse are similar to those on the Operations Manager database, but they can vary. Additionally, the workload put on the Reporting data warehouse by reporting is different from the load put on the Operations Manager database by Operations Console usage.

> **NOTE**
>
> This requirement is relatively new to OpsMgr 2007 and above, as in previous versions the data transfers from the Operations Manager database to the data warehouse database were batched. However, this caused reports to be out of date due to the lag in the transfer and also spikes in load when the transfers took place. Microsoft shifted to a real-time transfer, which improves reporting and increases performance, but it puts the data warehouse in the critical data path.

Factors that impact the Reporting data warehouse include the following:

▶ Volume of data collection

▶ Number of consoles generating reports

▶ Number of Service Level Dashboards open simultaneously

There is only one Reporting data warehouse per management group.

The minimum supported hardware configuration for the Reporting data warehouse component is as follows:

▶ 2.8GHz or faster x64 processor

▶ 4GB of RAM or more

▶ 100GB of available hard disk space

The software requirements for the Reporting data warehouse component consist of the following:

▶ Windows Server 2008 SP2 64 bit or Windows Server 2008 R2 SP1

▶ SQL Server 2008 SP1 or higher

▶ SQL Server 2008 R2 or higher

▶ .NET Framework 3.5 SP1

▶ .NET Framework 4.0

▶ SQL Collation—SQL_Latin1_General_CP1_CI_AS

▶ %SYSTEMDRIVE% formatted with the NTFS file system

▶ SQL Server Full Text Search

Reporting Server

The Reporting Server component is installed on a Reporting Services instance and provides the extensions needed for the Operations Manager reports. The reports are generated from the Reporting data warehouse and can be generated ad hoc, exported, or scheduled for email delivery.

The reports are accessed via the Operations Console and security is integrated with the Operations Manager roles.

Factors that impact the reporting server include the following:

▶ The size of the Reporting data warehouse database

▶ The number and complexity of reports being generated

The minimum supported hardware configuration for the Reporting Server component is as follows:

▶ 2.8GHz or faster x64 processor

▶ 2GB of RAM or more

▶ 20GB of available hard disk space

The software requirements for the Reporting Server component are as follows:

▶ Windows Server 2008 R2 SP1

▶ SQL Server Reporting Services 2008 SP1 or higher

▶ SQL Server Reporting Services 2008 R2 or higher

▶ .NET Framework 3.5 SP1

▶ .NET Framework 4.0

▶ At least 1024MB free hard disk space on %SYSTEMDRIVE% drive

▶ SQL Collation: SQL_Latin1_General_CP1_CI_AS

Operations Console

The Operations Console is used to monitor systems, run tasks, configure environmental settings, set author rules, subscribe to alerts, and generate and subscribe to reports. The console automatically scopes to the objects that an operator is authorized to manage in his or her user role. This allows the OpsMgr administrator to grant application owners full operator privileges to the Operations Console, but to a restricted set of objects. These restrictions are based on Active Directory security principles (users and security groups) and are respected by all consoles, APIs, and even the command shell.

Console performance can be a major issue to contend with in an OpsMgr infrastructure. The Operations Console places a substantial load on the operations database, more so than any other factor. This manifests itself in slow console performance, including delays in presenting information, updating views, or switching between views. Because this is the end-user-facing component, this can generate frustration for operators and administrators.

Factors that impact the Operations Console include the following:

▶ Disk latency on the Operations Manager database

▶ Number of consoles open simultaneously

There can be a maximum of 50 simultaneous open consoles on any management group, which includes the Operations Console, the Web console, and the command shell.

The minimum supported hardware configuration for the Operations Console component is as follows:

▶ 2.8GHz or faster processor

▶ 2GB of RAM or more

▶ 20GB of available hard disk space

The software requirements for the Operations Console component are as follows:

▶ Windows Vista, Windows 7, Windows Server 2008 64 bit, or Windows Server 2008 R2 SP1

▶ .NET Framework 3.5 SP1

▶ .NET Framework 3.5 SP1 hotfix KB976898

▶ .NET Framework 4.0

▶ Microsoft Windows PowerShell 2.0

▶ Microsoft Report Viewer 2008 SP1 Redistributable Package

▶ File system: %SYSTEMDRIVE% must be formatted with the NTFS file system

▶ Windows Installer version: at least Windows Installer 3.1

Web Console

The Web console is an optional component used to monitor systems, run tasks, and manage Maintenance mode from a web browser. The Web console is very similar to the Monitoring space in the Operations Console, but the Web console has some limitations such as only a 24-hour view of performance data.

> **NOTE**
>
> The default behavior of the Web console can be adjusted by making changes to the
> `web.config` file. See Chapter 7, "Operations Manager 2012 Implementation and
> Administration," for details on how to do this.

The Web console is an excellent choice for application administrators who need console access to the Operations Manager infrastructure, but don't want to go through the trouble of installing the full console.

Factors that impact the Web console include the following:

- Disk latency on Operations Manager database
- Number of consoles open simultaneously

There can be a maximum of 50 simultaneous open consoles on any management group, which includes the Operations Console, the Web console, and the command shell.

The minimum supported hardware configuration for the Web console component is as follows:

- 2.8GHz or faster x64 processor
- 2GB of RAM or more
- 20GB of available hard disk space

The software requirements for the Web console component are as follows:

- Windows Server 2008 R2 SP1
- .NET Framework 3.5 SP1
- .NET Framework 4.0
- Internet Information Services (IIS)
- ASP.NET

Command Shell

This optional component is built on PowerShell and provides full command-line management of the OpsMgr environment. A wide array of PowerShell cmdlets are available that allow for viewing configuration and operations data, as well as setting operational parameters.

Factors that impact the command shell include the following:

- Disk latency on the Operations Manager database
- Number of consoles open simultaneously

There can be a maximum of 50 simultaneous open consoles on any management group, which includes the Operations Console, the Web console, and the command shell.

The minimum supported hardware configuration for the command shell component is as follows:

- ▶ 2.8GHz or faster processor
- ▶ 2GB of RAM or more
- ▶ 20GB of available hard disk space

The software requirements for the command shell component are as follows:

- ▶ Windows Vista, Windows 7, Windows Server 2008, or Windows Server 2008 R2 SP1
- ▶ .NET Framework 3.5 SP1
- ▶ .NET Framework 4.0
- ▶ Microsoft Windows PowerShell 2.0

Gateway

This optional component provides mutual authentication through certificates for nontrusted systems in remote domains or workgroups.

The Gateway server is designed to improve management of devices in demilitarized zones (DMZs) or behind firewalls. The Gateway server aggregates communication from agents and forwards them to a management server inside the firewall. The Gateway server does not have direct access to the database, data warehouse, or Root Management Server. The most important resource on a Gateway server is the CPU; however, Gateway servers do not typically require high-end hardware.

Factors that impact the Gateway server include the following:

- ▶ Volume of data collection

Operations Manager can support a maximum of 1,500 Windows agents or 100 UNIX/Linux agents per Gateway server. OpsMgr does not have a hard-coded limit of Gateway servers per management group.

The minimum supported hardware configuration for the Gateway server component is as follows:

- ▶ 2.8GHz or faster processor
- ▶ 2GB of RAM or more
- ▶ 20GB of available hard disk space

The software requirements for the Gateway server component are as follows:

- ▶ Windows Server 2008 R2 SP1

- ▶ .NET Framework 3.5 SP1

- ▶ .NET Framework 4.0 (for UNIX/Linux management)

- ▶ Microsoft Windows PowerShell 2.0

- ▶ Microsoft Core XML Services (MSXML) 6.0

Audit Forwarder

Audit Collection Services (ACS) is an optional component used to collect security events from managed systems; this component is composed of a forwarder on the agent that sends all security events, a collector on the management server that receives events from managed systems, and a special database used to store the collected security data for auditing, reporting, and forensic analysis. ACS is a service that gathers Windows security log entries in real time and consolidates them in a database for easy access by security auditors. Audit Collection Services as implemented in Operations Manager 2012 will work on Windows servers, Windows clients, and UNIX/Linux cross-platform agents.

> **NOTE**
>
> The cross-platform support for ACS was released in December 2009 and requires additional setup of ACS agents on the UNIX/Linux computers. See Chapter 7 for details on how to do this.

The audit forwarder component resides on the managed computer. In Windows clients, the audit forwarder is a component of the agent and is disabled by default. In UNIX/Linux clients, the audit forwarder is a separately deployed agent. The agent collects security events from the local security events log and forwards them to the audit collector.

Factors that impact the audit forwarder include the following:

- ▶ Volume of security event data collection

- ▶ Level of audit logging

- ▶ If the client is a domain controller

The software requirements for the audit forwarder component are as follows:

- ▶ Microsoft Core XML Services (MSXML) 6.0

Audit Collector

The audit collector is a management server with the audit collector feature installed on it. This component receives security event data from the audit forwarders and inserts the data into the audit collection database.

The most important resource on an audit collection is the CPU; however, audit collection servers do not typically require high-end hardware.

Factors that impact the audit collector include the following:

▶ Volume of data collection

▶ Level of audit logging

▶ Number of domain controller audit forwarders

Ultimately, the audit collector is a management server. Operations Manager can support a maximum of 3,000 Windows agents or 500 UNIX/Linux agents per audit collector. There is only one audit collector per audit database.

The minimum supported hardware configuration for the audit collector management server component is as follows:

▶ 2.8GHz or faster x64 processor

▶ 2GB of RAM or more

▶ 50GB of available hard disk space

The software requirements for the audit collector management server component are as follows:

▶ Windows Server 2008 R2 SP1

▶ .NET Framework 3.5 SP1

▶ .NET Framework 4.0

▶ Microsoft Core XML Services (MSXML) 6.0

Audit Collection Database

The audit database is a SQL Server 2005/2008 database (OperationsManagerAC) and has similar requirements to the operations database and reporting database. The most critical resource used by the audit database is the I/O subsystem, but the CPU and RAM are also important.

The database handles a large number of operations due to the volume of security events collected. In addition, the database conducts daily maintenance at 2:00 a.m. every morning, which places an additional load on the server. The edition of SQL is an important factor in the maintenance; in SQL Server Standard Edition, the database is paused and in SQL Server Enterprise Edition, the database continues to accept data.

Factors that impact the audit collection database include the following:

▶ Volume of security event data collection

▶ Level of audit logging

▶ Number of domain controller audit forwarders

▶ Number and type of reports generated

▶ SQL Server version (Enterprise or Standard)

The audit collection database can only support one audit collector, which limits the audit collection database to 3,000 Windows agents or 500 UNIX/Linux agents.

The minimum supported hardware configuration for the audit collection database component is as follows:

▶ 2.8GHz or faster x64 processor

▶ 2GB of RAM or more

▶ 100GB of available hard disk space

The software requirements for the audit collection database component consist of the following:

▶ Windows Server 2008 SP2 or Windows Server 2008 R2 SP1

▶ Microsoft SQL Server 2005 or SQL Server 2008

▶ .NET Framework 3.5 SP1

▶ .NET Framework 4.0

Audit Collection Services Reporting

The ACS reporting component is installed separately from ACS and consists primarily of a reporting model and set of reports based on the audit collection database. These reports provide summaries and analysis of the security events that have been collected.

The ACS reporting component can be hosted on a separate server, the audit collection database server, Reporting data warehouse, or even the Reporting Server component. The security is fully integrated with the OpsMgr Reporting Services security module.

Factors that impact the Audit Collection Services reporting include the following:

▶ Number and type of reports generated

The ACS reporting component can be installed on as many SRS instances as needed.

TIP

For organizations that have stringent security requirements, it might not be acceptable to have OpsMgr administrators access the security data collected by ACS. In those cases, the ACS reporting component can be installed on a dedicated instance of SQL Reporting Services and tighter security can be configured in controlling access to reports.

The minimum supported hardware configuration for the ACS reporting component is as follows:

- 2.8GHz or faster x64 processor

- 2GB of RAM or more

- 20GB of available hard disk space

The software requirements for the ACS reporting component are as follows:

- Windows Server 2008 SP2 or Windows Server 2008 R2 SP1

- .NET Framework 3.5 SP1

- .NET Framework 4.0

- IIS

- Microsoft SQL Server 2008 R2 Reporting Services

Securing OpsMgr

Security has evolved into a primary concern that can no longer be taken for granted. The inherent security in any IT system is only as good as the services that have access to it; therefore, it is wise to perform a security audit of all systems that access information from servers. This concept holds true for management systems as well because they collect sensitive information from every server in an enterprise. This includes potentially sensitive event logs that could be used to compromise a system. Consequently, securing the OpsMgr infrastructure should not be taken lightly.

Role-Based Security Model

The Operations Manager infrastructure supports a role-based security model, which allows roles to be defined as profiles and assigned to Active Directory security principles.

NOTE

The built-in Operations Manager Administrator profile can only have group security principles assigned to it. Other built-in and custom profiles can have both group and user security principles assigned.

Seven different roles provide a range of authorization options. The roles are as follows:

▶ **Administrator**—The Administrator profile includes full privileges to Operations Manager. No scoping of the Administrator profile is supported.

> **NOTE**
>
> The local administrators group is placed in the Administrator profile at installation by default. This means that all members of the local administrators group are by default also Operations Manager administrators. Because the domain administrators group is normally a member of the local administrators group, all members of the Domain Admins group are also by default Operations Manager administrators.
>
> This can be changed by changing the groups in the Administrator profile.

▶ **Operator**—The Operator profile includes a set of privileges designed for users who need access to alerts, views, and tasks. A role based on the Operator profile grants members the ability to interact with alerts, execute tasks, and access views according to their configured scope.

▶ **Advanced Operator**—The Advanced Operator profile includes a set of privileges designed for users who need access to limited tweaking of monitoring configuration in addition to the Operator privileges. A role based on the Advanced Operator profile grants members the ability to override the configuration of rules and monitors for specific targets or groups of targets within the configured scope.

▶ **Read-Only Operator**—The Read-Only Operator profile includes a set of privileges designed for users who need read-only access to alerts and views. A role based on the Read-Only Operator profile grants members the ability to view alerts and access views according to their configured scope.

▶ **Report Operator**—The Report Operator profile includes a set of privileges designed for users who need access to reports. A role based on the Report Operator profile grants members the ability to view reports according to their configured scope.

▶ **Author**—The Author profile includes a set of privileges designed for authoring of monitoring configuration. A role based on the Author profile grants members the ability to create, edit, and delete monitoring configuration (tasks, rules, monitors, and views) within the configured scope. For convenience, Authors can also be configured to have Advanced Operator privileges scoped by group.

▶ **Report Security Administrator**—The Operations Manager Report Security Administrator profile is designed to enable the integration of SQL Server Reporting Services security with Operations Manager user roles. This gives Operations Manager administrators the ability to control access to reports. This role cannot be scoped.

For each of the roles, there is a profile created at installation that grants the role access across all objects. Additional profiles can be created for the Operator, Advanced Operator, Read-Only Operator, and the Author roles that narrow the scope of objects, allowing flexible access control to different users or groups of users.

> **NOTE**
>
> The access granted by profiles is cumulative. If a user is a member of two profiles, they will have the access granted by the combined profiles. There is no "deny" concept in the access controls within profiles.

The access is granted based on the user's account either directly or via group membership. The access controls are respected across all methods of access, including the Operations Console, Web console, command shell, and even API access.

A key part of any Operations Manager design is developing the administrative model that will grant users the appropriate console access they need.

Securing OpsMgr Agents

Each server that contains an OpsMgr agent and forwards events to management servers has specific security requirements. Server-level security should be established and should include provisions for OpsMgr data collection. All traffic between OpsMgr components, such as the agents, management servers, and database, is encrypted automatically for security, so the traffic is inherently secured.

> **NOTE**
>
> In environments with high-security requirements, the organization could investigate the use of encryption technologies such as IPSec to scramble the event IDs that are sent between agents and OpsMgr servers, to protect against eavesdropping of OpsMgr packets.

OpsMgr uses mutual authentication between agents and management servers. This means that the agent and management server must trust a common certificate authority, a simple requirement when the agents reside in the same forest as the management server. If the agent is located in a different forest or workgroup, client certificates can be used to establish mutual authentication. If an entire nontrusted domain must be monitored, the Gateway server can be installed in the nontrusted domain, agents can establish mutual authentication to the Gateway server, and certificates on the Gateway and management server are used to establish mutual authentication. In this scenario, you can avoid needing to place a certificate on each nontrusted domain member.

Understanding Firewall Requirements

OpsMgr servers that are deployed across a firewall have special considerations that must be taken into account. Port 5723, the default port for OpsMgr communications, must specifically be opened on a firewall to allow OpsMgr to communicate across it.

Table 6.1 describes communication ports for this and other OpsMgr components.

TABLE 6.1   OpsMgr Communication Ports

From	To	Port
Agent	Management server	5723
Agent	Gateway server	5723
Agent (ACS forwarder)	Management server ACS collector	51909
Management server	Network device	161, 162
Gateway server	Management server	5723
Gateway server	Management server	5723
Management or Gateway server	UNIX or Linux computer	1270
Management or Gateway server	UNIX or Linux computer	22
Management server	Operations Manager database	1433
Management server	Management server	5723, 5724
Management server	Reporting data warehouse	1433
Management server ACS collector	ACS database	1433
Operations Console	Management server	5724
Operations Console (reports)	SQL Server Reporting Services	80
Reporting Server	Management server	5723, 5724
Reporting Server	Reporting data warehouse	1433
Web console browser	Web console server	51908
Web console server	Management server	5724

The firewall port for the agents is the port that needs to be opened most often, which is only port 5723 from the agent to the management servers for monitoring. Other ports, such as 51909 for ACS, are more rarely needed. Figure 6.5 shows the major communications paths and ports between OpsMgr components.

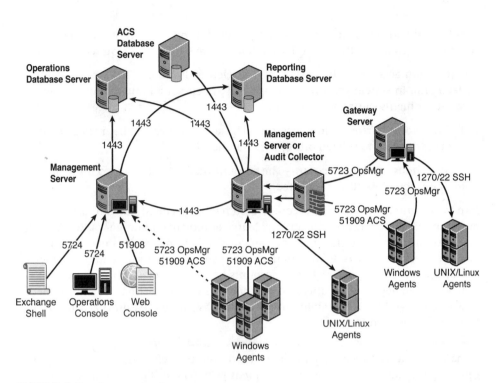

FIGURE 6.5   Communications ports.

NOTE

Note the directionality of the management server to UNIX/Linux arrow. This is because the management server collects information from the UNIX/Linux agents, rather than having the UNIX/Linux agents upload the information. This explains the lower scalability numbers for UNIX/Linux agents.

Action and RunAs Account Security

In addition to the aforementioned security measures, security of an OpsMgr environment can be strengthened by the addition of multiple service accounts and RunAs accounts to handle the different OpsMgr components and management packs. For example, the Management Server Action account and the SDK/Configuration service account should be configured to use separate credentials, to provide for an extra layer of protection in the event that one account is compromised.

▶ **Management Server Action account**—The account responsible for collecting data and running responses from management servers.

▶ **SDK and Configuration service account**—The account that writes data to the operations database; this service is also used for all console communication.

▶ **Local Administrator account**—The account used during the agent push installation process. To install the agent, local administrative rights are required.

▶ **Agent Action account**—The credentials the agent will run as. This account can run under a built-in system account, such as Local System, or a limited domain user account for high-security environments.

▶ **Data Warehouse Write Action account**—The account used by the management server to write data to the Reporting data warehouse.

▶ **Data Warehouse Reader account**—The account used to read data from the data warehouse when reports are executed.

▶ **RunAs accounts**—The specific accounts used by management packs to facilitate monitoring. Out of the box, Operations Manager provides a number of RunAs accounts and RunAs profiles, and you can create additional ones as necessary to delegate specific rights as defined in the management pack documentation. These accounts are then assigned as RunAs accounts used by the management pack to achieve a high degree of security and flexibility when monitoring the environment. New to OpsMgr 2012 is the ability to selectively distribute the RunAs account to just the agents that need them.

Various management packs have their own RunAs accounts, such as the Active Directory management packs and the Exchange management pack. These allow accounts with specific elevated privileges to be assigned to execute management pack scripts.

Securing DMZ Servers with Certificates

Servers in an organization's DMZ are usually not domain members and, thus, cannot do automatic mutual authentication with the OpsMgr server. However, these servers are the most exposed in the organization and, thus, a critical asset to be monitored. Thankfully, there is a well-defined process for using certificates to handle the mutual authentication. Certificates on both the management servers and the agents are used to mutually authenticate their communications.

The certificates used for mutual authentication must:

▶ Have the Name field match the computer name in the Computer Properties

▶ Be configured with Server (1.3.6.1.5.5.7.3.1) and Client (1.3.6.1.5.5.7.3.2) OIDs

▶ Be marked as Exportable

▶ Have their issuing CA trusted by the computer

The agent checks for these conditions at startup and will not use the certificate if these conditions are not satisfied.

See Chapter 7 for details on how to configure management servers and agents for mutual authentication.

Fault Tolerance and Disaster Recovery

The ability to recover from failures is critical to the proper function of any system, including Operations Manager. Although the two concepts are closely related, fault tolerance and disaster recovery are fundamentally different.

Fault tolerance is the ability to continue operating even in the event of a failure. This ensures that failures don't result in loss of service. Fault-tolerance mechanisms, such as clustering or load-balanced components, have activation times typically measured in seconds or minutes. These mechanisms typically also have high costs associated with them, such as duplicated hardware.

On the other hand, disaster recovery is the ability to restore operations after a loss of service. This ensures that failures don't result in the loss of data. Disaster recovery mechanisms, such as backups or log shipping, have activation times typically measured in hours or days. Disaster recovery mechanisms generally have lower costs associated with them, though failover sites in backup data centers can be expensive.

As IT organizations mature, the monitoring systems such as Operations Manager become more critical and, thus, require investment in fault tolerance.

> **NOTE**
>
> Depending on the organization, Operations Manager is sometimes considered to be a non-business-critical system and, thus, is not implemented with fault tolerance. The rationale for this is that if Operations Manager is down, business-critical systems would still be operational albeit without monitoring or alerting.

In addition to the scalability built in to OpsMgr, redundancy is built in to the components of the environment. Proper knowledge of how to deploy OpsMgr redundancy and place OpsMgr components correctly is important to the understanding of OpsMgr redundancy. The main components of OpsMgr can be made redundant through the following methods:

- ▶ **Management servers**—Management servers are automatically redundant and agents will failover and failback automatically between them. Simply install additional management servers into the resource pool for redundancy.

- ▶ **SQL databases**—The SQL database servers hosting the various databases can be made redundant using SQL clustering, which is based on Windows clustering. This supports failover and failback.

Figure 6.6 shows a fully fault-tolerant architecture.

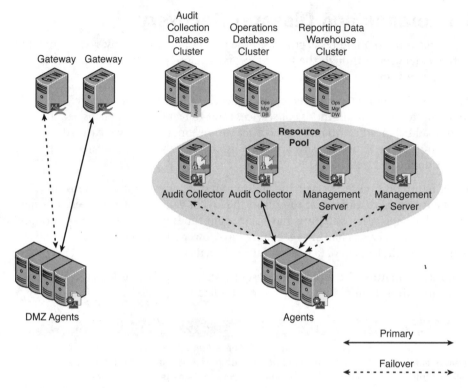

Figure 6.6   Operations Manager 2012 fault tolerance.

Management Group Redundancy

Having multiple management servers deployed across a management group allows an environment to achieve a certain level of redundancy. If a single management server experiences downtime, another management server within the management group will take over the responsibilities for the monitored servers in the environment. For this reason, it might be wise to include multiple management servers in an environment to achieve a certain level of redundancy if high uptime is a priority.

Resource Pools

Resource pools provide fault tolerance for the OpsMgr 2012 management group. However, they are used differently by different managed devices, such as Windows computers, UNIX computers, and network devices.

Windows computers work exactly as they did within OpsMgr 2007 and are assigned a primary management server. The difference with resource pools is that they will failover to management servers within the default resource pool, which is the All Management Servers Resource Pool. All management servers are members of this default resource pool and cannot be removed.

UNIX and Linux computers and network devices function differently. They can be manually assigned to resource pools and will failover between management servers within their resource pool. The OpsMgr administrator can create resource pools and assign management servers to those pools, allowing different devices to failover between different management servers.

Resource pools can also be used to control which management servers will send out notifications. The Notifications Resource Pool is created at installation and by default automatically includes all management servers. However, this resource pool can be converted to a manual resource pool, allowing the membership to be selected and thus controlling which management servers will send out notifications. Any management server within this group can send out notifications, allowing for fault tolerance.

Resource pools replace the Root Management Server (RMS) functionality, or limitations, present in OpsMgr 2007. The RMS component was a single point of failure and required complicated clustering to mitigate its loss. Resource pools in OpsMgr 2012 replace this functionality with an easily and automatically fault-tolerant service.

Clustering and Operations Manager

Because there can be only a single OpsMgr database and a single Reporting data warehouse per management group, the databases are a single point of failure and should be protected from downtime. Utilizing Windows Server 2008 R2 clustering for SQL databases helps to mitigate the risk involved with the OpsMgr and reporting databases.

> **NOTE**
>
> Geo-clusters (multisite clusters) are also supported; however, the maximum round-trip latency for the network heartbeat connection must be less than 500ms. This is a technology requirement for Microsoft Cluster Services (MSCS), but a violation of the requirement in an Operations Manager environment might result in inadvertent failover of components.

The following components can be clustered:

▶ Operations database

▶ Reporting data warehouse

▶ Audit collection database

Operations Manager only supports Microsoft Cluster Services quorum node clusters. The clusters should be single active-passive clusters dedicated to the respective components. This is the recommended cluster architecture.

Table 6.2 shows a sample cluster architecture with the components on separate dedicated clusters per recommended best practice.

TABLE 6.2   Sample Recommended Cluster Configuration

Component	Cluster	Node 1	Node 2
Operations database	CLUSTER01	Active	Passive
Reporting data warehouse	CLUSTER02	Active	Passive
Audit collection database	CLUSTER03	Active	Passive

The database components (operations database, Reporting data warehouse, and the audit collection database) can coexist on the same active node of an active-passive cluster. This could be all three or a combination of any two of the three database components. The cluster should be scaled up accordingly to avoid potential resource issues with having the multiple roles on a single node.

Other configurations are possible, but not recommended (for example, active-active SQL cluster configurations where there is a separate database component on each active node, such as the operations database on node 1 and the data warehouse on node 2). This is not recommended due to potential catastrophic performance issues when one of the nodes fails over. The concern is that if node 1 is running at 60% of resource utilization supporting the operations database and node 2 is running at 60% of resource utilization supporting the data warehouse, then when a node fails the single remaining node would suddenly be expected to be running at 120% of resource utilization supporting both components. This typically results in the failure of the second node in the cluster due to resource constraints.

> **NOTE**
>
> Management server clustering is not supported in OpsMgr 2012. This is a change from OpsMgr 2007, where clustering the RMS was the recommended approach to fault tolerance. Resource pools eliminated this need for clustering and are no longer supported.

Disaster Recovery

Disaster recovery in Operations Manager is critical to be able to recover in the event of the loss of any or all of the components. This includes the loss of a database, Root Management Server, or a management server.

The critical items to back up in an Operations Manager infrastructure, that is, the items needed to recover the environment, include the following:

▶ **Operations database (OperationsManager)**—The OperationsManager database contains almost all of the Operations Manager environment configuration settings, agent information, management packs with customizations, operations data, and other data required for Operations Manager to operate properly.

- ▶ **Reporting data warehouse database (OperationsManagerDW)**—The OperationsManagerDW database contains all of the performance and other operational data from your Operations Manager environment. SQL Reporting Services then uses this data to generate reports, such as trend analysis and performance tracking.

- ▶ **Audit collection database (OperationsManagerAC)**—The Audit Collection Services (ACS) database, OperationsManagerAC, is the central repository for events and security logs that are collected by ACS forwarders on monitored computers.

- ▶ **Master database**—The master database is a system database, which records all of the system-level information for a Microsoft SQL Server system, including the location of the database files. It also records all logon accounts and system configuration settings. The proper functionality of the master database is key to the operation of all of the databases in a SQL Server instance.

- ▶ **MSDB database**—The MSDB database, Msdbdata, is a SQL system database, which is used by the SQL Server agent to schedule jobs and alerts and for recording operators. The proper functionality of the MSDB database is key to the operation of all the databases in a SQL Server instance.

- ▶ **Internet Information Services**—The Internet Information Services (IIS) contains the custom settings for the Web console and the reporting database. Backing up the IIS 6.0 metabase in Windows Server 2003 or the IIS 7.x configuration in Windows Server 2008/R2 is necessary to restore the full functionality. Loss of this would require reconfiguring the Web console and the reporting database.

- ▶ **Override management packs**—These management packs contain the overrides that have been configured as part of tuning management packs. Loss of these management packs will reset the installed management packs to their default state and require all the overrides to be reentered.

- ▶ **Custom management packs**—These management packs contain all the custom development. Loss of these would require development to be redone.

Each of the components will have a different backup method and a different impact if the data is not recoverable. The most critical piece of OpsMgr, the SQL databases, should be regularly backed up using standard backup software that can effectively perform online backups of SQL databases. If integrating these specialized backup utilities into an OpsMgr deployment is not possible, it becomes necessary to leverage built-in backup functionality found in SQL Server. Table 6.3 lists the backup methods for each component.

TABLE 6.3   OpsMgr Component Backup Methods and Impacts

Component	Backup Method
Operations database (OperationsManager)	SQL Backup
Reporting data warehouse database (OperationsManagerDW)	SQL Backup
Audit collection database (OperationsManagerAC)	SQL Backup
Master database	SQL Backup
MSDB database	SQL Backup
IIS 6.0 Metabase or IIS 7.0 Configuration	IIS Backup
Override management packs	Operations Console
Custom management packs	Operations Console

The schedule of the backups is important. This is especially true as the databases can become quite large and the backup process time consuming, as well as expensive in terms of tapes and storage. The backup schedule suggested in Table 6.4 is based on a trade-off between the effort to back up and the impact of a loss.

TABLE 6.4   OpsMgr Component Backup Schedules

Component	Full Backup	Incremental Backup
Operations database (OperationsManager)	Weekly	Daily
Reporting data warehouse database (OperationsManagerDW)	Monthly	Weekly
Audit collection database (OperationsManagerAC)	Monthly	Weekly
Master database	Weekly	
MSDB database	Weekly	
IIS 6.0 Metabase or IIS 7.0 Configuration	Weekly	
Override management packs	Weekly and After Changes	
Custom management packs	Weekly and After Changes	

Given the volume of data in the Reporting data warehouse and the audit collection database, some organizations might choose to not perform backups of these components. The value of the long-term historical operational and security data might not be worth the storage requirements. Even if that is decided, the Operations Manager database should always be backed up to avoid loss of the valuable configuration, deployment, and tuning information.

> **TIP**
>
> The long-term operational, performance, and security information in the Reporting data warehouse and the audit collection database can be captured in reports as an alternative or supplement to database backups.
>
> Reports that summarize key metrics and information can be scheduled automatically in SQL Reporting Services and stored in a file share, allowing for long-term access to summarized data.

See Chapter 7 for details on how to configure backup procedures for each system component.

Understanding OpsMgr Component Requirements

OpsMgr's simple installation and relative ease of use often belie the potential complexity of its underlying components. This complexity can be managed with the right amount of knowledge of some of the advanced concepts of OpsMgr design and implementation.

Each OpsMgr component has specific design requirements, and a good knowledge of these factors is required before beginning the design of OpsMgr. Hardware and software requirements must be taken into account, as well as factors involving specific OpsMgr components, such as the management server, Gateway servers, service accounts, mutual authentication, and backup requirements.

Exploring Hardware Requirements

Having the proper hardware for OpsMgr to operate on is a critical component of OpsMgr functionality, reliability, and overall performance. Nothing is worse than overloading a brand-new server only a few short months after its implementation. The industry standard generally holds that any production servers deployed should remain relevant for three to four years following deployment. Stretching beyond this time frame might be possible, but the ugly truth is that hardware investments are typically short term and need to be replaced often to ensure relevance. Buying a less-expensive server might save money in the short term but could potentially increase costs associated with downtime, troubleshooting, and administration. That said, the following are the Microsoft-recommended minimums for any server running an OpsMgr 2012 server component:

▶ 2.8GHz processor or faster x64 architecture

▶ 20GB of free disk space

▶ 2GB of RAM

These recommendations apply only to the smallest OpsMgr deployments and should be seen as minimum levels for OpsMgr hardware. More realistic deployments would have the following minimums:

- ▶ Two to four 2.8GHz cores

- ▶ Windows 2008 R2 SP1 operating system

- ▶ 64-bit SQL Server

- ▶ 100GB free disk space on RAID 1+0 for performance

- ▶ 4–8GB of RAM

Operations Manager 2012 is one of Microsoft's most resource-intensive applications, so generous processor, disk, and memory are important for optimal performance. Future expansion and relevance of hardware should be taken into account when sizing servers for OpsMgr deployment, to ensure that the system has room to grow as agents are added and the databases grow.

NOTE

The specific hardware requirements per component are listed in the "OpsMgr Architecture Components" section of this chapter.

Determining Software Requirements

OpsMgr components can be installed only on Windows Server 2008 R2 SP1, which is only available in x64 versions. The database for OpsMgr must run on a Microsoft SQL Server 2008 server. The database can be installed on the same server as OpsMgr or on a separate server, a concept that is discussed in more detail in following sections.

OpsMgr itself must be installed on a member server in a Windows Active Directory domain. It is commonly recommended to keep the installation of OpsMgr on a separate server or set of dedicated member servers that do not run any other applications that could interfere in the monitoring and alerting process.

A few other requirements critical to the success of OpsMgr implementations are as follows:

- ▶ Microsoft .NET Framework 3.5 SP1 and 4.0 must be installed on the management server and the reporting server.

- ▶ Windows PowerShell 2.0.

- ▶ Microsoft Core XML Services (MSXML) 6.0.

- ▶ Client certificates must be installed in environments to facilitate mutual authentication between non–domain members and management servers.

- ▶ SQL Reporting Services must be installed for an organization to be able to view and produce custom reports using OpsMgr's reporting feature.

> **NOTE**
>
> The specific software requirements per component are listed in the "OpsMgr Architecture Components" section of this chapter.

Network Bandwidth Requirements

Each of the communications paths between OpsMgr components requires a certain minimum bandwidth to communicate properly.

Table 6.5 lists the communication bandwidth requirements between OpsMgr components.

TABLE 6.5   OpsMgr Minimum Communications Bandwidth

From	To	Minimum Bandwidth
Agent	Management server or gateway	64Kbps
Management server	Agentless	1024Kbps
Management server	Operations Manager database	256Kbps
Management server	Management server	64Kbps
Gateway server	Management server	64Kbps
Management server	Reporting data warehouse	768Kbps
Management server	Reporting Server	256Kbps
Reporting Server	Reporting data warehouse	1024Kbps
Operations Console	Management server	768Kbps
Operations Console	Reporting Server	768Kbps
Web console browser	Web console server	128Kbps
ACS collector	ACS database	768Kbps

The values given are minimum requirements, but actual requirements will be based on load factors as well. For example, although the minimum bandwidth for a Gateway server to a management server is given as 64Kbps, the actual bandwidth requirements will depend on the number of agents that the gateway is supporting and the workloads on the agents.

> **NOTE**
>
> The agentless bandwidth requirement clearly shows one of the issues with deploying agentless monitoring and why it does not scale. At 1024Kbps, the network requirement alone for agentless monitoring is 16 times that of an agent-based monitoring.

Figure 6.7 shows the communications bandwidth requirements graphically.

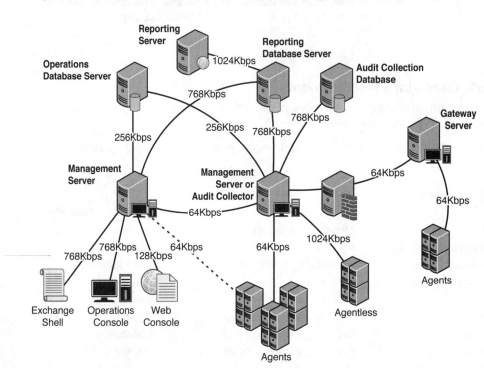

FIGURE 6.7   Communications bandwidth requirements.

Sizing the OpsMgr Databases

Depending on several factors, such as the type of data collected, the length of time that collected data will be kept, or the amount of database grooming that is scheduled, the size of the OpsMgr database will grow or shrink accordingly. It is important to monitor the size of the database to ensure that it does not increase well beyond the bounds of acceptable size. OpsMgr can be configured to monitor itself, supplying advance notice of database problems and capacity thresholds. This type of strategy is highly recommended because OpsMgr could easily collect event information faster than it could get rid of it.

The size of the operations database can be estimated through the following formula:

```
Number of agents x 5MB x retention days + 1024 overhead = estimated database size
```

For example, an OpsMgr environment monitoring 1,000 servers with the default seven-day retention period will have an estimated 36GB operations database:

```
(1000 agents * 5MB / day per agent * 7 day) + 1024MB = 36,024MB
```

The size of the reporting database can be estimated through the following formula:

```
Number of agents x 3MB x retention days + 1024 overhead = estimated database size
```

The same environment monitoring 1,000 servers with the default 400-day retention period will have an estimated 1.2TB reporting database:

```
(1000 agents * 3 MB / day per agent * 400 days) + 1024MB = 1,201,024MB
```

The size of the audit collection database can be estimated through the following formula:

```
Number of agents x 120MB x retention days + 1024 overhead = estimated database size
```

This assumes that 4% of the servers are domain controllers, that is, 40 domain controllers for the 1,000 servers. At that ratio, the domain controllers are contributing 45% of the database size due to their high volume of events.

The environment monitoring 1,000 servers with the default 14-day retention period will have an estimated 1.6TB audit collection database at steady state:

```
(1000 agents * 120MB / agent per day * 14 days) + 1024MB = 1,681,024MB
```

Table 6.6 summarizes the estimated daily database growth for each database for each agent.

TABLE 6.6   Database Growth Estimates

Database	Daily Growth Estimate (MB)
Operations Manager database	5MB/day per agent
Data warehouse	3MB/day per agent
Audit collection database	120MB/day per agent

NOTE

It is important to understand that these estimates are rough guidelines only and can vary widely depending on the types of servers monitored, the monitoring configuration, the degree of customization, and other factors.

For example, more or less domain controllers will have a huge impact on the audit collection database and a large proportion of Exchange servers will have a similar impact on the Operations Manager database size.

Monitoring Non–domain Member Considerations

DMZ, workgroup, and nontrusted domain agents require special configuration; in particular, they require certificates to establish mutual authentication. Operations Manager 2012 requires mutual authentication, that is, the server authenticates to the client and the client authenticates to the server, to ensure that the monitoring communications are not hacked. Without mutual authentication, it is possible for a hacker to execute a man-in-the-middle attack and impersonate either the client or the server. Thus, mutual authentication is a security measure designed to protect clients, servers, and sensitive Active Directory domain information, which is exposed to potential hacking attempts by the all-powerful management infrastructure. However, OpsMgr relies on Active Directory Kerberos for mutual authentication, which is not available to non–domain members.

> **NOTE**
>
> Workgroup servers, public web servers, and Microsoft Exchange Edge Transport role servers are commonly placed in the DMZ and are for security reasons not domain members, so almost every Windows Server 2008 R2 environment will need to deploy certificate-based authentication.

In the absence of Active Directory, trusts, and Kerberos, OpsMgr 2012 can use X.509 certificates to establish the mutual authentication. These can be issued by any Public Key Infrastructure (PKI), such as Microsoft Windows Server 2008 R2 Enterprise CA.

Installing agents on DMZ servers is discussed in Chapter 7.

OpsMgr Design Considerations

To be able to design an Operations Manager 2012 architecture, it is necessary to have a working understanding of not just the components of the architectures but also important design constraints. These include how Operations Manager handles data, how to connect management groups, and how Operations Manager behaves over the wide area network (WAN). One of the most critical design points is ensuring that the database components can handle the large volume of data, which is constrained by the disk subsystem and the version of SQL Server deployed.

Defining Management Groups

OpsMgr utilizes the concept of management groups to logically separate geographical and organizational boundaries. Management groups allow you to scale the size of OpsMgr architecture or politically organize the administration of OpsMgr.

At a minimum, each management group consists of the following components:

▶ A management server

▶ An operations database

▶ Management agents

▶ Management consoles

OpsMgr can be scaled to meet the needs of different-sized organizations. For small organizations, all the OpsMgr components can be installed on one server with a single management group. In large organizations, the distribution of OpsMgr components to separate servers allows the organizations to customize and scale their OpsMgr architecture. Multiple management groups provide load balancing and fault tolerance within the OpsMgr infrastructure. Organizations can set up multiple management servers at strategic locations, to distribute the workload among them.

> **NOTE**
>
> The general rule of thumb with management groups is to start with a single management group and add on more management groups only if they are absolutely necessary. Administrative overhead is reduced, and there is less need to re-create rules and perform other redundant tasks with fewer management groups.

Understanding How OpsMgr Stores Captured Data

OpsMgr itself utilizes two Microsoft SQL Server databases for all collected data. Both databases are automatically maintained through OpsMgr-specific scheduled maintenance tasks.

The operations database stores all the monitoring rules that are imported by management packs and operational data collected from each monitored system. Data in this database is retained for seven days by default. Data retention for the operations database is lower than the reporting database to improve efficiency of the environment. This database must be installed as a separate component from OpsMgr but can physically reside on the same server, if needed.

The reporting database stores data for long-term trend analysis and is designed to grow much larger than the operations database. Data in the reporting database is stored in three states: raw data, hourly summary, and daily summary. The raw data is only stored for 7 days, whereas both daily and hourly data are stored for 400 days. This automatic summarization of data allows for reports that span days or months to be generated very quickly.

Disk Subsystem Performance

The disk performance is a critical factor in the OpsMgr overall performance. Because of the volume of data that flows from the components into the various databases, data must make it into the databases quickly. However, for usability, console performance is the single most important factor. The console places a significant load on the server, primarily reading the data from the Operations Manager database. If this read access is slow, console performance will be impacted and users will be dissatisfied with Operations Manager.

> **NOTE**
>
> This usability measure is critical, as there is no point in collecting all this operational and performance data if the users cannot access it.

The key measure to watch is the average disk seconds per read (Avg. Disk Sec./Read counter) for the logical disk where the Operations Manager database is located (the OperationsManager.mdf file). This should not be higher than 0.030 seconds (30ms) on a sustained basis. This measure is independent of the number of agents in a management group, which makes it a very useful measurement across all scales of deployments.

If the disk subsystem is experiencing greater than 0.030-second read times on the Operations Manager database volume, the Operations Console will have performance issues.

For long-term trending, the Operations Manager data can be used to view the performance of the disk subsystem. Figure 6.8 shows the Avg. Disk Sec/Read for the operations database volume for a sample OpsMgr 2012 system for a period of 2 hours. The performance is frequently over the 0.030 sec or 30ms target line, which means that the disk subsystem is not performing well enough and there are likely to be delays in the console performance. As can be seen from the callout in the figure, there was a peak at 9:05 p.m. at 0.31 seconds. This peak is over an order of magnitude larger than the recommended value of .03 seconds.

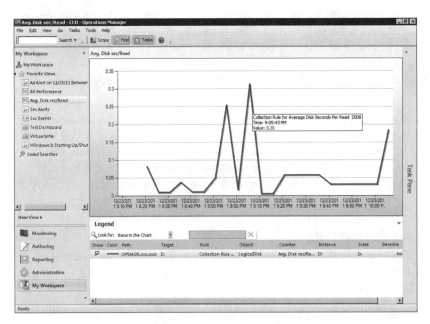

FIGURE 6.8   Avg. Disk Sec/Read for OpsMgr database disk.

NOTE

Because the console has a big impact on the database access, it is important to not use the console to measure the Avg. Disk Sec/Read counter while testing. Instead use the Performance Monitor to measure the counter. This prevents the console from impacting the measuring process.

However, it is good to use the console for reporting to generate reports on long-term trends to see how the disk is performing over the long run.

Choosing Between SAN and DAS

One of the common points of contention is what storage systems to use when deploying Operations Manager. The two main contenders are a storage area network (SAN) disk subsystem and a direct attached storage (DAS) disk subsystem. The SAN is typically a switched-based fiber-channel fabric and a large array of disks that is managed by a dedicated storage team. The SAN has high reliability and high performance, but also high cost. The DAS is a RAID subsystem of disks that are directly attached to the servers. Depending on the RAID configuration, this can have high reliability and high performance, but costs less than a SAN.

Choosing between a SAN and DAS can be tough, as there are competing claims as to which subsystem actually performs better. There are three important performance measures to look at when deciding on a disk subsystem:

- ▶ **I/Os Per Second (IOps)**—This indicates how many I/O requests can be handled in a second. This measure is impacted by the size of the requests, with larger requests reducing the number of requests that the system can handle in a second.

- ▶ **I/O Latency (Latency)**—This indicates how long it takes to handle a given request. This measure is also impacted by the size of the requests, with larger requests increasing the latency.

- ▶ **Megabytes Per Second (MBps)**—This indicates how many megabytes of data can be handled in a second. This measure is also impacted by the size of the requests, but larger requests actually increase the amount of data that can be handled (which is a good thing).

For small data transfers, the IOps and Latency are the critical measures. For large data transfers, the MBps is the critical measure. The OpsMgr database accesses are all large data transfers, so the MBps measurement is the critical measure for the performance and scalability of the system. SQL uses 8KB pages, leading to random and sequential 8KB I/O on the disks that host the databases, which are relatively large data requests.

In general, a SAN provides better performance than a DAS. This is especially true for large block-level data transfers, which is what the SQL database will be doing. The SAN provides a faster data transfer due to the higher MBps.

If possible, always implement the Operations Manager database server with SAN disk subsystems.

NOTE

The configuration of the SAN and the DAS can dramatically affect the performance of the two disk subsystems. For example, a DAS subsystem with six controllers, RAID 1+0, and a separate channel and disks for each set of databases and logs will outperform a standard SAN.

However, for most implementations, the SAN is going to be the better bet for performance.

If using DAS, the design of the DAS is critical to ensuring the performance of the disk subsystem. Choose the RAID appropriately, as not all RAIDs are created equal in terms of performance. The following bullets compare the common RAID choices and their performance:

▶ **RAID 1**—This is a pair of drives that are mirrored. RAID 1 provides no performance benefit, as the read/write performance is that of a single drive. The second drive in the RAID array is used simply for fault tolerance.

▶ **RAID 5**—This is a set of drives with the data striped across them and with one drive providing parity for fault tolerance. RAID 5 provides mostly read performance benefit, as the parity drive is a write bottleneck in the RAID array.

▶ **RAID 1+0**—The data is striped across half the drives in the RAID array and then mirrored to the other half of the drives in the array. There is both read and write performance benefit, which is a multiple of the number of disks in the RAID array divided by two.

Given the read and write performance benefits, RAID 10 is always the preferred method. An important benefit of RAID 10 is that the size of the array can be increased by adding spindles (that is, disks) and this also increases the performance of the array. As the Operations Manager system is scaled up and better performance is needed, the disk subsystem needs to be scaled to increase performance. This allows target performance (that is, IOps) to be reached.

A 10,000 RPM SCSI disk will be able to sustain approximately 125 IOps of random read/writes. Using this as a base, a target rate of IOps can be computed in terms of number of disks needed (because RAID-10 performance scales with the number of disks). The computation for the number of disks needed in the RAID-10 array is as follows:

```
Target IOps / (125 IOps per disk / 2) = Number of disk is RAID-10 array
```

For example, if a target of 500 IOps is needed, the computation is as follows:

```
500 IOps / (125 IOps per disk / 2) = 8 disks
```

A RAID 1+0 array of eight disks would be sufficient to meet the 500 IOps goal.

This allows designers to compute the sizing of RAID-10 arrays needed to achieve the desired performance in terms of IOps. For RAID 1 and RAID 5, the write performance is limited to that of a single drive, that is, 125 IOps.

Choosing SQL Versions

Another issue is the edition of SQL Server to use. For Operations Manager, which leverages the power of SQL Server heavily, there can be serious performance impacts in choosing the wrong edition of SQL Server. The current version of SQL Server 2008 R2 has significant performance improvements over previous versions, especially when combined with Windows Server 2008 R2. The R2 versions of Windows Server 2008 and SQL Server 2008 are really a better-together combination, which OpsMgr 2012 can really take advantage of.

Not only does the version make a difference, but the edition of SQL Server makes a difference as well. SQL Server Enterprise Edition is designed to scale to the largest of hardware platforms and handle large workloads, but has an associated high cost. SQL Server Standard Edition has built-in technology scalability limitations, but a much lower cost.

SQL Server Enterprise Edition supports more parallel operations, allowing multiple databases to coexist. Both SQL Server Enterprise and Standard Editions support parallel queries, but only SQL Server Enterprise Edition supports parallel index and consistency check operations. SQL Server Enterprise Edition has a host of other performance benefits, such as indexed views, table and index partitioning, dynamic memory management, and enhanced read-ahead and scanning. These enhancements allow SQL Server Enterprise Edition to handle much larger Operations Manager implementations and to handle multiple components on the same SQL server.

SQL Server Standard Edition has a limit of four CPUs, whereas SQL Server Enterprise Edition is only limited by the operating system. In other words, SQL Server Standard Edition limits parallel processing of queries to a maximum of four CPUs. This is a good example of when the difference between CPUs (that is, sockets on the motherboard) and cores is important. SQL Server Standard Edition counts the physical CPUs toward the limitation.

> **NOTE**
>
> The SQL Server license that is included in the Operations Manager Server 2012 with SQL Server Technology is a SQL Server 2008 R2 Standard Edition license.

In addition, SQL Server Enterprise provides better support for online operations. This is especially critical for ACS, which handles a large volume of data at all times. Every day at 2:00 a.m., the ACS database will perform maintenance. With SQL Server Standard Edition, the database has to pause. If the ACS collector queue fills up during this pause and the ACS forwarders disconnect, the data becomes backlogged. If the Windows security event logs roll over during this time, security events can be lost. With SQL Server Enterprise

Edition, the database does not pause during maintenance and there is no backlog problem.

> **NOTE**
>
> The ACS backlog issue does not have to persist for very long to have an impact. In one organization, the Windows security event logs would roll over every 60 seconds due to the level of auditing being performed. The ACS database being paused for 30 minutes for maintenance results in a significant loss of security data.

In general, the best-practice guidance is to use SQL Server Enterprise Edition when

▶ Multiple Operations Manager components will coexist on the same database server, as SQL Server Enterprise handles parallel processing more effectively and can take advantage of additional resources in a scaled-up server.

▶ Audit Collection Services is deployed, to avoid the maintenance pause.

▶ You have more than four CPU sockets, as SQL Server Enterprise can use the additional resources.

▶ Clustering is used, as the additional overhead of clustering can impact performance.

Given the cost differential, sometimes it will be necessary to deploy SQL Server Standard Edition. Best-practice guidance when using SQL Server Standard Edition is to

▶ Keep OpsMgr database components on separate SQL servers.

▶ Deploy 64-bit versions.

▶ Use extra memory in database servers to compensate.

Multiple Management Groups

As previously defined, an OpsMgr management group is a logical grouping of monitored servers that are managed by a single OpsMgr SQL database, one or more management servers, and a unique management group name. Each management group established operates completely separately from other management groups, although they can be configured in a hierarchical structure with a top-level management group able to see "connected" lower-level management groups.

The concept of connected management groups allows OpsMgr to scale beyond artificial boundaries and also gives a great deal of flexibility when combining OpsMgr environments. However, certain caveats must be taken into account. Because each management group is an island in itself, each must subsequently be manually configured with individual settings. In environments with a large number of customized rules, for example, such manual configuration would create a great deal of redundant work in the creation, administration, and troubleshooting of multiple management groups.

Deploying Geographic-Based Management Groups

Based on the factors outlined in the preceding section, it is preferable to deploy OpsMgr in a single management group. However, in some situations, an organization needs to divide its OpsMgr environment into multiple management groups. The most common reason for division of OpsMgr management groups is division along geographic lines. In situations in which WAN links are saturated or unreliable, it might be wise to separate large "islands" of WAN connectivity into separate management groups.

Simply being separated across slow WAN links is not enough reason to warrant a separate management group, however. For example, small sites with few servers would not warrant the creation of a separate OpsMgr management group, with the associated hardware, software, and administrative costs. However, if many servers exist in a distributed, generally well-connected geographical area, that might be a case for the creation of a management group. For example, an organization could be divided into several sites across the United States but decide to divide the OpsMgr environment into separate management groups for East Coast and West Coast, to roughly approximate their WAN infrastructure.

Smaller sites that are not well connected but are not large enough to warrant their own management group should have their event monitoring throttled to avoid being sent across the WAN during peak usage times. The downside to this approach, however, is that the reaction time to critical event response is increased.

Deploying Political or Security-Based Management Groups

The less-common method of dividing OpsMgr management groups is by political or security lines. For example, it might become necessary to separate financial servers into a separate management group to maintain the security of the finance environment and allow for a separate set of administrators.

Politically, if administration is not centralized within an organization, management groups can be established to separate OpsMgr management into separate spheres of control. This would keep each OpsMgr management zone under separate security models.

As previously mentioned, a single management group is the most efficient OpsMgr environment and provides for the least amount of redundant setup, administration, and troubleshooting work. Consequently, artificial OpsMgr division along political or security lines should be avoided, if possible.

Putting It All Together in a Design

To illustrate the concepts discussed in this chapter, three designs are presented. These design scenarios cover a range of organizations from small to medium to large. The profile of the three enterprises is as follows:

- **Small enterprise**—A total of 30 servers in 3 locations, a main office with a shared T1 to the branch offices, and 25% bandwidth availability.

- **Medium enterprise**—A total of 500 servers in 10 locations, a main office with a shared 11Mbps fractional T3 to the branch offices, and 25% bandwidth availability.

▶ **Large enterprise**—A total of 2,000 servers in 50 locations, a main office with a shared 45Mbps T3 to the branch offices, and 25% bandwidth availability.

Based on these sizes, designs were developed.

In these designs, DAS was used as a design constraint, rather than a SAN. This provides a more realistic minimum hardware specification. Performance could be further improved by using SAN in place of DAS.

Small Enterprise Design

The first design point is for a small enterprise consisting of the following:

▶ 30 servers

▶ Three locations, including a main office and two branch offices

▶ A shared T1 from the main office to the branch offices

▶ Approximately 25% bandwidth availability

For illustration and sizing, the numbers and types of servers at each location is listed in Table 6.7. Because the types of servers determine which management packs are loaded and determine database sizing, it is important to have some sense of the monitored servers.

TABLE 6.7   Small Enterprise Server Counts

Server Type	Central Office	Each Branch Office	Total
Windows servers	4	2	8
Exchange servers	5	0	5
SQL servers	5	0	5
IIS servers	4	2	8
Active Directory servers	2	1	4

Given the relatively small number of managed computers, a single-server design makes the most sense. The recommended design for the small enterprise is given in Table 6.8.

TABLE 6.8   Small Enterprise OpsMgr Design Recommendation

Server	Component(s)	Processors	Memory	Disk
OM01	Operations database, Reporting data warehouse, Reporting Server, and management server	4 cores	8GB RAM	4-disk RAID-10 data 2-disk RAID-1 logs

For the server software, the recommendations are as follows:

▶ Windows Server 2008 R2 SP1, Standard Edition 64-bit

▶ SQL Server 2008 R2 Enterprise 64-bit

Given that the components are all on the same server, the single-server option can really use the SQL Enterprise performance improvements. Also, using the Enterprise version of SQL allows the database server to add processors in the future if resource utilization dictates it.

Figure 6.9 shows the architecture for the small organization.

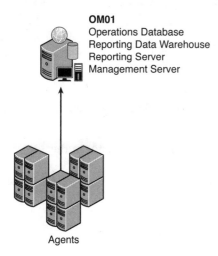

OM01
Operations Database
Reporting Data Warehouse
Reporting Server
Management Server

Agents

FIGURE 6.9   Operations Manager 2012 small enterprise architecture.

If adding Audit Collection Services to the design, dedicated systems are recommended. The specification is shown in Table 6.9.

TABLE 6.9   Small Enterprise ACS Design Recommendation

Server	Component(s)	Processors	Memory	Disk
ACS01	Audit collector	2 cores	4GB RAM	2-disk RAID 1
ACS02	Audit collection database	4 cores	4GB RAM	2-disk RAID-1 data 2-disk RAID-1 logs

For the server software, the recommendations are as follows:

▶ Windows Server 2008 R2 SP1, Standard Edition 64-bit

▶ SQL Server 2008 R2 Enterprise 64-bit

In the ACS design, the SQL Server 2008 R2 Enterprise Edition could be downgraded to Standard Edition with minimal impact. The downside would be a pause in the security event collection during nightly maintenance. The volume of data should be low enough that no data loss would occur during the pause.

The databases will grow to their steady state sizes proportional to the number of agents being monitored, all other things being equal. Table 6.10 lists the estimated database sizes for the small enterprise databases. These sizes are important for determining the drive sizes and sizing backup solutions.

TABLE 6.10   Small Enterprise Estimated Database Sizes

Database Size (GB)	Agents	MB/Agent/Day	Retention	Database
OperationsManager	30	5	7	1.05
OperationsManagerDW	30	3	400	36
OperationsManagerAC	30	120	14	50.4

These sizes would be changed by adjustments to the retention periods, managed computer configuration, and management packs.

When determining the sizing of the disk subsystems, it is important to factor in the following:

▶ Database sizes

▶ Local backup overhead

▶ Log overhead

▶ Operating system overhead

▶ Application overhead

Typically, there should be a cushion of at least three to four times the database size to account for the overhead factors. The RAID types and number of disks would be changed to accommodate the storage needs.

Medium Enterprise Design

The second design point is for a medium enterprise consisting of the following:

▶ 500 servers

▶ 11 locations, including a main office and 10 branch offices

▶ A shared 11Mbps fractional T3 from the main office to the branch offices

▶ Approximately 25% bandwidth availability

For illustration and sizing, the numbers and types of servers at each location are listed in Table 6.11. Because the types of servers determine which management packs are loaded and determine database sizing, it is important to have some sense of the monitored servers.

TABLE 6.11   Medium Enterprise Server Counts

Server Type	Central Office	Each Branch Office	Total
Windows servers	150	3	35
Exchange servers	10	1	8
SQL servers	50	1	10
IIS servers	185	3	35
Active Directory servers	5	2	12

Given the number of managed computers, a dual-server design makes the most sense. This would be a database server and a management server. The recommended design for the medium enterprise is given in Table 6.12.

TABLE 6.12   Medium Enterprise OpsMgr Design Recommendation

Server	Component(s)	Processors	Memory	Disk
OM01	Management Server	2 cores	4GB RAM	2-disk RAID 1
OM02	Operations database, Reporting data warehouse, and Reporting Server	4 cores	4GB RAM	6-disk RAID-10 data 2-disk RAID-1 logs

These are minimum specifications for performance and storage requirements. They can be revised upward based on additional requirements, such as backup storage.

For the server software, the recommendations are as follows:

▶ Windows Server 2008 R2 SP1, Standard Edition 64-bit

▶ SQL Server 2008 R2 Enterprise 64-bit

Given that the database components are all on the same server, the database server can really use the SQL Enterprise performance improvements. Also, using the Enterprise version of SQL allows the database server to add processors in the future if resource utilization dictates it. Using 64-bit versions similarly allows memory to be added and utilized without having to rebuild servers.

Figure 6.10 shows the architecture for the medium-sized organization.

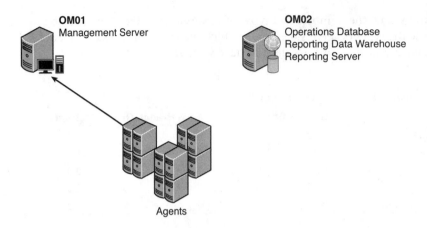

FIGURE 6.10   Operations Manager 2012 medium enterprise architecture.

If adding Audit Collection Services to the design, dedicated systems are recommended. The specification is shown in Table 6.13.

TABLE 6.13   Medium Enterprise ACS Design Recommendation

Server	Component(s)	Processors	Memory	Disk
ACS01	Audit collector	2 cores	4GB RAM	2-disk RAID 1
ACS02	Audit collection database	4 cores	4GB RAM	6-disk RAID-10 data 2-disk RAID-1 logs

The larger ACS data disk size is mainly to support the anticipated database size.

For the server software, the recommendations are for:

▶ Windows Server 2008 R2 SP1, Standard Edition 64-bit

▶ SQL Server 2008 R2 Enterprise 64-bit

In the ACS design, the SQL Server 2008 Enterprise Edition is an important factor. Given that there are 12 AD DCs and a total of 500 servers, the volume of security events will be significant and the SQL Enterprise Edition's ability to do online maintenance will be important.

The databases will grow to their steady state sizes proportional to the number of agents being monitored, all other things being equal. Table 6.14 lists the estimated database sizes for the medium enterprise databases. These sizes are important for determining the drive sizes and sizing backup solutions.

TABLE 6.14   Medium Enterprise Estimated Database Sizes

Database	Agents	MB/Agent/Day	Retention	Database Size (GB)
OperationsManager	500	5	7	17.5
OperationsManagerDW	500	3	400	600
OperationsManagerAC	500	120	14	840

These sizes would be changed by adjustments to the retention periods, managed computer configuration, and management packs. In the case of the medium enterprise design, the larger OperationsManagerAC database size drives a large RAID array for the ACS database server.

When determining the sizing of the disk subsystems, it is important to factor in the following:

▶ Database sizes

▶ Local backup overhead

▶ Log overhead

▶ Operating system overhead

▶ Application overhead

Typically, there should be a cushion of at least three to four times the database size to account for the overhead factors. The RAID types and number of disks would be changed to accommodate the storage needs.

Large Enterprise Design

The last design point is for a large enterprise consisting of the following:

▶ 2,000 servers

▶ 51 locations, including a main office and 50 branch offices

▶ A shared 45Mbps T3 from the main office to the branch offices

▶ Approximately 25% bandwidth availability

For illustration and sizing, the numbers and types of servers at each location is listed in Table 6.15. Because the types of servers determine which management packs are loaded and determine database sizing, it is important to have some sense of the monitored servers. This information can also be used with the System Center Capacity Planner tool.

6

TABLE 6.15   Large Enterprise Server Counts

Server Type	Central Office	Branch Office (Each)	Branch Offices (Total)
Windows servers	575	2	100
Exchange servers	15	2	100
SQL servers	300	2	100
IIS servers	600	2	100
Active Directory servers	10	2	100
Totals	1,500		500

Given the relatively large number of managed computers, a server per component design makes the most sense. This places each component on its own dedicated server, ensuring that there is no contention for resources between components. The recommended design for the large enterprise is given in Table 6.16.

TABLE 6.16   Large Enterprise OpsMgr Design Recommendation

Server	Component(s)	Processors	Memory	Disk
OM01	Management server	4 cores	12GB RAM	4-disk RAID 10
OM02	Operations database	4 cores	8GB RAM	8-disk RAID-10 data
				2-disk RAID-1 logs
OM03	Reporting data warehouse	4 cores	8GB RAM	16-disk RAID-10 data
				2-disk RAID-1 logs
OM04	Reporting Server	2 cores	4GB RAM	2-disk RAID 1
OM05	Management server	2 cores	4GB RAM	2-disk RAID 10

These are minimum specifications for performance and storage requirements. The 8-disk RAID-10 subsystem for the OperationsManager database is driven mainly by performance considerations, whereas the OperationsManagerDW 16-disk RAID 10 is driven mainly by storage requirements. They can be revised upward based on additional requirements, such as backup storage.

NOTE

This configuration could really benefit from SAN storage to improve performance and scalability. At the very least, the database servers will require external drive enclosures to support the large number of disks.

For the server software, the recommendations are as follows:

▶ Windows Server 2008 R2 SP1, Standard Edition 64-bit

▶ SQL Server 2008 R2 Enterprise 64-bit

Given the scale of the infrastructure, the 64-bit platforms are needed to take advantage of the larger memory and to increase the performance of the SQL database servers.

Figure 6.11 shows the architecture for the large-sized organization.

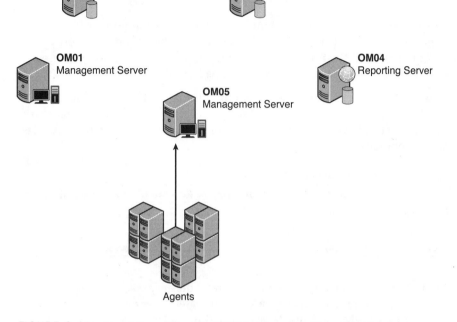

FIGURE 6.11   Operations Manager 2012 large enterprise architecture.

If adding Audit Collection Services to the design, dedicated systems are recommended. The specification is shown in Table 6.17.

TABLE 6.17   Large Enterprise ACS Design Recommendation

Server	Component(s)	Processors	Memory	Disk
ACS01	Audit collector	2 cores	4GB RAM	2-disk RAID 1
ACS02	Audit collection database	8 cores	8GB RAM	24-disk RAID-10 data 2-disk RAID-1 logs

The larger ACS data disk size is mainly to support the anticipated database size, rather than performance considerations.

NOTE

This configuration could really benefit from SAN storage to improve performance. At the very least, the database server will require an external drive enclosure to support the large number of disks.

For the server software, the recommendations are as follows:

▸ Windows Server 2008 R2 SP1, Standard Edition 64-bit

▸ SQL Server 2008 R2 Enterprise 64-bit

In the ACS design, the SQL Server 2008 R2 Enterprise Edition is an important factor. Given that there are 100 AD DCs and a total of 2,000 servers, the volume of security events will be quite large and the SQL Enterprise Edition's performance improvements, scalability, and ability to do online maintenance will be critical.

The databases will grow to their steady state sizes proportional to the number of agents being monitored, all other things being equal. Table 6.18 lists the estimated database sizes for the large enterprise databases. These sizes are important for determining the drive sizes and sizing backup solutions.

TABLE 6.18   Large Enterprise Estimated Database Sizes

Database	Agents	MB/Agent/Day	Retention	Database Size (GB)
OperationsManager	2,000	5	7	70
OperationsManagerDW	2,000	3	400	2400
OperationsManagerAC	2,000	120	14	3360

These sizes would be changed by adjustments to the retention periods, managed computer configuration, and management packs. In the case of the medium enterprise design, the larger OperationsManagerAC database size drives a large RAID array for the ACS database server.

NOTE

For these larger databases, larger drives can be used to reduce the number of spindles in the RAID-10 arrays. This reduces the performance, but should not be a problem for the Reporting data warehouse and the audit collection databases.

When determining the sizing of the disk subsystems, it is important to factor in the following:

▸ Database sizes

▸ Local backup overhead

▸ Log overhead

▸ Operating system overhead

▸ Application overhead

Typically, there should be a cushion of at least three to four times the database size to account for the overhead factors. This is more difficult with large enterprise organizations and their correspondingly large data sets. The RAID types and number of disks would be changed to accommodate the storage needs, especially if online backup to tape or replication to an offsite recovery site might be used instead of local backup.

Planning an Operations Manager Deployment

An Operations Manager project can be a small endeavor or a very large one, depending on the organization, requirements, and budget. Whatever the scale, appropriate planning is key to the success of any Operations Manager project.

> **NOTE**
>
> What "appropriate planning" means for any given organization or project will vary greatly. This could be a 100-page design and planning document. Or it could be a single-page design and plan outline. The important point is that it be done to the degree needed to ensure the success of the project.

A project is defined by its scope, timeline, and budget. The scope defines what's included in the project and, sometimes more important, what's not included in the project. The timeline defines when the project will start, end, and some level of detail on what occurs in between. The budget defines how much it will cost, which could be in terms of money, effort, resources, or a combination of all of these.

A typical Operations Manager project will have three to five phases. These phases are as follows:

1. Design principles training (optional)

2. Design and planning phase

3. Proof of concept phase (optional)

4. Pilot phase

5. Production phase

The design principles training and the proof of concept phases are optional and might not be needed for some implementations, especially smaller or less-complex ones. The other phases will almost always be needed, even if they vary in scope depending on the environment.

> **NOTE**
>
> Although projects can vary in scope and size, by and large Operations Manager projects will be compact projects. Ultimately, the project is deploying a monitoring platform to support the applications and is, thus, smaller than the application projects it is supporting.

This section looks at the following project elements:

- Major phases
- Major tasks
- Deliverables

These elements help define the project, ensuring that the project team can deliver the project scope on time and within the budget.

For the specifics steps on deploying Operations Manager 2012, see Chapter 7 and Chapter 8.

Design Principles Training

Before launching into the design and planning process, it is recommended to have an Operations Manager subject matter expert (SME) conduct a Microsoft Operations Manager training session for all team members. The session should introduce the technology components and principles of Operations Manager 2012 design, planning, and integration. The session helps to establish the basic criteria for the architectural elements of OpsMgr and bring all design participants up to the same level of knowledge. The session also allows for general Operations Manager technology questions to be addressed in advance of the design and planning sessions.

Design principles training for Operations Manager can be conducted in a daylong session, a 4-hour session, or even just an hour-long session. The length of the training very much depends on the scale of the project and the technological sophistication of the participants. For a large organization, a daylong session is recommended. For a small organization, an hour-long session is sufficient.

Conducting a design principles training session can make the design and planning sessions flow much smoother, as well as produce a much better design and plan.

Design and Planning Phase

During the design and planning phase, the project team works together to create an Operations Manager 2012 architecture and implementation plan that satisfies the business and technical requirements.

The architecture is usually created during a half-day to two-day design session that covers a host of Operations Manager design-related topics, including, but not limited to, the following:

- Business and technical goals and objectives
- Components
- Architecture
- Fault-tolerant strategy

- Disaster recovery strategy
- Configuration settings
- Integration
- Hardware specification
- Customization
- Administrative model
- Notification model
- Administration and maintenance procedures
- Documentation

The implementation plan is created during the planning session(s), which usually range from a half day to three days. The planning session covers the following topics:

- Phases
- Tasks
- Resources
- Timeline
- Risk identification and mitigation

The deliverable from the designand planning session is as follows:

- Design and planning document

The design and planning document communicates the results of the design and planning sessions. The outline of the design and planning document should include the following sections:

- Project overview
- Goals and objectives
- Architecture
- Configuration settings
- Integration
- Customization
- Administration model
- Notification model
- Fault tolerance and disaster recovery

- Project plan
- Phases
- Tasks
- Deliverables
- Resources
- Timeline
- Budget

The length of a design and planning document will vary according to the size of the organization and the complexity of the design and plan. A small organization might have 1–5 pages in length. Larger organizations and complex deployments will have a more detailed document of 20–50 pages in length.

Proof of Concept Phase

The proof of concept (POC) phase is essentially the lab phase, also known as the prototype phase. The POC phase begins with the building of a prototype lab. The prototype lab is typically an isolated simulated production environment. It should include all of the types of servers found in the production environment that could potentially affect connectivity and performance.

> **TIP**
>
> In today's modern IT environment, the POC lab can be built in a virtual environment even if the production environment will be all physical. This allows for the testing of the functionality of the design, but not the scalability of the design. It reduces the expense of the POC significantly to use virtual machines.

Some organizations might choose to forgo the expense of a POC and go directly into a production build. This makes sense for smaller organizations or projects with limited budgets.

> **NOTE**
>
> Operations Manager is a particularly good candidate for skipping the lab phase. The reason is that the Operations Manager infrastructure can be deployed into a production environment with little or no impact to the existing servers. Agents can be selectively deployed to only test systems, allowing the OpsMgr to be tested in production.

The POC lab should have a minimum set of servers needed to deploy Operations Manager and to test key management packs against application servers. The POC lab environment should include the following:

- ▶ Operations Manager servers

- ▶ Active Directory domain controllers

- ▶ Application servers

- ▶ Internet connectivity

The application servers can be servers such as Exchange or IIS servers, as well as LOB servers. Any application that requires testing should be included.

NOTE

The Operations Manager POC infrastructure does not need to be scaled to the full production environment depending on the scope of the POC. Some POCs will want to test and document deployment procedures, in which case a server configuration similar to the production environment is needed. If the POC is to test management pack functionality, a single OpsMgr server with all components can be deployed.

During the proof of concept phase, management packs will be tuned initially. These tuning options can be stored in override management packs, which can be exported and then imported into the production build.

Specific test plans will be developed during the lab build process. Testing areas should include the following:

- ▶ Interoperability

- ▶ Deployment

- ▶ Configuration

- ▶ Administration

- ▶ Notifications

- ▶ Failover capabilities

- ▶ Backup and recovery

The lab should exist throughout the entire project to allow testing and verification of configurations, with the primary usage during the POC phase. Once implementation completes, the lab can be scaled back as required.

The major tasks for the proof of concept phase include the following:

- ▶ Build servers in the lab

- ▶ Deploy Operations Manager infrastructure

- ▶ Create override management packs

- ▶ Create custom reports

▶ Create custom management packs

▶ Develop notification model

▶ Test functionality

▶ Test disaster recovery and fault tolerance

This list is definitely subject to change based on the specifics of the project, especially depending on the goals and objectives developed during the design and planning phase.

The deliverables for the proof of concept phase include the following:

▶ Working lab Operations Manager infrastructure

▶ Functionality (80%)

▶ Tuned management packs (50%)

▶ Build documentation

▶ Override management packs

▶ Notification model

▶ Administration model

▶ Issues database

The proof of concept phase, given its scaled-down nature, is unlikely to be able to deliver 100% of the production functionality due to missing applications and simplified architecture when compared with production. The 80% of functionality is a good target. The management pack tuning will likely only be at 50% at the end of the POC, as the production conditions that trigger alerts will not be seen in the lab.

It is also important to start an issues database during the POC phase, in which issues that arise are logged and solutions documented. This helps document the solutions and is a useful database to pass to the support teams, so they know what the solutions are to common problems. The issues log can be an actual SQL database or just an Excel spreadsheet. The issues log will be added to throughout the various phases.

> **NOTE**
>
> After building the lab environment, it frequently makes sense to leave the lab up and running. This lab provides a platform for testing deployments in a controlled setting before deploying them into production. The management packs can be tuned in the lab, the override settings exported, and then imported into the production Operations Manager environment. This reduces the risk of deploying new management packs or updates.

Pilot Phase

The goal of the pilot phase is to roll out the production Operations Manager 2012 infrastructure and deploy a subset of agents and sites in a limited production environment. This allows the functionality to be tested in the production environment and the impacts to servers assessed. Some key issues to assess include the following:

▶ Alert and notification noise

▶ Impact of agents on managed computers

▶ Performance of OpsMgr servers

▶ Database growth

Evaluating these and other metrics ensures that the Operations Manager infrastructure is performing as expected during the design and planning sessions.

The major tasks for the pilot phase include the following:

▶ Deploy production Operations Manager infrastructure

▶ Configure Operations Manager infrastructure

▶ Configure the administrative model

▶ Configure the notification model

▶ Import override management packs from proof of concept

▶ Deploy pilot agents (5%–10% of total servers)

▶ Conduct cross-training

▶ Tune management packs

Servers and sites scheduled for deployment in this phase should be a representative sample that includes extremes. The number of agents to deploy in the pilot phase can vary, but a good rule of thumb is to target 5%–10% of the total number of servers in production.

Management pack tuning is a critical task in this phase, while the number of agents is still low and the overall volume of alerts is low. This will pay big dividends when the balances of the agents are deployed in the production phase.

> **NOTE**
>
> The goal of management pack tuning is to get to a notification-to-trouble ticket ratio of 1:1. This means that every notification that is generated is an actionable alert and is not a false-positive or duplicated. In a real-world deployment, this can be a tough standard to meet as alerts and notification can be noisy. The more effectively tuned a management pack is, the closer it approaches the 1:1 ratio.

The deliverables for the pilot phase include the following:

▶ Working production Operations Manager infrastructure

▶ Agents deployed (5%–10%)

▶ Functionality (100%)

▶ Tuned management packs (80%)

▶ Updated documents

▶ Cross-training

▶ Issues database (90%)

All the functionality of the Operations Manager 2012 infrastructure should have been deployed by the end of the pilot phase. As there will be only 10% of the agents deployed, the tuning will only be at 80% or so.

Production Phase

With successful proof of concept and pilot phases, the production phase should be well understood and offer few surprises. The main purpose of the production phase is to deploy agents, which at this stage in the project should have relatively low risk. Any major issues or concerns will have been uncovered in the proof of concept and pilot phases.

The major tasks for the production phase include the following:

▶ Deploy agents

▶ Conduct cross-training

▶ Tune management packs

In this final phase, the various tasks that were in progress from previous phases (such as the management pack tuning, agent deployment, and issues database) will be finalized. The deliverables for the production phase include the following:

▶ Agent deployed (100%)

▶ Tuned management packs (100%)

▶ Cross-training

▶ Issues database (100%)

▶ Transition to support

By the conclusion of the production phase, the Operations Manager infrastructure should be completely tuned and ready to hand over to support. The transition to support is a critical point in the project, as the staff assuming the support and maintenance of the Operations Manager infrastructure should be cross-trained on the procedure to ensure that the infrastructure continues to operate at 100%.

> **NOTE**
>
> Even though the tuning is complete at the time of transitioning to support, management pack tuning is an ongoing process. As the production environment changes, servers are added, applications are changed, and management packs are updated, then alert and notification noise levels will rise. This requires additional tuning over time.

Time Estimates

The time needed per phase on any given project will vary according to the size of the organization, the organization culture, the scope of the project, and the complexity of the project.

Table 6.19 provides some estimates of times needed to execute the phase for small, medium, and large organizations.

TABLE 6.19   Sample Project Time Estimates

Phase	Small	Medium	Large
Design principles training	1 hour	4 hours	1 day
Design and planning phase	1 day	2 days	1 week
Proof of concept phase	N/A	N/A	2 weeks
Pilot phase	N/A	1 week	1 month
Production phase	1 week	2 weeks	1 month

For some of the organization sizes, certain phases are not normally done. For example, a small organization will likely move from the design phase directly into a production deployment phase. There would be no need for a proof of concept or pilot phase with a small organization. This is reflected in the table.

Summary

System Center Operations Manager 2012 is key to managing IT environments, and a solid design and plan are key to a successful Operations Manager infrastructure. Understanding the components of Operations Manager, their interactions, and their constraints is critical to designing and deploying an effective infrastructure. This type of functionality is instrumental in reducing downtime and getting the most out of an OpsMgr investment.

Best Practices

The following are best practices from this chapter:

▸ Always create a design and plan when deploying Operations Manager, even if it is a simple one.

▸ Take future expansion and relevance of hardware into account when sizing servers for OpsMgr deployment.

▸ Keep the installation of OpsMgr on a separate server or set of separate dedicated member servers that do not run any other separate applications.

▸ Start with a single management group and add on additional management groups only if they are absolutely necessary.

▸ Use Windows 2008 R2 SP1 and SQL 2008 R2 together to gain maximum performance from both.

▸ Use SQL Enterprise when combining components on the same server.

▸ Use SQL Enterprise when scaling up Operations Manager.

▸ Deploy ACS on separate servers if possible.

▸ Allocate adequate space for the databases depending on the length of time needed to store events and the number of managed systems.

▸ Leverage the reporting database to store and report on data over a long period.

▸ Always create disaster recovery processes to restore in the event of a failure.

▸ Deploy fault tolerance (that is, clusters) only when needed.

▸ Size the disk subsystems to provide sufficient IOps to support the anticipated data flows.

▸ Use SANs where possible for the improved IOps and throughput.

▸ Configure OpsMgr to monitor itself.

CHAPTER 7

Operations Manager 2012 Implementation and Administration

IN THIS CHAPTER

▶ Installing Operations Manager 2012

▶ Deploying OpsMgr Agents

▶ Monitoring DMZ Servers with Certificates

▶ Configuring Operations Manager 2012

▶ Administering Operations Manager 2012

▶ Backing Up OpsMgr 2012

▶ Best Practices

System Center Operations Manager (OpsMgr) 2012 provides the best-of-breed approach to monitoring and managing servers, applications, and devices. However, to ensure that OpsMgr is able to provide that best-of-breed functionality, it is critical that the OpsMgr infrastructure be properly

- ▶ Installed

- ▶ Configured

- ▶ Maintained

Without these three pillars, the OpsMgr infrastructure cannot be guaranteed to perform properly.

This chapter covers the installation, configuration, and administration of Operations Manager 2012. The installation is performed for two specific scenarios:

- ▶ Small organization

- ▶ Medium organization

These two scenarios were designed in Chapter 6, "Operations Manager 2012 Design and Planning." This chapter picks up where that chapter left off and implements those two designs. This chapter also includes the installation of the Audit Collection Services (ACS) to monitor security events.

The chapter also covers the common configuration points needed for all OpsMgr installations with best-practices guidance. Finally, the chapter covers best-practices maintenance and administration tasks needed to ensure a healthy OpsMgr infrastructure.

Installing Operations Manager 2012

Operations Manager 2012 is a multitier and multicomponent application that can be deployed in a variety of architectures. This allows OpsMgr to support scaling from a small organization to a very large enterprise.

Three different installations are performed in this section:

▶ A small organization install on a single server

▶ A small organization upgrade from a single server

▶ A medium-sized organization install on two servers

These installations correspond to the small and medium organization designs that were presented in Chapter 6.

In addition, the installation of ACS on a separate set of servers is performed.

Single-Server OpsMgr 2012 Install

This section steps through the install of OpsMgr and Reporting Server on a single-server configuration. There will be a single server named OM1 with all the components. Figure 7.1 shows the architecture for the small organization build.

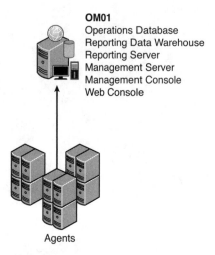

OM01
Operations Database
Reporting Data Warehouse
Reporting Server
Management Server
Management Console
Web Console

Agents

FIGURE 7.1   Operations Manager 2012 small enterprise architecture.

The specification for a single-server configuration of OM1 to support the small organization is as follows:

▶ 4 cores

▶ 8GB of RAM

▶ 4-disk RAID 10 for data and 2-disk RAID 1 for logs

These hardware requirements ensure that the system can perform to specification.

> **NOTE**
>
> If the configuration were to be virtualized on a Windows Server 2008 R2 Hyper-V host, a single-server configuration is not recommended. Instead, a two-server configuration is recommended and SQL Server 2008 R2 should be installed on the second server to balance the load. See the section "Multiserver OpsMgr 2012 Install" later in this chapter.

The steps in this section assume that the single server has been prepared with the following:

▶ Windows Server 2008 R2 SP1 operating system installed

▶ Microsoft Core XML Services (MSXML) version 6.0

▶ Microsoft Report Viewer 2008 SP1 Redistributable

▶ Web Server (IIS) role with the appropriate role services installed

▶ .NET Framework 3.5.1 feature installed

▶ .NET Framework 4.0

▶ SQL Server 2008 SP1, SQL Server 2008 R2, or SQL Server 2008 R2 SP1 with Reporting Services installed

▶ SQL Collation: SQL_Latin1_General_CP1_CI_AS

▶ SQL Server Full Text Search required

▶ An OpsMgr service account with local administrator rights to the server and system administrator rights to SQL Server 2008

> **NOTE**
>
> It is recommended to install the IIS role before installing .NET Framework 4.0; otherwise, the ASP.NET 4.0 will need to be registered with IIS manually. To register ASP.NET 4.0 manually, execute the following command:
> `c:\windows\Microsoft.NET\Framework64\v4.0.30319\aspnet_regiis.exe -r`

To support the OpsMgr 2012 Web Console role, the following Web Server role services are needed:

- ▶ Static Content
- ▶ Default Document
- ▶ Directory Browsing
- ▶ HTTP Errors
- ▶ HTTP Logging
- ▶ Request Monitor
- ▶ Request Filtering
- ▶ Static Content Compression
- ▶ ASP.NET
- ▶ ISAPI Extensions
- ▶ ISAPI Filters
- ▶ .NET Extensibility
- ▶ Windows Authentication
- ▶ IIS 6 Metabase Compatibility

The first eight (8) are selected by default when adding the Web Server role to Windows Server 2008; the other role services must be added manually.

This prepares the system for the install of OpsMgr 2012. Once the server meets all the prerequisites and is ready for installation, complete the following steps to run the install:

1. Log on with the OpsMgr service account.

2. Launch Setup.exe from the OpsMgr installation media.

3. Click Install Hyperlink.

4. Select the features to install; in this example, check all the boxes. These are Management Server, Management Console, Web Console, and Reporting Server.

5. Click Next.

6. Select the installation location and click Next.

7. The prerequisites will be checked. Remediate any issues or click Next to continue if passed.

NOTE

On the Prerequisites screen, the Review Full System Requirements link can be clicked to launch a browser window to see the full list of requirements for each component.

8. Type the management group name in the Management Group text box and click Next.

9. Accept the license agreement and click Next.

10. Enter the server name and the instance of SQL Server on which to install the Operations Manager 2012 operations database, and then click the Tab key to populate the database fields.

11. Leave the default database name "OperationsManager" and size of 1,000MB. Change the data and log file locations if appropriate, and then click Next.

12. Enter the server name and the instance of SQL Server on which to install the Operations Manager 2012 data warehouse database, and then click the Tab key to populate the database fields.

13. Leave the default database name "OperationsManagerDW" and size of 1,000MB. Change the data and log file locations if appropriate, and then click Next.

14. Choose the SQL Reporting Services instance and click Next.

15. Choose the Default website to use for the Web console and click Next.

16. Leave the default selection Use Mixed Authentication and click Next.

17. Enter the account information for the Management Server Action Account, Data Reader Account, and Data Writer Account, and then click Next.

> **NOTE**
>
> If there is an action account warning pop-up, click OK to clear the warning.

18. At the Health Improve Operations Manager 2012 screen, check the appropriate options and click Next to continue.

19. At the Microsoft Update screen, select the recommended On option button.

20. At the Installation Summary screen, review the selections and click Install to continue.

21. Once setup is complete, click Close to exit the installation wizard.

Operations Manager 2012 is now installed in a single-server configuration. Although the small organization design was created for 30 servers, this configuration can manage up to 250 servers.

Multiserver OpsMgr 2012 Install

This section steps through the install of OpsMgr and Reporting Server on a two-server configuration to support a medium-sized organization. The infrastructure is designed to support up to 500 agent systems, as specified in the medium organization design in Chapter 6. There will be two servers, with the management server named OM1 and the database server named OM2. Figure 7.2 shows the architecture for the medium-sized organization build.

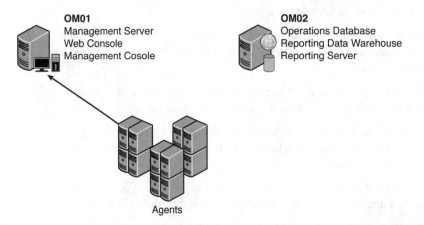

FIGURE 7.2   Operations Manager 2012 medium enterprise architecture.

The hardware specification for the management server OM1 configuration is as follows:

▶ 2 cores

▶ 4GB of RAM

▶ 2-disk RAID 1

The steps in this section assume that the management server OM1 has been prepared with the following:

▶ Windows Server 2008 R2 SP1 operating system installed

▶ MSXML version 6.0

▶ Web Server (IIS) role with the appropriate role services installed

▶ Microsoft Report Viewer 2008 SP1

▶ .NET Framework 3.5.1 feature installed

▶ .NET Framework 4.0

▶ An OpsMgr service account with local administrator rights to the server and system administrator rights to SQL Server 2008

NOTE

It is recommended to install the Internet Information Service (IIS) role before installing .NET Framework 4.0; otherwise, the ASP.NET 4.0 will need to be registered with IIS manually. To register ASP.NET 4.0 manually, execute the following command:
`c:\windows\Microsoft.NET\Framework64\v4.0.30319\aspnet_regiis.exe -r`

To support the OpsMgr 2012 Web Console role, the following Web Server role services are needed on the management server OM1:

▶ Static Content

▶ Default Document

▶ Directory Browsing

▶ HTTP Errors

▶ HTTP Logging

▶ Request Monitor

▶ Request Filtering

▶ Static Content Compression

▶ ASP.NET

▶ ISAPI Extensions

▶ ISAPI Filters

▶ .NET Extensibility Windows Authentication

▶ IIS 6 Metabase Compatibility

The first eight (8) are selected by default when adding the Web Server role to Windows Server 2008; the other role services must be added manually.

NOTE

The Web Console role requires that the ISAPI and CGI restrictions be allowed for ASP.NET 4.0. This can be done by selecting the web server in the IIS Manager tool and opening the ISAPI and CGI restrictions feature. Click the two ASP.NET v4.0.30319 options and select Allow for each one (as shown in Figure 7.3).

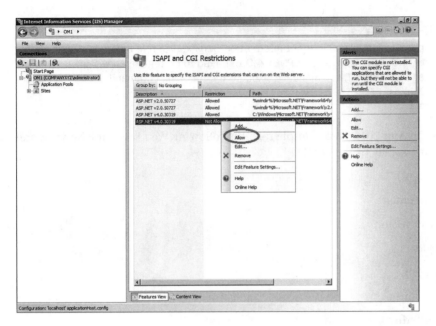

FIGURE 7.3   Allow ISAPI and CGI for ASP .NET 4.0.

The hardware specification for the database server OM2 configuration is as follows:

▶ 4 cores

▶ 4GB of RAM

▶ 6-disk RAID 10 for data and 2-disk RAID 1 for logs

These hardware requirements ensure that the system can perform to specification.

The steps in this section assume that the database server has been prepared with the following:

▶ Windows Server 2008 R2 SP1 operating system installed

▶ SQL Server 2008 with Reporting Services installed

▶ SQL_Latin1_General_CP1_CI_AS Collation selected

▶ SQL Server Full Text Search installed

▶ .NET Framework 3.5.1 feature installed

▶ .NET Framework 4.0

▶ An OpsMgr service account with local administrator rights to the server and system administrator rights to SQL Server 2008

This prepares the system for the installation of OpsMgr 2012.

Because the install is on separate servers, this requires that the installations take place in a specific order. The order of installation is in two parts:

1. Management Server, Management Console, and Web console components—This will also install the operational database and data warehouse database components.

2. Reporting Server component—This will install the report engine that pulls data from the data warehouse database. This step must be run on the server that will hold the Reporting Server role.

The first part is to install the Management Server, Management Console, and Web console components. Once the servers meet all the prerequisites and are ready for installation, the steps to run the install are as follows:

1. Log on to the management server (OM1 in this example) with the OpsMgr service account.

2. Launch Setup.exe from the OpsMgr installation media.

3. Click Install at the System Center 2012 Operations Manager splash screen, as shown in Figure 7.4.

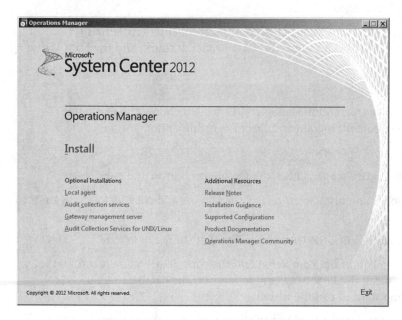

FIGURE 7.4   Operations Manager 2012 installation screen.

4. At the Select Features to Install screen, check off the options: Management Server, Management Console, and Web Console.

5. Click Next.

6. At the Select Installation Location screen, enter the installation location and click Next.

7. Verify the prerequisites have been met and remediate if necessary, and then click Next.

8. Enter a management group name, in this case **COMPANYXYZ**, and then click Next.

9. Accept the license agreement and click Next.

10. Enter the operational database server name and instance, in this case **OM2**. The wizard will automatically initiate a check of the target database server.

11. Leave the database name at the default OperationsManager. Change the data file and log file locations if necessary, and then click Next.

12. Enter the data warehouse database server name and instance, in this case **OM2**. The wizard will automatically initiate a check of the target database server.

13. Leave the database name at the default OperationsManagerDW. Change the data file and log file locations if necessary, and then click Next.

14. Leave the Default Web Site option selected and click Next.

15. Leave the Use Mixed Authentication option selected for the Web console authentication mode and click Next.

16. At the Configure Operations Manager Accounts screen, enter credentials for the Management Server Action Account, the Data Reader Account, and the Data Writer Account.

17. Click Next.

18. At the Help Improve Operations Manager 2012 screen, choose the Customer Experience Improvement Program and Error Reporting options.

19. Click Next.

20. At the Microsoft Update screen, check the On option button and click Next.

21. At the Installation Summary screen, review the choices and click Install to begin the installation.

22. Once setup completes, click the Close button to exit the Setup Wizard.

The first part of the installation has completed and the console will launch automatically. The second part is to install the Reporting components on the database server OM2. Complete the following steps to run the install:

1. Log on to the database server (OM2 in this example) with the OpsMgr service account.

2. Launch Setup.exe from the OpsMgr installation media.

3. Click Install at the System Center 2012 Operations Manager splash screen.

4. At the Select Features to Install screen, only check the Reporting Server option.

5. Click Next.

6. At the Select Installation Location screen, enter the installation location and click Next.

7. Verify the prerequisites have been met and remediate if necessary, and then click Next.

8. Enter a management server name, in this case **OM1**, and then click Next.

9. Choose the SQL Server instance for Reporting Services and click Next.

10. Enter the credentials for the Data Reader Account and click Next.

11. At the Help Improve Operations Manager 2012 screen, choose the Operational Data Reporting option and click Next.

12. At the Microsoft Update screen, check the On option button and click Next.

13. At the Installation Summary screen, review the choices and click Install to begin the installation.

14. Once setup completes, click the Close button to exit the Setup Wizard.

Operations Manager 2012 is now installed in a multiserver configuration. This configuration can manage up to 500 servers.

NOTE

The Operations Console will need to be closed and reopened to see the newly installed reports in the console.

Importing Management Packs

After the initial installation, OpsMgr only includes a few core management packs. The management packs contain all the discoveries, monitors, rules, knowledge, reports, and views that OpsMgr needs to be able to effectively monitor servers and applications. One of the first tasks after installing OpsMgr 2012 is to import management packs into the system.

A large number of management packs are in the Internet catalog on the Microsoft website. These include updated management packs, management packs for new products, and third-party management packs. It is important to load only those management packs that are going to be used, as each additional management pack increases the database size, adds discoveries that impact the performance of agents, and, in general, clutters up the interface.

The key management packs for a Windows environment are as follows:

- Windows Server Operating System MPs
- Active Directory Server MPs
- Windows Cluster Management MPs
- Microsoft Windows DNS Server MPs
- Microsoft Windows DHCP Server MPs
- Microsoft Windows Group Policy MPs
- Microsoft Windows Hyper-V MPs
- Windows Server Internet Information Services MPs
- Windows Server Network Load Balancing MPs
- Windows Server Print Server MPs
- Windows Terminal Services MPs
- SQL Server MPs (to monitor the OpsMgr database roles)

If the OpsMgr 2012 infrastructure will be supporting UNIX/Linux agents, then the appropriate System Center UNIX/Linux Monitoring management packs will need to be downloaded. These are organized by platform type and include the following:

- AIX Operating System MPs
- HP UNIX Operating System MPs
- Linux Operating Systems MPs
- Solaris Operating System MPs

The core UNIX monitoring management packs are loaded by default at installation, so only the specific platform management packs and language management packs need to be imported from the catalog.

> **NOTE**
>
> The specific UNIX/Linux platform management packs will need to be imported before installing the UNIX/Linux agents. Otherwise, the UNIX/Linux agent discovery will fail.

There might be other management packs that are appropriate for the environment, depending on the applications that are installed. For example, if the organization has deployed Exchange Server 2010 and HP Proliant server hardware, it would be good for the organization to deploy the Exchange management packs and the HP Proliant management packs.

For each of these management packs, it is important to load the relevant versions only. For example, if the environment includes Windows Server 2008 only, only load the Windows Server Core OS 2008 Management Pack. If the environment includes both Windows Server 2003 and Windows Server 2008, load both the Windows Server Core OS 2003 and the Windows Server Core OS 2008 Management Packs. In addition, a number of language packs don't need to be loaded unless those particular languages are supported by the organization at the server level.

Some collections of management packs require that all versions be loaded, but the Management Pack Import Wizard checks and warns if that's the case.

In versions of OpsMgr prior to 2007 R2, the management packs had to be downloaded from the Microsoft website one by one, the MSI installed one by one, and the management packs imported one by one. Dependencies would not be checked unless additional steps were taken to consolidate the management pack files prior to importing. This was a very labor-intensive process. Also, there was no easy way to check for updates to previously installed management packs.

In OpsMgr 2012, a new Management Pack Import Wizard was introduced. This wizard connects directly to the Microsoft management pack catalog and downloads, checks, and imports management packs. It even does version checks to ensure that the management packs are the latest versions. This is a huge improvement over the old method of importing management packs.

To import the key management packs, use the following steps:

1. Launch the Operations Console.

2. Select the Administration section.

3. Select the Management Packs folder.

4. Right-click the Management Packs folder and select Import Management Packs.

5. Click Add and select Add from Catalog.

6. Click the Search button to search the entire catalog.

> **NOTE**
>
> The View pull-down menu in the Management Pack Import Wizard includes four options, which are All Management Packs in the Catalog, Updates Available for Installed Management Packs, All Management Packs Released in the Last 3 Months, and All Management Packs Released in the Last 6 Months. The Updates option checks against the previously installed management packs and allows the download of updated versions of those.

7. Select the key management packs from the previous bulleted list and click Add for each of them. Each of the major management packs might include a number of submanagement packs for discovery, monitoring, and other breakdowns of functionality.

8. When done adding management packs, click OK.

9. The wizard now validates the added management packs, checking for versions, dependencies, and security risks. It allows problem management packs to be removed and dependencies to be added to the list.

10. Click Install to begin the download and import process. Progress is shown for each of the management packs being imported.

11. After all the management packs are imported, click Close to exit the wizard.

After the import completes, the management packs take effect immediately. Agents begin discovering based on the schedule specified in the management packs and monitors and rules begin deploying.

See Chapter 8, "Using Operations Manager 2012 for Monitoring and Alerting," for detailed instructions on installing management packs and configuring them for optimal performance.

OpsMgr 2012 Audit Collection Services Install

ACS collects security events from the security log of agents configured as alert forwarders. This can be quite a heavy load, so the ACS functionality is typically installed on separate servers to avoid impacting the operational data collection and alerting.

There will be two servers in this example, with the audit collection server named ACS1 and the audit database server named ACS2. To be able to launch ACS reports directly from the Operations Manager console, the ACS report model will be installed on the OpsMgr 2012 server with the Reporting Server role. In this case, that is the OM2 server.

Figure 7.5 shows the architecture for the ACS build.

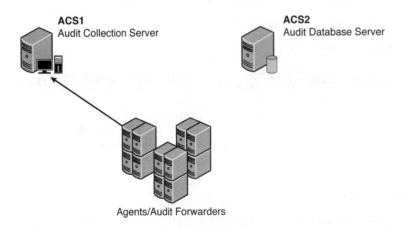

FIGURE 7.5   Operations Manager 2012 ACS architecture.

> **NOTE**
>
> The ACS architecture and build are essentially the same for small, medium, and even large organizations. The differences are only in the size and configuration of the audit database server disk subsystem.

The hardware specification for the ACS1 audit collection server configuration is as follows:

- ▶ 2 cores
- ▶ 4GB of RAM
- ▶ 2-disk RAID 1

The steps in this section assume that the audit collection server ACS1 has been prepared with the following:

- ▶ Windows Server 2008 R2 SP1 operating system installed
- ▶ Web Server (IIS) role
- ▶ .NET Framework 3.5.1 feature installed
- ▶ .NET Framework 4.0
- ▶ An OpsMgr service account with local administrator rights to the server and system administrator rights to SQL Server 2008 R2

The hardware specification for the ACS2 audit database server configuration is as follows:

- ▶ 4 cores
- ▶ 4GB of RAM
- ▶ 6-disk RAID 10 for data and 2-disk RAID 1 for logs

These hardware requirements ensure that the system can perform to specification.

The steps in this section assume that the database server ACS2 has been prepared with the following:

- ▶ Windows Server 2008 R2 SP1 operating system installed
- ▶ SQL_Latin1_General_CP1_CI_AS Collation selected
- ▶ SQL Server Full Text Search installed
- ▶ .NET Framework 3.5.1 feature installed
- ▶ .NET Framework 4.0
- ▶ An OpsMgr service account with local administrator rights to the server and system administrator rights to SQL Server 2008 R2

> **NOTE**
>
> Although the configuration will work with either SQL Server Enterprise or SQL Server Standard Edition, SQL Server Enterprise Edition is the preferred choice due to the performance improvements. See Chapter 6 for details.

There are three parts to the installation of the ACS functionality. These parts, in the order of execution, are as follows:

1. Management Server component install

2. Audit collection server install

3. ACS report model install

The first part is to install the OpsMgr 2012 Management Server component on the audit collection server ACS1, which is needed for the ACS collector to function. All ACS collectors are also management servers.

Once the audit collection server meets all the prerequisites and is ready for installation, complete the following steps to run the install:

1. Log on to the management server (ACS1 in this example) with the OpsMgr service account.

2. Launch `Setup.exe` from the OpsMgr installation media.

3. Click Install at the System Center 2012 Operations Manager splash screen.

4. At the Select Features to Install screen, check off the Management Server options.

5. Click Next.

6. At the Select Installation Location screen, enter the installation location and click Next.

7. Verify the prerequisites have been met and remediate if necessary, and then click Next.

8. At the Specify an Installation Option screen, choose the Add a Management Server to an Existing Management Group option, and then click Next.

9. Enter the operational database server name and instance, in this case `OM2`. The wizard will automatically initiate a check of the target database server.

10. In the Database Name drop-down, choose the OperationsManager database and click Next.

11. At the Configure Operations Manager Accounts screen, enter credentials for the Management Server Action Account, the Data Reader Account, and the Data Writer Account, and then click Next.

12. If there is a security warning, accept it and proceed.

13. At the Microsoft Update screen, check the On option button and click Next.

14. At the Installation Summary screen, review the choices and click Install to begin the installation.

15. When setup completes, click the Close button to exit the Setup Wizard.

The second part of the ACS installation is the audit collection server install on ACS1, which also creates the audit collection database.

> **NOTE**
>
> Before installing the audit collection database, firewall ports need to be opened per the Microsoft Knowledge Base article at http://support.microsoft.com/kb/968872.

Once the appropriate firewall ports have been opened, complete the following steps to install ACS:

1. Log on to the audit collection server (ACS1) with the OpsMgr service account.

2. Launch Setup.exe from the OpsMgr 2012 installation media.

3. From the Optional Installations section, click Audit Collection Services.

4. Click Next.

5. Accept the license agreement and click Next.

6. Select Create a New Database and click Next.

7. Leave the data source name at the default (OpsMgrAC) and click Next.

8. Enter the audit database server name (**ACS2** in this example), leave the default database name of OperationsManagerAC, and then click Next.

9. Select Windows Authentication and click Next.

10. Specify the database and log file locations. These need to be created beforehand. Then click Next.

11. On the Event Retention Schedule page, note that the daily database maintenance will take place at 2:00 a.m. and that the default number of days to retain data is 14. Accept the defaults by clicking Next.

> **WARNING**
>
> Changing the default retention can have a large impact on the size of the audit database. ACS collects large quantities of events, so increasing the retention window can create very large databases. Only change after careful review. See Chapter 6 for details on sizing the databases.

12. Leave the Time Stamp Format at Local and click Next.

13. Click Next to start the install.

14. At the SQL Server Login pop-up, click OK to use the existing credentials or enter credentials to use.

> **NOTE**
>
> These credentials are used to connect to the remote database server and set up the OperationsManagerAC database. They need appropriate rights to the remote database server.

15. Click Finish to exit the wizard.

The third part of the installation is the ACS Report Model install, which provides access to the database via reports. This is done on the Operations Manager Reporting Server (OM2 in this example) to allow for full integration into the Operations Manager console. The model install is done via command line, rather than a wizard. The command line takes the format:

```
UploadAuditReports.cmd {DatabaseServer\Instance} {ReportingServiceURL} {Report-
Folder}
```

In this example, the database server is the ACS2 audit database server, the Reporting Service URL is https://om2.companyabc.com/ReportServer, and the report folder is d:\ReportModels\acs. To install the reports, use the following steps:

1. Log on to the database server (OM2 in this example) with the OpsMgr service account.

2. Insert the OpsMgr installation media.

3. Copy the \ReportModels\acs\ files into a temporary folder c:\acs.

4. Open a command prompt, using Start, Run, cmd.

5. Enter the command **cd \acs** to change to the ACS report models directory.

6. Enter the command **UploadAuditReports "ACS2"** **"http://om2.companyabc.com/ReportServer"** **"C:\acs"** and press Enter to execute the command.

The results will be as follows:

```
C:\>cd \acs
C:\acs>cd \ReportModels\acs
C:\acs>UploadAuditReports "ACS2"
"https://om2/ReportServer" "C:\acs"
Warning(s) Loading file d:\ReportModels\asc\Models\Audit.smdl:
```

```
Warning(s) Loading file d:\ReportModels\asc\Models\Audit5.smdl:
c:\acs>
```

The warnings are normal and do not indicate a problem. After executing the command, in the Operations Manager console in the Reporting space, there will be a new folder named "Audit Reports" with 25 reports. The ASC infrastructure is now deployed and ready for use.

> **NOTE**
>
> Although the ACS infrastructure has been deployed, no audit forwarders have been configured and, thus, no security data will be collected. In the next section, agents are configured as audit forwarders to enable the collection of security events.

Deploying OpsMgr Agents

OpsMgr agents are deployed to all managed servers through the OpsMgr Discovery Wizard, or by using software distribution mechanisms such as Active Directory Group Policy Objects (GPOs) or System Center Configuration Manager 2012. Installation through the Operations Console uses the fully qualified domain name (FQDN) of the computer. When searching for systems through the Operations Console, you can use wildcards to locate a broad range of computers for agent installation. Certain situations, such as monitoring across firewalls, can require the manual installation of these components.

The Discovery Wizard can discover and configure monitoring for Windows computers, UNIX/Linux computers, and for network devices. It will push agents to Windows and UNIX/Linux computers, as long as the proper rights are provided, such as an account with local administrator rights or a root account.

Installing Windows Agents

Generally, there are three ways to deploy agents: The first is using software distribution such as Microsoft System Center Configuration Manager or Active Directory GPOs, the second is manual installation using the product media, and the third and most common way is using the System Center Operations Manager (SCOM) Discovery Wizard to search for and install agents on domain members by executing the following steps:

1. Launch the Operations Console and select the Administration section.

2. Right-click the top-level Administration folder and select Discovery Wizard.

3. Select Windows Computers and click Next.

4. Select Automatic Computer Discovery and click Next. This scans the entire Active Directory domain for computers.

5. Leave the Use Selected Management Server Action Account selected and click Discover. This starts the discovery process.

6. After the discovery process runs (this might take a few minutes), the list of discovered computers is displayed. Select the devices that should have agents deployed to them, as shown in Figure 7.6.

> **NOTE**
>
> The list only includes systems that do not already have agents installed. If a computer has an agent installed, the wizard excludes it from the list of devices.

FIGURE 7.6   Discovered computers.

7. Click Next.

8. Leave the Agent Installation Directory and the Agent Action Account at the defaults, and then click Finish.

9. The Agent Management Task Status window opens, listing all the computers selected and the progress of each installation. As shown in Figure 7.7, the agent installation task started for the selected computers. The ACS2, CM2, and VMM1 agents have been installed successfully and the others are in progress.

10. Click Close when the installation completes.

Even if the window is closed before the installs complete, the results of the installs can be viewed in Task Status view in the Monitoring section of the Operations Console.

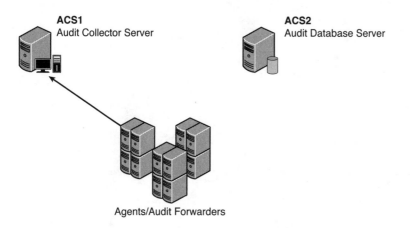

FIGURE 7.7   Agent installation progress.

The agent deployment is very efficient and a large number of computers can be selected for deployment without any issues. The agents start automatically and begin to be monitored as they are discovered.

After installation, it might be necessary to wait a few minutes before the information from the agents is sent to the management server.

During the next few minutes after installation, the agent contacts the management server and establishes a mutually authenticated, encrypted communication channel with the assigned management server. If the agent was pushed through a software delivery system such as System Center Configuration Manager 2012, the agent determines the management server through command-line options or Active Directory–integrated discovery.

Figure 7.8 shows the state of the agents after deployment. The computers show the Agent or Management Server state as healthy. However, the Windows Operating System state shows as Not Monitored. This is because there have been no additional management packs imported on this newly installed Operations Manager infrastructure. Management packs must be imported and configured for OpsMgr to monitor additional objects like the Windows operating systems. See Chapter 8 for detailed instructions on importing, configuring, and using management packs.

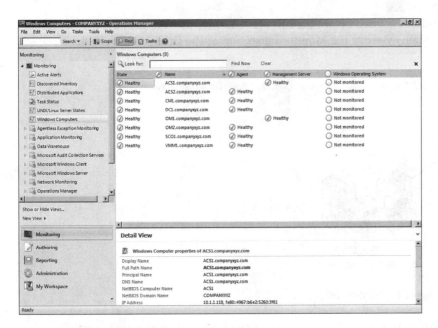

FIGURE 7.8   Agent state in a new infrastructure.

Once management packs are imported, the agent downloads rules to discover the various applications and components it's hosting, allowing the correct application-specific management packs to be applied.

This discovery process runs periodically to ensure the correct rules are always applied to the server.

Configuring Alert Forwarders

The Audit Collection Services does not start collecting security event data after installation of the audit collection server. The audit collection server install creates the following ACS components:

▶ Audit collection

▶ Audit collection database

It does not enable the third ACS component, which is the

▶ Audit forwarder

The audit forwarder is installed with each agent and the service is the System Center Audit Forwarding service, but is disabled by default, as shown in Figure 7.9. The service must be enabled through the console, which configures the audit forwarder to send security events to the correct audit collector and enables the service.

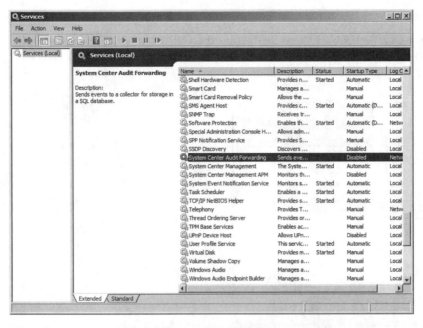

FIGURE 7.9   Disabled Audit Forwarding service.

The steps to enable the Audit Forwarder component and, thus, enable audit collection are done on an agent-by-agent basis. To enable audit collection, complete the following steps:

1. Launch the Operations Manager console.

2. Select the Monitoring space.

3. Expand the Operations Manager folder.

4. Expand the Agent Details folder.

5. Select the Agent Health State view.

> **NOTE**
>
> Management servers are not displayed in the Agent Health State view. To enable audit collection for management servers, select the Management Server, Management Server Health State view.

6. Select an agent in the Agent State pane.

7. Click on Enable Audit Collection in the Health Service Tasks in the Actions pane.

> **NOTE**
>
> Up to 10 agents can be enabled at the same time by holding down the Ctrl key and clicking to select agents, then clicking on the Enable Audit Collection action. However, if more than 10 agents are selected, the UI disables the action.

8. In the Run Task – Enable Audit Collection window, click the Override button.

9. In the Collection Server New Value field, enter the FQDN name of the audit collector (in this example, the audit collector is **ACS1.companyxyz.com**) and click Override to save. The window should look similar to Figure 7.10.

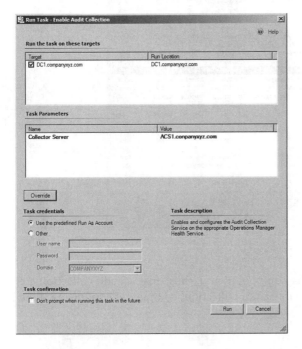

FIGURE 7.10   Enable Audit Collection task with override set.

10. Click the Run button to run the task to enable the Audit Forwarder component on the selected agent.

11. The Task Status window shows the progress of the task and eventually a status of Success.

12. Click Close to close the status window.

NOTE

The status window can be closed immediately without impacting the task execution. The status can be later reviewed in the top-level Task Status view in the console.

After the task completes, the Operations Manager Audit Forwarding service starts and is set to Automatic. The audit forwarders begin sending security events to the audit collector immediately. This includes security events that were logged prior to the service starting, so there will be an initial spike in traffic associated with the audit collection.

The status of the audit collector and audit forwarders can be viewed in the Operations Manager console. There are State views in the Collector folder and the Forwarder folder in the Microsoft Audit Collection Services folder in the Monitoring space of the Operations Console. These views do not report on the security events collected, but only on the state of the collection mechanisms.

The only access to the security information being collected is via the Reporting Services reports. See Chapter 9, "Using Operations Manager 2012 for Operations and Security Reporting," for details on how to generate ACS reports and review the security information.

Installing UNIX/Linux Agents

The OpsMgr UNIX/Linux agent can be deployed in much the same way as a Windows agent. The UNIX/Linux agent has dependencies that vary by the specific operating system. The dependencies can be found online on the Microsoft website at the following link: http://technet.microsoft.com/en-us/library/dd789030.aspx. These dependencies vary greatly from version to version and include the following required components:

▶ Packages

▶ Minimum versions

▶ Patches

Although the agent deployment is straightforward, getting the UNIX/Linux hosts up to the required levels might not be. These systems are frequently not kept updated after the initial deployments, so the UNIX/Linux application servers can get far behind in their patch levels over time.

> **NOTE**
>
> The agent install checks the dependencies and fails if they are not met. The error message helpfully lists the specific dependencies that failed.

By way of example, the dependencies for IBM AIX 5.3 and IBM AIX 6.1 are given in Tables 7.1 and 7.2.

TABLE 7.1   IBM AIX 5L 5.3 Dependencies

Required Package	Description	Minimum Version
OS version	Version of operating system	AIX 5.3, Technology Level 6, Service Pack 5
xlC.rte	XL C/C++ Runtime	9.0.0.2
openssl.base	OpenSSL Libraries; Secure Network Communications Protocol	0.9.8.4

TABLE 7.2   IBM AIX 6.1 Dependencies

Required Package	Description	Minimum Version
OS version	Version of operating system	AIX 6.1, any technology level and service pack
xlC.rte	XL C/C++ Runtime	9.0.0.5
OpenSSL/openssl.base	OpenSSL Libraries; Secure Network Communications Protocol	0.9.8.4

The UNIX/Linux agent installation is very similar to the Windows agent installation. They both use the Discovery Wizard and can be pushed from the Operations Console.

> **NOTE**
>
> This is in keeping with Microsoft's stated goal of having UNIX/Linux cross-platform agents be full citizens in the Operations Manager 2012 environment. There should be no fundamental difference between installing a Windows agent and installing a UNIX/Linux agent.

There are four tasks to UNIX agent installation, mainly due to separate root password issues. The tasks are:

1. Create RunAs accounts.

2. Associate RunAs accounts with RunAs profiles.

3. Distribute RunAs accounts to management pools.

4. Install UNIX/Linux agent.

Tasks 1 and 2 might be able to be skipped, if the credentials are the same as those for previous machines.

Before installing the UNIX agent, a couple key RunAs accounts need to be created. One is the monitoring account, which is the account used to access the UNIX system to monitor health and performance. The second is the agent maintenance account, which is the account used to maintain the agent including upgrading or restarting the agent. These RunAs accounts will contain the account credentials with elevated access to the UNIX systems, typically the root credentials.

To configure the UNIX RunAs accounts, complete the following steps:

1. Open the Operations Console with an account that is a member of the Operations Manager 2012 Administrator profile.

2. Select the Administration view.

3. Expand the Run As Configuration folder.

4. Choose the UNIX/Linux Accounts folder.

5. In the Tasks pane, click Create Run As Account.

6. In the Account Type screen, leave Monitoring Account selected and press Next.

7. Enter a display name, such as **UNIX Monitoring Account** and click Next.

> **NOTE**
>
> Given that UNIX/Linux systems generally do not have the benefit of a centralized direc-
> tory like Microsoft Active Directory, it is likely that most environments will need to
> create multiple RunAs accounts to handle different credential pairs. It helps to use a
> good naming convention for these RunAs accounts.

8. Enter the credentials, typically a root-level account if not the root account itself.

9. Click Next.

10. In the Distribution Security screen, leave the More Secure option selected and click Create.

11. Click Close.

12. In the Tasks pane, click Create Run As Account.

13. In the Account Type screen, choose Agent Maintenance Account and press Next.

14. Enter a display name, such as **UNIX Agent Maintenance Account** and click Next.

15. Choose the User Name and Password option in the Account Credentials screen.

16. Enter the credentials, typically a root-level account if not the root account itself.

17. Click Next.

18. In the Distribution Security screen, leave the More Secure option selected and click Create.

19. Click Close.

The next task is to associate the RunAs accounts with the RunAs profiles. The three default UNIX/Linux RunAs profiles are the UNIX/Linux Action Account, the UNIX/Linux Agent Maintenance Account, and the UNIX/Linux Privileged Account. Each of these needs to have the appropriate RunAs account associated with them. The monitoring account is associated with the UNIX/Linux Action Account and the UNIX/Linux Privileged Account. The agent maintenance account is associated with the UNIX/Linux Agent Maintenance Account profile, as might be expected from the name.

To associate the RunAs accounts with the RunAs profiles, complete the following steps:

1. Open the Operations Console with an account that is a member of the Operations Manager 2012 Administrator profile.

2. Select the Administration view.

3. Expand the Run As Configuration folder.

4. Choose the Profiles folder.

5. Right-click the UNIX/Linux Action Account profile and select Properties to start the Run As Profile Wizard.

6. At the Introduction screen, click Next.

7. At the General Properties screen, click Next.

8. At the Add Run As Accounts screen, click the Add link.

9. In the Run As Account pull-down, choose the appropriate RunAs account. In this case, the account is the UNIX Monitoring Account. Then click OK.

10. Click Save to save the setting and then click Close.

11. Right-click the UNIX/Linux Privileged Account profile and select Properties to start the Run As Profile Wizard.

12. At the Introduction screen, click Next.

13. At the General Properties screen, click Next.

14. At the Add Run As Accounts screen, click the Add link.

15. In the Run As Account pull-down, choose the appropriate RunAs account. In this case, the account is the UNIX Monitoring Account. Then click OK.

16. Click Save to save the setting and then click Close.

17. Right-click the UNIX/Linux Agent Maintenance Account profile and select Properties to start the Run As Profile Wizard.

18. At the Introduction screen, click Next.

19. At the General Properties screen, click Next.

20. At the Add Run As Accounts screen, click the Add link.

21. In the Run As Account pull-down, choose the appropriate RunAs account. In this case, the account is the UNIX Agent Maintenance Account. Then click OK.

22. Click Save to save the setting and then click Close.

The RunAs accounts are now associated with the appropriate RunAs profiles. The next task is to distribute the RunAs account to the management pool. This allows the RunAs profile to use that RunAs account to monitor or maintain the agent on the UNIX computer.

> **NOTE**
>
> The reason why the RunAs accounts for UNIX are distributed to the management pool is that the management servers remotely access the UNIX/Linux servers to monitor and manage them. This is fundamentally different than the agent-based management of Windows systems, which is done by the local agent itself.

To distribute the RunAs accounts to the management pool, run the following steps:

1. Open the Operations Console with an account that is a member of the Operations Manager 2012 Administrator profile.

2. Select the Administration view.

3. Expand the Run As Configuration folder.

4. Choose the UNIX/Linux Accounts folder.

5. Under the Type: Agent Maintenance section, right-click the appropriate agent maintenance account and select Properties. In this case, the account is the UNIX Agent Maintenance Account.

6. At the General Properties screen, click Next.

7. At the Account Credentials screen, click Next.

8. At the Distribution Security screen, click the Add link.

9. In the Option pull-down, choose the Search By Resource Pool Name option.

10. Click the Search button to list the available resource pools.

11. Choose the All Management Servers Resource Pool and click the Add button.

12. Click OK to save the selection.

13. Click Save and Close to exit the wizard.

14. Under the Type: Monitoring section, right-click the appropriate monitoring and select Properties. In this case, the account is the UNIX Monitoring Account.

The next task is to install the UNIX agent. To install the UNIX agent, complete the following steps:

1. Open the Operations Console with an account that is a member of the Operations Manager 2012 Administrator profile.

2. Select the Administration view.

3. Right-click Administration and select Discovery Wizard.

4. On the Computer and Device Management Wizard Discovery Type page, choose UNIX/Linux Computers, and then click Next.

5. On the Discovery Method page, click Add to specify criteria for discovering UNIX-based systems and Linux-based systems on your network. You can use the IP address, FQDN, or an address range.

6. Click the Set Credentials button.

7. Choose the User Name and Password option in the Account Credentials screen.

8. Enter the credentials, typically a root-level account if not the root account itself.

9. Leave the default (this account has privilege level).

10. Click OK.

11. Click the Save button.

12. Choose a target resource pool from the pull-down, in this case the All Management Servers Resource Pool, and click Discover to initiate system discovery.

13. If there is an invalid certificate on the discovered system or systems, the Certificate Status page opens. Select the systems that you want new certificates issued to, and then click Sign.

14. On the Discovery Results page, in the Manageable Computers list, select the check box for the system or systems that you want to manage, or click the Select All check box to include all discovered systems.

15. If there are systems listed in the Additional Results tab on the Discovery Results page that the wizard was unable to discover, you can click Details to get information about why the discovery failed. Correct the problems and repeat the discovery step.

16. After you have selected the systems you want to manage, click Manage to start the deployment.

17. On the Deployment Complete page, the Computer and Device Management Wizard displays the agent deployment status in the Status menu.

18. Click Done to close the wizard.

The UNIX agent will take a while to discover services, so give it approximately 30 minutes to complete the discovery and begin monitoring.

Removing the UNIX agent might be necessary for troubleshooting or if the UNIX server is being decommissioned. To delete the agent from the console, complete the following steps:

1. Launch the Operations Console.

2. Select the Administration space.

3. Select the UNIX/Linux Servers node.

4. Right-click on the UNIX agent and select Uninstall Agent.

5. Click Yes to uninstall the agent.

Sometimes an agent installation will fail due to missing prerequisites or rights. This can render the system in an incomplete state, where the agent cannot be installed from the console nor removed from the console. When attempting the failed installation again, the following misleading message will be shown:

```
Deployment Failed
Message: Installed Agent failed to initialize properly.
Details: Access is denied.
```

This situation requires a manual removal of the failed agent install. To remove the UNIX agent manually or due to a failed installation, use the version-specific process described at http://technet.microsoft.com/en-us/library/dd788958.aspx. To remove the agent from a Red Hat or SUSE Linux enterprise server, use the following procedure:

1. Log in via telnet or Secure Shell (SSH) to the UNIX host as root.

2. Type the command **rpm -e scx**.

3. Type the command **rm -rf /etc/opt/microsoft/scx**.

The agent should now be gone from the UNIX host. The agent can now be installed using the Discovery Wizard again.

Network Monitoring

Network management is not a new concept. Simple management of various network nodes has been handled for quite some time through the use of the Simple Network Management Protocol (SNMP). Quite often, simple or even complex systems that utilize SNMP to provide for system monitoring are in place in an organization to provide for varying degrees of system management on a network.

Operations Manager monitors network devices using SNMP. The devices are discoverable with the Discovery Wizard and the public SNMP community string. By default, the device information is gathered and up/down state is monitored. This monitoring can be extended to any available SNMP data, including the network interfaces and ports on those devices and the virtual LANs (VLANs) that they participate in. Chapter 8 details how to create a custom management pack to monitor other SNMP-based metrics.

Monitoring DMZ Servers with Certificates

Servers in an organization's demilitarized zone (DMZ) are usually not domain members and, thus, cannot do automatic mutual authentication with the OpsMgr server. However, these servers are the most exposed in the organization and, thus, critical to be monitored. Thankfully, there is a well-defined process for using certificates to handle the mutual authentication.

NOTE

This topic also applies to machines that are workgroup servers or servers that are members of domains where there is no trust to the OpsMgr domain.

Monitoring servers in the DMZ requires an install of certificate-based mutual authentication. This process has a lot of steps, but is straightforward. To install and configure certificates to allow the DMZ servers to use mutual authentication, the following five major steps need to be completed:

1. Create a certificate template to issue the correct format of X.509 certificates for Operations Manager to use for mutual authentication.

2. Request the root CA certificate to trust the certificate authority (CA) and the certificates it issues. This is done for each DMZ server and possibly for the management servers if not using an enterprise CA.

3. Request a certificate from the root CA to use for mutual authentication. This is done for each DMZ server and for each management server.

4. Install the Operations Manager agent manually. This is done for each DMZ server.

5. Configure the agent to use the certificate. This is done for each DMZ server and for each management server.

These various X.509 certificates are issued from a certificate authority, which could be a Windows Server 2008 R2 CA.

Creating a Certificate Template

This step creates a certificate template named Operations Manager that can be issued from the Windows Server 2008 R2 Certification Authority Web Enrollment page. The certificate template will support server authentication (OID 1.3.6.1.5.5.7.3.1) and client authentication (OID 1.3.6.1.5.5.7.3.2) as well as allow the name to be manually entered rather than autogenerated from Active Directory because the DMZ server will not be an Active Directory domain member.

To create the security template, complete the following steps:

1. Log on to the CA, which is CERT.companyaxyz.com in this example.

2. Launch Server Manager.

3. Expand Roles, Active Directory Certificate Services, and select Certificate Templates (*fqdn*).

4. Right-click the Computer template and select Duplicate Template.

5. Leave the version at Windows 2003 Server, Enterprise Edition and click OK.

6. On the General tab in the Template Display Name field, enter **Operation Manager**.

7. Select the Request Handling tab and mark the Allow Private Key to Be Exported option.

8. Select the Subject Name tab and select Supply in the Request option. Click OK at the warning.

9. Select the Security tab, select Authenticated Users, and check the Enroll right.

10. Click OK to save the template.

11. Select the Enterprise PKI to expose the CA.

12. Right-click the CA and select Manage CA.

13. In the certsrv console, expand the CA, right-click Certificates Templates, and then select New, Certificate Template to Issue.

14. Select the Operations Manager certificate template and click OK.

The new Operations Manager template will now be available in the Windows Server 2008 R2 Certification Authority Web Enrollment page.

Requesting the Root CA Server Certificate

This allows the DMZ server to trust the Windows Server 2008 R2 CA. This does not need to be done on the OpsMgr management servers because the Windows Server 2008 R2 CA is an enterprise CA and all domain members automatically trust it. If the CA is not an enterprise CA, the steps need to be completed for the management servers as well.

To request and install the root CA certificate on the DMZ server, execute the following steps:

1. Log on to a DMZ server with local administrator rights.

2. Open a web browser and point it to the certificate server, in this case https://cert.companyxyz.com/certsrv. Enter credentials if prompted.

3. Click the Download a CA Certificate, Certificate Chain, or CRL link (shown in Figure 7.11).

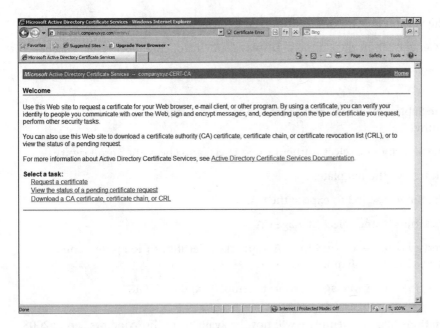

FIGURE 7.11   Downloading a root CA certificate.

4. Click Yes in the Web Access Confirmation dialog box.

5. Click the Download CA Certificate link. Note: If the certificate does not download, add the site to the Local Intranet list of sites in Internet Explorer.

6. Click Open to open the CA certificate.

7. Click Install Certificate to install the CA certificate.

8. On the Certificate Import Wizard page, click Next.

9. Select Place All Certificates in the Following Store option button.

10. Click Browse.

11. Click the Show Physical Stores check box.

12. Expand the Trusted Root Certification Authorities folder and select the local computer store.

13. Click OK.

14. Click Next, Finish, and OK to install the CA certificate.

15. Close any open windows.

Repeat the above for all DMZ servers. Now the DMZ servers will trust certificates issued by the certification authority. The next step is to request the certificates to use for the mutual authentication for all servers.

Requesting a Certificate from the Root CA Server

Each of the management servers and the servers in the DMZ need to be issued certificates to use for communication.

To request a certificate, complete the following steps:

1. Log on as an administrator, then open a web browser and point it to the certificate server (in this case, https://cert.companyabc.com/certsrv).

2. Click the Request a Certificate link.

3. Click the Advanced Certificate Request link.

4. Click the Create and Submit a Request to This CA link.

5. Click Yes in the Web Access Confirmation dialog box.

6. In the Type of Certificate Template field, select Operations Manager.

7. In the Name field, enter the full computer name of the target server.

> **NOTE**
>
> Go to the actual server to get the name! The full computer name for computers in the DMZ might or might not be the fully qualified domain name. Because DMZ computers are often not members of an Active Directory domain, the name might just be the NetBIOS name or the domain might be different than expected. If the name on the certificate does not match the full computer name, then mutual authentication will fail. Even the case of the name matters, so upper- and lowercase must match as well.
>
> To ensure the name is correct, on the target server, go to Computer Properties, Computer Name. Copy the full computer name and paste it into the Name field of the form.

8. Click Submit.

9. Click Yes when you get the warning pop-up.

10. Click Install This Certificate.

11. Click Yes when you see the warning pop-up. The certificate is now installed in the user certificate store.

> **NOTE**
>
> The certificate was installed in the user certificate store, but needs to be in the local computer store for Operations Manager. The ability to use web enrollment to directly place the certificate into the local computer store was removed from the Windows Server 2008 web enrollment, so the certificate needs to be moved manually.

12. Select Start, Run and then enter **mmc** to launch an MMC console.

13. Select File and then click Add/Remove Snap-In.

14. Select Certificates and click Add.

15. Select My User Account and click Finish.

16. Select Certificates again and click Add.

17. Select Computer Account and click Next.

18. Select the local computer, click Finish, and then click OK.

19. Expand the Certificates – Current User and Personal folders, and then select the Certificates folder.

20. In the right pane, right-click the certificate issued earlier and select All Tasks, Export. The certificate can be recognized by the certificate template name Operations Manager.

21. At the Certificate Export Wizard, click Next.

22. Select Yes, Export the Private Key. Click Next.

23. On the Export File Format screen, click Next.

24. Enter a password and click Next.

25. Enter a directory and filename and click Next.

26. Click Finish to export the certificate. Click OK at the pop-up.

27. Expand the Certificates (Local Computer) and Personal folders, and then select the Certificates folder.

> **NOTE**
>
> If this is the first certificate in the local computer store, the Certificates folder will not exist. Simply select the Personal folder instead and the Certificates folder will be created automatically.

28. Right-click in the right pane and select All Tasks, Import.

29. At the Certificate Import Wizard, select Next.

30. Click Browse to locate the certificate file saved earlier. Change the file type to Personal Information Exchange (.pfx) to see the file. Click Next.

31. Enter the password used earlier, select the Mark This Key as Exportable, and click Next.

32. Click Next.

33. Click Finish and then click OK at the pop-up to complete the import.

The preceding steps need to be completed for each DMZ server and for each management server.

Installing the Agent on the DMZ Server

The agent needs to be installed manually on each DMZ server. Normally, agents would be pushed by the Operations Manager console, but DMZ servers typically do not have the local security and network configuration to support agent push installation.

To manually install the agent, complete the following steps:

1. Log on as an administrator and insert the OpsMgr 2012 installation media.

2. At the AutoPlay menu, select Run Setup.exe.

3. Select Local Agent from the Optional Installation menu.

4. Click Next.

5. Click Next to accept the default directory.

6. Click Next to specify management group information.

7. Type in the management group name and FQDN of the management server. Keep the default management server port as 5723. The example shown in Figure 7.12 has COMPANYXYZ as the management group name and om1.companyxyz.com as the management server.

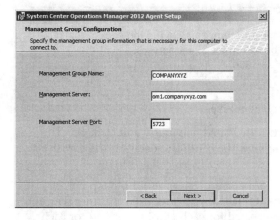

FIGURE 7.12   Manually entered management group information.

8. Click Next.

9. Click Next at the Agent Action Account page to leave the local system as the action account.

10. Use Microsoft Updates (Recommended) and then click Next.

11. Click Install to complete the installation.

12. When the installer is finished, click Finish.

The preceding steps need to be completed for each DMZ server.

The agent is installed, but will not communicate correctly with the management server. This is because the agent has not been configured to use the certificate for mutual authentication. This is done in the next section.

Configuring the Agent to Use the Certificate

After the agent is installed, the agent still needs to be configured to use the correct certificate. The OpsMgr installation includes a utility called MOMCertImport.exe that configures the agent to use certificates for authentication and specifies which certificate in the local computer store to use. The tool does not do any validation checking of the certificate itself, so care needs to be taken that the correct certificate is selected.

To configure the agent to use a certificate, complete the following steps:

1. Log on as an administrator on the DMZ server and insert the OpsMgr 2012 installation media.

2. Open Windows Explorer.

3. Select the OpsMgr 2012 installation media location.

4. Select the SupportTools directory and then the AMD64 directory.

> **NOTE**
>
> Windows Server 2008 R2 is a 64-bit operating system, so AMD64 is the correct folder for the 64-bit binaries. If the procedure is being run for 32-bit servers, select the appropriate directory for the binaries such as i386.

5. In the directory, double-click MOMCertImport.exe.

6. In the pop-up window, select the certificate issued previously and click OK. The View Certificate button can be used to view the certificate details if the correct certificate is not obvious.

The Operation Manager service will restart automatically to have the certificate selection take effect. The preceding steps need to be repeated for each DMZ server and for each management server.

The Operations Manager event log can be viewed with the Windows Event Viewer. It is named Operations Manager and is located in the Applications and Services Logs folder in the tool. Any problems with the certificate will be shown in the log immediately following the start of the System Center Management service.

> **NOTE**
>
> Sometimes, determining if the requisite port 5723 has been opened correctly can be difficult. An easy way to check to see if the port is open is to use the telnet client. The telnet client can be installed from the features of Windows 2008 R2. On the DMZ machine, run the command `telnet <management server> 5723`, where *<management server>* is the fully qualified domain name of the management server. For example, the command in our example would be: `telnet om1.companyxyz.com 5723`.
>
> If the port is open and the management server is reachable, then you'll get a blank screen. You can press the Enter key to exit. If the port is not open and the management server is unreachable, then you'll get a connect failed error.

Configuring Operations Manager 2012

After installing the Operations Manager 2012 infrastructure, several configuration steps should be taken to have the system monitor properly, generate Active Directory synthetic transactions, and send out email notifications of alerts.

Global Management Group Settings

After the installation of the Operations Manager infrastructure, several settings need to be configured for the management group. These settings are called global management group settings. They include a number of settings that control the security, data retention in the operations database, agent heartbeat interval, web addresses for alerts and consoles, and manual agent security. Figure 7.13 shows the Global Management Group Settings page.

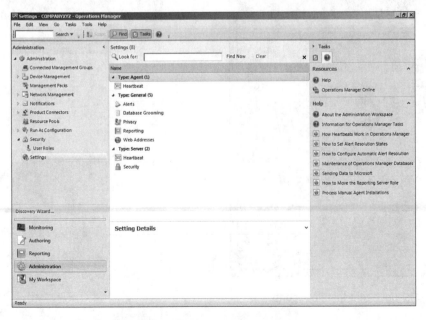

FIGURE 7.13   Global Management Group Settings.

The two key global management group settings that need to be configured are as follows:

▶ Manual Agent Install Security

▶ Database Grooming

The Manual Agent Install Security controls how Operations Manager handles manual agent installations. If an agent is installed manually—that is, not pushed out from the console—the management servers will by default reject the agent. This is done to ensure that rogue computers are not connecting to the management infrastructure. In reality, this is a relatively low-probability threat. For most organizations, it is more convenient to have the manual agents be automatically accepted.

To configure the management group to accept manual agents, complete the following steps:

1. Launch the Operations Console.

2. Select the Administration space.

3. Select the Settings folder.

4. Under the Type: Server section, right-click on Security and select Properties.

5. Select the Review New Manual Agent Installations in Pending Management View option.

6. Check the Automatically Approve New Manually Installed Agents check box. Figure 7.14 shows how the settings should appear.

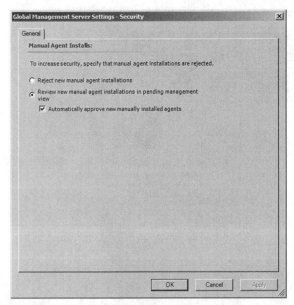

FIGURE 7.14   Manual Agent Install Security.

7. Click OK to save the settings.

Now manual agents will be accepted automatically.

The Database Grooming controls how long data is retained in the operations database, which, in turn, dictates how much data is visible in the Operations Console. Once the data retention period is reached, the data is groomed (that is, deleted) from the operations database. The default grooming settings are set for seven days, which means that after seven days the data is no longer available in the Operations Console. However, the data is available in summarized form in the Reporting data warehouse for the retention period of that database, which is approximately a year. This data can then be viewed with the reports.

The biggest impact of the operations database grooming settings is that by default only a week of data is available. When troubleshooting problems using the console, it is important to have more than a week's worth of data. This allows for comparing data week to week to ascertain trends and catch longer-term problems.

However, the longer the grooming settings, the larger the size of the OperationsManager database. Thus, it is important to balance the data retention against the size of the database.

The best-practice recommendation is to set the database grooming settings to 14 days to have 2 weeks' worth of data for troubleshooting without creating too large a database. These settings will essentially double the size of the OperationsManager database, which is manageable in most cases.

The settings to change are for the following records:

- Resolved Alerts
- Events Data
- Performance Data
- Task History
- Monitoring Job Data
- State Change Events Data
- Maintenance Mode History
- Availability History

WARNING

Do not adjust the Performance Signature grooming interval from the default of two days. This value is used to compute baselines. Changing it negatively affects performance baselines.

To adjust the Database Grooming settings, complete the following steps:

1. Launch the Operations Console.

2. Select the Administration space.

3. Select the Settings folder.

4. Under the Type: General section, right-click on Database Grooming and select Properties.

5. Select the record to change and click Edit.

6. Change the value to 14 and click OK.

7. Repeat for each of the remaining records. Do not change the Performance Signature record. Figure 7.15 shows how the configuration should look.

FIGURE 7.15   Database Grooming settings.

8. Click OK to save the configuration changes.

Now the data will be retained in the operations database for 14 days.

Agent Proxy Configuration

Operations Manager 2012 has a variety of security measures built in to the product to prevent security breaches. One measure in particular is the prevention of impersonation of one agent by another. That is, an agent SERVER1 cannot insert operations data into the database about a domain controller DC1. This could constitute a security violation, where

SERVER1 could maliciously generate fraudulent emergencies by making it appear that DC1 was having operational issues.

Although this is normally a good feature, this can be a problem if, in fact, SERVER1 is monitoring DC1 from a client perspective. The Operations Manager infrastructure would reject any information presented about DC1 by SERVER1. When this occurs, the system generates an alert to indicate that an attempt to proxy operations data has occurred. Figure 7.16 shows an example of the alert, where DC1.companyxyz.com is attempting to submit data for another computer. In the normal course of events, this alert is not an indication of an attack but rather a configuration problem.

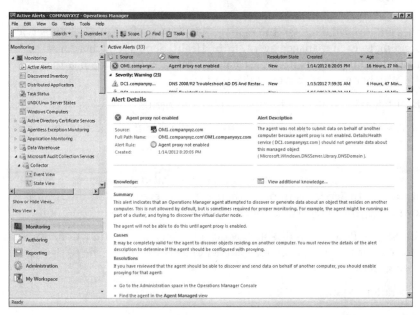

FIGURE 7.16   Agent Proxy alert.

To get around this problem, Agent Proxy can be selectively enabled for agents that need to be able to present operational data about other agents. To enable Agent Proxy for a computer, complete the following steps:

1. Open the Operations Manager 2012 console.

2. Select the Administration section.

3. Expand the Device Management folder and select the Agent Managed node.

4. Right-click the agent in the right pane, in this case DC1, and select Properties.

5. Click the Security tab.

6. Check the Allow This Agent to Act as a Proxy and Discover Managed Objects on Other Computers check box.

7. Click OK to save.

Repeat this for all agents that need to act as proxy agents.

Agent Restart Recovery

Agents will heartbeat every 60 seconds by default, contacting their management server to check for new rules and upload data. On the management server, there is a Health Service Watcher corresponding to each managed agent. If the Health Service Watcher for an agent detects three missed heartbeats in a row (that is, 3 minutes without a heartbeat), the Health Service Watcher executes a pair of diagnostics:

▶ First, the Health Service Watcher attempts to ping the agent.

▶ Second, the Health Service Watcher checks to see if the Health Service is running on the agent.

An alert is then generated for each of the diagnostics if they failed. If the agent is reachable via ping but the Health Service is stopped, there is a recovery to restart the Health Service. This allows the agent to recover automatically from stopped agent conditions.

The Restart Health Service Recovery is disabled by default. To enable the functionality, an override can be created for the Health Service Watcher objects. To enable the recovery, execute the following steps:

1. Open the Operations Manager 2012 console.

2. Select the Authoring space.

3. Expand the Management Pack Objects node.

4. Select the Monitors node.

5. Select View, Scope.

6. Click Clear All to clear the scope.

7. Type **health service watcher** in the Look For field and click the View All Targets option button.

8. Select the Health Service Watcher target. Don't pick the ones with additional information in parentheses.

9. Click OK.

10. Type **Heartbeat Failure** in the Look For field and click Find Now.

11. Right-click the Health Service Heartbeat Failure aggregate rollup node and select Overrides, Override Recovery, Restart Health Service, and For All Objects of Class: Health Service Watcher.

12. Check the Override box next to Enabled, and set the value to True.

13. In the Select Destination Management Pack pull-down menu, select the appropriate override management pack. If none exists, create a new management pack named "Operations Manager MP Overrides" by clicking New and then following the prompts to create a new management pack.

NOTE

Never use the Default Management Pack for overrides. Always create an override management pack that corresponds to each imported management pack.

14. Click OK to save the override.

Now if the Health Service is stopped on an agent, the management server automatically attempts to restart it.

Notifications and Subscriptions

When alerts are generated in the console, a wealth of information is available about the nature of the problem and how to troubleshoot and resolve it. However, most administrators will not be watching the console at all times. Operations Manager has a sophisticated notification mechanism that allows alerts to be forwarded to email, SMS, IM, or even a command-line interface. The most common method of alert notification is email.

However, Operations Manager generates a lot of alerts. If each one of these alerts were forwarded, this would overwhelm the average administrator's Inbox and prove totally useless. Operations Manager has two alert parameters to help categorize the alerts. Each alert has two parameters that help guide the notification process: severity and priority.

Alert Severity is the first and main parameter. There are three severity levels:

▶ **Critical (2)**—These alerts indicate that there is a problem that needs to be fixed immediately and is directly actionable (that is, there is something that can be done).

▶ **Warning (1)**—These alerts indicate that there is a problem, but that it might not be immediately impacting the environment or might not be directly actionable.

▶ **Information (0)**—These alerts indicate that there is something that is good to know, but might not be a problem nor is actionable.

By the nature of things, a lot more warning alerts are generated than critical alerts. In general, notifications should only be sent out for critical alerts. That is, an email should never be sent for a warning or informational alert.

Alert Priority is the second parameter that qualifies the alert status. The priority allows management pack authors to make some alerts more important than others. There are three levels of priority as well:

▶ High (2)

▶ Medium (1)

▶ Low (0)

In general, a high-priority, critical severity alert is very important. This includes events like an agent down or a security breach. A medium-priority, critical severity alert is important. Both are generally actionable.

The best practice is to create two Simple Mail Transfer Protocol (SMTP) channels to deliver the alert notification emails, which are as follows:

▶ **SMTP (High Priority)**—High-priority email to an SMTP gateway

▶ **SMTP (Normal Priority)**—Regular email to an SMTP gateway

Then, create two notification subscriptions that use the severity and the priority to select the emails to be sent:

▶ Notification for All Critical Severity High-Priority Alerts

▶ Notification for All Critical Severity Medium-Priority Alerts

This provides a configuration that delivers the very important alerts (high-priority, critical severity alerts) via high-priority email and important alerts (medium-priority, critical severity alerts) via regular email. All other alerts will be available in the console and no emails will be sent to notify of them.

The next sections set up the notification infrastructure described previously.

The first step is to set up a channel, that is, how the emails will be sent. To set up a channel, complete the following steps:

1. Launch the Operations Manager 2012 console.

2. Select the Administration space.

3. Expand the Notifications folder and select the Channels node.

4. Right-click the Channels node and select New Channel, E-Mail (SMTP).

5. Enter `SMTP Channel (High Priority)` for the channel name and click Next.

6. Click Add, enter the FQDN of the SMTP server, and click OK.

7. Enter a return SMTP address, such as `opsmgr@companyxyz.com`, and click Next.

8. Change the Importance to High and click Finish. Click Close to close the wizard.

9. Right-click the Channels node and select New Channel, E-Mail (SMTP).

10. Enter `SMTP Channel (Normal Priority)` for the channel name and click Next.

11. Click Add, enter the FQDN of the SMTP server, and click OK.

12. Enter a return SMTP address and click Next.

13. Leave the Importance at Normal and click Finish. Click Close to close the wizard.

The second step is to set up the subscriber, that is, to whom the emails will be sent. The steps are as follows:

1. Launch the Operations Manager 2012 console.

2. Select the Administration space.

3. Expand the Notifications folder and select the Subscribers node.

4. Right-click the Subscribers node and select New Subscriber.

5. Click the "..." button and select a user or distribution group. Click OK.

6. Click Next.

7. Click Next to always send notifications.

8. Click Add.

9. Type `Email` for the address name and click Next.

10. Select the Channel Type as E-Mail (SMTP), enter the delivery email address, and then click Next.

11. Click Finish.

12. Click Finish again to save the subscriber. Click Close to exit the wizard.

> **NOTE**
>
> It is a best practice to use distribution lists rather than user email addresses for subscribers.

The last step is to set up the subscriptions, that is, what to notify on. To set up the subscriptions, complete the following steps:

1. Launch the Operations Manager 2012 console.

2. Select the Administration space.

3. Expand the Notifications folder and select the Subscriptions node.

4. Right-click the Subscriptions node and select New Subscription.

5. Enter **Notification for All Critical Severity High Priority Alerts** for the subscription name and click Next.

6. Check the Of a Specific Severity and the Of a Specific Priority check boxes.

7. In the Criteria Description pane, click the Specific Severity link, check the Critical check box, and then click OK.

8. In the Criteria Description pane, click the Specific Priority link, check the High check box, and then click OK.

9. Click Next.

10. Click Add, click Search, select the subscriber, click Add, and then click OK.

11. Click Next.

12. Click Add, click Search, select the SMTP Channel (High Priority) channel, click Add, and then click OK.

13. Click Next, click Finish, and then click Close.

14. Right-click the Subscriptions node and select New Subscription.

15. Enter **Notification for All Critical Severity Medium Priority Alerts** for the subscription name and click Next.

16. Check the Of a Specific Severity and the Of a Specific Priority check boxes.

17. In the Criteria Description pane, click the Specific Severity link, check the Critical check box, and then click OK.

18. In the Criteria Description pane, click the Specific Priority link, check the Medium check box, and then click OK.

19. Click Next.

20. Click Add, click Search, select the subscriber, click Add, and then click OK.

21. Click Next.

22. Click Add, click Search, select the SMTP Channel (Normal Priority) channel, click Add, and then click OK.

23. Click Next, click Finish, and then click Close.

Now, the subscribers will get email notifications for alerts based on the severity and priority. These severities and priorities are based on the judgments of the authors of the management packs, which might or might not be optimal for any given organization. Later in the chapter, the priority and severity of alerts are used to tune the management packs to reduce alert noise.

Administering Operations Manager 2012

After Operations Manager 2012 has been installed and configured, ongoing work needs to be done to ensure that the product performs as expected. The two primary activities are to, first, tune the management packs to ensure that alerts are valid for the environment and that alert noise is reduced and, second, produce reports of the information that Operations Manager 2012 is collecting.

Dip Stick Health Check Tasks

Whenever a motorist is going for a drive, the conscientious driver goes through a set of basic automotive health checks, including the following:

- ▶ Check the oil level with the dip stick.

- ▶ Check the tire pressure.

- ▶ Check the gasoline level.

These are sometimes referred to as the "dip-stick health checks" because the oil level is checked with a dip stick.

Like any other complicated technology, Operations Manager 2012 can have problems in a variety of ways, ranging from running out of disk space, to failing to send email notifications, to having agents stopped, and so forth. To make sure that Operations Manager is functioning properly, a set of dip-stick health checks can be performed to make sure everything is running smoothly.

These are the health check tasks that the OpsMgr administrator should do every day to verify the health and proper operation of the OpsMgr infrastructure:

1. Verify that you have received notifications by email. Confirm that you are getting notifications within the normal range. Too many is a bad sign and too few (or none) is also a bad sign.

2. Review OpsMgr daily reports sent via email or in the console. If using the console, the reports are stored in the Favorites folder in the Reporting space. See Chapter 9 for how to set up these reports.

3. In the Operations Manager console, review the Active Alerts view. This shows you new alerts.

4. In the Operations Manager console, review the All Alerts view. This shows you both new and closed alerts.

5. In the Operations Manager console, review the Agent Health State view in the \Operations Manager\Agent Details node. Investigate any Critical, Warning, or Not Monitored states.

6. In the Operations Manager console, review the Active Alerts view in the \Operations Manager\Agent Details node. Investigate any Critical or Warning alerts.

7. In the Operations Manager console, review the Management Server Health State view in the \Operations Manager\Management Server node. Investigate any Critical, Warning, or Not Monitored states.

8. In the Operations Manager console, review the Active Alerts view in the \Operations Manager\Management Server node. Investigate any Critical or Warning alerts.

After reviewing the results of these health check tasks, an administrator can be pretty confident that the Operations Manager 2012 infrastructure is functioning properly.

Health check task #2 recommends reviewing the daily reports. The recommended Operations Manager health reports to review on a daily basis are as follows:

▶ **Alert Logging Latency report**—This report tells you the length of time between an event being raised to an alert being generated. This should be under 30 seconds.

▶ **Send Queue % Used Top 10 report**—This report tells you if agents are having trouble uploading their data to the management servers. These queues should be less than 1%.

▶ **Top 10 Most Common Alerts report**—This report analyzes the most common alerts that were generated and are good for identifying alert-tuning opportunities.

▶ **Daily Alert report**—This report gives you a complete list of all the alerts that were generated. This is very detailed, but is good for chasing down problems uncovered in other checks.

See Chapter 9 for detailed instructions on how to set up these reports.

These health check tasks should give a good sense of the operational health of the SCOM infrastructure.

Management Pack Updates

Management pack updates are released periodically by Microsoft. The Operations Console allows you to update installed management packs from the online catalog.

> **NOTE**
>
> Installing updates by definition changes the rules, alerts, and monitors that are deployed. This can have significant consequences on the alerts that are generated. Any updates should first be tested in a lab setting to ensure that there are no problems.

The online catalog should be checked for updates to the installed management packs on a monthly basis. To do this, complete the following steps:

1. Launch the Operations Console.

2. Go to the Administration space.

3. Select the Management Packs node.

4. Right-click on the Management Packs node and select Import Management Packs.

5. Click Add and select Add from Catalog.

6. In the View pull-down, select Updates Available for Installed Management Packs.

7. Click the Search button.

8. Review the results in the Management Packs in the Catalog pane.

9. Select the management packs to update and click Add to add them to the Selected Management Packs pane.

10. Click OK.

11. Review the select management packs, the version numbers, and any warnings or informational messages.

12. Click Install to download and import the management packs.

13. After download and import, click Close to close the Import Management Packs Wizard.

The management pack updates take effect immediately.

Notification and Alert Tuning

After deploying Operations Manager 2012, there are frequently complaints about the number of alert notifications that get generated. This can cause organizations to decommission the product, ignore the emails, or generally complain about what a bad product it is. In reality, the Operations Manager alert notifications just need to be tuned.

The following process helps tune the management pack quickly and effectively to reduce alert and email noise. This is done by adjusting parameters on the rules (Enable/Disable, Severity, and Priority) using overrides.

Alert Severity is the first parameter to be tuned. There are three levels:

▶ Critical (2)

▶ Warning (1)

▶ Information (0)

Alert Priority is the second parameter to be tuned. There are three levels of priority as well:

- ▶ High (2)
- ▶ Medium (1)
- ▶ Low (0)

There are two SMTP channels to deliver the emails:

- ▶ **SMTP Channel (High Priority)**—High-priority email to an SMTP gateway
- ▶ **SMTP Channel (Normal Priority)**—Regular-priority email to an SMTP gateway

---

NOTE

These channels were created earlier in the chapter.

There are two notification subscriptions that use the severity and priority to select the emails to be sent:

- ▶ Notification for All Critical Severity High-Priority Alerts
- ▶ Notification for All Critical Severity Medium-Priority Alerts

The channels and subscriptions automatically send email notifications for critical severity high- and medium-priority alerts.

NOTE

These notification subscriptions were created earlier in the chapter.

However, sometime the alerts that are generated are not appropriate for the environment. This is because the source alert is not appropriate or actionable, so the resulting email is not useful and can be considered noise.

When you get an email from an alert that you don't want, you need to tune the management pack monitor or rule. The basic decision tree is as follows:

1. **Alert is noise?** If no, this means that the alert is appropriate and actionable. In this case, the underlying cause of the alert needs to be addressed.

2. **Alert not needed?** If yes, create an override to disable the rule for either the instance of the object, the class of objects, or a group of the objects. This prevents the alert from being generated, so no console alerts and definitely no emails are generated.

3. **Alert severity too high?** If yes, create an override to change the alert severity to a warning. This keeps the alert in the console as a warning, but does not generate an email.

4. **Alert priority too high?** If yes, create an override to change the alert priority to low. This keeps the alert as a critical alert, but prevents an email from being .

Figure 7.17 shows the decision tree in a flowchart form.

FIGURE 7.17   Alert tuning flowchart.

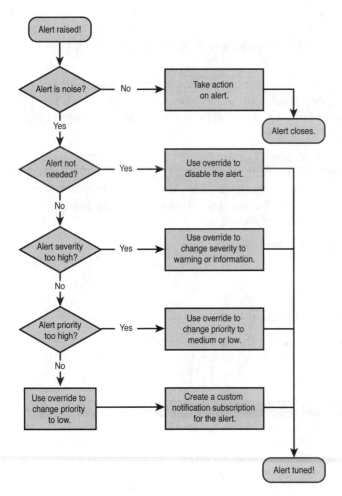

If these are not enough to narrow down the email notification behavior, a custom approach is needed. For example, if you want to get an email when mail flow alerts are generated but only after a couple are generated, do the following:

1. Change the alert priority to low using an override. This prevents the alert from generating a notification from the default subscriptions.

2. Create a notification subscription for the alert, but set an aging to longer than the test interval or whatever you want to wait before sending the email.

NOTE

When creating the custom notification subscription, make sure to have the With Specific Resolution State criteria checked and only "New" resolution states selected. If this is not done, the notification triggers after the aging. This is because even if the alert closes before the aging period is up, the "Closed" resolution state still triggers the notification.

This process takes care of the majority of cases and reduces spamming by the OpsMgr console.

These options can be taken for all objects of the target class, for just the specific instance that generated the alert, or for a group. The group would have to be created in advance and would have to contain objects of the type targeted by the monitor or rule generating the alert.

For example, let's say there is an Application of Group Policy critical alert that is occurring frequently in the environment. It is occurring on a number of Windows Server 2008 R2 servers and is generating a lot of email notifications. This alert is valid, but does not require immediate action. The alert needs to be tuned to change the severity from critical to warning. The steps to tune the alert are as follows:

1. Open the Operations Manager 2012 console.

2. Select the Monitoring space.

3. Select the Active Alerts view.

4. Locate and select the Application of Group Policy alert that is to be tuned.

5. Right-click the alert and select Overrides, Override the Monitor, and For All Objects of Class: Group Policy 2008 Runtime. This overrides the alert for all objects of that class.

NOTE

The alert is to be tuned for all objects, rather than any specific instances. If the alert is to be tuned for the specific instance that raised the alert, the For the Object option should be chosen. If it is a group of the objects, the For a Group option should be chosen. The group would have to be precreated and be a group of the target objects.

---

6. Check the Override box next to Alert Severity and set the value to Warning.

7. In the Select Destination Management Pack pull-down menu, select the appropriate override management pack. If none exists, create a new override management pack named **Group Policy MP Overrides** by clicking New and then following the prompts to create a new management pack.

> **NOTE**
>
> Never use the Default Management Pack for overrides. Always create an override management pack that corresponds to each imported management pack.

8. Click OK to save the override.

Now the next time the monitor triggers an alert, it will be of warning severity and will not generate a notification email. However, the alert can still be reviewed in the console.

This approach to tuning will address 90% of the noisy alerts that you get. To target the noisiest alerts, see the Most Common Alerts report in the next section. This helps identify the alerts that are responsible for the most noise. You'll frequently find that 50% of your alerts are coming from less than five rules or monitors. Tuning those gives you the most bang for your buck.

File Exclusions for Antivirus and Defragmentation Applications

When deploying management servers and agents, sometimes the following errors from the Health Service ESE Store come up:

```
Event Type:       Error
Event Source:     Health Service ESE Store
Event Category:   General
Event ID:         486
Description:      HealthService (2240) Health Service Store: An attempt to
move the file "C:\System Center Operations Manager 2012\Health Service
State\Health Service Store\edb03DAA.log" to "C:\System Center Operations
Manager 2012\Health Service State\Health Service Store\edbtmp.log" failed
with system error 5 (0x00000005): "Access is denied. ".  The move file
operation will fail with error -1032 (0xfffffbf8).
```

```
Event Type:       Error
Event Source:     Health Service ESE Store
Event Category:   Logging/Recovery
Event ID:         413
Description:      HealthService (2240) Health Service Store: Unable to create
a new logfile because the database cannot write to the log drive. The drive
may be read-only, out of disk space, misconfigured, or corrupted. Error -
1032.
```

7

These errors are followed by a restart of the Health Service. On the management servers, there is also a loss of data that can result in Performance view gaps and other issues. However, when troubleshooting the systems, there are no apparent disk problems or disk space issues.

The problem is due to antivirus or defragmentation application conflicts with the Operations Manager agent. When the agent attempts to move the log files and the antivirus/defragmentation application is accessing the log files, the agent is prevented from accessing the log file and throws the error. The service restarts and automatically deletes the log files and temporary databases, resulting in data loss.

To prevent this problem, the directory that hosts the OpsMgr agent queue and log files should be excluded from the antivirus and defragmentation applications. The directory for agents is by default:

```
C:\Program Files\System Center Operations Manager\Agent\Health Service State\Health
Service Store
```

The directory for management servers and gateways is by default:

```
C:\Program Files\System Center Operations Manager 2012\Server\Health Service
State\Health Service Store
```

This exclusion should be on the following components:

▶ Management server

▶ Gateways

▶ Agents

This also improves performance of the agents, which is particularly important on the management servers, gateways, and agents with heavy monitoring loads.

Web Console Performance View Time Frame

The Web console is a very useful tool, especially for application owners who use the console only occasionally and for OpsMgr operators who are away from their desks but need quick access to the console. However, the Web console has some built-in limitations. By default, the Web Console Performance views show the last 24 hours of data. There's no way to change that in the UI.

NOTE

The reasoning behind this is that beyond one day, users can request a lot of data, and that might have negative performance implications for the Web console.

This default can be changed, however. There is a Web.Config configuration file that controls a lot of the default behaviors of the Web console.

In the \Program Files\System Center Operations Manager 2012\Web Console\ WebHost\Web.Config file under <configuration> then <appSettings>, a number of keys control how the Web console displays information. A new key PerformanceHoursBefore can be added to control the hours displayed in all Performance views in the Web console.

> **NOTE**
>
> The key would need to be added to all management server computers that host the Web console component.

The following example sets the time span to 48 hours:

```
<configuration>
<appSettings>
...
<add key="PerformanceHoursBefore" value="48"/>
...
</appSettings>
</configuration>
```

Only the one line <add key="PerformanceHoursBefore" value="48"/> is added to the Web.Config file. The other text is to show where the line needs to be added. Save the file with the previous change. The IIS server hosting the Web console needs to be restarted and the Web console needs to be relaunched to see the effects, which will be that 48 hours of data are displayed rather than the default 24 hours.

> **NOTE**
>
> Changing this value changes the default time frame for all Performance views for all users of this Web console.

Backing Up OpsMgr 2012

In the event of a disaster, it is important to have backups of the components needed to restore the Operations Manager 2012 infrastructure. The components needed for disaster recovery include the following:

▶ OperationsManager database

▶ Reporting data warehouse database

▶ Audit collection database

▶ IIS 7.0 configuration

These components need to be backed up on different schedules. Table 7.3 lists the recommended schedule for the backups.

TABLE 7.3   OpsMgr Component Backup Schedules

Component	Full Backup	Incremental Backup
Operations database (OperationsManager)	Weekly	Daily
Reporting data warehouse database (OperationsManagerDW)	Monthly	Weekly
Audit collection database (OperationsManagerAC)	Monthly	Weekly
IIS 7.0 configuration	Weekly	

These backups are above and beyond the standard backups needed for servers, such as file-level backups, System State, and SQL Server backups.

OperationsManager Database Backup

The OperationsManager database contains most of the Operations Manager environment configuration settings, agent information, management packs with customizations, operations data, and other data required for Operations Manager to operate properly.

The loss of the OperationsManager database requires a complete rebuild of the Operations Manager 2012 infrastructure.

> **NOTE**
>
> During the backup, the OperationsManager database will be offline. However, the Operations Manager caches incoming data, and then inserts that data into the database when it comes back online.

The OperationsManager database should be backed up on a daily basis. The recommendation is to do a full backup weekly and a differential backup daily to reduce disk space requirements.

To set up the full and differential backups for the OperationsManager database, execute the following steps:

1. Launch SQL Server Management Studio on the operations database server.

2. Click the Connect button.

3. Expand the Databases folder.

4. Right-click the OperationsManager database, select Tasks, and click Back Up.

5. In the Back Up Database dialog box, type the name of the backup set in the Name box.

6. In the Destination section, click Add.

7. In the Select Backup Destination dialog box, type a path and a filename in the Destination on Disk box, click OK, and then click OK again.

> **NOTE**
>
> The destination location selected must have enough disk space to hold the backups.

8. In the Script pull-down list at the top of the window, select Script Action to Job.

9. In the Name field, enter a name for the job such as **Back Up Database - OperationsManager Full**.

10. In the New Job window, select the Schedules page and click New.

11. In the New Job Schedule dialog box, type **OperationsManager Weekly Full Backup** as the job name in the Name box, specify the job schedule as weekly, and then click OK.

12. Click OK.

13. At this point, click OK to execute a manual full backup or click Cancel to skip it.

14. Right-click the OperationsManager database, select Tasks, and click Back Up.

15. Select Differential in the Backup Type pull-down.

16. In the Back Up Database dialog box, type the name of the backup set in the Name box.

17. In the Destination section, click Add.

18. In the Select Backup Destination dialog box, type a path and a filename in the Destination on Disk box, click OK, and then click OK again.

> **NOTE**
>
> The destination location selected must have enough disk space to hold the backups.

19. In the Script pull-down list at the top of the window, select Script Action to Job.

20. In the Name field, enter a name for the job such as **Back Up Database - OperationsManager Differential**.

21. In the New Job window, select the Schedules page and click New.

22. In the New Job Schedule dialog box, type **OperationsManager Daily Differential Backup** as the job name in the Name box, specify the job schedule as daily, and then click OK.

23. Click OK.

24. Click OK to execute a manual differential backup right away or click Cancel to skip it.

> **NOTE**
>
> The full backup will have had to run before running the differential backup; otherwise, it will fail.

The OperationsManager database backup will now execute automatically according to the recommended schedule.

OperationsManagerDW Database Backup

The OperationsManagerDW database contains all of the historical performance and other operational data from the Operations Manager environment. To be able to restore reporting functionality and long-term historical data in case of failure, it is critical that the OperationsManagerDW database be backed up.

However, the OperationsManagerDW database is very large and can take up a large space. This large size needs to be balanced against the need to back up on a regular basis. The OperationsManagerDW database should be backed up on a weekly basis. The recommendation is to do a full backup monthly and a differential backup weekly to reduce disk space requirements.

To set up the full and differential backups for the OperationsManagerDW database, perform the following steps:

1. Launch SQL Server Management Studio on the operations database server.

2. Click the Connect button.

3. Expand the Databases folder.

4. Right-click the OperationsManagerDW database, select Tasks, and click Back Up.

5. In the Back Up Database dialog box, type the name of the backup set in the Name box.

6. In the Destination section, click Add.

7. In the Select Backup Destination dialog box, type a path and a filename in the Destination on Disk box, click OK, and then click OK again.

> **NOTE**
>
> The destination location selected must have enough disk space to hold the backups, particularly with the large Reporting data warehouse database.

8. In the Script pull-down list at the top of the window, select Script Action to Job.

9. In the Name field, enter a name for the job such as `Back Up Database - OperationsManagerDW Full`.

10. In the New Job window, select the Schedules page and click New.

11. In the New Job Schedule dialog box, type **OperationsManagerDW Monthly Full Backup** as the job name in the Name box, specify the job schedule as monthly, and then click OK.

12. Click OK.

13. At this point, click OK to execute a manual full backup or click Cancel to skip it.

14. Right-click the OperationsManagerDW database, select Tasks, and click Back Up.

15. Select Differential in the Backup Type pull-down.

16. In the Back Up Database dialog box, type the name of the backup set in the Name box.

17. In the Destination section, click Add.

18. In the Select Backup Destination dialog box, type a path and a filename in the Destination on Disk box, click OK, and then click OK again.

NOTE

The destination location selected must have enough disk space to hold the backups, particularly with the large Reporting data warehouse database.

---

19. In the Script pull-down list at the top of the window, select Script Action to Job.

20. In the Name field, enter a name for the job such as **Back Up Database - OperationsManagerDW Differential**.

21. In the New Job window, select the Schedules page and click New.

22. In the New Job Schedule dialog box, type **OperationsManagerDW Weekly Differential Backup** as the job name in the Name box, specify the job schedule as weekly, and then click OK.

23. Click OK.

24. Click OK to execute a manual differential backup right away or click Cancel to skip it.

NOTE

The full backup will have had to run before running the differential backup; otherwise, it will fail.

The OperationsManagerDW database backup will now execute automatically according to the recommended schedule.

OperationsManagerAC Database Backup

The ACS database, OperationsManagerAC, stores the security logs that are collected by ACS forwarders. The loss of the OperationsManagerAC database results in the loss of the historical security information.

Given the size of the database, the OperationsManagerAC database should be backed up on a weekly basis. The recommendation is to do a full backup monthly and a differential backup weekly to reduce disk space requirements.

To set up the full and differential backups for the OperationsManagerAC database, execute the following steps:

1. Launch SQL Server Management Studio on the operations database server.

2. Click the Connect button.

3. Expand the Databases folder.

4. Right-click the OperationsManagerAC database, select Tasks, and click Back Up.

5. In the Back Up Database dialog box, type the name of the backup set in the Name box.

6. In the Destination section, click Add.

7. In the Select Backup Destination dialog box, type a path and a filename in the Destination on Disk box, click OK, and then click OK again.

> **NOTE**
>
> The destination location selected must have enough disk space to hold the backups, particularly with the large audit collection database.

8. In the Script pull-down list at the top of the window, select Script Action to Job.

9. In the Name field, enter a name for the job such as **Back Up Database - OperationsManagerAC Full**.

10. In the New Job window, select the Schedules page and click New.

11. In the New Job Schedule dialog box, type **OperationsManagerAC Monthly Full Backup** as the job name in the Name box, specify the job schedule as monthly, and then click OK.

12. Click OK.

13. At this point, click OK to execute a manual full backup or click Cancel to skip it.

14. Right-click the OperationsManagerAC database, select Tasks, and click Back Up.

15. Select Differential in the Backup Type pull-down.

16. In the Back Up Database dialog box, type the name of the backup set in the Name box.

17. In the Destination section, click Add.

18. In the Select Backup Destination dialog box, type a path and a filename in the Destination on Disk box, click OK, and then click OK again.

> **NOTE**
>
> The destination location selected must have enough disk space to hold the backups, particularly with the large audit collection database.

19. In the Script pull-down list at the top of the window, select Script Action to Job.

20. In the Name field, enter a name for the job such as `Back Up Database - OperationsManagerAC Differential`.

21. In the New Job window, select the Schedules page and click New.

22. In the New Job Schedule dialog box, type `OperationsManagerAC Weekly Differential Backup` as the job name in the Name box, specify the job schedule as weekly, and then click OK.

23. Click OK.

24. Click OK to execute a manual differential backup right away or click Cancel to skip it.

> **NOTE**
>
> The full backup will have had to run before running the differential backup; otherwise, it will fail.

The OperationsManagerAC database backup will now execute automatically according to the recommended schedule.

IIS 7.x Configuration Backup

The IIS 7 `applicationHost.config` files include configuration information for the sites, applications, virtual directories, application pool definitions, and the default configuration settings for all sites on the web server.

To back up the IIS 7 configuration from a command prompt, complete the following steps:

1. Log on to the Windows Server 2008 computer that is hosting the Operations Manager 2012 Web console and Reporting components.

2. Open a command prompt by using the RunAs Administrator option and change the directory to `c:\system32\inetsrv`.

3. At the command prompt, type **appcmd add backup <backupname>**. If you do not include the name of the backup, the system will name it for you by using a date, time format.

The IIS 7 configuration is now backed up.

Summary

The installation, configuration, maintenance, and administration of the Operations Manager 2012 infrastructure is key to the long-term stability and performance of the monitoring platform. Following the guidance in this chapter helps ensure that the OpsMgr is able to perform its functions properly.

Best Practices

The following are best practices from this chapter:

▶ Deploy Operations Manager components on Windows 64-bit and SQL 64-bit for optimal performance.

▶ Use SQL Enterprise whenever possible to improve database performance, especially for the ACS components.

▶ Run the prerequisite checker before installing components and remediate all findings, including warnings.

▶ Take future expansion and relevance of hardware into account when sizing servers for OpsMgr deployment.

▶ Use a dedicated instance of SQL Reporting Services for Operations Manager reporting.

▶ The directory that hosts the OpsMgr agent queue and log files should be excluded from the antivirus and defragmentation applications.

▶ Keep the installation of OpsMgr on a separate server or set of separate dedicated member servers that do not run any other separate applications.

▶ Start with a single management group and add additional management groups only if they are absolutely necessary.

▶ Use a dedicated service account for OpsMgr.

▶ Allocate adequate space for the databases depending on the length of time needed to store events and the number of managed systems.

▶ Monitor the size of the OpsMgr database to ensure that it does not increase beyond the bounds of acceptable size.

▶ Leverage the reporting database to store and report on data over a long period.

▶ Modify the grooming interval to aggressively address environmental requirements.

▶ Do not modify the Performance Signature grooming interval, as this throws off the baseline calculations.

▶ Configure the management group to automatically approve manual agents.

▶ Ensure that the key OpsMgr components are backed up on the recommended schedules.

▶ When tuning, err on the side of fewer alerts. If nothing will be done about an alert, make sure it doesn't send a notification email.

CHAPTER 8

Using Operations Manager 2012 for Monitoring and Alerting

IN THIS CHAPTER

▶ Using OpsMgr Consoles

▶ Working with Management Packs

▶ Exploring the Operations Manager Management Pack

▶ Exploring the Windows Management Pack

▶ Exploring the Active Directory Management Pack

▶ Exploring the Exchange 2010 Management Pack

▶ Exploring the SQL Server Management Pack

▶ Exploring the Cross Platform Management Packs

▶ Management Pack Templates

▶ Custom Management Packs

▶ Best Practices

Out of the box, Operations Manager 2012 only monitors the basic health of the agents and the OpsMgr infrastructure. To really get the value from the monitoring platform, management packs (MPs) need to be deployed, configured, and tuned.

This chapter covers deploying the Microsoft management packs. Microsoft has a Common Engineering Criteria (CEC) that all their product development teams follow. The CEC specifies that all products they release must have an Operations Manager Management Pack to allow the product to be monitored.

> **NOTE**
>
> Although this is a great statement of intent, in practice the management packs are sometimes released well after the release date of the product, in violation of the CEC. For example, Windows Server 2008 was released and it was over six months before there was a corresponding management pack!

Each of the management packs has differing features, capabilities, and configuration requirements. This chapter discusses the core management packs in detail, specifically the following:

▶ Operations Manager Management Pack

▶ Windows Management Pack

- ▶ Active Directory Management Pack

- ▶ Exchange Management Pack

- ▶ SQL Server Management Pack

- ▶ Cross Platform Management Packs

For each of the management packs, the features, configuration, and tuning are covered.

In addition, this chapter looks at how to create custom monitoring using Management Pack Templates, custom management packs, Simple Network Management Protocol (SNMP), and distributed applications. These features help administrators extend Operations Manager 2012 to monitoring non-Microsoft products and applications.

Using OpsMgr Consoles

To understand how to use the management packs, it is important to understand how to use the OpsMgr consoles. Operations Manager 2012 has three main consoles that are used to access its functionality. These consoles have their advantages and disadvantages when compared with each other. The consoles are as follows:

- ▶ **Operations Console**—This is the full console and provides access to all the features and configuration of the Operations Manager 2012 platform.

- ▶ **Web console**—This is the lighter, web-based console and provides access to a subset of the operations space of the Operations Console.

- ▶ **Command shell**—This console, better yet shell, provides a PowerShell command-line interface into the functionality of Operations Manager.

These consoles allow administrators and operators to use the more appropriate form of access depending on their requirements. Also, the consoles present a unified security front and the same level of access regardless of which console is used, based on the user's credentials.

Using the Operations Console

The Operations Manager 2012 console introduces performance and User Interface (UI) improvements. The OpsMgr 2012 console is downward compatible with pre-R2 implementations of OpsMgr; however, non-R2 consoles will not be able to connect to an OpsMgr 2012 Management Server (MS).

The console attaches to the MS, and it is not recommended to go above 50 consoles as this adds a major strain on the MS and the database server—even assuming high-performance hardware. The full console can also be directed to other management groups via the MS by going to Tools and then to Connect in the full console.

> **NOTE**
>
> Although the performance of the UI has increased, the behavior of the `momcache.mdb` cache file is the same. This cache file has been seen to grow over 3GB and should be cleared from time to time. It is not recommended to clear the console frequently as the cache assists the console in performance. The console cache can be cleared by launching the console with `/clearcache` with the cache location in `%localappdata%\microsoft\microsoft.mom.ui.console`.

> **NOTE**
>
> To scale to more consoles, enterprise-sized organizations might choose to leverage a remote application with Windows Server 2008 R2 Terminal Services or Terminal Server jump points. Jump points are Terminal Servers configured with Terminal Services in Application mode, which allows more than two Remote Desktop Protocol (RDP) sessions. The Operations Manager console can be installed in the jump point, and then as many operators as needed can use the Remote Desktop Protocol (RDP) client to connect to the jump point and launch the console.

The Operations Manager console resembles the MMC 3.0 look and feel of previous versions. To recap, on the left is the console root containing the default views and management packs in addition to the Wonderbar-like bars containing additional views (that is, Authoring, Reporting, Administration, and My Workspace). The view in the center always reflects the data, with the right side containing any actionable items (that is, State Actions, Tasks, Reports, Help).

The console root hierarchy is divided into nine categories. The first six are detailed the list below with a high-level description of the category and purpose:

▶ **Folder**—Organizes views for ease of access. Unless created by a management pack, folders can be created and stored into a designated unsealed management pack (folders can live in the Default Management Pack, but folders cannot cross between management packs). Sealed management packs cannot be edited. Folders can contain the views. Applying filters within the views in OpsMgr 2012 can be compared with creating rules in Outlook.

▶ **Alert view**—Displays data specific to alerts.

▶ **Event view**—Displays data specific to collected events.

▶ **State view**—Displays the entity health of the managed object as it relates to the management pack, or personalized view in custom-created MP/views.

▶ **Performance view**—Displays collected performance statistics.

▶ **Task Status view**—Displays console-based and agent-based task history.

With these five views in the list above, data can be filtered by object, group, and then by conditions.

The other three of the nine view categories are more specialized and allow for composite views that display multiple types of objects in the same view. This is good for displaying a more holistic view of operational data and monitored objects. The three other view types are as follows:

▶ **Dashboard view**—Can be used to display multiple panes in a single view. The Dashboard view is much improved in OpsMgr 2012 and supports integration with SharePoint 2010.

▶ **Diagram view**—Can be used to display relationship information, using the Topology view in the Active Directory Management Pack (AD MP), for example. This Diagram view illustrates Active Directory forest properties on the domain monitored, as it relates to Active Directory sites, Active Directory site links, and Active Directory domains.

▶ **Web Page view**—Can be used to include an active Internet Explorer session within the console. This allows the OpsMgr console to become a portal to external utilities, such as an internal knowledge base/ticketing system or hardware manager like Hewlett Packard Systems Insight Manager (HP SIM).

Permissions are handled in the Administration view of the Operations Manager nested under Security, User Roles. By default, seven roles are available with the ability to filter them based on group scope, tasks, and views.

When configuring views for the consumer, it is recommended to tailor the views as needed (filtering for only the systems required for the consumer), test the views using an AD account, apply permissions on the views using AD groups (that is, users into the corresponding AD groups, and the corresponding AD groups into OpsMgr roles), and filter the views to only the custom set(s) created.

> **NOTE**
>
> While assigning a role, an often-overlooked feature is the View Group Members action, which launches a new window showing the highlighted group's members.
>
> This can be used to ensure targets within the group membership without having to restart the wizard.

Using the Web Console

The Web console can be thought of as a light mobile version of the full console, using forms-based authentication through Internet Information Services (IIS). Permission application does not happen at the IIS level, but through the Operations Manager console in the Administration view. The Web console does not cache any information, and is noticeably slower with data retrieving. Similar to the full console, the Web console attaches to the MS but with less overhead.

An additional option to interfacing with Operations Manager data is a web interface tailored to mobile devices. This interface provides high-level information on computers, distributed applications, and the ability to view the last 10 active alerts. By default, the interface for mobile devices can be reached at HTTP://<MANAGEMENTSERVER-NAME>:51908/Mobile.

With the new Web console, an operator has the ability to access the Health Explorer of the managed object. The Health Explorer can be accessed by using the same method as the full console, by right-clicking on the desired object and selecting Health Explorer.

> **NOTE**
>
> Although a link to the alert in the Web console URL is provided in the notification emails by default, users will not be able to access the information on the link if they are not granted rights to the Web console within Operations Manager.

Tasks can also be executed in the Web console. The Web console is limited to scripted tasks. Application-based tasks cannot be accessed through the Web console; however, it is possible to create a script to call the necessary application and have this available in the console.

Working with Management Packs

In working with management packs, the Operations Manager administrator will be performing many of the same administrative tasks for each management pack. This includes importing management packs, downloading management packs, exporting management packs, and tuning management packs.

> **NOTE**
>
> OpsMgr 2012 uses the same management packs as OpsMgr 2007 R2.

In the Administration view of the console is the Management Pack tree folder. This folder contains all management packs loaded into Operations Manager. With OpsMgr 2012, the administrator can download management packs directly from Microsoft's hosted catalog as opposed to manually downloading the bits, installing them, and then importing them. The System Center Operations Manager 2012 Catalog allows the operator to search for management packs based on a keyword, then download (and install if selected) the management pack. Although this feature is a step in the right direction, be wary of importing an entire management pack section. Using the Terminal Services Management Pack, for example, if the entire MP section is downloaded, undesired language packs are selected.

> **NOTE**
>
> A notable exception to the ability to download from the catalog is the Exchange 2010 Management Pack. This management pack must be downloaded separately and installed using an MSI package, due to some additional setup requirements.

It is recommended to only select the management packs required. In addition, with this feature, any supporting management packs will be downloaded if necessary.

It is also recommended to perform infrastructure-like changes (for example, management pack importing, rule/monitor creations/modifications/and so on) during nonbusiness hours because the rules are immediately propagated throughout the environment.

Importing a Management Pack from the Internet

A common administrative task is to import a management pack directly from the Web Service Catalog over the Internet.

To import the SQL Server Management Pack from the System Center Operations Manager 2012 Catalog, complete the following steps:

1. Navigate to the Administration view and select Management Packs.

2. In the Actions pane, select Import Management Packs.

3. In the Select Management Packs window, click the Add drop-down menu and select Add from Catalog.

4. For the example, the SQL Server Management Pack needs to be downloaded. In the Select Management Packs from Catalog window, type **SQL** in the Find field and click Search.

5. In the Management Packs in the Catalog section, expand the Microsoft folder, and then the SQL Server folder. There'll be a number of SQL Server–related management pack folders.

6. Expand the SQL Server 2008 folder. The actual management packs will be listed in the folder. In the status column, the status will be listed as Not Installed, Current, or Update Available depending on the management packs already installed. This is very helpful for determining which management packs need to be downloaded.

> **NOTE**
>
> Additional localized versions of the management packs, such as Chinese Simplified or French, are available in subfolders, which can be downloaded as the situation warrants.

7. Select the SQL Server 2008 (Discovery) Management Pack, and then click the Add button. Do the same for the SQL Server 2008 (Monitoring) Management Pack and the SQL Server Core Library Management Pack.

8. Verify the selected management packs (see Figure 8.1) and click OK.

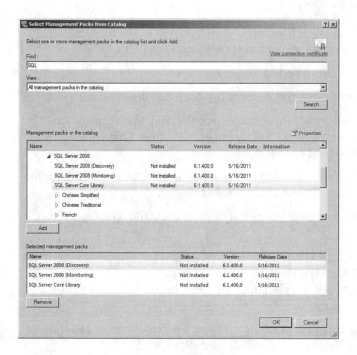

FIGURE 8.1   Importing a management pack from the Internet.

9. The Select Management Packs from Catalog section closes and the Import Management Packs window opens; verify the Import list and click Install.

NOTE

The management pack prerequisites and dependencies are checked, so any issues will be displayed here for resolution. For example, if one of the management packs had a dependency on another management pack that was not installed already, then the administrator could click on the error message to automatically import the required management pack.

---

10. All management packs will be downloaded, queued, and imported. Ensure there are no errors in the Import Status Detail window and click Close.

Now the management pack is installed and is immediately deployed to the relevant managed computers when their agents heartbeat.

Downloading a Management Pack from the Internet

Often, the OpsMgr administrator will download the management pack for review and archiving rather than import directly from the Internet. This is a good practice to ensure correct versioning or for lab testing prior to deployment in production. In the following example, the DHCP Management Pack is demonstrated.

To download (but not import) a management pack, complete the following steps:

1. Navigate to the Administration view and select Management Packs.

2. In the Actions pane, select Download Management Packs.

3. In the Select Management Packs window, click the Add drop-down menu.

4. For this example, the Forefront Threat Management Gateway Management Pack needs to be downloaded. In the Select Management Packs from Catalog window, type **Forefront** in the Find field and click Search.

5. In the Management Packs in the Catalog section, expand the Microsoft Corporation, Forefront, and then Forefront Threat Mgmt Gateway folder.

6. Select the Microsoft.Forefront.TMG Management Pack, click Add, and then click OK.

7. The Management Packs in the Catalog windows closes and the Import Management Packs window opens. Change the Download Management Pack to This Folder Location to c:\TEMP\MP_DL\ (if the path does not exist, create it using the Browse button), and click Download.

8. In the Download Management Packs window, ensure the management pack has a status of Downloaded (as shown in Figure 8.2), and click Close.

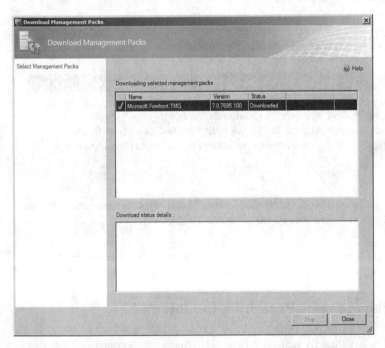

FIGURE 8.2   Downloading a management pack from the Internet.

Manually Installing a Management Pack from a Download

Assuming the MP files have been downloaded to the folder `c:\TEMP\MP_DL`, to manually import the downloaded management packs, complete the following steps:

1. Navigate to the Administration view and select Management Packs.

2. In the Actions pane, select Import Management Packs.

3. In the Select Management Packs window, click the Add drop-down menu and select Add from Disk.

4. The Online Catalog Connection window opens; click No for this window.

5. The Select Management Packs to Import window opens; browse to `c:\TEMP\MP_DL` and select the desired management pack files. Click Open when you are ready.

6. The Select Management Packs to Import window closes and the Import Management Packs window becomes active; confirm the Import list and click Install.

> **NOTE**
>
> The management pack prerequisites and dependencies are checked, so any issues will be displayed here for resolution. For example, if one of the management packs had a dependency on another management pack that was not installed already, then the administrator could click on the error message to automatically import the required management pack.

7. In the Import Management Packs window, ensure the objects have a status of Imported and click Close.

The management pack will take effect immediately, discovering new instances and automatically deploying monitors and rules. This import process is a useful procedure for both installing previously downloaded MPs and MPs from third-party vendors.

Exporting a Management Pack

A frequent administrative task for the OpsMgr administrator is to export a management pack. This is an easy way to back up a management pack or to move a custom management pack from the development/testing environment to production.

To export a management pack, complete the following steps:

1. Navigate to the Administration view and select Management Packs.

2. Select the desired unsealed management pack.

3. In the Actions pane, click Export Management Packs.

4. The Browse for Folder window opens; use the location `c:\TEMP\MP_EXP` (if the location does not exist, create it), click OK, and then click OK again.

8

> **NOTE**
>
> Only unsealed management packs can be exported.

Examining the management pack GUI further, information displayed through the full console does not reflect all of the information available. If more information is required, use the Operations Manager command shell `Get-SCOMManagementPack` cmdlet or PowerShell with the required OpsMgr add-in.

> **NOTE**
>
> Using the GUI interface, it is easier to view management pack dependencies.

In addition, report automation is recommended to ease change management and tracking of management packs. Operations Manager 2012 offers a Management Pack report in the Microsoft ODR Reporting Library that details the management packs installed to the management group as well as the overrides being applied. Custom-created management packs are not detailed in this report.

> **NOTE**
>
> Exporting a management pack is also a good way to manually edit the management pack XML file. This can be imported after changes are made to the XML file and the changes take effect on the managed agents.

Overrides and Override Management Packs

Monitors, rules, and tasks can have overrides; an override is used to apply value(s) other than the default. For example, if the alert is being generated for a condition that is not important to a particular organization, then the rule or monitor can be suppressed with an override. Or an override might become necessary during troubleshooting when data points need to be captured every 5 to 10 seconds, rather than the default 5 or 15 minutes as with some performance-capturing rules.

Three override methods are highlighted, as they are accessed in different places within Operations Manager.

The methods are as follows:

▶ **Method 1**—The first method is available in the Authoring view of the console. When browsing monitors, object discoveries, or rules, the Overrides button in the toolbar becomes available when an item is selected. Additionally, right-clicking on the item yields the Overrides option (as shown in Figure 8.3).

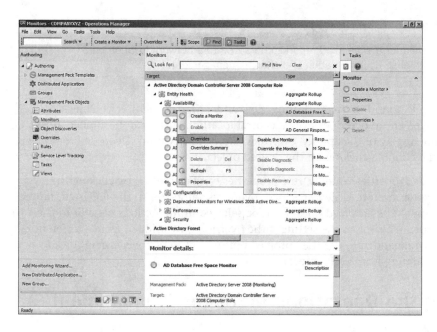

FIGURE 8.3   The Overrides option.

▶ **Method 2**—When browsing the Health Explorer for the monitored object, right-click on the monitor to access the properties, and then access the Overrides tab. Additionally, when viewing performance metrics through the Performance view, an Overrides option is available by right-clicking the selected object.

▶ **Method 3**—Within the Active Alerts view of the Monitoring view, monitors and rules that generate information can be issued an override by right-clicking an item and selecting Overrides.

It is recommended for overrides to be written to the management pack containing the overridden object. For sealed management packs, overrides should be saved to a custom management pack, typically named like the sealed MP with a suffix such as "Override MP". For example, the Exchange 2010 Management Pack Overrides would be stored in the management pack named Exchange 2010 Override MP. Override management becomes increasingly necessary, especially when Operations Manager management is performed by more than one individual.

Operations Manager includes integrated tools to manage/monitor overrides. The features provided can generate reports and ease management.

For reporting, Microsoft Generic Report Library has an Overrides report, which can be run against all management packs or a single management pack.

8

> **NOTE**
>
> It is recommended for a scheduled report to be saved to a network location on a monthly basis to ease documentation and change management.

The Overrides node, found in the Authoring view under Management Pack Objects, allows for management of overrides from a central location. Filters can be applied at the scope, easing the display of the applied overrides. From this location, Override Properties can be accessed by double-clicking on the desired object.

From the Override Properties window, rule properties can be accessed by clicking the Show Rule Properties button. Unless specified, overrides will be set to the Preferred, rather than Enforced, state. The Enforced option can be selected in the Actions pane or in the Override Properties—this forces the setting if the override is overridden from a different location. It is recommended to use the Enforced option, but to discover where the additional setting is coming from and remediate.

Exploring the Operations Manager Management Pack

The Operations Manager Management Pack monitors the overall health of the Operations Manager infrastructure. The Operations Manager infrastructure monitoring is divided into three major categories: Agent, Management Server(s), and Health Service. Within these categories, performance metrics are captured and console-based tasks can be executed.

> **NOTE**
>
> The Operations Manager Management Pack is imported during the installation, unlike the other management packs discussed in this chapter. The other management packs must be imported manually.

Updating this management pack is necessary as updates become available.

Eight component management packs make up the Operations Manager Management Pack:

- ▶ Microsoft.SystemCenter.OperationsManager.2007.mp
- ▶ Microsoft.SystemCenter.OperationsManager.AM.DR.2007.mp
- ▶ Microsoft.SystemCenter.OperationsManager.DataAccessService.mp
- ▶ Microsoft.SystemCenter.OperationsManager.Infra.mp
- ▶ Microsoft.SystemCenter.OperationsManager.Internal.mp
- ▶ Microsoft.SystemCenter.OperationsManager.Library.mp
- ▶ Microsoft.SystemCenter.OperationsManager.Reports.2007.mp
- ▶ Microsoft.SystemCenter.OperationsManager.SummaryDashboard.mp

After importing the management packs, some key configuration tasks should be performed to optimize the performance and operations of the management pack.

Configuring the Operations Manager Management Pack

A number of key Management Points in the Operations Manager Management Pack can be configured to optimize the behavior of the agents. They include monitors, diagnostic, and recovery changes. These are as follows:

- ▶ Management Server to Management Group Availability Health Rollup
- ▶ Health Service Heartbeat Failure Monitor
- ▶ Reinstall Health Service Recovery
- ▶ Restart Health Service Recovery
- ▶ Remote Data Access Service Check Monitor

The Management Server to Management Group Availability Health Rollup dependency rollup object rolls up the health from the Operational DB Watchers Group. Override the monitor to enable it for all objects of type Operations Manager management group. This monitors the space available in the operations database, in addition to checking operations database connectivity.

The Health Service Heartbeat Failure aggregate monitor checks the availability of each agent Health Service. The aggregate monitor includes a number of diagnostics and recoveries that can be triggered when problems are detected. Override the Resume Health Service recovery for all objects of type Health Service Watcher (Agent) to set the value of Enabled to True. This ensures that the Health Service will remain operational in the event a user with privileges has tampered with the Health Service by stopping it.

> **NOTE**
>
> All the Health Service Watcher monitors run on a management server and watch the agents. There is a Health Service Watcher for each agent making sure the agent is okay, just like its own personal guardian angel.

Also in the Health Service Heartbeat Failure aggregate monitor, override the Reinstall Health Service (triggered from Diagnostic) recovery for all objects of type Health Service Watcher (Agent) to set the value of Enabled to True. This feature is a time-saver, allowing the reinstallation of an agent from the alert if the agent has been uninstalled for some reason.

Also in the Health Service Heartbeat Failure aggregate monitor, override the Restart Health Service recovery for all objects of type Health Service Watcher (Agent) to set the value of Enabled to True. This ensures that the Health Service will remain operational in the event a user with privileges has stopped the service or if the service stops because of a resource problem.

> **NOTE**
>
> This is probably one of the most important overrides that an administrator can make. One of the most common problems found in an Operations Manager infrastructure review is that a number of agents are in an unmonitored state (gray) due to the agent service being stopped and never restarted. The Restart Health Service recovery ensures that those agents are restarted immediately.

The Remote Data Access Service Check monitor checks connectivity to the Data Access service. For the Collection Server objects, this is from each of the ACS collection management servers. Override the monitor for all objects of the class Management Server and set the Enabled value to True. This monitor detects when the MS is not reachable every 5 minutes with a 30-second timeout value.

Operations Manager Management Pack Views

The Operations Manager sealed management pack folder will appear in the Monitoring view tree.

Included by default at the top level of the tree is the Management Group Diagram view. This is a distributed application, detailing the Operations Manager management group infrastructure.

There are nine subfolders, categorizing the Operations Manager infrastructure by component. The most commonly used ones (Agent Details, Agent Performance, Health Service Configuration, Health Service Module Events, Management Server, and Management Server Performance) are discussed here.

The Agent Details folder contains three dashboards that are very important to use when monitoring or troubleshooting agent health. These are as follows:

- **Active Alerts**—Details open alerts for agents and their health watchers
- **Agent Health State**—Shows State view for agents and their health watchers
- **Agent Performance**—Shows four key performance metric views for agents

This Agent Health State dashboard is invaluable for troubleshooting agent issues. Health status can be accessed at a glance and from the Tasks pane on the right, a variety of useful tasks for diagnosing and repairing agents can be selected. Some of the more useful tasks that are available are as follows:

- Flush Health Service State and Cache
- Get the Agent Processor Utilization
- Reload Configuration
- Start Online Store Maintenance
- Trigger On Demand Discovery

For example, the Show Running Rules and Monitors for This Health Service task can be issued against the agent to show the rules and monitors actually running on the agent, which totals 1,363 for the DC1 domain controller, as shown in Figure 8.4.

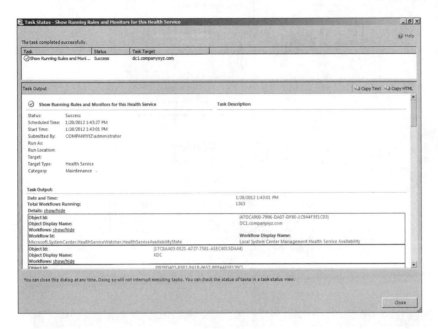

FIGURE 8.4   Show Running Rules and Monitors for This Health Service task.

The Agent Performance dashboard contains four Performance views, which are very useful for monitoring agent performance. The Agent Performance Dashboard views are as follows:

- Agent Processor Utilization
- Send Queue % Used
- Workflow Count
- Module Count

The Send Queue % Used view is particularly useful, as it shows in near–real time the agent queues that are backing up. This is always a sign of trouble. Figure 8.5 shows the Agent Performance view with the counters for DC1 selected. The view shows that the agent processor utilization averages around 1% to 2% and that the send queue % stays under 0.5%. These numbers show that the agent is performing well, as it is not consuming too much CPU time and the queues are not backed up at all.

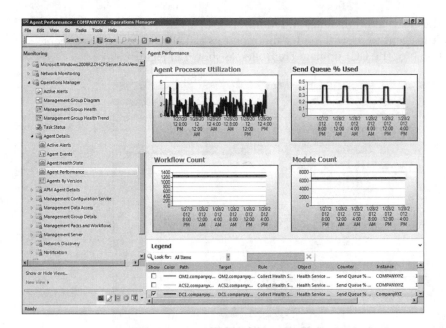

FIGURE 8.5   The Agent Performance view.

NOTE

Agent performance will vary depending on the workloads being monitoring, with a web server being a very light load and an Exchange server a heavy load. In general, look for the agent Send Queue % Used to stay under 1% and for Agent Processor Utilization to stay under 5%.

The top-level Management Server folder contains two views that help monitor and troubleshoot the management servers. This is very similar in function to the top-level Agent Details folder for agents. The views are as follows:

▶ **Active Alerts**—Filters for open management server alerts

▶ **Management Servers State**—Details the state of all management servers and Gateway servers in a four-pane dashboard

The Management Group Details folder contains a number of different views that show detailed events and performance data. There are five different Event views, which present filtering views from AEM Module Events to Notification Events. There is also a useful dashboard for displaying AD-based Agent Assigned Module events if the environment is using Active Directory agent assignment.

The Performance Data view in the Management Group Details folder (shown in Figure 8.6) displays the following performance metrics:

- ▶ Active File Uploads

- ▶ Agent Processor Utilization

- ▶ Batch and Data Item Metrics

- ▶ Dropped Item Counts per Item Type

- ▶ Total Errors and Errors/Sec per Item Type

- ▶ Queue Sizes and Percent Used

- ▶ Workflow Count

This is useful for correlating performance during troubleshooting.

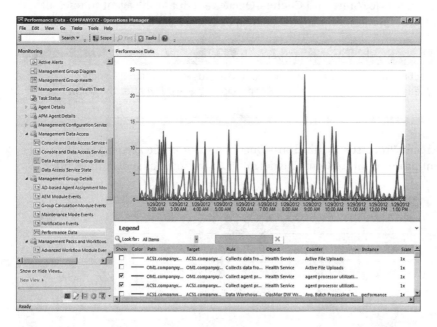

FIGURE 8.6   The OpsMgr MP Performance Data view.

NOTE

Each view in this sealed management pack reflects different information, as listed previously. The Agent Health State (under the Agent subfolder) is one of the most-used views. From this view, agent troubleshooting tools are made available by selecting an agent from the Agent State Dashboard view and selecting an action (for example, Flush Health Service State and Cache or Show Failed Rules and Monitors for This Health Service) from the Actions pane. In addition, the Management Server Health State (under the Management Server subfolder) is second in usefulness to the Agent Health State. From this view, troubleshooting actions can be processed against management servers from the Management Server State Dashboard view.

Operations Manager Management Pack Tasks

More than 19 Health Service tasks are included in the management pack and can be accessed in the Actions pane on the right when selecting an agent object. The tasks are as follows:

- ▶ **Computer Management**—Opens the Computer Management console with a remote connection to the selected computer.

- ▶ **Disable Audit Collection**—Queues a script at the agent to stop and disable the Audit Collection Service.

- ▶ **Enable Audit Collection**—Queues a script at the agent to enable and configure the Audit Collection Service.

- ▶ **Flush Health Service State and Cache**—Queues a script at the agent to reset all Health Service States (monitors, MPs cached, outbound data, rules, and so on).

> **NOTE**
>
> Because this action impacts the Health Service, the status will not update and will remain in a Queued status until timed out. Simply close the window after the script launches.

- ▶ **Get the Agent Processor Utilization**—Queues a script at the agent to get the real-time agent processor utilization. The default is 25 samples, as shown in Figure 8.7.

FIGURE 8.7   Get the Agent Processor Utilization task.

▶ **Get the Pool Member Monitoring a Top-Level Instance**—Returns the management server that is monitoring a top-level instance, that is, the computer.

▶ **Get Top-Level Instances Monitored by a Pool Member**—Returns the top-level instances (that is, computers) monitored by a management server.

NOTE

The pool tasks are new to OpsMgr 2012 and should be run against management server agents. They will generate errors when run against agents. In addition, the tasks have overrides that must be configured, including the `Pool ID` and the `ManagedEntityID`. The `Pool ID` is a GUID and can be obtained from the PowerShell command `get SCOMResourcePool`. The `ManagedEntityID` for an agent can be obtained from the `get-SCOMAgent` command. Not the easiest tasks to use.

▶ **Ping Computer (with Route)**—Runs trace route ping at the selected agent from the system running the console; opens a new window displaying the results to the MS.

▶ **Ping Computer Continuously (ping —t)**—Runs a continuous ICMP ping at the selected agent from the system running the console; opens a new window displaying the ping —t results to the MS.

▶ **Reload Configuration**—Queues a script at the agent to reload agent configurations.

▶ **Remote Desktop**—Launches an RDP client session at the selected computer.

▶ **Remote Desktop (Admin)**—Launches an RDP client session with the `/Admin` switch at the selected computer.

▶ **Remote Desktop (Console)**—Launches an RDP client session with the `/Console` switch at the object.

▶ **Show Failed Rules and Monitors for This Health Service**—Launches a script at the agent and returns a snapshot of the failed monitors/rules.

▶ **Show Enabled Rules and Monitors for This Health Service**—Launches a script at the agent and returns a snapshot of the enabled monitors/rules.

▶ **Start Audit Collection**—Launches a script at the agent to start the Audit Collection Service.

▶ **Start Online Store Maintenance**—Launches a script at the agent to start maintenance (Defrag) of the online store for the Health Service ESE store. Although the task is routinely processed at the agent, it can be launched as needed by this task.

▶ **Start WMI Service**—Launches a script at the agent to start the WMI service.

> **NOTE**
>
> Often an OpsMgr administrator will be asked to provide a report on the running OpsMgr processes on a managed agent. For this, the Show Running Rules and Monitors for This Health Service task is invaluable—information generated can be copied to text or HTML.

Exploring the Windows Management Pack

The Windows Management Pack discovers Windows 2000 Server, Windows Server 2003, and Windows Server 2008 to monitor availability, health, and performance. The management pack automatically detects, alerts, and responds to a wide range of critical events and performance metrics to ensure the long-term health and stability of the server operating systems.

> **NOTE**
>
> This management pack is also leveraged by other management packs, such as AD, Exchange, and SQL.

How to Configure the Windows Management Pack

With OpsMgr 2012, the management pack can be downloaded and imported directly from the Web Catalog. The location in the catalog is `Microsoft Corporation\Windows Server\Core OS\`. There are eight management packs and also additional language versions.

After downloading and installing this MP, usually the default location of the MP files is located in `c:\%Program Files%\System Center Management Packs\Windows Server Base OS System Center Operations Manager 2012 MP\`.

> **NOTE**
>
> When installing the MP via executing the downloaded MP source file (usually an MSI), content of the MSI is expanded into the default installation directory. Executing the MSI does not import the MP into Operations Manager.

The management packs that make up the Windows Core OS monitoring are as follows:

▶ `Microsoft.Windows.Server.2000.mp`

▶ `Microsoft.Windows.Server.2003.mp`

▶ `Microsoft.Windows.Server.2008.Discovery.mp`

▶ `Microsoft.Windows.Server.2008.Monitoring.mp`

▶ Microsoft.Windows.Server.2008.R2.Monitoring.BPA.mp

▶ Microsoft.Windows.Server.ClusterSharedVolumeMonitoring.mp

▶ Microsoft.Windows.Server.Library.mp

▶ Microsoft.Windows.Server.Reports.mp

The Microsoft.Windows.Server.Library.mp and Microsoft.Windows.Server.Reports.mp are common across all the Windows Server operating systems. The other operating system–specific management packs can be imported as needed.

In the event a manual import is required, the following order of import should be followed:

▶ First, the Microsoft.Windows.Server.Library.MP

▶ Second, the Microsoft.Windows.Server.2008.Discovery.MP

Afterwards, any operating system–specific MPs (such as the Microsoft.Windows.Server.2000.MP, Microsoft.Windows.Server.2003.MP or Microsoft.Windows.Server.2008.Monitoring.MP) can be imported.

The installed agent should be configured to use the Local System account. Using this account grants the agent the ability to process discovery, monitors, rules, tasks, and other Operations Manager–related tasks.

Tuning the Windows Management Pack

During Windows Management Pack deployment, a couple of items must be tuned to mitigate alerting storms and for baseline monitoring. The tuning points are as follows:

▶ Logical Disk Free Space Monitor

▶ Total Processor % Interrupt Time Rule

The Logical Disk Free Space Monitor for both Windows Server 2003 Logical Disk and the Windows Server 2008 Logical Disk should be tuned. The way the Logical Disk Free Space is configured, there are two sets of values for error and warning: % Threshold and MByte Threshold. Rather than a logical OR operator, the management pack uses a logical AND operator. Both the % Threshhold and the MByte Threshold must be true for the alert to trigger. By configuring one of the value sets to always be true, the monitor is effectively set to trigger on the other value set. Configure overrides for the following items:

▶ Error Mbytes Threshold for Non-System Drives to Value 10240

▶ Warning Mbytes Threshold for Non-System Drives to Value 10240

▶ Warning Mbytes Threshold for System Drives to Value 10240

8

Setting those to 10GB allows the % Threshold values to trigger alerts properly.

The Rule node contains several rules covering memory and interrupts that should be tuned. By default, many of the performance rules are disabled. This reduces the size of the database, but at the expense of details performance metrics. To take full advantage of OpsMgr 2012, it is a best practice to enable many of these collection rules using overrides for the respective objects.

Each version of the operating system will have its own object, such as Windows Server 2008 Core Operating System or Windows Server 2003 Core Operating System. Each object will have its own set of rules, which need to have the overrides configured to enable the rules. In the following examples, the objects and rules for the Windows Server 2008 operating system will be used. If Windows Server 2000 or Windows Server 2003 Management Packs are in use, then the corresponding overrides will need to be configured.

For the Windows Server 2008 Core Operating System object, five main rules need to be enabled. These rules can be found in the Authoring section of the console in the Management Pack Objects\Rules folder. The rules will be under the Type: Windows Server 2008 Core Operating System class. The rules to override are as follows:

▶ Page File Percentage Use 2008

▶ Total Processor % Interrupt Time 2008

▶ Memory Page Writes per Second 2008

▶ Memory Page Reads per Second 2008

▶ Memory % Committed Bytes in Use 2008

There are 10 disk-related rules that should be enabled to properly monitor disk activity. These are rules that target the Windows Server 2008 Logical Disk object. These rules can be found in the Authoring section of the console in the Management Pack Objects\Rules folder. The rules will be under the Type: Windows Server 2008 Logical Disk class. The specific rules to override are as follows:

▶ Collection Rule for Average Logical Disk Seconds per Write 2008

▶ Collection Rule for Disk Writes per Second 2008

▶ Collection Rule for Disk Reads per Second 2008

▶ Logical Disk Read Bytes per Second 2008

▶ Collection Rule for Average Disk Seconds per Read 2008

▶ Average Logical Disk Read Queue Length 2008

▶ Collection Rule for Average Disk Queue Length 2008

▶ Average Logical Disk Write Queue Length 2008

▶ Collection Rule for Disk Bytes per Second 2008

▶ Logical Disk Write Bytes per Second 2008

To properly monitor network activity, a number of rules need to be enabled for the Windows Server 2008 Network Adapter object. These rules can be found in the Authoring section of the console in the Management Pack Objects\Rules folder. The rules will be under the Type: Windows Server 2008 Network Adapter class. The specific rules to override are as follows:

▶ Network Adapter Bytes Sent per Second 2008

▶ Percent Bandwidth Used Write

▶ Percent Bandwidth Used Read

▶ Network Adapter Bytes Received per Second 2008

Enabling the previous rules for the class of objects will allow detailed performance metrics to be collected for the processor, disk, memory, and network for the Windows Server operating system. This will also enable the Windows Management Pack views (discussed in the next section) and reports to show useful information.

Windows Management Pack Views

Upon importing this management pack, a Microsoft Windows Server sealed management pack folder will appear in the Monitoring view tree.

Included by default are four top-level views in the Microsoft Windows Server:

▶ Active Alerts

▶ Operating System Performance (shown in Figure 8.8)

▶ Task Status

▶ Windows Server State

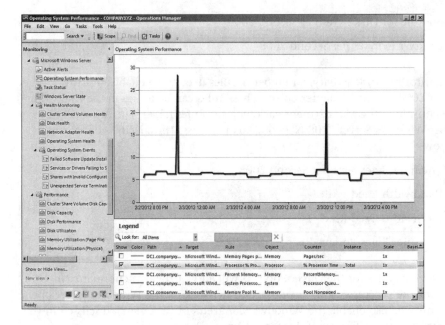

FIGURE 8.8 The Operating System Performance view.

In addition, a Health Monitoring subfolder contains the following four Dashboard views, one for each component:

- ▶ Cluster Shared Volumes Health
- ▶ Disk Health
- ▶ Network Adapter Health
- ▶ Operating System Health

Each of these component Dashboard views has two panes—the top pane shows the state of each discovered instance and the bottom pane shows any related alerts.

The Operating System Events subfolder under Health Monitoring contains Event views for Failed Software Updates Installations, Services or Drivers Failing to Start, Shares with Invalid Configuration, and Unexpected Service Terminations. These Event views are useful for detecting failure events.

NOTE

The Operating System Health Dashboard view located in this subfolder is the best location to view operating system health and mitigate open alerts.

For monitoring and graphing performance, the Performance subfolder contains the following eight performance Dashboard views:

- ▶ Cluster Share Volume Disk Capacity

- ▶ Disk Capacity

- ▶ Disk Performance

- ▶ Disk Utilization

- ▶ Memory Utilization (Page File)

- ▶ Memory Utilization (Physical)

- ▶ Network Adapter Utilization

- ▶ Processor Performance

The views nested under the Performance and Health Monitoring combine like performance captures allowing like data to be viewed from one location.

> **NOTE**
>
> The Performance subfolder of this sealed management pack is heavily used for troubleshooting. From this location, in-depth performance metrics for the past seven days can be viewed.

In the sample image in Figure 8.9, each quadrant of the Disk Performance Dashboard view must be selected and subvalues must be defined in the legend.

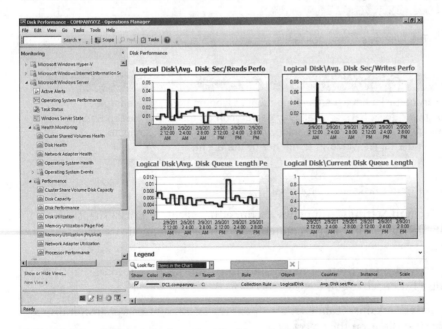

FIGURE 8.9   The Disk Performance Dashboard view.

Windows Management Pack Tasks

More than 10 Windows Computer tasks are included in the management pack and can be accessed in the Actions pane on the right when selecting a Windows Computer object. In addition, a subset of the Health Service tasks is available (Ping Computer, Remote Desktop, and so on), as shown in Figure 8.10.

FIGURE 8.10   The Windows Computer tasks.

> **NOTE**
>
> The Health Service tasks have a small blue monitor icon on them, whereas the Windows Computer tasks have a small grey server icon on them. The Health Service tasks are executed on the console machine, whereas the Windows Computer tasks are executed on the target Windows Computer by the agent.

The Windows Computer tasks are as follows:

▶ **Display Account Settings**—Launches a script at the agent; returns a snapshot displaying the current password requirements, settings, and applied server roles for the object

▶ **Display Active Connections**—Launches a script at the agent; returns a snapshot displaying a list of active connections (netstat)

▶ **Display Active Sessions**—Launches a script at the agent; returns a snapshot displaying the open sessions on the object

▶ **Display Local Users**—Launches a script at the agent; returns a snapshot enumerating the local users

▶ **Display Network Shares**—Launches a script at the agent; returns a snapshot displaying the shares on the object

▶ **Display Server Statistics**—Launches a script at the agent; returns a snapshot displaying the network statistics of the Server service on the object

▶ **Display Workstation Statistics**—Launches a script at the agent; returns a snapshot displaying the network statistics of the Workstation service on the object

▶ **Ipconfig**—Launches a script at the agent; returns a snapshot displaying the results of IPCONFIG /ALL

▶ **List Processes**—Launches a script at the agent; returns a snapshot displaying all running processes, session name, PID, and memory consumption, as shown in Figure 8.11

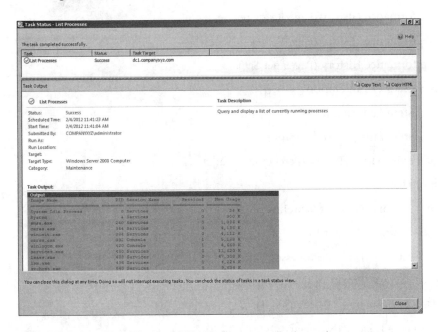

FIGURE 8.11   The Windows MP List Processes task results.

▶ **List Services**—Launches a script at the agent; returns a snapshot displaying all active services

▶ **RoutePrint**—Launches a script at the agent; returns a snapshot displaying the results of RoutePrint

> **NOTE**
>
> The State views always contain tasks in the Actions pane, when an object with tasks is selected.

These tasks are among the most useful tasks when troubleshooting. In particular, the List Processes, the Display Active Connections, and the Display Active Sessions are very helpful for gathering information.

Windows Management Pack Reports

By default, the Windows Management Pack contains 17 reports for Windows Server 2008. The included reports are as follows:

- ▶ Disk Performance Analysis (shown in Figure 8.12)
- ▶ Memory Performance History (Available MB)
- ▶ Memory Performance History (Page Reads per Sec)
- ▶ Memory Performance History (Page Writes per Sec)
- ▶ Memory Performance History (Pages per Sec)
- ▶ Operating System Configuration
- ▶ Operating System Performance
- ▶ Operating System Storage Configuration
- ▶ Paging File Performance History (Percentage Usage)
- ▶ Performance History
- ▶ Performance History (Context Switches per Sec)
- ▶ Performance History (Percent Interrupt Time)
- ▶ Performance History (Percent Processor Time)
- ▶ Performance History (Processor Queue Length)
- ▶ Physical Disk Performance History (Avg Disk Queue Length)
- ▶ Pool Performance History (Nonpaged Bytes)
- ▶ Pool Performance History (Paged Bytes)

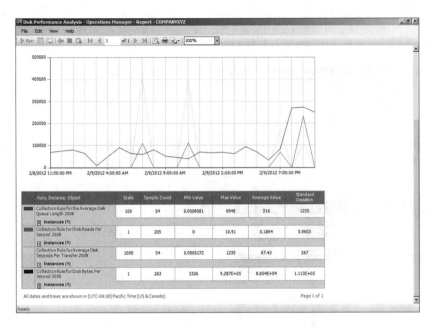

FIGURE 8.12   The Disk Performance Analysis report.

In addition to the operating system–specific reports, there are two generic reports for all Windows Server operating systems. These two reports provide a summary of operating system performance by system and a ranking of utilization across systems. The two reports are as follows:

▶ Performance by System

▶ Performance by Utilization

You can generate these reports by browsing to the Windows Server Operating System Reports.

The Performance by System report gives a summary of utilization, including processor, memory, logical disk, and network, for each system included in the report. Each server is given its own section in the report. The report can be generated for an individual Windows Computer or for a group of Windows Computer class objects. This report is good for analyzing the performance of individual systems.

The Performance by Utilization report gives a ranking of Windows Computer class objects across processor, memory, logical disk, and network metrics. This report allows you to target a large number of Windows Computer objects, for example the All Windows Computers group, and specify the top number that you want to select for each of the metrics. The top three might be different for each metric, as the top ranking systems are selected from the entire group. This report is very useful for determining which systems are experiencing the most utilization.

Figure 8.13 shows a sample Performance by Utilization report for the All Windows Computers group with the top three most utilized selected.

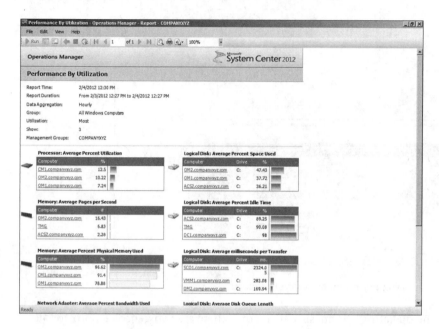

FIGURE 8.13 The Performance by Utilization report.

If you are getting the "too many arguments specified" error when generating the Performance By Utilization report, this is caused by the Windows 2003 MP. It also contains the stored procedure definition for Microsoft_SystemCenter_Report_Performace_By_Utilization, however the definition in the Windows 2003 MP is missing the "@DataAggregation INT," variable. Depending on the MP import process, it is possible that the stored procedure from the Microsoft.Windows.Server.Reports.mp will not be deployed, which does contain this variable. In order to resolve this issue, we need to modify the existing stored procedure.

NOTE

Ensure you back up your Data Warehouse database FIRST, and if you are not comfortable editing stored procedures, open a case with Microsoft on this issue.

To modify the stored procedure:

1. Launch SQL Studio Manager

2. Expand Databases

3. Expand OperationsManagerDW database

4. Expand Programmability

5. Expand Stored Procedures

6. Right-click on dbo.Microsoft_SystemCenter_Report_Performance_By_Utilization stored procedure and select Modify

7. Add the "@DataAggregation INT," line just below the "Alter procedure" line.

8. Click "execute" to save the stored procedure.

The report will now run without any error.

Exploring the Active Directory Management Pack

The Active Directory Management Pack is designed to monitor the health of an AD deployment, providing out-of-the-box monitoring and alerting, with plenty of config-urable options. The Active Directory Management Pack monitors vital processes, such as ADWS, ADMGS, Domain Controller locator, FRS, KDC, LDAP, LSASS, and so forth.

Configuring the Active Directory Management Pack

With OpsMgr 2012, the management pack can be downloaded and imported directly from the Web Catalog. (Reference the instructions on how to download and install MPs earlier in this chapter.)

In the event a manual import is required, the following order of import should be followed. After downloading and installing this MP, the default location of the MP files is located in `c:\Program Files (x86)\System Center Management Packs\Active Directory Operations Manager 2012 MP`. The management packs in that directory should be imported in the following order:

▸ Active Directory Server Common Library

▸ Active Directory Server 2000 Discovery

▸ Active Directory Server 2003 Discovery

▸ Active Directory Server 2008 Discovery

▸ Active Directory Server 2008 Monitoring

▸ Active Directory Server Client Monitoring

This management pack is also dependent on the `Microsoft.Windows.Server.Library`, which needs to be installed before importing the AD Management Packs. This MP file can be found in the Windows Server Operating System Management Pack. The latest version of the management pack supports Windows Server 2000, Windows Server 2003, Windows Server 2003 R2, Windows Server 2008, and Windows Server 2008 R2 in an agent-managed capacity. Agentless monitoring is not supported.

Several prerequisite tasks need to be completed before importing the management pack. These tasks are as follows:

- ► Each domain controller must have an agent installed.

- ► Each domain controller to be monitored must have a proxy enabled.

- ► Each domain controller to be monitored must have the Active Directory Management Pack Helper Object installed. This is normally installed with the agent automatically.

NOTE

The Active Directory Management Pack Helper Object installation files are located in the HelperObjects folder in the installation media, categorized by the CPU architecture. If the helper is installed manually, copy the MSI file to `c:\Program Files\System Center Operations Manager 2012\HelperObjects` or any other agent installation location with the HelperObjects folder.

Post importing management pack tasks include creating a RunAs account that must be associated with the AD MP Account RunAs Profile. Tables 8.1, 8.2, and 8.3 list the monitoring category, the list of scripts in the category, and the minimum required permissions.

TABLE 8.1   Client-Side Monitoring Scripts

Script Name	Required Permissions
AD_Client_Connectivity.vbs	Local Admin
AD_Client_GC_Availability.vbs	Domain User
AD_Client_PDC_Response.vbs	Local Admin
AD_Client_Serverless_Bind.vbs	Domain User
AD_Client_Update_DCs.vbs	Local User
ADClientPerspective.vbs	Local Admin

TABLE 8.2   Domain Controller Monitoring Scripts

Script Name	Required Permissions
AD_Database_and_Log.vbs	Local User
AD_DC_Demoted.vbs	Local Admin
AD_DNS_Verification.vbs	Domain User
AD_Enumerate_Trusts.vbs	Domain User
AD_General_Response.vbs	Domain User
AD_Global_Catalog_Search_Response.vbs	Domain User
AD_Lost_And_Found_Object_Count.vbs	Domain User
AD_Monitor_Trusts.vbs	Domain User
AD_Op_Master_Response.vbs	Domain User
AD_Replication_Monitoring.vbs	Local Admin
AD_Replication_Monitoring_Helper1.vbs	Local User
AD_Replication_Monitoring_Helper2.vbs	Local User

TABLE 8.2   Continued

Script Name	Required Permissions
AD_Replication_Partner_Count.vbs	Domain User
AD_Replication_Partner_Op_Master.vbs	Domain User
AD_Server_Moved_Site.vbs	Domain User
AD_Sysvol_Share_DataSource.vbs	Local User
AD_Time_Skew.vbs	Domain User
AD_Validate_Server_Trust_Event.vbs	Domain User
DCLocatorRunning.vbs	Local User
GeneralResponseCheck.vbs	Domain User

TABLE 8.3   Domain Controller Discovery

Script Name	Required Permissions
ADLocalDiscovery.vbs	Local Admin
ADRemoveTopologyDiscovery.vbs	Domain User
ADTopologyDiscovery.vbs	Domain User
PrepareEssentialDiscData*.vbs	Local User

The tables are useful for identifying rights problems in scripts and for troubleshooting script failure issues when deploying the Active Directory Management Pack.

Active Directory Client Monitoring Configuration

Although monitoring performance of Active Directory services is done by the domain controllers using a variety of measures, sometimes what really matters is how clients perceive the performance of the domain services. To measure that, the Active Directory Management Pack can generate synthetic transactions from selected client systems. These transactions include ADSI bind and search times, LDAP ping and bind times, global catalog search times, and PDC ping and bind times. The clients execute tests and log the results, as well as alert on slow performance.

The Active Directory Server Client object discovery is disabled by default. The object discovery has to be overridden to discover objects that will then run the rules. To selectively override the Active Directory Server Client object discovery, complete the following steps:

1. Open the Operations Manager 2012 console.

2. Select the Authoring view.

3. Expand the Management Pack Object node.

4. Select the Object Discoveries node.

5. Select View, Scope.

6. In the Look For field, type **Client Perspective**. This narrows down the selections.

8

7. Check the Active Directory Client Perspective target and click OK.

8. Right-click the AD Client Monitoring Discovery and select Overrides, Override the Object Discovery, and For a Specific Object of Class: Windows Computer.

9. A list of Windows Computer objects will be displayed. Select the computer that will act as an Active Directory client and click OK.

> **NOTE**
>
> The selected Windows computer should not be a domain controller. In addition, for each selected managed system to be used for the client perspective, the agent proxy must be enabled.

10. Check the Override box next to Enabled and set the value to True.

11. In the Select Destination Management Pack pull-down menu, select the appropriate override management pack. If none exists, create one for the Active Directory Management Pack by clicking New.

> **NOTE**
>
> Never use the Default Management Pack for overrides. Always create an override management pack that corresponds to each imported management pack.

12. Click OK to save the override.

13. Repeat for each Windows computer that will be an Active Directory Server Client Agent.

After a period of time, the selected agents will begin to generate Active Directory client perspective data and alerts. As a best practice, key Exchange servers are often selected as Active Directory Server Client Agents. It is also a best practice to select at least one agent in each location to be an Active Directory Server Client Agent as well.

Active Directory Replication Monitoring Configuration

The Active Directory Management Pack can monitor the replication latency between domain controllers in Active Directory. It uses sources and targets domain controllers, where the source domain controllers create objects in the OpsMgrLatencyMonitors container. These objects are read by the targets, which log performance data in the OpsMgr databases. There is a replication counter for each domain partition, for the DomainDNSZones partition, and for the ForestDNSZones partition between each source and target pair. There is also a counter for minimum replication latency and average replication latency.

To configure the OpsMgrLatencyMonitors container object, complete the following steps:

1. Open ADSI Edit.

2. Right-click on ADSI Edit in the left pane and select Connect To.

3. With the option button on Select a Well-Known Naming Context, select Configuration from the drop-down menu, and click OK.

4. Expand Configuration [<dcname.fqdn>], expand CN=Configuration,DC=<domain>,DC=<domain designation>, and look for OpsMgrLatencyMonitors.

5. If the container object OpsMgrLatencyMonitors exists, go to step 9. Otherwise, right-click on CN=Configuration,DC=<domain>,DC=<domain designation> and select New, Object.

6. In the Create Object window, select the container class and click Next.

7. In the Value Input field, type **OpsMgrLatencyMonitors**, and click Next.

8. Bypass the wizard to set additional attributes by clicking Finish.

9. In the CN=Configuration,DC=<domain>,DC=<domain designation> tree in the left pane, right-click the container object CN=OpsMgrLatencyMonitors and select Properties.

10. In the CN=OpsMgrLatencyMonitors Properties window, navigate to the Security tab and add the OpsMgr Action Account.

11. Click the Advance tab for OpsMgrLatencyMonitors on the newly added action account. Choose Edit to get the Permission Entry for OpsMgrLatencyMonitors window, navigate to the Object tab, and change the Apply To drop-down menu to This Object and All Descendant Objects.

12. Navigate to the Properties tab in the same Permission Entry for OpsMgrLatencyMonitors window, check the Write adminDescription value to Allow, and click OK.

13. In the Advanced Security Settings for OpsMgrLatencyMonitors window, click OK.

14. In the CN=OpsMgrLatencyMonitors Properties window, click OK.

The Active Directory Management Pack has the sources and targets disabled by default due to the number of counters that can potentially be created. Overrides need to be created for each source and each target domain controller to get the replication monitoring to function.

It is a best practice to reduce the number of sources and targets to a minimum, due to the number of counters that get created. An example of a source-target model might be to make all branch offices sources and a single central office DC as the target. Another example might be to pick a single DC in each site to be in both the source and target groups, assuming there are a limited number of sites.

To set the source overrides, complete the following steps:

1. Launch the Operations Manager 2012 console.

2. Select the Authoring view.

3. Expand the Management Pack Objects node.

4. Select the Rules node.

5. Ensure that the console is not scoped for any objects.

6. In the Look For field, enter **sources** and click Find Now.

7. Select the rule AD Replication Monitoring Performance Collection (Sources) in the Type: Active Directory Domain Controller Server 2008 Computer Role.

8. Right-click the rule and select Overrides, Override the Rule, and For a Specific Object of Class: Active Directory Domain Controller Server 2008 Computer Role.

9. The Select Object window opens and shows matching objects. Select the domain controller that will be the source and click OK.

> **NOTE**
>
> Groups can also be used to house the sources. If a group is used, override the rule for a group.

10. Check the Override check box next to Enabled and set the value to True.

11. In the Select Destination Management Pack drop-down menu, select the appropriate override management pack. If none exists, create a new management pack named Active Directory MP Overrides by clicking New.

> **NOTE**
>
> Never use the Default Management Pack for overrides. Always create an override management pack that corresponds to each imported management pack.

12. Click OK to save the override.

13. Repeat for each domain controller that will be a source.

To set the target overrides, complete the following steps:

1. Launch the Operations Manager 2012 console.

2. Select the Authoring view.

3. Expand the Management Pack Objects node.

4. Select the Rules node.

5. Ensure that the console is not scoped for any objects.

6. In the Look For field, enter **targets**, and click Find Now.

7. Select the rule AD Replication Monitoring Performance Collection (Targets) in the Type: Active Directory Domain Controller Server 2008 Computer Role.

8. Right-click the rule and select Overrides, Override the Rule, and For a Specific Object of Class: Active Directory Domain Controller Server 2008 Computer Role.

9. The Select Object window opens and shows matching objects. Select the domain controller that will be the target and click OK.

NOTE

Groups can also be used to house the targets. If a group is used, override the rule for a group.

---

10. Check the Override check box next to Enabled and set the value to True.

11. In the Select Destination Management Pack drop-down menu, select the appropriate override management pack. Use the same one from the previous steps when selecting the sources.

12. Click OK to save the override.

13. Repeat for each domain controller that will be a target.

NOTE

In the OpsMgrLatencyMonitors container, a folder for each object specified in the override should appear. If not, verify the permissions on the container object, then check the Operations Manager event log on the target/source DC agents for additional information.

After a period of time, monitoring will begin. Counters will be measuring the replication latency between the partitions. In addition, replication latency alerts will be triggered if latency falls below the predefined thresholds.

The AD Replication Monitoring Performance Collection (Target/Source) rule is configured by default to process every 3,600 seconds (1 hour). If replication latency data does not appear in the Replication Latency Performance view, found in the Microsoft Windows Active Directory node in the Replication Monitoring folder, then use the following steps to mitigate the issue:

1. Create a new RunAs Action Account.

2. Assign the newly created RunAs Action Account the same rights using the method listed in step 10 of the previous OpsMgrLatencyMonitors steps.

3. Change the Default Action Account RunAs Profile on the DCs used in the override for the rule to the newly created RunAs Action Account.

4. Check the Operations Manager event log on the DCs modified in the previous step and look for event ID 7026, with the following description: "The Health Service successfully logged on as the Run As account <account created in step 1> for management group <management group name>."

5. Allow for more than 3,600 seconds to elapse and check the Replication Latency Performance view under Monitoring view, Active Directory Server 2008, Replication Monitoring.

This sets the sources and targets for Windows Server 2008 domain controllers. For other versions, such as Windows Server 2003 and Windows 2000 Server domain controllers, the overrides need to be created for those domain controllers separately. Also, the replication latency mechanism does not support cross-version replication latency measurement.

NOTE

It might be tempting to make all domain controllers both sources and targets. Each domain controller would then be connected to every other domain controller. This is also known as a full mesh. However, the problem is that the number of connections grows as a power of 2. The general function for the number of connections in a full mesh is:

$$f(x) = (x^2 - x)/2$$

where x is the number of domain controllers and f(x) is the number of connections.

This means that 2 DCs will have 1 connection, 3 DCs will have 3 connections, 4 DCs will have 6 connections, and so on. By the time you get to 20 domain controllers, you have 190 connections. The connections are bidirectional and there are at least 5 counters that are collected per source-target pair, so for 20 DCs in a full mesh, there would be 1,900 performance counters (190 connections x 2 bidirectional x 5 counters) gathering data. Full mesh is bad!

Active Directory Domain Controller Performance Collection

The AD DC Performance Collection metric for NTDS DRA rules is disabled by default for discovered Active Directory Domain Controller Computer roles and Windows Domain Controller roles; this rule impacts the Replication Inbound Bytes/Sec and Intersite Replication Traffic in Monitoring View, Active Directory Server 2003/2008, Replication Monitoring.

In Windows Server 2003, the Performance object was categorized under NTDS. In Windows Server 2008 R2, the Performance object is categorized under DirectoryServices. The views Replication Inbound Bytes/Sec and Intersite Replication Traffic with the filters applied do not display information pertaining to Windows Server 2008 R2.

To enable this data collection for the Performance view, complete the following steps:

1. Open the Operations Manager 2012 console.

2. Select the Authoring view.

3. Expand Management Pack Objects and select Rules.

4. Change the scope to the Active Directory Domain Controller Computer role.

5. In the search, look for DRA. In this example, the AD DC Performance Collection—Metric NTDS DRA Inbound Bytes Total/Sec is overridden, which impacts the Replication Inbound Bytes/Sec Performance view.

6. Right-click on AD DC Performance Collection—Metric NTDS DRA Inbound Bytes Total/Sec and select Overrides, Override the Rule, For All Objects of Another Class: Active Directory Domain Controller Computer Role.

> **NOTE**
>
> There should be eight performance rules with DRA. To impact the Intersite Replication Traffic Performance view, override the rules that indicate traffic between sites For All Objects of Another Class: Windows Domain Controller.
>
> To impact the Replication Inbound Bytes/Sec Performance view, override the rule matching NTDS object name containing DRA Inbound counter name For All Objects of Class: Active Directory Domain Controller Computer Role. This only applies to versions previous to Windows Server 2008, as the object name changes and the views filter on the object in the sealed MP.

7. In the Override Property window, check the box for the parameter Enabled, change the Override Value to True, click Enforced, select the MP, and then click OK.

> **NOTE**
>
> All eight rules listed with DRA are configured to process every 15 minutes. For data to appear in the Performance view, allow more than 15 minutes to elapse.

To create a Performance view to display the metrics for Windows Server 2008 and above, complete the following steps:

1. Navigate to the Monitoring view and right-click the top-level tree object labeled Monitoring.

2. Select New, Folder.

3. Call the folder something relating to AD; for this example, use the name **AD_MP** and save to the Active Directory Management Pack Override MP Management Pack along with all the overrides configured.

4. Right-click on the newly created AD_MP folder and select New, Performance View.

5. For this example, enter **Replication Monitoring 2008** in the Name field. For the
   Show Data Related To field, select Active Directory Domain Controller Computer
   Role. Check the With a Specific Object Name check box, with a value of
   DirectoryServices; check the With a Specific Counter Name check box, with a value
   of DRA; and check the With a Specific Instance Name check box, with a value of
   NTDS. This should look something like Figure 8.14.

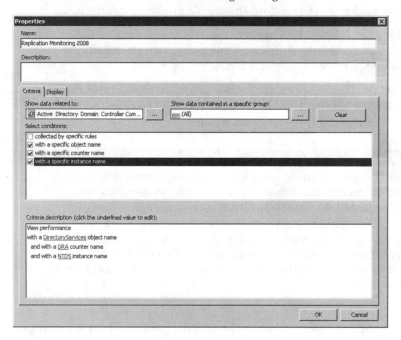

FIGURE 8.14   The Performance view setup.

Active Directory Management Pack Views

Upon importing this management pack, a Microsoft Windows Active Directory sealed
management pack folder will appear in the Monitoring view tree.

Included by default at the top level are the following views:

▶ **DC Active Alerts**—An Alert view filtering information relating to Active Directory
  Domain Controller Computer and does not have a 255 resolution state

▶ **DC Events**—An Event view filtering information relating to Active Directory
  Domain Controller Computer displaying all events

▶ **DC Performance Data**—A Performance view filtering information relating to Active
  Directory Domain Controller Computer and displaying all collected performance
  metrics

▶ **DC State**—A State view filtering information relating to Active Directory Domain Controller Computer displaying all states from an AD perspective, as shown in Figure 8.15

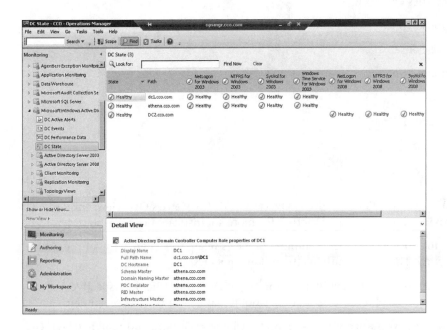

FIGURE 8.15   The DC State view.

The Active Directory Server 2008 subfolder, which is similar to the subfolder for Active Directory Server 2003, contains the following:

▶ **DC Server 2008 Active Alerts**—An Alert view filtering information relating to Active Directory Domain Controller Server 2008 role and does not have a 255 resolution state

▶ **DC Server 2008 Events**—An Event view filtering information relating to Active Directory Domain Controller Server 2008 role displaying all events

▶ **DC Server 2008 State**—A State view filtering information relating to Active Directory Domain Controller Server 2008 role displaying state information from an AD perspective

There is also a Performance subfolder containing 12 Performance views showing AD performance metrics. These views and dashboards are as follows:

▶ AD DIT/Log Free Space

▶ All Performance Data

▶ Database and Log Overview

▶ Database Size

▶ DC OS Metrics Overview

▶ DC Response Time

▶ DC/GC Response

▶ GC Response Time

▶ Log File Size

▶ LSASS Processor Time

▶ Memory Metrics

▶ OpsMaster Performance

The three dashboards—Database and Log Overview, DC OS Metrics Overview, and DC/GC Response—provide groups of related metrics for more sophisticated troubleshooting.

In the Client Monitoring subfolder, a number of views relate to a client view of the health of Active Directory. The folder contains the following views:

▶ **Client Alerts**—An Alert view filtering for Active Directory Client Perspective watcher, with a resolution state that does not equal 255 in the last seven days

▶ **Four Client Performance views**—Views for Client ADSI Bind and Search, Client GC Search Time, Client LDAP Ping and Bind, and Client PDC Ping and Bind Time

▶ **Client State**—A State view filtering for Active Directory Client Perspective watcher displaying all states

▶ **Client Performance Overview**—A dashboard combining the four Performance views in this folder into one view, as shown in Figure 8.16

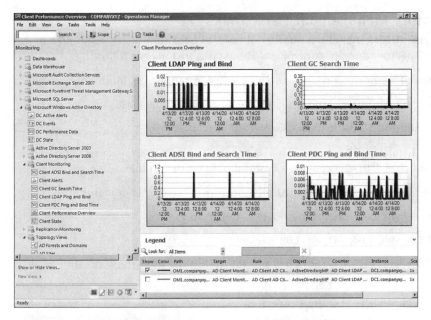

FIGURE 8.16   The Client Performance Overview dashboard.

In the Replication Monitoring subfolder, there are views containing the following:

▶ **Replication Alerts Last 7 Days**—An Alert view filtering information relating to Active Directory Domain Controller Computer displaying alerts not equal to a 255 resolution state, in the last seven days

▶ **Intersite Replication Traffic**—A Performance view displaying data for all versions previous to 2008

▶ **Replication Inbound Bytes/Sec**—A Performance view displaying data for all versions previous to 2008

▶ **Replication Latency**—A Performance view showing replication latency between domain controllers

▶ **Replication Performance Overview**—A Dashboard view combining the four views in this folder into one view

---

NOTE

Of the available views, the following views are heavily utilized during AD monitoring:

▶ Database and Log Overview

▶ DC OS Metrics Overview

▶ DC/GC Response Time

▶ Client Performance Overview

▶ Replication Performance Overview

Active Directory Management Pack Tasks

The AD Management Pack includes a number of tasks to help administer, test, and troubleshoot Active Directory domain controllers. These tasks include the following:

- **AD Generated Response Task**—Launches a script to output DC Bind Time

- **AD Users and Computers Snap-in Console Task**—Opens `DSA.MSC`

- **ADSI Edit Snap-in Console Task**—Opens `ADSIEDIT.MSC`

- **DCDIAG**—Requires `c:\Program Files\Support Tools\DCDIAG.exe.exe` to be present; launches `DCDIAG.Exe` with a customizable set of command-line parameters

- **Enumerate Trusts**—Enumerates trust relationships between AD domains

- **GP Update**—Launches a script to update Group Policy

- **LDP Tool Console Task**—Opens `LDP.exe.exe`

- **List Top Processes on DC**—Launches a script to find the top processes using more than 1% processor time in two samples

- **NETDIAG**—Runs NETDIAG diagnostic tool

- **NETDOM**—Runs NETDOM tool; requires `c:\Program Files\Support Tools\NETDOM.exe.exe` to be present

- **NETDOM Query FSMO**—Runs NETDOM Query FSMO command and outputs the results; requires `c:\Program Files\Support Tools\NETDOM.exe.exe` to be present

- **NLTEST**—Requires `c:\Program Files\Support Tools\NLTEST.exe.exe` to be present; launches `NLTEST.exe.exe`

- **REPADMIN Replsum**—Requires `c:\Program Files\Support Tools\REPADMIN.exe.exe` to be present; launches REPADMIN with `/Replsum`

- **REPADMIN**—Requires `c:\Program Files\Support Tools\REPADMIN.exe.exe` to be present; launches REPADMIN

- **SETSPN**—Requires `c:\Program Files\Support Tools\SETSPN.exe.exe` to be present; launches SETSPN with `L <Target>`

- **SPN Health**—Requires `c:\Program Files\Support Tools\SETSPN.exe.exe` to be present; launches SETSPN with `/test:MachineAccount /v`

> **NOTE**
>
> When one of the preceding tasks executes with an error regarding the path, it becomes necessary to override the support tool location and/or command-line string values. An override can be done in the Run Task window that opens when a task is executed. Look for the Override button above the task credentials and adjust as necessary. Windows 2008 and above should have the directory overridden to `c:\windows\system32` for example.

Active Directory Management Pack Reports

The Active Directory Management Pack ships with eight reports nested under Active Directory Server Common Library; these reports are as follows:

▶ AD Domain Changes

▶ AD Domain Controllers

▶ AD Machine Account Authentication Failures

▶ AD Replication Site Links

▶ AD Role Holders

▶ AD SAM Account Changes

▶ DC Replication Bandwidth (Deprecated)

> **NOTE**
>
> The DC Replication Bandwidth report has been deprecated and replaced with version-specific reports in separate folders by version. There is a report folder named Active Directory Server 2008 (Monitoring) that contains the new report AD 2008 DC Replication Bandwidth, as well as a corresponding folder and report for Active Directory 2003.

▶ DC Disk Space Chart (shown in Figure 8.17)

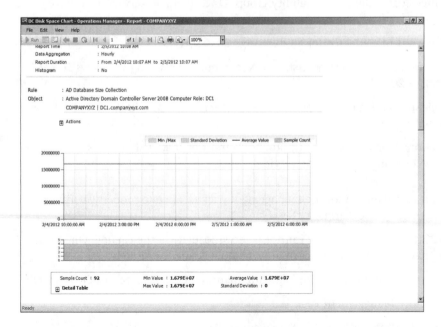

FIGURE 8.17   The DC Disk Space Chart report.

Of the available reports, the DC Disk Space Chart report is selected to generate an automated report to the AD application owner and operational support lead as a proactive measure. For audit and documentation purposes, the AD Domain Controllers and AD Role Holders reports are used.

Exploring the Exchange 2010 Management Pack

The Exchange Server 2010 Management Pack for Operations Manager 2012 uses an extensive set of monitors, rules, scripts, and knowledge to manage the Exchange 2010 messaging environment. The management pack is one of the most sophisticated management packs produced by Microsoft.

Unlike the Exchange 2007 MP for OpsMgr 2007 SP 1, the Exchange 2010 MP is refreshed and easier to use. This management pack provides monitoring on all facets essential to the overall health of the Exchange 2010 infrastructure.

Preparing to Install the Exchange 2010 Management Pack

In part due to the sophistication of the Exchange 2010 Management Pack, there are more preparation steps and requirements to installing it than for most management packs.

The prerequisites for the management pack are as follows:

▶ All Exchange 2010 servers must use the default LocalSystem as the agent action account.

▶ All Exchange 2010 database availability group (DAG) member servers must have agents.

▶ Agent proxy must be enabled for all Exchange 2010 servers.

▶ The Correlation service must be installed on a computer running Windows Server 2003, 2008, or 2008 R2.

▶ The Correlation service must have network connectivity to the RMS, and ideally be deployed on the RMS server itself.

▶ The Operations Manager Administration Tools must be installed on the server running the Exchange Correlation service.

These prerequisites are required for the management pack to operate properly, without which it might generate false alarms.

The Exchange 2010 Management Pack cannot be downloaded via the catalog. One of the prerequisites is that the management pack must be downloaded separately.

In addition, it is recommended that the following management packs be installed as well:

▶ Active Directory Management Pack

▶ Internet Information Services (IIS) Management Pack

- ▶ Domain Name System (DNS) Management Pack

- ▶ Windows Server Management Pack

These management packs monitor supporting services, which can impact the overall health of the Exchange 2010 system.

NOTE

There is a bug in the Exchange Server 2010 Management Pack version 14.2.71.0 that prevents it from discovering Edge server roles. To work around the problem, create a registry key in `HKLM\System\CurrentControlSet\Services\Netlogon\Parameters` named **Site-Name** of type string (REG_SZ). The value should be the name of the Active Directory site name that the Exchange 2010 organization lives in. This can be done before or after the management pack is deployed.

Correlation Engine Service

A common complaint about Exchange 2007 management pack was about the number of alerts it generated. The most common cause for too many alerts was the same root cause problem affecting multiple Exchange 2007 components, each of which would generate its own alert or set of alerts. The Exchange 2010 Management Pack introduced the Correlation Engine service to address this and reduce alerts.

The Correlation Engine service acts as a buffer between events that would raise alerts and Operations Manager. The Event Correlation service intercepts state change events and evaluates them based on the Exchange 2010 health state model stored in Operations Manager. Correlated events that are generated by the same root cause are suppressed and a single correlated alert is generated. The service also delays alerts by 90 seconds to allow correlated impacts to be detected before learning, thus also reducing the alert volume.

The service uses key health indicators (KHI), non-service impacting (NSI), and forensic categories to decide how to alert. The key health indicator category includes those alerts that will impact the health of the Exchange 2010 service. The non-service impacting category includes those alerts that might impact one or two users rather than the entire service. And the forensic category includes alerts that may not directly be impacting service, but will be useful for troubleshooting.

The Correlation Engine service is typically installed on a management server, but can also be installed on any server. Accordingly, it comes in both a 64-bit and a 32-bit version. If installed on an OpsMgr 2012 management server, then the 64-bit version must be used as Operations Manager 2012 only runs on Windows 2008 R2 SP1 (a 64-bit operating system).

The Correlation Engine service installer is included in the downloaded Exchange 2010 Management Pack.

NOTE

The Correlation Engine service installer is the main reason that the Exchange 2010 Management Pack cannot be installed through the catalog. The catalog can only install management pack files (*.mp) and cannot install the necessary service; hence, a separate download is needed for the Exchange 2010 Management Pack.

The Correlation Engine service makes use of custom fields in the alerts to track correlation information. This includes information such as if the alert is service impacting or non-service impacting, is actionable or nonactionable, is urgent or nonurgent, and the call-related problem ID. This information is recorded in the following custom fields in the alert:

- ▶ Custom Field 5

- ▶ Custom Field 6

- ▶ Custom Field 7

- ▶ Custom Field 8

- ▶ Custom Field 10

These custom fields should not be used or have their values changed for any Exchange alerts.

Installing the Exchange 2010 Management Pack

The Exchange 2010 Management Pack can be downloaded from the following link: http://www.microsoft.com/download/en/details.aspx?id=692 or by searching for "Exchange 2010 Management Pack download" for the latest version. Make sure to download the appropriate version, usually the 64-bit version. The management pack guide can also be downloaded from the same link.

Once the management pack MSI has been downloaded, install it by following instructions on the management server that will host the Correlation Engine service:

1. Launch the downloaded MSI.

2. At the security warning, click Run.

3. Accept the license agreement and click Next.

4. Note the installation directories, change as necessary, and then click Extract.

NOTE

The Correlation Engine service will be installed in this step.

5. Click Close to exit the installation wizard.

•

Now that the Correlation Engine service has been installed and the management packs unpacked, the management packs need to be imported. The two management packs are as follows:

▶ `Microsoft.Exchange.2010.mp`

▶ `Microsoft.Exchange.2010.Reports.mp`

To import the management packs, complete the following steps:

1. Launch the Operations Manager console.

2. Go to the Administration section.

3. Go to the Management Packs folder.

4. Right-click on the Management Packs folder and choose Import Management Packs.

5. Click Add and select Add From Disk.

6. Click No.

7. Browse to the management pack directory noted earlier (`c:\Program Files\System Center Management Packs` by default) and select the two `Microsoft.Exchange.2010` management packs.

8. Click Open.

9. The management packs will be evaluated and you'll see a security warning in the status, which can be safely ignored. Click Install.

10. At the pop-up security warning, click Yes.

11. Once the management pack is done importing, click Close.

After the management pack is imported, discovery will be started and Exchange 2010 servers in objects will be discovered automatically.

Test Mailbox Configuration

The Exchange 2010 Management Pack runs synthetic transactions to generate performance metrics for the Exchange 2010 infrastructure. These include Outlook Web Application, ActiveSync, and Exchange Web Services. The management pack leverages the native Exchange 2010 PowerShell test cmdlets to run the synthetic transactions. The PowerShell cmdlets that are used to generate the synthetic transactions are:

▶ `Test-OwaConnectivity`

▶ `Test-ActiveSyncConnectivity`

▶ `Test-WebServicesConnectivity`

If these commands have been used before, then a test mailbox will need to be created to allow the cmdlets to function properly.

To create the test mailbox, complete the following steps:

1. Log on to an Exchange 2010 mailbox server with Exchange administrator credentials.

2. Launch the Exchange Management Shell.

3. Enter the command `Set-Location "C:\Program Files\Microsoft\Exchange Server\V14\Scripts"`.

4. Enter the command `.\New-TestCasConnectivityUser.ps1`.

5. At the password prompt, enter a password and press Enter. The specific password doesn't matter, as it will be changed automatically by Exchange on a periodic basis.

> **NOTE**
>
> Although the specific password does not matter, the password complexity does matter. If the temporary password you select does not meet the domain password complexity requirements, the script will fail.

6. Press Enter to create the mailbox.

After the test mailbox is created, the synthetic transactions will run without error.

> **NOTE**
>
> If the test mailbox is not created properly, the management pack will generate a warning alert with the text "The test mailbox was not initialized. Run new-TestCasConnectivityUser.ps1 to ensure that the test mailbox is created." Simply use the previous steps to create a test mailbox should you get this alert.

Synthetic Transaction Event Collection

By default, events generated by the synthetic transactions are not recorded. Because the synthetic transaction generates a number of events, recording those events into the database can increase the size of the database. However, successful and unsuccessful events contain a wealth of data.

To populate the synthetic transaction Event views, script event collection must be enabled. To enable this, use the following steps:

1. Launch the Operations Manager console.

2. Choose the Authoring space.

3. Expand the Management Pack Objects folder.

4. Choose the Rules folder.

5. Click on Scope.

6. In the Look For field, enter `"Exchange Server 2010"` and select View All Targets.

7. Click Select All and then click OK.

8. In the Look For field, enter `"script event collection"` and click Find Now.

9. The first rule found will be in the ActiveSync type. Right-click on that rule and select Overrides, Override the Rule, for All Objects of Class ActiveSync.

10. Check the Override check box and change the Override Value to True.

11. Choose a management pack for the override and then click OK to save the override.

12. Repeat the override for the remaining rules for which events are needed.

Events will begin to be generated after a period of time and can be seen in the appropriate views.

Exchange 2010 Management Pack Views

Upon importing this management pack, a Microsoft Exchange Server sealed management pack folder will appear in the Monitoring view tree and in that folder will be an Exchange 2010 folder. The views are organized into folders by role, which helps control the number of objects within a given folder.

Included in the top-level views are the following:

▶ **Alerts view**—Details alerts that do not have a 255 resolution state for all systems discovered as Exchange 2010 All Entities Group.

▶ **Event view**—Shows events relates to the Exchange Server role.

▶ **Organization State view**—Displays the state of the Exchange 2010 organization with summary states for each Exchange 2010 service.

▶ **Performance view**—Displays all of the performance counters collected by the management pack. This allows Performance views across different counters for comparison and correlation.

▶ **Server State view**—Displays the discovered role health.

▶ **Service State view**—Displays the state of all Exchange 2010 services, including individual instances, as shown in Figure 8.18.

▶ **Task Stats**—Shows the status of all Exchange-related tasks that have been run. This view is somewhat useless, as the Exchange 2010 Management Pack doesn't include tasks any longer.

8

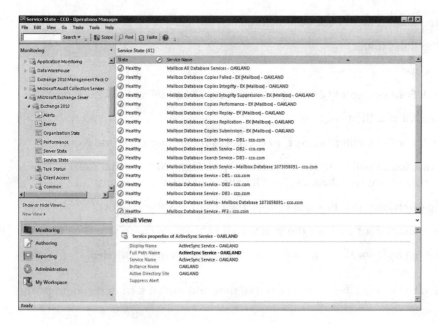

FIGURE 8.18   The Exchange 2010 Service State view.

For the Client Access role, the Client Access subfolder contains the following views:

▶ **Alerts view**—Displays alerts that do not have a 255 resolution state for all systems discovered with the role

▶ **Event view**—Shows events related to the role

▶ **Performance view**—Displays all the performance counters related to the role

▶ **State view**—Displays the state for all systems discovered with the role

Within the Client Access subfolder, a subfolder contains views related to the synthetic transactions:

▶ ActiveSync Connectivity

▶ ECP Connectivity

▶ IMAP4 Connectivity

▶ Outlook Client RPC

▶ Outlook Connectivity

▶ OWA Connectivity

▶ POP3 Connectivity

▶ Web Service Connectivity

Each of the folders contains Performance views of the synthetic transaction metrics (such as ActiveSync latency shown in Figure 8.19) and Event views of the scripts that generate the transactions. The Event views will not display any events by default, unless overridden as discussed in the section "Synthetic Transaction Event Collection."

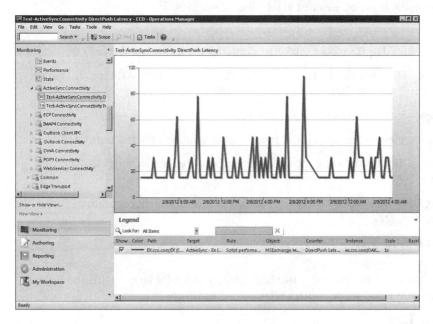

FIGURE 8.19   The Exchange 2010 ActiveSync Connectivity view.

The Outlook Client RPC subfolder under the Client Access subfolder contains the following Performance views:

▶ **Client: Latency > # secRPCs**—There are three Performance views that show the counts of client latency that are greater than 2 seconds, 5 seconds, and 10 seconds for each mailbox server.

▶ **Client: RPCs Succeeded**—This is a Performance view that shows the number of successful RPC connections for each mailbox server.

These views are very useful for understanding how the client response time is, but they require careful interpretation. The counters are counts since the last restart, so they will always be increasing. The different rates of increase or ratios are what are important. If there is a significant number of RPC latency over 10 seconds compared with 2 seconds, the system might be running below par. Or if the ratio changes in the wrong direction, that could be a sign of a problem.

8

> **NOTE**
>
> A good ratio is something like 1:3:15 for 10 seconds to 5 seconds to 2 seconds RPC latency. In other words, a well-performing system will have an approximately 1:15 ratio of RPC request latency greater than 10 seconds to those greater than 2 seconds. Most RPC requests should be serviced in less than 2 seconds.

For the Edge role, an Edge Transport subfolder contains the following views:

- ► **Alerts view**—Displays alerts that do not have a 255 resolution state for all systems discovered as Exchange 2010 Edge Transport role

- ► **Event view**—Shows events related to the role

- ► **Performance view**—Displays all the performance counters related to the role

- ► **State view**—Displays the state for all systems discovered as Exchange 2010 Edge Transport role

- ► **Transport DSN view**—Displays performance counters for Delivery Status Notifications (DSNs)

- ► **Transport Queues view**—Displays performance counters for queues

In addition, an Agents subfolder under the Edge Transport subfolder contains the following Performance views that show metrics related to the anti-spam agents:

- ► Attachment Filter

- ► Connection Filter

- ► Content Filter

- ► Protocol Analysis

- ► Recipient Filter

- ► Sender Filter

- ► Sender ID

The Hub Transport role has a corresponding Hub Transport subfolder containing the following:

- ► **Alerts**—Displays alerts that do not have a 255 resolution state for all systems discovered as Exchange 2010 Hub Transport role

- ► **Event view**—Shows events related to the role

- ► **Performance view**—Displays all the performance counters related to the role

- **State**—Displays the state for all systems discovered as Exchange 2010 Hub Transport role

- **Transport DSN**—Shows the transport DNSs

- **Transport Queues**—Shows the transport queues

An Agents subfolder under the Hub Transport subfolder contains the following Performance views that show metrics related to the anti-spam agents:

- Connection Filter

- Content Filter

- Protocol Analysis

- Recipient Filter

- Sender Filter

- SMS

- Sender ID

The Mailbox role has a corresponding Mailbox subfolder containing the following:

- **Alerts**—Displays alerts that do not have a 255 resolution state for all systems discovered as Exchange 2010 Mailbox role

- **Database Service State**—Shows the state of all databases across the organization, including number of copies

- **Event view**—Shows events related to the role

- **Performance view**—Displays all the performance counters related to the role

- **State**—Displays the state for all systems discovered as Exchange 2010 Mailbox role

The Mailbox role has an Information Store subfolder containing two subfolders, Database and RPC, that contain Performance Metric views.

A Database subfolder under the Information Store subfolder contains Performance views related to database read/write performance per second and in averages such as I/O Database Reads Average Latency (shown in Figure 8.20).

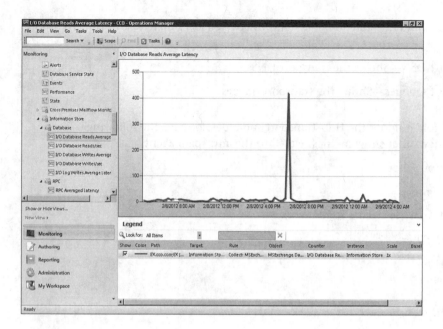

FIGURE 8.20   The Exchange 2010 I/O Database Reads Average Latency view.

A RPC subfolder under the Information Store subfolder contains the following:

▶ RPC Average Latency

▶ RPC Requests

The Unified Messaging role subfolder contains the following:

▶ **Alerts**—Displays alerts that do not have a 255 resolution state for all systems discovered as Exchange 2010 Unified Messaging role.

▶ **Event view**—Shows events related to the role.

▶ **Performance view**—Displays all the performance counters related to the role.

▶ **Performance Reporting**—Contains all the UM performance counters collected. This is a legacy view that duplicates the Performance view.

▶ **State**—Displays the state for all systems discovered as Exchange 2010 Unified Messaging role.

After the Exchange 2010 Management Pack has been deployed, Exchange administrators heavily utilize the ExBPA, Active Alerts, and Server State views for daily health check status reports. The views are used as opposed to stating a green or healthy status based on the fact that an issue has not occurred before the morning health check.

In addition, the Exchange 2010 Topology view has been used for documentation. The Client Access CAS Synthetic Transaction State view can be used for an at-a-glance health check on client connectivity and mail flow, and the EDGE performance counters under the Agents subfolder of Edge Transport can be used to tune the EDGE server.

Exchange 2010 Management Pack Reports

The Exchange Server 2010 Management Pack ships with 17 reports, which are as follows:

▸ **CAS**—This report shows the Protocol Availability numbers.

▸ **Client Performance**—The Client Performance report (shown in Figure 8.21) shows the percentage of successful RPC client/server operations between clients (2003 and newer) and Exchange 2010 during the specified time period. Any operations that take less than or equal to 2 seconds are considered successful. The Client RPC Latency and RPC count columns are calculated from the data generated by clients and sent to the Exchange server.

▸ **Machine Level Capacity Trending**—The Machine Level Capacity Trending Report provides capacity utilization information at the server level.

▸ **Cross Premises Mail Flow Monitoring**—The Cross Premises Mail Flow Monitoring report is used to measure mail flow in a cross-premises topology where your organization uses both Outlook Live and on-premises Microsoft Exchange servers. The report shows latency between on-premises Internet egress sites and Outlook Live datacenters, and the status of test messages over the reporting interval.

▸ **Performance Counter View**—The Performance Counter View report graphs performance counters for a number of selectable metrics.

▸ **Performance Counter View Raw**—The Performance Counter View Raw report lists the performance counters data points for a number of selectable metrics.

▸ **Performance Nutrition**—The Performance Nutrition report shows the detailed % Processor Time, Private Bytes, and Working Set statistics for computers hosting a number of services.

▸ **Protocol Downtime Details**—The Protocol Downtime Details report shows daily downtimes and impacting alerts that affected protocol availability of service entities on a given day.

▸ **Remote PowerShell Service**—This report shows the availability numbers for the Remote PowerShell service.

▸ **Role Level Capacity Trending**—This report shows capacity trending for the various Exchange 2010 roles over the course of a month.

▸ **SLA**—This report shows the SLA availability numbers.

▸ **SMTP Availability**—The SMTP Availability report provides client SMTP submission availability data as measured by synthetic transactions.

▶ **Transport Platform Distribution Group Usage**— Transport Platform Distribution Group Usage report provides usage data for distribution groups.

▶ **Transport Platform Hourly Server Statistics**—The Transport Platform Hourly Server Statistics report provides statistics from message tracking logs to provide information about mail flow latency by the hour.

▶ **Transport Platform Server Statistics**—The Transport Platform Server Statistics report provides statistics from message tracking logs to provide information about mail flow latency by the day.

▶ **Transport Platform Top Users**—Transport Platform Top Users report provides usage data for the clients that send the most messages, receive the most messages, and experience the most failures.

▶ **UM Local Service**—This report shows the UM availability numbers.

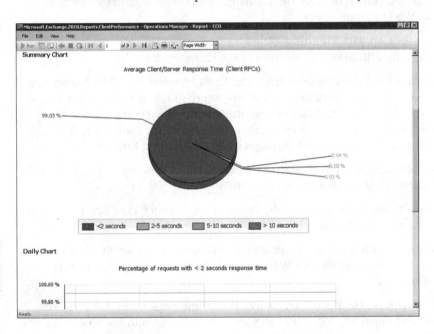

FIGURE 8.21   The Exchange 2010 Client Performance report.

Exploring the SQL Server Management Pack

The SQL Server Management Pack is produced by Microsoft to monitor the health of SQL Server 2005, 2008, and 2008 R2 installations via monitors and rules. Subject matter expertise from Microsoft on SQL is passed in the form of the management pack, on what should be monitored, for example, within the database or database engine. The management pack provides out-of-the-box views to access the default performance rules that capture metrics, such as database free space, transaction log free space, connected users, and so on. In addition, Microsoft provides a number of out-of-the-box reports, for example, detailing SQL Server Lock Analysis.

> **NOTE**
>
> Microsoft dropped support for SQL 2000 in this edition of the management pack. SQL 2000 servers are no longer detected or monitored.

Configuring the SQL Server Management Pack

With OpsMgr 2012, the management pack can be downloaded and imported directly from the Web Catalog. (Reference the instructions on how to download and install MPs earlier in this chapter.)

In the event a manual import is required, the following order of import should be followed. After downloading and installing this MP, the default location of the MP files is located in c:\Program Files (x86)\System Center Management Packs\Microsoft SQL Server System Center Operations Manager 2012 MP\.

Version 6.1.400.0 includes the following files:

▶ Microsoft.SQLServer.Library.mp

▶ Microsoft.SQLServer.2005.Discovery.mp

▶ Microsoft.SQLServer.2005.Monitoring.mp

▶ Microsoft.SQLServer.2008.Discovery.mp

▶ Microsoft.SQLServer.2008.Monitoring.mp

When monitoring SQL Server 2008, ensure that the SQL Distributed Management Objects feature is installed. The installation file is located within the Microsoft SQL Server 2008 feature pack.

8

> **NOTE**
>
> A limitation of the SQL management pack is that it expects that 64-bit operating systems will be running 64-bit versions of SQL. If a 32-bit version of SQL is installed on a 64-bit operating system, then performance counters will not be monitored correctly. This is due to inherent limitations in collecting performance data across architectures. This condition will generate a series of 10102 errors in the Operations Manager event log and then a 1103 message indicating that rules have been disabled.

SQL Cluster Configuration

For the most part, the SQL Management Pack detects and monitors SQL clusters. There are a couple of prerequisites and suggested changes to effectively monitor the clusters.

When monitoring clustered SQL installations, ensure that each node of the cluster has an OpsMgr agent installed. In addition, the Agent Proxy setting must be enabled per node in the cluster. This allows the nodes to discover and report on the virtual instances of SQL.

Key monitors in the SQL Management Pack check the state of services. These monitors have the parameter "Alert Only If service Startup Type Is Automatic" that is set to True by default, which means that it checks services that are set to start automatically. On servers in a cluster, the startup type for the services is set to manual. If you are monitoring a SQL Server cluster, override the parameter "Alert Only If Service Startup Type Is Automatic," setting it to False for the following monitors:

- SQL Server Windows Service (for both objects, SQL DB Engine and SQL DB)
- SQL Server Reporting Services Windows Service
- SQL Server Analysis Services Windows Service
- SQL Server Integration Services Windows Service
- SQL Server Full Text Search Service Monitor
- SQL Server Agent Windows Service

This allows the management pack to correctly monitor services on active and inactive cluster nodes.

What to Tune in the SQL Server Management Pack

The SQL Server Management Pack has several areas to tune, specifically discoveries, thresholds, and alert enabling. The tuning points are as follows:

- Discover SQL 200x Agent Jobs Discovery
- Transaction Log Space Free (MB) Monitor
- SQL Server Service Broker Manager Has Shutdown Rule
- Discover Replication Components
- SQL 200x Replication Publications and Subscriptions Discovery Provider
- Job Failures
- Restart of DB Engine
- Full Text Configuration

By default, the following SQL agent job discovery is not enabled. This means that jobs will not be monitored for successful completion. Depending on the SQL version in the environment, the following discoveries need to be enabled:

▶ **Discover SQL 2005 Agent Jobs**—Override the discovery for all objects of class SQL 2005 Agent.

▶ **Discover SQL 2008 Agent Jobs**—Override the discovery for all objects of class SQL 2008 Agent.

These discoveries can be found in the Authoring area of the console in the Object Discoveries folder. For the discovery object overrides, the IntervalSeconds is defaulted to 6,000 seconds or 100 minutes. Adjust this value if information is required sooner—then adjust the IntervalSeconds to a higher value after the initial discovery so as to not saturate the discovery tasks for objects of the class SQL 2005 Agent.

The SQL Server Service Broker Manager Has Shutdown rule enables alerting when the SQL Server Service Broker Manager has shut down. Use this rule when SQL SSBM requires monitoring. Override the rule for all objects of class SQL 2005DB Engine and all objects of class SQL 2008 DB Engine. There will be a separate rule for each object class, so there would be two overrides.

By default, the management pack does not discover SQL replication components or SQL publications/subscriptions. The rationale for shipping these important discoveries disabled is that most organizations are not using SQL replication, so enabling them by default would incur a performance penalty for the discoveries without any benefit. However, for organizations that are using SQL replication, the following discoveries should be enabled to allow the SQL management to monitor SQL replication:

▶ Discover Replication Components for SQL 2005 DB Engine objects

▶ Discover Replication Components for SQL 2008 DB Engine objects

▶ SQL 2005 Replication Publications and Subscriptions Discovery Provider for SQL 2005 DB Engine objects

▶ SQL 2008 Replication Publications and Subscriptions Discovery Provider for SQL 2008 DB Engine objects

Override the values for the Enabled property to True when replication monitoring is required.

Although the SQL management pack monitors the SQL agent by default, it does not monitor for failed jobs that the agent runs. To get alerts for failed jobs, enable the rule "A SQL Job Failed to Complete Successfully" via an override.

NOTE

Make sure that the option "Write to the Windows Application Event Log When the Job Fails" is selected for all SQL jobs you want to monitor. This is configured in the SQL job properties in SQL Server Management Studio.

The availability of DBEngine is monitored by monitor SQL Server Windows Service for the object SQL DB Engine. This monitor does not reflect the service restart. To be notified about each restart of DBEngine, you can enable the rules "SQL Server 2008 DB Engine Is Restarted" and "SQL Server 2005 DB Engine Is Restarted." These can be found in the Authoring space in the Rules folder.

The Full Text Search is not installed; the alerts will be generated by the management pack. To avoid false positive alerts regarding the Full Text Search, these monitors should be overridden to disable them. For SQL Server 2005 servers that do not have the SQL Server Full Text Search service installed, disable the monitor SQL Server Full Text Search Service Monitor. For SQL Server 2008 servers that do not have the SQL Server Full Text Filter Daemon Launcher service installed, disable the monitor SQL Server Full Text Search Service Monitor. Make sure to set the overrides on a per instance basis, to ensure that SQL servers with Full Text Search are properly monitored.

SQL Server Management Pack Views

Upon importing this management pack, a Microsoft SQL Server sealed management pack folder will appear in the Monitoring view tree.

The following are included by default at the top level:

- **Active Alerts**—Details all active alerts pertaining to the SQL role

- **Computers**—Details entity health state for discovered DB engines

- **Task Status**—Details task status pertaining to the SQL role

There are six subfolders categorizing SQL Server. These subfolders are useful for drilling in on specific components during analysis or troubleshooting.

The Databases folder views are as follows:

- **Database Free Space**—Shows the free space counters for all databases

- **Transaction Log Free Space**—Shows the transaction log free space for all databases

- **Database State**—Details the entity health of the discovered databases, as shown in Figure 8.22

> **NOTE**
>
> The Database State view can be personalized to include other discovered information, such as Database Autogrow settings and Database Size. This is useful for seeing the database information at a glance.

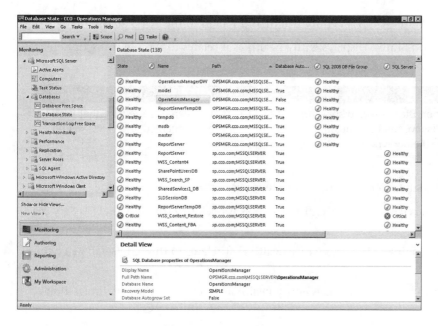

FIGURE 8.22   The SQL MP Database State view.

The Health Monitoring subfolder contains two views relating to health monitoring of database engines and agents:

▶ **Agent Health**—A dashboard displaying discovered SQL Server agents and open alerts

▶ **Database Engine Health**—A dashboard displaying discovered database engines and open alerts

The Performance subfolder contains four Performance views:

▶ **All Performance Data**—Combines 25 SQL-related performance counters, which allows comparisons across the counters

▶ **Database Free Space**—Details the free space per discovered database

▶ **Transaction Log Free Space**—Details the free space per discovered transaction log

▶ **User Connections**—Details the user connections counter per server

The Replication subfolder contains four state views covering the state of replication:

▶ **Distributor State**—Displays entity health as it relates to the SQL Distributor and discovered databases

▶ **Publication State**—Displays entity health as it relates to the SQL Publication

▶ **Publisher State**—Displays entity health as it relates to the SQL Publisher

▶ **Subscription State**—Displays entity health as it relates to the SQL Subscription

> **NOTE**
>
> The Replication State views display replication objects discovered, so require that the replication discoveries be enabled. If the discoveries are not enabled, the views will be blank even if the servers are participating in replication.

The Server Roles subfolder contains four state views covering the state of the SQL roles:

▶ **Analysis Services**—Displays entity health as it relates to the SQL Analysis Services role

▶ **Database Engines**—Displays entity health as it relates to the SQL Database Engines role

▶ **Integration Services**—Displays entity health as it relates to the SQL Integration Services role

▶ **Reporting Services**—Displays entity health as it relates to the Reporting Services role

The SQL Agent subfolder contains two state views covering the state of agents and jobs:

▶ **SQL Agent Job State**—Displays entity health as it relates to the SQL agent jobs

▶ **SQL Agent State**—Displays entity health as it relates to the SQL agent

Of the listed views, while deploying the SQL Server Management Pack with enterprise DBA teams, the SQL Agent Job State view in the SQL Agent subfolder of the sealed management pack is heavily used. The DBAs enjoy being able to review all configured job status and Last Run Status from one location. In addition, the Database State view located in the Databases subfolder of the sealed management pack is another heavily used location for the ability to view all discovered SQL databases in the environment and their discovered attributes (for example, Recovery Model, DB Size, Log Size, Database AutoGrowth Setting).

SQL Server Management Pack Tasks

The SQL Server Management Pack includes a number of tasks to help administer, test, and troubleshoot SQL servers, including the following:

▶ **Check Catalog (DBCC)**—Launches a script to check the online DB's catalog consistency

▶ **Check Database (DBCC)**—Launches a script to check the allocation, logical integrity, and structure of the objects in the target DB

- ▶ **Check Disk (DBCC)**—Launches a script to check the allocation structure consistency of the disk space of the target DB

- ▶ **Set Database Offline**—Launches a script to set the database to an OFFLINE state, using ALTER DATABASE (target DB) SET OFFLINE

- ▶ **Set Database Online**—Launches a script to set the database to an ONLINE state, using ALTER DATABASE (target DB) SET ONLINE

- ▶ **Set Database to Emergency State**—Launches a script to set the database to an emergency state, using ALTER DATABASE (target DB) SET EMERGENCY

- ▶ **SQL Management Studio**—Requires the SQLWB.exe.exe executable to be present as this launches the SQL Management Studio application with the S <target DB> -d <DB Name>

- ▶ **SQL Profiler**—Requires the profiler90.exe executable to be present as this launches the Profiler with the /S <target DB> /D <DB Name> /E parameters

- ▶ **Global Configuration Setting**—Launches SQLCMD.exe.exe with parameters against the discovered database engine

- ▶ **Start/Stop SQL Agent Service**—Tasks to start and stop the SQL Agent Service

- ▶ **Start/Stop SQL Agent Service on Cluster**—Tasks to start and stop the SQL Agent Service on a cluster

- ▶ **Start/Stop SQL Integrations Services Service**—Tasks to start and stop the SQL Integrations Services Service

- ▶ **Start/Stop SQL Integrations Service on Cluster**—Tasks to start and stop the SQL Integrations Service on a cluster

- ▶ **Start/Stop SQL Reporting Services Service**—Tasks to start and stop the SQL Reporting Services Service

- ▶ **Start/Stop SQL Reporting Services Service on Cluster**—Tasks to start and stop the SQL Reporting Services Service on a cluster

- ▶ **Start/Stop SQL Analysis Services Service**—Tasks to start and stop the SQL Analysis Services Service

- ▶ **Start/Stop SQL Analysis Services Service on Cluster**—Tasks to start and stop the SQL Analysis Services Service on a cluster

NOTE

The State views always contain tasks in the Actions pane. Different tasks will be available per discovered object, as the tasks are context sensitive. For example, if a SQL database is selected, then tasks such as Set Database Offline or Check Database (DBCC) become available.

SQL Server Management Pack Reports

The SQL Server Management Pack ships with 10 reports for 2005 and 2008.

For SQL Server 2005/2008, the reports are as follows:

- ▶ SQL Broker Performance
- ▶ SQL Server Configuration
- ▶ SQL Server Database Engine Counters (shown in Figure 8.23)
- ▶ SQL Server Lock Analysis
- ▶ SQL Server Service Pack
- ▶ SQL User Activity
- ▶ Top 5 Deadlocked Databases
- ▶ User Connections by Day
- ▶ User Connections by Peak Hours
- ▶ SQL Database Space

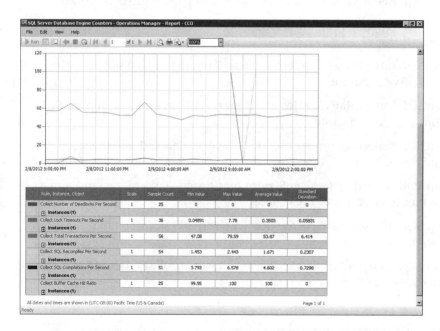

FIGURE 8.23   The SQL Server Database Engine Counters report.

All of the reports shipped with the management pack are valuable. One report in particular has been shown to be extremely beneficial, which is the SQL Server Service Pack report.

With database sprawl, it becomes a daunting task to track SQL version and patch levels throughout the enterprise, not to mention the servers with SQL installed. The SQL Server Service Pack report is an invaluable time-saver for the DBA and operational support teams. When using this report, add the object class `SQL DB Engine` or `MSSQLSERVER` object.

Exploring the Cross Platform Management Packs

Cross Platform Management Packs allow for AIX, HPUX, Red Hat Linux, SUSE Linux, and Solaris agent-based management from Operations Manager 2012.

Agent deployment is covered in Chapter 7, "Operations Manager 2012 Implementation and Administration." This section covers the management packs that support the cross-platform agents.

How to Configure the Cross Platform Management Packs

The management pack files can be found in `c:\Program Files\System Center Management Packs`, assuming a default OpsMgr 2012 installation. The Cross Platform Management Packs are divided into two groups, the UNIX library management packs, which are common to all the managed operating systems, and the operating system–specific management packs.

The UNIX library management packs are as follows:

- ▶ Unix Core Library

- ▶ Image Library (Unix)

- ▶ Unix LogFile Template Library

- ▶ Unix Service Template Library

- ▶ Unix View Library

These management packs are used across all Cross Platform Management Packs in the operating system–specific management packs that are dependent on them.

The operating system–specific management packs, using SUSE Linux as an example, are as follows:

- ▶ Linux Operating System Library

- ▶ SUSE Enterprise Operating System Library

- ▶ SUSE Enterprise Server 9 Operating System

- ▶ SUSE Enterprise Server 10 Operating System

- ▶ SUSE Enterprise Server 11 Operating System

For each of the operating system–specific management packs, there will be a library management pack for the operating system and a separate management pack for each version of the operating system. In the case of SUSE Linux, it uses the Linux library management pack and then a separate management pack for each of the supported versions (9, 10, and 11).

Import the management pack items from the online catalog (the easiest method) or from those found in `c:\Program Files\System Center Management Packs`, assuming a default OpsMgr 2012 installation.

Cross Platform Management Pack Views

Upon importing the Cross Platform Management Packs, a UNIX/Linux Servers sealed management pack folder appears in the Monitoring view tree.

There are four subfolders in UNIX/Linux Servers separating the views for AIX, HPUX, Linux, and Solaris. Each of the subfolders contains the same set of views but is filtered by the respective operating systems.

The respective operating system folders (AIX, HPUX, Linux, and Solaris) contain the following top-level views:

- ▶ **Computers Diagram**—A Diagram view showing the computers graphically
- ▶ **Server State**—A State view showing the state of all the operating system servers
- ▶ **Logical Disk State**—A State view showing the logical disk state for all discovered logical disks
- ▶ **Network Adapter State**—A State view showing the state of all discovered network adapters
- ▶ **Physical Disk State**—A State view showing the state of all discovered physical disks
- ▶ **Operating System Performance**—A view containing all the performance counters detailing operating system metrics for each server

In each operating system folder, there is a Health folder containing four Dashboard views. Each of the Dashboard views show the state of the monitored object and any alerts related to the object. The views are as follows:

- ▶ Logical Disk Health
- ▶ Network Adapter Health
- ▶ Operating System Health
- ▶ Physical Disk Health

In each operating system folder, there is a Performance folder containing six Dashboard views. The Dashboard views present the various operating system counters in different panes, allowing for easy correlation of performance. The Dashboard views are as follows:

▶ Logical Disk Capacity

▶ Memory Paging

▶ Memory Utilization

▶ Network Adapter Performance (not available with HPUX)

▶ Physical Disk Performance

▶ Processor Performance (shown in Figure 8.24)

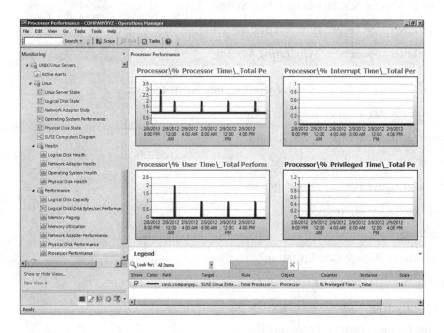

FIGURE 8.24   The Cross Platform Processor Performance overview.

In addition, there is one Performance folder view, Logical Disk\Disk Bytes/Sec Performance, that is not in the AIX operating systems views.

Cross Platform Management Pack Reports

The Cross Platform Management Pack ships with a number of reports. Separated by the operating system and version, the report folders are as follows:

▶ AIX 5.3

▶ AIX 6.1

▶ HPUX 11iv2

▶ HPUX 11iv3

▶ Red Hat Enterprise Linux Server 4 Operating System

▶ Red Hat Enterprise Linux Server 5 Operating System

▶ Red Hat Enterprise Linux Server 6 Operating System

▶ Solaris 8 Operating System

▶ Solaris 9 Operating System

▶ Solaris 10 Operating System

▶ SUSE Linux Enterprise Server 11 Operating System

▶ SUSE Linux Enterprise Server 10 Operating System

▶ SUSE Linux Enterprise Server 9 Operating System

Nested within each report folder are similar reports; they are as follows:

▶ Memory Performance History (Available MB)

▶ Memory Performance History (Page Reads per Sec)

▶ Memory Performance History (Page Write per Sec)

▶ Memory Performance History (Pages per Sec)

▶ Operating System Configuration

▶ Operating System Performance

▶ Operating System Storage Configuration

▶ Performance History, shown in Figure 8.25

▶ Total Percent IO Wait Time (Percentage Usage)

▶ Performance History (Percent Processor Time)

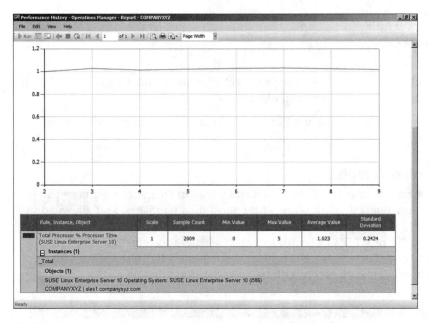

FIGURE 8.25   The Cross Platform Performance History report.

Management Pack Templates

Management Pack Templates provide an easy way to create custom management packs based on templates. These management packs can monitor a variety of different objects, including the following:

- Web Application Transaction Monitoring
- OLE DB Data Source
- Process Monitoring
- Windows Service
- TCP Port Monitor

In addition to the built-in Management Pack Templates, key management packs also add new Management Pack Templates. For example, the Exchange, ASP.NET, and Cross Platform Management Packs add the following Management Pack Templates:

- Exchange Client Access Server Monitoring
- Exchange Intra-Organization Mail Flow Monitoring
- UNIX/Linux Log File Monitoring
- UNIX/Linux Service

▶ ASP.NET Application

▶ ASP.NET Web Service

Management Pack Templates simplify the process of creating complex logic within Operations Manager to monitor common objects.

The text in this section defines the monitor, and then provides examples on how to configure the most common Management Pack Templates.

Web Application Template

Website response time metrics can be recorded and stored in Operations Manager using the Web Application Template. This is one of the most-used templates, as it allows administrators to monitor website performance from a client perspective. The template can target a straight HTTP or HTTPS URL with success criteria that can include HTTP result code, text matching, or latency. Or the template can capture a browser session with steps, logon credentials, and separate success criteria for each stage.

> **NOTE**
>
> The capture mode only supports 32-bit platforms. If the components are running on a 64-bit platform, then install the Operations Console on a 32-bit workstation and capture from that system.

The template also shows detailed results on the pages returned, including HTTP result codes, times, links, resources, and other interesting information. During troubleshooting, this can be very useful.

To create a Web monitor:

1. Navigate to the Authoring view, expand Authoring if not expanded, and expand and select Management Pack Templates.

2. Right-click on any of the subtree items and select Add Monitoring Wizard.

3. On the Add Monitoring Wizard page, select Web Application Transaction Monitoring and click Next.

4. On the General Properties page, for this example, use `Test-WebApplication` as the Name, save this to MP1 in the Select Destination Management Pack drop-down menu, and click Next.

5. On the Web Address page, use `www.cco.com` as the Test URL and click Test, as shown in Figure 8.26. If a timeout window appears, click Yes to continue waiting. Click the Details button to review the information collected and click Close when you are finished viewing the additional details. On the Web Address page, click Next.

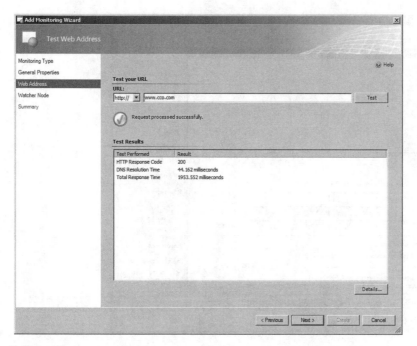

FIGURE 8.26   A Web Application test result.

6. On the Watcher Node page, select OM1.companyxyz.com and TMG, and click Next.

7. On the Summary page, review the settings and click Create.

8. Double-click on the newly created monitor to open the Web Application Editor (shown in Figure 8.27); from this location, configurations can be modified or added—configurations such as synthetic transactions, alerting criteria, performance counters, custom warning and error conditions, HTTP methods, and so on. Close the window without making any changes.

8

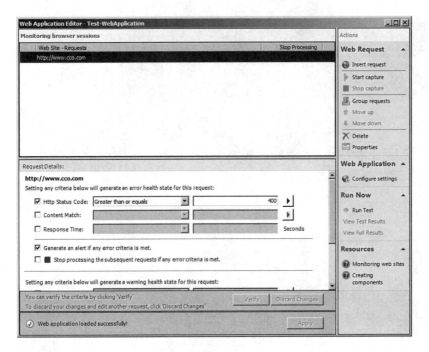

FIGURE 8.27 The Web Application Editor.

9. Wait for the rule to become active in the environment.

10. Navigate to the Monitoring view, Web Application and select Web Applications State.

For performance information, right-click on the newly created rule with the path from OM1.companyxyz.com, and select Open, Performance View.

Windows Service Template

The Windows Service Template monitors a Windows service, with an automatic or manual state. Performance data is also captured and stored. In the example, a group is created for the monitor to target. The group is created to dynamically include DC1.companyxyz.com and DC2.companyxyz.com.

To create a group, complete the following steps:

1. Navigate to the Authoring view in the console.

2. Select Groups, right-click on Groups, and select Create a New Group.

3. For the example, use **Group-WindowsServiceMonitoring** as the Name and select/create MP1.

4. Click Next on the Explicit Group Members page.

5. On the Dynamic Members page, click Create/Edit Rules. Add Windows Computer and select NetBIOS Computer Name for the Property and Matches Regular Expression for the Operator and [Dd][Cc] for the Value ([] signifies characters in range, and in this example looking for lower- and uppercase D and C).

NOTE

Not all regular expressions will function in the Value field. Use the option selector present when in the Value input box to see the available expressions.

---

6. Click Next at the Subgroups and Excluded Members page and, finally, click Create.

To create a monitor, complete the following steps:

1. Navigate to the Authoring view, expand Authoring if not expanded, and expand and select Management Pack Templates.

2. Right-click on any of the subtree items and select Add Monitoring Wizard.

3. On the Add Monitoring Wizard page, select Windows Service and click Next.

4. On the General Properties page, for the example, use `Test-WindowsService` as the Name, save this to MP1 in the Select Destination Management Pack drop-down menu, and click Next.

5. On the Service Details page, use Print Spooler Service (Spooler), select Group-WindowsServiceMonitoring as the Targeted group, and click Next.

6. On the Performance Data page, check the Generate an Alert If the CPU Usage Exceeds the Specified Threshold and the Generate an Alert If Memory Usage Exceeds the Specified Threshold for the Memory Usage check boxes, change the value to 100, and click Next.

7. On the Summary page, verify the configuration and click Create.

8. Wait for the rule to become active in the environment.

9. Disable the Print Spooler on DC1.companyxyz.com to test the monitor.

10. Monitor the results by navigating to the Monitoring view, Windows Service and Process Monitoring, and select Windows Service State.

NOTE

Notice the ability to Check Dependent NT Services in the Actions pane. The Start NT Service and Stop NT Service tasks will target the services being monitored.

---

11. For health information, right-click on the newly created monitor, and select Open, Health Explorer, as shown in Figure 8.28.

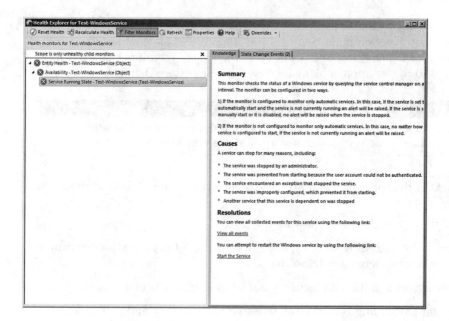

FIGURE 8.28   The Windows Service Health Explorer.

12. For performance information, right-click on the newly created monitor, and select Open, Performance View.

The GUI interface for the Windows Service cannot be configured to monitor for a memory value of more than 100MB. If configured to greater than 100MB, the GUI defaults back to 100MB when the setting is applied.

To configure the monitor to trigger on thresholds over 300MB, follow these steps:

1. Navigate to the Authoring view, expand Authoring, select Management Pack Templates, and select Windows Service.

2. Right-click on the newly created Windows Service monitor called Test-WindowsService, select View Management Pack Objects, and select Monitors.

3. In the Monitors window, expand Test-WindowsService, Entity Health, and then Performance. Right-click on Windows Service Memory Usage Monitor and then select Properties.

4. In the Windows Service Memory Usage Monitor Properties window, go to the Configuration tab. Click the Edit button and the Xml Configuration window opens, as shown in Figure 8.29.

FIGURE 8.29   Editing Windows Service threshold.

5. Change the value in the Threshold tag from 100000000 to 300000000 and click OK.

6. At the Windows Service Memory Usage Monitor Properties window, click OK. This effectively changes the threshold value from 100MB to 300MB.

NOTE

The monitor can no longer be modified through the GUI interface once these steps have been followed.

OLE DB Data Source Template

The OLE DB Data Source Template provides the ability to test OLE DB connectivity by initiating a connection to a specified database and executing a custom query. Natively, the following providers are supported: Microsoft OLE DB Provider for Analysis Services 9.0, Microsoft OLE DB Provider for Indexing Service, Microsoft OLE DB Provider for SQL Server, Microsoft OLE DB Simple Provider, MSDataShape, Microsoft OLE DB Provider for Microsoft Directory Services, SQL Native Client, SQLXMLOLEDB, and SQLXMLOLEDB 4.0.

For this example, an OLE DB monitor is configured against the OperationsManager DB. One monitor is configured for database connectivity, and another is configured to execute a query.

To create an OLE DB monitor, complete the following steps:

1. Navigate to the Authoring view, expand Authoring if not expanded, and expand and select Management Pack Templates.

2. Right-click on any of the subtree items and select Add Monitoring Wizard.

3. On the Add Monitoring Wizard page, select OLE DB Data Source and click Next.

4. On the General Properties page, for the example, use **Test-OLEDBDS** as the Name, save this to MP1 in the Select Destination Management Pack drop-down menu, and click Next.

5. On the Connection String page, click on the Build button. For this example, use the Provider Microsoft OLE DB Provider for SQL Server, DB1 as the computer or device, and OperationsManager as the database. The results are shown in Figure 8.30. Click OK when you are finished.

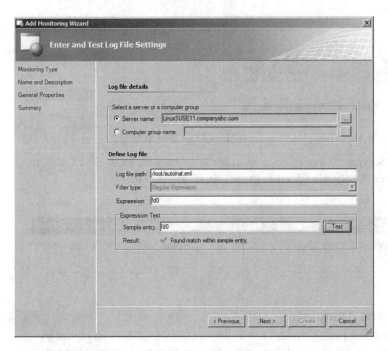

FIGURE 8.30   Building a connection string.

6. On the Connection String page, click the Test button to initiate a test. Notice that a green circled check mark appears stating Request Processed Successfully; click Next.

7. For testing purposes, change the database name to **JulianV** and click Test; notice that a red circled x now appears stating Cannot Open Database JulianV Requested by the Login. The login failed—the wizard's Test feature does not return false data. Change the database back to OperationsManager and continue.

8. The Query Performance page is where error and warning thresholds are configured. Leave this at the default (blank) for the purposes of this exercise and click Next.

9. The Watcher Node page enables the OLE transaction to be processed from one or more agent-managed computers. For the purposes of this exercise, select both OM1.companyxyz.com and OM2.companyxyz.com, and click Next when this has been completed.

NOTE

In real-world situations, the MS database is not recommended to be used as a watcher node (unless you are troubleshooting or are in other extreme situations).

10. Review the summary, and click Create if all options are satisfactory.

11. Browse to the Synthetic Transaction tree object in the Monitoring view. The Test-OLEDBs should appear; if it did not appear for a long time, restart the console or try launching the console with the `/clearcache` switch.

NOTE

Depending on the environment, the monitor will appear when the workflows have been distributed and started.

12. To view the captured performance metrics, right-click on the Test-OLEDBs with the path OM1.companyxyz.com, and select Open, Performance View. When a new window opens, click the Show check box in the Legend pane to begin viewing the collected data.

NOTE

Additional providers can be made available by installing the correct communication toolsets. An example is the SQL Server Native Client, which adds SQL Native Client to the OLE DB list of providers.

Process Monitoring Template

The Process Monitoring Template allows for monitoring of wanted and unwanted processes against a target group; the monitor can be configured based on the amount of spawned processes and duration, or configured if the spawned process runs for more than a certain duration of time. Performance data can also be collected, including CPU and memory metrics with definable polling cycles.

In this example, let's assume that we don't want Notepad.exe to run.

To create a process monitor to detect if this unwanted process is running, complete the following steps:

1. Navigate to the Authoring view, expand Authoring if not expanded, and expand and select Management Pack Templates.

2. Right-click on any of the subtree items and select Add Monitoring Wizard.

3. On the Add Monitoring Wizard page, select Process Monitoring and click Next.

4. On the General Properties page, for the exercise, use **Test-ProcessMonitor** as the Name, save this to MP1 in the Select Destination Management Pack drop-down menu, and click Next.

5. Select the Monitor Only Whether the Process Is Running (for Unwanted Process) option button.

6. For the Process Name, use **notepad.exe** and for the Target Group, use All Windows Computers, and click Next.

> **NOTE**
>
> In real-world scenarios, a group should be created to house the target systems. All Windows Computers is not a recommended group.

7. On the Running Processes page, there are no options to be selected. Click Next.

8. On the Performance Data page, there are no options to be selected. Click Next.

9. On the Summary page, verify the data and click Create.

10. Wait for the rule to become active in the environment.

11. Once the rule has integrated into the OpsMgr infrastructure, launch **notepad.exe** on one of the agent-managed systems.

12. Navigate to the Monitoring view, Windows Service and Process Monitoring, and select Process State, as shown in Figure 8.31. Open the Health Explorer for more information.

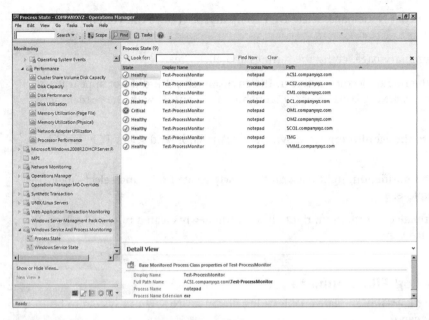

FIGURE 8.31   The Process State view.

TCP Port Template

The TCP Port Template enables TCP/IP port monitoring against an IP or hostname from more than one watcher node. The monitor attempts to open the port on a timed basis, ensuring that the port is responding. If the service or server supporting the port fails, the port will stop responding.

In this example, the goal will be to monitor that the RDP server is responding. By default, the RDP protocol uses port 3389.

To create a TCP port monitor, complete the following steps:

1. Navigate to the Authoring view, expand Authoring if not expanded, and expand and select Management Pack Templates.

2. Right-click on any of the subtree items and select Add Monitoring Wizard.

3. On the Add Monitoring Wizard page, select TCP Port and click Next.

4. On the General Properties page, for the exercise, use **Test-TCPPort** as the Name, save this to MP1 in the Select Destination Management Pack drop-down menu, and click Next.

5. On the Target and Port page, for the purposes of this exercise, use **OM2.companyabc.com** as the Computer or Device Name with 3389 as the Port. Test to make sure that the target accepts incoming RDP requests. Click Next.

6. On the Watcher Node page, select DC1.companyabc.com as the Watcher Node and click Next.

7. On the Summary page, verify the settings and click Create.

8. Wait for the rule to become active in the environment; if it did not appear for a long time, restart the console or try launching the console with the `/clearcache` switch.

9. Navigate to the Monitoring view, Synthetic Transaction and select TCP Port Check State.

10. For health information, right-click on the newly created rule, and select Open, Health Explorer.

11. For performance information, right-click on the newly created rule, and select Open, Performance View.

UNIX/Linux Log File Template

The UNIX/Linux Log File Template enables a log file on a UNIX/Linux system to be queried for a keyword.

In this example, the lab sles1.companyxyz.com virtual machine is used.

To create the log file monitor, complete the following steps:

1. Navigate to the Authoring view, expand Authoring if not expanded, and expand and select Management Pack Templates.

2. Right-click on any of the subtree items and select Add Monitoring Wizard.

3. On the Add Monitoring Wizard page, select UNIX/Linux LogFile and click Next.

4. In the Name and Description field, use **Test-NonMSFTLogfile** as the Name, select MP1 in the Select Destination Management Pack drop-down menu, and click Next.

5. On the Provide the Log File Monitoring Details page, select the computer running Linux.

6. For the Log File path, use **/root/autoinst.xml**; for the expression, use **fd0** and click Test; use **fd0** for both the regular and sample entry; and click Test again. Figure 8.32 shows a successful test. Click Next when the test is successful.

7. On the Summary page, review the settings and click Create.

When the fd0 is encountered in the log file, an alert will be raised.

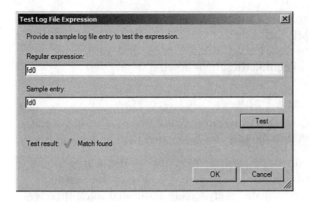

FIGURE 8.32   Test UNIX/Linux log file results.

UNIX/Linux Service Template

The UNIX/Linux Service Template allows the monitoring of a UNIX/Linux service.

To create the Unix/Linux service monitor, complete the following steps:

1. Navigate to the Authoring view, expand Authoring if not expanded, and expand and select Management Pack Templates.

2. Right-click on any of the subtree items and select Add Monitoring Wizard.

3. In the Add Monitoring Wizard window, select UNIX/Linux Service and click Next.

4. In the Name and Description field, use **Test-NonMSFTService** as the Name, select MP1 in the Select Destination Management Pack drop-down menu, and click Next.

5. Select the desired Linux server, select the Bash service, and click Create.

The Bash service will now be monitored and alerts will be generated if the service is stopped.

Custom Management Packs

Although Microsoft provides a number of management packs and Management Pack Templates to facilitate monitoring servers, applications, and systems, there is still the need to create custom management packs to monitor in-house applications or third-party applications.

Authoring Console

The Authoring Console is a separate installation and is included with the System Center Operations Manager 2007 R2 Authoring Resource Kit. The link to download the kit is: http://www.microsoft.com/download/en/details.aspx?id=18222. Microsoft did not change the format of management packs in OpsMgr 2012, so the Authoring Console remains the same as for OpsMgr 2007 R2.

Contained within the Authoring Console are a number of tools to aid in the creation of a management pack. Tools such as the MP Spell Checker, MPBPA, and Cookdown Analysis are included in the Authoring Resource Kit. The Authoring Console and Authoring Resource Kit should be installed prior to completing the following steps.

Creating a Custom Management Pack

Custom management packs can be created using the Authoring Console. Outside of the Authoring Console's GUI interface, an XML file can also be created with an XML editor.

For this example, a custom management pack is authored looking for the RootVer value to not equal 1 in the Registry. Demonstrated in the example is how to create a clean management pack, create a discovery, test the discovery, create additional rules, then seal and save the management pack.

To create a custom management pack, complete the following steps:

1. Launch the Authoring Console.

2. Go to File, and then to New.

3. At the New Management Pack window, select Windows Application Registry from the System Center installed templates, name the management pack **IdentityTest**, and then click Next.

4. For the Display Name, use **TestDN** and click Next.

5. At the Windows Application, leave the ID as the default and use **TestWA** as the Display Name—this helps differentiate the fields and how they relate within the MP—click Next to continue.

6. At the Discovery Schedule, change the unit of measure from seconds to hours and click Next.

7. At the Specify the Registry Attribute to Be Collected, click Add.

8. In the Edit Attribute Properties window, select the option button next to Value; in the Name field, use **RootVer**; for the Path field, use **Software\Microsoft\ASP.NET**; for the Attribute Type, use Check If Exists; and click OK. Then click Next.

9. At the Expression Filter, click the Insert button, select Expression, click the ellipses (...) in the Parameter Name, select RootVer (the value should autopopulate as Values/RootVer), select Does Not Equal for the Operator with a Value of 1, and then click Create.

10. In the Authoring Console, click the Health Model, click Discoveries, double-click the newly created discovery, and navigate to the Discovered Classes tab. Then click Add in Discovered Classes and Their Attributes and then click Add Discovered Type.

11. In the Management Pack Class Chooser, expand System.Device then select System.Computer and click OK.

12. Right-click on Computer in the Discovered Classes and Their Attributes section. Click Add Type Property on the shortcut menu, and then click DisplayName (System.Entity), as shown in Figure 8.33, and click OK.

FIGURE 8.33 Object discovery configuration.

13. Right-click the newly created discovery, and select Simulate.

NOTE

If the Simulate option is not available, the OpsMgr 2007 R2 Authoring Resource Kit must be installed. This can be downloaded directly from Microsoft at http://www.microsoft.com/download/en/details.aspx?displaylang=en&id=18222.

14. In the Test window, click the right triangle next to the Target Expressions text to resolve the target.

15. Enter the name of the MS. This MS must house an agent that can validate the values, as configured previously. For this exercise, use `OM1.companyxyz.com`. Click Connect when you are finished.

16. A new window opens prompting for a target selection; for this exercise, select OM1.companyxyz.com, and click Choose.

17. There should now be green circled check mark icons next to Target Expressions and Overridable Parameters; click Start Simulation.

18. Ensure the desired results and close the Test Simulation window.

19. In the Authoring Console, click the Health Model, then right-click Rules in the middle pane. Select New, Collection, Event Based, Windows Event Collection.

20. In the Windows Event Collection window, use **Test1** as the Display Name. From the Target drop-down menu, select the discovery created in the previous steps. For the example, this should read Test.NewElement and click Next.

21. For the Log name, use the default Application and click Next.

22. In the Build Event Expression, delete the line item Event Source and use 1704 as the Event ID Equals value. Click Finish.

23. Save the file as Standard Management Pack; click File, Save As and select Standard Management Pack.

To save as a sealed and signed management pack, a .SNK file must be generated. This process assumes that sn.exe is available; see the upcoming "Sealing a Management Pack Via Command Line" section if the executable is not available. Complete the following the steps to generate the .SNK file to be used during the seal and sign process:

1. Open the command prompt and type **sn k lab1.snk**.

2. Save the file as a sealed and signed management pack; click File, Save As and select Sealed and Signed Management Pack.

3. Select the destination where the management pack will be saved and the filename.

NOTE

The filename of the management pack must match management pack identity. If it does not, an error message appears during the sign and seal process.

4. A new window opens called Sealing Management Pack; for this exercise, use **companyxyz** as the Company Name, select the .SNK file created in the previous steps, and click OK.

Like any other management pack, this new custom management pack will need to be imported into a management group using the Operations Console to begin monitoring objects.

Modifying an Existing XML Management Pack File

Unsealed management packs are created in an XML format. At times, it can become necessary to modify the XML using the Authoring Console GUI interface. In the following example, an unsealed MP is exported. A value is modified, and the MP is imported into Operations Manager.

To edit an existing management pack XML file, complete the following steps:

1. Open the Authoring Console.

2. Go to File, Open.

3. In the Open Management Pack window, browse to c:\TEMP\MP_EXP, select MP2.XML, and click Open.

4. Expand the Health Model, and then select Rules.

5. Notice the name of the rule is prefixed with MOMUIGeneratedRule...; all rules created though the GUI interface will have a MOM prefix value.

6. Right-click the rule and select Properties.

7. Navigate to Modules and click Edit.

8. Change the Frequency value to 300; this value is calculated in seconds.

9. Click OK and OK again at the Rule Property window.

10. Go to File, Management Pack Properties and increment the Version field by one.

11. Save the management pack and import it back into Operations Manager using the steps found in the "Working with Management Packs" section.

12. Find the rule and verify that the Frequency value has changed.

Modifying the XML management pack is an easy way of adjusting the management pack properties.

Sealing a Management Pack Via Command Line

To seal a management pack, a .SNK file is required, which stands for Strong Name Key and is a part of the .NET assembly. Included with the .NET SDK is the SN.exe.exe, which aids in the creation of the key pair.

Once a .SNK file is available, signing and sealing can happen in the Authoring Console, or using MPSEAL.exe.exe (a tool located in the SupportTools directory of the installation media).

Using SN.ESE to create a .SNK file, the -k option is required, followed by a filename.

Using MPSEAL.exe.exe requires the XML version of the management pack; in addition, any MP libraries used must be within the path for MPSEAL.exe to find.

For the purposes of this exercise, MPSEAL.exe was copied into c:\Program Files\System Center 2012\Operations Manager\Server with the .SNK file located in c:\Source along with the standard XML of the management pack. Sealing a management pack with the command-line tool is shown in Figure 8.34.

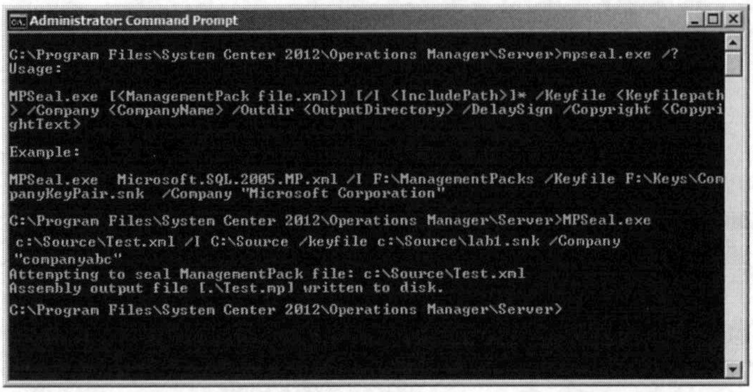

FIGURE 8.34   Sealing a management pack via command line.

Summary

Operations Manager provides the best approach to monitoring Microsoft-based infrastructure. By leveraging the core management packs, Operations Manager can provide key insight into the environment, thus eliminating guesswork and aiding troubleshooting efforts, creating repeatable responses to known issues, and creating a central company knowledge base.

Operations Manager requires active involvement by way of administration. Alerts should be mitigated or disabled if not actionable. In an ideal scenario, responsibilities within Operations Manager will be delegated; for example, all SQL alerts will be resolved or overridden by the DBA team. Custom management packs are used in one-off scenarios, with distributed applications created to monitor end-to-end scenarios for the Network Operations Center (NOC) to view and alert from.

Best Practices

The following are best practices from this chapter:

▶ If there are users who will receive alerts but won't have access to the Web console, create a notification channel that doesn't include an alert link in the body of the SMTP message.

▶ Before performing maintenance work on Operations Manager itself, disable notification subscriptions. That prevents alerts from being generated during the maintenance.

▶ When creating new rules and monitors, create them as disabled by default. Then create overrides to enable the rules and monitors for specific instances of objects.

▶ Use the Look For feature of the console when searching for discoveries, monitors, and rules to override or edit.

▶ Be sure to back up custom management packs, Management Pack Templates, and override management packs using the Export Management Pack function.

▶ Take the time to explore, configure, and tune any management packs that are deployed. Each management pack operates differently and has different tuning requirements to optimize its performance.

▶ Be sure to keep the management packs updated, as Microsoft routinely releases updates to the core management packs.

▶ Use Management Pack Templates to create monitoring for web applications, database sources, services, processes, and ports.

▶ Create custom management packs with the Authoring Console for more sophisticated applications or for publication.

Using Operations Manager 2012 for Operations and Security Reporting

IN THIS CHAPTER

▶ Reporting from OpsMgr

▶ Generating and Scheduling Reports

▶ OpsMgr 2012 Maintenance Reports

▶ Audit Collection Services Reporting

▶ Service Level Tracking

▶ OpsMgr 2012 Dashboards

▶ Publishing Dashboards into SharePoint 2010

▶ Best Practices

System Center Operations Manager (OpsMgr) 2012 not only monitors and collects information on the performance and health of monitored servers and applications, but also provides a myriad of ways to view that information. One of the key features of the OpsMgr platform is to provide a flexible reporting system. The Reporting data warehouse keeps a long-term historical record of the data collected and provides a mechanism to generate trending, availability, and security reports in a variety of formats and delivery mechanisms.

> **NOTE**
>
> Management packs frequently include reports that are installed when the management pack is imported. This includes Windows Server, Active Directory, Exchange, SQL, and the cross-platform management packs. These reports are discussed in Chapter 8, "Using Operations Manager 2012 for Monitoring and Alerting."

This chapter focuses on using the generic reports, security reports, and dashboards, including the following:

▶ Performance reports

▶ Alert reports

▶ Availability reports

▶ Service Level Tracking reports

▶ OpsMgr 2012 Dashboards

Dashboards in particular provide an exciting new method of delivering Operations Manager information to a wider range of audiences through publishing to SharePoint 2010.

Reporting from OpsMgr

The reporting in Operations Manager is based on SQL Reporting Services. This is a flexible reporting engine and allows reports to be viewed ad hoc, saved to favorites, exported, or delivered.

Reports that are generated ad hoc can also be exported to the following:

▶ Word

▶ Adobe Acrobat PDF

▶ Comma-separated value (CSV)

▶ TIFF

▶ MHTML (web archive)

▶ Excel

▶ XML

NOTE

Reports cannot be exported before generating the report ad hoc. Exporting a report regenerates the report. In other words, the report export process generates the report twice. This can be a significant factor when exporting a complex report. If this is an issue, a report can be scheduled with a one-time schedule and delivered to a file share.

Reporting Services can generate and deliver reports on a schedule. This is very helpful, as it eliminates the need for the administrator to remember to generate reports and, instead, delivers them automatically. Reports can be delivered to the following:

▶ Email

▶ Windows file share

▶ Null (used to create a cache of the report)

Delivered reports (file share or email) can be delivered in the same formats as exporting, but also support three additional formats:

▶ RPL Renderer

▶ Data Feed

▶ HTML 4.0

The HTML 4.0 format is useful for generating web pages for dashboard-type sites in combination with the Windows file share delivery format. The Data Feed format generates Atom-compliant data feeds of the report data and can be used by applications such as PowerPivot client. The Report Page Layout (RPL) Renderer format is a special binary format that supports Report Builder 2.0 and interactive viewing of the generated report.

OpsMgr management packs commonly include a variety of preconfigured reports to show information about the operating system or the specific application they were designed to work with. These reports are run in SQL Reporting Services. The reports provide an effective view of systems and services on the network over a custom period, such as weekly, monthly, or quarterly. They can also help you monitor your networks based on performance data, which can include critical pattern analysis, trend analysis, capacity planning, and security auditing. Reports also provide availability statistics for distributed applications, servers, and specific components within a server.

Availability reports are particularly useful for executives, managers, and application owners. These reports can show the availability of any object within OpsMgr, including a server (shown in Figure 9.1), a database, or even a service such as Active Directory that includes a multitude of servers and components. The Availability report shown in Figure 9.1 indicates that the SP server was down on 2/5/2012 for about 7.21% of the time or almost 2 hours. The rest of the time it had been up.

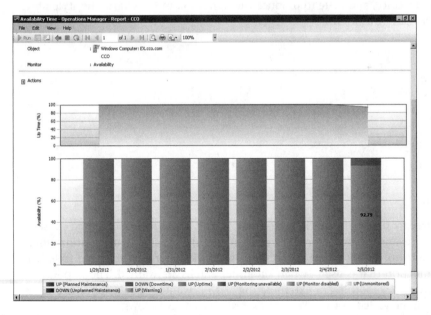

FIGURE 9.1   The Availability report.

The reports can be run on demand or at scheduled times and delivered via email. OpsMgr can also generate HTML-based reports that can be published to a web server and viewed from any web browser. Vendors can also create additional reports as part of their management packs.

Generating and Scheduling Reports

The Operations Manager 2012 infrastructure collects many Windows Server 2008 R2 data points. This information can be presented in reports, which can be generated ad hoc or scheduled. The scheduling option is very useful, as it reduces the need to actively open the console; instead, the reports are delivered via email.

Performance Reports

Performance reports are useful for graphing performance counters and data, which OpsMgr collects in droves. The Performance report can be used to create multiple charts of multiple series of performance data. Any data collected by Operations Manager can be graphed. The performance data is automatically summarized by hour and by day to reduce the size of the database and the time to generate reports.

The Performance reports are composed of charts and series within the charts. A Performance report can have multiple charts, each with a different set of series. For example, there could be a chart of disk performance series and a chart of processor performance series. Or there could be a chart for each server with performance counters for the server as the series.

The series are essentially the data collected by a performance collection rule. They can be formatted by style, color, and scale to produce the right look in the chart. The style of each of the series can be as follows:

- ▶ Area
- ▶ Column
- ▶ Line
- ▶ Point
- ▶ Spline
- ▶ Spline area
- ▶ Step line

The style can vary by series within the same chart, so the column style could be chosen for one series (for example, processor performance) and line for the memory utilization. This can be used to create important distinctions in the chart series. The spline style is a mathematical function that is useful when smoother graphs are wanted. The step line style is used when no smoothing or extrapolating at all is wanted. The color of the series within a chart can be varied as well. The colors available are as follows:

- ▶ Light Blue
- ▶ Dark Green
- ▶ Light Red

▶ Yellow

▶ Black

▶ Dark Blue

▶ Light Green

▶ Orange

▶ Light Gray-Blue

▶ Brown

The user interface cycles through the colors as series are added and loops back up to the top as more series are added to the chart. The colors can be chosen manually as well.

Finally, the series scale can be adjusted to format the chart properly. The counter can be scaled up by choosing a scale value larger than 1.0000 (the default) such as 10.0000, or can be scaled down by choosing a value smaller than 1.0000 such as 0.1000.

The series in the chart do not have to be the same and can be mixed and matched as needed. One important point is that the object selected must match or be contained as the rule selected as the basis of the series.

For example, an administrator or application owner might want to get a weekly graph of the Processor/% Processor Time, Paging File/% Usage, and Memory/% Committed Bytes in Use for a given system.

To schedule this report on a System Center Operations Manager server for email delivery, use the following steps:

1. Launch the Operations Manager 2012 console.

2. Select the Reporting space.

3. Select the Microsoft Generic Report Library node.

4. Select the Performance report and click Open.

5. In the From field, select Advanced.

6. Change the Offset to - (minus) and the number of days to 7. Click the green check mark (OK) to save the selections. The From field will show "Today -7 day(s)."

7. Change both the From and the To times to 12:00 AM.

8. In the Objects section, click the Change button to select what to graph.

9. In the Settings pop-up window, click the New Chart button.

6

NOTE

A Performance report can have multiple charts on the same report. For this example, the report has a single chart with multiple counters.

---

10. With the [Chart] highlighted, enter **DC1 Performance Chart** in the Chart Title field in the Details section.

11. With the [Chart] highlighted, click New Series to add a new data series to the chart.

NOTE

The series within a chart defaults to the line style and a scale of 1.0000, with each series taking the next color available starting with Light Blue.

---

12. With the series highlighted, click the Browse button in the Details section.

13. Select the Search By Counter tab.

14. Select the Processor performance object and the % Processor Time counter in the pull downs, and then click Search.

15. The search will likely return multiple rules that collect the counter. Select the rule that corresponds to the operating system, in this case Processor % Processor Time Total 2008. Take note of the Rule Target column, which shows that the rule targets the Windows Server 2008 Operating System. This will be needed later.

NOTE

If the rule selected does not match the object selected, the report returns no data. This is by far the most common problem with reports. Make sure that the object, or group of objects, selected is targeted by the rule.

---

16. Click OK to save the rule selection. If there were multiple instances of this counter, they would be displayed in the Rule section.

17. Click the Add Object button in the Details section.

18. Enter **Windows Server 2008** in the Object Name field and click Search. Don't enter the full rule target noted previously, as it will return an empty search result.

19. Select the server name in the Path column and click Add. Figure 9.2 shows the results.

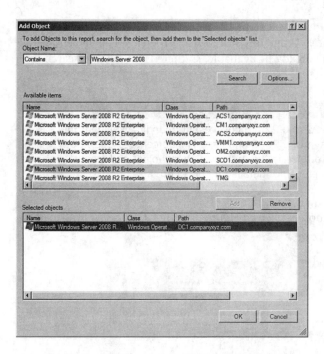

FIGURE 9.2   Adding a performance target object.

NOTE

The OpsMgr's inconsistent object-naming conventions make this a very tricky yet crucial step. The rule target was listed as Windows Server 2008 Operating System, yet the search of the objects showed a name of Microsoft Windows Server 2008 R2 Enterprise and a class of Windows Operating System. Either a detailed understanding of the OpsMgr schema or a bit of trial and error is needed to hunt down the correct object.

20. Click OK to save the object selection.

NOTE

It might be tempting to select multiple objects in this step. However, this results in the total of the objects in a single series (that is, line) on the chart. If separate series are wanted, they need to be defined separately.

21. Click the New Series button and repeat steps 12 through 20. Change the Object/Counter to Memory/% Committed Bytes in Use and select the Memory % Committed Bytes in Use 2008 rule. The object will already be available, so there is no need to search as was done in step 18.

22. Click the New Series button and repeat steps 12 through 20. Change the Object/Counter to Paging File/% Usage in Use and select the Page File Percentage Use 2008 rule. The object will already be available, so there is no need to search in step 18.

NOTE

If the counters described in steps 21 and 22 are not present, then it's likely that the rules (Memory % Committed Bytes in Use 2008 and Page File Percentage Use 2008) are not enabled. Search for the two rules in the Authoring\Rules folder and create overrides to enable them. See Chapter 8 for details on how to do this.

---

23. The results should look like those shown in Figure 9.3. Click OK to save the chart settings.

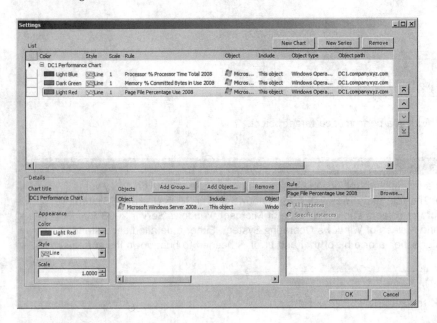

FIGURE 9.3   Performance chart settings.

24. Click Run to view the report. The report should look similar to Figure 9.4.

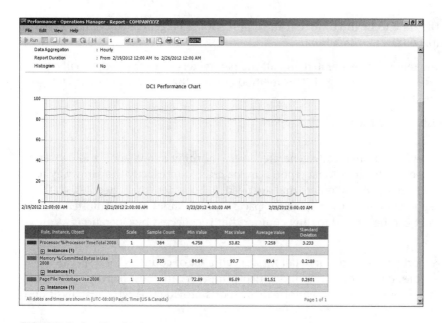

FIGURE 9.4   The Performance report.

The Performance report not only graphs the three selected counters, but also gives a statistical analysis of the data, including the sample count (that is, how many data points were collected in the report period), minimum value, maximum value, average value, and standard deviation from the average.

To have the report delivered on a scheduled basis, complete the following steps:

1. With the generated report still on the page, select File, Schedule.

2. In the Description field, enter **DC1 Performance Report**.

3. In the Delivery Method field, select Email.

NOTE

The Email option will only be available if it is configured correctly using the SQL Reporting Services Configuration Manager console.

4. In the To field, enter the SMTP address of the recipient.

5. In the Subject field, replace @ReportName with **DC1 Performance Report**. The variable name is unfortunately very long and ugly, so it's best to replace it.

6. Click Next.

7. Change the schedule to Daily.

8. Change the time to be the time that the report should be generated on a daily basis, for example 6:00 a.m. Click Next.

9. Because the report was generated and all the parameters were selected initially, no parameters need to be changed. This method ensures that the email report will match expectations.

10. Click Finish to save the scheduled report.

The report will now be automatically generated every morning at 6:00 a.m. and delivered via email to the recipients. Additional reports can be created in exactly the same way for the recommended rules and any others that are needed. To review the schedules, go to the Scheduled Reports node in the Reporting space. The schedules can be adjusted as well. This type of report can be created for any counter that is collected by Operations Manager.

Although this report provides lots of detail for a specific set of counters for a specific computer, sometimes it's important to find which computers are most heavily utilized or running low on a resource. The Top Performance reports provide this type of analysis and are discussed in the next section, "Top X Performance Reports."

Top X Performance Reports

When managing a number of agents, it can be difficult to pinpoint the problem systems. For example, which systems are the most heavily utilized? A report showing a graph of all the resources would be very messy and difficult to read even in a medium-sized organization with a small number of servers. Operations Manager 2012 has a set of reports that address this specific concern, the Performance Top Objects and Performance Top Instances. These reports take data from performance collection rules, perform some statistical analysis, and list the top systems.

For example, Figure 9.5 shows the top five systems with the most processor utilization. It is based on the Processor % Processor Time Total rule. It shows the top five heaviest processor utilization systems for the previous week. The report ranks the objects in descending order based on average value (the blue bar in the report) with standard deviation markings centered on the average value. The table gives the name of the object and some additional statistical information, such as sample count and max/min values.

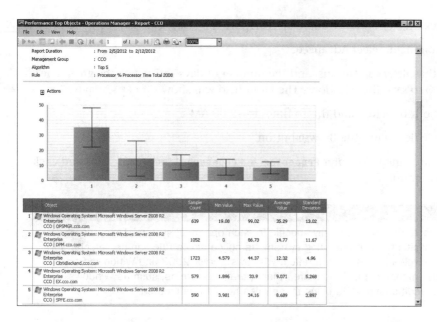

FIGURE 9.5   The Top Five Processor Utilization report.

This report is one of the reports in the Microsoft Generic Report Library and can be used against any performance counter. The report can pick the top (the default) or bottom objects, as well as vary the number of objects to return (the default is five).

The best-practice recommendation is to generate daily reports spanning the previous week for the following rules:

- Processor % Processor Time Total

- Page File Percentage Use

- Memory % Committed Bytes in Use

- Network Adapter Bytes Total per Second

- % Logical Disk Free Space

The Performance Top Objects report for each of these rules gives a good overview of the performance issues (or lack thereof) over the collection of all the monitored systems. These should be delivered on a daily basis in an email, published in SharePoint, or saved to a file share.

To schedule a report for email delivery, complete the following steps:

1. Launch the Operations Manager 2012 console.

2. Select the Reporting space.

3. Select the Microsoft Generic Report Library node.

4. Right-click the Performance Top Objects report and select Open.

5. In the From field, select Advanced.

6. Change the Offset to - (minus) and the number of days to 7. Click the green check mark (OK) to save the selections. The From field will show "Today -7 day(s)."

7. Change both the From and the To times to 12:00 AM.

8. In the Rule field, click the Browse button.

9. In the Rule Name field, enter **Processor % Processor Time Total 2008** and click the Search button.

NOTE

The performance rules are generally specific to each operating system. Thus, the reports are specific to each operating system, as only a single rule can be selected for the report. The rules in this section reflect Windows Server 2008 and Windows Server 2008 R2 performance data. If there are other operating systems, such as Windows Server 2003, additional reports using those rules need to be created.

---

10. In the Available Items pane, select the rule and click OK.

11. Click Run and confirm that the report looks good.

12. Select File, Schedule.

13. In the Description field, enter **Processor % Processor Time 2008 Total Report**.

14. In the Delivery Method field, select Email.

15. In the To field, enter the SMTP address of the recipient.

16. In the Subject field, replace @ReportName with **Processor % Processor Time Total 2008 Report**. The variable name is unfortunately very long and ugly, so it's best to replace it.

17. Click Next.

18. Change the schedule to Daily.

19. Change the time to be the time that the report should be generated on a daily basis, for example 6:00 a.m. Click Next.

20. Because the report was generated and all the parameters were selected initially, no parameters need to be changed. This method ensures that the email report will match expectations.

21. Click Finish to save the scheduled report.

The report will generate an email on the scheduled basis, at 6:00 a.m. every morning.

Windows Server Performance Reports

While the Top X Performance Reports are very flexible and can report on any performance counter, a separate report is needed for each counter. This can be unwieldy and result in a large number of reports. For the Windows operating systems, there are really just a set of four metrics that are critical to understand: processor, memory, disk, and network. The Windows core OS management packs include a pair of reports that do a great job of presenting this information. The two reports are Performance By System and Performance By Utilization.

The Performance By System shows performance metrics for each system included in the report in its own section, allowing an administrator to drill into the performance of the system quickly in a single report. The systems are listed in subreports sequentially in the master report. Each individual systems subreport has a breakdown of each of the four key metrics for the system. The metrics are color-coded to denote healthy (green), warning (yellow), and critical (red) states.

The Performance By Utilization report is very similar to the Top X Performance report, but for each of the four key metrics across the selected systems. The worst-performing systems are listed in each key metric, so it might be that different systems are listed in different metrics. Once again, the metrics are color-coded to denote healthy (green), warning (yellow), and critical (red) states.

For example, Figure 9.6 shows the Performance By Utilization report for the All Windows Computers group for the top three worst performers. The top three processor utilization systems are not the same as the top three memory page utilization systems. And the report also shows that processor utilization is clearly not a problem as it is showing healthy, but that the memory page utilization for two of the systems might be a problem.

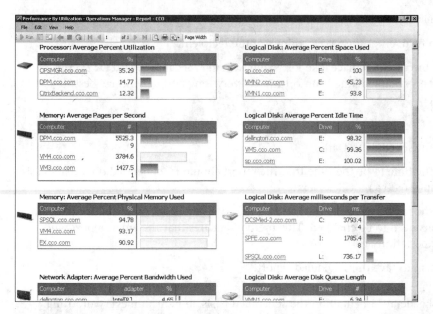

FIGURE 9.6   The Performance By Utilization report.

The Performance By Utilization report is a very useful summary, as it lets an administrator see at a glance what the top utilized systems are and if that utilization is a problem. It is recommended that this report be generated every day against all Windows computers.

To schedule the Performance By Utilization report for email delivery, complete the following steps:

1. Launch the Operations Manager 2012 console.

2. Select the Reporting space.

3. Select the Windows Server Operating System Reports node.

4. Right-click the Performance By Utilization report and select Open.

5. In the From field, select Advanced.

6. Change the Offset to - (minus) and the number of days to 7. Click the green check mark (OK) to save the selections. The From field will show "Today -7 day(s)."

7. Change both the From and the To times to 12:00 AM.

8. In the Group pull-down, choose all Windows computers.

9. Leave the Utilization pull-down at Most.

10. Leave the Number Of Systems at 10.

11. Click Run and confirm that the report looks good.

12. Select File, Schedule.

13. In the Description field, enter **Performance by Utilization Report**.

14. In the Delivery Method field, select Email.

15. In the To field, enter the SMTP address of the recipient.

16. In the Subject field, replace @ReportName with **Performance By Utilization Report**. The variable name is unfortunately very long and ugly, so it's best to replace it.

17. Click Next.

18. Change the schedule to Daily.

19. Change the time to be the time that the report should be generated on a daily basis, for example, 6:00 a.m. Click Next.

20. Because the report was generated and all the parameters were selected initially, no parameters need to be changed. This method ensures that the email report will match expectations.

21. Click Finish to save the scheduled report.

The report will generate an email on the scheduled basis, at 6:00 a.m. every morning.

Alerts Reports

Alerts reports can summarize the alerts that have been generated for a specific object or set of objects. This report is useful for summarizing reports for which notifications have been sent and for all alerts, many of which might not have had notifications sent.

The reports can show alerts from a single object like a Windows computer or even a database. They can also show alerts from groups of objects like the Exchange Server 2010 All Server Computers group or SQL Server 2008 DB Engine Group. Multiple objects and groups can be specified in the selection, and custom groups can be created to contain specific sets of monitored objects if needed.

The alerts can also be filtered by severity (Information, Warning, and Critical) and by priority (Low, Medium, and High) in any combination. This allows the Alerts reports to be tailored very precisely for the target audiences.

To create an Alerts report that shows the critical Exchange Server 2010 computer alerts from the previous day, complete the following steps:

1. Launch the Operations Manager 2012 console.

2. Select the Reporting space.

3. Select the Microsoft Generic Report Library node.

4. Right-click the Alerts report and select Open.

5. In the From field, select Yesterday.

6. Change both the From and the To times to 12:00 AM.

7. Click the Add Group button.

8. In the Group Name field, enter **Exchange Server 2010** and click the Search button.

9. Select the Microsoft Exchange 2010 All Server Computers and click Add.

10. Click OK to save the selections.

11. In the Severity section, uncheck the Warning and Information severity boxes.

12. Click Run and confirm that the report looks good.

The resulting report shows the critical severity alerts for all the Windows Computer objects in the Exchange Server 2010 All Server Computers group. The report is sorted by alert severity, though clicking on other columns changes the sort order. The sample report in Figure 9.7 shows the critical severity alerts: an AD Client Monitoring alert indicating that response times were slow and a database copy alert indicating that the log volume is low on disk space.

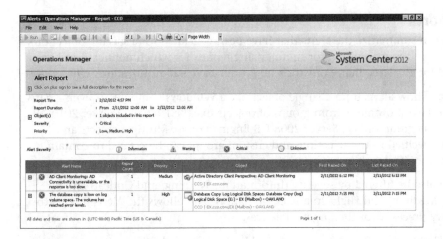

FIGURE 9.7   The Critical Severity Alert report for the Exchange Server 2010 All Server
Computers Group.

Different groups and objects can be selected to tailor the report to the target audience.

NOTE

If the report shows no data, it could be because there were no alerts generated for the
selected objects during the time period. It could also be that the wrong object or group
was selected. Confirm that there have been alerts generated and expand the time
range of the report to test if the report does return the alerts. Once the report is
confirmed, put the time range back to the desired time range.

The Alert report can be scheduled to be delivered on a daily or weekly basis to administrators or application owners using the steps in the previous section. To have the report
delivered on a scheduled basis, use the following steps:

1. With the generated Alert report still on the page, select File, Schedule.

2. In the Description field, enter **Exchange 2010 Computers Critical Alert Report**.

3. In the Delivery Method field, select Email.

NOTE

The Email option will only be available if it is configured correctly using the SQL
Reporting Services Configuration Manager console.

---

4. In the To field, enter the SMTP address of the recipient.

5. In the Subject field, replace @ReportName with **Exchange 2010 Computers Critical
   Alert Report**. The variable name is unfortunately very long and ugly, so it's best to
   replace it.

6. Click Next.

7. Change the schedule to Daily.

8. Change the time to be when the report should be generated on a daily basis, for example 6:00 a.m. Click Next.

9. Because the report was generated and all the parameters were selected initially, no parameters need to be changed. This method ensures that the email report will match expectations.

10. Click Finish to save the scheduled report.

The Critical Alerts report will now be automatically generated every morning at 6:00 a.m. and delivered via email to the recipients.

TIP

One way to leverage the Alert report is to create a report that summarizes all alerts generated after hours and deliver it first thing every morning. For example, if an IT organization has a support policy that dictates that support is provided from 6:00 a.m. to 8:00 p.m., no notifications are sent to pagers during the 8:00 p.m. to 6:00 a.m. off-hours period. To ensure that IT support can respond to any issues that occurred during the off-hours, generate an Alert report every morning at 6:00 a.m. that includes alerts that were raised from 8:00 p.m. to 6:00 a.m.

Availability Reports

The bane of every IT manager and executive is not knowing when systems and services were available and unavailable. They are typically at the mercy of the IT technical staff in faithfully reporting when systems are down. Famously, when the CEO or business unit managers are asked about IT reliability, they report far more outages than the IT technical staff reported.

Operations Manager solves this dilemma by providing Availability reports that can be delivered automatically to the Inboxes of IT managers and executives. This includes the availability of servers, services, applications, and even specific objects like databases. Availability reports can be generated for any object in Operations Manager.

The report determines the availability on the basis of the following six categories of state:

▶ **Unplanned Maintenance (default)**—This is essentially a critical state (red) outside of a maintenance window. Any time in this state is counted against the availability.

▶ **Warning**—This option can be selected if the Warning state should count against the availability.

▶ **Monitoring Unavailable**—This option counts the lack of a state to be downtime.

▶ **Planned Maintenance**—Planned Maintenance is the time in which the object is placed in Maintenance mode. Normally, objects are placed in Maintenance mode specifically to prevent the state from impacting the availability.

▶ **Monitor Disabled**—This option counts the disabled monitoring as unavailability.

▶ **Unmonitored**—Finally, Unmonitored is the state before an object has been discovered or if the underlying monitoring rules are disabled.

In most cases, the default of Unplanned Maintenance is sufficient. This means that if the object is in a critical state, it is considered unavailable.

The Availability Summary report shows downtime as a percentage bar (not by time) color-coded to show the state. The color codes are as follows:

▶ Uptime (Green)

▶ Downtime (Red)

▶ Warning (Yellow)

▶ Planned Maintenance (Blue)

▶ Unplanned Maintenance (Black)

▶ Unmonitored (White)

▶ Monitor Disabled (Light Gray)

▶ Monitoring Unavailable (Dark Gray)

The horizontal bar displays the percentage availability and multiple objects can be selected to present a summary of availability. This report shows the availability in terms of a percentage bar and stats such as Uptime and Downtime in both percentages and in hours:minutes:seconds format.

The report also contains links such as the Availability Tracker link, which can be used to drill into the availability of an object per aggregation period (daily or hourly). In fact, the Drill-Down Availability report (reached by clicking on the Availability Tracker link) is often a much more useful presentation of the availability.

The following links are available on the Availability Summary report:

▶ **Availability Tracker report**—This report shows the percentage availability per time period.

▶ **Downtime report**—This report shows the downtime on a horizontal timeline.

▶ **Monitor Availability report**—This report shows the monitor's time in state. Particularly interesting is the Expand Monitor Hierarchy option, which shows the time in state for the monitor hierarchy.

▶ **Configuration Changes report**—This report shows any configuration changes that are captured.

Each of these linked reports can be scheduled or exported as with any other report in Operations Manager.

The best way to get the Availability report is to find the application, server, or object in the Operations Console and then generate the Availability report from there. That ensures that the correct object is selected without having to search for it in the report interface.

To get an Availability report for the Exchange service, complete the following steps:

1. Launch the Operations Manager console.

2. Select the Monitoring space.

3. Select the Distributed Application folder.

4. Select the Exchange service.

5. Select the Tasks menu, Report Tasks, and then the Availability report.

NOTE

The Availability report is a generic report that can be generated for any object in Operations Manager. This includes distributed applications, servers, databases, or even a network interface card.

6. In the From field, select Advanced.

7. Change the Offset to - (minus) and the number of days to 7. Click the green check mark (OK) to save the selections. The From field will show "Today -7 day(s)."

8. Change both the From and the To times to 12:00 AM.

NOTE

There is a check box for Use Business Hours. This option is particularly useful for the Availability report. If the application has an availability requirement of certain core hours, such as 6:00 a.m. to 6:00 p.m. Monday through Friday, then it would be incorrect to generate an Availability report that covers the hours outside of the core hours.

Checking the Use Business Hours check box and then configuring the business hours provides a more accurate representation of the availability of the application from a business perspective.

9. The Exchange service object is already selected in the Objects section and doesn't need to be changed.

10. The Down Time section has Unplanned Maintenance selected. Change if needed.

11. Click Run to generate the report. The resulting report is shown in Figure 9.8.

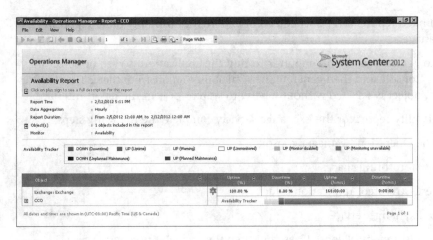

FIGURE 9.8   The Availability Summary report for the Exchange 2010 Service.

12. In the body of the report, click the Availability Tracker hyperlink to drill into the
    Availability report by time period, which in this case is seven days. There will be a
    report with a vertical availability bar for each day and a graph charting the availabil-
    ity. The report is shown in Figure 9.9.

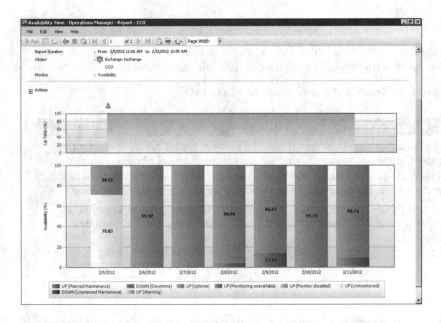

FIGURE 9.9   The Availability Tracker report for the Exchange 2010 Service.

13. In the menu bar, click the small blue left-pointing arrow, which is the Back to
    Parent Report control. This takes the browser back to the previous report, the
    Availability Summary report.

14. Click the plus symbol (+) in the first column next to the object name. This expands to show additional links within the report.

15. Click the Object Monitor Availability Detail to launch the report.

16. In the resulting report, click the Expand Monitor Hierarchy link above the table. After a bit of time, the report regenerates with an availability bar for each monitor in the health hierarchy of the Exchange 2010 Service.

NOTE

The resulting report can be quite long due to the number of monitors in the hierarchy. For a simple environment, this could be seven pages long. This would be shorter for less-complicated, distributed applications than the Exchange 2010 Service.

---

17. Click the Back to Parent Report control twice to get back to the Availability Summary report.

These Availability reports allow application owners and administrators to see the availability of any monitored object or group of objects. This information can be in summary form, by time period, or even monitor by monitor.

Any of the reports or linked reports can be generated ad hoc or scheduled using the techniques shown earlier in this section.

OpsMgr Scheduled Reports Don't Show Charts

Sometimes there is a problem where the OpsMgr scheduled reports run and display the correct text and numeric data, but no charts. The Reporting Server generates the following error at the same time:

```
Log Name: Application
Source: Report Server Windows Service (MSSQLSERVER)
Date: 2/11/2012 9:34:21 PM
Event ID: 108
Task Category: Extension
Level: Error
Keywords: Classic
User: N/A
Computer: <computername>
Description:
Report Server Windows Service (MSSQLSERVER) cannot load the EnterpriseManage-
mentChartControl extension.
```

This is caused by a problem with the loading of the charting extension. To resolve this problem, add the following information to the ReportingServicesService.exe.config file in the %Program Files%\Microsoft SQL Server\MSRS10.MSSQLSERVER\Reporting Services\ReportServer\bin\ directory:

```
<dependentAssembly>
<assemblyIdentity name="Microsoft.ReportingServices.ProcessingCore"
publicKeyToken="89845dcd8080cc91" culture="neutral" />
<bindingRedirect oldVersion="9.0.242.0" newVersion="10.0.0.0" />
</dependentAssembly>
<dependentAssembly xmlns="urn:schemas-microsoft-com:asm.v1">
<assemblyIdentity name="Microsoft.ReportingServices.ProcessingCore"
publicKeyToken="89845dcd8080cc91" culture="neutral" />
<bindingRedirect oldVersion="9.0.242.0" newVersion="10.0.0.0" />
</dependentAssembly>
```

Just paste in the text below the existing <dependentAssembly> entries. The SQL Reporting Services service will need to be restarted for the changes to take effect. After this, the charts will generate properly in the emails.

OpsMgr 2012 Maintenance Reports

There are also reports on Operations Manager 2012 that should be generated to ensure that the health and performance of the infrastructure are good. The reports to generate are as follows:

▶ **Most Common Alerts report**—This report is useful for determining what alerts are the noisiest and might be spamming the Inboxes of notification subscribers. The report shows which alerts are most common and gives additional statistical analysis.

▶ **Alert Logging Latency report**—This report is useful for determining the health of the OpsMgr infrastructure, as measured by the time an event occurs on a managed computer to the time an alert is raised. If this is too long (that is, greater than 30 seconds), it indicates that there is a problem.

▶ **Send Queue % Used Top 10 report**—This report tells you if agents are having trouble uploading their data to the management servers. These queues should be less than 1%.

▶ **Daily Alert report**—This report gives you a complete list of all the alerts that were generated. This is very detailed, but is good for chasing down problems uncovered in other checks.

▶ **SQL Database Space report**—This report shows the database space and growth of SQL databases. This is generated against the OpsMgr databases to monitor the growth.

These reports should be generated on a weekly basis (for example, Monday at 6:00 a.m.) spanning the previous week and be sent to the Operations Manager administrators.

Most Common Alerts Report

This report analyzes the most common alerts that were generated and is good for identifying alert-tuning opportunities. The Most Common Alerts report is based on the management packs that are installed. By default, the report selects all of the installed management packs and shows the top five most common alerts. To schedule the Most Common Alerts report, execute the following steps:

1. Launch the Operations Manager 2012 console.

2. Select the Reporting space.

3. Select the Microsoft Generic Report Library node.

4. In the reports pane, right-click the Most Common Alerts and select Open.

5. In the From field, select Advanced.

6. Change the Offset to Minus and the number of days to 7. Click the green check mark (OK) to save the selections. The From field will show "Today -7 day(s)."

7. Change both the From and the To times to 12:00 AM.

8. Click Run and confirm that the report looks good.

> **NOTE**
>
> The report is generated for all the installed management packs by default. This report can also be generated against a single or group of management packs, such as Exchange or Active Directory, by unselecting all but those management packs. This allows the alerts from a particular management pack to be evaluated.

9. Select File, Schedule.

10. In the Description field, enter **Most Common Alerts Report**.

11. In the Delivery Method field, select Email.

> **NOTE**
>
> The Email option will only be available if it is configured correctly using the SQL Reporting Services Configuration Manager console.

12. In the To field, enter the SMTP address of the recipient.

13. In the Subject field, replace @ReportName with **Most Common Alerts Report**.

14. Click Next.

15. Change the schedule to Weekly and ensure that only Mon is checked.

16. Change the time to be the time that the report should be generated on a daily basis, for example, 6:00 a.m. Click Next.

17. Because the report was generated and all the parameters were selected initially, no parameters need to be changed. This method ensures that the email report will match expectations.

18. Click Finish to save the scheduled report.

Figure 9.10 shows an example of the Most Common Alerts report. The most common alert for the previous week was that the WMI memory usage high, with 57.00% of alerts. This alert could be tuned to reduce the volume of alerts or the problem resolved.

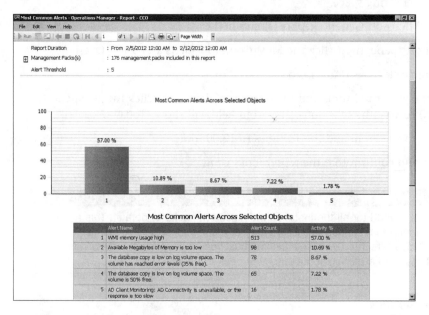

FIGURE 9.10   The Most Common Alerts report.

Alert Logging Latency Report

This report tells you the length of time between an event being raised on a managed computer to an alert being generated in the Operations Console. This should be under 30 seconds in a healthy OpsMgr environment.

> **NOTE**
>
> If the alert logging latency is too high, it means that problems can occur and alerts will not be generated fast enough for IT to be notified in advance of user notification mechanisms to kick in. The user notification mechanisms are those users calling in to the help desk to complain about systems being down. You never want to be the IT professional who is the last to hear about an outage.

The Alert Logging Latency report is based on the objects selected. The report does not include any objects by default, so the objects must be selected. It is a best practice to select the groups of agents, agentless, and agent watchers objects. To schedule the Alert Logging Latency report, execute the following steps:

1. Launch the Operations Manager 2012 console.

2. Select the Reporting space.

3. Select the Microsoft Generic Report Library node.

4. In the reports pane, right-click the Alert Logging Latency and select Open.

5. In the From field, select Advanced.

6. Change the Offset to Minus and the number of days to 7. Click the green check mark (OK) to save the selections. The From field will show "Today -7 day(s)."

7. Change both the From and the To times to 12:00 AM.

8. Click the Add Group button.

9. In the Group Name field, enter **agent** and click the Search button.

10. Select the Operations Manager Agent Managed Computer Group, the Operations Manager Agents, the Agentless Managed Computer Group, and the Microsoft.SystemCenter.AgentWatchersGroup and click Add.

11. Click OK to save the selections.

12. Click Run and confirm that the report looks good. The report should look similar to Figure 9.11. The report shows that a significant percentage of alerts on 2/5/2012 and 2/9/2012 took longer than 30 seconds.

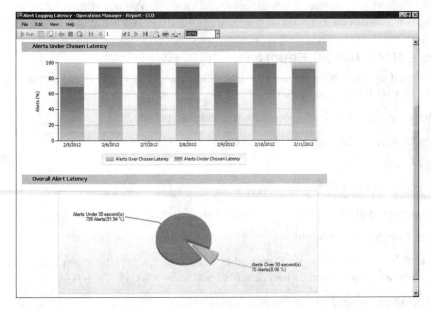

FIGURE 9.11   The Alert Logging Latency report.

13. Select File, Schedule.

14. In the Description field, enter **Alert Logging Latency Report**.

15. In the Delivery Method field, select Email.

> **NOTE**
>
> The Email option will only be available if it is configured correctly using the SQL
> Reporting Services Configuration Manager console.

16. In the To field, enter the SMTP address of the recipient.

17. In the Subject field, replace @ReportName with **Alert Logging Latency Report**.

18. Click Next.

19. Change the schedule to Weekly and ensure that only Mon is checked.

20. Change the time to be the time that the report should be generated on a daily basis,
    for example, 6:00 a.m. Click Next.

21. Because the report was generated and all the parameters were selected initially, no
    parameters need to be changed. This method ensures that the email report will
    match expectations.

22. Click Finish to save the scheduled report.

The Alert Logging Latency report will now generate on a weekly basis and be emailed to
the recipients. The report has two pages with lots of statistical analysis of the alert latency.
It is one of the more sophisticated reports in the OpsMgr library of reports.

Send Queue % Used Top 10 Report

This report tells you if agents are having trouble uploading their data to the management
servers. These queues should be less than 1%.

To schedule a report for email delivery, complete the following steps:

1. Launch the Operations Manager 2012 console.

2. Select the Reporting space.

3. Select the Microsoft Generic Report Library node.

4. In the report pane, right-click the Performance Top Objects and select Open.

5. In the From field, select Advanced.

6. Change the Offset to - (minus) and the number of days to 7. Click the green check
   mark (OK) to save the selections. The From field will show "Today -7 day(s)."

7. Change both the From and the To times to 12:00 AM.

8. Change the N field from 5 to 10 to return the Top 10.

> **NOTE**
>
> In larger organizations, it might be better to use a higher number such as the top 20. For smaller organizations, it might be better to use a smaller value like the top 5.

9. In the Rule field, click the Browse button.

10. In the Rule Name field, enter **Send Queue % Used** and click the Search button.

11. In the Available Items pane, select the Collect Health Service Management Group\Send Queue % Used rule and click OK.

12. Click Run and confirm that the report looks good.

13. Select File, Schedule.

14. In the Description field, enter **Send Queue % Used Top 10 Report**.

15. In the Delivery Method field, select Email.

> **NOTE**
>
> The Email option will only be available if it is configured correctly using the SQL Reporting Services Configuration Manager console.

16. In the To field, enter the SMTP address of the recipient.

17. In the Subject field, replace @ReportName with **Send Queue % Used Top 10 Report**.

18. Click Next.

19. Change the schedule to Daily.

20. Change the time to be the time that the report should be generated on a daily basis, for example, 6:00 a.m. Click Next.

21. Because the report was generated and all the parameters were selected initially, no parameters need to be changed. This method ensures that the email report will match expectations.

22. Click Finish to save the scheduled report.

The report generates on the scheduled basis, 6:00 a.m. every morning. If any of the send queue percentages get too high, this is cause for immediate investigation. See the sample report in Figure 9.12. This report shows that the Health Service for ex.cco.com had a max value of 98.87%, which indicates that the agent had problems, although they seem to have been temporary as the average value over the week was only 9.306%. This is still high, as a more healthy value would be 1% or lower.

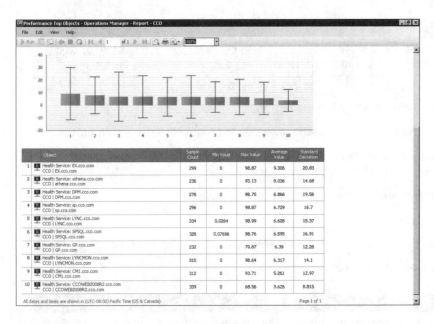

The following table appears within the report image:

	Object	Sample Count	Min Value	Max Value	Average Value	Standard Deviation
1	Health Service: EX.cco.com CCO | EX.cco.com	299	0	98.87	9.306	20.83
2	Health Service: athena.cco.com CCO | athena.cco.com	236	0	93.13	8.036	14.68
3	Health Service: DPM.cco.com CCO | DPM.cco.com	278	0	98.75	6.866	19.56
4	Health Service: sp.cco.com CCO | sp.cco.com	296	0	98.87	6.729	16.7
5	Health Service: LYNC.cco.com CCO | LYNC.cco.com	334	0.0264	98.99	6.628	15.37
6	Health Service: SPSQL.cco.com CCO | SPSQL.cco.com	328	0.07696	98.76	6.595	16.91
7	Health Service: GP.cco.com CCO | GP.cco.com	232	0	79.87	6.39	12.28
8	Health Service: LYNCMON.cco.com CCO | LYNCMON.cco.com	315	0	98.64	6.317	14.1
9	Health Service: CM1.cco.com CCO | CM1.cco.com	312	0	93.71	5.261	12.97
10	Health Service: CCOWEB2008R2.cco.com CCO | CCOWEB2008R2.cco.com	339	0	68.56	3.626	8.815

FIGURE 9.12   The Send Queue % Used report.

Daily Alerts Report

This report gives you a complete list of all the alerts that were generated. This is very detailed, but is good for chasing down problems uncovered in other checks.

To create an Alerts report that shows all the agent alerts from the previous day, complete the following steps:

1. Launch the Operations Manager 2012 console.

2. Select the Reporting space.

3. Select the Microsoft Generic Report Library node.

4. In the reports pane, right-click Alerts and select Open.

5. In the From field, select Yesterday.

6. Change both the From and the To times to 12:00 AM.

7. Click the Add Group button.

8. In the Group Name field, enter **agent** and click the Search button.

9. Select the Operations Manager Agent Managed Computer Group, the Operations Manager Agents, the Agentless Managed Computer Group, and the Microsoft.SystemCenter.AgentWatchersGroup, and click Add.

10. Click OK to save the selections.

11. In the Severity section, uncheck the Warning and Information severity boxes.

12. Click Run and confirm that the report looks good.

The resulting report shows the critical severity alerts for all the agent objects in the management group. The report is sorted by alert severity, though clicking on other columns changes the sort order. The sample report in Figure 9.13 shows the Critical Severity Alert report. There is only one page to the report. The report can be sorted by last raised by clicking on the Last Raised On column heading.

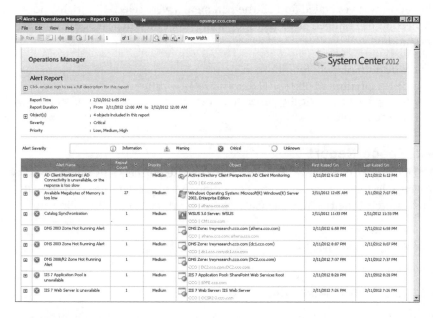

FIGURE 9.13   The Daily Critical Alert report.

The Alert report can be scheduled to be delivered on a daily or weekly basis to administrators or application owners using the steps in the previous section. To have the report delivered on a scheduled basis, use the following steps:

1. With the generated alert report still on the page, select File, Schedule.

2. In the Description field, enter **Daily Critical Alert Report**.

3. In the Delivery Method field, select Email.

NOTE

The Email option will only be available if it is configured correctly using the SQL Reporting Services Configuration Manager console.

4. In the To field, enter the SMTP address of the recipient.

5. In the Subject field, replace @ReportName with **Critical Daily Critical Alert
   Report**. The variable name is unfortunately very long and ugly, so it's best to
   replace it.

6. Click Next.

7. Change the schedule to Daily.

8. Change the time to be the time that the report should be generated on a daily basis,
   for example 6:00 a.m. Click Next.

9. Because the report was generated and all the parameters were selected initially, no
   parameters need to be changed. This method ensures that the email report will
   match expectations.

10. Click Finish to save the scheduled report.

The Alert report will now be automatically generated every morning at 6:00 a.m. and
delivered via email to the recipients.

SQL Database Space Report

Finally, the SQL Database Space report is based on the database objects. This report does
not have any objects selected by default, so the Operations Manager database objects will
need to be selected. To schedule the SQL Database Space report, complete the following
steps:

1. Launch the Operations Manager 2012 console.

2. Select the Reporting space.

3. Select the SQL Server 2008 (Monitoring) node.

4. In the report pane, right-click the SQL Database Space report and select Open.

5. In the From field, select Advanced.

6. Change the Offset to - (minus) and the number of days to 7. Click the green check
   mark (OK) to save the selections. The From field will show "Today -7 day(s)."

7. Change both the From and the To times to 12:00 AM.

8. Click the Add Object button.

> **NOTE**
>
> When the Add Object window opens, note that there is a caution triangle with the text
> "Filter Options Have Been Applied." The objects returned will only be those that match
> the report criteria, in the case of SQL database objects. This is new to Operations
> Manager 2012; before this, all object classes would be returned and it was difficult to
> ensure that the correct objects were included in the report. Many times, reports would
> be returned without any data at all due to the incorrect objects being selected. This is
> a huge improvement in OpsMgr 2012.

9. In the Object Name field, enter **Operations** and click the Search button.

10. Select all the OperationsManager databases and click Add.

11. Click OK to save the selections.

12. Click Run and confirm that the report looks good.

13. Select File, Schedule.

14. In the Description field, enter **Operations Manager Database Space Report**.

15. In the Delivery Method field, select Email.

NOTE

The Email option will only be available if it is configured correctly using the SQL
Reporting Services Configuration Manager console.

---

16. In the To field, enter the SMTP address of the recipient.

17. In the Subject field, replace @ReportName with **Operations Manager Database
    Space Report**.

18. Click Next.

19. Change the schedule to Weekly and ensure that only Mon is checked.

20. Change the time to be the time that the report should be generated on a daily basis,
    for example 6:00 a.m. Click Next.

21. Because the report was generated and all the parameters were selected initially, no
    parameters need to be changed. This method ensures that the email report will
    match expectations.

22. Click Finish to save the scheduled report.

The SQL Database Space report will be delivered every week on Monday at 6:00 a.m.

These five reports help ensure that the Operations Manager 2012 infrastructure is healthy
and performing well.

Audit Collection Services Reporting

Audit Collection Services (ACS) doesn't generate any security alerts or even store any of
its data in the OperationsManager database, so the data cannot be viewed from within
the monitoring space of the Operations Console. The ACS data is stored in the
OperationsManagerAC database. The only way to access the data is using the ACS reports.

The ACS reports are somewhat rudimentary. For example, they don't include the capability of using relative dates, which makes it difficult to schedule them. In this section, a
workaround to this problem is presented, which is to create a duplicate custom report and
schedule that.

The ACS Report Model was installed in Chapter 7, "Operations Manager 2012 Implementation and Administration." This section assumes that this has been completed successfully.

Reports in the ACS Report Model

The ACS reports are somewhat different from the other Operations Manager reports. They all generate by default, rather than prompting for parameters the way the standard OpsMgr reports do. The date ranges they span are usually two days, though this can be adjusted.

The reports are organized into several categories, as follows:

▶ Access Violation

▶ Account Management

▶ Forensic

▶ Planning

▶ Policy

▶ System Integrity

▶ Usage

The report-naming conventions and format in ACS leaves quite a bit to be desired. The naming convention uses underscores and dashes as separators, which results in a very ugly name for the reports.

The Access Violation reports look for failed logons. They consist of the following:

▶ **Access_Violation_-_Account_Locked**—This report details all account lockout events. This shows potential password-guessing attempts.

▶ **Access_Violation_-_Unsuccessful_Logon_Attempts**—This report details all failed logons. The report can be quite long, but shows potential password-cracking attempts.

The Account Management reports show the account management events, such as user creation, password resets, and administrator changes. The Account Management ACS reports consist of the following:

▶ **Account_Management_-_Domain_and_Built-in_Administrators_Changes**—This report shows the changes in membership to domain admins and the built-in administrators groups.

▶ **Account_Management_-_Password_Change_Attempts_by_Non-owner**—This report shows password resets by administrators.

▶ **Account_Management_-_User_Accounts_Created**—This report lists the user accounts created.

▶ **Account_Management_-_User_Accounts_Deleted**—This report lists the user accounts deleted.

The Forensic reports provide a more comprehensive view of all events for a user, a computer, or a specific event ID. These are useful when trying to understand everything that was done. The Forensic reports consist of the following:

▶ Forensic_-_All_Events_For_Specified_Computer

▶ Forensic_-_All_Events_For_Specified_User

▶ Forensic_-_All_Events_With_Specified_Event_ID

The Planning reports allow the administrator to understand the flow of events, which can be quite large. The ACS Planning reports consist of the following:

▶ **Planning_-_Event_Counts**—This report shows a count of all events generated in the past day. It shows the specific event IDs, the number of those events, and the percentage of the total, both numerically and graphically.

▶ **Planning_-_Event_Counts_by_Computer**—This report shows the count of events by computer. It shows the specific event IDs, the number of those events, and the percentage of the total, both numerically and graphically.

▶ **Planning_-_Hourly_Event_Distribution**—This report shows the count of events by hour. It shows the specific event IDs, the number of those events, and the percentage of the total, both numerically and graphically.

▶ **Planning_-_Logon_Counts_of_Privileged_Users**—This report shows the number of times that privileged users have logged on.

The Policy reports consist of the following:

▶ Policy_-_Account_Policy_Changed

▶ Policy_-_Audit_Policy_Changed

▶ Policy_-_Object_Permissions_Changed

▶ Policy_-_Privilege_Added_Or_Removed

The System Integrity reports consist of the following:

▶ **System_Integrity_-_Audit_Failure**—This report lists the times that systems failed to log security events due to a lack of resources.

▶ **System_Integrity_-_Audit_Log_Cleared**—This report shows audit log cleared events.

The Usage reports consist of the following:

- **Usage_-_Object_Access**—This report shows all object access–related audit events.

- **Usage_-_Privileged_logon**—This report shows the logon counts of privileged users.

- **Usage_-_Sensitive_Security_Groups_Changes**—This report lists all the sensitive security group changes.

- **Usage_-_User_Logon**—This report shows the logons by specified user.

These reports provide a comprehensive view of the security events being collected by the Audit Collection Services.

Generating ACS Reports

Generating reports from the ACS database (OperationsManagerAC) is straightforward for ad hoc reports. The report parameters have none of the complexity associated with the standard OpsMgr reports, and instead only have Start Date and End Date parameters.

By way of example, suppose an administrator has been requested to show all password resets that have been done in the past week. This would be those password changes done by an administrator on behalf of a user. Unauthorized password resets are an abuse of privilege and can be used to stage an elevation of privilege attack, so it is important to monitor these events.

To generate the Password Change Attempts report for the previous two weeks, complete the following steps:

1. Launch the Operations Console.

2. Select the Reporting space.

3. Select the Audit Reports folder.

4. Select the Account_Management_-_Password_Change_Attempts_by_Non-owner report.

5. Select Open to launch the report.

6. The report generates, but only for the current day (12:00 a.m. yesterday to 12:00 a.m. tomorrow).

7. Click View and select parameters to show the Start Date and End Date.

8. Change the Start Date to two weeks earlier and then click Run.

NOTE

The date that was selected was an actual date and there was no option to select a relative date like "Yesterday" or "Previous Week." This is a serious limitation of the built-in ACS reports as it prevents them from being run on a schedule.

---

9. A list of all the password reset events is displayed, as shown in Figure 9.14. Clearly, there was a rash of password changes on 2/12/2012.

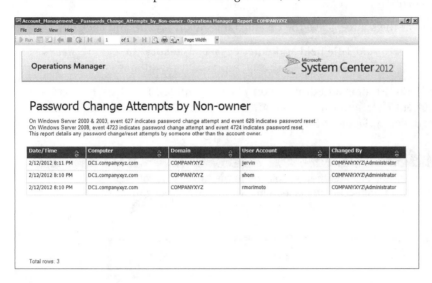

FIGURE 9.14   The Password Change Attempts by Non-Owner report.

This is a common pattern with all the ACS reports, in that they generate for the previous day by default and have to be changed.

Creating Custom ACS Reports

Although it is fine to generate reports on an ad hoc basis when requested, one of the strengths of the Operations Manager platform is to automate routine events to reduce the administrative burden. In the previous example, it would be better to schedule the Password Change Attempts by Non-Owner report to be delivered automatically on a weekly basis.

Unfortunately, the ACS reports do not facilitate this. The parameters control only allows fixed dates. When scheduling the report, the Report Parameters Section does not have any relative scheduling options.

To schedule the Password Change Attempts by Non-Owner report for delivery via email every week, a new custom report needs to be created. In Windows Server 2003, event 628 corresponds to password resets by another user. In Windows Server 2008, that event is 4724. The report needs to show these events.

The Reporting Service Report Builder 1.0 can be used to create a new ACS report. This is a very flexible report builder and ACS includes a model to facilitate creating new reports. To create a new custom report for Password Resets, complete the following steps:

1. Launch the Operations Manager 2012 console.

2. Select the Reporting workspace.

3. Click the Design a New Report link in the Actions pane.

4. Provide credentials if needed.

5. Select Audit as the source, leave the default Table report layout, and click OK.

6. Select the Click to Add Title field and enter **Password Resets in Last 2 Weeks Report**.

7. From the Fields list, drag and drop Logon Time, Computer, Target User, Target Domain, Client User, and Client Domain to the table. The report should look like the report design in Figure 9.15.

NOTE

The fields automatically align as they are placed in the table. Also, after placing the first field, subsequent fields can be placed simply by double-clicking them.

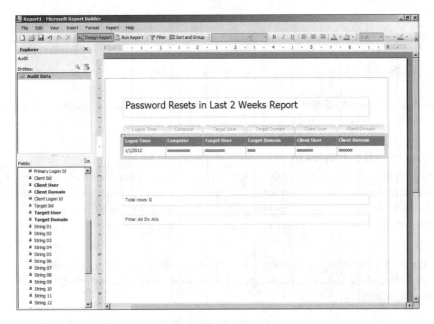

FIGURE 9.15 Custom ACS report design.

8. Click Filter on the Report menu.

9. In the Filter Data window, from the Fields list, drag and drop Event ID to the Dv Alls With box. Select event ID 628 in the drop-down menu.

10. In the Filter Data window, from the Fields list, drag and drop Event ID to the Dv Alls With box. Click the "and" option between the Event Id fields and select "or". Select event ID 4724 in the drop-down menu.

> **NOTE**
>
> If the event is not in the database, it will not be in the pull-down list of events. The event number can be typed into the field as well.

11. In the Filter Data window, from the Fields list, drag and drop Logon Time to the Dv Alls With box. Click the "equals" option, select Relative Dates, select Last (n), and select Days (including today). Enter **14** into the Days field.

12. The end result of the additions to the Filter Data window should look like Figure 9.16. Click OK when you are finished.

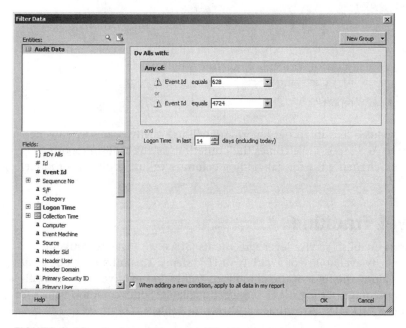

FIGURE 9.16   Custom ACS report Filter Data window.

13. Click Run Report to see what the report will look like.

14. Click File, Save to save the report to the report server. Select the Audit Reports folder.

15. Enter **Password Resets in Last 2 Weeks** for the Name and click Save.

16. Select File, Exit to exit the Report Designer.

17. In the Operations Console, select the Reporting space and then the Audit Reports folder.

18. The new report should be listed. If not, refresh the view.

19. Select the Password Resets in Last 2 Weeks report and select Open. The report should look like the built-in ACS report, as shown in Figure 9.17.

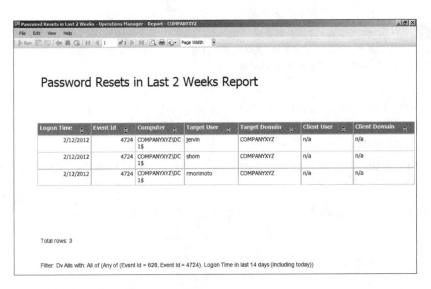

FIGURE 9.17   Custom ACS report.

The report can be scheduled like any other report and will use relative dates when generating. Creating custom ACS reports overcomes the limitations of the built-in reports, allowing relative dates, changing the format, adding columns, or just adding a corporate logo.

Service Level Tracking

Many IT organizations establish service-level agreements (SLAs) with the executives or business units that specify availability of a variety of IT systems. This might include availability measurements along the lines of the ubiquitous "nines," as in "five nines of availability." This is the percentage of time that a service is available. Some common values for this percentage and the associated downtime are shown in Table 9.1.

TABLE 9.1   The Nines and Downtime Per Year

Availability Percentage	Nines Terminology	Downtime Per Year
90%		876 hours
95%		438 hours
99%		87.6 hours
99.9%	Three nines	8.76 hours
99.99%	Four nines	52.56 minutes
99.999%	Five nines	5.256 minutes
99.9999%		31.536 seconds

Or the metric might be in terms of response time of the messaging system or of the Active Directory infrastructure. However, even with these SLAs in place, most IT organizations have no real way of measuring these SLAs in any objective fashion.

Until Operations Manager 2012, that is. OpsMgr is already gathering key availability and performance information via the management packs. Now, OpsMgr 2012 includes a feature named Service Level Tracking (SLT) that can measure availability against agreed-upon SLAs.

Service Level Objectives

Service Level Objectives (SLOs) match monitored objects with service-level goals, such as availability or performance metrics. For example, an OpsMgr administrator might want to define a Service Level Tracking for the Exchange Server 2010 Service. This is a distributed application created by the Exchange Server 2010 management pack that shows the availability of the Exchange Server 2010 messaging system as a holistic service.

In the example, the administrator configures Service Level Tracking (SLT) objectives to define the availability and performance goals for Exchange Server 2010. This includes an Availability Monitor SLO that is based on availability (99.0% uptime) and defines two Collection Rule SLOs that are based on a performance rule (Logon Latency less than 60 seconds and OWA Average Response Time less than 60 seconds). These SLOs are created in the Service Level Tracking (SLT) objectives mechanism.

To define the Exchange Server 2010 Service Level Objective, execute the following steps:

1. In the Operations Console, from the Authoring view, click Management Pack Objects and then click Service Level Tracking in the Authoring navigation tree.

2. In the Tasks pane, click Create.

3. Type a name for the service level that you are defining, which in this example is **Exchange 2010 Services SLT**. Optionally, provide a description. Click Next.

4. Under Targeted Class, click Select to specify the class for the service level, such as Distributed Application. You can search for a class by typing it into the Look For field. Select the Exchange distributed application for the service level and click OK.

5. Optionally, change the scope for the service level by targeting all objects in a class or by targeting a specific group. In most cases, the application will have a distributed application and no group targeting is needed.

6. Select the management pack where this service level will be saved. You can use an existing management pack or create a new one such as Exchange SLT MP.

NOTE

By default, Operations Manager saves the setting to the Default Management Pack. As a best practice, you should never use the Default Management Pack.

7. Click Next.

8. On the Service Level Objectives page, click Add, and then click Monitor State SLO to create a new monitor. This monitor tracks the availability of the application.

9. Type a name for the Service Level Objective. For this scenario, type **Availability**.

10. Under Monitor, choose the specific monitor that you want to use to measure the objective. For this scenario, choose Availability.

11. For the Service Level Objective goal, provide the numerical measure for your objective. For example, select 99.0 to indicate that your goal is 99.0% availability.

12. By default, only critical states impact availability. You can refine what the monitor tracks as available by selecting or clearing any of the following state criteria:

   ▶ Unplanned Maintenance

   ▶ Unmonitored

   ▶ Monitoring Unavailable

   ▶ Monitor Disabled

   ▶ Planned Maintenance

   ▶ Warning

13. Click OK.

14. On the Service Level Objectives page, click Add, and then click Collection Rule SLO to create a new collection rule. This rule tracks the performance of the application.

15. Define the performance collection rule.

16. Type a name for the Service Level Objective. For this scenario, type **Logon Latency**.

17. Specify the target class for the rule. For this scenario, select Mailbox Monitoring and click OK.

> **NOTE**
>
> This class must be contained in the distributed application, that is, the master class chosen for the Service Level Tracking object.

18. Specify the performance collection rule to use. For this scenario, choose the second option `Script performance collection: Execute: Test-MAPIConnectivity diag-nostic cmdlet. (Report Collection)`.

19. Choose one of the following aggregation methods:

   ▶ Average

   ▶ Min

   ▶ Max

In this example, the Average is chosen.

20. Define the Service Level Objective goal by choosing either Less Than or More Than and entering a value. For this scenario, choose Less Than and 120. This indicates that the performance goal is to never exceed 60 seconds. Click OK.

> **NOTE**
>
> Unfortunately, there is no easy way to tell what the units of measure are for the rule in this interface. It is important to research the rules that will be needed in advance to set the SLOs properly.

21. On the Service Level Objectives page, click Add, and then click Collection Rule SLO to create a new collection rule.

22. Type a name for the Service Level Objective. For this scenario, type `OWA Response`.

23. Specify the target class for the rule. For this scenario, select OWA.

24. Specify the performance collection rule to use. For this scenario, choose `Script performance collection: Execute: Test-OwaConnectivity (External) diagnostic cmdlet`.

25. Choose the Average aggregation method.

26. Choose Less Than and 120. This indicates that the performance goal for the average OWA response is to never exceed 60 seconds. Click OK.

27. On the Service Level Objectives page, click Next.

28. Review the summary, and click Finish.

29. When the Completion page opens, click Close.

This SLT is now available for reporting and for dashboards.

> **NOTE**
>
> If looking at daily aggregations on a recently created SLT in either a report or a Service Level Dashboard, the information is not displayed until one day after the SLT is created. The report or the dashboard gives an error indicating the information in not available. The hourly aggregation works fine.

Service Level Tracking Reports

Once Service Level Objectives are defined, Service Level Tracking reports can be generated against those SLOs. This provides a measurement of the performance of the application, service, or server against the desired goals. The results are shown starkly in red and green, indicating failure to meet objectives (red) or success in meeting the objectives (green).

To generate a Service Level Tracking report against the Exchange 2010 Service SLT defined in the previous section, complete the following steps:

1. Launch the Operations Manager console.

2. Select the Reporting space.

3. Select the Microsoft Service Level Report Library folder.

> **NOTE**
>
> Although the folder is called a "Library," there is really only one report in the folder.

4. Select the Service Level Tracking Summary Report and click Open.

5. In the From field, select Advanced.

6. Change the Offset to Minus and the number of days to 7. Click the green check mark (OK) to save the selections. The From field will show "Today -7 day(s)."

7. Change both the From and the To times to 12:00 AM.

8. In the Service Levels section, click Add.

9. Click the Search button in the Add Service Levels window.

10. Select the appropriate Service Level Objective, in this example Exchange 2010 Service SLT.

11. Click Add and then click OK to save the selection.

12. In the Additional Time Intervals section, uncheck the Report Duration. Check the Last 24 Hours, Last 7 Days, and Last 30 Days.

13. Click Run to generate the report.

14. Click the plus symbol (+) next to the name of the SLT to view the details.

The results can be seen in Figure 9.18, with each of the chosen time intervals shown in a separate column. Unfortunately, the Exchange 2010 Service is not meeting the Service Level Objectives, specifically due to the OWA response time not meeting the defined SLO of under 60 seconds. The OWA Response section has been expanded to show the Service Level Tracking for each time range. The line through the SLT bars is the 60-second service-level agreement target, which has clearly been exceeded.

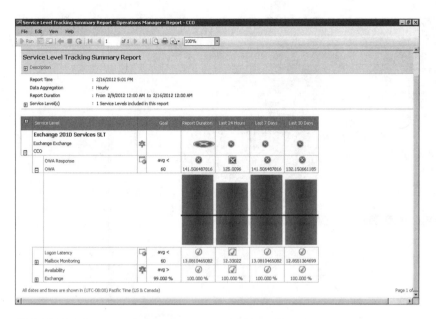

FIGURE 9.18   The Service Level Tracking Summary report.

The Service Level Tracking Summary report provides a good view of the overall performance of the Service Level Tracking object, which includes one or more Service Level Objectives. There is also a drill-down view, which shows the Service Level Objective Detail report.

After generating the Service Level Tracking report, click one of the hyperlinks for the Service Level Objectives. In this example, the failing OWA response time will be drilled into. For each of the time frames selected and the individual Service Level Objectives, there is a hyperlink that will drill into that SLO for that time period.

In the sample report generated in Figure 9.18, clicking on the Last 30 Days OWA Response hyperlink generates the SLO Detail report for the OWA Response for the Last 30 Days, as shown in Figure 9.19. The report has a cool graph for the time frame (showing that the OWA response time spikes to over 1500 on one occasion), a thermometer type indicator, and a speedometer showing where the average falls (in this case, on the 132-second mark). The graph also includes a black line that marks the SLO, which is difficult to see due to the spike.

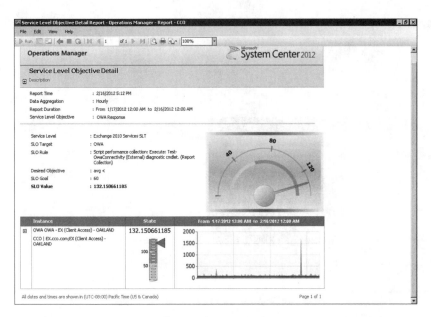

FIGURE 9.19   The Service Level Objective Detail report.

These reports can be scheduled for automatic delivery, as shown earlier in the chapter.

OpsMgr 2012 Dashboards

According to the Wikipedia entry on "Dashboard," a dashboard is an executive information system user interface that is designed to be easy to read. The benefits of dashboards
are in their visual presentation of complex performance and state information.
Dashboards were one of the most requested feature enhancements to OpsMgr 2007.
Operations Manager 2012 now includes brand-new dashboard functionality that allows
more sophisticated dashboards to be created and published in the console, Web console,
and in SharePoint 2010.

New Dashboard Functionality

The OpsMgr 2012 dashboards essentially replace the Service Level Dashboards (SLD) 2.0
Solution Accelerator, a popular SharePoint bolt-on addition to OpsMgr 2007 that used
Service Level Tracking. The new OpsMgr 2012 dashboards are much more flexible and
customizable; in addition, the new OpsMgr 2012 dashboards can be published in both
consoles and in SharePoint.

NOTE

Dashboards can be created and edited in both the full console and in the Web console. This functionality is new to the Web console, which in the past did not allow users to edit their views. Now Web console users, with the appropriate rights, can create their own custom dashboards.

The dashboard layout can be either a column or grid format, with each column or cell in a grid containing a widget. If the column format is chosen, there can be a maximum of five columns in the layout. The column format defaults to a widget in each column. However, additional cells can be added to the column format, which in effect creates a column of cells. Each cell is the same size within the column dashboard. Figure 9.20 shows an example of a SQL performance metrics three-column dashboard with six cells. In the figure, the Processor % spike has been selected and the value of that data point (62.9778% at 12:38 AM) is displayed.

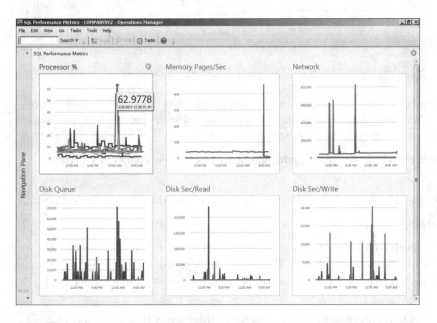

FIGURE 9.20   SQL Performance Metrics Column Dashboard.

If the grid format is chosen, then there can be between one and nine cells in the grid. The cells in the grid can be laid out in a variety of formats, depending on the number of cells chosen. Because of the layout limitations for the grid format, the number of cells in a grid dashboard are limited to 1, 2, 3, 4, 5, 6, and 9. The advantage of the grid format over the column format is that the grid format allows different sized cells within the same view. Figure 9.21 shows a three cell grid format dashboard with SQL state, alerts, and processor information.

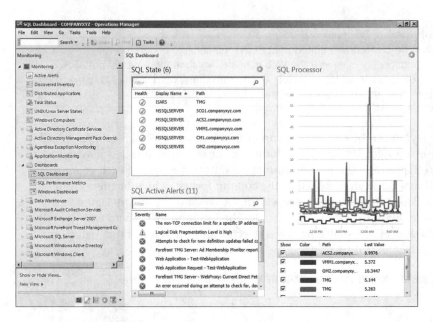

FIGURE 9.21   SQL Grid Dashboard.

Widgets specify what content to display in the cells or columns. This can be state, performance, or alert data. The data to be displayed can be scoped to include specific groups and objects. The available widgets are as follows:

▶ **Performance widget**—Displays performance graphs and gets data from the data warehouse.

▶ **Alert widget**—Displays a list of alerts and gets data from the operations database.

▶ **State widget**—Displays states and gets data from the operations database.

▶ **Objects by Performance widget**—The object by performance widget shows the top x or bottom x performance objects. This is useful for seeing just the best or worst performing objects, such as processor or memory, from a large pool of potential objects.

▶ **Instance Details widget**—The instance details widget show the details of an object. This object is static based on the widget configuration. This is useful for hard coding an object to display details for, such as the Active Directory Service or Exchange Service.

▶ **Details widget**—The details widget dynamically shows the details of any object selected in the other dashboard views. This is similar to the details windows in built-in OpsMgr views.

Different widgets can be combined in a single dashboard, though any cell in a dashboard can contain only a single widget. As can be seen from the preceding list, different widgets get their data from different OpsMgr 2012 databases.

Creating Dashboards in OpsMgr 2012

Dashboards are simple to create in OpsMgr 2012. To illustrate, suppose a database team needs a dashboard to show the status of SQL servers. To create a basic SQL dashboard, follow these steps:

1. Launch the OpsMgr 2012 console.

2. In the monitoring space, right-click on the top-level Monitoring folder and select New, Dashboard View.

3. Choose Grid Layout, and click Next.

4. Type **SQL Servers Dashboard** and click Next.

5. Choose the number of cells, in this example 3 cells.

6. Choose the second layout template, as shown in Figure 9.22, and then click Next.

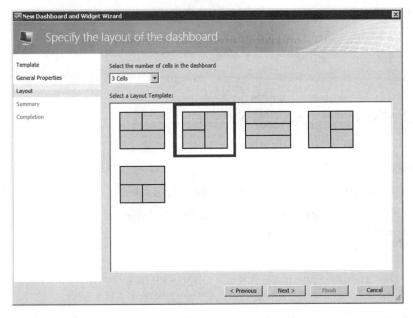

FIGURE 9.22   Dashboard layout.

7. Click Create to create the dashboard.

8. Once the dashboard is created, click Close to exit the wizard.

The dashboard has been created, but is not displaying any information as widgets have not been selected for each of the cells. To choose the widgets for each of the cells, execute the following steps.

To add a state widget to the dashboard, complete the following steps:

1. Choose the SQL Servers Dashboard that was just created. The blank dashboard will be shown, but each of the cells will contain a Click to Add Widget link.

2. In the upper-left cell, click the Click to Add Widget link.

3. Choose the State Widget template and click Next.

4. Type **SQL State** and click Next.

5. At the Specify the Scope screen, click on the Add button to select a group.

6. Choose the SQL Computers group, click Add to select, and click OK to save the selection. You can filter the list by entering text in the Filter field.

7. Click Next.

8. At the Specify the Criteria screen, leave the default to display all states and click Next.

9. At the Specify Display Preferences screen, leave the defaults and click Next.

10. Click Create to add the widget to the cell.

11. Click Close to close the wizard.

To add an alert widget to the dashboard, follow these steps:

1. In the lower-left cell, click the Click to Add Widget link.

2. Choose the Alert Widget template and click Next.

3. Type **SQL Alerts** and click Next.

4. At the Specify the Scope screen, click on the "…" button to select a group.

5. Choose the SQL Computers group and click OK to save the selection. You can filter the list by entering text in the Filter field.

6. Click Next.

7. At the Specify the Criteria screen, make sure the Display Alerts Only with the Specified Resolution States and New(0) check boxes are selected. Click Next.

8. At the Display screen, leave the default and click Next.

9. Click Create to add the widget to the cell.

10. Click Close to close the wizard.

To add a performance widget to the dashboard, follow these steps:

1. In the right cell, click the Click to Add Widget link.

2. Choose the Performance Widget template and click Next.

3. Type **SQL Processor** and click Next.

4. At the Specify the Scope and Counters screen, click on the "…" button to select a group.

5. Choose the SQL Computers group and click OK to save the selection. You can filter the list by entering text in the Filter field.

6. Click the Add button to add counters.

7. In the Object pull-down, choose Processor.

8. In the Available Items window, choose the % Processor Time counter and the _Total instance. Click the Add button to add the counter to the selected items and click OK to save the selection.

9. Click Next.

10. In the Time Range screen, leave the default 24 hours and click Next.

11. In the Specify the Chart Preferences screen, leave the defaults and click Next.

12. Click Create to add the widget to the cell.

13. Click Close to close the wizard.

The SQL Servers Dashboard now displays state, alerts, and processor performance for all SQL servers.

Viewing Dashboards

Dashboards can be viewed in the console and the Web console simply by selecting them, as with any other console view. The Dashboard views automatically refresh periodically. In both consoles, the dashboard can be customized and used in exactly the same way.

Once created, the dashboard can be customized by selecting the gear icon in the upper-right corner of the dashboard. Clicking on it shows a Configure pop-up, which can be used to modify the dashboard configuration. For example, the name of the dashboard in the grid layout can be modified. However, the number of cells or columns cannot be modified.

More usefully, each widget can be customized by selecting the gear icon in the upper-right corner of the widget cell. Clicking in the gear icon shows a more extensive menu of options, including the following:

▸ **Clear Contents**—Clears the widget from the cell, allowing the new widget to be selected and configured.

▸ **Swap with Next Widget**—Swaps the position of this widget with the next widget.

▸ **Swap with Previous Widget**—Swaps the position of this widget with the previous widget.

▸ **Configure**—Modify the configuration of the widget for all users.

▸ **Personalize**—Modify the configuration of the widget for just the current user.

6

One nice feature of the OpsMgr 2012 dashboards is the ability to organize the widget cells. Swapping widgets allows individuals to put the views within a dashboard in exactly the order they prefer.

When viewed in the full console, the states, alerts, and counters are all active objects in the dashboard. This means that objects can be manipulated and explored using the Health Explorer, views, reports, and properties. Right-clicking on an object or counter will bring up a submenu of options, depending on the object class. For example, right-clicking on the processor performance spike shown in Figure 9.23 brings up a submenu which includes Entity Properties, showing detailed properties of the object that is generating the spike. In this case, the object CM1 experienced the high processor utilization.

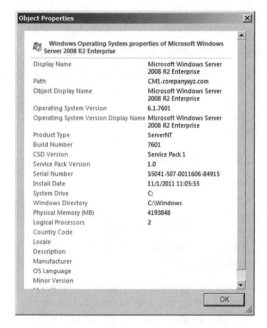

FIGURE 9.23   Dashboard object menus.

Other menu options shown when right-clicking an object in the dashboard include the following:

- Entity Properties
- Health Explorer
- Navigation Submenu
- Reports Task Submenu

The navigation submenu includes the Alert View, Diagram View, Event View, Network Vicinity Dashboard, Performance View, and State View. The Reports Task submenu includes the reports that are appropriate for that specific object selected, which can vary greatly depending on the object class.

> **NOTE**
>
> The object menus are not available in the Web console view of the dashboard.

Publishing Dashboards into SharePoint 2010

Most organizations do not want to have to train users on either the OpsMgr 2012 full console or even the Web console. However, there is a need to publish the dashboard information to a wide audience within the organization. This includes executives, directors, and managers who simply need visual access to key information technology performance metrics. Publishing dashboards in SharePoint 2010 is the answer to this need. OpsMgr 2012 includes the Operations Manager Dashboard Viewer web part to allow users to view dashboards in SharePoint 2010 sites.

Dashboards published in SharePoint are essentially read-only, with no ability to modify the dashboard configuration, link to other dashboards or reports, or run tasks. This feature serves the single-purpose function of displaying information. Although this might be considered a limitation, it is actually appropriate for the low access generally granted to dashboard users. If more elevated rights or functionality is needed, then the full console or Web console is recommended.

Preparing the SharePoint infrastructure to publish dashboards requires several steps, including deploying the web part, configuring the web part, adding web parts to SharePoint pages, and configuring shared credentials.

Deploying the Web Part

The first step in the process of publishing OpsMgr 2012 dashboards into SharePoint 2010 is to install the Operations Manager Dashboard Viewer web part.

To deploy the web part, execute the following steps on the SharePoint 2010 server:

1. Log on to the SharePoint 2010 server with SharePoint admin credentials.

2. From the OpsMgr 2012 installation media, copy the `\Setup\Amd64\SharePoint` folder to a local directory on the SharePoint 2010 server. For this example, the local directory will be `c:\OpsMgr2012\SharePoint\`.

3. Launch the SharePoint 2010 Management Shell.

4. Change the directory to the OpsMgr 2012 SharePoint folder, in this example `c:\OpsMgr2012\SharePoint\`.

5. Run the PowerShell command script `.\install-OperationsManager-DashboardViewer.ps1`.

6. Enter the name of the OpsMgr 2012 SharePoint folder, in this example `c:\OpsMgr2012\SharePoint\`, and press Enter.

7. To install on all sites, press Enter.

8. The installation script will install the Operations Manager Dashboard Viewer web part and enable it for all existing SharePoint sites.

NOTE

This procedure will need to be repeated if future sites are installed on the SharePoint server.

Now that the web part is installed, it needs to be configured to connect to the OpsMgr 2012 Web console to be able to access dashboards.

Configuring the Web Part to Connect to the Web Console

The web part needs to be configured to connect to the Web console. Fortunately, there is a PowerShell script to do this. To configure the web part to connect to the Web console, follow these steps:

1. Log on to the SharePoint 2010 server with SharePoint admin credentials.

2. Launch the SharePoint 2010 Management Shell.

3. Change directory to the OpsMgr 2012 SharePoint folder, in this example `c:\OpsMgr2012\SharePoint\`.

4. Run the PowerShell command script `.\ add-OperationsManager-WebConsole-Environment.ps1 –title <Dashboard Title> –webconsoleUnc <path to Web Console web.config>`. For this example, the command would be: `.\ add-OperationsManager-WebConsole-Environment.ps1 -title "CCO Dashboard" -webconsoleUnc "\\opsmgr\d$\Program Files\System Center Operations Manager 2012\WebConsole\WebHost"`.

5. The script runs and pulls configuration information from the `web.config` file to properly configure the web part.

The server-level configuration is now complete. The web part is installed and configured, ready for use in a SharePoint page.

Adding a Web Part to a SharePoint Page

To display an OpsMgr 2012 dashboard in a SharePoint 2010 page, the web part needs to be added to the page and configured for the proper dashboard.

To add the web part to a SharePoint page, execute the following steps:

1. Launch Internet Explorer and connect to a SharePoint site.

2. Create a new page by clicking on Site Actions and then New Page.

3. Give the page and name, for this example **SQL Servers Dashboard** and click Create.

4. Add the OpsMgr 2012 dashboard web part by clicking on Insert, Web Part, Microsoft System Center, Operations Manager Dashboard Viewer, and then click Add. The web part will be inserted at the top of the page, as shown in Figure 9.24.

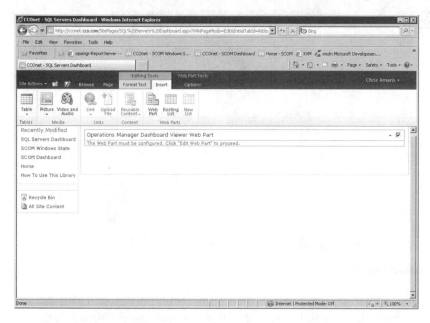

FIGURE 9.24   Adding a dashboard web part to a page.

Now that the dashboard has been added to the SharePoint page, it needs to be configured to show the proper dashboard. In this case, it will show the SQL Servers Dashboard.

To configure the dashboard web part, do the following:

1. Launch the OpsMgr 2012 Web console in Internet Explorer.

2. Navigate to the appropriate dashboard for the web part, in this case the SQL Servers Dashboard.

3. Once the dashboard is displayed, copy the URL from the address bar in Internet Explorer. It should look something like the following:
   http://opsmgr/OperationsManager/#/dashboard(type=Microsoft.SystemCenter.OperationsManager.DefaultUser!UIGenerated_454e2063fad9432ca027155b05a91076_SQLServersDashboard.

4. Back on the SharePoint page, select the Operations Manager Dashboard Viewer web part.

5. In the right corner of the web part, open the pull-down and select Edit Web Part (as shown in Figure 9.25).

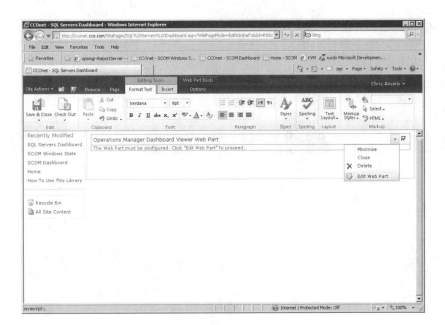

FIGURE 9.25   Editing the web part.

6. In the Operations Manager Web Console Environments pull-down, select the environment previously configured. In the case of this example, the environment that was configured was the "CCO Dashboard" environment.

7. In the Dashboard Link field, paste the SQL Servers Dashboard URL copied from the Web console.

8. Click the OK button to save the edits.

The SharePoint web page now shows the OpsMgr 2012 dashboard, as shown in Figure 9.26.

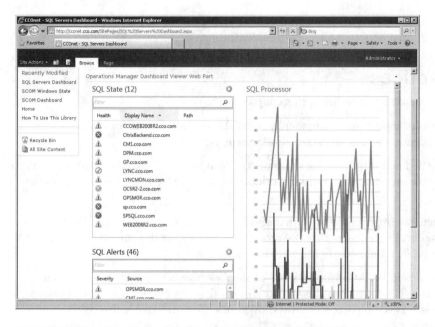

FIGURE 9.26   SharePoint web page with OpsMgr 2012 dashboard.

In exploring the web part, certain features are preserved from the console view of the SharePoint and some are not. The order of the cells in the dashboard can be rearranged using the swap widget function, available by selecting the gear icon in the upper-right corner of the cell. In the chart, selecting a point on the graph shows the value of the data point as well as highlights the target in the legend of the graph. However, there is no right-click functionality in the dashboard, such as Health Explorer or views.

When crafting dashboards for publishing SharePoint 2010, it is critical to carefully think out the information that users of the dashboards will need as they will be unable to do much customization themselves.

Summary

The information collected by Operations Manager 2012 is extensive and can best be displayed using scheduled reports and dashboards. This allows the information to get to the targeted end users automatically, in the case of scheduled reports, and ensures that the summarized data is presented to them and that the users don't have to take action to see the information on a normal basis.

OpsMgr 2012 dashboards provide exciting new functionality for delivering visual information to a wider range of users than previously possible. The ability to show the same view across the full console, Web console, and SharePoint websites allows for coherent view of the same information across all users.

9

These features make Operations Manager 2012 the best platform for capturing and presenting operational data in a business-friendly format.

Best Practices

The following are best practices from this chapter:

- ▶ Use scheduled reports to automatically distribute operational reports to administrators, application owners, managers, and executives.

- ▶ Use the scheduled Windows file share distribution to post reports to directories that link to web pages. Use the Overwrite option to have the web pages update automatically.

- ▶ Always generate reports in the format and time period ad hoc first, and then schedule the report. This ensures that the reports are targeted at the correct objects, return the appropriate data, and are formatted as expected.

- ▶ Locate objects in the Monitoring space of the Operations Console, and then select the reports to generate from there. This ensures that the correct objects and reports are matched, as the reports will only show in the user interface if they work with those objects.

- ▶ Use SQL Server Reporting Services to produce custom ACS reports using OpsMgr's Reporting feature.

- ▶ Duplicate the existing ACS reports with custom reports to be able to schedule the reports with relative dates.

- ▶ Schedule the OpsMgr Maintenance reports for weekly delivery to easily monitor the health and performance of Operations Manager.

- ▶ Leverage the reporting database to store and report on data over a long period.

- ▶ When tuning, use the Most Common Alerts report to see which alerts are the most valuable targets for tuning.

- ▶ Use dashboards instead of the Operations Console or Web console as a way of presenting Operations Manager data to a wider audience without impacting the performance of the alerting.

CHAPTER 10

Data Protection Manager 2012 Design, Planning, Implementation, and Administration

IN THIS CHAPTER

▶ What Is System Center Data Protection Manager?

▶ Data Protection Manager Background

▶ Data Protection Manager Prerequisites

▶ Planning a Data Protection Manager Deployment

▶ Deploying Data Protection Manager

▶ Completing Required Configuration Tasks

▶ Creating Protection Groups

▶ Administrating Data Protection Manager

▶ Best Practices

When we think about the many different applications used in enterprises, backup systems are probably the most important. Being both loved and hated, backup systems are a definitive requirement for any adequate data protection scheme. Once deployed correctly, they typically sit in the background backing up data, which can then be easily retrieved if some future calamity causes the real data to be lost. However, if they are not deployed correctly and some type of backup failure occurs, the ramifications associated with this failure can be huge. After all, data is a very important asset to any organization, and the assumption that a backup exists if needed leads organizations to heavily depend on their backup system in a catastrophe. Although the physical aspects of IT infrastructure can be easily replaced, data can be either irreplaceable or very hard to reproduce, so having a backup system that works is a key factor in a well-managed IT environment.

Sadly, despite being a very important part of disaster recovery, many backup systems are often ill-planned or not deployed at all due to the amount of effort (both human and infrastructure) that is required to maintain them. To try and negate or meet some of these challenges, Microsoft developed System Center Data Protection Manager (DPM) to manage disk-based and tape-based data protection and recovery for machines across an entire organization.

What Is System Center Data Protection Manager?

Microsoft's System Center DPM is part of the System Center line of products that is designed to help organizations manage their IT infrastructure. DPM itself is a hybrid data replication and archival solution that utilizes features commonly found in everyday backup solutions to provide centralized data protection management for a variety of Microsoft-based application servers, file servers, and end-user workstations, including, but not limited to, the following:

▶ Exchange Server 2003 SP2, Exchange Server 2007, and Exchange Server 2010

▶ SQL Server 2000 SP4, SQL Server 2005 SP1 or later, SQL Server 2008, and SQL Server 2008 R2

▶ SharePoint Portal Server 2003, SharePoint Server 2007, Windows SharePoint Services, SharePoint Server 2010, and SharePoint Foundation Services

▶ Windows-based PCs (from Windows XP to Windows 7 versions)

▶ Files and application data on regular or clustered servers

▶ System State for protected file and application servers

▶ Hyper-V (including support for both guest-based and host-based protection)

DPM is different from most backup solutions in use today, which tend to only provide a purely tape-based protection scheme. DPM provides a disk-to-disk, disk-to-tape, and disk-to-disk-to-cloud data backup and recovery solution. Additionally, these processes are coupled with the concept of Continuous Data Protection (CDP), which automatically and constantly saves a copy of every change made to a protected data set. To better understand the advantages associated with using DPM, the following sections outline common data recovery needs and how DPM can be used to address those needs.

Understanding Modern Data Recovery Needs

Businesses today operate in an environment that is drastically different from even just 10 years ago. Information systems and the data managed by the systems are important to business operations. However, in the past, the *how* and *when* that information had to be available tended to not be as critical to the overall productivity of an organization as it is today. Most organizations now operate under the *now* pretense in which information must be readily accessible at all times regardless of the time of day. Combined with the fact that businesses are under constant pressure to lower costs, improve efficiency, and do more with less, this has introduced a number of new data recovery needs that IT professionals must contend with. Consider the following:

▶ **Quick recovery from system outages**—In today's 24/7 business environment, any decrease in productivity equates to direct financial lost. Coupled with the fact that many organizations now heavily depend on their information systems for operations, IT professionals must increasingly ensure that the recovery time from system outages is as short as possible.

▶ **Shrinking backup and restore windows**—Like with system outages, the time windows for backup and restore operations are also shrinking, meaning that data protection activities might not have the luxury of executing within a defined window of time. Instead, IT professionals must employ a solution that can quickly complete backups or on-demand restores.

▶ **Data protection in branch and remote offices**—Data in an organization is not always centralized, as in the case where each branch office might have its own unique data repository that needs to be protected but tend to lack the needed IT infrastructure and personnel resources needed to host and manage a traditional dedicated tape-based backup solution. Any data protection solution that is employed must be able to handle remote locations by either working "over the wire" or requiring as few dedicated resources as possible.

▶ **Tape-based reliability and resource requirements**—Tape-based backup options are not always reliable. Common perception is that there is a direct correlation to the reliability of a tape-based solution and the resources needed to manage that solution. In particular, dedicated resources are often needed for storing and recovering tapes, ensuring software backup catalogs are not corrupt, and routinely testing backup devices to confirm media is readable. Given that most organizations tend to be very resource-constrained, their backup and recovery solutions should minimize the amount of resources required to be dedicated to their operation and support.

▶ **Cost reduction**—Controlling costs is always a primary requirement for the deployment of any IT solution. When this is combined with today's economic challenges, the need to do more with less is even more paramount. Any data protection solution that is deployed should remove complexity from the environment, be simple to manage, and be affordable to use.

How Data Protection Manager Meets Today's Data Recovery Needs

Most organizations use magnetic tape for backup of systems and data because tape-based data protection solutions offer two distinct advantages. First, the combination of media and long-term storage cost tends to be comparatively low. Second, tape-based technologies are very mature and a large number of different tape-based data protection solutions and many IT professionals who understand those solutions are readily available.

Although tape-based solutions have proven to be an effective means to protect data for well over 50 years, the underlying technology associated with magnetic tape recording solutions has not drastically changed since it was first developed. Therefore, tape as a near-term backup and recovery medium suffers from a number of different constraints:

▶ **Tape-based solutions tend to be slow**—When compared with the speed and I/O bandwidth of disk-based data protection solutions, tape-based solutions have a huge speed disadvantage. This speed weakness is only further exacerbated by the need to locate and mount tapes and build indexes when performing restores.

10

▶ **Tape-based solutions tend to be complex**—More moving parts, such as robotic tape changers, are needed to move a tape than a disk-based storage solution. Coupled with the fact that the usability of tapes is subject to physical wear and damage due to environmental storage conditions, the chances that some aspects of a tape-based data protection solution will experience failure are far greater than that of a disk-based solution.

▶ **Tape-based solutions tend to lack effective centralization**—Tape-based data protection solutions tend to lack any type of effective means for the centralization of backup and restore processes. Additionally, when the centralization deficit is addressed, the tape-based solution either requires a large amount of bandwidth between a remote site and the central backup site, or a local tape drive must be deployed into the remote site, which introduces its own set of management challenges.

▶ **Tape-based solutions tend to lack disk-based backup integration**—In the past, tape-based data protection solutions tended to lack any type of integration with disk-based solutions. Therefore, IT organizations had to manage several different vendors if they wanted a complete data protection solution that combined the benefits of a disk-based solution with that of a tape-based solution.

To address the issues found with tape-based data protection solutions, DPM employs a combination of disk-based, tape-based, and cloud-based storage processes, interlaced with the concept of CDP for Microsoft-based application and file servers. The following subsections explain how these various components of the DPM architecture are used to protect data.

Disk-Based Storage

Also called *disk-to-disk*, or D2D for short, disk-based storage is a backup where data from one computer is duplicated and stored on the hard disk of another computer. The primary advantage of using this type of backup is the potential time savings associated with backing up and restoring data. Instead of having to locate a specific tape, loading the tape, and positioning the tape to the correct starting point, with a D2D recovery job, you just need to identify the data, and DPM locates the data and retrieves it. Other benefits of using D2D include the lower failure rate of disk drives when compared with tapes. Additionally, using a D2D protection strategy allows for incremental data replication versus all-at-once backups/restores, which reduces the impact of network-based backup and restore operations.

Tape-Based Backup and Archive

Also called *disk-to-tape*, or D2T for short, tape-based backup and archive is the traditional method of backing up data from one computer to storage media such as tape. As before, the usage of magnetic tape still provides the same inexpensive and portable form of data protection, which is very convenient for long-term storage. However, the real benefit of D2T support in DPM becomes evident when it is combined with D2D. In this configuration, called disk-to-disk-to-tape (D2D2T), you have the rapid recovery and replication benefits of disk-based storage in addition to the long-term ability to archive data using a medium that can be kept offsite.

Cloud-Based Storage

Also called *disk-to-disk-to-cloud*, or D2D2C for short, cloud-based storage is a new storage feature that was first introduced in DPM 2007 SP1. When using D2D2C, you still protect data using D2D, but you can then also store that data in the cloud for longer-term protection using either Microsoft's Azure or third-party cloud services that support this DPM feature.

Continuous Data Protection

CDP is a continuous backup or real-time backup in which every change that is made to a data set is replicated to a separate storage location, typically over the network. This differs from a traditional backup scheme in that the copies of data are not based on a *single point in time* when a backup was taken; instead, logical objects, such as files, mailboxes, messages, database files, logs, and so on, can be recovered from *any point in time* based on the replicated data.

Because it is based on the CDP concept, DPM protects Windows application and file servers by continuously capturing data changes with application-aware, byte-level agents installed on protected servers. When data is modified on a data source, the agent creates a replica, or copy, of the data. These data replicas are then stored in the storage pool (a set of disks) or custom volumes on the DPM server. As further changes are made to the data source, the agent tracks the changes and then updates the replica by synchronizing the changes to the DPM server at regular defined intervals, which can be used to create a recovery point.

In DPM, replicas of data are divided into protection groups. A protection group is a collection of data sources that share the same protection configuration, such as the following:

▶ A volume, share, or folder on a desktop computer, file server, or server cluster

▶ Exchange databases on an Exchange server or server cluster

▶ A database of an instance of SQL Server or server cluster

▶ A SharePoint farm

▶ A group of workstations

A separate replica is kept for each member of a protection group. Because members have the same protection configuration, they also share the same settings that are common to a protection group (protection policy, disk allocations, replica creation method, and so on).

To track changes on a data source, a DPM protection agent continuously watches for block-level changes using the volume filter. This filter is just a bitmap that lives in paged pool memory and includes one bit for every block on the protected volume. As blocks are modified in the volume, a bit is flipped in the bitmap. If the data source is file data, the protection agent uses the volume filter in conjunction with the operating system change journal to track which files have changed (modifications, creations, and deletions) since the last synchronization job (by default, every 15 minutes). If a file has changed, the agent transfers only the changed blocks of data to the DPM server, which are then synchronized with the replica.

If the data source is considered application data (Exchange, SQL Server, SharePoint, and so forth), the protection agent either performs an express full backup or an incremental synchronization (if the application supports it). When the protection agent performs an express full backup (typically once a day), the following process is followed:

1. The volume filter is used to generate a bitmap related to the application data files.

2. Next, the VSS writer is instructed to create a VSS snapshot of what is basically a frozen set of blocks.

3. Then, the resulting VSS snapshot is compared with the last volume filter bitmap since the initial replica creation or the last express full backup to identify the data that has been modified.

4. The protection agent then synchronizes all of the changed blocks to the DPM server, the VSS snapshot is released, and a recovery point is created on the DPM server.

For transactional-based applications (like SQL Server, Exchange, and SharePoint), the protection agent also does an incremental synchronization every 15 minutes by default. The method by which an incremental synchronization is performed depends on the application that is being protected because the protection agent is application aware. For example:

▶ For Exchange, an incremental VSS snapshot is created using the Exchange VSS writer. The protection agent then uses the incremental snapshot to copy committed, sequential transaction logs to the DPM server.

▶ For SQL Server and effectively SharePoint because it stores data in SQL Server, the protection agent just copies closed transaction logs to the DPM server.

Data Protection Manager Background

Data Protection Manager is in its fourth major edition with the 2012 release of the product. Additionally, service packs in earlier editions have introduced new functionality in minor editions of DPM. Details about each major release and the intermediate service pack releases are as follows.

Data Protection Manager 2006

Data Protection Manager was released September 27, 2005. This first version introduced the world to Microsoft's vision of Continuous Data Protection for application and file servers using seamlessly integrated disk and tape media; however, this version was limited to protecting file servers residing in the same Active Directory domain. Although it was a starting point, DPM's initial release had very little market traction because of its limited scope.

Data Protection Manager 2006 SP1

In October 2006, Microsoft released SP1 for Data Protection Manager 2006, which included the following:

- ▶ Support for 64-bit protection
- ▶ Support for Windows Server 2003 R2
- ▶ Support for clustered servers
- ▶ Protection for SIS-enabled servers
- ▶ Microsoft Update opt-in support
- ▶ Changes to the disk allocation formula

DPM 2006 SP1's support for backing up the ever-growing 64-bit server market and clustered servers that was the mainstay of enterprise data server environments headed the product in the right direction. However, still with a lack of support to back up more than just file systems, even Service Pack 1 of DPM 2006 made very little dent in the needs and demands of enterprises.

Data Protection Manager 2007

Released in October 2007, Data Protection Manager 2007 drastically improved the capabilities of the DPM product line, adding support for Exchange Server, SQL Server, and SharePoint. In addition, DPM 2007 also introduced native support for tape backups and the concept of zero data loss application recovery. Some of the new features or changes included in this release are as follows:

- ▶ Built-in support for tape-based backup and archive
- ▶ Protection of:
    - ▶ Exchange Server 2003 SP2 and Exchange Server 2007, including Cluster Continuous Replication (CCR) and Local Continuous Replication (LCR) clusters
    - ▶ SQL Server 2000 SP4 and SQL Server 2005 SP1 or greater, including 2005-based mirrored clusters
    - ▶ Office SharePoint Server 2007 and WSS 3.0
    - ▶ Virtual Server 2005 R2 SP1 and its virtual machines
    - ▶ Windows Server 2008
    - ▶ Files on Windows-based PCs, including Windows XP Professional SP2 and all Windows Vista Editions except the Home Edition

10

> ▶ Files and application data on clustered servers

> ▶ System State for protected file and application servers

▶ Introduction of zero data loss restoration for application data

▶ Support for protection across domains

▶ Disaster recovery support (DPM protecting a DPM server)

▶ Introduction of the PowerShell-based DPM Management Shell

▶ Support for end-user-based recoveries

▶ Support for bare-metal recoveries

▶ Functional changes from DPM 2006, including:

> ▶ Increased synchronization frequency from hourly to every 15 minutes

> ▶ Administrators group membership required to access the DPM Administrator Console

> ▶ Dropping of support for Windows 2000-based file servers

> ▶ Support for RAID using the new custom volumes feature

NOTE

Workstations and laptops protected using DPM 2007 not only had to be domain members, but they also had to be consistently connected to the corporate network at all times through a reliable network connection. For the workloads of Exchange, SQL, and SharePoint that are domain-based applications and are always connected to the network, this requirement was not a deterrent for organizations looking to choose DPM as their backup solution.

DPM 2007's support for business-critical applications was the first step that helped organizations decide to adopt DPM as their backup solutions. DPM 2007 now supported the backup of domain controllers, file servers, Exchange, SharePoint, and SQL, which for the most part addressed the backup needs of an entire enterprise. Many organizations that experienced failed tape backups and/or data loss, or wanted a digital backup system instead of a tape backup system, began deploying DPM 2007 as their backup system.

Data Protection Manager 2007 SP1

In January 2009, Microsoft released SP1 for Data Protection Manager 2007, which includes the following:

▶ Support for SharePoint Server 2003 and WSS 2.0

▶ Enhancements to how Office SharePoint Server and WSS are protected, including index protection, significant catalog optimization, and support for mirrored content databases

- ▶ Support for both Hyper-V guest-based and host-based protection

- ▶ Support for Exchange Server Standby Continuous Replication

- ▶ Support for SQL Server 2008, including support for parallel backups of databases within a single instance and the ability to move data from SQL Server 2005 to SQL Server 2008 for migration scenarios

- ▶ Introduction of local data source protection where DPM can now protect its own file services and virtualization hosting

- ▶ Support for cross-forest data protection

- ▶ Support for cloud-based third-party vaulting partners

NOTE

In addition to the server pack, Microsoft also released a DPM management pack, which allowed System Center Operations Manager 2007 to monitor and manage DPM deployments.

The release of the service pack for DPM 2007 was a pleasant addition to organizations that had selected to use DPM 2007 as their backup product. Although the service pack in itself did not include any additional major enhancement to bring over organizations still set on their "old way" of backing up by tape, the feature set in DPM 2007 SP1 began to provide functions critical to enterprise backup needs.

Data Protection Manager 2010 and DPM 2010 Service Pack 1

The next major version, Data Protection Manager 2010, released during the first half of 2010, contained a number of improvements over the 2007 SP1 release of DPM, including improved client protection, which can take place while the machines are online or offline. In addition, this version can protect virtual machines that are moved across Cluster Shared Volumes on Windows Server 2008 R2 Hyper-V using the Live Migration feature. Other new features or changes included in this release include the following:

Continuous Data Protection of Windows application and file servers:

- ▶ Windows Server from 2003 through 2008 R2

- ▶ SQL Server 2000 through 2008

- ▶ Exchange Server 2003 through 2010

- ▶ SharePoint Server 2003 through 2010

- ▶ Dynamics AX 2009

- ▶ Essential Business Server 2008 and Small Business Server 2008

- ▶ SAP running on SQL Server

New protection and recovery capabilities:

▶ For SQL Server, a single DPM server can protect up to 2,000 databases. Authorized DBAs can restore data themselves using the new self-service restore capability. Also, entire instances of SQL Server can be protected where all new databases are automatically protected.

▶ For SharePoint, all new content databases are automatically protected. Additionally, for SharePoint 2010 servers, a recovery farm is no longer needed to do individual item recovery.

▶ The ability to protect machines that are in a workgroup or in an untrusted domain.

Protection and recovery support for the following Microsoft virtualization environments:

▶ Microsoft Virtual Server 2005 R2

▶ Windows Server 2008 through R2 with Hyper-V

▶ Protection of Live Migration–enabled servers running on CSV in Hyper-V R2

▶ Protection of virtual machines from Windows guests or from the hypervisor host

▶ Ability to restore virtual machines to an alternate host

▶ Support for single-item restores from host-based backups

Windows client protection:

▶ Protection of Windows XP through Windows 7

▶ Centralized policy management from DPM 2012, supporting backups while laptops are online or offline

▶ Ability to perform restores while online or offline

▶ Improved intelligent and customizable filtering to ensure relevant data is protected

Scalability, reliability, and manageability:

▶ Capacity for a single DPM server to protect up to 100 servers, 1,000 laptops, or 2,000 databases

▶ Improved autoprotection, autohealing, and reduced alerting for a more "fire-and-forget" experience

▶ Enhanced disaster recovery options

DPM 2010 and the release of Service Pack 1 for DPM 2010 has truly made DPM an enterprise-ready backup solution, finally providing function in DPM that is not available in other backup solutions. Some of the key technologies include the ability for an organization to back up SharePoint 2010 in the middle of the day, and restore a SharePoint library, table, or single file to the running SharePoint 2010 environment in the middle of the day, a very important feature for organizations needing to be able to recover accidentally deleted or corrupted content in SharePoint. Additionally, DPM 2010 SP1 is smart enough to know that when an organization backed up an Exchange 2010 Database Availability Group (DAG) replica, that DPM would properly flush the logs on the primary copy of the mail, something that took other vendors upwards of over a year to achieve.

DPM 2010 clearly showed that Microsoft's knowledge of Microsoft applications SharePoint, Exchange, and SQL Server made it more apt, aware, and capable of supporting their backup and recovery requirements. With DPM 2010, organizations now had a compelling reason to select DPM as the organization's primary backup solution because it was better than other alternatives available in the marketplace.

Data Protection Manager 2012

Data Protection Manager 2012, the topic of this and the next chapter, expands on the core functionality built over the previous generations of the product, further enhancing administration and backup support. Specifically, the following features are new to DPM 2012:

- ▶ **Centralized management**—New to DPM 2012 is its ability to centrally monitor and provide remote administration and recovery capabilities for administrators. With earlier releases of DPM, each DPM server had its own console for administration of servers backed up by the specific DPM system. With DPM 2012, an administrator can install the Central Console on a system and monitor multiple DPM 2012 and DPM 2010 servers, conduct remote administration of the local and remote DPM servers, and initiate the recovery of guest sessions and data from the Central Console.

- ▶ **Role-based access**—DPM 2012 also provides the ability to designate and delegate administration tasks to other individuals, including the ability to have other administrators, such as an Exchange or SharePoint administrator, receive alerts and notifications from System Center Operations Manager or other monitoring systems concerning the status of DPM backups and restores, and the ability to distribute administrator tasks to other individuals.

- ▶ **Restoral of item-level content of SharePoint 2010 data**—Although DPM 2010 SP1 provided the ability for an administrator to back up SharePoint data and recover it directly to an existing SharePoint 2010 server, eliminating the need to set up a separate recovery lab server to perform the restore, the restoration process was a full content database recovery. With DPM 2012, content can now be restored at the item level, such as a document library, list, or a specific file, directly to an operational SharePoint 2010 server.

- ▶ **SQL Filestream support**—DPM 2012 provides SQL Filestream support, a data storage mechanism included in SQL 2008 that provides the ability to store data files, such as documents, images, and audio/video content, to a file server, yet have SQL manage the content. SharePoint 2010 takes advantage of SQL Filestream in its implementation of SharePoint Remote Blog Storage (RBS), where SharePoint data is

10

stored outside of the SQL database. SharePoint RBS solved a long-standing problem in SharePoint where organizations storing massive amounts of image files, large computer-aided design (CAD) files, video files, or the like caused the SharePoint SQL servers to be unmanageably large. But with SharePoint RBS, the data can be redirected to write directly to a server or SAN's file storage system. DPM 2012 now has the ability to back up and recover this SQL Filestream data in a managed and organized manner that maintains the integrity of the stored information.

▶ **Certificate-based protection of non–Active Directory machines**—Early releases of DPM required that the target system be a domain-joined system, preventing organizations from being able to back up kiosks, DMZ-based servers, standalone Hyper-V hosts, and the like. DPM 2010 SP1 added the ability to back up Windows workgroup members by preinstalling an agent on the remote system and targeting it for backup. DPM 2012 can now back up a non-domain-joined system based on a Secure Sockets Layer (SSL) certificate issued to the system to support authentication.

▶ **Support for multiple DPM servers to share a single SQL instance**—Previous versions of DPM supported only a single DPM server per SQL instance. DPM 2012 now provides the ability to allow multiple DPM servers to share a single SQL instance for DPM management, allowing organizations to better leverage their SQL Server environments.

Data Protection Manager Prerequisites

This section describes the hardware, operating system, and software requirements that must be met before installing and using System Center 2012 Data Protection Manager.

Hardware Requirements

Table 10.1 shows the minimum and recommended hardware requirements for Data Protection Manager 2012.

TABLE 10.1   DPM 2012 Hardware Requirements

Component	Requirement
Processor speed	Minimum: 1GHz
	Recommended: 2.33GHz quad-core or faster
Memory	Minimum: 512MB
	Recommended: 4GB
	DPM with SQL installed: 4GB + 2.5GB per SQL instance running on the server
Disk space	System volume: 1GB
	DPM installation: 1.2GB
	Database files drive: 900MB

Supported Operating Systems

The following operating systems are supported as the base operating systems that Data Protection Manager 2012 runs on the following:

- Windows Server 2008, Standard and Enterprise Editions
- Windows Server 2008 SP2, Standard and Enterprise Editions
- Windows Server 2008 R2, Standard and Enterprise Editions
- Windows Server 2008 R2 SP1, Standard and Enterprise Editions

Remote SQL Instance Requirements

Data Protection Manager 2012 supports the following versions of SQL Server where DPM writes configuration information and utilizes it to report of the status of DPM jobs:

- SQL Server 2008, Standard or Enterprise Editions
- SQL Server 2008 R2, Standard or Enterprise Editions

NOTE

Clustered installations of SQL Server are not supported.

Software Requirements

The following software requirements must be met before installing Data Protection Manager 2012 on a Windows server:

- Microsoft PowerShell 2.0
- Microsoft .NET Framework 3.5 Service Pack 1
- Windows Installer (MSI) 4.5
- Windows Single Instance Store (SIS)
- Virtual C++ 2008 Redistributable

NOTE

To install Data Protection Manager, the computer must be a member of a domain, it cannot be a Microsoft System Center Operations Manager management server or an Active Directory domain controller, and cluster services must not be enabled. Additionally, you must have administrative privileges to the server.

10

Planning a Data Protection Manager Deployment

Deploying any information system can be a very challenging task and DPM is no exception. Many different factors, both business and technical related, need to be considered when planning a DPM deployment, and any DPM deployment plan needs to be well thought out to be successful. Although Microsoft has attempted to make DPM as easy as possible to deploy and use, this also happens to be its Achilles' heel. It is very easy for an IT professional to get DPM up and working very quickly, and get to a point where the storage sizing, DPM server performance, protection groups, and so on are all afterthoughts, thus causing administration issues or, worse, resulting in data loss.

This section describes the steps that should be taken to plan a Data Protection Manager deployment. The steps that are provided include step-by-step instructions and best-practice design advice with the goal of helping IT professionals avoid planning mistakes that can prove to be costly and difficult to correct.

Step One: Understand the Environment

The first step of the DPM planning process is to understand the environment into which the product is being deployed. To complete this step, you should review the architecture for information systems in your organization by reviewing their relevant design documents, performing discovery sessions with the owners of systems, and reviewing the status of the systems in real time. Items that you should pay particular attention to during this phase of the design include the following:

- The current Active Directory forest design

- The current network topology and available bandwidth

- A thorough understanding of any existing data protection solutions

- A thorough understanding of any planned/pending organizational changes such as business acquisitions or diversifications

- Awareness of applications that will be retired, replaced, or upgraded

- Awareness of any new applications that will be introduced into the environment

The key to having this understanding of the state of the environment is that far too many times backup administrators jump right into setting up the backup solution and start backing up a key one or two applications, later to realize that the backup of key systems were not being performed because of a lack of awareness that the other systems even existed in the enterprise. Everyone assumes that if they build a system, "someone" will be backing it up. And although that might have been the case with an old tape backup system years ago, when the tape backup system died and the new DPM server was implemented, that system was no longer being backed up.

With the proliferation of virtual guest sessions and "server sprawl" in the enterprise, new servers pop up every month (or every week), and unless someone is specifically told to back up the system, the system is left unmanaged. Additionally, it is common for an organization to buy enough backup space for the one or two applications that the organization starts to back up with DPM, but as new applications are identified, the organization quickly runs out of backup space to back up all of the target applications in the environment.

Having a holistic view of the enterprise and its applications, and truly understanding what each server and virtual guest session is, what it's running, and who the application owner is, helps the organization ensure it has a true handle on successfully backing up all business-critical applications.

> **NOTE**
>
> When asked how to find out who owns an application running on some physical or virtual server, or to know whether anyone is using the server, the simple answer is to just unplug the server from the network or pause the virtual guest session. If someone is using the application, you will hear from that person pretty quickly. There are obviously more elegant ways to identify application ownership and usage monitoring access to the system, even by sending a message out to query the organization if anyone knows who is administering, managing, or using an application. However, there comes a point where the disconnect/pause message returns a much faster approach.

Step Two: Define the Project Scope

The next step of the DPM-planning process is to define the scope of the DPM deployment project. While completing this task, it is important to ensure that the goals of the project are aligned to the business requirements for data protection, business continuity, and disaster recovery. To begin this process, use the information gathered from the first step of the planning process to identify the information systems that should be protected using DPM. Once you have completed that task, you should then meet with the owners of those systems and determine the business requirements for protecting data. At this stage of the planning process, the requirements that you should be gathering for each system include the following:

▶ **Data loss tolerance**—What is the acceptable amount of data loss that can be tolerated by the information system? The value for this parameter should be specified in a unit of time (minutes, hours, or days).

▶ **Retention range**—How long should the protected data be stored? The value for this parameter should be specified in a unit of time and based on what the recovery requirements are for the data that is being protected. For example, in some cases, regulatory and compliance requirements might require the data to be retained for years.

▶ **Data recovery speed**—What is the acceptable data recovery speed? Again, the value for this parameter should be specified in a unit of time. However, to accurately represent this parameter, you need to take into consideration the difference between a system being restored to a serviceable level and the recovery of that system's data. In some cases, these might be two different recovery objectives.

10

▶ **End-user recovery**—Is there a requirement to allow end users to recover their data?

▶ **Disaster recovery**—Is DPM being deployed as part of a business continuity plan (BCP) or disaster recovery plan (DRP)? This is very important to understand because the information contained in a BCP or DRP will help determine when a system needs to be operational again, where recovery data should be stored, and if DPM itself will need to be protected.

▶ **Protected data**—Last, but not least, work with the system owners to develop a very clear understanding for the data that must be protected and its location. After all, DPM is not a general-purpose backup tool. As such, you need to be able to map the capabilities of DPM into the data protection needs of the information system you are trying to protect.

NOTE

Just as important as documenting the applications that are being backed up and managed by DPM, it is important for an IT administrator to clearly document the systems and applications that are not being backed up by DPM. This information should be signed off by IT management so that someone is aware of the applications that are not being backed up by DPM—that either should be backed up by a different solution or that are clearly not going to be backed up at all.

Step Three: Design the Protection Groups

The third step in the DPM planning process is to map out a logical design for the membership and configuration of the protection groups. To complete this step, the first task you need to complete is to take the data sources that DPM will be protecting (identified in step two) and then group them together (protection groups), for example:

▶ The System State for a certain collection of servers

▶ A collection of ERP databases that resides on a SQL Server cluster

▶ An Exchange Server 2010 DAG

▶ File data that resides on a collection of Windows 7 and Windows Vista machines

▶ File data that resides in a DFS namespace

▶ A SharePoint 2010 farm

Once you have outlined your protection groups, your next task is to determine what the recovery goals should be for each group. Keep in mind that not every data source has the same requirements for backup and recovery. Therefore, the level of protection for each protection group should be based on realistic recovery goals based on the business needs for protection of the data.

> **NOTE**
>
> The remaining planning steps in this section imply that D2D2T data protection is being used. Although it is perfectly feasible to use a D2T2T or D2D2C data protection, most enterprise data protection scenarios are better served using short-term, disk-based protection.

For example, based on the information that was collected during the second step of the DPM design process, you might have the following requirements for Exchange data:

▶ A data loss tolerance of only 30 minutes

▶ A data retention requirement of five years

▶ A system recovery requirement with some data of one day

Based on this information, you need to define your short-term disk recovery goals in terms of retention range, synchronization frequency, and recovery point schedule:

▶ **Retention range**—The value for this parameter should be specified as a unit of time, which controls how long a recovery point should be retained by the DPM server. Once the age of a recovery point has exceeded the specified retention range, it is deleted from the storage pool.

▶ **Synchronization frequency**—The value for this parameter should be specified as a unit of time, which controls how often the protection agent will send the block-level updates to the DPM server. Synchronization for a protection group can occur as frequently as every 15 minutes or much longer depending on the stated data loss tolerance requirement for the data that is being protected.

▶ **Recovery point schedule**—The value for this parameter should be specified as a unit of time, which controls how often recovery points are created. Recovery points for a protection group can be created as frequently as every 15 minutes or much longer depending on the stated data loss tolerance requirement for the data that is being protected.

It is important to remember, as discussed in the "What Is System Center Data Protection Manager?" section, that the synchronization process and the resulting recovery point schedule differ slightly in DPM depending on the type of data that is being protected. Additionally, DPM tries to guide you through the process of defining these values, both based on what is technically possible and what makes sense.

For example, there are certain VSS limitations that help shape what the retention range, synchronization frequency, and recovery point schedule can be. With VSS, there can only be up to 512 snapshots that simultaneously exist for the same volume. Of these 512 snapshots, a maximum of 64 snapshots can be used for the shadow copies for the Shared Folders feature. So the total number of recovery points is limited to 512 for application servers and 64 for file servers. Additionally, of the 512 snapshots available to applications,

10

DPM reserves the ability to use 64 snapshots for any file protection that might occur in a storage group that is being used to protect application data. Therefore, recovery goal options for short-term disk protection are limited to the values shown in Table 10.2.

Table 10.2   Short-Term Disk Recovery Options

Protection Method	Recovery Goals
Retention range	1–448 days
Synchronization frequency	Between 15 minutes and 24 hours, or just before a recovery point
Recovery points	For files, recovery points are created based on the defined schedule and for applications they are created after each synchronization

Next, you need to define the long-term recovery goals in terms of retention range, frequency of backup, and recovery point schedule:

▶ **Retention range**—The value for this parameter is a unit of time (between 1 day and 99 years), which controls how long a recovery point should be retained on a tape.

▶ **Frequency of backup**—The value for this parameter is a unit of time, which controls how often full backups are performed. If the retention range is 1–99 years, backups can occur daily, weekly, biweekly, monthly, quarterly, half-yearly, or yearly. For a retention range between 1 and 11 months, backups can occur daily, weekly, biweekly, or monthly. And, for a retention range of 1–4 weeks, backups can occur daily or weekly.

▶ **Recovery point schedule**—Depending on the retention range and backup frequency, DPM recommends a recovery point schedule. If needed, you can further customize the recovery point schedule to meet your needs.

The last step in planning your protection groups is to describe their configuration using a logical format based on the information that you have gathered so far. For example, you might want to use a form, as shown in Table 10.3.

TABLE 10.3   Protection Group Planning Checklist

Parameter	Value
Protection group name	The name for the protection group
Machines/Resources	A list of machine or resource names that hold the data that will be protected by this protection group
Type of data	Application data or file data
Approximate size	An estimate of the current size of the data
Rate of change	An estimate of how often the data changes
Protection method	D2D2T or D2T2T
Short-term retention range	The predetermined short-term retention range value
Short-term synchronization frequency	The predetermined short-term synchronization frequency value

Parameter	Value
Short-term recovery point schedule	The predetermined short-term recovery point schedule value
Long-term retention range	The predetermined long-term retention range value
Long-term frequency of backup	The predetermined long-term frequency of backup
Replica creation method	Automatic or Manual
Custom volume requirement	True or False

NOTE

The more frequently you back up information and the longer you want to retain the information, the more storage space is required. The good news about DPM is that it has the ability to maintain a copy of the information you specify; however, the bad news is that DPM could take up dozens if not hundreds (or thousands) of terabytes of storage to support chosen settings. Although having a backup every 15 minutes of information would be extremely helpful for an 8–12 hour business window, having 15-minute increments of data that is three days old is completely unnecessary. Prior to implementing DPM, most organizations only backed up their systems once a night, so their data loss tolerance used to be 24 hours of data with only a nightly copy of information—and in some cases only a weekly backup of information. So take consideration in the reality of retention and recovery so that the proper balance between recovery points and backup storage space is appropriate for the organization.

Step Four: Calculate the Storage Requirements

The fourth step in the DPM planning process is to calculate the storage requirement for the DPM deployment. Unfortunately, correctly calculating the exact amount of storage that DPM will require happens to be a bit of a dark art. To help administrators through this very difficult process with Data Protection Manager, the DPM product team provided a set of storage calculators and a volume sizing tool. Starting with Data Protection Manager 2010, a number of underlying changes have been designed to increase the scalability of a single DPM server, for example:

▶ Support for growth of storage volumes as required

▶ Support for hundreds of servers, thousands of laptops/desktops, and tens of thousands of SQL databases per DPM server

▶ An overall increase in the ability to fan-in a large number of data sources

As noted previously, DPM 2012 now provides central administration of multiple DPM servers, thus allowing an organization to distribute the backup of data across multiple backup systems, and thus improving backup performance and scalability of backup data states.

10

NOTE

DPM can be deployed onto a virtual machine. However, when a virtual machine is used, the storage pool (where backups are stored) should be connected by using pass-through disks or other connected storage. Because backup space in a DPM environment is typically calculated in terabytes, connected storage better meets the storage needs.

Step Five: Design the DPM Server

The last step in the DPM planning process is to design the DPM server. To complete this step, you must first determine how many DPM servers are required and where they should be physically located in relation to the data they are protecting. The best method to calculate the number of servers needed is to again use the DPM 2012 storage calculators. These calculators are Excel spreadsheets where you can enter information about the application data you are protecting and they will then provide recommendations such as the following:

▶ The recommended number of DPM servers needed

▶ The recommended number of processor cores per DPM server needed to support DPM

▶ The recommended RAM configuration per DPM server needed to support the DPM activities

▶ The recommended virtual memory configuration per DPM server needed to support DPM activities

▶ The total storage capacity needed

When using these storage calculators, remember that they are application-specific. Therefore, the recommendations that they make only apply to protecting the application data that the storage calculator was created for. For example, the Exchange storage calculator only provides recommendations about protecting Exchange data, the SharePoint storage calculator only provides recommendations for SharePoint data, and so on.

With this in mind, combine the data from these storage calculators to determine a base set of requirements for your DPM servers and modify them to include other considerations such as the following:

▶ Operating system limitations

▶ Unsupported installation scenarios (where DPM cannot be installed on):

    ▶ Domain controllers

    ▶ Exchange servers

    ▶ Operations Manager management or Gateway servers

- ▶ The criticality of the data that a DPM server will be protecting
- ▶ Performance bottleneck and load distribution associated with synchronization frequencies and restoration activities
- ▶ Legal or compliance reasons for data separation
- ▶ Proximity to data sources and storage systems
- ▶ Ease of administration
- ▶ Any disaster recovery requirements

All of these steps are intended to help the backup administrator more clearly understand the organization's needs in terms of planning, protecting, and properly supporting the backup needs of the organization. There are undoubtedly variations to these steps depending on the size of the organization or the stated requirements for DPM, for example, "We are buying DPM only to back up Exchange and SharePoint." However, as noted in this planning section, it is just as important to document what isn't being backed up and managed in addition to specifically what is.

Deploying Data Protection Manager

This section covers the steps needed to perform a basic Data Protection Manager 2012 deployment as well as the software requirements along with what is involved to install the DPM application software, deploy the protection agent, configure the storage pool, and complete other required DPM configuration tasks for a basic deployment.

Preparing the Data Protection Manager Server

Before the DPM installation can be started, the base Windows operating system needs to be installed. With the Data Protection Manager 2012 release, the preferred server operating system is Windows Server 2008 R2. However, as noted in the "Supported Operating Systems" section earlier in this chapter, Data Protection Manager 2012 can also be installed on Windows Server 2008.

After the base server operating system has been installed and the latest updates have been applied, the next task is to join the server to the domain and then ensure all of the software requirements are met, as noted in the "Software Requirements" section earlier in this chapter.

NOTE

The DPM installation wizard will install the Windows Single Instance Store (SIS), Microsoft .NET Framework, and Visual C++ Redistributable components if any of these components are not installed beforehand.

10

Preparing the Remote SQL Instance

If you plan to use a remote SQL instance for your DPM installation (that is, SQL Server that is running on a system other than the local DPM server you are installing), you need to ensure that the following features are installed on the target SQL server:

▶ Database Engine services (both subsections)

▶ Reporting Services

▶ Management Tools—Basic

▶ Management Tools—Complete

▶ SQL Client connectivity SDK

Once the remote SQL instance has been installed, ensure the following:

▶ Reporting Services is configured and linked to the remote SQL instance.

▶ The SQL Agent service is running and set to Automatic startup.

▶ A Windows Firewall exception is created for `SQLServer.exe`.

▶ The Named Pipes protocol is enabled.

▶ The DPM SQLPrepInstaller package has been installed.

> **NOTE**
>
> During the installation of DPM 2012, there is a prerequisite and configuration valida-
> tion process that will test the target server and SQL server to ensure the required and
> supported versions of files are installed properly. If components are missing, DPM will
> prompt you to install the components and then retry or restart the installation process.
> Many IT administrators will just run the DPM installer and let the DPM installer prompt
> the administrator to install the needed versions of components rather than reading
> this section or the prerequisite notes that come with DPM. So preconfiguring the DPM
> or SQL server is not really necessary, only helps to minimize having to continuously
> add components, updates, features, or patches during the DPM installation process.

Running the Data Protection Manager Installation

After meeting all of the hardware, operating system, and software requirements, the next step in your deployment is to execute the DPM Setup Wizard to complete a basic DPM installation. To start the installation, log on to the DPM server using a domain user account that is a member of the local administrators group. Then execute the DPM Setup Wizard (`setup.exe`) from the installation media or an ISO file, or use a copy of the setup files from a shared network location. Once the wizard has started, use the following steps to complete the installation:

1. In the Data Protection Manager 2012 window, as shown in Figure 10.1, select the Install Data Protection Manager option.

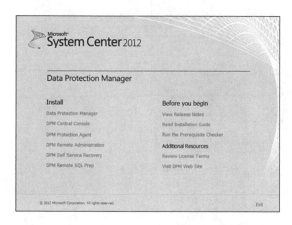

FIGURE 10.1   Starting the DPM Setup Wizard.

2. When prompted with the Microsoft Software License Terms dialog box, select the I Accept the License Terms and Conditions check box, and then click OK. This starts the DPM Setup Wizard.

3. On the Welcome page, click Next.

4. On the Prerequisites Check page, two SQL Server database options are presented. If you plan to use a new dedicated local instance of SQL Server for DPM, use the default SQL Server option. However, if you plan to use a remote SQL instance, select the Use an Existing Instance of SQL Server option, then provide the name for the remote SQL instance and the user credentials that will be used to connect to that instance. Once the SQL option has been selected, click on the Check and Install button to initiate the prerequisites check. Once the check has finished, the Setup Wizard either permits the installation to continue by displaying a confirmation and allowing you to click Next to continue, or if one or more requirements or recommendations have not been met, the Setup Wizard displays a warning or error message. If this occurs, you are either allowed to continue the installation by clicking Next, or you are prevented from continuing until any noted requirements have been met. An example of this behavior is shown in Figure 10.2.

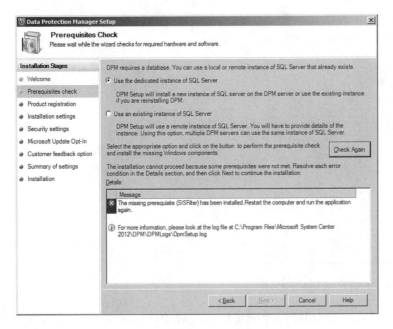

FIGURE 10.2   The Prerequisites Check page.

If the DPM Setup Wizard installs any prerequisite software and a restart is required, restart the DPM server and then restart the DPM Setup Wizard again.

5. On the Product Registration page, enter the product registration information for your organization, and then click Next.

6. On the Installation Settings page, you can either use the default folder location for the program files or modify the installation path to meet your needs. If you chose the option to install a local SQL database, the location for the database files can also be changed if necessary. Once you have chosen the desired file locations, click Next.

7. On the Security Settings page, provide a strong password for the DPMR$<computer name> account and then click Next.

If you choose to use the local SQL instance, you will be prompted to provide a strong password for the restricted MICROSOFTDPMAcct and DPMR$<computer name> local user accounts. The first account, MICROSOFTDPMAcct, is used to run the SQL Server and SQL Server Agent services, whereas the DPMR$<computer name> account is used to securely generate reports. When you use a remote SQL instance, the Setup Wizard will only create the DPMR$<computer name> account.

8. On the Microsoft Update Opt-In page, select the desired Microsoft Update service option, and then click Next.

9. On the Customer Experience Improvement Program page, select the desired Customer Experience Improvement Program option, and then click Next.

10. On the Summary of Settings page, review the summary of installation settings, and then click Install (accept the security warning if prompted).

11. Once the installation has completed, the Installation page is shown. Click Close to complete the installation.

Completing Required Configuration Tasks

Before DPM can be used to protect data in your environment, you must complete the following required configuration tasks.

Adding Disks to the Storage Pool

As mentioned previously in this chapter, DPM stores replicas and recovery points of protected data using a storage pool (a set of disks). When adding a new storage pool, keep the following requirements in mind:

▶ A USB/1394 "removable storage" disk cannot be used.

▶ The disk cannot have the DPM installation on it.

▶ The disk can only use space on volumes that are created for the storage pool.

NOTE

Setting up the target storage space for DPM is sometimes confusing. DPM partitions the storage space itself from space that is available on the target disk. If you point DPM to store backups at a partition that has already been partitioned and/or is otherwise accessed as a drive (for example, E>, F>), DPM will tell you that you don't have adequate space for DPM backups. DPM will not prompt you that the target storage space you are specifying needs to be unpartitioned, nor will DPM unpartition a disk. So when setting up the target DPM backup space, the storage destination needs to be a completely unpartitioned target.

Use the following steps to add a new disk to the storage pool using the DPM 2012 Administrator Console:

1. Log on to the DPM server using a domain user account that is a member of the local administrators group.

2. Next, open the DPM 2012 Administrator Console using either the desktop or Start menu icon.

3. Once the console has loaded, on the left side, click Management, and then select the Disks link.

4. From the ribbon toolbar at the top, click Add.

5. Once the Add Disks to Storage Pool dialog box opens, select the desired disk, click Add, and then click OK.

6. The disk is then added as the DPM storage pool, as shown in Figure 10.3.

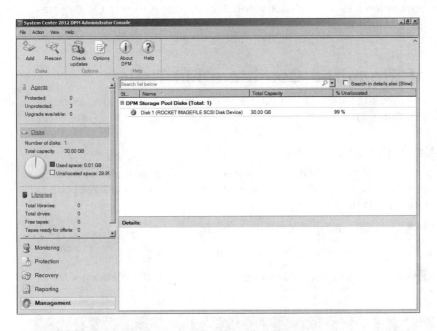

FIGURE 10.3   Adding a disk to the DPM storage pool.

You can also add a new disk to the storage pool using the DPM Management Shell:

1. Log on to the DPM server using a domain user account that is a member of the local administrators group.

2. Next, open the DPM 2012 Management Shell using either the desktop or Start menu icon.

3. Now execute the following command:

```
Get-DPMDisk -DPMServerName <DPM server name>
```

4. Using the `NtDiskID` value from the desired disk object that is returned from the `Get-DPMDisk` cmdlet, execute the following command:

```
Get-DPMDisk -DPMServerName <DPM server name> | where {$_.NTDiskID -eq <NtDiskId
Value>} | Add-DPMDisk
```

5. Lastly, verify that the disk has been added to the storage pool using the following command:

```
Get-DPMDisk -DPMServerName <DPM server name> | where {$_.NTDiskID -eq <NtDiskId
Value>} | select Name, NtDiskID, IsInStoragePool
```

NOTE

If you plan to only use disk-to-tape protection or custom volumes to protect data, adding a disk to the storage pool is not a requirement.

Configuring Tape Libraries

If you plan to use tape libraries or standalone tape drives for short-term and long-term data protection on tape, you need to physically attach the tape devices to the DPM server. Next, complete the following steps to add the tape library or standalone tape drives using the DPM 2012 Administrator Console:

1. Log on to the DPM server using a domain user account that is a member of the local administrators group.

2. Next, open the DPM 2012 Administrator Console using either the desktop or Start menu icon.

3. Once the console has loaded, on the left side, click Management, and then select the Libraries link.

4. From the tool ribbon at the top, click Rescan, then click Yes at the acknowledgment prompt to proceed with the rescan.

The rescan operation might take a couple of minutes; let the scan complete. During a rescan, DPM examines the attached tape devices and updates the information that is displayed on the Libraries tab in the DPM Administrator Console, as shown in Figure 10.4. If at any point you add or remove a tape device, the rescan operation will need to be rerun.

10

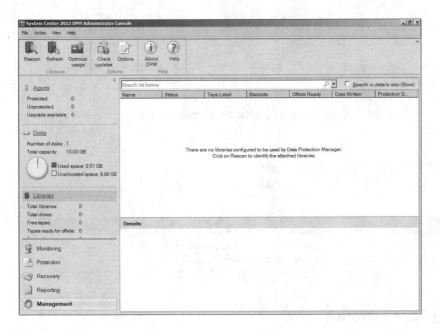

FIGURE 10.4   Scanned tape library.

Deploying the Protection Agent Using the DPM Administration Console

Before data from a data source (machine) can be protected, you must first install a protection agent. These agents are responsible for identifying data that can be protected, tracking changes to that data, and transferring the changes from the protected data source to the DPM server. To deploy the protection agent, you must first ensure that the intended computer meets the following set of prerequisites:

▶ The computer must have a supported version of Windows for the protection agent, as noted in the "Data Protection Manager Background" section earlier in this chapter.

▶ Protected volumes must be formatted as NTFS and be at least 1GB.

▶ A protected computer's fully qualified domain name (FQDN) should not have more than 400 characters.

▶ For Windows Server 2003 and Windows XP machines, you might need to apply KB940349 ("Availability of a Volume Shadow Copy Service (VSS)") update rollup package for Windows Server 2003 to resolve some VSS snapshot issues.

▶ Also for Windows Server 2003 and Windows XP machines, you might need to install the Shadow Copy Client (ShadowCopyClient.msi).

After meeting the prerequisites, you can deploy the protection agent to computers using two different methods. The steps for the first method, using the DPM 2012 Administrator Console, are as follows:

1. Log on to the DPM server using a domain user account that is a member of the local administrators group.

2. Next, open the DPM 2012 Administrator Console using either the desktop or Start menu icon.

3. Once the console has loaded, on the left side, click Management, and then select the Agents link.

4. From the tool ribbon at the top, click Install. This starts the Protection Agent Installation Wizard.

5. On the Select Agent Deployment Method page, you are given two options, as shown in Figure 10.5. The Install Agents option is used to completely install the protection agent on a computer. The Attach Agents option is used to just add a protected computer's object to the DPM server. This option is useful for scenarios that require the agent to be installed manually. For the purpose of this procedure, select the Install Agents option and click Next.

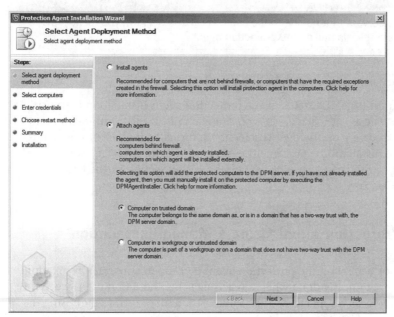

FIGURE 10.5   Protection Agent Installation Wizard.

6. On the Select Computers page, you can either select 1 to 50 computers from the Computer Name list or enter the name of the computer in the Computer Name box and then click Add. Once you have added all of the desired computer names to the Selected Computers list, click Next.

10

> **NOTE**
>
> To find a computer from a different domain, you must use the FQDN to be able to successfully resolve the DNS name of the target server.

7. On the Enter Credentials page, provide the credentials for a domain user account that has local administrator rights on all the computers being added, and then click Next.

8. If you selected a node in a server cluster or Exchange 2010 Database Availability Group, DPM detects the additional nodes in the cluster or DAG and displays the Select Cluster Nodes page. On this page, select the option that you want DPM to use for selecting the remaining nodes in the cluster, and then click Next.

9. On the Choose Restart Method page, select the option you want DPM to use to restart the computers after the protection agent is installed, and click Next. All computers (except a DPM server) must be restarted when the protection agent is installed. A restart is required so that the DPM volume filter can be loaded. Until this filter is loaded, you cannot start protecting data on a computer.

> **NOTE**
>
> DPM will not restart servers that belong to a cluster. For these servers, you must manually restart them after installing the protection agent.

10. On the Summary page, click Install to begin the installation.

11. On the Installation page, the status of the protection agent installation is shown. At any time during the agent installation, you can click Close and continue to monitor the installation progress on the Agents screen. Additionally, if an error is encountered during the installation, you can either review the error message on the Installation page or in the Alerts area of the Monitoring section in the DPM Administrator Console.

Deploying the Protection Agent Using a Manual Installation Process

The second method for deploying the protection agent is through a manual installation. Manual installations are typically done when a machine is behind a firewall, the agent is being incorporated into a server image, or the remote installation of the agent using the DPM Administrator Console is not possible. An example of such a scenario is shown in Figure 10.6.

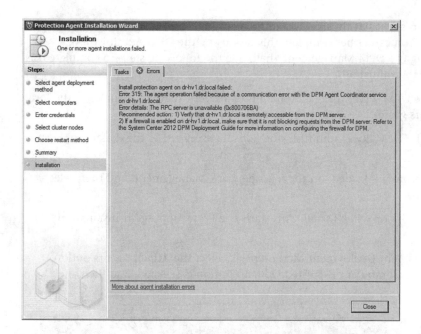

FIGURE 10.6   Remote protection agent installation failure.

In Figure 10.6, the protection agent installation failed on dr-hv1 because Windows Firewall is enabled without the needed rules to allow the remote installation to proceed. To work around this issue, you can either modify the Windows Firewall settings on dr-hv1 or perform a manual installation. To complete a manual installation of the protection agent, use the following steps:

1. Copy the protection agent installer (`DPMAgentInstaller_x86.exe` or `DPMAgentInstaller.exe_x64`) from the Agents folder in the DPM 2012 installation media to the intended machine (in this case, dr-hv1).

2. Next, open a command prompt as an administrator and execute the installer using the following command:

```
DPMAgentInstaller_x86.exe or DPMAgentInstaller.exe_x64 <DPM server name>
```

> **NOTE**
>
> Performing a manual installation of the protection agent does the following:
>
> ▶ Installs the protection agent prerequisites and the DPM protection agent
> ▶ Configures the target computer to be managed from the specified DPM server name
> ▶ Makes any needed Windows Firewall changes to allow outbound and inbound communications with the DPM server

10

Once the protection agent has finished installing, you then need to attach the computer to the DPM server. You can either complete this task using the DPM Administrator Console or by using the DPM Management Shell. Use the following steps to complete this task using the DPM Administrator Console:

1. Log on to the DPM server using a domain user account that is a member of the local administrators group.

2. Next, open the DPM 2012 Administrator Console using either the desktop or Start menu icon.

3. Once the console has loaded, on the left side, click Management, and then select the Agents link.

4. From the tool ribbon, click Install. This starts the Protection Agent Installation Wizard.

5. On the Select Agent Deployment Method page, select the Attach Agents option, ensure that the Computer on Trusted Domain option is selected, and then click Next.

NOTE

If the machine you are adding is in a workgroup or in an untrusted domain, use the Computer in a Workgroup or Untrusted Domain option. This option can be used to protect workgroup machines and systems in untrusted domains within your intranet for the following scenarios:

- File servers
- System State
- SQL Server
- Exchange Server
- Hyper-V
- Small business server

You cannot use this option for the following scenarios:

- Clustered servers (except for Exchange Server 2010)
- Mirrored servers
- SharePoint
- Laptops
- Bare metal restores
- End-user recovery

---

6. On the Select Computers page, you can either select up to 50 computers from the Computer Name list or enter the name of the computer in the Computer Name box and click Add. Once you have added all of the desired computer names to the Selected Computers list, click Next.

7. On the Enter Credentials page, provide the credentials for a domain user account that has local administrator rights on all the computers being added, and then click Next.

8. On the Summary page, click Attach to complete the attachment process.

9. On the Installation page, the status of the protection agent attachment is shown. At any time during the agent installation, you can click Close and continue to monitor the installation progress on the Agents screen. Additionally, if an error is encountered during the installation, you can either review the error message on the Installation page or in the Alerts area of the Monitoring section in the DPM Administrator Console.

Deploying the Protection Agent Using Certificates

Data Protection Manager 2012 added the support of protecting target servers through the use of certificates. Instead of requiring a target server to be a member server of a domain, or using a local administrator account on the target system, organizations can issue a certificate to the target server and have DPM identify the target server by the certificate. The certificate method of backup is perfect for DMZ-resident servers such as web or Gateway servers. Additionally, certificate-based backups are useful for target devices like appliances, kiosks, or data acquisition devices that are not part of a domain but would benefit from being backed up. Non-domain-joined Hyper-V host servers in a DMZ serving multiple virtual guest sessions like edge servers and gateways can have a certificate installed and targeted as the backup host where all of the guest sessions on the host can be backed up.

> **NOTE**
>
> The certificate-based protection agent option can be used to protect machines of the following type:
> - File servers
> - SQL Server
> - Hyper-V
>
> You cannot use this option for the following scenarios:
> - Exchange Server
> - Client computers
> - SharePoint servers
> - Bare metal recovery
> - System State

10

To deploy the protection agent using certificates, install a certificate on the DPM server with a metadata file that will be used during the installation of certificates on all certificate-based target systems. To generate the DPM server certificate and metadata file, do the following:

1. Generate an X.509 v3 certificate for client authentication and server authentication, a key length of at least 1024 bits, a key type of exchange from a certificate authority for the DPM server. Because this certificate is used only for computer-to-computer purposes, it is perfectly fine to issue the certificate from your own Windows certificate authority and save the cost of a public certificate.

2. Log on to the DPM server using a domain user account that is a member of the local administrators group.

3. Import the certificate into the personal certificate store of the Local Computer account.

4. Run set-DPMCredentials in the DPM Management Shell, which generates a metadata file that will be used when installing the certificate in each certificate-based target system.

To deploy the protection agent on a target server using certificates, do the following:

1. Generate a certificate (X.509 v3 certificate with client authentication and server authentication, key length of at least 1024 bits, key type should be exchange) from a certificate authority for the target server you want DPM to protect. Have a copy of this certificate and the metadata file created in the previous series of steps from the DPM server.

2. Log on to the target server on which you want to install the certificate using a user account that is a member of the local administrators group.

3. Import the certificate into the personal certificate store of the Local Computer account.

4. Run setup.exe from the DPM 2012 installation media and choose to install the DPM protection agent on the system.

5. Run setDPMServer.exe from c:\Program Files\Microsoft Data Protection Manager\DPM\bin to create a certificate metadata file that will later be added to the DPM server to complete the certificate-based association between the DPM server and the target server.

To add the target server to the DPM server to enable the DPM server to back up the target server, do the following:

1. Log on to the DPM server using a domain user account that is a member of the local administrators group.

2. Launch the DPM Management Shell.

3. Run the PowerShell script c:\Program Files\Microsoft System Center 2012\DPM\DPM\bin\Attach-ProductionServerwithCertificate.ps1, which is in the c:\Program Files\Microsoft System Center 2012\DPM\DPM\bin directory on the DPM server.

4. When prompted for the DPM server name, type in the name of the DPM server, and then press Enter.

5. When prompted for the PSCredential, enter in the name of the file that was generated on the target server using setDPMServer.exe, and then press Enter.

The target system will be added to the DPM server you have specified.

Attaching a Protection Agent Using PowerShell

Another method to attach a manually deployed agent to the DPM server is to use the DPM Management Shell and the Attach-ProductionServer.ps1 script, as described in the following process:

1. Log on to the DPM server using a domain user account that is a member of the local administrators group.

2. Next, open the DPM 2012 Management Shell using either the desktop or Start menu icon.

3. Now execute the following command:

```
.\Attach-ProductionServer.ps1 <DPM server name> <production server name> <user
name> <password> <domain>
```

Creating Protection Groups

As mentioned previously in this chapter, a protection group is a collection of data sources that share the same protection configuration. Before data can be protected by DPM, you must create at least one protection group, in which you specify the target servers you want to back up, the backup frequency, and the data retention frequency among other backup setting parameters. Backups can be deemed short term or long term, where short-term storage provides for real-time immediate recovery of information, whereas long-term storage is for archival purposes.

Creating a Protection Group with Short-Term or Long-Term Storage

All DPM backups are initially configured to support short-term storage needs. This allows a backup to be used to immediately recover a lost or corrupt server or data set. Long-term storage such as writing week-old short-term data to tape can be configured using the same process. To create a protection group for short-term or long-term storage, you need to use the Create New Protection Group Wizard, which guides you through the process of setting up a new protection group. The steps involved with using this wizard are as follows:

1. Log on to the DPM server using a domain user account that is a member of the local administrators group.

2. Next, open the DPM 2012 Administrator Console using either the desktop or Start menu icon.

3. Once the console has loaded, on the left side click Protection, and then from the tool ribbon click New.

4. The Create New Protection Group Wizard starts, as shown in Figure 10.7. On the Welcome to the New Protection Group Wizard page, click Next.

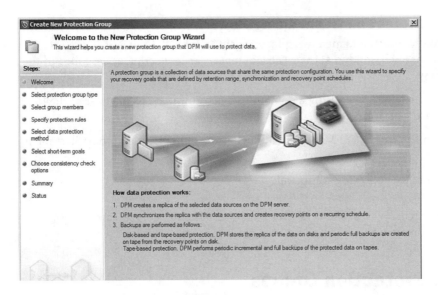

FIGURE 10.7   Create New Protection Group Wizard.

5. On the Select Protection Group Type page, you are given the option of creating two different kinds of protection groups. For the purpose of these steps, select the Servers option, and then click Next.

NOTE

Specific steps for creating protection groups for Exchange Server, SQL Server, SharePoint, clients, and so on are provided in Chapter 11, "Using Data Protection Manager 2012 to Protect File Systems, Exchange, SQL, and SharePoint." For the purpose of these steps, a protection group is being created for a generic file server.

6. On the Select Group Members page, use the interface to add members into the protection group. To do this, expand the desired server node to expose its data sources. Next, select each data source that you want to add into the protection group by placing a check mark in the box next to it. An example of this process is shown in Figure 10.8.

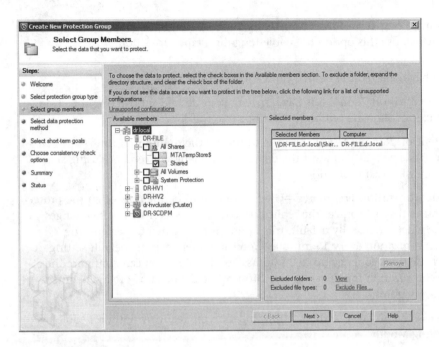

FIGURE 10.8   Adding members to a protection group.

When adding members to a protection group, the following considerations or recommendations should be noted:

▶ Data sources already added to another protection group are displayed but cannot be selected.

▶ For data that is on a system volume, it is recommended that the individual folders or shares be protected instead of the entire volume.

▶ SQL Server database snapshots cannot be protected.

▶ SharePoint databases cannot be protected as a SQL Server data source. Instead, they should be included as part of a SharePoint protection group.

▶ A separate individual tape is required for each protection group as they cannot share.

7. Once you have finished selecting the desired data sources, click Next.

8. On the Select Data Protection Method page, type a new name for the protection group in the Protection Group Name box, and then choose one of the following options as the desired protection method:

▶ **I Want Short-Term Protection Using**—Use this option to enable short-term protection and select the desired media.

10

> ▸ **I Want Long-Term Protection Using Tape**—If you have a tape device
> attached, use this option to enable long-term tape protection.

9. After you have selected the desired protection method, click Next.

10. On the Specify Short-Term Goals page, specify your desired short-term protection
    goals using the following options or sections:

    > ▸ **Retention Range**—Use this option to specify the duration of time (between 1
    > and 64 days) that you want the data to be available for recovery using short-
    > term, disk-based protection.

    > ▸ **Synchronization Frequency**—Use this option to define how often the protec-
    > tion agent synchronizes the replica on your DPM server with data changes
    > from a data source. By default, this option is configured to perform the
    > synchronization every 15 minutes. You can either keep the default setting or
    > increase the frequency up to 24 hours. Additionally, you can configure the
    > synchronization frequency to synchronize the data just before a scheduled
    > recovery point.

    > ▸ **Recovery Points**—Use this section to define the recovery point schedule by
    > clicking Modify.

NOTE

For the purpose of these steps, a protection group is using disk-based, short-term
protection. When you use tape-based, short-term protection, the steps in the wizard
are slightly different to handle the scheduling options for the tape backup jobs. More
information about these differences is provided later in this section.

---

11. After you have specified the desired short-term protection goals, click Next.

12. On the Review Disk Allocation page, review the disk allocations that DPM recom-
    mends for the protection group. If you need to make any modifications to these
    allocations, click Modify.

13. After you have reviewed the disk allocations and made any needed changes, click
    Next.

14. If you have a tape device attached, the Specify Long-Term Protection page is shown.
    Use this page to specify your long-term protection goals using tape backups based
    on the following sections:

    > ▸ **Recovery Goals**—Use this section to specify the retention range and backup
    > frequency. The settings you define here determine the long-term recovery
    > point schedule. If needed, you can also create a custom schedule by clicking
    > Customize.

▶ **Backup Schedule**—Use this section to customize the long-term full backup schedule by clicking Modify. The scheduling options that are shown in this section depend on the retention range and backup frequency settings that have been defined in the Recovery Goals section.

15. After you have specified the desired long-term protection goals, click Next.

16. If you have a tape device attached, the Select Library and Tape Details page is also shown. Use this page to specify the library and configuration options for the backup tapes based on the following options:

   ▶ **Library**—This option is used to select the tape library that will be used.

   ▶ **Drives Allocated**—This option is used to define how many drives are allocated for the tape backups.

   ▶ **Copy Library**—This option is used to select the library you want to use for multiple backup copies.

   ▶ **Tape Options for Long-Term Protection**—This option is used to define if the tape data should be compressed or encrypted.

NOTE

To encrypt data on tape for long-term protection, a valid encryption certificate must be imported into the DPMBackupStore.

17. After you specified the desired library and tape details, click Next.

18. On the Choose Replica Creation Method page, use the Replica in DPM Server section to define how the initial replica of the protected data should be created. A replica can either be created over the network by immediately copying the data or scheduling the initial copy to some later time. Or, you can manually create a replica using some form of removable media such as tape. However, when creating the replica manually, it is critical that aspects of the data like directory structure, time stamps, security permissions, and so on are retained from the protected data.

19. After you have specified the desired replica creation method, click Next.

20. On the Consistency Check Options page, specify the desired option for how the consistency check for the protection group will be handled, and then click Next.

21. On the Summary page, review the information about the protection group and then click Create Group.

22. Next, the status and results of the protection group creation process are shown on the Status page, as shown in Figure 10.9. Once the protection group has been created, click Close to exit the wizard.

10

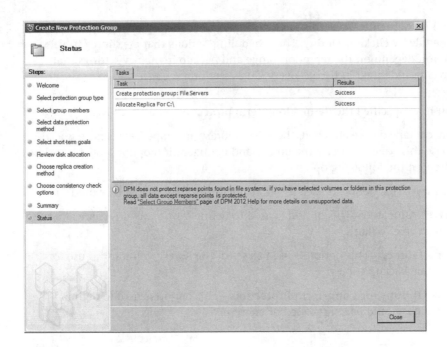

FIGURE 10.9   Protection group creation status.

Using Tape both for Short- and Long-Term Protection

When creating a new protection group, you have the option of choosing tape both for short-term and long-term protection methods. If this choice is made, the steps in the Create New Protection Group Wizard differ slightly in that you need to define the full backup schedule for the short-term protection goal on tape. It is recommended that the short-term, tape-based, full backups be executed just prior to the long-term backups. The reason is that DPM creates copies of the latest short-term, tape-based, full backup to generate the long-term backup. By scheduling the short-term, tape-based, full backup just before the long-term backup, you ensure that the latest version of the protected data is protected.

Administrating Data Protection Manager

Administrating any type of information system can often be a very broad topic and, unfortunately, Data Protection Manager is no exception. For example, DPM administrators must monitor performance, manage tapes, monitor the DPM server operations, perform recoveries, and diagnose agent communication issues. Because administrating DPM is such a broad scope, this section, in keeping with the theme of this book, focuses on DPM administration topics that are either critical to DPM operations or in need of greater explanation due to the lack of available information. For example, items covered in this section include the DPM management interfaces, how to use custom volumes, and recovering data.

DPM Administrator Console

The DPM Administrator Console is a Microsoft Management Console (MMC) snap-in that is used to manage a DPM server that by default is installed when you install Data Protection Manager. To access it, you must be interactively logged on to the DPM server using a domain account that has local administrator privileges. The only method to remotely access the console is to use a Remote Desktop connection.

In the DPM Administrator Console, management tasks are logically grouped together based on related function within the navigation bar. These groupings or task areas are Monitoring, Protection, Recovery, Reporting, and Management, as shown in Figure 10.10.

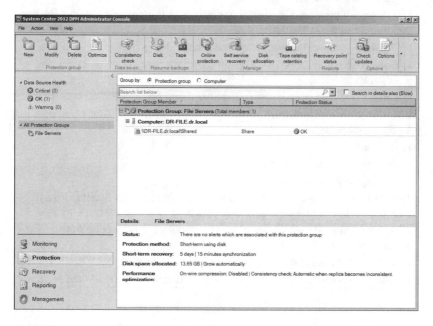

FIGURE 10.10   DPM Administrator Console.

Except for Recovery, each task area consists of two panes: the unlabeled display pane, details pane, as well as the Actions toolbar. The toolbar shows the different management activities that can be completed with the currently selected task or item selected in the display pane. To better understand this relationship, a breakdown of each task area and its associated management activities is shown in Table 10.4.

10

TABLE 10.4   DPM Administrator Console Tasks

Task Area	Usage
Monitoring	The Monitoring task area is used to monitor the status of data protection, data recovery, and other related DPM operations. In this task area, there are two tabs: ▶ **Alerts**—Shows errors, warnings, and informational messages ▶ **Jobs**—Shows the status of jobs and their associated tasks
Protection	The Protection task area is used to manage protection groups. Using this task area, you can: ▶ Create, modify, and manage protection groups ▶ Manage online protection ▶ Modify disk allocations and perform consistency checks ▶ Manage recovery points ▶ Optimize performance
Recovery	The Recovery task area is used to recover data from recovery points. In this task area, there are two tabs: ▶ **Browse**—Browse for recoverable data by protected computer and date ▶ **Search**—Search for recoverable data by data type, location, origin, and recovery point date
Reporting	The Reporting task area is used to manage and review DPM reports. Using this task area, you can: ▶ Schedule reports ▶ Edit reports ▶ Generate and view reports ▶ Manage report subscriptions
Management	The Management task area is used to manage protection agents, storage pool disks, and tape libraries. In this task area, there are three tabs: ▶ **Agents**—Manage, deploy, remove, and update the protection agents and agent licenses ▶ **Disks**—Manage, add, and remove disks in the storage pool ▶ **Libraries**—Manage tape libraries, tape devices, and tapes in the library

DPM Management Shell

The DPM Management Shell is a command-line management interface for Data Protection Manager. This management shell is built using Windows PowerShell, which is a .NET Framework–based, object-oriented, command-line shell and associated scripting language. Using the DPM Management Shell, you have access to DPM-related commands, also known as cmdlets, which can be used as an alternative interface to the DPM Administrator Console to perform data protection management tasks, as shown in Figure 10.11.

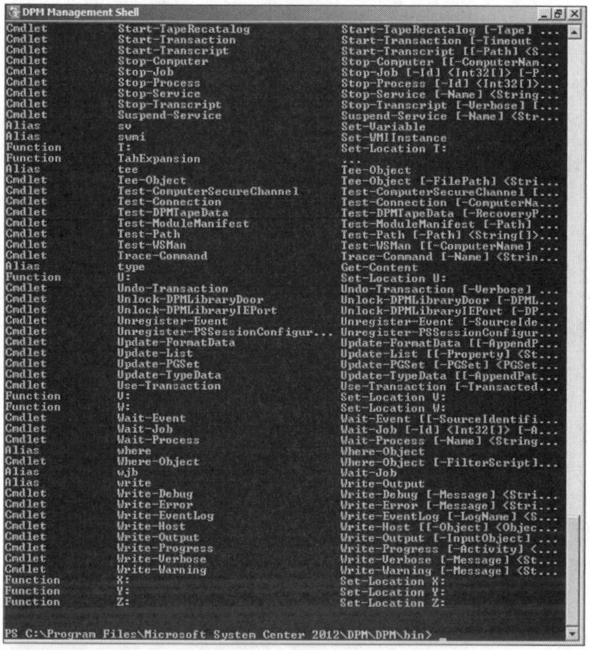

FIGURE 10.11   DPM Management Shell.

In fact, any task that you can perform using the DPM Administrator Console can be completed using the DPM Management Shell and in some scenarios, the shell provides additional features that the MMC-based console does not. Unlike the DPM Administrator Console, which can only be accessed directly from the DPM server, the DPM Management Shell can be installed on computers other than the DPM server, which means that you can use the management shell to remotely manage multiple DPM servers. Lastly, because the management shell is based on PowerShell, you can automate routine management tasks using the PowerShell scripting language.

> **NOTE**
>
> Being able to automate DPM tasks is a very key concept to understand. By using the DPM Management Shell, you can integrate data protection and recovery tasks with the rest of the System Center Enterprise Suite applications.

To discover the supported cmdlets in the DPM Management Shell, open the management shell and execute the Get-DPMCommand cmdlet. This cmdlet produces a command list that shows only the cmdlets belonging to DPM. For each cmdlet, Help documentation can be accessed by using the Get-Help or help cmdlet, as shown in the following example:

```
Get-Help <cmdlet name>
```

10

If more information is needed about a cmdlet, you can use the -Full or -Detailed parameters for the Get-Help cmdlet. For example:

```
Get-Help Get-DPMVolume -Detailed
```

Like the DPM Administrator Console, the DPM cmdlets are technically logically divided into task areas. However, the division is not necessarily very apparent. Microsoft frequently publishes updated DPM Administrator Console guides on the DPM Blogsite that are helpful in leveraging the latest command-line or scripted processes available.

Using DPM Central Console for Administration

Data Protection Manager 2012 added an additional method for administering DPM using the Central Console. The Central Console has two functions, a server component and a client component. The Central Console server component allows System Center Operations Manager (SCOM) to receive alerts and status of all DPM servers for centralized monitoring. The Central Console client component provides a single administration view and management controls for multiple DPM servers. From the central console client component, protection groups can be centrally created, backup jobs can be initiated, recovery processes can be initiated, and the status of all protection groups can be monitored.

The DPM Central Console client component can be installed on a system that is not a DPM server, so it can be installed on a Windows XP SP3, Windows Vista, or Windows 7 workstation or a server designated as a central DPM client console system. The Central Console server component needs to be installed on a server running SCOM 2012 as the server components add the monitoring and alerting functions for DPM to the SCOM server. The Central Console server and client components can be installed on the same SCOM server so that the SCOM server monitors and alerts the DPM server as well as acts as the Central Console client for managing DPM servers. The server system on which the Central Console client is installed cannot be a target server for DPM backups, meaning that if you want your SCOM server to be the Central Console client server, it cannot be backed up by DPM. Many organizations choose to install the Central Console server components on the SCOM server, and install the Central Console client components on a Windows 7 workstation.

For organizations that leverage SCOM alerting on the health of systems in the environment, the ability to issue DPM alerts to SCOM simplifies and centralizes notifications. The most common alert is consistency checks of DPM backups. When a DPM server is having problems backing up a target destination, a DPM alert is generated. Additionally, when the data on a DPM server gets out of sync with the target server, manual intervention is required to initiate a consistency check of the DPM protection group.

All of these alerts are sent to SCOM, and SCOM actions can be used to page or alert an administrator to check on the status of a target server or the DPM server, or a consistency check of the DPM protection group can be initiated to ensure backups are being processed properly.

To install the DPM Central Console on a system, log on to the system on which you want to install the DPM Central Console by using a domain user account. The domain user account needs to be a member of the local administrators group of the system. Execute the DPM Setup Wizard (`setup.exe`) from the installation media or an ISO file, or use a copy of the setup files from a shared network location. Once the wizard has started, use the following steps to complete the installation:

1. In the Data Protection Manager 2012 window, select the Install DPM Central Console option.

2. Read and select the I Accept the License Terms and Conditions option, and then click OK.

3. At the Welcome screen, click Next.

4. Then select Install Central Console Server-Side and Client-Side Components (if you are sitting at the SCOM server and you want it to be both the SCOM monitoring server for DPM alerts as well as a central DPM administration console) or Install Just the Central Console Server Side-Components or Just the Central Console Client-Side Components, and then click Next.

5. If you are installing the Central Console server-side, you will be prompted to install the DPM Discovery and Monitoring and the DPM Library management packs. The management packs are `Microsoft.SystemCenter.DataProtectionManager.2011.Discovery.mp` and `Microsoft.SystemCenter.DataProtectionManager.2011.Library.mp` from the `c:\Program Files\Microsoft DPM\Management Packs\` directory that were copied onto the SCOM server in step 2. After installation of the management packs, continue with the installation.

6. After installation of the Central Console server-side components, click Close, and then start the System Center Operations Manager Console. SCOM will have an Alert view and a State view for DPM servers. A sample State view of DPM protection groups in SCOM is shown in Figure 10.12.

10

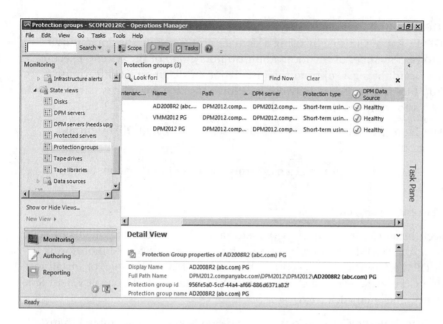

FIGURE 10.12   State view of DPM 2012 protection groups in SCOM.

7. For a system with the Central Console client-side components install, launch the DPM 2012 Central Console to manage all DPM servers and protection groups.

NOTE

Once the DPM Central Console server components have been installed on the SCOM server, you need to make override changes on the server running SCOM. The changes are noted in Table 10.5

TABLE 10.5   SCOM Override Parameters

	Default	Override Value
Health Service Handle Count Threshold	2,000	8,000
Health Service Private Bytes Threshold	100MB	1GB
Monitoring Host Handle Count Threshold	2,000	8,000
Monitoring Host Private Bytes Threshold	100MB	1GB

To override the Operations Manager monitors, do the following:

1. Log on to the SCOM server with a user account that is a member of the Operations Manager Advanced Operator role.

2. In the SCOM Console, click on the Authoring button.

3. In the authoring pane, click to expand the Management Pack Objects, and then click Monitors.

4. On the SCOM Console toolbar, click Overrides, and then select Override the Monitor.

5. After you choose which group of objects you want to override, the Override Properties dialog box opens.

6. Click to place a check mark in the Override column next to each setting you want to override.

7. Select a management pack from the Select Destination Management Pack option.

8. Make the override changes noted in Table 10.5.

9. Click OK when completed.

Running administration tasks from the central console is the same as running administration tasks from the default DPM Administrator Console and is detailed in Chapter 11 on specifically targeting application servers like Exchange, SharePoint, and SQL for backup, recovery, and administration.

Using Custom Volumes

In certain cases, you might want to store protected data using a location outside of the DPM storage pool. For example:

▶ Regulatory requirements specify that data needs to be partitioned off and isolated.

▶ Data criticality requires it to be separated onto a high-performance LUN.

▶ Performance limitations can only be solved by separating the I/O-intensive DPM workloads across multiple spindles.

To handle these situations, and others, you can assign a custom volume to a protection group member (data source) in place of the DPM storage pool. A custom volume is any volume that is attached to the DPM server that doesn't contain system and program files. To use a custom volume for a protection group member, two custom volumes must be available for use. One volume is used to store the replica, whereas the other stores recovery points.

Use the following steps to assign a custom volume when creating a new protection group:

1. Log on to the DPM server using a domain user account that is a member of the local administrators group.

2. Using Disk Management, create two volumes of the desired size and name.

3. Next, open the DPM 2012 Administrator Console using either the desktop or Start menu icon.

4. Once the console has loaded, on the taskbar, click New and select Create Protection Group.

5. On the Welcome to the New Protection Group Wizard page, click Next.

6. On the Select Protection Group Type page, choose the desired protection group type, and then click Next.

7. On the Select Group Members page, select the desired protection group members, and then click Next.

8. On the Select Data Protection Method page, ensure that the desired data protection method is selected, and then click Next.

9. On the Specify Short-Term Goals page, specify your desired short-term protection goals, and then click Next.

10. On the Review Disk Allocation page, click Modify.

11. In the Modify Disk Allocation dialog box, change the storage type to Custom Volume on the desired data source, and then define the replica volume, recovery volume, and format option.

NOTE

If the custom volume is used in a storage network, do not choose to format the volume.

12. When you are finished defining the custom volumes, click OK and then click Next.

13. Complete the Create New Protection Group Wizard and on the Summary page, click Create Group.

When using custom volumes, it is important to understand that the selection of a storage pool or custom volume for a protection group member cannot be modified after the group is created. To change the storage location for a group member, that member must first be removed from a protection group and then added back to the protection group as a new member. Therefore, as a general rule, you can only specify the usage of a custom volume for new members that are being added to the protection group.

Recovering Data

One of the main features of DPM, when short-term disk protection is used, is the ease with which administrators can find and recover data. Perform the following steps to find and recover data:

1. Log on to the DPM server using a domain user account that is a member of the local administrators group.

2. Next, open the DPM 2012 Administrator Console using either the desktop or Start menu icon.

3. Once the console has loaded, on the left side, click Recovery.

4. Using either the Browse or Search sections, find the recovery item that needs to be recovered, as shown in Figure 10.13.

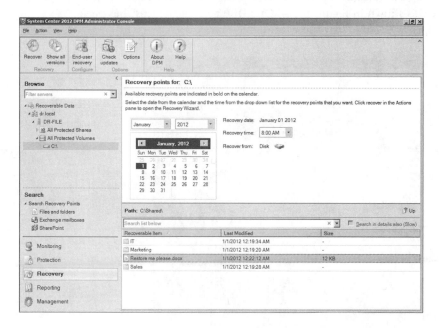

FIGURE 10.13   Finding protected data to recover.

5. Once you have selected the recovery item to recover, click Recover in the tool ribbon.

6. After the Recovery Wizard has started, the Review Recovery Selection page is shown. Review the recovery selections and then click Next.

7. On the Select Recovery Type page, select the Recover to the Original Location option, and then click Next. Alternatively, you can also recover a recovery item to an alternate location or copy the data to tape. These options are useful if you need to verify or analyze the data that is being recovered.

> **NOTE**
>
> If you use the Copy to Tape option, the entire volume will be copied to tape and more data than what was selected will be restored.

8. On the Specify Recovery Options page, ensure that the Overwrite and the Apply Security Settings of the Destination Computer options are selected. By choosing these two options, any existing items will be overwritten and then inherit the security settings from the target or parent folder.

10

9. Once you have finished choosing the specific recovery options, click Next.

10. On the Summary page, review the recovery settings, and then click Recover.

11. Next, the status and results of the recovery process are shown on the Recovery Status page, as shown in Figure 10.14. Once the recovery process has been completed, click Close to exit the wizard.

FIGURE 10.14   Recovery Status page.

Summary

This chapter, dedicated to Data Protection Manager 2012, hopefully provided you with a better understanding of the DPM product. Everything from DPM's background, to planning a deployment, to installing the solution, to basic administration tasks was covered. After reading this chapter, you should now also understand that DPM is an extremely powerful tool that is designed to simplify the backup and recovery of data for Microsoft applications and servers. In doing so, DPM attempts to ensure your data is continuously protected regardless of the organization's size and complexity. Chapter 11 extends the basic concepts covered in this chapter to specific guidance on backing up Microsoft Exchange, SharePoint, and SQL Server.

Best Practices

The following are best practices from this chapter:

▶ Do not install DPM on domain controllers, Exchange servers, or Operations Manager management or Gateway servers.

▶ For most enterprise deployments, the recommended protection method is to use D2D2T or D2D2C.

▶ DPM can be deployed onto a virtual machine. However, when a virtual machine is used, the storage pool needs to be connected by using pass-through disks or iSCSI.

▶ Although the DPM Installation Wizard attempts to install prerequisite software, it is always a best practice to understand what requirements need to be met before installing a server application.

▶ Spend time mapping out your DPM deployment. Failure to fully understand the business requirements and then designing a DPM installation to meet those requirements might result in data loss or worse.

▶ If you plan to only use tape-based protection, you do not need to plan for DPM disk storage requirements.

▶ When creating a storage group and adding members, plan the selection of a storage pool or custom volume because these attributes of a data source cannot be modified once storage pool or custom volume is added as a member of a storage group.

▶ For data that is on a system volume, protect the individual folders or shares instead of the entire volume.

▶ SharePoint databases cannot be protected as a SQL Server data source. Instead, they should be included as part of a SharePoint protection group.

▶ Plan to use a separate individual tape for each protection group.

▶ When planning to encrypt tape data, ensure that the proper encryption certificate has been imported and you are managing the life cycle of that certificate.

▶ Being able to automate DPM tasks is a key concept to understand. By using the DPM Management Shell, you can integrate data protection and recovery tasks with the rest of the System Center Enterprise Suite applications.

▶ Consider using the DPM Central Console in conjunction with SCOM 2012 if you are managing and administering multiple DPM servers. The Central Console can assist in consolidating administrative tasks for protection groups from multiple DPM host servers.

10

▶ Integrate DPM with System Center Operations Manager to leverage the capabilities of SCOM for monitoring and alerting the state of DPM backups and data consistency.

▶ If the custom volume is used in a storage network, choose not to to format the volume.

▶ Plan volume deployment in advance. Keep in mind that protected volumes must be NTFS with a minimal partition size of at least 1GB.

CHAPTER 11

Using Data Protection Manager 2012 to Protect File Systems, Exchange, SQL, and SharePoint

IN THIS CHAPTER

▶ Protecting File Servers

▶ Protecting System State

▶ Protecting Exchange Servers

▶ Protecting SQL Servers

▶ Protecting SharePoint Farms

▶ Protecting Virtualized Environments

▶ Best Practices

For most Microsoft operating systems and server applications, the act of managing backup and restore processes can prove challenging for an IT administrator. It's not that solutions such as SharePoint are hard to back up and restore. Instead, each solution from Microsoft tends to have its own quirks, gotchas, and processes that need to be taken into account when trying to protect its data. As such, the need to customize backup and restoration processes for each solution is what makes protecting them more difficult than it should be.

In Chapter 10, "Data Protection Manager 2012 Design, Planning, Implementation, and Administration," you were introduced to Data Protection Manager (DPM), how it protects data, and how to install and manage it. With this chapter, the focus now shifts toward how DPM can be used to effectively protect Microsoft solutions such as the Windows file system, Exchange Server, SQL Server, and SharePoint farms. As you learn in this chapter, for each of these solutions, DPM has been tailored to meet their data protection needs, from being able to protect Exchange Server 2010 Database Availability Groups (DAG) to performing full-farm SharePoint recoveries. DPM is a very powerful data protection tool when it comes to protecting Microsoft solutions. By using DPM, you can significantly improve your backup and recovery processes in a Microsoft-centric environment and hopefully reduce the headaches that you might now be experiencing.

Protecting File Servers

As discussed in Chapter 10, DPM has supported replication and data protection for file server data since the initial DPM 2006 release of the product. In fact, with that release of DPM, file server data was pretty much all it protected. With the DPM 2012 release, the number of different Microsoft technologies that DPM can protect has vastly increased, but at its core, DPM still offers file server data protection for Windows Server from 2003 through 2008 R2.

The primary benefit of using DPM to protect file server data is its support for file versioning based on previous VSS snapshots taken from various points in time. Obviously, this differs from most backup solutions that rely on versions of data based on a single point in time (typically once a day or once a week). Also, as expected, when using DPM to protect file server data, you are not just limited to protecting individual files. You can, in fact, protect and recover entire volumes, shares, and folders. To illustrate this, a matrix between the allowed file server data sources and the data that can be recovered from them is shown in Table 11.1.

TABLE 11.1   File Server Data Sources and Recoverable Data

Allowed Data Sources	Recoverable Data
Volume	Volume
Share	Share
Folder	Folder
	File data (versions)

When adding a data source as a member of a protection group, any child objects (data sources) under that data source are then also automatically selected. This is a key concept to understand when protecting file data because it means you can just select a top-level data source to protect entire volumes and folder hierarchies. Additionally, you can also specify exclusions by either unselecting child data sources under a top-level data source or defining file exclusions, as shown in Figure 11.1.

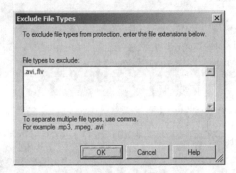

FIGURE 11.1   Defining file type exclusions.

If you use exclusions, it simply tells the DPM protection agent not to synchronize the data you have excluded. However, it is important to remember that when items are excluded they cannot be protected by DPM at all. This is because once a data source is a member of a protection group, that data source will then be unavailable for selection into additional protection groups. By design, data sources can only be members of one protection group at a time. However, this doesn't preclude placing different data sources on the same file server into different protection groups.

> **NOTE**
>
> A computer that is protected by DPM can have multiple protection groups protecting data sources. However, all these protection groups must be from one DPM server. In other words, a protected computer can only be protected by a single DPM server regardless of how many DPM servers have been deployed.

In addition to file server data that you can manually exclude from a data source, the DPM protection agent also automatically excludes the following:

- Recycle Bin, paging files, System Volume Information folder

- Volumes that are not formatted with NTFS

- Encrypted files and unencrypted files within encrypted folders

- Reparse points, including Distributed File System (DFS) links, Single Instance Store (SIS) files, and junction points

- NTFS hard links

DPM can also be used to protect file server data located on clusters, in DFS namespaces, and on mount points. The details about these supported scenarios and how they are protected are as follows.

Data in a DFS Namespace

When protecting data in a DFS namespace, you cannot protect file shares through their DFS namespace paths. Instead, DPM can only protect data located in a DFS namespace by using server-specific local paths. This is because DFS is designed to provide location transparency and redundancy by allowing shares in multiple different locations to be logically grouped under one folder. In other words, the data that is located in a DFS namespace is somewhat redundant because if a server fails, a Windows client will transparently select a different server to use and the data is replicated between the different servers that are hosting the data. Therefore, if DPM were DFS aware, and it attempted to protect each target under the same root or link, there might be the possibility of synchronization issues and a huge increase in the amount of storage needed to protect DFS-based data. Instead, the recommended approach to protecting data in a DFS namespace is to only protect a single "copy" of the data located on a server-specific local path.

Data on a File Server Cluster

Because DPM is cluster aware, you can also protect data that is located on file servers that have been clustered using Microsoft Cluster Service (MSCS) or the Failover Clustering feature on Windows Server 2008. To do this, you need to ensure that the protection agent is installed on each node in the cluster that owns the file data resources that you intend to protect. Once this requirement has been met, DPM will be able to continue protecting the data even if a failover happens in the cluster.

> **NOTE**
>
> DPM cannot be used to protect a cluster's quorum disk.

Data on Mount Points

Mount points are a subset of NTFS5 reparse point functionality, which allows you to connect a volume at a mount point directory within a parent volume without having to assign a drive letter to that volume. As a result, you can consolidate multiple volumes under one drive letter. A typical use for mount points is in very large Exchange Server deployments that call for fast recovery times. In these deployments, it is common practice to place each database and transaction log pair on its own set of logical unit numbers (LUNs). For example, with an Exchange Server 2007 mailbox server, there can be a maximum of 50 storage groups and each storage group would have its own transaction log LUN and database LUN. In these cases, the number of available drive letters would be quickly exhausted and mount points would have to be used to handle the number of LUNs.

Luckily, DPM can protect data that is located on a mount point. However, DPM will not protect the mount point metadata. This means that to recover data that is located on a mount point, you must first manually re-create the mount point hierarchy before you can attempt to recover the data.

> **NOTE**
>
> DPM does not support the protection of mount points within mount points (nested mount points).

Protecting System State

The System State is a collection of system-specific data that is maintained by Windows and can be backed up as a single unit, including items such as the Registry, COM+ Class Registration database, boot files (including the system files), and system files that are under Windows File Protection. A System State backup is not an entire system backup, but a backup is designed to return a computer to a known state should the need arise.

If a computer already has the protection agent installed, DPM can be used to protect its System State. Just like file server data, a protected computer's System State is shown as a data source, which can be added as a member of a protection group. An example of this is shown in Figure 11.2.

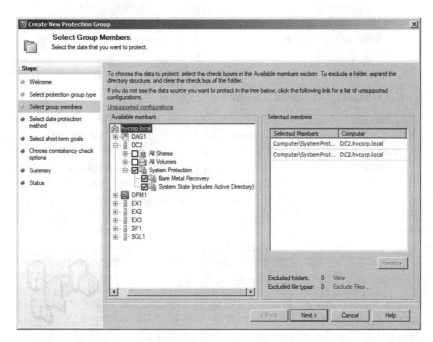

FIGURE 11.2   Adding System State data sources.

To back up the System State, DPM leverages Windows Backup to generate a System State backup and a resulting (.bkf) file. This file is then copied to the DPM server and saved to the specified medium defined by the protection group. Depending on if the computer is just a workstation or a server that has different server roles, the resulting System State backup will include different data, as shown in Table 11.2.

TABLE 11.2   System State Data

Computer Type or Role	System State Data
Base Server or Workstation	Boot files
	The COM+ Class Registration database
	Registry hives
Active Directory Domain Services	Active Directory (NTDS) files
	The system volume (SYSVOL)
Active Directory Certificate Services	Certificate Services database
Cluster Node	Cluster Service metadata

Lastly, it is generally recommended that System State backups be placed in their own protection groups. This recommendation is made because System State data tends not to change very often. As such, it might be more efficient to have a less-frequent backup schedule for System State backups when compared with backups of file and application data. However, in certain recovery scenarios, it might make more sense to protect a computer's System State data in the same protection group with the rest of its data so that the entire server can be reliably restored to a known state along with its data should the need arise.

Protecting Exchange Servers

One of the hardest aspects of managing any Exchange Server environment is ensuring that the related data is always protected and recoverable. It is not that the act of protecting or recovering Exchange data is necessarily difficult. Instead, because the Exchange Server database architecture is transaction based, any backup and recovery solution that is being used needs to be tailored toward Exchange itself. Although many solutions have been used over the years to handle protecting Exchange data, the previous norm has mostly been to rely on bulky brick-level backups, complex recovery processes, and large data gaps and to expect a lack of backup and restore granularity. When compounded with Exchange's often notorious reputation for suffering from "database inconsistencies during a disaster," there was a huge void that needed to be filled to help administrators take better control of protecting their Exchange data.

Therefore, it seems only logical, as with protecting System State and file server data, that DPM can also be used to protect Exchange Server 2003 through 2010. By using DPM, you can utilize its lossless recovery abilities to ensure that recoverable data includes not only last night's backup, but also the most recent transactions. To do this, a protection agent performs a full backup (typically once a day) and uses the resulting VSS snapshot to identify what data has changed. Then, the agent synchronizes all of the changed blocks to the DPM server. Next, to ensure that administrators can recover Exchange data using DPM up to the latest recovery point (as often as 15 minutes), the protection agent performs an incremental VSS snapshot to copy committed sequential transaction logs to the DPM server. Lastly, during a recovery operation, DPM also has the ability to play back any other surviving Exchange transaction logs, thus ensuring as little data is lost as possible.

In addition to DPM's lossless abilities, its feature set also tackles the need to conduct single mailbox restores. In the past, if an individual mailbox had to be restored, either the entire database had to be restored, or administrators had to use third-party solutions. With DPM, administrators can select an individual mailbox and restore it to an Exchange 2010 recovery database or Exchange 2003 or 2007 recovery storage group, and then use native Exchange tools to move the mailbox data back to a production database. To better illustrate DPM's ability to granularly recover Exchange data, a matrix of allowed data sources and the data that can be recovered is shown in Table 11.3.

TABLE 11.3   Exchange Server Data Sources and Recoverable Data

Exchange Server Version	Allowed Data Sources	Recoverable Data
Exchange Server 2003 (SP2)	Storage group	Storage group Database
Exchange Server 2007		Mailbox
Exchange Server 2010	DAG/database Database	Database Mailbox

Protecting Exchange Databases

The steps used to protect Exchange Server 2010 databases using DPM are almost identical regardless of whether you are trying to only protect databases on a standalone mailbox server or an entire DAG. For the purposes of this example, the following steps describe how to protect databases on servers in a DAG:

1. While logged on to the DPM server as a domain user account that is a member of the local administrators group, open the DPM 2012 Administrator Console.

2. Next, ensure that all members of the DAG have the protection agent installed and the agent is reachable with a normal status.

> **NOTE**
>
> With DPM 2012, you can split the protection of DAG nodes between DPM servers. In other words, within a DAG that has five nodes, you can have one DPM server protect two nodes, and then have the other DPM server protect the other three nodes. However, for the purposes of these steps, all the nodes of the DAG are being protected by a single DPM server.

3. Now, click Protection on the navigation bar, and then click New in the toolbar.

4. Once the Create New Protection Group Wizard has started, click past the Welcome page, select the Servers Protection Group Type option, and then click Next.

5. On the Select Group Members page, use the interface to add the database copies that you want to protect into the protection group, as shown in Figure 11.3.

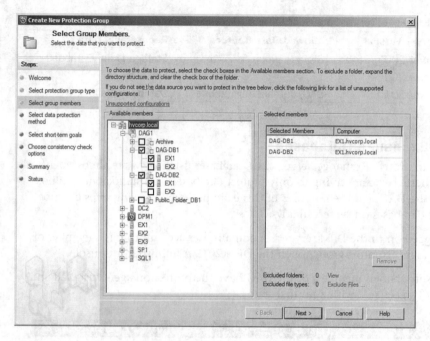

FIGURE 11.3   Adding database copies.

NOTE

In this example, you should notice that each of the two mailbox servers that are part of the DAG named DAG1 are hosting a copy of the databases DAG1-DB1 and DAG1-DB2. However, only one copy of each database is being added into the protection group. Technically, this is all you need because individual databases in Exchange Server 2010 are not tied to a particular Exchange server. Therefore, you can recover a database by using backups from different database copies on different servers in the same DAG. Or, you can also add additional copies of the database into the protection group. Ultimately, the choice is yours as to how many protected copies you want of the same database and associated log files.

6. Once you have finished selecting the desired database copies, click Next.

7. On the Select Data Protection Method page, type a new name for the protection group in the Protection Group Name box, choose the desired protection methods, and then click Next.

8. On the Specify Exchange Protection Options page, choose if you want DPM to run the Exchange Server Database Utilities (Eseutil.exe) tool to check the integrity for both a database and its log files or just for its log files. For DAG servers, it is recommended that the ESEUTIL tool only be run for the log files.

> **NOTE**
>
> Before configuring the Eseutil integrity check option, you must first copy the
> `Eseutil.exe` and the supporting DLL (`ese.dll`) from an Exchange server to the DPM
> server (`c:\Program Files\Microsoft Data Protection Manager\DPM\bin`).
> Additionally, the `Eseutil.exe` and `ese.dll` versions must be from the most recent
> edition of Exchange Server. If these files are updated on an Exchange server (either
> through an upgrade or by installing an update), you must then update these files on
> the DPM server as well.

9. Once you have finished selecting the desired Eseutil integrity check option, click Next.

10. On the Specify Exchange DAG Protection page, specify which database copies should be selected for a full backup and which copies should be selected for a copy backup. If you have selected multiple copies of a database to be protected by DPM, only one copy should be selected for full backup, as shown in Figure 11.4.

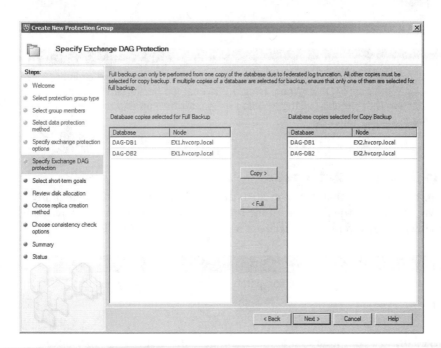

FIGURE 11.4   Specifying Exchange DAG protection.

11. Once you have finished configuring the desired DAG protection, click Next.

12. On the Specify Short-Term Goals page, specify your desired short-term protection goals, and then click Next.

13. On the Review Disk Allocation page, review the disk allocations that DPM recommends for the protection group, and then click Next.

14. If you have a tape device attached, the Specify Long-Term Protection page is shown. Use this page to specify your long-term protection goals, and then click Next.

15. Next, if you have a tape device attached, the Select Library and Tape Details page is also shown. Use this page to specify the library and configuration options for the backup tapes, and then click Next.

16. On the Choose Replica Creation Method page, use the Replica in DPM Server section to define how the initial replica of the protected data should be created, and then click Next.

17. On the Consistency Check Options page, specify the desired option for how the consistency check for the protection group will be handled, and then click Next.

18. On the Summary page, review the information about the protection group and then click Create Group.

19. Next, the status and results of the protection group creation process are shown on the Status page. Once the protection group has been created, click Close to exit the wizard.

> **NOTE**
>
> As a general rule, Exchange Server databases should not be configured to use circular logging when being protected by DPM. When using a VSS-enabled backup utility such as DPM in conjunction with circular logging, you can encounter backup and recovery issues, up to and including data loss.

Restoring an Exchange Database

The steps used to recover an Exchange Server 2010 database using DPM differ depending on if you are trying to restore the database to the original location or to an alternate location. Use the following steps to restore a database to the original location:

> **NOTE**
>
> This method overwrites an existing production database and therefore may destroy data.

1. While logged on to a computer as a domain user account that is a member of the Exchange Organization Management and Server Management groups, open the Exchange Management Shell (EMS).

2. Next, execute the following command against the targeted database to allow restoring a database from a backup:

```
Get-MailboxDatabase -Identity <database name> | Set-MailboxDatabase
-AllowFileRestore $True
```

3. Next, open the DPM 2012 Administrator Console.

4. Once the console has loaded, click Recovery on the navigation bar.

5. Select All Protected Exchange Data for the server whose backup from which the database is to be restored, as shown in Figure 11.5.

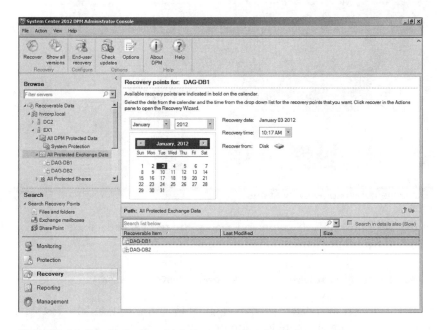

FIGURE 11.5   Choosing which Exchange database to recover.

6. Once you have selected the database to recover, click Recover in the toolbar.

7. After the Recovery Wizard has started, the Review Recovery Selection page is shown. Review the recovery selections and then click Next.

8. On the Select Recovery Type page, the Recover to Original Exchange Server Location option is already selected (as it is the only available option if the latest recovery point has been chosen); click Next to continue.

9. On the Specify Recovery Options page, ensure that the Mount the Databases After They Are Recovered option is selected, and then click Next.

10. On the Summary page, review the recovery settings, and then click Recover.

11. Next, the status and results of the recovery process are shown on the Recovery Status page, as shown in Figure 11.6. Once the recovery process has been completed, click Close to exit the wizard.

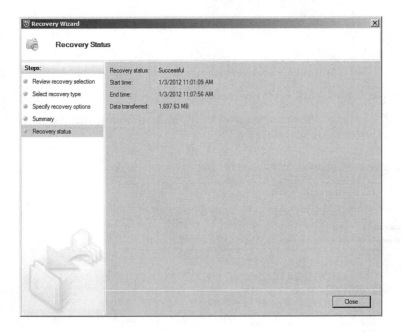

FIGURE 11.6   Exchange database recovery status.

12. Finally, execute the following EMS command against the recovered database to set
the `AllowFileRestore` property to `False`:

```
Set-MailboxDatabase -Identity <database name> -AllowFileRestore $False
```

In addition to being able to restore a database to its original location, you can also restore
a database to any of the following alternate location options:

▶ **Recover to Another Database on an Exchange Server**—Use this option to recover
the database to another Exchange server. This option might be used in scenarios
where restoring to the original Exchange server is not feasible and you want to use
the database portability feature to remap users to the restored database on another
server.

▶ **Recover to a Recovery Database**—Use this option to recover the database to a
recovery database. Once recovered, you can then mount the database and extract
data as part of a recovery operation to restore individual mailboxes or individual
items in a mailbox. This method does not overwrite an existing mailbox database,
so it is nondestructive. This option is the most commonly used method in Exchange
administration.

▶ **Copy to a Network Folder**—Use this option to recover the database and its log files
to a network location. This option is useful if you are trying to recover the database

into a lab environment, if you are recovering to another Exchange server and want to bring the database to a clean shutdown, or if you are planning to do some form of forensic analysis on the database. However, keep in mind that the recovery destinations (network locations) available for this option can only be volumes or shares that are protected by DPM.

▶ **Copy to Tape**—Use this option to recover the database to a tape. This option is useful if you need to recover the database to a medium that can be shipped offsite.

> **NOTE**
>
> The alternate location options are not available if you use the latest recovery point to recover from. Instead, you must either choose an earlier recovery point or a database copy that is only being protected using a copy backup.

How to Restore a Mailbox

To recover a mailbox, the process is the same regardless of whether you are trying to recover a mailbox that is located in a DAG or in a single mailbox database. To complete such a recovery, complete the following steps:

1. While logged on to a computer as a domain user account that is a member of the Exchange Organization Management and Server Management groups, open the EMS.

2. Next, execute the following command to create a recovery database:

```
New-MailboxDatabase -Recovery -Name <new database name> -Server <Exchange Server
Name> -EdbFilePath <path to EDB file> -LogFolderPath <path to log file folder>
```

> **NOTE**
>
> If you use an existing recovery database, you may need to execute the following command against the targeted data-base to allow restoring a database from a backup:
>
> ```
> Set-MailboxDatabase -Identity <recovery database name> -AllowFileRestore
> $True
> ```

3. Now, open the DPM 2012 Administrator Console.

4. Once the console has loaded, click Recovery on the navigation bar.

5. In the results pane, for Recovery time, change Latest to the desired recovery point time.

6. Expand the server whose backup from which the mailbox is to be restored and select the database, and then in the lower results pane, scroll to find and select the mailbox to be restored as shown in Figure 11.7.

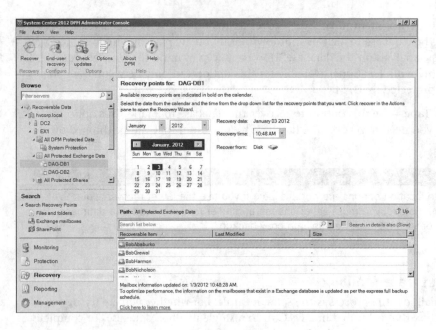

FIGURE 11.7   Choosing which mailbox to recover.

7. Once you have selected the mailbox to recover, click Recover in the toolbar.

8. After the Recovery Wizard has started, the Review Recovery Selection page is shown. Review the recovery selections and then click Next.

9. On the Select Recovery Type page, select the Recover Mailbox to an Exchange Server Database option, and then click Next to continue.

NOTE

If needed, you can also choose to recover the mailbox to either a network folder or to a tape.

10. On the Specify Destination page, browse to the Exchange server that has the intended recovery database and then provide the recovery database name that you created in step 2, as shown in Figure 11.8.

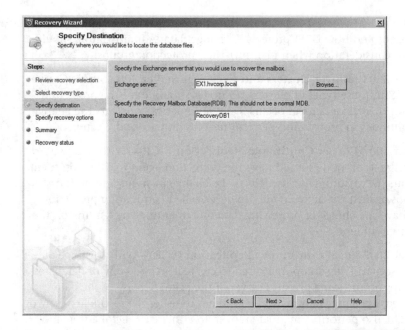

FIGURE 11.8   Specifying the recovery database information.

11. Once you have provided the recovery database information, click Next.

12. On the Specify Recovery Options page, click Next.

13. On the Summary page, review the recovery settings, and then click Recover.

14. Next, the status and results of the recovery process are shown on the Recovery Status page. Once the recovery process has been completed, click Close to exit the wizard.

15. Once the mailbox has been restored, use the following EMS commands to complete the recovery process:

```
Mount-Database -Identity <recovery database name>
Restore-Mailbox -Identity <mailbox name> -RecoveryDatabase <recovery database name>
```

In the Restore-Mailbox command, you may add any of several selection parameters to restore a subset of the content instead of all of it, which may be useful if you want to restore specific items.

Exchange High-Availability Caveats

Although DPM is a cluster-aware data protection solution and will continue protecting Exchange data even if an unplanned failover happens or if resources are shifted between cluster nodes, there are some caveats in relation to the different Exchange high-availability configurations and how DPM protects Exchange data. Administrators should take the following into consideration when planning their protection groups:

▶ **Exchange Server 2003 failover clusters and Exchange Server 2007 Single Copy Cluster (SCC)**—With these types of clusters, all nodes should have the protection agent installed on them. If a failover occurs, DPM automatically detects the change in status and continues to protect and perform restores only from the active node.

▶ **Exchange Server 2007 Cluster Continuous Replication (CCR)**—With this two-node type of cluster, each node should have the protection agent installed on them. If a failover occurs, DPM automatically detects the change in status and performs restore operations against the active node. However, when configuring protection, administrators have the choice of protecting data on either node depending on the needs of their environment.

▶ **Exchange Server 2007 Local Continuous Replication (LCR)**—With this type of high-availability scenario, log shipping is used to create a second copy of databases and storage groups on the same physical server. If the primary copy of the data becomes corrupted, Exchange automatically switches to using the secondary copy or administrators can also perform a manual failover. In either case, DPM automatically continues to protect the data using the active copy.

▶ **Exchange Server 2007 Standby Continuous Replication (SCR)**—With DPM, you can protect Exchange mailbox storage group replicas on SCR target nodes. However, as a general recommendation, protection of SCR target nodes should be done using a DPM server located within the same recovery site as the target. Generally, a backup of an SCR target should not be considered a replacement of a backup of the primary server or one of the cluster nodes.

▶ **Exchange Server 2010 DAG**—When protecting a DAG, the Create New Protection Group Wizard does not indicate which database copy is the active copy. Once the protection group has been created, changing the active database copy has no impact as DPM still continues protecting data using a passive database copy. However, changing the active database copy does affect the recovery process as DPM cannot perform database recoveries against a passive database copy. Therefore, before initiating a recovery, administrators must know which database copy is the active one. Lastly, the recovery process to an active database is the same as recovering to a standalone database. Then once the database has been recovered, the passive copies need to be synchronized with the recovered active database using the Resume-MailboxDatabaseCopy cmdlet.

Additional Considerations

Lastly, when using DPM to protect Exchange Server data, administrators should be aware of the following considerations:

- ▶ **Creating new storage groups or databases**—If you create a new Exchange 2003 or 2007 database within an already protected storage group, DPM automatically updates the protection group and protects the new database. However, if you create a new Exchange 2003 or 2007 storage group or a new Exchange 2010 database, you need to manually update the protection group or create a new protection group to protect these new data sources.

- ▶ **Changing storage group or database file paths**—After changing the file paths for a storage group or database, you need to run a consistency check on the protection group or replica to resume protection.

- ▶ **Dismounted databases**—While a database is dismounted, protection jobs for that database will fail.

- ▶ **Renaming storage groups or databases**—Storage groups and databases can be renamed without any additional steps that need to be taken.

- ▶ **Moving databases**—You can move Exchange 2003 or 2007 databases between storage groups; however, if the storage group is not protected, the database becomes unprotected. Additionally, if you are moving from an unprotected storage group to a protected storage group, the database becomes protected after a consistency check has been performed.

Protecting SQL Servers

Traditionally, there have been several different methods for protecting SQL Server databases. The first method is to ensure that no transactions can occur by taking the database offline and then backing up the database files. The second method is to use SQL Server's native backup tool, which relies on VSS and the SQL Server VSS writer to perform an online backup. The final method is to use a third-party backup tool, which might or might not employ VSS to perform a SQL Server backup.

In either case, most of the solutions that are designed to protect SQL Server databases all rely on single-point-in-time backups. However, like Exchange Server, SQL Server is a transaction-based application. Therefore, the data that is contained in a SQL Server database is constantly being updated and modified. Further complicating matters is the fact that SQL Server databases tend to host applications and data that are mission critical for organizations. In other words, there is a strong need to ensure that the data within these databases is continuously protected and can be recovered at any given time; the need for protecting SQL Server databases is a gap that DPM can easily fill thanks to its Continuous Data Protection features.

> **NOTE**
>
> Before you can start protecting data on a SQL Server 2005 SP1 instance, you must first enable and then start the SQL Server VSS Writer Service.

How to Protect SQL Server Databases

The steps used to protect SQL Server databases using DPM are almost identical regardless of whether you are trying to only protect databases on a standalone SQL Server instance or on a SQL Server cluster. For the purposes of this example, the following steps describe how to protect a database located on a standalone SQL Server instance:

1. While logged on to the DPM server as a domain user account that is a member of the local administrators group, open the DPM 2012 Administrator Console.

2. Next, ensure that the SQL Server has the protection agent installed and the agent is reachable with a normal status.

> **NOTE**
>
> When protecting a SQL Server cluster, all nodes of the cluster should have the DPM protection agent installed on them.

3. Now, click Protection on the navigation bar, and then click New in the taskbar.

4. Once the Create New Protection Group Wizard has started, click past the Welcome page, select the Servers Protection Group Type option, and then click Next.

5. On the Select Group Members page, use the interface to add the database, databases, or entire SQL Server instances that you want to protect into the protection group, as shown in Figure 11.9. On a nonclustered SQL server, the SQL objects are under the server object, whereas on a clustered SQL server, you will find the SQL objects under the cluster name.

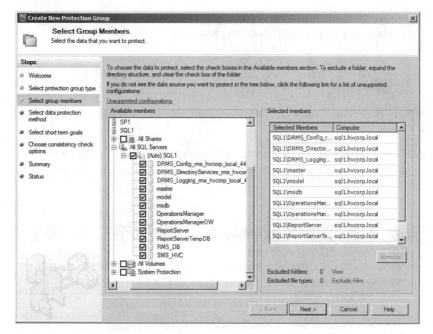

FIGURE 11.9   Adding SQL databases.

NOTE

For databases that are located in a SQL Server cluster, DPM represents the databases as part of the cluster in the Create New Protection Group Wizard.

6. Once you have finished selecting the desired database(s) or SQL Server instances, click Next.

7. On the Select Data Protection Method page, type a new name for the protection group in the Protection Group Name box, choose the desired protection methods, and then click Next.

8. On the Specify Short-Term Goals page, specify your desired short-term protection goals, and then click Next.

9. On the Review Disk Allocation page, review the disk allocations that DPM recommends for the protection group, and then click Next.

10. If you have a tape device attached, the Specify Long-Term Protection page is shown. Use this page to specify your long-term protection goals, and then click Next.

11. Next, if you have a tape device attached, the Select Library and Tape Details page is also shown. Use this page to specify the library and configuration options for the backup tapes, and then click Next.

12. On the Choose Replica Creation Method page, use the Replica in DPM Server section to define how the initial replica of the protected data should be created, and then click Next.

13. On the Consistency Check Options page, specify the desired option for how the consistency check for the protection group will be handled, and then click Next.

14. On the Summary page, review the information about the protection group and then click Create Group.

15. Next, the status and results of the protection group creation process are shown on the Status page. Once the protection group has been created, click Close to exit the wizard.

> **NOTE**
>
> Being able to protect an entire SQL Server instance is a new feature in DPM 2012. If you choose to protect an entire SQL Server instance, all new databases added to that instance are automatically protected.

Restoring a SQL Server Database

The steps used to recover a SQL Server database using DPM differ slightly depending on if you are trying to restore the database to its original instance of SQL Server or to an alternate location. Use the following steps to restore a database to its original instance of SQL Server:

1. While logged on to the DPM server as a domain user account that is a member of the local administrators group, open the DPM 2012 Administrator Console.

2. Once the console has loaded, click Recovery on the navigation bar.

3. Using either the Browse or Search tabs, find the database that needs to be recovered, as shown in Figure 11.10.

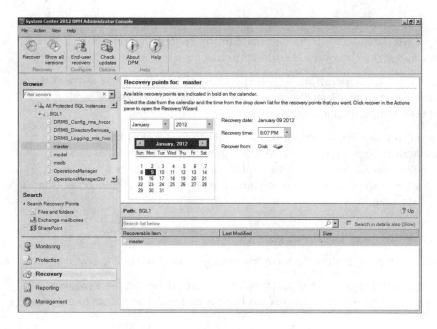

FIGURE 11.10   Choosing which SQL database to recover.

4. Once you have selected the database to recover, in the details pane, for Recovery time select the desired recovery point (do not select Latest), and then click Recover in the toolbar.

5. After the Recovery Wizard has started, the Review Recovery Selection page is shown. Review the recovery selections and then click Next.

6. On the Select Recovery Type page, select the Recover to Original Instance of SQL Server (Overwrite Database) option, and then click Next to continue.

NOTE

When you recover a SQL database to its original instance of SQL Server, the original database is overwritten using the replica that was chosen to recover the database with. If you are trying to attempt a lossless recovery, you then need to restore the database using the latest recovery point, and have DPM replay any residual live transactions from the SQL Server log files (LDF).

Relationships between databases must also be taken into account when planning database protection and recovery to maintain data integrity.

7. On the Specify Database State page, select either the Leave Database Operational option or Leave Database Non-Operational But Able to Restore Additional Transaction Logs, and then click Next to continue.

   ▶ **Leave Database Operational**—When you use this option, DPM recovers the database using the selected recovery point, replays necessary transaction logs, and then remounts the database.

   ▶ **Leave Database Non-Operational But Able to Restore Additional Transaction Logs**—When you use this option, DPM recovers the database using the selected recovery point, replays necessary transaction logs, but does not remount the database so that you can replay additional transaction logs (if you have them).

8. On the Specify Recovery Options page, click Next.

9. On the Summary page, review the recovery settings, and then click Recover.

10. Next, the status and results of the recovery process are shown on the Recovery Status page. Once the recovery process has been completed, click Close to exit the wizard.

In addition to being able to restore a database to its original SQL Server instance, you can also restore a database to any of the following alternate location options:

▶ **Recover to Any Instance of SQL Server**—Use this option to recover the database to another instance of SQL Server. This option is particularly useful if you need to test recovery procedures, want to create a lab environment, or are trying to migrate the database to a new instance of SQL Server. However, keep in mind that when you recover a database to a different instance of SQL Server, DPM will not be able to perform a lossless recovery by replaying the transaction logs.

▶ **Copy to a Network Folder**—Use this option to recover the database and its log files to a network location. This option is useful if you need physical access to the database and log files.

▶ **Copy to Tape**—Use this option to recover the database to a tape. This option is useful if you need to recover the database to a medium that can be shipped offsite.

How to Conduct a Self-Service Restore

In DPM 2012, a new feature called the DPM Self Service Recovery Tool allows authorized SQL Server database owners to perform self-service database recoveries without the need of intervention by a DPM administrator. To configure this feature, the DPM administrator must first create a DPM role, which grants authorized SQL Server database owners the needed DPM rights to perform recovery operations for databases that they own. To create the DPM role, complete the following steps:

1. While logged on to the DPM server as a domain user account that is a member of the local administrators group, open the DPM Management Shell.

2. Next, execute the following command to create the DPM role:

```
$Role = New-DPMRole –Name "SQL Self-Service Restore" –Description "Perform self-
service restores of SQL Server databases on server SERVERNAME" –DPMServerName <DPM
server name>
```

3. Now, add a domain security group to the role, which should have the ability to recover databases:

```
Add-DPMSecurityGroup -DpmRole $Role -SecurityGroups "<Domain NetBIOS Name>\
<Security Group Name>"
```

4. Next, use the following commands to identify the databases that the SQL administrators can recover and then add them to the role:

```
$DatabasesForEndUserRecovery = $null
$ListOfPGs = Get-ProtectionGroup –DPMServerName <DPM Server Name>
$ListOfPGs | ForEach-Object {if ($_.FriendlyName -eq "<Protection Group Name>") {$PG
= $_ ; break}}
$DatasourcesInPG = Get-Datasource $PG
$DatasourcesInPG | ForEach-Object {if ($_.LogicalPath -eq "<Database Instance
Name>") {$DatabasesForEndUserRecovery += ,$_}}
Add-DPMRecoveryItem  -DPMRole $Role -type SQLDatabase -Datasources
$DatabasesForEndUserRecovery
Add-DPMRecoveryItem  -DPMRole $Role -type SQLINSTANCE -SqlInstances "<SQL Server
Instance Name>"
```

5. Lastly, save the role using the following command:

```
Set-DPMRole -DpmRole $Role
```

> **NOTE**
>
> Alternatively, DPM roles can be created and managed using the Self Service Recovery Tool for SQL Server in the DPM Administrator Console.

After you have created the DPM role, SQL administrators can now use the DPM Self Service Recovery Tool to perform recoveries of SQL Server databases that are protected by a DPM server. Use the following steps to use the DPM Self Service Recovery Tool to complete a database recovery:

> **NOTE**
>
> If your Active Directory environment has the Schema Master FSMO role hosted in a
> different domain from the DPM server such as a forest root domain, the Active
> Directory schema will need to be extended by running the
> DPMADSchemaExtension.exe tool on the domain controller that hosts the Schema
> Master role in the other domain, using an account that is a member of the schema
> admins group. This utility is located on the DPM server in the folder c:\Program
> Files\Microsoft System Center 2012\DPM\DPM\End User Recovery.

1. Have the SQL administrator install the DPM Self Service Recovery Tool. By default,
   the installation packages are located on the DPM 2012 installation CD in the
   DPMSqlEURInstaller folder.

2. Once the DPM Self Service Recovery Tool has been installed, have the SQL administrator open the DPM Self Service Recovery Tool. This console can be used to list
   recovery jobs for SQL Server databases and start recoveries, rerun recoveries, or stop
   recoveries, as shown in Figure 11.11.

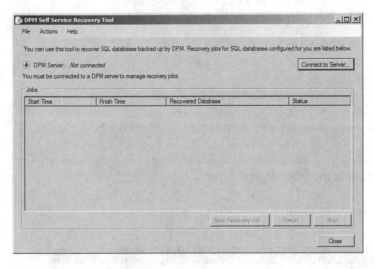

FIGURE 11.11   The DPM Self Service Recovery Tool.

3. After the console has opened, click Connect to Server, provide the DPM server
   name, and then click Connect.

4. Next, click New Recovery Job. This opens the Recovery Wizard, as shown in Figure
   11.12, and SQL administrators can then complete the database recovery as already
   described earlier in this section.

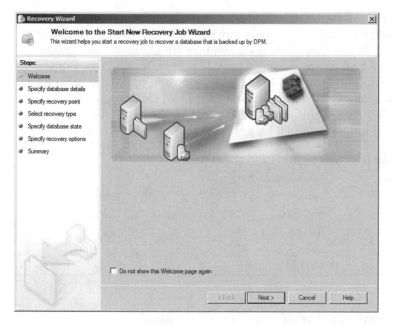

FIGURE 11.12   Completing a database recovery using the DPM Self Service Recovery Tool.

> **NOTE**
>
> The SQL End User Recovery feature uses TCP port 11313 to communicate with the DPM server. To use this feature, you need to ensure that Windows Firewall has been configured to allow incoming connections on this port.

Protecting SharePoint Farms

Unfortunately, certain components in a SharePoint farm rely on other components for the farm to function. For example, the configuration database and the Central Administration content database of a SharePoint farm must be in sync. Naturally, keeping these two databases in perfect sync tends to add a certain amount of complexity when it comes to backup and recovery procedures. That is why until DPM introduced the ability to protect an entire SharePoint farm, the options for SharePoint data protection were a bit limited.

In the past, you could use the tools included with SharePoint to back up and restore a SharePoint farm. For example, the Central Administration website contains a UI-based tool to perform backup and recovery processes. Or, if you were more command-line inclined, you could also use the Stsadm tool to do the same thing. When combined with Windows Scheduler, the Stsadm tool could be used to schedule regular backups, giving you an almost complete backup solution. Additionally, you could also rely on SQL Server tools to back up the SharePoint databases or also turn to third-party backup solutions.

Sadly, the issue with all of the aforementioned data protection solutions (except possibly third-party solutions that have done their homework to integrate with SharePoint and Windows Server Volume Shadow Copy Service) is that they fail to provide end-to-end protection from an entire farm down to a single item. In a sense, they all lack a single streamlined approach, which is a gap that DPM fills by being able to provide data protection for not only a SharePoint farm, but also its related content databases, search data, sites, and files or lists. To illustrate this, a matrix between the allowed SharePoint data sources and the data that can be recovered from them is shown in Table 11.4.

TABLE 11.4   SharePoint Data Sources and Recoverable Data

Allowed Data Sources	Recoverable Data
Farm	Farm
	Database
	Search data
	Site
	File or list

Preparing SharePoint for Protection

The first step in preparing SharePoint for protection by DPM is to ensure that the protection agent has been installed on all servers that have content you intend to protect. For example, in a simple SharePoint farm that consists of two Web Front End (WFE) servers, one index server, and a two-node clustered SQL Server instance, you would install the protection agent on both nodes in the SQL Server cluster, on the index server (if you are planning on protecting search content), and on only one of the WFE servers.

> **NOTE**
>
> WFE servers do not host content. Therefore, technically only one Web Front End server needs to have the protection agent installed in a SharePoint farm because it needs to serve as an entry point for DPM to protect the SharePoint farm and it contains any customizations that have been made to SharePoint, which should be protected as part of the farm.

After installing the protection agent, the next step is to configure the SharePoint farm for DPM protection using the `ConfigureSharePoint.exe` utility. This utility is used to configure the WSS Writer Service and the `WSSCmdletsWrapper` with the correct credentials needed to access the farm to perform backups and recoveries. Use the following steps to configure a SharePoint farm for protection:

1. Log on to the WFE on which you have installed the protection agent as a SharePoint farm administrator and local administrator.

2. Next, open PowerShell command console and CD to `c:\Program Files\Microsoft Data Protection Manager\DPM\bin`.

3. Now, execute the following command to configure the SharePoint farm for protection:

```
.\ConfigureSharepoint.exe -EnableSharePointProtection
```

4. When prompted, provide the correct credentials required to access the SharePoint farm for backup and recovery purposes.

By executing the `ConfigureSharePoint.exe` utility, the Windows SharePoint Services VSS Writer service is configured to use the specified credentials and then is started. Additionally, the utility configures the `WSSCmdletsWrapper` process with the needed credentials to access the SharePoint farm using the SharePoint Object Model. The `WSSCmdletsWrapper` is a DCOM application that runs on the WFE and is used as a bridge between the data in the SharePoint farm and the DPM replication agent (DPMRA) service.

Protecting a SharePoint Farm

The steps used to protect SharePoint data using DPM are almost identical regardless of whether you are trying to only protect Windows SharePoint Services or an entire SharePoint farm. For the purposes of this example, the following steps describe how to protect a SharePoint farm:

1. While logged on to the DPM server as a domain user account that is a member of the local administrators group, open the DPM 2012 Administrator Console.

2. Next, click Protection on the navigation bar, and then click New in the toolbar.

3. Once the Create New Protection Group Wizard has started, click past the Welcome page, select the Servers Protection Group Type option, and then click Next.

4. On the Select Group Members page, use the interface to locate the WFE server object, expand the WFE server object, and you will then see a SharePoint object. Expand this object and you will see the SharePoint farm represented in the name format: `<database server name>\<Config Database Name>...`, as shown in Figure 11.13. Select this object.

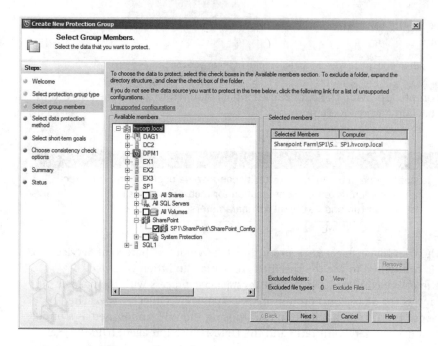

FIGURE 11.13   Adding a SharePoint farm.

5. Once you have finished selecting the desired SharePoint farm, click Next.

6. On the Select Data Protection Method page, type a new name for the protection group in the Protection Group Name box, choose the desired protection methods, and then click Next.

7. On the Specify Short-Term Goals page, specify your desired short-term protection goals, and then click Next.

8. On the Review Disk Allocation page, review the disk allocations that DPM recommends for the protection group, and then click Next.

9. If you have a tape device attached, the Specify Long-Term Protection page is shown. Use this page to specify your long-term protection goals, and then click Next.

10. Next, if you have a tape device attached, the Select Library and Tape Details page is also shown. Use this page to specify the library and configuration options for the backup tapes, and then click Next.

11. On the Choose Replica Creation Method page, use the Replica in DPM Server section to define how the initial replica of the protected data should be created, and then click Next.

12. On the Consistency Check Options page, specify the desired option for how the consistency check for the protection group will be handled, and then click Next.

13. On the Summary page, review the information about the protection group and then click Create Group.

14. Next, the status and results of the protection group creation process are shown on the Status page. Once the protection group has been created, click Close to exit the wizard.

Recovering a SharePoint Farm

Recovering SharePoint data using DPM can be broken down into the following scenarios:

- ▶ Recovering an entire SharePoint farm

- ▶ Recovering a content database

- ▶ Recovering a Shared Services Provider (SSP) and its search data or recovering Office SharePoint Server Search data

- ▶ Recovering item-level objects, such as sites, lists, and items

- ▶ Restoring customizations and configuration settings outside of SharePoint databases

Depending on the SharePoint recovery scenario you are attempting to execute, the processes that you should follow are different and each has its own supportability implications and prerequisites. For example, if you are planning to restore the SharePoint farm configuration database and associated Central Administration website content database, this can only be done, as in supported, by completing a full-farm recovery. In other words, these databases must be recovered in conjunction with all other databases in the SharePoint farm to the same point in time. Luckily, thanks to DPM's usage of VSS, you can accomplish a full-farm recovery using a point-in-time snapshot of all the databases in a SharePoint farm.

To perform a full SharePoint farm recovery while the farm is still available, complete the following steps:

1. First, ensure that the following are true:

   - ▶ All WFE servers are configured as they were when the recovery point was created. If the configuration is different, the recovery operation will fail.

   - ▶ The SQL Server instances must be configured with the same names that were in place when the recovery point was created. If the instance names are different, the recovery operation will fail.

2. Next, while logged on to the DPM server as a domain user account that is a member of the local administrators group, open the DPM 2012 Administrator Console.

3. Once the console has loaded, click Recovery on the navigation bar.

4. On the Browse tab, under the Recoverable Data section, expand the SharePoint server that contains the SharePoint farm to be recovered. Then under the server name, select the All Protected SharePoint Data object. This displays the farm name in the lower-right pane, as shown in Figure 11.14.

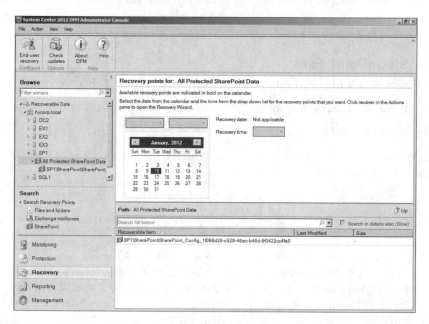

FIGURE 11.14   Selecting a SharePoint farm for recovery.

5. Now, in the calendar display, select the date and time the recovery point was created and then select the SharePoint farm object to be recovered under the Recoverable Item field.

6. Once you have selected the SharePoint farm, click Recover in the toolbar.

7. After the Recovery Wizard has started, the Review Recovery Selection page is shown. Review the recovery selections and then click Next.

8. On the Select Recovery Type page, select the Recover All SharePoint Content and Components to perform a full SharePoint farm recovery. If you need to restore the farm for auditing or other purposes, select the Copy All SharePoint Content and Components to a Network Folder. Additionally, you can choose the Copy the Windows SharePoint Services Farm to Tape option to restore the related farm data to tape.

9. After making the recovery type selection, click Next to continue.

10. On the Specify Recovery Options page, click Next.

11. On the Summary page, review the recovery settings, and then click Recover.

12. Next, the status and results of the recovery process are shown on the Recovery Status page. Once the recovery process has been completed, click Close to exit the wizard.

Once the recovery operation has been completed, it will take about 15–30 minutes (depending on the size of the SharePoint farm) before search services become available. However, users are able to access the SharePoint farm and its content immediately after the completion of a recovery operation.

In the event that you need to perform a SharePoint farm recovery and the farm is not available because of some catastrophic failure, the steps are slightly different from a recovery when the farm is available, as follows:

1. Ensure that any new hardware (WFE servers and SQL Server instances) have the same name as the servers that existed when the recovery point was created.

2. Next, install any necessary prerequisite software and the DPM protection agent.

3. Now, ensure that the DPM protection agent is communicating with the DPM server and then use the ConfigureSharePoint.exe utility to configure the WSS Writer Service and the WSSCmdletsWrapper.

4. From within the DPM Administrator Console, complete a recovery of the SharePoint farm using the DPM Recovery Wizard.

5. After the recovery operation has completed, run the SharePoint Products and Technologies Configuration Wizard and disconnect all of the front-end web servers from the farm.

6. Next, on each WFE server in the SharePoint farm, use the Internet Information Services (IIS) Manager console to delete all website and application pool entries for the farm being restored. Then run the SharePoint Products and Technologies Configuration Wizard and select the option to connect to an existing SharePoint farm. When prompted, provide the server name and database name used at the start of this process (these names must be the same as when the recovery point was created).

7. On the Completing the SharePoint Products and Technologies Configuration Wizard page, click Advanced Settings, and then click Next.

8. Then on the Advanced Settings page, select the option Use This Machine to Host the Web Site, and complete the wizard.

Recovering a Content Database

Despite being protected as part of the SharePoint farm, content databases can be recovered individually just like any other SQL Server database. The only difference from a SQL Server database recovery is that the content database recovery object needs to be selected from under the <database server name>\<Config Database Name> object that is used to represent the SharePoint farm within the DPM Administrator Console, as shown in Figure 11.15.

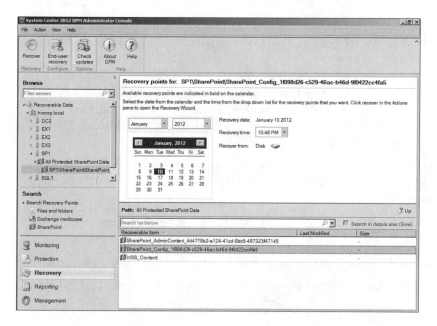

FIGURE 11.15   Selecting a content database for recovery.

> **NOTE**
>
> After completing a content database recovery operation, be sure to detach and reat-tach the database using the Central Administration website to force an update to the sitemap table in the SharePoint farm configuration database.

Recovering Sites, Lists, and Items

The term for recovering SharePoint sites, lists, and items using DPM is called item-level recovery. In relation to SharePoint object hierarchy, item-level objects are objects that are stored within a SharePoint content database. Therefore, recovering these objects is only supported by using the SharePoint Object Model. Failure to use the object model—for example, if you attempted to perform a direct extraction—can lead to corruption of the database and the items/data in the database.

This is why item-level data protection has always been a very difficult task to accomplish in relation to protecting a SharePoint farm. To help farm administrators overcome this challenge, the DPM product team introduced the ability to perform SharePoint item-level recovery in DPM 2007 SP1. Although the introduction of item-level recovery support was a step forward in easing the difficulties associated with protecting SharePoint data, making this feature work required the use of a SharePoint recovery farm to host a recov-ered version of the content database, which would hold the SharePoint object being recovered. From there, the object could be exported and imported using the SharePoint Object Model back into the production SharePoint farm.

Needless to say, although the support of item-level recovery was a great leap forward in SharePoint data protection, the need for a recovery farm placed an additional burden on SharePoint administrators just trying to recover single items, thus slowing down the entire recovery process for potentially critical data. Thankfully, this issue is addressed in SharePoint 2010 with DPM 2012 with the ability to perform item-level recovery directly to the existing SharePoint farm in the middle of the day.

Use the following steps to perform an item-level recovery operation:

1. While logged on to the DPM server as a domain user account that is a member of the local administrators group, open the DPM 2012 Administrator Console.

2. Once the console has loaded, click Recovery on the navigation bar.

3. On the Search tab under the Search Parameters section, complete the following, as shown in Figure 11.16:

    ▶ Change the Search drop-down parameter to SharePoint.

    ▶ In the SharePoint Search section, choose either the Search Site or Search Documents option.

    ▶ Then provide the search string of the site or document you are trying to recover for the Name parameter.

    ▶ Lastly, in the Recovery Points section, define the recovery point range within which your search should be performed.

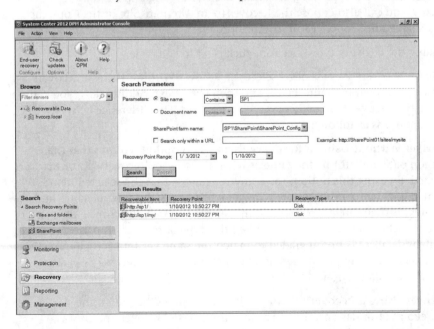

FIGURE 11.16   Defining SharePoint recovery search parameters.

4. Once you have defined the search parameters, click Search.

5. After the search results are displayed in the Search Results panel, locate the recoverable item that you want to recover, select it, and then click Recover.

6. Alternately, if the SharePoint site has been indexed, when you are on the Recovery tab and drill down through the SharePoint server, expand the All Protected SharePoint Data, and expand the SharePoint Config; in the lower right of the DPM console under Recoverable Item, you can drill down through the SharePoint server directory to specifically find the file(s) you are looking to restore.

NOTE

The SharePoint index from a DPM backup is performed once a day, so if you are trying to restore information, you may need to force a creation of the index of the information that is backed up and available on DPM. To create an index of the SharePoint index, do the following on the DPM server. Launch the DPM Management Shell, and run `get-ProtectionGroup dpmserver.yourdomain.com |get-datasource |where-object {$_.type -like "*sharepoint*"} | start-createcatalog`. You can highlight the file you want to recover and click Recover in the toolbar menu.

---

7. After the Recovery Wizard has started, the Review Recovery Selection page is shown. Review the recovery selections and then click Next.

8. On the Select Recovery Type page, select the Recover to Original Site option. Additionally, you can also choose the Recover to an Alternate Site or the Copy the Windows SharePoint Services Farm to Tape options.

9. After making the recovery type selection, click Next to continue.

10. On the Select Recovery Process page, select the Recover Without Using a Recovery Farm option, as shown in Figure 11.17, and then click Next. Additionally, you can also choose the Recover Using a Recovery Farm option. The difference between these two options is as follows:

   ▶ **Recover Without Using a Recovery Farm**—This option requires that the version of SharePoint be the same as when the selected recovery point was created. By using this option, the content database that the selected item is located in is temporarily restored and attached to a SQL Server instance and the item is then directly restored to the targeted SharePoint farm. This is called an unattached database recovery. When this type of recovery is performed, the content database is not upgraded to match the same version as the production farm version. Therefore, if there is a version mismatch, a recovery operation might cause corruption.

   ▶ **Recover Using a Recovery Farm**—This option should be used if the SharePoint farm has been updated since the selected recovery point was created. By using this option, the content database is temporarily restored and attached to a temporary SharePoint recovery farm. From there, the selected items are extracted and restored to the targeted SharePoint farm.

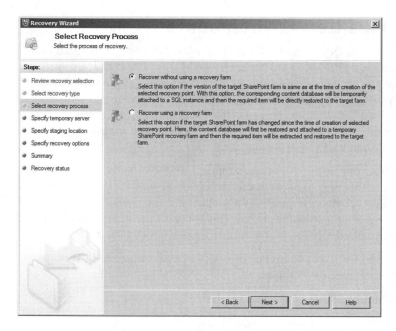

FIGURE 11.17   Selecting the item-level recovery process.

> **NOTE**
>
> To perform an item-level restore without the use of a recovery farm is only possible with a SharePoint 2010 farm. The concept of unattached database recovery is a new feature in SharePoint 2010, which is required to perform an item-level recovery without the use of a SharePoint recovery farm.

11. On the Specify Temporary Server page, define a SQL Server instance to temporarily stage the content database prior to recovery. Then define a file location where the database files can be copied to (these are deleted after the recovery operation has been completed), and then click Next.

12. On the Specify Staging Location page, define a temporary file location on the WFE where DPM can extract the files from the recovered database and then import them into the production database, and then click Next.

13. On the Specify Recovery Options page, click Next.

14. On the Summary page, review the recovery settings, and then click Recover.

15. Next, the status and results of the recovery process are shown on the Recovery Status page. Once the recovery process has been completed, click Close to exit the wizard.

Protecting Virtualized Environments

Like Exchange and SQL Server, DPM can also be used to protect Hyper-V virtualized environments. When protecting a virtualized environment, DPM uses VSS to take a complete snapshot for each protected virtual machine and its associated configuration information. For virtual machines whose operating systems (like Windows 2000 Server and Linux) do not support VSS, DPM performs what is called an offline backup. With this type of backup, the DPM protection agent pauses the virtual machine, takes a snapshot, unpauses the virtual machine, and then backs up the snapshot.

For virtual machines whose operating systems do support VSS, DPM performs an online backup. When performing this type of backup, the protection agent uses VSS to quiesce (make inactive) application activity and produces a snapshot of the virtual machine and its data in a stable and usable state. Needless to say, this is one of the main benefits of using DPM to protect virtualized environments over other data protection methods.

With DPM 2012, protection for Hyper-V environments can be performed for a various number of deployment scenarios, for example:

▶ Cluster Shared Volumes (CSV)

▶ Highly available virtual machines on a failover cluster

▶ Standalone hosts

▶ Windows Server/Server Core and Microsoft Hyper-V Server and Local Data Source Protection

Protecting Hyper-V Virtual Machines

The steps used to protect Hyper-V virtual machines using DPM are almost identical regardless of whether you are trying to only protect virtual machines on a standalone Hyper-V host or virtual machines located on a high-availability deployment using CSV or a failover cluster. For the purposes of this example, the following steps describe how to protect virtual machines located on a standalone Hyper-V host:

1. While logged on to the DPM server as a domain user account that is a member of the local administrators group, open the DPM 2012 Administrator Console.

2. Next, ensure that the Hyper-V host has the protection agent installed and the agent is reachable with a normal status.

3. Now, click Protection on the navigation bar, and then click Create Protection Group in the Actions pane.

4. Once the Create New Protection Group Wizard has started, click past the Welcome page, select the Servers Protection Group Type option, and then click Next.

5. On the Select Group Members page, find the Hyper-V server that hosts the virtual machines you intended to protect and expand its object out. Next, expand the HyperV node to see a list of virtual machines that can be protected. Using this list, select the virtual machines that are to be protected, as shown in Figure 11.18.

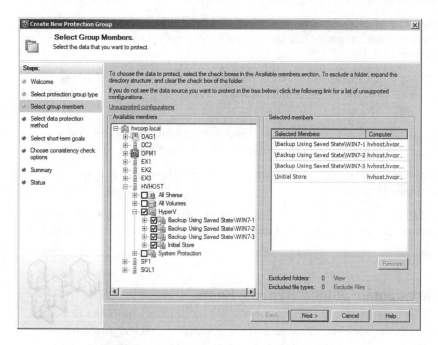

FIGURE 11.18   Adding virtual machines.

NOTE

In Figure 11.18, notice that some of the virtual machines state "Backup Using Saved State." This status indicates the virtual machine will be backed up using an offline backup. If a virtual machine supports an online backup, its status message would be "Backup Using Child Partition." However, if the virtual machine is off or in a saved state at the time you are modifying a protection group's members, the state of the virtual machine will be "Backup Using Saved State."

---

6. Once you have finished selecting the desired virtual machines, click Next.

7. On the Select Data Protection Method page, type a new name for the protection group in the Protection Group Name box, choose the desired protection methods, and then click Next.

8. On the Specify Short-Term Goals page, specify your desired short-term protection goals, and then click Next.

9. On the Review Disk Allocation page, review the disk allocations that DPM recommends for the protection group, and then click Next.

10. If you have a tape device attached, the Specify Long-Term Protection page is shown. Use this page to specify your long-term protection goals, and then click Next.

11. If you have a tape device attached, the Select Library and Tape Details page is also shown. Use this page to specify the library and configuration options for the backup tapes, and then click Next.

12. On the Choose Replica Creation Method page, use the Replica in DPM Server section to define how the initial replica of the protected data should be created, and then click Next.

13. On the Consistency Check Options page, specify the desired option for how the consistency check for the protection group will be handled, and then click Next.

14. On the Summary page, review the information about the protection group, and then click Create Group.

15. Next, the status and results of the protection group creation process are shown on the Status page. Once the protection group has been created, click Close to exit the wizard.

Protecting Nondomain Joined Hyper-V Hosts

With DPM 2012, an organization has the ability to protect nondomain joined Hyper-V hosts servers through the use of certificates. Many organizations have Hyper-V hosts managing edge servers, servers in their demilitarized zone (DMZ), servers in branch offices, or utility servers that are not part of the organization's Active Directory domain. By leveraging certificate-based backups covered in Chapter 10 under the section "Deploying the Protection Agent Using Certificates," the organization can target Hyper-V hosts (and the guest sessions running on the host servers) simply by creating a certificate-based relationship between the DPM 2012 server and the target Hyper-V host system.

Targeting a Hyper-V Host Across a Firewall

DPM 2012 uses a number of DCOM (Distributed Component Object Model) commands to deploy DPM agents, back up and restore data, and retrieve DPM agent statuses. Because DCOM uses a combination of static and dynamic network ports, DPM may not be able to communicate with a Hyper-V host that is behind a firewall. In order to ensure that DPM can communicate with a host across a firewall, several key points must be addressed specific to the configuration of the firewall and the DPM server. The points that should be reviewed are as follows: Review the existing rules on the firewall to ensure that communication is allowed between the DPM server and the Hyper-V host on the static network ports listed in Table 11.5.

Because DCOM uses dynamic TCP ports above 1024 for server-agent communication, the intervening firewall may block communication between server and agent on these dynamic high ports. It is possible to configure the DPM server to use a static range of TCP high ports using these procedures from Microsoft: http://support.microsoft.com/kb/154596. To ensure that the static port range that you select does not conflict with TCP ports used by other applications, it is recommended to use a static port range above 50000 for DPM communication (for example, 50000 through 50050). The current list of all registered network ports is available from IANA (Internet Assigned Numbers Authority) at http://www.iana.org/assignments/service-names-port-numbers/service-names-port-numbers.xml.

Once the DPM server has been assigned to use a static range of TCP high ports for DCOM, configure a rule on the intervening firewall to allow the DPM server to communicate with the Hyper-V server over the selected static port range.

After configuring the DPM server and firewall using the steps above, run the `wbemtest` utility to verify that the DPM server can communicate with the Hyper-V host using DCOM. Launch the `wbemtest` utility on the DPM server, click the Connect button, enter `\\HyperVHostName\root\cimv2` in the Connect field (substituting the actual name of the Hyper-V host) and click the Connect button again. If the connection is successful, click the Enum Classes button and click OK in the dialog box to return a list of WMI classes from the Hyper-V host.

Once communications between the DPM server and Hyper-V host have been verified, the DPM agent can be deployed to the Hyper-V host using the DPM Protection Installation Wizard.

TABLE 11.5   Network Protocols and Ports Used By DPM 2012

Protocol	Ports	Description
DCOM	TCP 135 TCP Dynamic (1024-65536)	DCOM is used by the DPM server and DPM agents to issue commands and indicate responses.
TCP	TCP 5718 TCP 5719	DPM communicates with the agent coordinator on port 5718 and with the protection agent on port 5719.
DNS	UDP 53	DNS is used by the DPM server and agents for name resolution.
Kerberos	TCP 88 UDP 88	Kerberos is used by the DPM server and agents for authentication.
LDAP	TCP 389 UDP 389	LDAP is used by the DPM server for directory queries.
NetBIOS	UDP 137 UDP 138 TCP 139 TCP 445	NetBIOS is used by the DPM server and agents for miscellaneous operations.

Recovering Hyper-V Virtual Machines

The steps used to recover a virtual machine using DPM are almost identical regardless of whether you are trying to only recover the virtual machine to a standalone Hyper-V host or to high-availability deployment using CSV or a failover cluster. For the purposes of this example, the following steps describe how to recover a virtual machine located on a standalone Hyper-V host:

1. While logged on to the DPM server as a domain user account that is a member of the local administrators group, open the DPM 2012 Administrator Console.

2. Once the console has loaded, click Recovery on the navigation bar.

3. Using either the Browse or Search tabs, find the virtual machine that needs to be recovered, as shown in Figure 11.19.

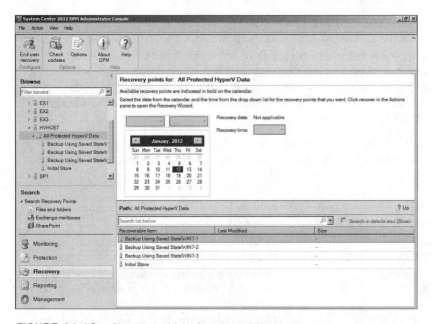

FIGURE 11.19   Choosing which virtual machine to recover.

NOTE

Be sure to select the All DPM Protected Data node and then choose the virtual machine in the Recoverable Item list to recover. If you select the virtual machine object under Recoverable Data, the Recoverable Item list then shows a list of virtual hard disks (VHDs). At this point, if you selected the VHD to do a recovery, you would be recovering just the VHD and not the virtual machine.

4. Once you have selected the virtual machine to recover, click Recover in the Action pane.

5. After the Recovery Wizard has started, the Review Recovery Selection page is shown. Review the recovery selections and then click Next.

6. On the Select Recovery Type page, select the Recover to Original Instance option, and then click Next to continue. Additionally, you can also choose to perform a recovery using either of the Recover to an Alternate Location, Copy to a Network Folder, or Copy to Tape options. A breakdown for all of the options on this page is as follows:

   ▶ **Recover to Original Instance**—This option restores the virtual machine onto the original Hyper-V host or cluster. The source virtual machine is overwritten with the virtual machine from the recovery point when this recovery option is used.

   ▶ **Recover to an Alternate Location**—This option, called alternate location recovery or ALR, is new to DPM 2012 and allows you to recover the virtual machine to an alternate Hyper-V host or cluster. When using this option, the virtual machine is automatically registered and configured with the targeted Hyper-V host or cluster.

   ▶ **Copy to a Network Folder**—Similar to an ALR recovery, however, only the virtual machine files are restored to the alternate host. If you target a Hyper-V host or cluster, DPM does not register and configure the virtual machine. Instead, this task must be done manually or through some automated procedure.

   ▶ **Copy to Tape**—Use this option to recover a virtual machine to a tape. This option is useful if you need to recover the virtual machine to media that can be taken offsite.

7. On the Specify Recovery Options page, click Next.

8. On the Summary page, review the recovery settings, and then click Recover.

9. Next, the status and results of the recovery process are shown on the Recovery Status page. Once the recovery process has been completed, click Close to exit the wizard.

Performing Item-Level Recovery on Virtual Machines

With DPM 2007, you could protect both a Hyper-V host and its guests by performing a host-level backup. However, when it came to meeting more granular data protection needs, administrators had to resort to installing the protection agent directly on a virtual machine. In some cases, like protecting Exchange data, installing the protection agent directly on a virtual machine made sense. But, when it came to just protecting files, folders, volumes, and so forth, many administrators wished that just a host-level backup would suffice.

In DPM 2012, you can now perform host-level backups and then from those backups, perform item-level recovery (ILR) for things such as files, folders, volumes, and VHDs. Although this is a great feature, a couple of limitations need to be taken into consideration when using ILR:

▶ Items can only be restored to a network share or a volume on a DPM-protected server.

▶ The Hyper-V role must be enabled on the DPM server to perform item-level recoveries. This is a requirement because DPM has to mount the VHDs of the protected virtual machines to extract the data from them.

▶ You cannot use ILR to recover an item to its original location.

Table 11.6 describes the supported and unsupported recovery scenarios that can be used for ILR.

TABLE 11.6   Hyper-V ILR Recovery Scenarios

Scenario	Volumes or Files/ Folders Recovery	Virtual Hard Disk (VHD) Recovery
From a virtual machine that has snapshots	Yes	
(Only to Windows Server 2008 R2)	Yes	
From a secondary DPM server	Yes	Yes
From tape backup	Yes	Yes
From NTFS volumes	Yes	N/A
From non-NTFS volumes	No	Entire VHD only
From a VHD that is partitioned using dynamic disk partitioning	No	Entire VHD only

Summary

This chapter focused on how System Center Data Protection Manager 2012 can be used to protect Microsoft operating systems and server applications. As shown in this chapter, DPM can be used to protect a wide number of Microsoft solutions, including, but not limited to, Exchange Server, SQL Server, and SharePoint farms. Based on the information provided in this chapter, you should now have a better understanding as to how these solutions each have their own special data protection needs. For example, when protecting a SharePoint farm, the only supportable method for recovering the configuration database and the Central Administration content database is to perform a full-farm recovery. As you have seen with SharePoint, and the rest of the Microsoft solutions discussed in this chapter, DPM has been tailored to meet each of their needs, thus making it a very compelling data protection solution for a Microsoft-centric environment.

Best Practices

The following are best practices from this chapter:

▶ A computer that is protected by DPM can have multiple protection groups protecting data sources. However, all these protection groups must be from one DPM server.

▶ When protecting data in a DFS namespace, use DPM to only protect a single "copy" of the data located on a server-specific local path.

▶ Do not use DPM to protect a cluster's quorum disk.

▶ Because System State data tends not to change very often, System State backups should be placed in their own protection groups.

▶ Always ensure that the `Eseutil.exe` and `ese.dll` versions on the DPM server are from the most recent edition of Exchange Server.

▶ Exchange Server databases should not be configured to use circular logging when being protected by DPM.

▶ After recovering an Exchange database that is in a DAG, the passive copies need to be synchronized with the recovered active database using the `Resume-MailboxDatabaseCopy` cmdlet.

▶ Before you can start protecting data on a SQL Server 2005 SP1 instance, you must first enable and then start the SQL Server VSS Writer Service.

▶ When protecting a SQL Server cluster, all nodes of the cluster should have the DPM protection agent installed on them.

▶ When using DPM 2012, you can choose to protect an entire SQL Server instance, and all new databases added to that instance will be automatically protected.

▶ When you recover a SQL database to its original instance of SQL Server, the original database is overwritten using the replica that was chosen to recover the database with. If you are trying to attempt a lossless recovery, you then need to restore the database using the latest recovery point, and have DPM replay any residual live transactions from the SQL Server log files (LDF).

▶ The SQL End User Recovery feature uses TCP port 11313 to communicate to the DPM server. To use this feature, you need to ensure that Windows Firewall has been configured to allow incoming connections on this port.

▶ WFE servers do not host content. Therefore, technically only one Web Front End server needs to have the protection agent installed in a SharePoint farm.

▶ The `ConfigureSharePoint.exe` utility can also be used to enable protection for Search and configure a temp folder location for recoveries by using the `EnableSPSearchProtection` and `SetTempPath` parameters.

▶ After completing a content database recovery operation, be sure to detach and reattach the database using the Central Administration website to force an update to the sitemap table in the SharePoint farm configuration database.

▶ Item-level restore without the use of a recovery farm is only possible with a SharePoint 2010 farm.

CHAPTER 12

Virtual Machine Manager 2012 Design, Planning, and Implementation

IN THIS CHAPTER

▶ Understanding Virtual Machine Manager

▶ Virtual Machine Manager Background

▶ What's New in System Center Virtual Machine Manager 2012

▶ Virtual Machine Manager Prerequisites

▶ Planning a Virtual Machine Manager Deployment

▶ Deploying Virtual Machine Manager

▶ Best Practices

Once an organization understands and adopts the value of system virtualization, IT administrators will naturally look for improved ways to deploy, control, and administer their virtual infrastructures. To help fill this gap, administrators can turn to Microsoft's System Center Virtual Machine Manager 2012 (VMM). VMM provides a System Center common management interface for the virtualized data center that allows increased server utilization and dynamic resource allocation. It also works across multiple virtualization platforms, including those from Microsoft, VMware, and Citrix.

VMM also takes a holistic approach to managing an organization's "fabric," which includes LAN networking, WAN networking, and storage subsystems. When creating and allocating resources for virtual guest sessions, VMM examines and rates the infrastructure to determine the best placement of virtualized guest sessions. It compares the infrastructure against a set of criteria and rates the suitability of the virtual machine (VM) to be deployed on the set of fabric and host resources where it can be deployed.

Understanding Virtual Machine Manager

The VMM product line provides administrators with the ability to centrally administer and manage their virtual infrastructures. By using VMM, organizations can further increase physical server utilization, rapidly provision new virtual machines, and delegate management of these virtual machines to authorized self-service end users. The topics in this section provide you with an overview of VMM features and functionality.

The Value VMM Brings to the Enterprise

VMM greatly enhances the administration and management capabilities of virtual guest sessions over the built-in Hyper-V management console that comes with Hyper-V. This solution also allows organizations to more easily manage centralized servers and organize them in a manner that helps administrators delegate access and administration rights to those that need access to specific servers or groups of servers. These benefits to an enterprise and more are described in the following list:

▶ **Centralized management**—VMM offers a centralized management solution for the entire virtual enterprise. Using one tool, the administrator can manage, create, deploy, move, copy, or delete any virtual machine in the enterprise. It makes no difference whether the host or virtual machine is running Microsoft Hyper-V, VMware ESX, or Citrix XenServer.

▶ **Decreased server sprawl**—VMM prevents virtual machine server sprawl by managing all the host servers in the enterprise. Due to the ease of deploying virtual machines, virtual server sprawl can become a real issue if not managed. Virtual machines can be deployed to the wrong host servers, and precious network resources can be squandered. VMM provides a way to take control of the virtual infrastructure and deploy virtual machines in the best way, based on resource and performance needs.

▶ **Integration with System Center Operations Manager**—Tight integration with System Center Operations Manager 2007 R2 or 2012 (SCOM) provides the capability to monitor and manage the virtual network like never before. SCOM offers VMM and Hyper-V management packs to provide real-time monitoring of host and virtual servers. It provides both alerting and built-in knowledge that aids the administrator in troubleshooting and recovery. In addition, administrators also gain access to PRO (Performance and Resource Optimization), which is an enhanced monitoring and management feature that is enabled when VMM is paired with SCOM. It helps guide administrators by outlining ways to more efficiently deploy and run both physical and virtual resources. PRO can even move a virtual machine from a problem host to another or perform a specified action on a virtual machine or host in response to an error condition.

▶ **Profiles and templates that make provisioning easier**—VMM provides the administrator with a complete, yet simple, server provisioning process. Multiple hardware and operating system profiles can be stored in the VMM library. Hundreds of virtual machine templates can be stored and grouped together for easy deployment. Templates also aid in server standardization, an important aspect in any environment. Troubleshooting is minimized when the administrator can be sure that each VM based on the same template will be configured the same way.

> ► **Self-service provisioning**—Self-Service Users can deploy the virtual machines they have access to without the need to understand the underlying physical infrastructure. By using the Self-Service Portal, these users can automatically deploy VMware, Hyper-V, and XenServer virtual machines to the most suitable server, based on the criteria set by the administrator. For developers, this makes building or rebuilding test servers extremely easy, thus allowing them to spend more time writing code and less time worrying about the infrastructure to test that code.

> ► **Disaster recovery and business continuity**—One of the most important promises of virtualization is the increased ability to perform disaster recovery operations. To make this promise a reality, VMM offers several features that increase server uptime and provide business-continuity protection. Because VMM is cluster aware, it can automatically move highly available (HA) virtual machines from one cluster node to another, without an administrator having to worry about which host is appropriate for that particular virtual machine. The administrator can also define the suitability criteria of each host to help guide other administrators or Self-Service Users to use the correct host.

> ► **Optimized resource allocation**—By knowing and understanding the resource requirements and constraints of each physical host and virtual machine server, VMM can make the best use of the hardware available. With this knowledge, more virtual machines can be placed on existing host servers, realizing an even greater value from the virtual environment.

> ► **Physical and virtual server conversions**—VMM provides both physical-to-virtual (P2V) and virtual-to-virtual (V2V) conversion capabilities. The P2V process is used to rapidly convert a physical server to a Hyper-V or VMware virtual server, preserving the existing operating system, applications, and data. This is useful when the administrator needs to virtualize an existing physical server, but the configuration is too complex or the application software is no longer available. In some instances, this conversion can even occur while the server is online, reducing downtime during the conversion process.

> ► **Role-based access control**—The VMM role-based access control (RBAC) model, along with administrator delegation, allows VMM Administrators to provide more autonomy and less administrative overhead in managing and working with the virtual infrastructure. Using this feature, department and regional VMM Administrators can be granted the appropriate rights to manage and deploy the virtual machines needed, without the need to engage a higher administrator.

Technical Problems Addressed by VMM

VMM offers many advanced virtual machine management features, while emphasizing ease of use and automation. The three management interfaces (the Administrator Console, the command shell, and the Self-Service Portal) offer a variety of ways for VMM Administrators and users to create, deploy, and manage their virtual machines, addressing the following technical problems in an IT organization:

▶ **Delegated administration**—IT environments with delegated administration and permissions models require a flexible and granular management solution to manage and control their virtual environment. VMM offers this flexibility via its RBAC model, which provides better control and granularity in administration and user delegation.

▶ **Meeting ITIL requirements**—Enterprises that utilize Information Technology Infrastructure Library (ITIL) concepts and techniques will benefit from the service-based management that VMM provides. For example, a VMM Administrator can provide a higher level of service to other departments and users thanks to VMM. Additionally, the Self-Service Portal can be used to provide a controlled way for users to deploy their own virtual machines without having to worry about the infrastructure needed to support those virtual machines.

▶ **Disaster recovery and business continuity**—Any IT environment with a need for server disaster recovery or line-of-business continuity will appreciate the high-availability features built in to VMM. For example, thanks to VMM's native awareness of Windows and VMware clusters, it is an ideal management solution that can automatically move HA virtual machines from one host cluster node to another when the situation warrants.

▶ **Dynamically changing environments**—Every IT environment has finite resources. VMM provides dynamic virtual server placement based on physical constraints. Administrators define scores for physical hosts that define the suitability of a virtual machine for each host. VMM then displays the score of each potential host in an easy-to-understand five-star rating. As resources change on these hosts, the rating changes, thus providing for the most optimal virtual machine placement based on the current resources available within the virtual infrastructure.

▶ **Highly leveraged virtual infrastructure**—Enterprises with a need for rapid deployment and virtualization can take full advantage of the tremendous cost savings that virtualization provides. For organizations beginning to incorporate Hyper-V servers into their VMware environment, VMM provides the perfect management platform for managing both environments. For organizations just starting down the virtualization path, VMM provides the advanced management capabilities that ensure rapid, controlled deployment of virtual machines into their IT environment.

▶ **Meeting virtual machine conversion requirements**—IT environments that require physical or virtual server conversions will enjoy VMM conversion capabilities. VMM can convert physical servers to virtual servers (P2V) and VMware ESX virtual servers to Microsoft Hyper-V virtual servers (V2V). P2V conversions allow organizations to get rid of old hardware running on legacy systems, which provides a way to rapidly virtualize physical infrastructure, whereas V2V conversions allow organizations to rapidly convert potentially expensive-to-license VMware ESX virtual machines to Hyper-V-based virtual machines.

▶ **Dealing with heterogeneous environments**—Current VMware ESX and VirtualCenter customers who want to use Hyper-V can use VMM 2012 to manage both environments. This heterogeneous management solution reduces administrative overhead and complexity. VMM provides the same functionality as VMware VirtualCenter and VMotion for both VMware and Hyper-V environments, all in the same virtual machine management solution.

Components of VMM

Virtual Machine Manager is a series of components that includes Windows Server, SQL Server, a locally installed agent, an administrative console, and an optional self-service console. The components that make up VMM include the following:

▶ A Windows Server 2008 SP2 or later server on which the VMM service (Server component) is installed.

▶ A SQL Server 2008 or later instance to host the VMM database and its related data.

▶ A collection of servers on which the VMM Agent is installed. These servers act as hosts on which to deploy virtual machines using VMM.

▶ A server or servers on which the VMM Agent is installed that act as VMM library servers. Library servers store resources for the VMM environment.

▶ One or more computers on which the VMM Administrator Console is installed. These computers or servers provide the administrative GUI and command shell to manage the physical and virtual infrastructure.

▶ One or more web servers that act as Self-Service Portals, which allow designated users to create or manage their own virtual machines.

> **NOTE**
>
> VMM components can be combined on the same server or split among several different servers and workstations depending on the needs of the deployment.

VMM Server

The VMM server has the Virtual Machine Manager service (VMMService), but it can also include the VMM database and the VMM library depending on how you are deploying VMM. The VMMService service provides the needed interfaces to run and manage VMM, communicating with and storing its configuration in the SQL database. This service also monitors the health of virtual machines and hosts. When necessary, it moves virtual machines between host servers to ensure the availability of virtual machines that are being managed by VMM.

VMM Administrator Console

The Administrator Console is a Microsoft Management Console (MMC) that is built upon
Windows PowerShell. This console provides an administrative interface to the VMM
server and it offers complete management of the virtual environment, including creating,
managing, and deploying virtual machines and virtual local area networks (VLANs);
managing host servers; configuring user roles; and so forth. VMM Administrators can
manage all virtual machines and the VMM organizational settings using this console,
whereas VMM Delegated Administrators can manage only the virtual machines that have
been delegated to them.

VMM Self-Service Portal

The VMM Self-Service Portal provides a web-based interface that allows Self-Service Users
to provision virtual machines from the VMM library. It also allows Self-Service Users to
store virtual machines in the library if they have sufficient rights. The most common use
of the Self-Service Portal is to provide an environment for developers and testers to create
and manage their own virtual labs. Depending on an organization's needs, multiple types
of Self-Service User roles can be provisioned by a VMM Administrator to facilitate the
deployment and management of virtual machines using the Self-Service Portal.

VMM Agent

The VMM Agent is the agent software that allows VMM to monitor and manage Windows
Server 2008 and Windows Server 2008 R2 Hyper-V host servers. It can be installed
remotely using the VMM Administrator Console or manually using the VMM software
media. All Windows host servers must also be joined to a domain. This can either be the
same domain as the VMM server or in a different domain that is either trusted or
nontrusted.

VMM Library

The VMM library is a centralized repository for all Windows-based and VMware-based
virtual machine–related objects. These objects are the building blocks of the virtual
machines that will be created and include the following: hardware profiles, guest OS
profiles, templates, virtual hard disks (VHDs), CD-ROM images (ISOs), and so on. The
VMM Library consists of the following:

> ► **Hardware profiles**—These profiles make up the virtual hardware components of a
> virtual machine. BIOS boot order (CD-ROM, hard drive, floppy, and so on), CPU
> count and type, physical RAM, floppy drive, and serial (COM) ports are all part of
> the hardware profile. IDE and SCSI adapters and virtual DVD drives are part of the
> bus configuration. One or more network adapters can be added and the network
> type (external, internal, or private) or VLAN can be specified.

> ► **Guest OS profiles**—These profiles are used to configure the name, administrator
> password, Windows product key, time zone, and Windows operating system type of
> the virtual machine. Networking allows the administrator to choose which
> Windows workgroup or domain to join. To join a domain, the virtual machine must

have at least one virtual network adapter attached to a virtual network. The guest OS profile can also include a Sysprep answer file or GUIRunOnce commands. A Sysprep answer file is used to configure additional settings in the virtual machine not specified in the guest OS profile, such as assigning regional settings or languages. Sysprep scripts must be stored on a VMM library share.

▶ **Disk images and ISO image files**—The VMM library also stores Hyper-V and Virtual Server virtual hard disks (VHD files) and VMware virtual hard disks (VMDK files). Virtual disks can be either blank or contain data, such as a preconfigured operating system or generic data used by applications. Additionally, the VMM library can be used to store CD-ROM and DVD-ROM disks. This is achieved by creating a single file image (ISO image) of the optical disk and copying it to the VMM library share. ISOs can then be mounted by virtual machines either during the virtual machine creation or at any time after the virtual machine is deployed. ISOs can also be configured to run directly from the VMM library or copied to the local virtual machine folder on the host.

▶ **VM templates**—Templates are used to create new virtual machines. They usually consist of a VHD (one that is either stored in the library or from a virtual machine currently located on a host), a hardware profile, and an OS profile. After a VM template has been created, it can be deployed to a host server that is either a standalone server for non-HA virtual machines or a host cluster for HA virtual machines.

PowerShell Support

Like Microsoft Exchange Server 2007 and Exchange Server 2010, VMM is written completely on top of Windows PowerShell. Any task that can be completed using the Administrator Console or the Self-Service Portal user interfaces can also be completed using PowerShell. As a matter of fact, each task that is performed using these consoles is actually completed using PowerShell. In other words, when an administrator performs an action from a console, that action or command, shown in Figure 12.1, is passed down to PowerShell for execution.

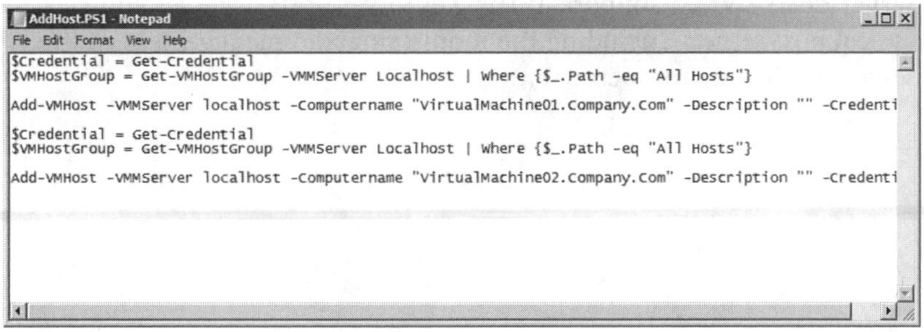

FIGURE 12.1   PowerShell command sequence.

The commands shown in the figure were generated using the Administrator Console. When an administrator attempts to complete an action using the console, a button is available that, when clicked, displays the PowerShell commands that will be executed to complete the action. This allows an administrator to copy, modify, and save the PowerShell script, which can easily be used to automate future tasks either through direct interaction with the command shell or via an automation script.

Heterogeneous VM Management

As evident with Microsoft's continued investment in virtualization technologies, it is almost a given that Hyper-V virtualization will be leveraged by IT departments. However, a large number of companies have already invested in VMware virtualization, using VMware ESX server and proprietary VMware VirtualCenter for management. Adding Hyper-V to the virtual landscape can increase the complexity and time required to manage the physical and virtual infrastructure for these companies. Thankfully, Microsoft designed VMM to be a heterogeneous management system that reduces the complexity of managing different physical and virtual systems in the enterprise by providing the ability to manage the following host systems:

▶ **Hyper-V hosts**—VMM supports hosts running Windows Server 2008 and Windows Server 2008 R2 that have the Hyper-V server role enabled. Additionally, if an administrator adds a Windows Server 2008 and R2 host to VMM and the Hyper-V server role has not been enabled, VMM enables the Hyper-V server role automatically as it adds the server as a host managed by VMM. VMM can also import a Windows Server 2008 or R2 computer that is already configured as a Hyper-V host and will import any Hyper-V virtual machines that are already deployed on that host.

▶ **VMware hosts**—VMM supports connecting to a VMware virtualization manager server. It imports its data (including the host servers that it manages and the virtual machines deployed on those hosts) into the VMM library database. VMM then integrates the imported VMware objects into its set of Windows-based objects. From an administrator's point of view, the Windows-based and VMware-based objects are managed in the same way using the same VMM Administrator Console.

▶ **Citrix XenServer hosts**—VMM supports Citrix XenServer hosts as target and managed physical host servers, including the monitoring and management of the target host servers in the environment.

Cluster Support in VMM

Clusters are an important resource in the virtual enterprise because they offer a highly available platform to host mission-critical virtual machines. After all, if a single host system is responsible for hosting an enterprise's most critical systems, then that host becomes a single point of failure. To fill this gap, VMM supports both Windows Server 2008 failover clusters and VMware ESX host clusters. Using VMM's native cluster support, administrators can move virtual machines from one physical node of a cluster to another, either manually or automatically. Being able to move virtual machines allows an administrator to patch the active node or bring it down for maintenance without impacting the mission-critical virtual machines hosted on the server. It also provides automatic fault tolerance in the event of an unexpected server failure. Additionally, VMM's cluster support allows administrators to reduce costs by consolidating different clustered host systems into a common managed collection of resources.

VMM can manage up to 16 node host clusters that are configured using the Windows Failover Cluster management console. VMM takes advantage of the many cluster management improvements available in Windows Server 2008/2008 R2, making cluster configuration and management much easier for administrators. Because of this tight integration, VMM can automatically detect the addition or removal of a node within the host cluster. Furthermore, if one host in the host cluster becomes unavailable, the virtual machines on that host are automatically moved to another host in the same host cluster.

VMM's support for host clusters ensures the virtual machines deployed on hosts in that cluster are highly available. Virtual machines deployed on host clusters are called highly available virtual machines, or HA virtual machines. Configuring a virtual machine as an HA virtual machine can be done using an option in its hardware profile. Once enabled as an HA virtual machine, that virtual machine can then be placed only on an available host cluster, ensuring the high availability of the VM resource.

> **NOTE**
>
> Virtual machines marked as highly available can only be placed on host clusters. Likewise, VMM does not place virtual machines that are not marked as highly available on host clusters.

Role-Based Access Control

Permissions in VMM are based on *user roles*, which can be scoped to increase or limit the
objects that a user role can access, as shown in Figure 12.2.

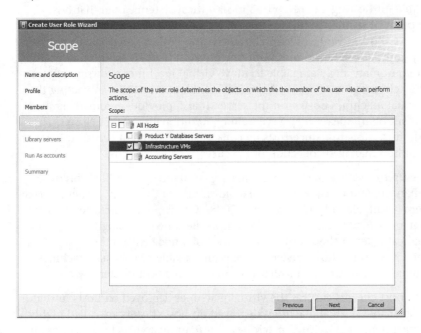

FIGURE 12.2   Creating a user role.

User roles are similar to security groups in Active Directory. They are made up of domain
accounts or groups and have a particular set of permissions granted to them. There are
three basic user role types in VMM:

▶ **VMM Administrator**—This user role has complete, unlimited access to VMM and
the objects in the VMM library. Members of this role can be Active Directory users
or groups. VMM Administrators can add or remove members to this role, but
because only one VMM Administrator role exists, it cannot be created, deleted, or
modified. Members of the VMM Administrator role can use the Administrator
Console and the command shell, but cannot access the Self-Service Portal unless
they are also members of a Self-Service User role.

▶ **VMM Delegated Administrator**—This user role is scoped to a particular set of VMM
objects (determined during role configuration). Members can be Active Directory
users or groups. VMM Delegated Administrators cannot add themselves to the VMM
Administrator role or configure global settings across the VMM environment. They
can, however, perform all operations on all VMM objects within the specified scope.
Scopes are made up of one or more host groups or library servers. Members of a
VMM Delegated Administrator role can use the Administrator Console and the
command shell, but cannot access the Self-Service Portal unless they are also
members of a Self-Service User role.

▶ **Self-Service User**—This user role is made up of Active Directory users or groups who can perform all allowed operations on a specific set of virtual machines deployed on one or more hosts within specified host groups. Self-Service Users can be granted the right to store their own virtual machines on a VMM library server. Administrators can limit their access to one or more specified library shares on a server. Members can access the Self-Service Portal interface and the command shell, but cannot access the Administrator Console unless they are also a member of at least one of the Administrator roles listed previously. Furthermore, VMM allows Self-Service Users to work with any virtual machine in either Hyper-V or VMware to check out or deploy virtual machines to the proper host, without having to know which host to use. It is completely transparent to the end user.

When working with virtual machine permissions in relation to Hyper-V hosts, VMM now preserves changes that are made to role definitions and role members within the root scope of the Hyper-V authentication store. All other changes to any other scopes are over-written every half hour by the VMM user role refresher. This process differs from how role processing was handled in VMM 2008, where access to virtual machines, hosts, and resources was determined based only on the rights and permissions associated with VMM user roles, in effect ignoring the Hyper-V authorization store for hosts and virtual machines that it managed.

Virtual Machine Manager Background

Although virtual servers and clients have helped organizations minimize the number of physical systems they have, the challenge has been to manage these virtual systems. However, it wasn't until 2007 that Microsoft finally had a product that was dedicated to virtual machine management, which has then led to the current release covered in this book, Virtual Machine Manager 2012.

Early Virtualization Management Techniques

In the beginning, virtual machine management was performed by the system administrator using the standard Windows monitoring and management techniques: viewing event logs, performance counters, and system properties of both the virtual machine and the host that runs it. With the proliferation of virtual machines in the data center, there grew a need to centralize virtual machine management, including their placement, and provide disaster-recovery options for these guests.

Virtual Machine Manager 2007

Microsoft's answer to this need was Virtual Machine Manager 2007. With this initial release, VMM was available in three versions: System Center Virtual Machine Manager 2007, System Center Virtual Machine Manager 2007 Workgroup Edition, and System Center Essentials 2007. VMM 2007 provided comprehensive support for consolidating 32-bit physical servers onto virtual infrastructures and the rapid provisioning and deployment of new 32-bit virtual machines. Providing additional support to IT administrators,

VMM 2007 also featured a library to centrally manage the building blocks of the
virtual data center, including virtual hard drives, VMM templates, and support for P2V
conversions.

Virtual Machine Manager 2008

Released in September 2008, Virtual Machine Manager 2008 further improved the capabilities of the VMM product line. It replaced VMM 2007 while adding many new features,
including full Hyper-V support, 64-bit virtual machine support, and the ability to manage
both Microsoft and VMware virtual infrastructures. Some of the other new features or
changes included in this release are as follows:

▶ Extended support for virtual machine hosts to both Hyper-V and VMware hosts

▶ Integrated native support for Windows Server 2008 failover clusters

▶ Increased options for securing access to VMM resources using role-based access
  control (RBAC)

▶ Improved integration with Operations Manager 2007 to optimize physical resources

▶ Enhanced networking support, including VLANs, for virtual networking and
  isolation

▶ Improved disk and DVD management for VMs

▶ Expanded VMM library functionality

Backward Compatibility and Enhancements in VMM 2008

VMM 2008 was backward compatible with the earlier version of Microsoft Virtual
Machine Manager, VMM 2007.

Command Console Cmdlets

The more than 30 VMM 2007 cmdlets were improved to work with Hyper-V, and another
30+ new cmdlets were introduced in VMM 2008. Most of these cmdlet changes provide
Hyper-V and role-based access control support.

Virtual Machine Manager 2008 R2

The next major version, Virtual Machine Manager 2008 R2, was released in August of
2009. This release contained a number of improvements over the VMM 2008 release. For
example, Windows Server 2008 R2 Hyper-V host support allowed VMM Administrators
using VMM 2008 R2 to take advantage of the significant feature improvements made to
Hyper-V, such as the following:

▶ Live migration between Windows Server 2008 R2 clustered hosts. By using live
  migration, administrators were able to migrate a virtual machine between nodes in a
  Windows Server 2008 R2 failover cluster without any downtime.

▶ Support for both Virtual Machine Queue (VMQ) and TCP Chimney Offload features in Windows Server 2008 R2. Using these features, VMM 2008 R2 was able to perform network optimization during virtual machine placement. For example, with the VMQ feature, a unique network queue was able to be created for each virtual network adapter that was connected directly to the virtual machine's memory. This connection allowed packets to be routed directly from the hypervisor to the virtual machine. By using the TCP Chimney Offload feature, the processing of network traffic was able to be off-loaded from the physical NIC on the host computer, thus reducing CPU load and improving network performance.

▶ Support for the addition and removal of virtual hard disks (VHDs) while a virtual machine was running.

▶ Support for the Windows Server 2008 R2 Cluster Shared Volume (CSV) feature. By using CSV, all hosts in a Windows Server 2008 R2 failover cluster were able to have parallel access to the same virtual machine files on a single, shared logical unit number (LUN). In other words, because all nodes in a cluster access a single shared LUN, there was more complete transparency about which node controls each file. CSV support was a key component that allowed live migration of virtual machines.

In addition to enhancements based on Windows Server 2008 R2 Hyper-V features, the following sections discuss other features or changes included in VMM 2008 R2.

Hosts Can Be Placed in Maintenance Mode

Maintenance mode in VMM 2008 R2 is a feature that allowed Windows-based hosts to be placed into a state that allowed administrators to perform maintenance tasks on the host, such as applying updates or replacing a physical component. When placing hosts that are nodes in a Windows Server 2008 R2 cluster into Maintenance mode, an administrator was able to do either of the following for its highly available virtual machines:

▶ When available, use live migration to evacuate all virtual machines to other hosts on the same cluster.

▶ Place all virtual machines on the host into a saved state.

For standalone hosts or hosts that are nodes in a Windows Server 2008 R2 cluster that have any non-highly available virtual machines that are placed into Maintenance mode, VMM automatically places these virtual machines into a saved state.

When Maintenance mode is started on any host, VMM automatically did the following:

▶ Blocked virtual machine creation operations on the host

▶ Excluded the host from the host ratings during placement

▶ Displayed a host status of In Maintenance Mode in Host view of the VMM Administrator Console

Then when a host was taken out of Maintenance mode, VMM 2008 R2 reversed these changes. However, VMM did not automatically do a live migration to move highly available virtual machines back onto the original host in a Windows Server 2008 R2 cluster, nor did it restart any of the virtual machines on a host. Instead, these tasks had to be completed manually by an administrator.

Enhanced Support for SAN Transfers

Virtual Machine Manager 2012 supports a faster method of transferring virtual machines from one host to another without the need to replicate the data from host to host. This is done through storage area network (SAN) transfers where the local unit number (LUN) on the SAN hosting the virtual guest session is remapped from the source host to a destination host. In this manner, the destination Hyper-V host sees the guest session without the guest session data having to actually be replicated from host to host, which is very time consuming. The following items are the SAN transfer enhancements that were made in VMM 2008 R2:

▶ **SAN migration into and out of clustered hosts**—Using this feature, administrators were able to migrate virtual machines and highly available virtual machines into and out of clustered hosts using a SAN transfer, which automatically configured the cluster nodes to recognize and support the new workload.

▶ **Expanded support for iSCSI SANs**—With VMM 2008 R2, administrators were able to perform SAN transfer for virtual machines that used initiator-based iSCSI target connections. In previous VMM versions, only one LUN could be bound to a single iSCSI target. With VMM 2008 R2, LUN masking was possible, which allowed for multiple LUNs per iSCSI target .

Sanbolic Clustered File System Support

In VMM 2008 R2, the support for the Sanbolic Clustered File System (CFS) was added. By using this third-party share volume solution, administrators were able to perform quick migration on hosts running Windows Server 2008 with Hyper-V and live migration on hosts running Windows Server 2008 R2 with Hyper-V.

Veritas Storage Foundation for Windows Support

VMM 2008 R2 also added support for the Veritas Storage Foundation 5.1 for Windows (SFW), which was able to be used as an online storage management solution for creating virtual storage devices from physical disks and arrays. During virtual machine placement or migration, an SFW volume that was created as part of a cluster resource group was able to be selected. However, an SFW volume was limited to one virtual machine.

VMware Port Groups for Virtual Switches

For virtual machines deployed to a VMware ESX Server host, VMM 2008 R2 allowed support for using any existing VMware port groups that were available for virtual switches.

Windows PowerShell 2.0

VMM 2008 R2 added support for Windows PowerShell 2.0 while continuing support for Windows PowerShell 1.0.

What's New in System Center Virtual Machine Manager 2012

Out of all of the System Center 2012 updates, System Center Virtual Machine Manager 2012 has had the most radical changes in terms of look and feel to the IT professional. VMM 2012 was completely rewritten with a focus on the cloud and fabric as the overall look and structure of the tool. VMM 2012 starts off with the premise that in order to build and deploy virtual images, the organization needs to have the appropriate storage subsystems and networking fabric in place. As such, the changes and additions to VMM 2012 over previous versions are pretty extensive. Some of the top new functions in VMM 2012 that are covered in this book include the following:

▶ **Inclusion of fabric management**—With the focus on being able to manage virtual machines and a mixed private and public cloud infrastructure, Virtual Machine Manager 2012 starts with the configuration and management of fabric resources. VMM 2012 allows for the ability to create and manage Hyper-V clusters, use Citrix XenServers as target virtual hosts, and discover physical host systems and automatically make the host into a Hyper-V managed host server. VMM also allows for the configuration of network and storage resources, including creating logical networks, IP address pools, load balancing, storage logical units, and storage pools.

▶ **Simplification of host provisioning**—VMM 2012 allows for the provisioning of systems, including host servers from bare metal to Hyper-V hosts, and the inclusion of Hyper-V hosts to highly available clusters.

▶ **Allocation of logical networks and address management**—VMM 2012 allows for the creation of VLANs and subnets within a data center, as well as management of the IP addresses, load balancing VIPs, and MAC addresses for host systems, guest sessions, and networks.

▶ **Storage management and storage classification**—Beyond just managing virtual hosts and guest sessions, VMM 2012 added the ability to also manage storage systems using SMI-S, a storage management standard. Additionally, storage was able to be classified based on storage performance and storage subsystem capabilities.

▶ **Support for private cloud configurations**—VMM 2012 allows for the creation of private clouds, including combining hosts, networks, storage subsystems, and resource libraries to identify a private cloud environment. Application profiles can then be created to automatically install server application virtualization (Server App-V), Web-deployed applications, Microsoft SQL data-tier applications (DACs), and creation of virtual guest sessions from virtual machine templates. A service template designer has been included to improve the template build process combined with automated deployment of templates to build private cloud infrastructure as required by the organization.

▶ **Administration improvements**—VMM 2012 adds administration improvements, including several new roles, such as the Delegated Administrator, Read-Only Administrator, and Self-Service User roles. Additionally, the ability to create and use RunAs accounts allows an organization to delegate administration and management tasks without having to directly give each role administrator critical credential access information.

▶ **Improvements in scalability and high availability**—Additions in VMM 2012 provide improvements for scalability by providing the ability to add additional virtual machines to a deployed service as well as update a service within a private cloud for dynamic growth as required by the application or needs of an organization. Additionally, VMM 2012 provides the ability to install a highly available VMM management server so that the management of VMM services can keep up with the demands and needs for reliability in an enterprise environment.

Virtual Machine Manager Prerequisites

This section describes the hardware, operating system, and software requirements for each of the VMM components, which must be met before installing and using System Center Virtual Machine Manager 2012.

VMM Server

The following are the system requirements for installing the VMM Server component.

Hardware Requirements

Table 12.1 shows the minimum and recommended hardware requirements for a VMM server that is managing up to 150 hosts.

TABLE 12.1   VMM Server Hardware Requirements

Component	Requirement
Processor speed	Minimum: Pentium 4, 2GHz (x64 bit only) Recommended: Dual-Processor, Dual-Core, 2.8GHz (x64) or greater
Memory	Minimum: 2GB Recommended: 4GB
Disk space (with a local VMM database)	Minimum: 2GB Recommended: 50GB
Disk space (using a local, full version of SQL Server)	Minimum: 80GB Recommended: 150GB

> **NOTE**
>
> If you are also using the VMM server as a library server, the disk space requirements will vary greatly depending on the number and size of virtual machine templates, virtual hard disks, virtual floppy disks, ISO images, scripts, hardware profiles, guest operating system profiles, and stored virtual machines. Additionally, if you are planning to manage more than 150 hosts, you should conduct a VMM sizing operation to ensure that your infrastructure is sized accordingly to support the number of desired hosts.

Supported Operating Systems

The following operating systems are supported by the VMM Server component:

▶ Windows Server 2008 R2 SP1 x64, Standard and Enterprise Editions or more current

Remote SQL Instance Requirements

The VMM Server component supports the following versions of SQL Server:

▶ SQL Server 2008, Standard or Enterprise Editions (32-bit or 64-bit)

▶ SQL Server 2008 R2, Standard, Enterprise, or Datacenter Editions (32-bit or 64-bit)

Software Requirements

The VMM Server component has the following software requirements:

▶ Microsoft .NET Framework 3.51 SP1

▶ Windows Automated Installation Kit (WAIK) for Windows 7 (x64)

VMM Administrator Console

The VMM Administrator Console can be installed on other computers to remotely access and manage a VMM deployment. However, it is recommended that the Administrator Console also be installed on the same machine that is hosting the VMM Server component. In fact, if you are planning to use the VMM Reporting feature, the Administrator Console must be installed on the VMM server.

Hardware Requirements

Table 12.2 shows the minimum and recommended hardware requirements for the Administrator Console.

TABLE 12.2   VMM Administrator Console Hardware Requirements

Component	Requirement
Processor speed	Minimum: Pentium 4, 550MHz Recommended: Pentium 4, 1GHz or greater
Memory	Minimum: 512MB Recommended: 1GB
Disk space	Minimum: 512MB Recommended: 2GB

NOTE

As you manage more hosts with your VMM deployment, the hardware requirements for the Administrator Console will continue to increase.

Supported Operating Systems

The VMM Administrator Console supports the following operating systems:

▶ Windows Server 2008 R2 SP1 (full installation), Standard, Enterprise, or Datacenter Editions (x64 only)

▶ Windows 7 SP1 Professional, Enterprise, or Ultimate (x86 or x64)

Software Requirements

The Administrator Console has the following software requirements:

▶ Windows PowerShell 2.0

▶ Microsoft .NET Framework 3.51 SP1

VMM Self-Service Portal

The following are the system requirements for installing the VMM Self-Service Portal on a dedicated machine. The actual requirements for this VMM component will vary depending on the number of concurrent self-service connections being made on the web server.

Hardware Requirements

Table 12.3 shows the minimum and recommended hardware requirements for the Self-Service Portal for maintaining up to 10 concurrent connections.

TABLE 12.3   VMM Self-Service Portal Hardware Requirements

Component	Requirement
Processor speed	Minimum: Pentium 4, 2.8Ghz Recommended: Pentium 4, 2.8GHz or greater
Memory	Minimum: 2GB Recommended: 2GB
Disk space	Minimum: 512MB Recommended: 20GB

NOTE

Installation of the Self-Service Portal on a domain controller is not supported.

Supported Operating Systems

The VMM Self-Service Portal supports the following operating systems:

▶ Windows Server 2008 R2 SP1 x64, Standard and Enterprise Editions or more current

Software Requirements

The VMM Self-Service Portal has the following software requirements:

▶ Windows PowerShell 2.0

▶ Microsoft .NET Framework 3.51 SP1

▶ Web Server (IIS) role must be installed along with the following server role services:

   ▶ .NET Extensibility

   ▶ ASP.NET

   ▶ Default Document

   ▶ Directory Browsing

   ▶ HTTP Errors

   ▶ IIS 6 Metabase Compatibility

   ▶ IIS 6 WMI Compatibility

   ▶ ISAPI Extensions

   ▶ ISAPI Filters

   ▶ Request Filtering

   ▶ Static Content

Virtual Machine Hosts

The following are the system requirements for virtual machine hosts that can be managed by VMM:

- ▶ Windows Server 2008 R2 SP1 (full installation or ServerCore), Enterprise/Datacenter Editions (x64 only)

- ▶ Windows Server 2008 SP2 (full installation or ServerCore), Enterprise/Datacenter Editions (x64 only)

- ▶ Hyper-V 2008 R2 (x64 only)

- ▶ VMware vCenter v4.1 with the following hosts:

  - ▶ ESX 4.1

  - ▶ ESXi 4.1

  - ▶ ESX 3.5

  - ▶ ESXi 3.5

- ▶ Citrix XenServer 6.0 (with Citrix XenServer Integration Suite supplemental pack for System Center Virtual Machine Manager)

> **NOTE**
>
> From time to time, Microsoft updates the support for various versions of host systems as well as support for Windows, VMM, and SQL database. Check with the latest Microsoft TechNet posting on the most current system configuration support.

Planning a Virtual Machine Manager Deployment

Deploying any information system can be a very challenging task. VMM is no exception as there are many different things, both business and technical related, that need to be considered when planning a VMM deployment. This section describes the steps that should be taken to plan a Virtual Machine Manager deployment. The steps that are provided include step-by-step instructions and best-practice design advice with the goal of helping IT professionals avoid planning mistakes that can prove to be costly and difficult to correct.

Step One: Understand the Environment

The first step of the VMM planning process is to understand the environment in which the deployment will take place. To complete this step, review the relevant design documents for information systems in your organization, perform discovery sessions with the owners of systems, and review the status of the systems in real time. Items that you should pay particular attention to during this phase of the design include the following:

▶ The current Active Directory forest design

▶ The current network topology and available bandwidth

▶ The existing virtual infrastructure, including locations of already deployed virtual machine hosts and current virtualization technologies that are being used

▶ Any planned/pending organizational changes (business acquisitions or diversifications), including the desired management model, whether centralized or decentralized

▶ Applications that will be retired, replaced, or upgraded

▶ Any new applications that will be introduced into the environment

Step Two: Define the Project Scope

The next step of the VMM planning process is to define the scope of the VMM deployment project. While completing this task, it is important to ensure the goals of the project are aligned to the business requirements for virtualization, fault tolerance, capacity, performance, and disaster recovery. To complete this step, use the information gathered from the first step of the planning process to answer the following questions:

▶ **What part of the organization is in scope?**—To answer this question, you need to determine if VMM is being deployed to manage your organization's entire virtual infrastructure or just a part of it.

▶ **What virtualization technology and management solution is currently being used?**—This is a very important question as it will help you determine the size and placement for VMM instances, related web servers, and library servers in the organization. To answer this question, you need to understand where virtualization is currently being used, how that virtualization solution is being managed, and the location for any existing virtualization hosts and their related virtual machines.

▶ **Is virtualization being used as part of a disaster recovery solution?**—Virtualization can be a key component for facilitating a rapid recovery from a disaster. As such, VMM can further enhance the recoverability of a virtualization deployment in response to a disaster. Understanding if this is a business requirement for your VMM deployment will help you determine its criticality to business operations and just how fault tolerant the deployment needs to be.

▶ **Will self-service provisioning be used?**—Using the Self-Service Portal, users can provision and manage their own virtual machines. To answer this question, you need to determine if self-service provisioning is a requirement and at which locations this requirement must be met. Based on the answer to this question, you will be able to better determine the sizing and placement for VMM-related web servers.

▶ **What is the desired management model for virtualization?**—Every organization
manages their environments differently. When answering this question, you need to
determine if the desired virtualization management model is one that consists of a
centralized management approach or if management responsibilities should be
distributed, or delegated, across the organization. Based on how this question is
answered, you then use the information to determine the RBAC model for your
VMM deployment.

Step Three: Determine Operations Manager Integration

The third step in the VMM planning process is to determine if System Center Operations
Manager should be integrated with the VMM deployment. For VMM to make intelligent
placement recommendations for where virtual machines should be deployed or automatically moved to, the VMM Agent collects performance data from host server(s) and sends
it to the VMM server every 9 minutes. To further enhance VMM's ability to make intelligent decisions about virtual machine placements, you can also deploy Operations
Manager Agents to host servers and their virtual machine guests to gather additional
performance information using the Operations Manager Server Virtualization
Management Pack.

When you have deployed Operations Manager in this manner, you can then configure
the Administrator Console so that it connects to Operations Manager as a reporting user
to access the additional performance information using Operations Manager reports.
Once configured in this manner, an Administrator Console user can then seamlessly drill
down from Performance views for a host server to further drill down and examine performance data (operating system and applications) for each virtual machine guest running
on that host.

If you choose to integrate Operations Manager and VMM in this manner, you also
need to determine which of the following integration options best suits your VMM
deployment:

▶ Create an Operations Manager management group for each VMM instance.

▶ Dedicate a single Operations Manager management group to manage all of the
deployed VMM instances.

> **NOTE**
>
> An Operations Manager management group can manage multiple instances of the
> version of VMM (either VMM 2008/2008 R2 or VMM 2012). However, each VMM
> instance can only be managed by one Operations Manager management group.

Step Four: Determine the Number of VMM Instances

The fourth step in the VMM planning process is to determine the number of VMM instances that should be deployed. A VMM instance is a single installation of VMM Server, which has the following considerations:

▶ Each VMM instance must have its own separate SQL Server database instance.

▶ Each managed host server can only be managed by a single VMM instance.

▶ There is no relationship between VMM instances. Therefore, they cannot be integrated nor can they share data.

Based on these considerations, you need to use the information that was gathered during the previous steps in this planning process to best answer the following questions to determine if more than one VMM instance is required:

▶ **Are there isolated networks?**—Sometimes an organization might have isolated networks for various purposes. For example, a lab deployment tends to be isolated from production networks. Therefore, depending on the virtualization needs for those networks, you need to deploy a separate VMM instance.

▶ **Is self-service provisioning a requirement?**—If you are planning to use self-service provisioning, you choose to deploy different VMM instances to facilitate a clear separation between self-service-related virtual machines and virtual machines that are considered sensitive or secure. Additionally, it is generally recommended that each VMM instance that is using self-service be limited to 1,000 or less virtual machines dedicated for use by Self-Service Users. If there is a requirement to support more than this number of dedicated virtual machines, additional VMM instances should be deployed.

▶ **Does the management model call for a centralized or decentralized deployment?**—During the scoping step of this planning process, you should have determined the intended management model for your VMM deployment. If you have chosen to follow a decentralized model, a separate VMM instance should be deployed for each location and requires a virtualization management solution. For a centralized model, barring any additional sizing limitations, you can deploy a single VMM instance.

▶ **Are there any organizational requirements that must be met?**—In certain cases, there might be political or organizational considerations that might require that additional VMM instances be deployed. For example, if there is a clear separation between two different business groups, there might be a requirement that the same separation also exists for the virtual infrastructure.

▶ **What number of host servers and virtual machines must the deployment support?**—As a general rule of thumb, each VMM instance can only support up to 400 host servers and 8,000 virtual machines. If you need to support more host servers or virtual machines, additional VMM instances need to be added to your deployment.

Step Five: Design the VMM Server

The fifth step in the VMM planning process is to design the VMM server infrastructure. By definition, the VMM server is the central hub for what defines a VMM managed host set and how the various VMM components interact with that set. As such, the VMM server performs most of the functions that are critical to the functionality of a VMM deployment. However, despite its key nature, the number of different tasks a VMM server has to perform only results in a relativity light workload for the server this component is deployed on. Therefore, the recommended hardware configuration for a VMM server that is supporting up to 8,000 virtual machines and 400 host servers is a dual-processor or dual-core, 3.6GHz or greater (x64) with 8GB of RAM.

Step Six: Design the Database Server and Database

The sixth step in the VMM planning process is to create and document the VMM database server and database design. The VMM database is used to store the configuration information for a VMM instance and any performance data that might be collected by VMM. In general, the workload impact to a SQL Server instance that is hosting the VMM database is relatively light. Therefore, the recommended hardware configuration for a database server that is supporting up to 8,000 virtual machines and 400 host servers is a dual-core machine with 8GB of RAM and 200GB of available disk space.

> **NOTE**
>
> Unlike the VMM server, the VMM database is stateful so the database server that is hosting it can be configured such that it is fault tolerant.

Step Seven: Design the Self-Service Portal Web Server(s)

The seventh step in the VMM planning process is to determine the Self-Service Portal web server design. As discussed previously in this chapter, the Self-Service Portal allows users to provision and manage their own virtual machines with administrator intervention. Like other VMM components, the Self-Service Portal is a relatively lightweight application. Therefore, the recommended hardware configuration is a dual-core machine with 2GB of RAM.

Step Eight: Design the Infrastructure Fabric

The eighth step in the VMM planning process is to design the infrastructure fabric, specifically the LAN and WAN network infrastructure and the storage subsystem. Because VMM 2012 has the ability to manage more than just virtual hosts and guests, and actually reach into the management of the fabric, the planning process needs to include fabric management.

Fabric management involves identifying the bandwidth requirements and the bandwidth capacity of the virtualized environment. If the demands exceed the capacity, a well-planned management platform will provide the needed information to detect the change and increase capacity as needed. VMM 2012 supports storage management for SMI-S storage subsystems, and thus the provisioning, management, capacity planning, and storage extension needs to be planned and prepared for as part of the VMM 2012 rollout.

Step Nine: Design the Library Servers and Libraries

The ninth and final step in the VMM planning process is to determine the library servers and library's design. As discussed earlier in this chapter, a VMM library is a collection of resources that includes such items as:

▶ VM templates

▶ Disk images and ISO image files

▶ Guest OS profiles

▶ Hardware profiles

A library server is a file server with one or more shares that is used to store the previously listed items. Although each VMM instance must have at least one library server, you can deploy more than one library server depending on the needs of your VMM deployment.

The primary function for a library server is to act as a storage depot, which host servers can then use to retrieve the mentioned items as part of a virtual machine provisioning task. As some of these items can be fairly large, the primary design considerations that should be taken into account for library servers are as follows:

▶ **The storage configuration**—A library server can use all forms of direct attached storage (DAS) and supports Fibre Channel or an iSCSI SAN. The appropriate configuration will vary depending on the number and size of the items that are stored in the library.

▶ **The amount of network traffic**—Specifically consider traffic that is generated when items are transferred to a host server during a virtual machine provisioning task. As a general recommendation, library servers should be placed in the same location as the host servers that they will service.

▶ **The type of fault tolerance used for library shares**—You can either choose to use Distributed File System (DFS) or a file server cluster to provide fault tolerance for your library shares.

Deploying Virtual Machine Manager

This section covers the steps needed to perform a basic Virtual Machine Manager 2012 deployment. After completing this section, you will understand how to meet any software requirements, install the VMM application software, and complete any other required VMM configuration tasks for a basic deployment.

Preparing the Virtual Machine Manager Server

Before the VMM installation can be started, the base Windows operating system needs to be installed. After the base server operating system has been installed and the latest updates have been applied, join the server to the domain and then ensure all of the software requirements are met, as noted in the VMM Server "Software Requirements" section earlier in this chapter.

Depending on a variety of factors, VMM can be deployed on a single server that hosts the VMM server, SQL database, and Administrator Console, or these components can be deployed across separate, single-purpose servers. The decision about how to deploy VMM in the enterprise depends on the physical and virtual environment and, to a lesser degree, the administration of these environments.

> **NOTE**
>
> The computer where VMM is installed must be joined to an Active Directory Domain
> Services domain.

Single-Server Deployment

A single-server deployment is often used in small environments where physical resources are tight and the virtual environment is small. In this type of deployment, a single server hosts the VMM server and the SQL Server database, the Administrator Console, and possibly even the Self-Service Portal. A single-server deployment is recommended for a virtual infrastructure environment (both the VMM server and host servers) that doesn't span a wide area network (WAN).

Multiple-Server Deployment

A multiple-server deployment is usually used in larger, high-performance VMM environments or where the virtual environment spans across a WAN. VMM performance is improved by installing the different components on separate servers and placing these servers closest to the resources they access the most. Typically, this involves using a dedicated (or at least separate) SQL Server database server and placing VMM libraries close to the host servers where the virtual machines will be deployed. Often, the Administrator Console is installed on separate servers or workstations to facilitate administration. The Self-Service console can also be deployed on its own server or on another underutilized web server or it can even be virtualized itself.

Installing the Virtual Machine Manager Server

After meeting all of the hardware, operating system, and software requirements, the next step in your deployment is to execute the VMM Setup Wizard to complete a basic single-server VMM installation. To start the installation, log on to the VMM server using a domain user account that is a member of the local administrator's group. Then execute the VMM Setup Wizard (`setup.exe`) from the installation media, an ISO file, or a copy of the setup files from a shared network location. Once the Setup Wizard has started, use the following steps to complete the installation:

1. In the Virtual Machine Manager 2012 window, as shown in Figure 12.3, select Install. This starts the VMM Setup Wizard.

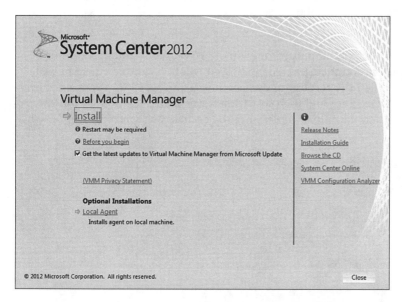

FIGURE 12.3   Starting the VMM Setup Wizard.

2. On the first page of the wizard, Select Features to Install, select VMM Management Server, which automatically also selects VMM Console.

3. On the Product Registration page, provide the product registration information for your organization, and then click Next.

4. On the License Terms page, select the I Have Read, Understood, and Agree with the Terms of the License Agreement option, and then click Next.

5. On the Customer Experience Improvement Program page, select the desired Customer Experience Improvement Program (CEIP) option, and then click Next.

6. On the Microsoft Update page, select the desired Microsoft Update option, and then click Next.

7. On the Installation Location page, you can either use the default folder location or modify the installation path to meet your needs. After choosing the desired installation location, click Next.

8. On the Prerequisites Check page, a prerequisites check is automatically performed by the Setup Wizard. After the prerequisites check has completed, review any alerts or warnings about hardware that does not meet the minimum or recommended requirements, or missing software prerequisites, and then click Next.

NOTE

You can continue the installation if you receive warnings, but you must resolve all
alerts before you can proceed with the installation.

9. On the Database Configuration page, provide the server name and port for the
remote SQL instance and the user credentials that will be used to connect to that
instance (if other than the account under which you are logged in). Next, select the
desired SQL Server instance and then select the New Database option, as shown in
Figure 12.4. After you have finished defining the desired SQL Server settings, click
Next.

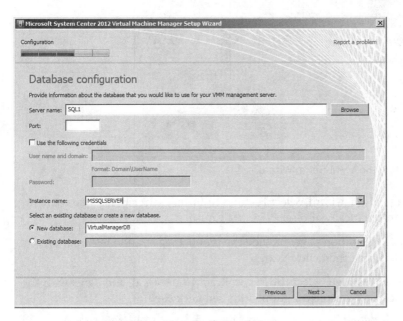

FIGURE 12.4   Defining the SQL Server Settings.

NOTE

When using a SQL Server instance and database, the SQL Server 2008 Management
Tools – Basic or Command Line Utilities must be preinstalled on the intended VMM
server.

10. On the Configure Service Account and Distributed Key Management page, for the VMM service account, you can either choose to use the LocalSystem account or define and use a domain account. When using a domain account, that account should be an account that is specifically designated to be used for VMM (failure to do so might cause unexpected results or result in the VMM installation being less secure). If you are planning a high-availability installation of VMM server, make sure to use an account to create containers in Active Directory and select the option to Store My Keys in Active Directory. After you have defined the desired installation settings, click Next.

On the Port Configuration page, it is recommended that you select the default port settings for the VMM server installation.

NOTE

If you plan to use shared ISO images with Hyper-V virtual machines or if VMM is being installed into an environment with a disjointed namespace, a domain account must be used as the VMM service account. When using a domain account, that account must also be a member of the VMM server's local administrators group.

11. On the Library Configuration page, choose to either create a new default library share on the VMM server or use an existing share on the VMM server as a library share. If you choose to create a new library share, the default share name is MSSCVMMLibrary and its folder is located at %SYSTEMDRIVE%\ProgramData\Virtual Machine Manager Library Files. Once you have chosen or defined the desired library share settings, click Next.

NOTE

You can always add other library shares to the default library server or other library servers on different computers. However, neither the default library server nor its library share can be removed or relocated.

12. On the Installation Summary page, review the summary of installation settings, and then click Install.

13. On the Installing Features page, the Setup Wizard installs any missing software prerequisites if necessary, and then installs the VMM Server and VMM Console components, as shown in Figure 12.5. The installation might take several minutes, depending on the options that were selected. Once the installation has finished, click Close.

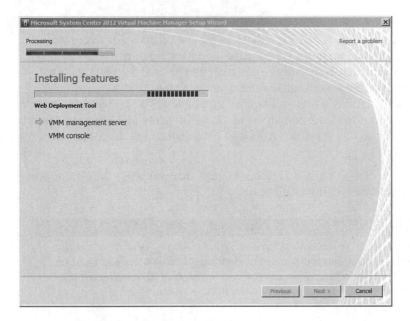

FIGURE 12.5   VMM Server installation progress.

Installing the VMM Administrator Console

During the install of the VMM Server component, the installation wizard installs the
VMM Administrator Console automatically. In addition to this, however, you might also
want to install additional Administrator Console instances on other computers as needed.
To complete this task, use the following steps:

1. Execute the VMM Setup Wizard (setup.exe) from the installation media, an ISO
   file, or a copy of the setup files from a shared network location.

2. In the Virtual Machine Manager 2012 window, select the Install Option to start the
   VMM Setup Wizard.

3. On the first page of the wizard, Select Features to Install, select VMM Console and
   click Next.

4. On the License Terms page, select the I Agree with the Terms of This Notice check
   box, and then click Next.

5. On the Customer Experience Improvement Program page, click Next.

6. On the Microsoft Update page, select the desired Microsoft Update option, and then
   click Next.

7. On the Installation Location page, you can either use the default folder location or
   modify the installation path to meet your needs. After choosing the desired installation location, click Next.

8. On the Port Assignment page, it is recommended that the default port settings are used for the Administrator Console installation. After you have defined the desired port assignment, click Next.

9. On the Port Configuration page, change the port number for the Administrator Console if you did not install it with the default, and then click Next.

10. On the Installation Summary page, review the summary of installation settings, and then click Install.

11. On the Installing Features page, the Setup Wizard installs any missing software prerequisites, if necessary, and then installs the Administrator Console, as shown in Figure 12.6. The installation might take several minutes, depending on the options that were selected. Once the installation has finished, click Close.

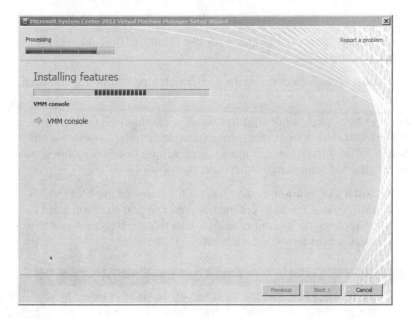

FIGURE 12.6   Administrator Console installation progress.

The first time you launch the Administrator Console, you will be prompted with the Connect to Server dialog box. If you are running the Administrator Console on the same computer as the VMM server, just click Connect. For installations where the Administrator Console has been installed on a different computer, type the name of the VMM server followed by a colon and the connection port that you assigned during the installation of that VMM server.

NOTE

The default port for the Administrator Console to communicate with the VMM server is 8100.

Installing the Self-Service Portal

The VMM Self-Service Portal is an optional component that can be installed to allow users to create and manage their own virtual machines. If you are planning to use this component, the next step in the VMM deployment process is to install the Self-Service Portal. To complete this task, perform the following steps while logged on to the VMM server as a local administrator:

1. Execute the VMM Setup Wizard (`setup.exe`) from the installation media, an ISO file, or a copy of the setup files from a shared network location.

2. In the Virtual Machine Manager 2012 window, select the Install option. This starts the VMM Setup Wizard.

3. On the first page of the wizard, What Would You Like to Do?, select Add Features.

4. On the Select Features to Add page, select VMM Self-Service Portal and click Next.

5. On the License Terms page, select the I Agree with the Terms of This Notice check box, and then click Next.

6. On the Microsoft Update page, select the desired Microsoft Update option, and then click Next.

7. On the Prerequisites Check page, a prerequisites check is automatically performed by the Setup Wizard. After the prerequisites check has completed, review any alerts or warnings about hardware that does not meet the minimum or recommended requirements or missing software prerequisites, and then click Next.

8. On the Self-Service Portal Configuration page, specify the name of the VMM server you want the VMM Self-Service Portal to connect to, and the port that you want the VMM Self-Service Portal to use for communications with that server. Once you have specified the desired web server settings, click Next.

> **NOTE**
>
> If you plan to install the Self-Service Portal on the VMM server, you need to either specify a different TCP port (other than 80) or define a host header for the portal.

9. On the Installation Summary page, review the summary of installation settings, and then click Install.

10. On the Installing Features page, the Setup Wizard installs any missing software prerequisites if necessary, and then installs the Self-Service Portal. The installation might take several minutes, depending on the options that were selected. Once the installation has finished, click Close.

Securing the Self-Service Portal

After you complete the base installation of the Self-Service Portal, you should complete some additional tasks to ensure that the portal is secure. These tasks are as follows.

Configure SSL for the Self-Service Portal

As a best practice, you should always configure Secure Sockets Layer (SSL) on the Self-Service Portal. Depending on how you are using the portal, the SSL certificate can either be issued by a publicly trusted certificate authority or from a certificate authority that is part of your organization's internal Public Key Infrastructure (PKI).

Enable Integrated Windows Authentication

By default, the Self-Service Portal uses forms-based authentication (FBA) to control access to the website. When logging on to the portal using FBA, users have a cached credentials option called Store My Credentials. If this option is selected, VMM securely caches the credentials on the web server for the duration of the session. These cached credentials are then used for remote connections, which are initialized from inside the portal.

To reduce the risks associated with cached credentials and the confusion this option might cause for users who are not aware of it, you can enable Integrated Windows Authentication on the portal. By enabling this method of authentication, users will no longer be prompted for their credentials when they access the Self-Service Portal. Instead, when a user attempts to access the portal, his or her current Windows credentials are used and the user is only prompted for credentials if additional authorization is needed.

> **NOTE**
>
> If the Self-Service Portal has been deployed on a different computer from the VMM server and Integrated Windows Authentication has been enabled, you also need to configure Kerberos constrained delegation for the VMM service account.

Installing the VMM Agent

After installing the required VMM components, the next step in the VMM deployment process is to install the VMM Agent on the host servers. For host servers that are members of a domain, you can "push" the agent to them using the following steps:

1. Log on to a computer that has the Administrator Console installed as a domain user account that is a member of the VMM Administrator role.

2. Next, open the Administrator Console using either the desktop or Start menu icon.

3. Once the console has loaded, in the VMs and Services pane, right-click All Hosts and select the virtual host type that you want to add to the console. This starts the Add Resource Wizard, as shown in Figure 12.7.

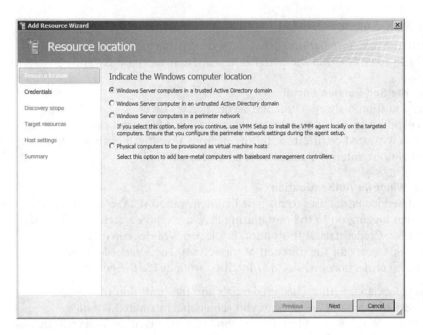

FIGURE 12.7   The Add Resource Wizard.

4. On the first page of the wizard, Resource Location, select the Windows Server
   Computers in a Trusted Active Directory Domain option and select Next.

5. On the Credentials page, provide the credentials that will be used to connect to the
   host, and then click Next.

NOTE

For credentials, the VMM 2012 administrator can use a RunAs account created in the
administration functions of VMM. This minimizes sharing key administrative accounts
and passwords, and instead just allows the use of accounts for elevated privilege
functions.

6. On the Discovery Scope page, provide the name of the host server in the Computer
   Names box and then click next, as shown in Figure 12.8.

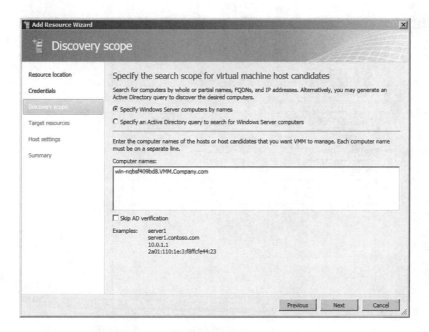

FIGURE 12.8   The Discovery Scope page.

7. On the Target Resources page, select the computers that have been discovered by the VMM Console based on the input on the Discovery Scope page, and select Next.

8. On the Host Settings page, select the desired host group and host reassociation options, and then click Next.

9. On the Summary page, review the information for the host servers that will be added, and then click Finish. Additionally, you can click View Script to see the commands that will be executed by the Administrator Console to add the selected host servers.

NOTE

VMM not only installs the VMM Agent, but, if needed, it also installs or enables the required virtualization software and creates a Windows Firewall exception.

10. Next, the Jobs dialog box is displayed showing the agent installation progress, as shown in Figure 12.9.

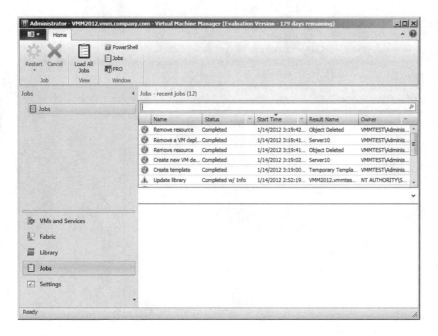

FIGURE 12.9   The Jobs dialog box.

Manually Installing the VMM Agent

For host servers that are within the DMZ or if there was some issue with the agent push, you can opt to perform a manual installation of the VMM Agent. To manually install the VMM Agent, complete the following steps:

1. Execute the VMM Setup Wizard (setup.exe) from the installation media, an ISO file, or a copy of the setup files from a shared network location.

2. In the Virtual Machine Manager 2012 window, select the Local Agent option. This starts the VMM Agent Setup Wizard.

3. On the first page of the wizard, License Terms, select the I Accept the Terms of This Notice, and then click Next.

4. On the Destination Folder page, you can either use the default folder location or modify the installation path to meet your needs, and then click Next.

5. On the Security File Folder page, if the host server is on a perimeter network, enable the This Host Is on a Perimeter Network option and define the following values:

   ▶ **Security File Encryption Key**—Provide a string that will be used as the encryption key to create the security file. Be sure to note the string that you use as the encryption key. That string will need to be entered again when you are adding the host using the Administrator Console.

> ▶ **Export Security File To**—If needed, click Change to modify the folder path where the security file will be exported to.

> ▶ **Use a CA Signed Certificate for Encrypting Communications**—By default, the VMM Agent Setup Wizard generates a self-signed certificate that is used to encrypt communications between the host server and the VMM server. If you want to use a certificate that has been signed by a trusted CA, enable this option and provide the thumbprint of the certificate.

6. Once you have defined the desired Security File Folder settings, click Next.

7. On the Configuration Settings page, use the default port settings, and then click Next.

8. On the Ready to Install page, click Install.

9. On the Completed the Microsoft System Center Virtual Machine Manager Agent (x64) Setup Wizard page, click Close.

10. Navigate to the folder where the security file is stored (by default, that location is `c:\Program Files\Microsoft System Center Virtual Machine Manager 2012` and the name of the file is `SecurityFile.txt`).

11. Next, copy the `SecurityFile.txt` file to the VMM server.

12. Log on to a computer that has the Administrator Console installed as a domain user account that is a member of the VMM Administrator role.

13. Next, open the Administrator Console using either the desktop or Start menu icon.

14. Once the console has loaded, in the Actions pane, click Add Host. This starts the Add Hosts Wizard.

15. On the first page of the wizard, Select Host Location, select the Windows Server-Based Host on a Perimeter Network option, and then click Next.

16. On the Select Host Servers page, for each host server that you are adding to VMM, provide the host server name or IP address, the encryption key, and the path to the `SecurityFile.txt`, as shown in Figure 12.10. After providing these details, click Add. Once you have finished selecting all of the host servers that you plan to add into VMM, click Next.

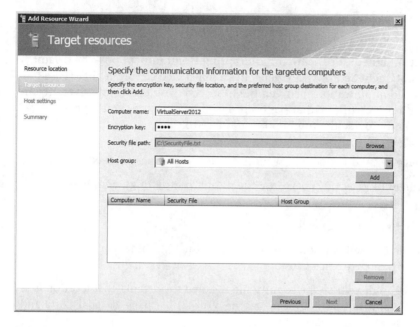

FIGURE 12.10   Selecting host servers to add to VMM.

17. On the Host Properties page, leave the default settings and then click Next.

18. On the Summary page, review the information for the host servers that will be
added, and then click Add Hosts.

Summary

This chapter, dedicated to Virtual Machine Manager 2012, hopefully provided you with
an advanced understanding of the overall VMM solution offering. Everything from
VMM's background, planning a deployment, and installing the solution were covered.
After reading this chapter, you should now also understand that VMM is an extremely
powerful addition to Microsoft's virtualization offerings. By using VMM, organizations
have the ability to manage virtual machines across multiple hosts and to delegate the
administration and management of the virtual machines on the same host or on other
virtual hosts in the organization. However, VMM not only supports the management of
Microsoft-based virtualization platforms, but it also provides connectivity and support for
management of virtual machines running on other platforms such as VMware.

Best Practices

The following are best practices from this chapter:

- ▶ Organizations using Hyper-V should use VMM 2012 instead of previous versions of VMM to get the most out of the virtual management environment.

- ▶ VMM 2012 can only be installed on Windows Server 2008 x64, Standard and Enterprise Editions or Windows Server 2008 R2 x64, Standard and Enterprise Editions.

- ▶ Ensure the system that VMM is being installed on is attached to a Windows domain.

- ▶ For most deployments, VMM can be installed on the same system as the SQL Server instance that hosts the VMM database.

- ▶ Use the Self-Service Portal to allow end users or developers to create and manage their virtual machines.

- ▶ Use the Administrator Console to manage Microsoft Hyper-V, VMware ESX, and Citrix XenServer hosts.

- ▶ Organizations that deploy VMM Server components in a redundant configuration should ensure that VMM libraries are made redundant, too.

- ▶ VMM libraries should be placed on clustered file servers when fault tolerance of the library is required.

- ▶ Multiple geographically placed VMM library servers should be configured for organizations with multiple host servers in different locations.

- ▶ Create hardware profiles to define the hardware used in common virtual machines (for example, a dual-processor server with 2GB of RAM and a DVD-ROM).

- ▶ Create guest OS profiles to define the operating system profile used in common virtual machines (for example, Windows Server 2008 x64 Standard Edition).

- ▶ Use VMM to reduce the complexity of managing multiple virtualization platforms.

- ▶ Learn the VMM command shell cmdlets for command-line management of the virtual environment.

- ▶ Use host clusters to host mission-critical virtual machines to provide a higher level of fault tolerance.

- ▶ Store common CD images (ISOs) in the VMM library for easy access from the VMM Administrator Console.

- ▶ Ensure that only highly available virtual machines are marked as such in the VM's settings. Doing so ensures that the virtual machine can only be placed on host clusters.

▶ The VMM Administrator role cannot be limited so create additional administrative
  roles to further delegate VMM administrative rights.

▶ Use a single-server deployment for VMM and SQL Server in a relatively simple environment; split the VMM components in a large, enterprise environment.

CHAPTER 13

Managing a Hyper-V Environment with Virtual Machine Manager 2012

IN THIS CHAPTER

▶ Understanding the VMM Private Cloud

▶ Using the VMM Management Interfaces

▶ Understanding Virtual Machine Conversions

▶ Managing VMM User Roles

▶ Deploying Virtual Machines

▶ Migrating Virtual Machines

▶ Understanding and Implementing Server App-V

▶ Best Practices

In Chapter 12, "Virtual Machine Manager 2012 Design, Planning, and Implementation," you were introduced to Virtual Machine Manager (VMM), how it is structured, and how to install it. In this chapter, the focus now shifts toward understanding the VMM management interfaces and how they can be used to manage a Hyper-V environment. This chapter discusses the new VMM private cloud concepts, how VMM can be used to perform virtual machine (VM) conversions, how VMM management rights can be delegated, how to deploy virtual machines, how to migrate those virtual machines between host servers or storage locations, and how to use Server App-V to sequence applications for use in a private cloud. As you learn in this chapter, VMM is a very effective management tool for your virtual infrastructure. By using VMM, you can significantly improve your management capabilities over a virtual infrastructure that includes Microsoft, VMware, and Citrix hosts, while enabling rapid provisioning of new virtual machines by VMM Administrators or authorized Self-Service Users.

Understanding the VMM Private Cloud

Virtual Machine Manager 2012 introduces a number of new concepts focused on the use of VMM as a private cloud solution. From the perspective of a VMM Administrator, the term private cloud can be loosely defined as a group of resources that is provisioned and managed on-premise by an organization, using the organization's own hardware. The purpose of the VMM private cloud is to present a service-oriented model for provisioning resources to end users, as opposed to the classic infrastructure-focused model, which is often not well understood by the end user.

The key architectural concept behind the private cloud is the fabric, which is an abstraction layer that shields the underlying technical complexities of the resources that make it up, allowing the resources to be defined as a whole and presented to end users in a simple, typically on-demand fashion. The VMM Administrator Console is used to build the private cloud by defining and configuring the resources that make up the fabric. Once defined, the private cloud can then be assigned to Self-Service Users to meet their business requirements, as described later in this chapter.

From the above description, it should be evident that the VMM private cloud concept will be most advantageous to larger organizations with many resources to manage, as well as any organization with a business requirement to present VMM resources to end users using an on-demand service-oriented model. However, regardless of whether private cloud features are leveraged, the same Administrator Console and associated terminology are used for all VMM deployments. With that in mind, it makes sense for all VMM Administrators to become familiar with the various fabric resources that are exposed via the VMM Administrator Console.

Although much more could be written regarding the concept of the private cloud and how it can be leveraged within VMM, this chapter provides an overview of the new concepts that are presented in VMM 2012 related to the private cloud and fabric resources, which will help you gain an understanding of how this technology can be leveraged.

VMM Fabric Resources

On a high level, there are three resource pools that make up the fabric, as follows:

- Servers

- Networking

- Storage

Within these three major resource areas, a number of individual elements can be discovered, defined, and configured, collectively making up the fabric that powers a private cloud. Figure 13.1 shows these resource areas displayed within the VMM Administrator Console. The following sections provide an overview of these three resource pools and the types of individual resource elements that can be defined within each.

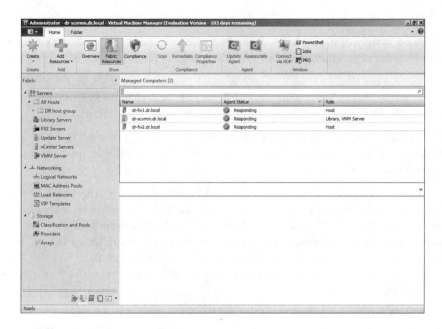

FIGURE 13.1   Fabric resources.

Servers

In addition to Hyper-V hosts, VMM 2012 allows two other host server platforms to be included as part of a private cloud: VMware ESX/ESXi (versions 3.5 and 4.1) and Citrix XenServer (version 6.0 and above). The following are the VMM fabric resources that make up the Servers resource pool:

- ▶ **Host groups**—Collections of host servers that serve as destinations where virtual machines can be deployed

- ▶ **Library servers**—Repositories for resources that can be used to build virtual machines, such as ISO files, VM templates, and hardware templates

- ▶ **PXE servers**—Systems used to automatically deploy images and boot VMs from a bare-metal state via the network, using the Preboot Execution Environment (PXE)

- ▶ **Update servers**—Systems used for automatically patching and updating VMs based on compliance policies

- ▶ **vCenter servers**—VMware management servers used to allow interoperability between VMM and VMware ESX/ESXi hosts

- ▶ **VMM server**—Authorized VMM servers that form the backbone of the VMM 2012 platform

Networks

VMM 2012 provides a variety of networking resources that can be used to quickly service the network requirements of the private cloud. The following are the VMM fabric resources that make up the Networking resource pool:

▶ **Logical networks**—User-defined groupings of IP subnets and virtual local area networks (VLANs) used to organize and simplify VM network assignments.

▶ **MAC address pools**—Static collections of MAC addresses that can be used to creatively manage network address assignments for Windows-based VMs running on any managed Hyper-V, VMware ESX/ESXi, or Citrix XenServer host.

▶ **Load balancers**—Hardware load balancers that can be integrated with the VMM Console and used to load-balance the network traffic for VMs that make up a service tier. In addition to Microsoft Network Load Balancing (NLB), hardware load balancers are supported for integration with VMM if the vendor supplies a configuration provider, which is a VMM plug-in that translates VMM PowerShell commands to application programming interface (API) calls that are specific to a load balancer manufacturer and model.

▶ **Virtual IP (VIP) templates**—A collection of load balancer–related configuration settings for a specific type of network traffic. When creating a service that requires load balancing, VMM users (including Self-Service Users) can select a VIP template that matches the load balancing requirements of the application being deployed.

Storage

VMM 2012 provides some interesting new features that allow an administrator to discover, classify, and provision remote storage on supported storage arrays. The new Microsoft Storage Management Service, which is automatically installed during the installation of VMM 2012, is used to communicate with external storage arrays that leverage Storage Management Initiative – Specification (SMI-S). SMI-S is a storage standard developed and maintained by the Storage Networking Industry Association (SNIA), with the main objective of enabling broad interoperable management of heterogeneous storage vendor systems. Once an SMI-S compatible storage array has been made available, the storage array can be added to VMM 2012 and used to automate and track storage assignments to Hyper-V hosts and host clusters.

At this time, the number of storage arrays that feature SMI-S and support the new storage automation features of VMM 2012 is somewhat limited. Although the number of supported arrays will no doubt increase in the future, it is important to note that VMM still recognizes both local and remote storage arrays for which an SMI-S provider is not available. However, you cannot perform active management operations on those storage arrays through VMM. For example, you cannot use VMM to perform operations such as logical unit number (LUN) creation and deletion, nor for the assignment of storage to host groups, hosts, and host clusters. For an array that does not support the new storage management features, these tasks must be performed using the storage vendor's management utilities as opposed to using the VMM Administrator Console.

NOTE

The new storage automation features of VMM 2012 are only supported for Hyper-V hosts, and cannot be used with VMware ESX/ESXi or Citrix XenServer.

Like earlier versions of the product, VMM also supports Virtual Disk Service (VDS) to connect to storage hardware that uses a VDS provider. Support for VDS is provided mainly for backward compatibility to allow storage area network (SAN) transfer functionality for these devices; however, support for VDS hardware providers has been deprecated and will therefore not be supported with future releases.

Following are the VMM fabric resources that make up the Storage resource pool:

▶ **Classifications and pools**—User-defined labels applied to storage, typically used to differentiate the various storage pools by quality of service

▶ **Providers**—SMI-S providers that can be discovered and integrated with VMM

▶ **Arrays**—SMI-S storage arrays that can be discovered and selected for use with VMM

Using the VMM Management Interfaces

Virtual Machine Manager provides an interface to manage virtual guest sessions through an Administrator Console, command-line interfaces, or Self-Service Portals, allowing flexibility in the access method used to manage virtual systems. The following sections provide details on each of these management interfaces and how each can be leveraged to administer the VMM environment.

VMM Administrator Console

As discussed in Chapter 12, the Administrator Console is a Microsoft Management Console (MMC) that is built upon Windows PowerShell and can be used to complete the following tasks:

▶ Adding hosts

▶ Creating host groups

▶ Managing hosts

▶ Managing host clusters

▶ Configuring the VMM library

▶ Creating private clouds

▶ Creating VMs

▶ Deploying and migrating VMs

▶ Managing VMs

- ▶ Configuring the Self-Service Portal

- ▶ Monitoring and reporting

- ▶ Administering and managing roles

You can either install the Administrator Console on the same computer as the VMM server or on a number of different computers. An Administrator Console installation also installs the VMM command shell, which allows you to manage the VMM environment from the command line.

The Administrator Console, shown in Figure 13.2, consists of the tool ribbon across the top, the navigation pane on the lower left, the workspace area above the navigation pane, the results pane on the top right, and the details pane below the results pane.

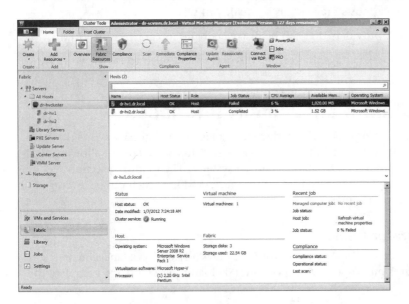

FIGURE 13.2   VMM Administrator Console.

Creating Host Groups

Host groups allow the administrator to group together collections of similar hosts, such as perimeter hosts, domain hosts, or other host categories. To create a host group, complete the following steps:

1. Log on to a computer that has the Administrator Console installed using a domain user account that is a member of the VMM Administrator role.

2. Next, open the Administrator Console using either the desktop or Start menu icon and connect to your VMM server.

3. Once the console has loaded, in the navigation pane, click the Fabric icon to open the Fabric workspace.

4. In the Fabric workspace, expand Servers, then right-click All Hosts, and select Create Host Group.

5. VMM creates a new host group with the generic name *New Host Group*, with the group name highlighted. Enter a new name, and press Enter to complete the host group configuration.

NOTE

Host groups can also be moved, renamed, or deleted by selecting the appropriate action from the right-click context menu for a given host group.

Managing Hosts

After installing the VMM Agent on a host server and then adding it to the VMM server (as discussed in Chapter 12), it can then be managed from either the Fabric workspace or the Hosts pane in the Administrator Console. To manage host servers, complete the following steps:

1. Log on to a computer that has the Administrator Console installed using a domain user account that is a member of the VMM Administrator role.

2. Next, open the Administrator Console using either the desktop or Start menu icon and connect to your VMM server.

3. Once the console has loaded, in the navigation pane, click the Fabric icon to open the Fabric workspace.

4. In the Fabric workspace, select All Hosts. The hosts managed by this VMM server display in the results pane. Alternately, expand All Hosts, and the same list of hosts will also appear within the Fabric workspace.

5. From either the results pane or the Fabric workspace, select any host, and a choice of actions appears within the tool ribbon. The same set of actions can also be selected by right-clicking on the host in either location. The administrator can move the host to a host group, refresh the host in the details pane, remove the host from the VMM server, access the host properties, and more.

NOTE

The Properties page allows the administrator to view or configure the host summary, host status, VM status, hardware configuration, reserved resources (for example, CPU and RAM), networking, VM placement path, storage, remote connection port, and more.

Managing Host Clusters

Host clusters are Windows or VMware ESX clusters that provide high availability and fault tolerance. The actions for host clusters allow the administrator to move a Hyper-V host cluster to a different host group, delete a host cluster from VMM, monitor host clusters, and modify the host cluster properties. To manage host clusters, complete the following steps:

1. Log on to a computer that has the Administrator Console installed using a domain user account that is a member of the VMM Administrator role.

2. Next, open the Administrator Console using either the desktop or Start menu icon and connect to your VMM server.

3. Once the console has loaded, in the navigation pane, click the Fabric icon to open the Fabric workspace.

4. In the Fabric workspace, expand All Hosts. The clusters managed by this VMM server appear within the Fabric workspace.

5. Select any cluster, and then from the tool ribbon click the Host Cluster tab to reveal a choice of actions. The same set of actions can also be selected by right-clicking on the cluster in the Fabric workspace. The actions available for managing the host cluster include optimizing resource usage, moving the cluster to a host group, adding cluster nodes, and more.

When a node is added to a failover cluster outside of VMM, the new node is automatically discovered and added to the host cluster within VMM. However, until you add the node to VMM as a host, the new node displays in the Hosts view with a Pending status. If a highly available virtual machine fails over to the pending host, that virtual machine will then have a Missing status in VMM. To prevent this from happening, add the host into VMM by right-clicking on the host with a Pending status, and then selecting Add to Host Cluster.

In addition, VMM also detects when a node has been evicted from a failover cluster. When this happens, VMM then sets the Clustered property of the node to False and begins managing the host server as a regular, nonclustered host. To stop managing the host and remove it from VMM, use the Remove Host action to remove the host from VMM.

Configuring the VMM Library

The VMM library is a Windows share that hosts the resources used by VMM to create virtual machines. The library contains files (Virtual Hard Disks [VHDs], ISOs, and so on). To add or remove libraries from VMM, complete the following steps:

1. Log on to a computer that has the Administrator Console installed using a domain user account that is a member of the VMM Administrator role.

2. Next, open the Administrator Console using either the desktop or Start menu icon and connect to your VMM server.

3. Once the console has loaded, in the navigation pane, click the Library icon to open the Library workspace.

4. Select Library Servers in the Library workspace. The library contents display in the results pane.

5. Additional VMM libraries can be added to the Administrator Console by clicking the Add Library Server action in the tool ribbon. A library can be removed by right-clicking the library and selecting Remove.

If Windows PowerShell scripts are stored in the VMM library, they can be viewed, edited, removed, and even executed from the Library view. In addition, entire virtual machines can be stored in the VMM library. From here, they can be cloned, deployed, and removed. VMware virtual machines stored in the library can be converted to a VMM virtual machine. However, the VMware virtual machine's configuration files must be stored in the library before you can convert it using this method.

NOTE

VMM libraries can be stored on Windows clusters to increase the availability and fault tolerance of the library resources.

Creating Private Clouds

A new concept in VMM 2012 is the private cloud, which is a group of resources that is provisioned and managed on-premise by an organization, using an organization's own hardware. Private clouds can be created from host groups that contain resources from Hyper-V hosts, VMware ESX hosts, and Citrix XenServer hosts. To create a private cloud, complete the following steps:

1. Log on to a computer that has the Administrator Console installed using a domain user account that is a member of the VMM Administrator role.

2. Next, open the Administrator Console using either the desktop or Start menu icon and connect to your VMM server.

3. Once the console has loaded, in the navigation pane, click the VMs and Services icon to open the VMs and Services workspace.

4. From the tool ribbon, click Create Cloud. This starts the Create Cloud Wizard, as shown in Figure 13.3.

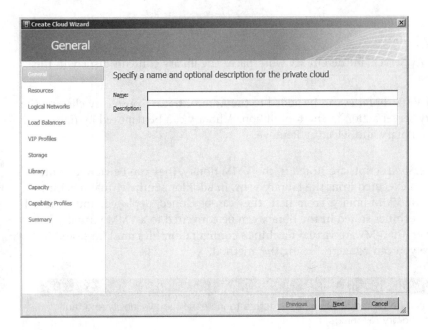

FIGURE 13.3   Create Cloud Wizard.

5. Once the Create Cloud Wizard has started, define the following variables on the General page:

   ▶ **Name**—Enter the name for the new private cloud.

   ▶ **Description**—Enter a useful description for the new cloud.

6. Once you have defined the desired general information for the new private cloud, click Next.

7. On the Resources page, select either the VMM host groups or VMware resource pools that will be available for users of the private cloud, and then click Next.

8. On the Logical Networks page, select the logical networks that will be available for users of the private cloud, and then click Next.

9. On the Load Balancers page, select the load balancers that will be available for users of the private cloud, and then click Next.

10. On the VIP Profiles page, select the VIP templates that will be available for users of the private cloud, and then click Next.

11. On the Storage page, select the storage classifications that will be available for users of the private cloud, and then click Next.

> **NOTE**
>
> Only the logical networks, load balancers, and storage classifications that are associated with the selected host groups will appear in the lists for possible selection in the Create Cloud Wizard.

12. On the Library page, configure the following resources, if required:

    ▶ **Stored VM path**—Click Browse, then expand the library server, and select the library share or folder in a library share that will be used as the location for Self-Service Users to store virtual machines.

    ▶ **Read-only library shares**—Click Add, and then select one or more library shares where administrators can provide read-only resources to cloud users.

13. Once you have finished defining the desired VM paths and library shares, click Next.

14. On the Capacity page, set the capacity limits for the private cloud by either accepting the default values or clearing one or more of the Use Maximum check boxes and then setting an alternate quota for a particular resource. The following resources are available for configuration on the Capacity page:

    ▶ **Virtual CPUs**—Sets a limit on processing capacity within the private cloud that is equivalent to the capacity that can be provided by a specific number of CPUs.

    ▶ **Memory**—Sets a quota on memory (in gigabytes) that is available to virtual machines that are deployed in the private cloud.

    ▶ **Storage**—Sets a quota storage capacity (in gigabytes) that is available to virtual machines that are deployed in the private cloud.

    ▶ **Custom quota (points)**—Sets a quota on virtual machines that are deployed in the private cloud based on total quota points that are assigned to the VMs through their VM templates. Custom quotas are provided for backward compatibility with Self-Service User roles that were created in VMM 2008 R2.

    ▶ **Virtual machines**—Limits the total number of virtual machines that can be deployed on the private cloud.

15. Once you have defined the Capacity settings for the new private cloud, click Next.

16. On the Capability Profiles page, select the capability profiles that match the type of hypervisor platforms that are running in the host groups selected for this private cloud, and then click Next.

17. On the Summary page, carefully review the settings, and then click Finish to proceed with the creation of the private cloud, or click Previous to go back and change the configuration.

18. Once you click Finish, the Jobs dialog box opens showing the progress of the private cloud creation. Use this dialog box to monitor the progress of the task and confirm that the private cloud is migrated successfully. If the job fails, read the error message in the details pane for information about the cause of the failure and the recommended course of action to resolve the issue.

Managing VMs

Virtual machines in the VMM inventory can be fully managed within the Administrator Console. To manage virtual machines, complete the following steps:

1. Log on to a computer that has the Administrator Console installed using a domain user account that is a member of the VMM Administrator role.

2. Next, open the Administrator Console using either the desktop or Start menu icon and connect to your VMM server.

3. Once the console has loaded, in the navigation pane, click the VMs and Services icon to open the VMs and Services workspace.

4. In the VMs and Services workspace, select a host. The VMs hosted on that host display in the results pane.

Using the Administrator Console, you can start, pause, stop, save the state, shut down, or connect to any managed virtual machines. Other actions include migrating the virtual machine, creating and managing checkpoints, repairing the virtual machine, installing guest services, cloning the virtual machine, storing it in a VMM library, removing the virtual machine, and configuring its properties.

Monitoring and Reporting

VMM allows the capability to monitor the health and performance of virtual machines by integrating VMM with System Center Operations Manager (SCOM) and enabling Performance and Resource Optimization (PRO). With VMM 2012, Microsoft has simplified the process of integrating VMM with SCOM by providing an integration wizard within the VMM Administrator Console. This integration procedure automatically imports into SCOM the VMM management packs that are required to provide this functionality. Once the integration is completed, the SCOM management console can be used to configure monitoring and reporting of the entire VMM environment.

Integration with SCOM also allows VMM to leverage this relationship to provide PRO tips. Several of the VMM management packs imported into SCOM are PRO-enabled. Whenever a monitor within one of these management packs identifies an opportunity for optimization, a PRO tip is generated in VMM, which allows an administrator to either manually or automatically implement the tip to provide remediation.

Administering and Managing VMM

The entire VM infrastructure can be administered from the VMM Administrator Console or by using the VMM command shell. VMM administration includes managing user roles, managing agents on managed servers, adding non-Microsoft virtualization managers to VMM, and configuring VMM settings. To manage VMM, complete the following steps:

1. Log on to a computer that has the Administrator Console installed using a domain user account that is a member of the VMM Administrator role.

2. Next, open the Administrator Console using either the desktop or Start menu icon and connect to your VMM server.

3. Once the console has loaded, go to the Administration view by clicking the Settings button in the navigation pane.

From within the Administration view, you have the following options for administering and managing VMM:

▶ The General settings allow the administrator to configure global settings in VMM, such as guest agent settings, the database connection, library settings, network settings, remote control, and the self-service administrator email address.

▶ The Security section contains two components. First, user roles allow the administrator to manage user roles and create new user roles, such as Delegated Administrators and Self-Service Users. Each of these roles can be scoped to a particular set of virtual machines, libraries, and so on. For example, the VMM Administrator can configure Self-Service User roles to perform only certain actions. Second, RunAs accounts allow the administrator to configure sets of credentials that can then be used throughout the VMM infrastructure. This not only facilitates the use of common credentials in various locations and simplified account maintenance, but also allows the delegation of the use of various accounts to other roles.

▶ System Center Settings provides a way for the administrator to configure SCOM integration to enable reporting along with PRO functionality. Physical Resource Optimization (PRO) provides workload- and application-aware resource optimization for Hyper-V host clusters.

▶ Servicing Windows provides a way to create and view servicing windows, which allow the scheduling of servicing outside VMM for System Center 2012.

▶ Configuration Providers allows a way to view the status and other details of configuration providers, which are VMM plug-ins.

VMM Command Shell

The VMM command shell is built on Microsoft Windows PowerShell, an administrator-focused interactive command-line shell and scripting platform that is integrated into the Windows platform. The VMM command shell is installed with the VMM Administrator Console. Administrators can use the VMM command shell as an alternative to, or in addition to, the Administrator Console for centralized management of the physical and virtual system infrastructure. Anything that can be done in the Administrator Console can be done using the VMM command shell. The Administrator Console even enables you to view the command shell commands that the console will run before actually executing them.

The command shell provides commands (called cmdlets, shown in Figure 13.4) that administrators can use to perform simple administrative tasks or in combination with other cmdlets or command-line elements to perform more complex tasks.

FIGURE 13.4   VMM command shell.

In fact, any task that you can perform using the Administrator Console can be completed using the command shell, and in some scenarios the shell provides additional features that the MMC-based console does not. Additionally, because the management shell is based on PowerShell, you can automate routine management tasks using the PowerShell scripting language. To discover the supported cmdlets in the VMM Management Shell, open the command shell and execute the `Get-Command *-vmm*` command. This command produces a command list that shows only the cmdlets belonging to VMM. For each cmdlet, help documentation can be accessed by using the `Get-Help` or `help` cmdlet, as shown in the following example:

```
Get-Help <cmdlet name>
```

If more information is needed about a cmdlet, you can use the `-Full` or `-Detailed` parameters for the `Get-Help` cmdlet. For example:

```
Get-Help Get-VMMManagedComputer -Detailed
```

Understanding Virtual Machine Conversions

Using VMM, administrators can convert existing physical computers into VMs. This process is known as a physical-to-virtual, or P2V, conversion. Additionally, VMM can also be used to convert virtual machines from other virtualization platforms, such as VMware ESX and Microsoft Virtual Server to Windows Hyper-V. This process is known as virtual-to-virtual, or V2V, conversion. Details about each of these types of conversion processes are provided in the following sections.

> **NOTE**
>
> In VMM 2012, Microsoft now supports virtual machine conversions from Citrix XenServer to Hyper-V. However, unlike VMware VM conversions, XenServer VM conversion uses the P2V process. VMM only supports the conversion of XenServer VMs that are running supported Windows-based guest operating systems (see Table 13.1).

Working with P2V Conversions

There are two methods for converting physical computers to virtual machines. The first method, called an online P2V conversion, is performed using the Volume Shadow Copy Service (VSS) to copy data while the server continues to service user requests. During this type of conversion, the operations of the source computer are not interrupted, which might cause data consistency issues depending on what that computer is being used for. The second conversion method, called an offline P2V conversion, is performed by restarting the source computer into the Windows Preinstallation Environment (Windows PE) and VMM then clones the physical disk or disks to VHD format. Once the cloning process is complete, the source computer is then restarted and returned to operations. Unlike an online P2V conversion, an offline P2V conversion does not suffer from data consistency issues and should be used depending on the type of source computer you plan to convert.

To perform a P2V conversion, the source computer must meet the following requirements:

- ▶ Must have at least 512MB of RAM

- ▶ Cannot have any volumes larger than 2040GB

- ▶ Must have an Advanced Configuration and Power Interface (ACPI) BIOS; Vista WinPE will not install on a non-ACPI BIOS

- ▶ Must be accessible by VMM and by the host computer

Table 13.1 shows the supported operating systems that VMM can convert using the P2V process.

TABLE 13.1   Supported Operating Systems for P2V Conversion

Operating System	P2V Online	P2V Offline
Windows Server 2008 with Hyper-V	No	No
Windows Server 2008	Yes	Yes
Windows Server 2008 x64	Yes	Yes
Windows Server 2008 R2 x64	Yes	Yes
Windows Web Server 2008 R2	Yes	Yes
Windows Server 2003 SP2 or later	Yes	Yes
Windows Server 2003 x64 SP2 or later	Yes	Yes
Windows 2000 SP4 or later	No	Yes

TABLE 13.1   Continued

Operating System	P2V Online	P2V Offline
Windows XP SP2 or later	Yes	Yes
Windows XP x64 SP2 or later	Yes	Yes
Windows Vista SP1 or later	Yes	Yes
Windows Vista x64 SP1 or later	Yes	Yes
Windows 7 all versions	Yes	Yes

NOTE

VMM does not support P2V conversion of Windows NT Server 4.0 source computers. These computers can be migrated using the Microsoft Virtual Server 2005 Migration Toolkit (VSMT) or third-party solutions.

Performing a P2V Online Conversion

To simplify the P2V conversion process, VMM provides a task-based wizard. Additionally, the P2V process can be completely scripted so that you can perform large-scale P2V conversions using the Windows PowerShell command line. To complete a P2V online conversion using the Convert Physical Server Wizard, complete the following steps:

1. Ensure that the source computer meets the operating system and additional requirements listed earlier in this section for P2V conversions.

2. Next, log on to a computer that has the Administrator Console installed using a domain user account that is a member of the VMM Administrator role.

3. Next, open the Administrator Console using either the desktop or Start menu icon and connect to your VMM server.

4. Once the console has loaded, in the navigation pane, click the VMs and Services icon to open the VMs and Services workspace.

5. From the tool ribbon, click Create Virtual Machine, and then select Convert Physical Machine from the drop-down menu. This starts the Convert Physical Server Wizard, as shown in Figure 13.5.

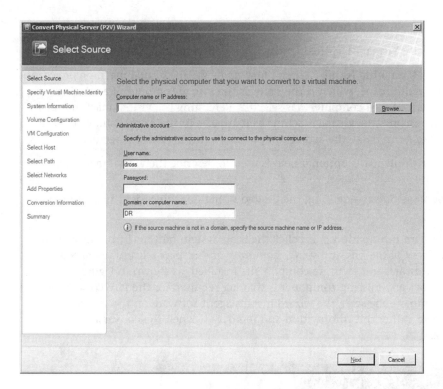

FIGURE 13.5   Convert Physical Server (P2V) Wizard.

6. Once the Convert Physical Server Wizard has started, define the following variables on the Select Source page:

> **Computer Name or IP Address**—Enter the name of the physical computer or click the Browse button to locate the computer object to convert in Active Directory.

> **User Name**—Enter a username of an account with local administrator rights on the source computer.

> **Password**—Enter the password for the local administrator user account.

> **Domain or Computer Name**—Enter the domain of the local administrator user account if it is not already populated, or the machine name or IP address if the computer is not a domain member.

NOTE

You should perform a disk defragmentation on the source computer's hard drives to help minimize the time required for the cloning process. Also, ensure that a fast network connection exists between the source and the VMM server.

---

7. Once you have finished defining the desired source information, click Next.

8. On the Specify Virtual Machine Identity page, define the following variables:

   ▶ **Virtual Machine Name**—Enter a new name for the virtual machine or accept the default name, which is the same as the source computer if an Active Directory–based computer was selected. Renaming the virtual machine name only renames the virtual machine as it appears in the Administrator Console. It does not rename the actual computer account in Active Directory.

   ▶ **Description**—This optional field is used to describe the virtual machine.

9. Once you have finished defining the desired virtual machine identity information, click Next.

10. On the System Information page, click the Scan System button. By doing so, you begin a survey of the physical source computer and display a list of operating system, hardware, and software components installed, as shown in Figure 13.6. It also identifies any missing components that are required for the P2V conversion to run. To complete the scan, the wizard installs agent software on the source computer to gather this information and removes it when the conversion is complete.

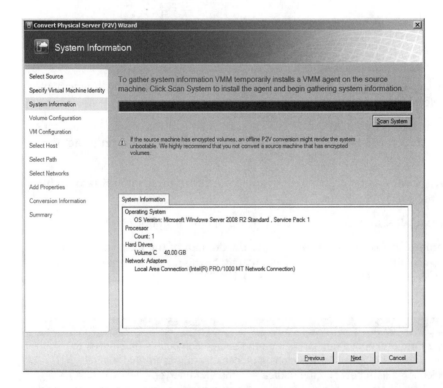

FIGURE 13.6   System Information page.

NOTE

If the scan fails, ensure that the winmgmt (Windows Management Instrumentation) service is running on the source computer and that a firewall is not blocking HTTP and WMI traffic to the VMM server. A firewall exception will be created for the remote administration service (RemoteAdmin) if a firewall is installed on the source computer. The administrator can remove this exception after the conversion operation is complete.

11. Once the scan has completed and the System Information Results window displays the operating system, hard drives, and network adapter information gathered from the survey, click Next.

12. On the Volume Configuration page, review the list of disk volumes detected and make changes, if required:

    ▶ Deselect volumes that should not be included in the new virtual machine.

    ▶ Increase the size of the VHD for each volume. The size of a VHD can be increased, but not decreased. The minimum size is determined by the size of actual data on the volume.

    ▶ Choose to configure the VHD type to be dynamic (the default) or fixed. Dynamic VHDs automatically grow as more data is saved to the disk. Fixed VHDs are created with the full allocated disk space as configured by the administrator.

    ▶ Configure the channel that the VHD will use. Options include up to 2 IDE channels and up to 62 SCSI channels each on 4 virtual SCSI buses (providing up to 250 separate channels total). Click Next to continue.

13. Once you have finished defining the desired volume configuration settings, click Next.

14. On the Virtual Machine Configuration page, select the number of processors and RAM to use on the new virtual machine. The number of processors available for selection is limited by the number of physical processors available in the source computer. The default amount of memory initially specified by the wizard is equal to the amount of physical RAM in the source computer.

15. Once you have finished defining the desired virtual machine configuration settings, click Next.

16. On the Select Host page, select the most suitable host server to deploy the new virtual machine to, as shown in Figure 13.7. Each host has a star rating (from zero to five stars) indicating its suitability to host the new virtual machine.

    ▶ The Details tab displays the status, operating system, virtualization software platform, virtualization software status, and names of the virtual machines running on the selected host.

▶ The Rating Explanation tab explains what the star rating means for the selected host and tells what requirements are met for the virtual machine by this host.

▶ The SAN Explanation tab describes the suitability of the host to connect to a SAN for virtual machine storage. Items listed here include Fibre Channel host bus adapters (HBAs) installed and iSCSI initiators installed.

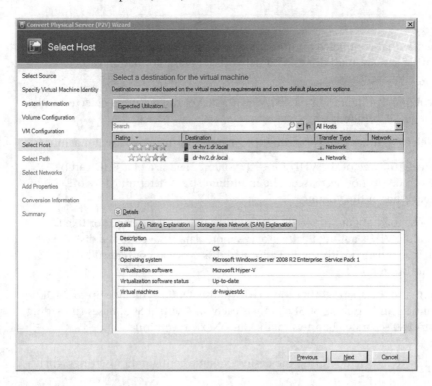

FIGURE 13.7   Selecting the virtual machine host server.

NOTE

The ratings can be customized using the Expected Utilization button. Here, the administrator can select multiple criteria and change the anticipated resource utilization for each component, such as CPU utilization, required disk space, expected disk I/O per second, and expected network utilization.

17. Once you have finished selecting the desired host server, click Next.

18. On the Select Path page, select the folder where the files associated with the new virtual machine should be placed. Either accept the default location or click Browse to select a different path. After selecting the desired path, click Next.

19. On the Select Networks page, the Virtual Network drop-down menu displays all the current networks available on the selected host server. Select Not Connected or the appropriate virtual network for the virtual machine to use. After selecting the desired virtual network connection, click Next.

20. On the Add Properties page, configure the following:

    ▶ **Automatic Start Action**—Select the action to perform for this virtual machine when the physical host starts. Available actions are as follows: Never Automatically Turn On the Virtual Machine, Always Automatically Turn On the Virtual Machine, or Automatically Turn On the Virtual Machine If It Was Running When the Physical Server Stopped.

    ▶ **Automatic Stop Action**—Select the action to perform for this virtual machine when the physical host server stops. Available actions are as follows: Save State, Turn Off Virtual Machine, or Shut Down Guest OS.

21. On the Conversion Information page, any issues that were encountered while checking the source computer for P2V conversion suitability are displayed. If no issues were detected, click Next. Otherwise, review the issues that were detected by the wizard. These issues must be resolved before the P2V conversion can succeed. Each issue listed is accompanied by a solution that explains how to resolve it. After all issues have been resolved, click the Check Again button to rerun the survey until no issues are found.

22. The Summary page displays a summary of the settings selected in the Convert Physical Server Wizard. Carefully review these settings and click Create to proceed with the P2V conversion or click Previous to go back and change the configuration.

    ▶ An optional check box can be selected to start the virtual machine immediately after deploying it to the host.

    ▶ As with many actions performed from the VMM Administrator Console, the Convert Physical Server Wizard offers a View Script button. This option enables the administrator to view, modify, and save the PowerShell commands that the wizard will execute to perform the P2V conversion, as shown in Figure 13.8.

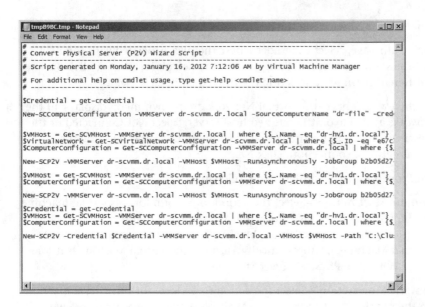

FIGURE 13.8   Convert physical server script.

23. Once you click Create, the results pane displays a summary of the P2V conversion. Clicking the Jobs icon in the navigation pane displays a more detailed view of the progress of the conversion, as shown in Figure 13.9. Use this screen to monitor the progress of the P2V conversion and confirm that the virtual machine is created successfully. If the job fails, read the error message in the details pane for information about the cause of the failure and the recommended course of action to resolve the issue. Be patient; the conversion process takes several minutes or longer and consists of the following steps:

▶ Collect the machine configuration information.

▶ Add the source machine agent.

▶ Create the virtual machine.

▶ Copy the hard disk.

▶ Deploy the file (using the Background Intelligent Transfer Service, BITS).

▶ Make the operating system virtualizable.

▶ Start the virtual machine.

▶ Install the virtual machine components.

▶ Stop the virtual machine.

▶ Remove the source machine agent.

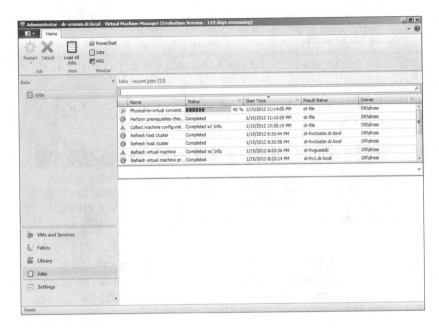

FIGURE 13.9   The Jobs screen.

Working with V2V Conversions

During a V2V conversion, an existing VMware ESX virtual machine configuration file and its associated virtual disk files are converted to Hyper-V-related formats. When conducting this type of conversion, VMM Administrators do not need administrative rights on the VMware virtual machine to complete the process because the V2V conversion is just converting files to another type of virtual machine file. Instead, the VMware virtual machine is simply turned off, and the files are copied to the VMM library for the conversion.

Performing a V2V Conversion

To simplify the V2V conversion process, VMM provides a task-based wizard. Additionally, the V2V process can be completely scripted so that you can perform large-scale V2V conversions using the Windows PowerShell command line. To complete a V2V conversion using VMware files that have been copied to a library share, complete the following steps:

1. Copy the VMX and VMDK files of the VMware virtual machine that you intend to convert to the library share on the appropriate VMM library server (by default, the share name for the first library share is MSSCVMMLibrary).

2. Next, log on to a computer that has the Administrator Console installed using a domain user account that is a member of the VMM Administrator role.

3. Next, open the Administrator Console using either the desktop or Start menu icon and connect to your VMM server.

4. Once the console has loaded, open the Library workspace by clicking the Library icon in the navigation pane.

5. In the Library workspace, expand the library server, right-click the library share where the VMware files were copied, and then click Refresh.

NOTE

By clicking Refresh, all the files on the share are immediately indexed by VMM and are added to the Library view. Conversely, you can also wait for the library refresher to automatically complete a full re-index of the file-based resources on all library shares. By default, the library refresher completes a re-index every hour.

---

6. In the navigation pane, click the VMs and Services icon to open the VMs and Services workspace. From the tool ribbon, click Create Virtual Machine, and then select Convert Virtual Machine from the drop-down menu. This starts the Convert Virtual Machine Wizard.

7. Once the Convert Virtual Machine Wizard has started, click the Browse button on the Select Source page; this opens the Select Virtual Machine Source dialog box, as shown in Figure 13.10.

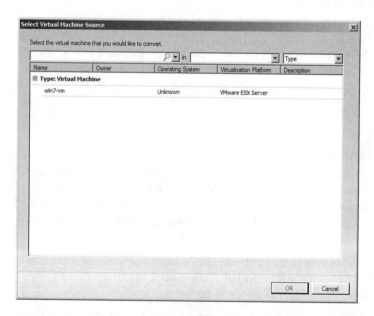

FIGURE 13.10   The Select Virtual Machine Source dialog box.

8. Use the Select Virtual Machine Source dialog box to find the virtual machine that you intend to convert, and then select the virtual machine and click OK.

9. Once you have selected the desired source virtual machine, click Next.

10. On the Specify Virtual Machine Identity page, define the following variables:

    ▶ **Virtual Machine Name**—Enter a new name for the virtual machine or accept the default name, which is the display name of the source files added to the library share. Renaming the virtual machine name only renames the virtual machine as it appears in the Administrator Console. It does not rename the actual host name of the computer.

    ▶ **Description**—This optional field is used to describe the virtual machine.

11. Once you have finished defining the desired virtual machine identity information, click Next.

12. On the Virtual Machine Configuration page, select the number of processors and RAM to use on the new virtual machine. Both settings are configured based on the configuration of the source virtual machine that was added to the library share.

13. Once you have finished defining the desired virtual machine configuration settings, click Next.

14. On the Select Host page, select the most suitable host server to host the virtual machine. Each host has a star rating (from zero to five stars) indicating its suitability to host the virtual machine.

    ▶The Details tab displays the status, operating system, virtualization software platform, virtualization software status, and names of the virtual machines running on the selected host.

    ▶The Rating Explanation tab explains what the star rating means for the selected host and tells what requirements are met for the virtual machine by this host.

    ▶The SAN Explanation tab describes the suitability of the host to connect to a SAN for virtual machine storage. Items listed here include Fibre Channel HBAs installed and iSCSI initiators installed.

NOTE

The ratings can be customized using the Expected Utilization button. Here, the administrator can select multiple criteria and change the anticipated resource utilization for each component, such as CPU utilization, required disk space, expected disk I/O per second, and expected network utilization.

---

15. Once you have finished selecting the desired host server, click Next.

16. On the Select Path page, select the folder where the files associated with the new virtual machine should be placed. Either accept the default location or click Browse to select a different path. After selecting the desired path, click Next.

17. On the Select Networks page, the Virtual Network drop-down menu displays all the current networks available on the selected host server. Select Not Connected or the appropriate virtual network for the virtual machine to use. After selecting the desired virtual network connection, click Next.

18. On the Additional Properties page, configure the following:

   ▶ **Automatic Start Action**—Select the action to perform for this virtual machine when the physical host starts. Available actions are as follows: Never Automatically Turn On the Virtual Machine, Always Automatically Turn On the Virtual Machine, or Automatically Turn On the Virtual Machine If It Was Running When the Physical Server Stopped.

   ▶ **Automatic Stop Action**—Select the action to perform for this virtual machine when the physical host server stops. Available actions are as follows: Save State, Turn Off Virtual Machine, or Shut Down Guest OS.

19. The Summary page displays a summary of the settings selected in the Convert Virtual Machine Wizard. Carefully review these settings and click Create to proceed with the V2V conversion or click Previous to go back and change the configuration.

   ▶ An optional check box can be selected to start the virtual machine immediately after deploying it to the host.

   ▶ As with many actions performed from the VMM Administrator Console, the Convert Virtual Machine Wizard offers a View Script button. This option enables the administrator to view, modify, and save the PowerShell commands that the wizard will execute to perform the V2V conversion, as shown in Figure 13.11 .

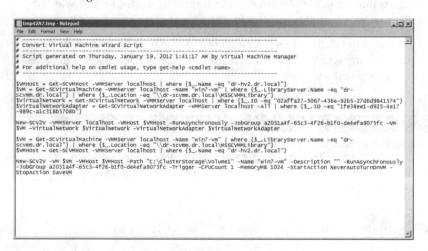

FIGURE 13.11   Convert virtual machine script.

20. Once you click Create, the results pane displays a summary of the V2V conversion. Clicking the Jobs icon in the navigation pane displays a more detailed view of the progress of the conversion. Use this screen to monitor the progress of the V2V conversion and confirm that the virtual machine is created successfully. If the job fails, read the error message in the details pane for information about the cause of the failure and the recommended course of action to resolve the issue. Be patient; the conversion process takes several minutes or longer and consists of the following steps:

- ▶ Collect the machine configuration information from the VMX file.

- ▶ Create the virtual machine.

- ▶ Convert the VMDK file to a VHD file.

- ▶ Deploy the file (using the LAN).

- ▶ Make the operating system virtualizable.

- ▶ Start the virtual machine.

- ▶ Install the virtual machine components.

- ▶ Stop the virtual machine.

- ▶ Remove the source VMX machine configuration.

Managing VMM User Roles

As discussed in Chapter 12, VMM implements a role-based access control (RBAC) model for managing administrative permissions. Using this model, each VMM Administrator and Self-Service User is assigned a role. Each role consists of an administrative profile that determines which actions a role member can perform and the scope for which virtual infrastructure objects these rights are applicable.

Four types of user roles are available in VMM, as follows:

- ▶ **Administrator**—Users who are assigned the Administrator role have full rights to the virtual infrastructure and can perform all actions in the VMM Administrator Console. These administrators can create new Delegated Administrator and Self-Service User roles. Only members of this role can add additional members to the Administrator role. The Administrator role is created when VMM is installed for the first time in the domain. The user who installs VMM is automatically added to the Administrator user role during installation. There is only one Administrator user role in each domain.

- ▶ **Delegated Administrator**—Users who are assigned the Delegated Administrator role can perform all actions in the VMM Administrator Console that apply, or are scoped, to them. The scope of objects is defined during the creation of the role. The Delegated Administrator user role does not exist by default. There can be zero or more Delegated Administrator roles in each domain. Delegated Administrator roles are created by users who have the Administrator user role. Members of this user role can create new Delegated Administrator and Self-Service User roles, but only within the scope of objects that apply to them.

▶ **Read-Only Administrator**—Users who are assigned the Read-Only Administrator role can view properties, status, and job status of objects in the VMM Administrator Console that apply, or are scoped, to them. As indicated by the title of the role, the Read-Only Administrator cannot modify any of the objects in VMM. The scope of objects is defined during the creation of the role. The Read-Only Administrator user role does not exist by default. There can be zero or more Read-Only Administrator roles in each domain. Read-Only Administrator roles are created by users who have the Administrator user role or Delegated Administrator role. One of the primary purposes of the Read-Only Administrator role is to grant required access to auditors within VMM without allowing the configuration to be modified.

▶ **Self-Service User**—Users who are assigned the Self-Service User role can be granted rights to operate, create, manage, store, create checkpoints for, and connect to VMs in their scope using the Self-Service Portal. This role is scoped by a member of the Administrator or Delegated Administrator role to pertain to a specific set of virtual infrastructure objects. Users with this role cannot manage their role or any other role in VMM. They also cannot create new user roles.

> **NOTE**
>
> Users who are assigned the Administrator or a Delegated Administrator role cannot access the Self-Service Portal unless they are also assigned to one or more Self-Service User roles.

Managing the Administrator User Role

To manage the Administrator user role, complete the following steps:

1. Log on to a computer that has the Administrator Console installed using a domain user account that is a member of the VMM Administrator role.

2. Next, open the Administrator Console using either the desktop or Start menu icon and connect to your VMM server.

3. Once the console has loaded, click the Settings icon in the navigation pane to open the Settings workspace, and then expand Security and select User Roles.

4. Select the Administrator user role in the results pane. The current members of the Administrator user role are then displayed in the details pane.

5. In the results pane, right-click the Administrator role and select Properties to display the properties of the role.

6. The Administrator Properties dialog box opens. If desired, you can use the Name and Description tab to modify the description for the Administrator user role.

7. Click the Members tab. The current members are listed, as shown in Figure 13.12.

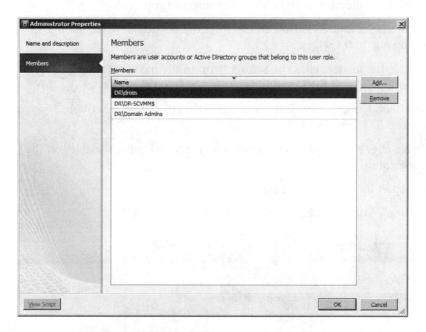

FIGURE 13.12   Managing members of the Administrator user role.

8. To remove members from the Administrator user role, select the user to remove and click the Remove button.

NOTE

There must be at least one member of the Administrator user role at all times. VMM does not allow you to remove all members of the Administrator user role.

---

9. To add members to the Administrator user role, click Add and enter the name or names of the users or security groups to add. Click the Check Names button to resolve the users or groups. Members must be users or security groups in the Active Directory domain that the VMM server is a member of, or a domain where a full two-way trust exists.

10. Click OK to close the Administrator Properties window.

Creating a Delegated Administrator User Role

To create a Delegated Administrator user role, complete the following steps:

1. Log on to a computer that has the Administrator Console installed using a domain user account that is a member of the VMM Administrator role.

2. Next, open the Administrator Console using either the desktop or Start menu icon and connect to your VMM server.

3. Once the console has loaded, click the Settings icon in the navigation pane to open the Settings workspace, and then expand Security and select User Roles.

4. From the tool ribbon, click Create User Role. This starts the Create User Role Wizard, as shown in Figure 13.13.

5. Once the Create User Role Wizard has started, define the following variables on the Name and Description page:

   ▶ **Name**—Enter the name for the new user role.

   ▶ **Description**—Enter a useful description for the new user role.

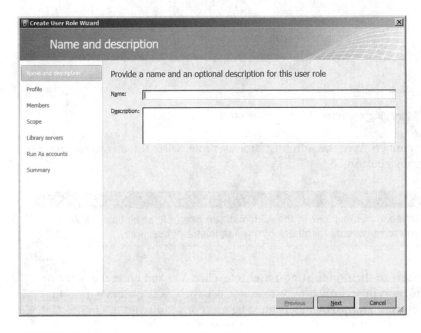

FIGURE 13.13   The Create User Role Wizard.

6. Once you have defined the desired general information for the new role, click Next.

7. On the Profile page, select the option for Delegated Administrator, and then click Next.

8. On the Add Members page, click Add to add new members to the role. Enter the name or names of the users or security groups to add. Click the Check Names button to resolve the users or groups. Members must be users or security groups in the Active Directory domain that the VMM server is a member of, or a domain where a full two-way trust exists.

> **NOTE**
>
> You may also choose to not populate the members of the new Delegated Administrator user role at this time. Members may be populated after the role is created.

9. Once you have finished adding the desired members to the new Delegated Administrator user role, click Next.

10. On the Scope page, as shown in Figure 13.14, select the objects that members of the new user role can manage. This process is called scoping; when scoping your virtual infrastructure, Delegated Administrators will not be able to view or monitor objects from the Administrator Console that are not selected on this page.

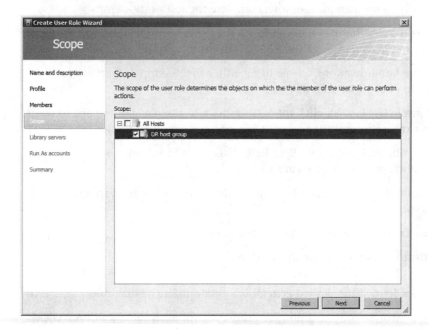

FIGURE 13.14   Scoping the objects for the Delegated Administrator user role.

11. After you have finished scoping the objects for the new Delegated Administrator user role, click Next.

12. On the Library Servers page, click Add and select one of the available library servers to allow the new Delegated Administrator user role to use the specified library server.

13. After you have finished choosing a library server, click Next.

14. On the Run As Accounts page, if needed, click Add and select one or more of the available RunAs accounts to allow the new Delegated Administrator user role to use the specified RunAs accounts.

NOTE

It is also possible to create a new RunAs account that will be used by the Delegated Administrator user role by clicking the Create Run As Account button.

---

15. After you have finished choosing the RunAs accounts to use, click Next.

16. On the Summary page, carefully review the settings and then click Finish to proceed with the creation of the Delegated Administrator role, or click Previous to go back and change the configuration.

Creating a Read-Only Administrator User Role

To create a Read-Only Administrator user role, complete the following steps:

1. Log on to a computer that has the Administrator Console installed using a domain user account that is a member of the VMM Administrator role.

2. Next, open the Administrator Console using either the desktop or Start menu icon and connect to your VMM server.

3. Once the console has loaded, click the Settings icon in the navigation pane to open the Settings workspace, and then expand Security and select User Roles.

4. From the tool ribbon, click Create User Role. This starts the Create User Role Wizard, as shown previously in Figure 13.13.

5. Once the Create User Role Wizard has started, define the following variables on the Name and Description page:

   ▸ **Name**—Enter the name for the new user role.

   ▸ **Description**—Enter a useful description for the new user role.

6. Once you have defined the desired general information for the new role, click Next.

7. On the Profile page, select the option for Read-Only Administrator, and then click Next.

8. On the Add Members page, click Add to add new members to the role. Enter the name or names of the users or security groups to add. Click the Check Names button to resolve the users or groups. Members must be users or security groups in the Active Directory domain that the VMM server is a member of, or a domain where a full two-way trust exists.

NOTE

You may also choose to not populate the members of the new Read-Only Administrator user role at this time. Members may be populated after the role is created.

9. Once you have finished adding the desired members to the new Read-only Administrator user role, click Next.

10. On the Scope page, as shown in Figure 13.14, select the objects that members of the new user role can view. This process is called scoping; when scoping your virtual infrastructure, Read-Only Administrators will not be able to view or monitor objects from the Administrator Console that are not selected on this page.

11. After you have finished scoping the objects for the new Read-Only Administrator user role, click Next.

12. On the Library Servers page, click Add and select one of the available library servers to allow the new Read-Only Administrator user role to view the specified library server.

13. After you have finished choosing a library server, click Next.

14. On the Run As Accounts page, if needed, click Add and select one or more of the available RunAs accounts to allow the new Read-Only Administrator user role to view the specified RunAs accounts.

NOTE

It is also possible to create a new RunAs account that will be viewed by the Read-Only Administrator user role by clicking the Create Run As Account button

15. After you have finished choosing the RunAs accounts to use, click Next.

16. On the Summary page, carefully review the settings and then click Finish to proceed with the creation of the Read-Only Administrator role, or click Previous to go back and change the configuration.

Creating a Self-Service User Role

To create a Self-Service User role, complete the following steps:

1. Log on to a computer that has the Administrator Console installed using a domain user account that is a member of the VMM Administrator role.

2. Next, open the Administrator Console using either the desktop or Start menu icon and connect to your VMM server.

3. Once the console has loaded, click the Settings icon in the navigation pane to open the Settings workspace, and then expand Security and select User Roles.

4. From the tool ribbon, click Create User Role. This starts the Create User Role Wizard, as shown previously in Figure 13.13.

5. Once the Create User Role Wizard has started, define the following variables on the Name and Description page:

   ▶ **Name**—Enter the name for the new user role.

   ▶ **Description**—Enter a useful description for the new user role.

6. Once you have defined the desired general information for the new role, click Next.

7. On the Profile page, select the option for Self-Service User, and then click Next.

8. On the Add Members page, click Add to add new members to the role. Enter the name or names of the users or security groups to add. Click the Check Names button to resolve the users or groups. Members must be users or security groups in the Active Directory domain that the VMM server is a member of, or a domain where a full two-way trust exists.

NOTE

You may also choose to not populate the members of the new Self-Service User role at this time. Members may be populated after the role is created.

---

9. Once you have finished adding the desired members to the new Self-Service User role, click Next.

10. On the Scope page, select the private clouds that members of the new user role can manage. Also, select the Show PRO Tips option if the members of the user role should be allowed to receive and implement PRO tips.

11. Once you have finished selecting the scope for the new Self-Service User role, click Next.

12. On the Resources page, configure the following settings:

    ▶ **Resources**—Click Add to select the specific resources that the Self-Service User role can use during virtual machine creation. Resources that can be assigned include hardware profiles, operating system profiles, virtual machine templates, application profiles, SQL server profiles, and service templates.

    ▶ **Specify User Role Data Path**—Click Browse, and then select one of the available library shares that members of the user role can use to upload and share their own resources, as shown in Figure 13.15.

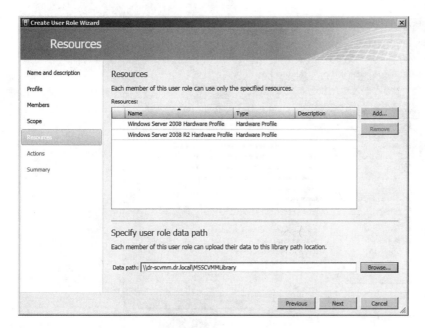

FIGURE 13.15   Defining Resources.

13. Once you have finished selecting the resources assigned to the new Self-Service User role, click Next.

14. On the Actions page, configure one of the following:

- ▶ Click Select All to permit this Self-Service User role to perform all available VMM tasks, as shown in Figure 13.16.

- ▶ Select individual permitted actions. Table 13.2 lists all the actions available for the Self-Service User to run. Use the tasks in this list to scope the rights that Self-Service Users have on their virtual machines.

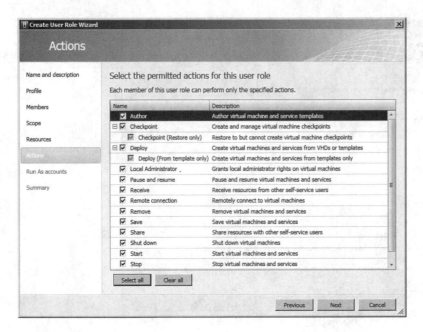

FIGURE 13.16   Defining permitted actions.

TABLE 13.2 Self-Service User Virtual Machine Tasks

Task	Description
Author	Allows the user to author virtual machines and service templates.
Checkpoint	Allows the user to manage checkpoints on a virtual machine.
Checkpoint (Restore Only)	Allows the user to restore to, but not create, virtual machine checkpoints.
Deploy	Allows the user to create VMs or service from VHDs or templates.
Deploy (From Template Only)	Allows the user to create VMs or service from a template only.
Local Administrator	Grants the user local administrator permission on virtual machines they create.
Pause and Resume	Allows the user to pause processing a virtual machine and resume processing after the virtual machine has been paused.
Receive	Grants permission to receive resources from other Self-Service Users.
Remote Connection	Allows the user to connect to and control the virtual machine remotely. This is also known as Virtual Machine Remote Control (VMRC) access.
Remove	Allows the user to delete and discontinue management of a virtual machine from VMM.
Save	Allows the user to save the state of VMs or services.

Task	Description
Share	Allows the user to share resources with other Self-Service Users.
Shut Down	Allows the user to shut down virtual machines.
Start	Allows the user to start virtual machines and services.
Stop	Allows the user to stop processing of a virtual machine.
Store and Re-deploy	Allows the users to store VMs in the library, and then redeploy those VMs.

15. Once you have finished defining the desired actions, click Next.

16. On the Run As Accounts page, if needed, click Add and select one or more of the available RunAs accounts to allow the new Self-Service User role to use the specified RunAs accounts.

NOTE

It is also possible to create a new RunAs account that will be used by the Self-Service User role by clicking the Create Run As Account button

17. After you have finished choosing the RunAs accounts to use, click Next.

18. On the Summary page, carefully review the settings, and click Finish to proceed with the creation of the Self-Service User role or click Previous to go back and change the configuration.

Modifying User Roles

To modify user roles, complete the following steps:

1. Log on to a computer that has the Administrator Console installed using a domain user account that is a member of the VMM Administrator role.

2. Next, open the Administrator Console using either the desktop or Start menu icon and connect to your VMM server.

3. Once the console has loaded, click the Settings icon in the navigation pane to open the Settings workspace, and then expand Security and select User Roles.

4. In the results pane, right-click the user role that you want to modify, and then click Properties to display the properties of the role.

5. The Properties dialog box opens. Using the following tabs, you can define the various settings for the user role:

   ▶ **Name and Description**—Use this tab to modify the name or description of the user role.

   ▶ **Members**—Use this tab to add or remove members as needed.

▶ **Scope**—Use this tab to define which objects this role has rights to. This is only valid for Delegated Administrator, Read-Only Administrator, and Self-Service User roles.

▶ **Resources**—Use this tab to define which resources the members of this role can use, along with the library shares that can be used to upload and share resources. This is only valid for Self-Service User roles.

▶ **Library Servers**—Use this tab to define which library servers the members of this role can use. This is only valid for Delegated Administrator, Read-Only Administrator, and Self-Service User roles.

▶ **Run As Accounts**—Use this tab to define which RunAs accounts the members of this role can use. This is only valid for Delegated Administrator, Read-Only Administrator, and Self-Service User roles.

6. Once you have finished defining desired user role settings, click OK.

Removing User Roles

To remove a user role, complete the following steps:

1. Log on to a computer that has the Administrator Console installed using a domain user account that is a member of the VMM Administrator role.

2. Next, open the Administrator Console using either the desktop or Start menu icon and connect to your VMM server.

3. Once the console has loaded, click the Settings icon in the navigation pane to open the Settings workspace, and then expand Security and select User Roles.

4. In the results pane, right-click the user role that you want to modify, and then click Delete.

5. When the confirmation prompt is displayed, click Yes to remove the user role.

Deploying Virtual Machines

This section describes how to deploy virtual machines on managed hosts using VMM. In this section, the process of virtual machine placement is discussed, you learn how to customize host ratings during placement, and you examine the procedures for deploying and migrating virtual machines to another host.

Virtual Machine Placement

The process of selecting the most suitable host upon which to deploy a virtual machine is called virtual machine placement. When you attempt to deploy a virtual machine using VMM, a list is created of all the managed host servers where the virtual machine can be placed. Each host is given a star rating, from zero to five stars, indicating its suitability for the given virtual machine. This star rating is based on the VM's hardware and resource requirements and each host's ability to fulfill these requirements. Host ratings also take resource maximization, fault tolerance, and load balancing into consideration.

> **NOTE**
>
> If a virtual machine has been configured using the Make This VM Highly Available option, it can only be placed on Hyper-V host clusters. Hosts that are not clusters cannot host HA VMs.

Automatic Placement

For certain situations, when a user or administrator attempts to deploy a virtual machine, VMM automatically determines which host server is the most suitable to be used for the deployment. This feature is called Automatic Placement and applies to the following scenarios:

▸ When virtual machines are deployed by Self-Service Users from the Self-Service Portal, the virtual machine is automatically deployed to the most suitable host server in the specified host group.

▸ When the drag-and-drop method of migration within the Administrator Console is used, the virtual machine is automatically deployed to the most suitable host server in the target group.

Customizing Host Ratings for a Virtual Machine

If needed, you can customize the host ratings when executing specific VMM wizards that affect the state of a virtual machine. When doing this, you override the global criteria used to create host ratings for the virtual machine–related action that is being performed. The VMM wizards where this behavior applies are as follows:

▸ Create Virtual Machine Wizard

▸ Convert Physical Server (P2V) Wizard

▸ Convert Virtual Machine Wizard

▸ Deploy Virtual Machine Wizard

▸ Migrate Virtual Machine Wizard

To override the placement settings for a virtual machine during placement on a host, follow these steps on the Select Host page of the listed wizards:

1. Click the Expected Utilization button.

2. The VM Load screen appears, as shown in Figure 13.17. Use this screen to refine the host ratings by adjusting the workload characterization of the virtual machine, using the following settings:

▶ CPU: Expected CPU Utilization

▶ Disk: Required Physical Disk Space (GB)

▶ Disk: Expected Disk I/O per Second (IOPS)

▶ Network: Expected Utilization (Megabits per Second)

3. Click OK to continue the wizard.

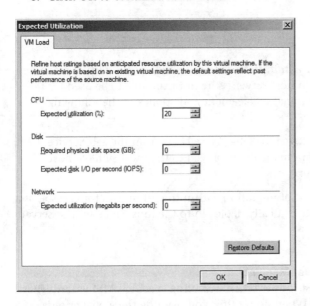

FIGURE 13.17   Customizing host ratings for a virtual machine.

Deploying Virtual Machines Using the Administrator Console

To deploy a virtual machine that's stored in the library using the VMM Administrator
Console, complete the following steps:

1. Log on to a computer that has the Administrator Console installed using a domain
user account that is a member of the VMM Administrator role.

2. Next, open the Administrator Console using either the desktop or Start menu icon
and connect to your VMM server.

3. Once the console has loaded, click the Library icon in the navigation pane to open
the Library workspace.

4. In the Library workspace, expand the Library Servers node and the appropriate
library server that holds the virtual machine that you want to deploy.

5. Next, select the Stored Virtual Machines and Services node to display the available
virtual machines, as shown in Figure 13.18.

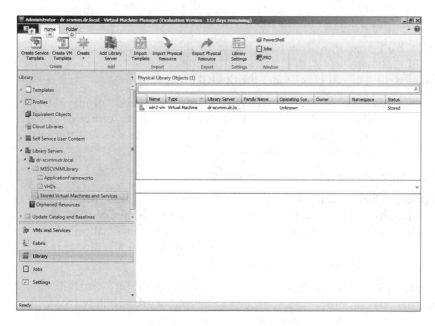

FIGURE 13.18   Examining available VMs stored in a library.

6. In the results pane, select the virtual machine that you want to deploy.

7. From the tool ribbon, click Deploy. This starts the Deploy Virtual Machine Wizard.

8. On the Select Host page, select the most suitable host server to deploy the new virtual machine to. Each host has a star rating (from zero to five stars) indicating its suitability to host the new virtual machine (the Make This VM Highly Available check box should be selected to ensure appropriate availability of the system).

   ▶ The Details tab displays the status, operating system, virtualization software platform, virtualization software status, and names of the virtual machines running on the selected host.

   ▶ The Rating Explanation tab explains what the star rating means for the selected host and tells what requirements are met for the virtual machine by this host.

   ▶ The SAN Explanation tab describes the suitability of the host to connect to a SAN for virtual machine storage. Items listed here include Fibre Channel HBAs installed and iSCSI initiators installed.

NOTE

The ratings can be customized using the Expected Utilization button. Here, the administrator can select multiple criteria and change the anticipated resource utilization for each component, such as CPU utilization, required disk space, expected disk I/O per second, and expected network utilization.

9. Once you have finished selecting the desired host server, click Next.

10. On the Select Path page, select the folder where the files associated with the new virtual machine should be placed. Either accept the default location or click Browse to select a different path. After selecting the desired path, click Next.

11. On the Select Networks page, the Virtual Network drop-down menu displays all the current networks available on the selected host server. Select Not Connected or the appropriate virtual network for the virtual machine to use. After selecting the desired virtual network connection, click Next.

12. On the Add Properties page, configure the following:

   ▶ **Automatic Start Action**—Select the action to perform for this virtual machine when the physical host starts. Available actions are as follows: Never Automatically Turn On the Virtual Machine, Always Automatically Turn On the Virtual Machine, or Automatically Turn On the Virtual Machine If It Was Running When the Physical Server Stopped.

   ▶ **Automatic Stop Action**—Select the action to perform for this virtual machine when the physical host server stops. Available actions are as follows: Save State, Turn Off Virtual Machine, or Shut Down Guest OS.

13. The Summary page displays a summary of the settings selected in the Deploy Virtual Machine Wizard. Carefully review these settings and click Deploy to proceed with the virtual machine deployment or click Previous to go back and change the configuration.

   ▶ An optional check box can be selected to start the virtual machine immediately after deploying it to the host.

   ▶ As with many actions performed from the VMM Administrator Console, the Deploy Virtual Machine Wizard offers a View Script button. This option enables the administrator to view, modify, and save the PowerShell commands that the wizard will execute to perform the virtual machine deployment.

14. Once you click Deploy, the results pane displays a summary of the virtual machine deployment. Clicking the Jobs icon in the navigation pane displays a more detailed view of the progress of the deployment. Use this screen to monitor the progress of the deployment, and confirm that the virtual machine is created successfully. If the job fails, read the error message in the details pane for information about the cause of the failure and the recommended course of action to resolve the issue.

Creating a Virtual Machine Using the Self-Service Portal

To create a new virtual machine using the Self-Service Portal, complete the following steps:

1. The Self-Service User opens the Self-Service Portal by entering the following URL in Internet Explorer:

   ▶ If the Self-Service Portal website is using a dedicated port, type **http://** followed by the computer name of the web server, a colon (**:**), and then the port number (for example, **http://vmm2008:8080**).

   ▶ If the Self-Service Portal is configured to use host headers, type **http://** followed by the host header name.

2. When prompted, enter a valid Self-Service User **<domain>\<username>** and password, and click the Log On button. The Self-Service Portal displays in the browser, as shown in Figure 13.19.

FIGURE 13.19   The VMM Self-Service Portal.

3. Once the portal has loaded, click New Computer in the Actions pane. This opens the New Virtual Machine window.

4. Select the correct private cloud to use from the Target Cloud drop-down menu at the top of the New Virtual Machine window, as shown in Figure 13.20.

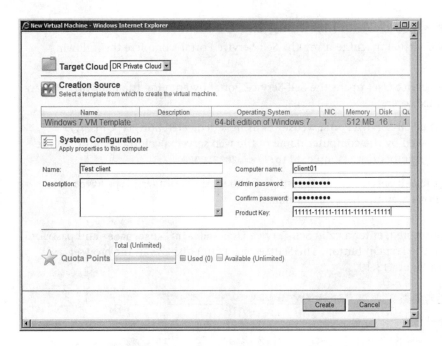

FIGURE 13.20   The New Virtual Machine window.

5. In the Creation Source section, select the template from which to create the new virtual machine.

6. In the System Configuration section, define the following variables:

   ▸ **Name**—Type a friendly name for the new virtual machine (for example, **Windows Server 2008 x64 Accounting Server**).

   ▸ **Description**—Type a description for the new virtual machine.

   ▸ **Computer Name**—Type the computer name of the new virtual machine (for example, **SF-ACCT03**).

   ▸ **Administrator Password/Confirm Password**—Enter and confirm the local administrator password for the new virtual machine.

   ▸ **Product Key**—Type the Microsoft product key for the new virtual machine.

NOTE

The number of quota points, if any, is displayed at the bottom of the New Virtual Machine window. This indicates how many quota points the user has available. If the user does not have enough quota points available for this virtual machine, the user will be unable to deploy it.

7. After clicking the Create button, the new virtual machine is created and deployed. The Self-Service Portal updates to show the status of the deployment of the new virtual machine. The deployment might take a few minutes as files are copied to the host server and the virtual machine needs to be configured.

> **NOTE**
>
> Details about the progress of the virtual machine deployment can be monitored by selecting the virtual machine in the Self-Service Portal, clicking Properties in the Actions pane, and then selecting the Latest Job tab.

Migrating Virtual Machines

VMM provides the capability to move, or migrate, virtual machines quickly and easily between host servers. These migrations are performed using methods that are split into two categories. The first category is called a virtual machine migration, in which the virtual machine is moved from one host server to the other, or between cluster nodes. Details about the supported virtual machine migration technologies in VMM are shown in Table 13.3.

TABLE 13.3 Supported Virtual Machine Migration Technologies

Migration Type	Technologies Used	Migration Time
Live Migration	Windows Server 2008 R2 Hyper-V	None
	Windows Server 2008 Failover Cluster	
	ESX/ESXi 3.5 and 4.1 with VMotion	
	Citrix XenServer 6.0 with Microsoft SCVMM XenServer Integration Suite	
Quick Migration	Windows Server 2008 Hyper-V or greater Windows Server 2008 Failover Cluster	**Under a minute** (Virtual machine is placed into a saved state while being moved between cluster nodes.)
SAN Migration	Windows Server 2008 Hyper-V or greater Virtual Server 2005 R2 Virtual Disk Service (VDS) Hardware Providers	**Under a minute** (Virtual machine is placed into a saved state while being moved between hosts using unmasking and masking operations at the SAN level.)
	N-Port Identification Virtualization (NPIV) on Emulex and QLogic Fibre Channel HBAs iSCSI on EMC, HP, Hitachi, NetApp, EqualLogic arrays	

TABLE 13.3 Supported Virtual Machine Migration Technologies

Migration Type	Technologies Used	Migration Time
Network Migration	Windows Server 2008 Hyper-V or greater Virtual Server 2005 R2 BITS for Virtual Server and Hyper-V	**Minutes or hours** (For Windows Server 2008 or Virtual Server hosts, the virtual machine needs to be stopped or in a saved state for the entire duration of transfer.)
	ESX/ESXi 3.5, 4.1 sFTP for ESX XenServer 6.0	**Under a minute** (For Windows Server 2008 R2 Hyper-V host, the virtual machine remains in a running state during the transfer of its virtual disks. However, to move the virtual machine's memory state and associated differencing disks, it is placed into a saved state.)

The second category is called a storage migration; when performing this type of migration, a virtual machine's files are moved to a different storage location on the same host server. Details about the supported storage migration technologies in VMM are shown in Table 13.4.

TABLE 13.4 Supported Storage Migration Technologies

Migration Type	Technologies Used	Migration Time
Storage VMotion	ESX/ESXi 3.5 and 4.1 with Storage VMotion	None
Quick Storage Migration	Windows Server 2008 R2 Hyper-V BITS for Hyper-V	**Under a minute** (The virtual machine remains in a running state during the transfer of its virtual disks. However, to move the virtual machine's memory state and associated differencing disks, it is placed into a saved state.)

Using the Migrate Action

The Migrate Virtual Machine Wizard enables the administrator to migrate a virtual machine to another host using a VMM wizard, as follows:

1. Log on to a computer that has the Administrator Console installed using a domain user account that is a member of the VMM Administrator role.

2. Next, open the Administrator Console using either the desktop or Start menu icon and connect to your VMM server.

3. Once the console has loaded, click the VMs and Services icon in the navigation pane to open the VMs and Services workspace.

4. In the VMs and Services workspace, select either the host group, cluster, or host that contains the VM to be migrated.

5. In the results pane, select the virtual machine to migrate, and then click Migrate Virtual Machine from the tool ribbon. This starts the Migrate Virtual Machine Wizard.

6. On the Select Host page, select the most suitable host server to migrate the virtual machine to. Each host has a star rating (from zero to five stars) indicating its suitability to host the virtual machine.

   ▶ The Details tab displays the status, operating system, virtualization software platform, virtualization software status, and names of the virtual machines running on the selected host.

   ▶ The Rating Explanation tab explains what the star rating means for the selected host and tells what requirements are met for the virtual machine by this host.

   ▶ The SAN Explanation tab describes the suitability of the host to connect to a SAN for virtual machine storage. Items listed here include Fibre Channel HBAs installed and iSCSI initiators installed.

NOTE

The ratings can be customized using the Expected Utilization button. Here, the administrator can select multiple criteria and change the anticipated resource utilization for each component, such as CPU utilization, required disk space, expected disk I/O per second, and expected network utilization.

---

7. Once you have finished selecting the desired host server, click Next.

8. On the Select Path page, select the folder where the files associated with the new virtual machine should be placed. Either accept the default location or click Browse to select a different path. After selecting the desired path, click Next.

9. On the Select Networks page, the Virtual Network drop-down menu displays all the current networks available on the selected host server. Select Not Connected or the appropriate virtual network for the virtual machine to use. After selecting the desired virtual network connection, click Next.

10. The Summary page displays a summary of the settings selected in the Migrate Virtual Machine Wizard. Carefully review these settings, and click Move to proceed with the virtual machine migration or click Previous to go back and change the configuration.

   ▶ As with many actions performed from the VMM Administrator Console, the Migrate Virtual Machine Wizard offers a View Script button. This option enables the administrator to view, modify, and save the PowerShell commands that the wizard will execute to perform the virtual machine deployment.

11. Once you click Move, the results pane displays a summary of the migration. Clicking the Jobs icon in the navigation pane displays a more detailed view of the progress of the migration. Use this screen to monitor the progress of the migration and confirm that the virtual machine is created successfully. If the job fails, read the error message in the details pane for information about the cause of the failure and the recommended course of action to resolve the issue.

Using the Migrate Storage Action

The Migrate Storage action is used to perform a storage migration. To complete a storage migration for a virtual machine, complete the following steps:

1. Log on to a computer that has the Administrator Console installed using a domain user account that is a member of the VMM Administrator role.

2. Next, open the Administrator Console using either the desktop or Start menu icon and connect to your VMM server.

3. Once the console has loaded, click the VMs and Services icon in the navigation pane to open the VMs and Services workspace.

4. In the VMs and Services workspace, select either the host group, cluster, or host that contains the VM to be migrated.

5. In the results pane, select the powered off virtual machine to migrate, and then click Migrate Storage from the tool ribbon. This starts the Migrate Virtual Machine Wizard.

6. On the Select Path page, select the folder where the files associated with the new virtual machine should be placed, as shown in Figure 13.21. Either accept the default location or click Browse to select a different path. After selecting the desired path, click Next.

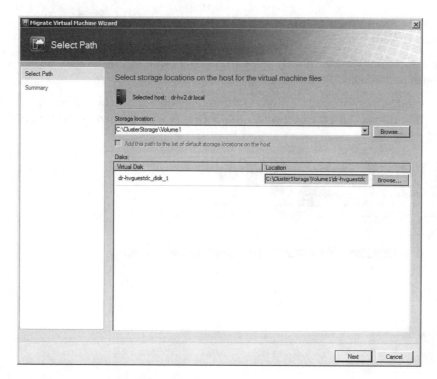

FIGURE 13.21   The Select Path page.

7. The Summary page displays a summary of the settings selected in the Migrate Virtual Machine Wizard. Carefully review these settings, and click Move to proceed with the storage migration or click Previous to go back and change the configuration.

8. Once you click Move, the results pane displays a summary of the migration. Clicking the Jobs icon in the navigation pane displays a more detailed view of the progress of the migration. Use this screen to monitor the progress of the migration and confirm that the virtual machine is created successfully. If the job fails, read the error message in the details pane for information about the cause of the failure and the recommended course of action to resolve the issue.

Dragging and Dropping the Virtual Machine onto a Host Server

In addition to using the Migrate Virtual Machine Wizard to move a virtual machine from one host server to another, you can also just drag and drop virtual machines between host servers. To drag and drop a virtual machine onto a host server, complete the following steps:

1. Log on to a computer that has the Administrator Console installed using a domain user account that is a member of the VMM Administrator role.

2. Next, open the Administrator Console using either the desktop or Start menu icon and connect to your VMM server.

3. Once the console has loaded, click the VMs and Services icon in the navigation pane to open the VMs and Services workspace.

4. In the VMs and Services workspace, expand the various host groups, as shown in Figure 13.22, until you find the host server to which you want to migrate the virtual machine.

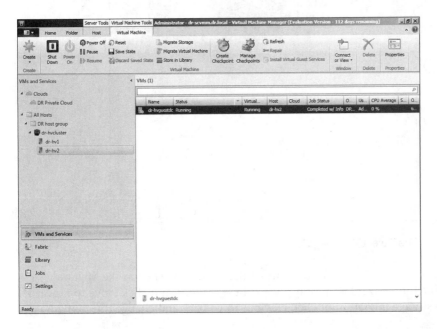

FIGURE 13.22   Locating the host server on which to migrate the virtual machine.

5. Next, in the results pane, select the virtual machine to migrate and drag and drop it onto the new host.

6. The Migrate Virtual Machine dialog box appears, displaying the host ratings for the selected target host, along with additional information. To begin the migration, click Migrate VM. The VM is then migrated to the new host.

Dragging and Dropping the Virtual Machine onto a Host Group

This process is the same as dragging and dropping the virtual machine onto a host server, as described previously, with a few differences. Instead of dropping the virtual machine onto a specific host, the virtual machine is dropped onto a host group that contains one or more hosts. Then Automatic Placement, as explained earlier in this chapter, automatically places the virtual machine on the most suitable host in the selected host group. Host selection is based on host ratings.

Understanding and Implementing Server App-V

A new feature of VMM 2012 is the ability to leverage virtual application packages created using Server Application Virtualization (Server App-V). Virtual application packages are images of applications that can be copied to a system running the Server App-V Agent and started without requiring a local installation. Server App-V builds on the application virtualization (App-V) technology used to streamline desktop deployments by separating the application configuration and state from the underlying operating system, resulting in an effective method of reducing hardware and operational costs that are associated with application deployment. For example, Server App-V can be used to significantly reduce the number of images that need to be managed, and can be used to automate deployment of applications across the data center.

> **NOTE**
>
> Not all applications are supported for use with Server App-V. It is primarily designed for use with business applications. Some examples of applications that are not supported for Server App-V are antivirus software, Microsoft SQL Server, and Microsoft SharePoint. In cases like SQL or SharePoint, there are built-in native application methods for high availability and scalability, such as load balancing, clustering, database replication, and the like. Therefore, the architecture of scalability, redundancy, and high availability should be taken into account in selecting the right technology to meet the needs of the organization.

Server App-V Basics

To get started with Server App-V, there are a few terms that you need to be familiar with, primarily the following:

▶ **Sequencer**—A software utility used to create virtual application packages by monitoring and recording the entire installation and setup process for an application.

▶ **Virtual application package**—An application packaged by the Sequencer to run in a self-contained, virtual environment. The virtual environment contains the information necessary to run the application on the client without installing the application locally.

▶ **Deployment configuration file**—An .xml file that contains customized settings that are applied to a specific virtual application package when the package is run on a target computer.

▶ **Virtual environment**—A runtime container that defines the resources available to application processes that are launched from a sequenced application package.

▶ **Server App-V Agent**—Agent software installed on Server App-V clients, used to accept and then set up virtualization packages on the target system.

Server App-V Sequencer Installation

The Server App-V Sequencer is supported for installation on the following operating system versions (note that the Sequencer is available for both 32- and 64-bit installations):

▶ Windows Server 2003 SP2, Standard and Enterprise Editions

▶ Windows Server 2003 R2 SP2, Standard and Enterprise Editions

▶ Windows Server 2008 SP2, Standard and Enterprise Editions

▶ Windows Server 2008 R2, Standard and Enterprise Editions

After meeting the operating system requirements, the next step is to copy the Server App-V Sequencer installation file to the system where the software will be installed, using the file version that matches the processor architecture of the system (x86 or x64). The Server App-V Sequencer installation file is named SeqSetup.exe, and can be found in the x86 or x64 subdirectory under the following path on the VMM Server: Program Files\Microsoft System Center 2012\Virtual Machine Manager\SAV. To start the installation, log on to the system where the Sequencer will be installed using an account that is a member of the local administrators group. Then execute the SeqSetup.exe file to start the Microsoft Server Application Virtualization Sequencer Setup Wizard. Once the wizard has started, use the following steps to complete the installation:

1. On the Welcome page, click Next.

2. When prompted with the License Agreement dialog box, select the I Accept the License Terms check box, and then click Next.

3. On the Customer Experience Improvement Program page, select the desired Customer Experience Improvement Program option, and then click Next.

4. On the Destination Folder page, either use the default folder location or modify the installation path to meet your needs, and then click Next.

5. At the Ready to Install page, click Next to begin the installation.

6. Once the installation is complete, click Finish to exit the wizard.

Server App-V Agent Installation

The Server App-V Agent must be installed on any target system that will be used to run the application packages that are created using the Server App-V Sequencer. To install the agent, the first step is to copy the Server App-V Agent installation file to the system where the agent will be installed, using the file version that matches the processor architecture of the system (x86 or x64). The Server App-V Agent installation file is named AgentSetup.exe, and can be found in the x86 or x64 subdirectory under the following path on the VMM Server: `Program Files\Microsoft System Center 2012\Virtual Machine Manager\SAV`. To start the installation, log on to the system where the agent will be installed using an account that is a member of the local administrators group. Then execute the `AgentSetup.exe` file to start the Microsoft Server Application Virtualization Agent Setup Wizard. Once the wizard has started, use the following steps to complete the installation:

1. On the Welcome page, click Next.

2. When prompted with the License Agreement dialog box, select the I Accept the License Terms check box, and then click Next.

3. On the Microsoft Update Opt-In page, select the desired Microsoft Update option, and then click Next.

4. On the Destination Folder page, either use the default folder location or modify the installation path to meet your needs, and then click Next.

5. At the Ready to Install page, click Next to begin the installation.

6. Once the installation is complete, click Finish to exit the wizard.

Creating a New Server Application Package

An application package is created by using the Sequencer to monitor the installation and setup process for an application and then record the information that is necessary for the application to run in a virtual environment. The following steps are used to create a new server application package:

1. Log on to the system where the Server App-V Sequencer is installed using an account that is a member of the local administrators group.

2. Start the Server App-V Sequencer by clicking on Start, pointing to All Programs, pointing to Microsoft Application Virtualization, and then clicking on Microsoft Application Virtualization Sequencer.

3. At the opening screen, select the option for Create a New Virtual Application Package, as shown in Figure 13.23.

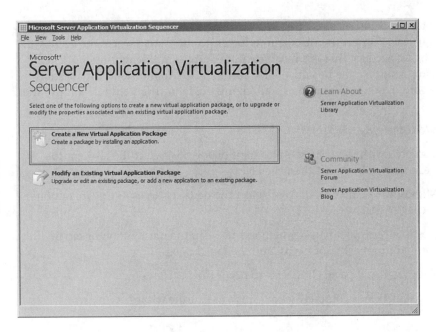

FIGURE 13.23   Creating a new virtual application package.

4. On the Prepare Computer page, any issues which could cause the package creation to fail will automatically be listed. Review any listed issues and resolve these before continuing with the package creation. For example, it might be necessary to disable antivirus scanning software prior to continuing. After remediation, you can check to see if a particular conflict has been resolved by clicking Refresh to update the information displayed. After fixing any issues that are listed, click Next to continue with the package creation.

5. At the Select Installer page, click Browse, and then navigate to and select the application to be sequenced. Alternately, if the application does not have an installer file and you plan to perform all installation steps manually, click Select This Option to Perform a Custom Installation. Once you have selected the installer file, click Next.

6. At the Package Name page, specify a name that will be associated with the package. Also the Primary Virtual Application Directory will automatically be selected as the root of the App-V virtual drive (typically Q:\). Although it is possible to adjust the Primary Virtual Application Directory location by selecting the Edit (Advanced) option, this is typically not necessary, as the default path is recommended for most applications. Once the package name has been specified, click Next to continue.

7. Once the Installation page appears, the Sequencer will then automatically initiate the application installation routine. Follow through with the installation of the application as you would normally, with one important exception: When the option to change the destination folder appears, select the Primary Virtual Application Directory identified in the previous step as the target destination for the

application, which will allow the Sequencer to monitor the installation process. This will typically be the folder at the root of the App-V virtual drive named after the package; see Figure 13.24 for an example of how this configuration might appear for a typical installation of the Adobe Acrobat Reader application.

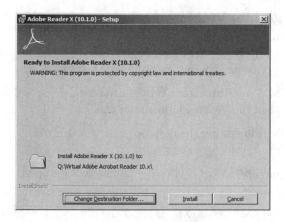

FIGURE 13.24   Installing an application to the virtual application directory.

8. After the application installation routine is complete, the Installer page will display a Run option, which can be used to specify any additional installation files that must be run as part of the installation. If there are additional installation files that are required, select Run, and then navigate to and select the additional installation files. Once all installations have been completed for the application, select I Am Finished Installing, and then click Next.

NOTE

It is also possible to minimize the Sequencer and perform any additional required installation steps directly on the system where the Sequencer is running. This is possible because the Sequencer monitors all system activity, regardless of whether it originates from the Sequencer user interface.

---

9. On the Configure Software page, the programs that are contained in the package will be listed. It is possible to run one or all of these programs on this screen in order to complete any configuration tasks that must be captured within the package. For example, it might be necessary to configure license agreements, set user preferences, or disable automatic updates for the application. To run one of the listed programs, select the program from the list and click Run Selected. To run all of the listed programs, click Run All. After all required configuration tasks have been completed, click Next, and then wait for the package to be created.

10. On the Completion page, review the information displayed in the Virtual Application Package Report pane, and then click Close.

11. The Sequencer console now appears, with the newly sequenced application now listed. To save the package files, select the File menu, click Save, and then choose a location to save the package files.

Importing an Application Package into VMM

Once an application package is created using the Server App-V Sequencer, it can be imported into the VMM library for use in a variety of public cloud configurations. The following procedure is used to import an application package into the VMM library:

1. Log on to a computer that has the VMM Administrator Console installed using a domain user account that is a member of the VMM Administrator role.

2. Next, open the Administrator Console using either the desktop or Start menu icon and connect to your VMM server.

3. Once the console has loaded, in the navigation pane, click the Library icon to open the Library workspace.

4. In the Library workspace, expand Library Servers, and then select the library server that will be used to import the application package.

5. From the tool ribbon, click Import Physical Resource.

6. At the Import Library Resources dialog box, click Add Resource, and then navigate to and select the .osd file representing the application package to be imported. At the bottom of the Import Library Resources dialog box, click Browse, and then select the target library server and folder that will be used to host the application package. Once the package and the target have been specified, click Import to import the package into the library.

Summary

This chapter focused on how Virtual Machine Manager 2012 can be used to manage an organization's virtual infrastructure. As shown in this chapter, VMM can be managed using the Administrator Console and the command shell. By using these interfaces, administrators can execute such VMM-related tasks as performing virtual machine conversions (P2V and V2V), managing user roles, deploying new virtual machines, and migrating virtual machines to new host servers or new storage locations. VMM is a powerful management tool that has a lot of great features built in to it. For example, virtual machines can easily be deployed using both the Administrator Console and the Self-Service Portal. Virtual machine migration can be performed easily using wizards or simple drag-and-drop methods. Lastly, Hyper-V virtual machines can be created from physical servers using P2V conversion. This process can be performed online without disrupting the physical server by using the VSS, and can be used to reduce the number of physical servers in the organization's environment.

Best Practices

The following are best practices from this chapter:

▶ Use VMM's P2V function to convert physical computers or Citrix XenServer virtual machines to Hyper-V virtual machines.

▶ Use VMM's V2V function to convert virtual machines created on VMware ESX to Hyper-V virtual machines.

▶ Use the online P2V process to convert physical computers to virtual machines without disrupting the online server.

▶ Use the offline P2V process to convert offline physical computers to Hyper-V virtual machines.

▶ Use the Microsoft Virtual Server 2005 Migration Toolkit to convert Windows NT Server 4.0 computers to virtual machines.

▶ Perform a disk defragmentation on the source computer before performing the P2V conversion.

▶ Ensure that a fast network connection exists between the source computer and the VMM server.

▶ Use the owner property of a virtual machine to identify the owner or contact person for the virtual machine.

▶ Ensure that the WMI service is running on the source computer and that a firewall is not blocking HTTP and WMI traffic to the VMM server.

▶ Remove the RemoteAdmin firewall exception, if necessary, after the conversion is complete to increase server security.

▶ Increase the size of a VHD to allocate more space for the virtual machine if necessary.

▶ Use the Jobs view to monitor the progress of P2V and V2V conversions.

▶ Review the details in the Jobs view for errors and to determine the cause of failures and the recommended course of action to resolve issues.

▶ Pay special attention to collect any data that was changed on the source server after an online conversion process was begun.

▶ Copy VMware ESX VMX and VMDK files to a VMM library that is closest to the host server to speed virtual machine conversion.

▶ Always refresh the VMM library server after adding files to the library.

▶ Use the P2V process to create a virtual copy of the organization's production environment for testing.

▶ Use RBAC to define the administrator roles in VMM.

▶ Because the Administrator user role has full access to the VMM infrastructure, limit the number of members of this group as much as possible.

▶ Use the Delegated Administrator user role to scope administrators to a specific set of objects in VMM.

▶ Create a VMM Administrators group in Active Directory and add that group to the Administrator role in VMM. This is better than adding an individual user account, in case that user account is deleted.

▶ Create security groups in Active Directory and use these groups to define members of the Delegated Administrator and Self-Service User roles in VMM.

▶ Monitor the membership of the Delegated Administrator user roles because Delegated Administrators can manage the groups they are members of.

▶ Add Administrators or Delegated Administrators to the Self-Service User role if Self-Service Portal access is required.

▶ Run wizards, such as the Create Virtual Machine Wizard, to view, customize, and save the PowerShell scripts that the wizard will run.

▶ Build a collection of PowerShell scripts that perform commonly used VMM administration tasks.

▶ Scope the VMM library resources that Self-Service Users can access by creating their own folders in the VMM library share.

▶ Use a common virtual machine path on all host servers to ensure that virtual machine migrations will succeed.

▶ Use quota points for Self-Service Users to control the number of virtual machines they can deploy to hosts.

▶ Monitor the progress of virtual machine migrations using the Jobs view in the Administrator Console or the Properties page of the virtual machine in the Self-Service Portal.

▶ Notify users of an active virtual machine before migrating it to a new host because the virtual machine might be temporarily stopped during the migration.

▶ Use Automatic Placement of migrated virtual machines by using the "drag and drop onto a host group" method.

▶ Consider the goals and architecture of server-based applications to determine whether Server Application Virtualization (App-V) is appropriate for a given application.

▶ Use native high availability, data replication, clustering, and load-balancing technologies instead of Server App-V when the application is better designed with other technologies that meet the needs of the organization.

CHAPTER 14

Service Manager 2012 Design, Planning, and Implementation

IN THIS CHAPTER

▶ What's New in Service Manager 2012

▶ Explaining How Service Manager Works

▶ Service Manager Design Parameters

▶ Putting It All Together in a Service Manager Design

▶ Planning a Service Manager Deployment

▶ Deploying Service Manager

▶ Deploying Service Manager Connectors

▶ Backing Up Service Manager 2012

▶ Best Practices

Information technology (IT) has become central to the success of the organizations it serves, while at the same time becoming evermore complex. To meet modern economic pressures, IT departments have to become more efficient and do more with less. To meet these challenges, organizations are turning to service management processes and the frameworks that describe them. These frameworks include the following:

▶ Microsoft Operations Framework (MOF)

▶ ITIL

▶ Control Objectives for Information and Related Technology (COBIT)

▶ International Organization for Standardization (ISO) 2000

These frameworks help organizations integrate people, processes, and technologies into a uniform process. System Center Service Manager 2012 is a comprehensive tool for automating and tracking those service management processes. SvcMgr includes a number of predefined service management processes and provides a platform for developing others. The included processes are as follows:

▶ Incident and problem management

▶ Change control

▶ Asset management

Service Manager (SM) integrates information from a variety of sources, including the following:

▶ Active Directory

▶ Configuration Manager

▶ Operations Manager

▶ System Center Orchestrator

This information is integrated in a configuration management database (CMDB). This is, in turn, integrated into a variety of processes, enabling best-practices enforcement and tracking.

In particular, SvcMgr addresses a common request from Microsoft users for an incident-tracking system that automatically generates trouble tickets (that is, incidents) for issues that are discovered by the System Center family members—Operations Manager and Configuration Manager. These incidents automatically associate the affected services and items, displaying key information about those services and items from the CMDB. This level of synthesis of operations and configuration data into an incident-tracking system is extremely helpful for IT professionals.

What's New in Service Manager 2012

Service Manager 2012 (SCSM 2012) incorporates a number of new features and incremental improvements. New features in Service Manager 2012 include the following:

▶ **Data warehouse reporting**—A key component of SCSM 2012 is the new data warehouse feature. The data warehouse collects data from multiple sources (such as Configuration Manager, Operations Manager, and Service Manager as well as other sources, such as Oracle or SAP (Systems, Applications, and Products in Data Processing)) and provides access to the collected data through OLAP (online analytical processing) cubes defined in Service Manager, which can be used to create drag-and-drop reports using SharePoint, Excel, or other business intelligence (BI) solutions.

▶ **Orchestrator and VMM integration**—Service Manager 2012 introduces connectors for System Center Orchestrator (formerly Opalis) and Virtual Machine Manager (VMM). The Orchestrator connector is used to import task sequences called runbooks into Service Manager so they can be accessed from within SCSM, and the VMM connector imports information on virtual machines and VM templates. These new connectors allow Orchestrator and VMM components to be integrated into service offerings in SCSM.

▶ **Service requests and release management**—In Service Manager 2012, service requests are a new type of work item that allow users to select from predefined entries in the SCSM service catalog. Service requests provide a framework for user request fulfillment and tracking. Similarly, the new Release Management feature provides the ability to consolidate multiple changes and deploy them in a controlled and understandable manner.

▶ **Self-Service Portal**—The Self-Service Portal has been completely reengineered for SCSM 2012. The SCSM 2012 portal integrates directly with the SCSM service catalog to provide service offerings to users based on their Active Directory security group memberships. Users can also post comments on their own active work items through the portal to update their incidents. The Self-Service Portal in SCSM 2012 uses Microsoft Silverlight components together with SharePoint Foundation 2010 to allow extensive portal customization through the use of familiar SharePoint administration tools.

Improvements in Service Manager 2012 include the following:

▶ **Accessing information in closed work items**—SCSM 2012 allows users to access documents attached to closed work items, which was not possible in SCSM 2010.

▶ **Parallel activity support**—In SCSM 2010, workflows were only performed sequentially (one task following another). This has been improved in SCSM 2012 to support activities that occur in parallel. The workflow designer now has a graphical user interface, which improves on the table-based interface in SCSM 2010.

▶ **Parent-child support for incident and release management**—SCSM 2012 now allows parent/child relationships to be defined for incidents and releases. This allows child incidents to be automatically closed when the parent incident is closed.

▶ **PowerShell functionality**—Service Manager 2012 now includes 122 PowerShell cmdlets, which support Service Manager and data warehouse functions (up from 28 cmdlets in Service Manager 2010). Microsoft has also added the capability to launch a PowerShell session from within the Service Manager console. Finally, the Service Manager cmdlets support a new -online parameter for retrieving the most current online help information, using the syntax Get-help <cmdlet-name> -online.

▶ **Service-level agreements (SLA) for incidents**—Service Manager 2012 now allows calendars to be created for service-level agreements so that SLAs can be monitored based on predefined support hours. Multiple calendars can be configured to support different SLAs for different user groups.

▶ **Upgrade path from SCSM 2010**—Service Manager 2012 supports upgrading an existing SCSM 2010 environment to SCSM 2012. *Please note*: The SCSM 2010 portal will *not* function in an SCSM 2012 environment, so the new SCSM 2012 portal must be used instead.

Explaining How Service Manager Works

Service Manager 2012 is the second iteration of service management product for Microsoft. It enhances the functionality introduced in System Center 2010 and moves the System Center suite up from the technical processes of monitoring systems, gathering inventory, and deploying applications to the business processes of change management, interacting with end users, and enforcing policies.

SvcMgr Processes

Service management processes are central to any modern IT organization. Standardizing, tracking, automating, and reporting on processes is critical to the success of the IT organization. Service Manager manages the following three major IT processes out of the box:

▶ Incident management

▶ Problem management

▶ Change management

These processes are embodied in Process Management Packs. These management packs include workflows, forms, reports, and templates to instrument and automate the processes.

The incident management process is designed to drive the identification and resolution of service and system outages. The management pack provides integrated access to synthesized configuration and operational data, relationships between other systems, a search engine that accesses the collective database of IT assets, and automatic generation of incidents from Operations Manager and Configuration Manager. The incidents can be routed, escalated, reported on, and attached to problems.

The problem management process is designed to drive the identification and resolution of root causes. These root causes might be the source of multiple incidents or change requests. The Problem Management Pack integrates incidents and allows flagging of problems that are in process as well as actions taken to diagnose and resolve the problems. This facilitates resolving incidents while working toward a long-term solution to the root causes.

The Change Management Pack is designed to ensure that changes are evaluated and approved before implementation, thus ensuring that the IT systems are stable and documented. The management pack enforces the creation of requests for change (RFC), automatically generates RFCs from incidents, provides a routing and review process, and even automates the changes themselves.

In addition to the built-in service management processes, Service Manager can be extended with additional management packs and custom management packs can be developed.

A key new feature in Service Manager 2012 is the integration with System Center Orchestrator 2012. Service Manager 2012 provides an option to connect to an Orchestrator server and import *runbooks* into the CMDB. A *runbook* is a collection of IT processes that are performed in sequence to complete a business goal. For example, a business might create a runbook to assist in troubleshooting a production web server outage, to perform log file consolidation across several servers, or to deploy a new virtual machine. By storing runbooks within the CMDB, it is possible for Service Manager 2012 to perform automated actions based on a variety of conditions, such as an Operations Manager alert or a user-generated service request. This chapter provides an overview of Orchestrator in the context of Service Manager 2012. The installation, configuration, and use of Orchestrator 2012 are discussed in detail in Chapter 17, "Orchestrator 2012 Implementation and Automation."

> **NOTE**
>
> The term *runbook automation* was created by Gartner Research. Runbook automation is analogous to the term *IT Process Automation* or *ITPA*, which is used by other research firms.

SvcMgr Technologies

The Service Manager platform is built around a set of key technologies. These technologies enable the Service Manager capabilities.

The technologies are as follows:

- **Workflow engine**—The workflow engine automates IT processes and facilitates the integration with System Center products, such as Operations Manager and Configuration Manager.

- **Data warehouse**—The data warehouse consolidates data and allows consolidated reporting across the System Center products.

- **Connector Framework**—The Connector Framework provides integration with System Center products like Operations Manager, Configuration Manager, and Orchestrator as well as Active Directory and third-party products.

- **Configuration management database**—The CMDB provides a central view of managed assets and relationships between objects.

- **Self-Service Portals**—The Self-Service Portals provide a web-based interface that allows users to reset their passwords, request software, and request support.

- **Knowledge base**—The knowledge base (KB) is a repository of solutions from both within the organization and from the industry at large. This knowledge base grows over time as incidents and problems are resolved.

These technologies help tie together the people, processes, and technologies central to the success of the organization.

SvcMgr Architecture Components

The Service Manager architecture consists of six major components. These are the components that can reside on different systems and must be accounted for when designing a Service Manager system.

NOTE

All Service Manager components must be installed on Active Directory domain systems in the same forest. No Service Manager components can reside on workgroup systems or in other Active Directory forests.

The Service Manager components are as follows:

- ▶ **Service Manager management server**—The Service Manager management server is the component that runs the workflow engine, manages the CMDB, runs the connectors, and to which the console connects.

- ▶ **Service Manager database**—The Service Manager database, also known as the CMDB, is the storage for all the service management information, including objects, configuration information, relationships, and processes, such as the problems, incidents, and change management. The CMDB is a superset of the database in Operations Manager. The Service Manager database is appropriately named ServiceManager.

- ▶ **Service Manager data warehouse management server**—The data warehouse management server hosts the server components of the data warehouse, such as the reporting engine.

- ▶ **Service Manager data warehouse database**—This database stores the long-term historical data from the Service Manager database and provides reporting on long-term trends and history. The data warehouse is composed of three separate databases: the DWStagingAndConfig, DWRepository, and DWDataMart databases.

- ▶ **Service Manager console**—The Service Manager console provides administrators, analysts, and help desk staff access to the functionality of Service Manager, such as incidents, change management, reports, and administration.

- ▶ **Service Manager Self-Service Portal**—The Self-Service Web Portal provides browser-based access to Service Manager for end users. The Service Manager 2012 portal can be accessed through the URL https://*servername*/SMPortal, where *servername* is the name of the server hosting the portal.

The Service Manager 2012 architecture is shown in Figure 14.1, with all the major components and their data paths.

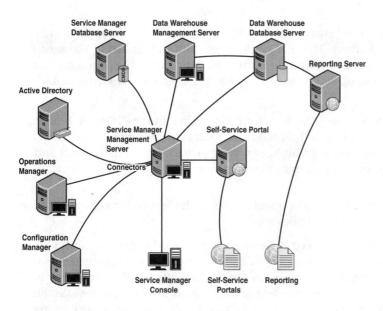

FIGURE 14.1   The Service Manager 2012 architecture.

The databases that make up the Service Manager data warehouse perform very specific roles in the data warehouse. Data travels in a three-stage process through the databases. This is the Extraction, Transformation, and Loading (ETL) process, which moves data from the Service Manager database into the data warehouse. The stages are as follows:

▶ **Extraction**—The data is extracted from the ServiceManager database and is populated into the DWStagingAndConfig database.

▶ **Transformation**—The data in the DWStagingAndConfig database is transformed into the proper format and stored in the DWRepository database.

▶ **Loading**—The data in the DWRepository database is finally loaded into the DWDataMart database .

Data warehouse reports are generated from the DWDataMart database.

Other key components are operational rather than architectural components. These operational components are as follows:

▶ **Workflows**—These are sequences of activities defined in management packs that model and enforce service management processes. These workflows are run by the Windows Workflow Foundation in Microsoft .NET Framework 3.5.

▶ **Templates**—Templates are predefined forms that allow the system to collect data. These can be both manually entered and automatically populated. Templates include constraints that help reduce errors and enforce policies.

▶ **Connectors**—Connectors provide links to other repositories of information, such as Active Directory, Operations Manager, Orchestrator, and Configuration Manager. The connectors transfer and synchronize data into the CMDB. The connectors can leverage templates and workflows to automatically start processes based on the incoming data.

▶ **Knowledge base (KB)**—The KB is the information stored in the CMDB on how to resolve problems and incidents. This can come from external sources such as Microsoft TechNet and also from internal sources such as the IT professionals and the organization's own incident and problem history.

These architectural and operational components make up the Service Manager application and deliver the functionality of the application.

A key new feature of the data warehouse in Service Manager 2012 is the accessibility of warehoused data through OLAP (online analytical processing) cubes that are generated and refreshed from within Service Manager. The Service Manager OLAP functionality is designed to provide efficient analysis across significantly sized sets of data—for example, identifying adherence to service-level agreements (SLAs) for all incidents created during the last business quarter. Service Manager 2012 includes a number of preconfigured OLAP cubes, which can be viewed by users in Microsoft Excel and also as SharePoint dashboards. It is also possible for users to create their own customized OLAP cubes for the data sources that they are interested in, and then include these authored OLAP cubes in custom management packs. Because the Service Manager data warehouse can consume data from sources internal and external to System Center (such as Oracle and SAP), the Service Manager 2012 data warehouse provides true business intelligence capabilities for reporting across all aspects of the enterprise.

The following example describes how to use Excel to view and analyze one of the predefined Service Manager OLAP cubes:

> **NOTE**
>
> For this example to work as described, Excel must be installed on the same machine where the Service Manager 2012 console is installed.

1. In the Service Manager console, click Data Warehouse, expand the Data Warehouse node, and then click Cubes.

2. In the Cubes pane, select a cube name, and then under Tasks, click Analyze Cube in Excel. For example, select SystemCenterWorkItemsCube and analyze it.

3. Excel will open and display a PivotTable Field List. You can drag and drop fields from this list to create slices and charts. For example, if you want to see the total number of incidents currently open, expand IncidentDimGroup, and then select Incidents Opened.

4. You can add additional fields to generate a more complex analysis. For example, you can add computers from the ComputerDim dimension by selecting the DisplayName field to see the number of incidents that affect different computers.

5. Optionally, you can save the workbook to a shared folder or other shared location.

Service Manager Design Parameters

SvcMgr's simple installation and relative ease of use belies the potential complexity of its underlying components. This complexity can be managed with the right amount of knowledge of some of the advanced concepts of SvcMgr design and implementation.

Each SvcMgr component has specific design requirements, and a good knowledge of these factors is required before beginning the design of SvcMgr. Hardware and software requirements must be taken into account as well as factors involving specific SvcMgr components, such as the management servers, databases, connectors, and backup requirements.

Exploring Hardware Requirements

Having the proper hardware for SvcMgr to operate on is a critical component of SvcMgr functionality, reliability, and overall performance. Nothing is worse than overloading a brand-new server only a few short months after its implementation. The industry standard generally holds that any production servers deployed should remain relevant for three to four years following deployment. Stretching beyond this time frame might be possible, but the ugly truth is that hardware investments are typically short term and need to be replaced often to ensure relevance. Buying a less-expensive server might save money in the short term but could potentially increase costs associated with downtime, troubleshooting, and administration. That said, the following are the Microsoft-recommended minimums for any server running a SvcMgr 2012 server component:

▶ 2.66GHz 64-bit processor or faster

▶ 2 cores

▶ 8GB of random access memory (RAM)

These recommendations apply only to nonproduction or very small SvcMgr deployments and should be seen as minimum levels for SvcMgr hardware. Most production deployments would have the following minimums:

▶ 2.66GHz 64-bit processor or faster

▶ 2–8 cores

▶ 8–16GB of RAM

Service Manager 2012 has relatively heavy database access requirements, so generous processor, disk, and memory are important for optimal performance. Future expansion and relevance of hardware should be taken into account when sizing servers for SvcMgr deployment, to ensure that the system has room to grow as agents are added and the databases grow.

If the Service Manager 2012 components are to be virtualized, the minimum requirements for the virtual machines are as follows:

▶ 2 virtual CPUs

▶ 8GB of RAM

This includes the Service Manager management server, the data warehouse management server, and the Self-Service Web Portal. However, the SQL servers should always be installed on physical hardware due to the loads placed on them.

The minimum hardware requirements given in Table 14.1 are those needed to run the basic Service Manager components.

TABLE 14.1   Minimum Hardware Requirements

Component	Processor	Cores	Memory	Disk
Service Manager management server	2.66GHz 64-bit	2	8GB	RAID 1
Service Manager database	2.66GHz 64-bit	2	8GB	RAID 10
Service Manager data warehouse management server	2.66GHz 64-bit	2	8GB	RAID 1
Service Manager data warehouse database	2.66GHz 64-bit	2	8GB	RAID 10
Service Manager Self-Service Portal	2.66GHz 64-bit	2	8GB	RAID 1
Service Manager console	2.0GHz 32-bit	1	1GB	RAID 1

The minimum requirements are typically not enough for optimal performance. To get good console and reporting performance, the recommendations in Table 14.2 should be followed.

TABLE 14.2   Recommended Hardware Requirements

Component	Processor	Cores	Memory	Disk
Service Manager management server	2.66GHz 64-bit	8	8GB	RAID 1
Service Manager database	2.66GHz 64-bit	8	8–16GB	RAID 10
Service Manager data warehouse management server	2.66GHz 64-bit	2	8GB	RAID 1

TABLE 14.2   Continued

Component	Processor	Cores	Memory	Disk
Service Manager data warehouse database	2.66GHz 64-bit	8	8–16GB	RAID 10
Service Manager Self-Service Portal	2.66GHz 64-bit	2	8GB	RAID 1
Service Manager console	2.0GHz 32-bit	2	2GB	RAID 1

As can be seen from the recommendations, the Service Manager components have a relatively heavy memory and processing requirement. See the sample designs later in this chapter for recommendations based on specific numbers of users and computers.

Determining Software Requirements

SvcMgr components must be installed on 64-bit versions of the operating system and database. However, the console can be installed on a 32-bit platform. The database can be installed on the same server as SvcMgr or on a separate server, a concept that is discussed in more detail in following sections.

The software requirements critical to the success of SvcMgr implementations are given in Table 14.3.

TABLE 14.3   Software Requirements

Component	Software
Service Manager management server	Windows Server 2008 R2 64-bit with SP1
Microsoft .NET Framework 3.5 with SP1	
ADO.NET Data Services Update for .NET Framework 3.5 SP1	
Windows PowerShell 2.0	
Microsoft Report Viewer Redistributable	
Service Manager database	Windows Server 2008 R2 64-bit with SP1
SQL Server 2008 64-bit (SP1 or SP2) or SQL Server 2008 R2 64-bit	
SQL Server Reporting Services	
Microsoft .NET Framework 3.5 with SP1	
Service Manager data warehouse management server	Windows Server 2008 R2 64-bit with SP1
Microsoft .NET Framework 3.5 with SP1	
Windows PowerShell 2.0	
Service Manager data warehouse database	Windows Server 2008 64-bit or Windows Server 2008 R2 64-bit
SQL Server 2008 64-bit (SP1 or SP2) or SQL Server 2008 R2 64-bit	
SQL Server Reporting Services	

TABLE 14.3   Continued

Component	Software
Microsoft .NET Framework 3.5 with SP1	
Service Manager Self-Service Portal Server 2008 R2 64-bit Internet Information Services 7	Windows Server 2008 64-bit or Windows
IIS 6 Metabase Compatibility	
ASP.NET 2.0	
Microsoft .NET Framework 4.0	
Microsoft Analysis Management Objects (AMOs)	
SSL Certificate	
Microsoft SharePoint Foundation 2010	
Excel Services for SharePoint 2010	
Microsoft Silverlight	
Service Manager console	Windows Server 2008, Windows Server 2008 R2 with SP1, Windows Vista Ultimate or Enterprise with SP2, or Windows 7 Professional or Ultimate with SP1
Microsoft Report Viewer Redistributable	
Windows PowerShell 2.0	
Microsoft .NET Framework 3.5 with SP1	
ADO.NET Data Services Update for .NET Framework 3.5 SP1	
Microsoft Analysis Management Objects (AMOs)	

NOTE

Service Manager infrastructure components must be installed on either Standard or Enterprise Editions, including both the operating system and SQL Server. In addition, SQL servers that host the Service Manager database, the data warehouse database, or the Reporting Services database must all use the same SQL Server collation. The default SQL collation (SQL_Latin1_General_CP1_CI_AS) is acceptable for Service Manager as long as Service Manager will only support the English language. If Service Manager will be required to support multiple languages, the appropriate SQL collation should be selected from the list of approved collations at http://technet.microsoft.com/en-us/library/hh495583.aspx.

SvcMgr components must be installed on a member server in a Windows Active Directory domain. It is commonly recommended to keep the installation of SvcMgr on a separate server or set of dedicated member servers that do not run any other applications that could interfere in the monitoring and alerting process.

Disk Subsystem Performance

Disk performance is a critical factor in the SvcMgr overall performance. Because of the volume of data that flows from the components into the various databases, data must make it into the databases quickly. However, for usability, console performance is the single most important factor. The console places a significant load on the server, primarily reading the data from the Service Manager database. If this read access is slow, console performance will be impacted and users will be dissatisfied with Service Manager.

> **NOTE**
>
> This usability measure is critical, as there is no point in collecting all this incident, change management, relationship, and configuration data if the users and analysts cannot access it.

The key measure to watch is the average disk seconds per read, that is, Avg. Disk sec/Read counter and the Avg. Disk sec/Write counter for the logical disk where the ServiceManager database is located, the `ServiceManager.mdf` file. These should not be higher than 0.020 seconds (20ms) on a sustained basis. Ideally, the time should be less than 10ms for optimal performance.

If the disk subsystem is experiencing greater than 0.020 second read or write times on the ServiceManager database volume, the Service Manager console will have performance issues.

Choosing Between SAN and DAS

If possible, always implement the Service Manager database servers with storage area network (SAN) disk subsystems. For information on choosing between SAN and direct attached storage (DAS), see the section "Choosing Between SAN and DAS" in Chapter 6, "Operations Manager 2012 Design and Planning."

Choosing SQL Versions

For Service Manager implementations, the best option is the Server Plus CAL licensing. Service Manager has very low client access license (CAL) requirements because the consoles do not require CALs. Purchasing per processor licensing is not recommended, as a typical SvcMgr database server will have a lot of CPUs and would not benefit from unlimited CALs.

In general, the best-practice guidance is to use SQL Server Enterprise Edition in the following scenarios:

▶ Multiple Service Manager components will coexist on the same database server, as SQL Server Enterprise Edition handles parallel processing more effectively and can take advantage of additional resources in a scaled-up server.

▶ You have more than four CPU sockets, as SQL Server Enterprise Edition can use the additional resources. This should not be confused with cores.

▶ Clustering is used, as the additional overhead of clustering can impact performance.

Given the cost differential, sometimes it will be necessary to deploy SQL Server Standard Edition. Best-practice guidance when using SQL Server Standard Edition is to

- Keep SvcMgr database components on separate SQL servers.

- Deploy 64-bit versions. This is a requirement for Service Manager components.

- Use extra memory in database servers to compensate.

In addition, the collation chosen at the installation of SQL Server 2008 is critical for multilanguage installations of Service Manager. The default collation for SQL Server 2008 is SQL_Latin_CP1_CI_AS, but is not supported by Service Manager for multilingual installations. The SQL collation is selected at installation time of SQL Server 2008 and cannot be changed without a complete reinstall of SQL.

If the default SQL collation was chosen, then the Service Manager install will show a warning that the unsupported collation will cause problems with multilingual installations.

The supported collations for multilanguage installations are as follows:

- Latin1_General_100_CI_AS for English

- Chinese_Traditional_Stroke_Count_100_CI_AS for Chinese Taiwan

- Chinese_Simplifies_Pinyin_100_CI_AS for Chinese PRC

- French_100_CI_AS for French

- Latin1_General_100_CI_AS for German

- Latin1_General_100_CI_AS for Italian

- Japanese_XJIS_100_CI_AS for Japanese

- Korean_100_CI_AS for Korean

- Latin1_General_100_CI_AS for Portuguese or Brazilian

- Cyrillic_General_100_CI_AS for Russian

- Traditional_Spanish_100_CI_AS for Spanish

Using one of the supported collations will allow Service Manager to run in multilingual environments without any issues.

NOTE

The collation warning can safely be ignored if the Service Manager installation will only use the English language.

Putting It All Together in a Service Manager Design

To illustrate the concepts discussed in this chapter, three designs are presented. These design scenarios cover a range of organizations from small to medium to large. The profile of the three enterprises is given in the following list:

▸ **Small enterprise**—A total of 100 servers in 3 locations, a main office with a shared T1 to the branch offices, and 25% bandwidth availability

▸ **Medium enterprise**—A total of 500 servers in 10 locations, a main office with a shared 11Mbps fractional T3 to the branch offices, and 25% bandwidth availability

▸ **Large enterprise**—A total of 2,000 servers in 50 locations, a main office with a shared 45Mbps T3 to the branch offices, and 25% bandwidth availability

Based on these sizes, designs were developed.

In these designs, DAS was used as a design constraint, rather than a SAN. This provides a more realistic minimum hardware specification. Performance could be further improved by using SAN in place of DAS.

> **NOTE**
>
> The Service Manager server and the data warehouse management server components cannot be installed on the same server. Any Service Manager design must have at least two servers.

For any Service Manager design that incorporates a data warehouse, there will be two Service Manager management groups. One is for the Service Manager and one is for the Service Manager data warehouse. These two need to be named differently, for example:

▸ Company ABC SM

▸ Company ABC DW

> **WARNING**
>
> If the Service Manager and the data warehouse management groups have the same name, it is not possible to register the Service Manager management group with the data warehouse.

The Service Manager management group names should also be different from the Operations Manager management group name.

Small Enterprise Design

The first design point is for a small enterprise consisting of the following:

▶ 500 users

▶ 100 servers

For illustration and sizing, the number of incidents, change requests, and concurrent consoles at each location are listed in Table 14.4. Because these are the primary metrics and loading that determine database sizing, it is important to have some sense of the workload.

TABLE 14.4   Small Enterprise Workload Counts

Server Type	Counts
Incidents/month	500
Change requests/month	50
Concurrent consoles	2

Given the relatively small number of managed computers, a single-server design makes the most sense. The recommended design for the small enterprise is as given in Table 14.5.

> **NOTE**
>
> Service Manager can be installed on a single physical server. However, the server would have to host the data warehouse server in a virtual guest session running on the physical host.

TABLE 14.5   Small Enterprise SvcMgr Design Recommendation

Server	Component(s)	Processors	Memory	Disk
SM1	Service Manager management server, Service Manager database, data warehouse database, console, Self-Service Portal	8 cores	16GB RAM	4-disk RAID-10 data
				2-disk RAID-1 logs
SM2 (virtual)	Data warehouse management server	2 virtual CPUs	4GB RAM	

The SM2 server hosting the Data Warehouse Management Server role would be a virtual server running on the SM1 server. For the server software, the recommendations are for the following:

- Windows Server 2008 R2 Standard Edition 64-bit

- SQL Server 2008 Enterprise 64-bit

Given that the components are all on the same server, the single-server option can really use the SQL Server Enterprise performance improvements. Also, using SQL Server Enterprise allows the database server to add processors in the future if resource utilization dictates it.

> **NOTE**
>
> The SQL database instance would be installed on the SM1 host server and would contain all four of the Service Manager databases, which are the ServiceManager, DWStagingAndConfig, DWRepository, and DWDataMart.

Figure 14.2 shows the architecture for the small organization.

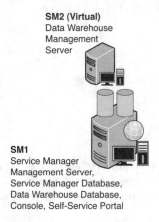

SM2 (Virtual)
Data Warehouse
Management
Server

SM1
Service Manager
Management Server,
Service Manager Database,
Data Warehouse Database,
Console, Self-Service Portal

FIGURE 14.2   The Service Manager 2012 small enterprise architecture.

The databases will grow to their steady state sizes proportionally to the number of work items and computers, all other things being equal. Table 14.6 lists the estimated database sizes for the small enterprise databases. These sizes are important for determining the drive sizes and sizing backup solutions.

TABLE 14.6   Small Enterprise Estimated Database Sizes

Database	Retention	Database Size (GB)
ServiceManager	90 days	3
DWStagingAndConfig, DWRepository, and DWDataMart	365 days	15

These sizes would be changed by adjustments to the retention periods and work items, such as incidents and change requests.

When determining the sizing of the disk subsystems, it is important to factor in the following:

▶ Database sizes

▶ Local backup overhead

▶ Log overhead

▶ Operating system overhead

▶ Application overhead

Typically, there should be a cushion of at least two times the database size to account for the overhead factors. The RAID types and number of disks would be changed to accommodate the storage needs.

Medium Enterprise Design

The second design point is for a medium enterprise consisting of the following:

▶ 2,000 users

▶ 500 servers

For illustration and sizing, the number of incidents, change requests, and concurrent consoles at each location are listed in Table 14.7. Because these are the primary metrics and loading that determine database sizing, it is important to have some sense of the workload.

TABLE 14.7   Medium Enterprise Workload Counts

Server Type	Counts
Incidents/month	2,000
Change requests/month	200
Concurrent consoles	10

Given the number of managed computers, a dual-server design makes the most sense. This would be a Service Manager server and a data warehouse server. The recommended design for the medium enterprise is as given in Table 14.8.

TABLE 14.8   Medium Enterprise SvcMgr Design Recommendation

Server	Component(s)	Processors	Memory	Disk
SM1	Service Manager management server, Service Manager database, console, Self-Service Portal	8 cores	8GB RAM	2-disk RAID 1
SM2	Data warehouse management server, data warehouse database	8 cores	4GB RAM	2-disk RAID 1

These are minimum specifications for performance and storage requirements. They can be revised upward based on additional requirements, such as backup storage.

> **NOTE**
>
> The servers can be virtual in this design.

For the server software, the recommendations are for the following:

▶ Windows Server 2008 R2 Standard Edition 64-bit

▶ SQL Server 2008 Enterprise 64-bit

Given that the database components are all on the same server, the database server can really use the SQL Server Enterprise performance improvements. Also, using SQL Server Enterprise allows the database server to add processors in the future if resource utilization dictates it. Using 64-bit versions similarly allows memory to be added and utilized without having to rebuild servers.

Figure 14.3 shows the architecture for the medium-sized organization.

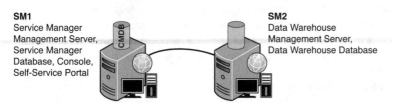

SM1
Service Manager
Management Server,
Service Manager
Database, Console,
Self-Service Portal

SM2
Data Warehouse
Management Server,
Data Warehouse Database

FIGURE 14.3   The Service Manager 2012 medium enterprise architecture.

The databases will grow to their steady state sizes proportionally to the number of work items and computers, all other things being equal. Table 14.9 lists the estimated database sizes for the medium enterprise databases. These sizes are important for determining the drive sizes and sizing backup solutions.

TABLE 14.9   Medium Enterprise Estimated Database Sizes

Database	Retention	Database Size (GB)
ServiceManager	90 days	4
DWStagingAndConfig, DWRepository, and DWDataMart	365 days	20

These sizes would be changed by adjustments to the retention periods and work items, such as incidents and change requests.

When determining the sizing of the disk subsystems, it is important to factor in the following:

- Database sizes
- Local backup overhead
- Log overhead
- Operating system overhead
- Application overhead

Typically, there should be a cushion of at least two times the database size to account for the overhead factors. The RAID types and number of disks would be changed to accommodate the storage needs.

Large Enterprise Design

The last design point is for a large enterprise consisting of the following:

- 10,000 users
- 2,000 servers

For illustration and sizing, the numbers and types of servers at each location are listed in Table 14.10. Because the types of servers determine which management packs are loaded and the database sizing, it is important to have some sense of the monitored servers. This information can also be used with the System Center Capacity Planner tool.

TABLE 14.10   Large Enterprise Workload Counts

Server Type	Counts
Incidents/month	7,500
Change requests/month	1,000
Concurrent consoles	25

Given the relatively large number of work items, computers, and users, a server-per-component design makes the most sense. This places each component on its own dedicated server, ensuring that there is no contention for resources between components. The recommended design for the large enterprise is as given in Table 14.11.

TABLE 14.11   Large Enterprise SvcMgr Design Recommendation

Server	Component(s)	Processors	Memory	Disk
SM1	Service Manager management server, console, Self-Service Portal	8 cores	8GB RAM	2-disk RAID 1
SM2	Service Manager database	8 cores	8GB RAM	4-disk RAID-10 data 2-disk RAID-1 logs
SM3	Data warehouse management server	8 cores	8GB RAM	2-disk RAID 1
SM4	Data warehouse database	8 cores	8GB RAM	4-disk RAID-10 data 2-disk RAID-1 logs

These are minimum specifications for performance and storage requirements. The 4-disk RAID-10 subsystem for the database servers is driven mainly by performance considerations. These specifications can be revised upward based on additional requirements, such as backup storage.

> **NOTE**
>
> This configuration could really benefit from SAN storage to improve performance and scalability. At the very least, the database servers will require external drive enclosures to support the large number of disks.

For the server software, the recommendations are for the following:

▶ Windows Server 2008 R2 Standard Edition 64-bit

▶ SQL Server 2008 Enterprise 64-bit

Given the scale of the infrastructure, the 64-bit platforms are needed to take advantage of the larger memory and to increase the performance of the SQL database servers. SQL Server Enterprise Edition is also a welcome improvement for a scenario of this size because it supports improved performance and scalability for large environments.

Figure 14.4 shows the architecture for the large-sized organization.

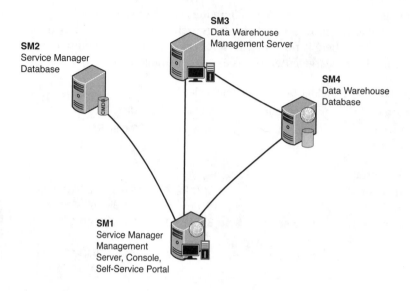

FIGURE 14.4   The Service Manager 2012 large enterprise architecture.

The databases will grow to their steady state sizes proportionally to the number of work items and computers, all other things being equal. Table 14.12 lists the estimated database sizes for the large enterprise databases. These sizes are important for determining the drive sizes and sizing backup solutions.

TABLE 14.12   Large Enterprise Estimated Database Sizes

Database	Retention	Database Size (GB)
ServiceManager	90 days	15
DWStagingAndConfig, DWRepository, and DWDataMart	365 days	60

These sizes would be changed by adjustments to the retention periods and work items, such as incidents and change requests.

When determining the sizing of the disk subsystems, it is important to factor in the following:

- ▶ Database sizes
- ▶ Local backup overhead
- ▶ Log overhead
- ▶ Operating system overhead
- ▶ Application overhead

Typically, there should be a cushion of at least three to four times the database size to account for the overhead factors. This is more difficult with large enterprise organizations and their correspondingly large data sets. The RAID types and number of disks would be changed to accommodate the storage needs; online backup to tape or replication to an offsite recovery site might be used instead.

Planning a Service Manager Deployment

A Service Manager project can be a small endeavor or a very large one, depending on the organization, requirements, or budget. Whatever the scale, appropriate planning is key to the success of any Service Manager project.

> **NOTE**
>
> What *appropriate planning* means for any given organization or project will vary greatly. This could be a 100-page design and planning document. Or it could be a single-page design and planning outline. The important point is that it be done to the degree needed to ensure the success of the project.

A project is defined by its scope, timeline, and budget. The scope defines what's included in the project and, sometimes more important, what is not included in the project. The timeline defines when the project will start, end, and some level of detail on what occurs in between. The budget defines how much it will cost, which could be in terms of money, effort, resources, or a combination of all of these.

A typical Service Manager project will have three to five phases, as follows:

1. Design Principles Training phase (optional)

2. Design and Planning phase

3. Proof of Concept phase (optional)

4. Pilot phase

5. Production phase

The Design Principles Training and the Proof of Concept phases are optional and might not be needed for some implementations, especially smaller or less-complex ones. The other phases will almost always be needed, even if they vary in scope depending on the environment.

> **NOTE**
>
> Although projects can vary in scope and size, by and large Service Manager projects will be compact projects. Ultimately, the project is deploying a management platform to support the applications and is, thus, smaller than the application projects it is supporting.

This section looks at the following project elements:

▶ Major phases

▶ Major tasks

▶ Deliverables

These elements help define the project, ensuring that the project team can deliver the project scope on time and within the budget.

Design Principles Training Phase (Overview Of Service Manager Components and Integration)

Before launching into the Design and Planning phase, it is recommended to have a Service Manager subject matter expert (SME) conduct a Microsoft Service Manager training session for all team members. The session should introduce the technology components and principles of Service Manager 2012 design, planning, and integration. The session helps to establish the basic criteria for the architectural elements of SvcMgr and bring all design participants up to the same level of knowledge. The session also allows for general Service Manager technology questions to be addressed in advance of the design and planning sessions.

Design principles training for Service Manager can be conducted in a daylong session, a four-hour session, or even just an hour-long session. The length of the training very much depends on the scale of the project and the technological sophistication of the participants. For a large organization, a daylong session would be recommended. For a small organization, an hour-long session would be sufficient.

Conducting a design principles training session can make the design and planning sessions flow much smoother, as well as produce a much better design and plan.

Design and Planning Phase (Plan the Service Manager Architecture)

During the Design and Planning phase, the project team works together to create a Service Manager 2012 architecture and implementation plan that satisfies the business and technical requirements.

The architecture is usually created during a half-day to two-day design session that covers a host of Service Manager design-related topics, including, but not limited to, the following:

▶ Business and technical goals and objectives

▶ Components

▶ Architecture

▶ Fault-tolerant strategy

▶ Disaster recovery strategy

- Configuration settings
- Integration
- Hardware specification
- Workflows (incident, problem, and change request)
- Templates
- Customization
- Administrative model
- Notification model
- Administration and maintenance procedures
- Documentation

14

The implementation plan is created during the planning session(s), which usually range from a half day to three days. The planning session covers the following topics:

- Phases
- Tasks
- Resources
- Timeline
- Risk identification and mitigation

The deliverable from the design and planning session is the

- Design and planning document

The design and planning document communicates the results of the design and planning sessions. The outline of the design and planning document should include the following sections:

- Project Overview
- Goals and Objectives
- Architecture
- Configuration Settings
- Integration
- Customization
- Incident and Problem Processes
- Change Request Processes

▶ Administration Model

▶ Notification Model

▶ Fault Tolerance and Disaster Recovery

▶ Project Plan

▶ Phases

▶ Tasks

▶ Deliverables

▶ Resources

▶ Timeline

▶ Budget

The length of a design and planning document will vary according to the size of the organization and the complexity of the design and plan. A small organization might have 1–5 pages in length. Larger organizations and complex deployments will have a more detailed document 20–50 pages in length.

Proof of Concept Phase (Build the Service Manager Prototype Lab)

The Proof of Concept (POC) phase is essentially the lab phase, also known as the prototype phase. The POC phase begins with the building of a prototype lab. The prototype lab is typically an isolated simulated production environment. It should include all of the types of servers found in the production environment that could potentially affect connectivity and performance.

TIP

In today's modern IT environment, the POC lab can be built in a virtual environment even if the production environment will be all physical. This allows for the testing of the functionality of the design, but not scalability of the design. It reduces the expense of the POC significantly to use virtual machines.

Some organizations might choose to forgo the expense of a POC and go directly into a production build. This makes sense for smaller organizations or projects with limited budgets.

NOTE

Service Manager is a particularly good candidate for skipping the lab phase. The reason is that the Service Manager infrastructure can be deployed into a production environment with little or no impact to the existing servers. Connectors can be deployed and workflows can be tested without impacting the environment.

The POC lab should have a minimum set of servers needed to deploy Service Manager and to test key management packs against application servers. The POC lab environment should include the following:

- ▶ Service Manager servers
- ▶ Active Directory domain controllers
- ▶ Operations and Configuration Manager servers
- ▶ Internet connectivity

Much of the testing will be on the Service Manager configuration, connector configuration, testing workflows, and developing templates.

> **NOTE**
>
> The Service Manager POC infrastructure does not need to be scaled to the full production environment depending on the scope of the POC. Some POCs will want to test and document deployment procedures, in which case a server configuration similar to the production environment is needed. If the POC is to test management pack functionality, a single SvcMgr server with all components can be deployed.

Specific test plans will be developed during the lab build process. Testing areas should include the following:

- ▶ Deployment
- ▶ Configuration
- ▶ Administration
- ▶ Incident workflow
- ▶ Problem workflow
- ▶ Change request workflow
- ▶ Connectors
- ▶ Notifications
- ▶ Self-Service Web Portal
- ▶ Data warehouse
- ▶ Failover capabilities
- ▶ Backup and recovery

The lab should exist throughout the entire project to allow testing and verification of configurations, with the primary usage during the POC phase. Once implementation completes, the lab can be scaled back as required.

14

The major tasks for the Proof of Concept phase include the following:

▶ Build servers in the lab

▶ Deploy Service Manager infrastructure

▶ Develop workflow models for incidents, problems, and change requests

▶ Create templates

▶ Create custom reports

▶ Create custom management packs

▶ Develop the notification model

▶ Test the functionality

▶ Test disaster recovery and fault tolerance

This list is definitely subject to change based on the specifics of the project, especially depending on the goals and objectives developed during the Design and Planning phase.

The deliverables for the Proof of Concept phase include the following:

▶ Working lab Service Manager infrastructure

▶ Functionality (80%)

▶ Tuned workflows (50%)

▶ Build documentation

▶ Templates

▶ Workflows

▶ Notification model

▶ Administration model

▶ Issues database

The Proof of Concept phase, given its scaled-down nature, is unlikely to be able to deliver 100% of the production functionality due to missing applications and simplified architecture when compared with production. The 80% of functionality is a good target. The workflow development will likely only be at 50% at the end of the POC, as the production conditions that trigger incidents, problems, and change requests will not be seen in the lab.

It is also important to start an issues database during the POC phase, in which issues that arise are logged and solutions are documented. This helps document the solutions and is a useful database to pass to the support teams, so they know what the solutions are to common problems. The issues log can be an actual SQL database or just an Excel spreadsheet. The issues log will be added to throughout the various phases.

> **NOTE**
>
> After building the lab environment, it frequently makes sense to leave the lab up and running. This lab provides a platform for testing new templates and processes in a controlled setting before deploying them into production.

Pilot Phase

The goal of the Pilot phase is to roll out the production Service Manager 2012 infrastructure and deploy consoles in a limited production environment. This allows the functionality to be tested in the production environment and the impacts to users and servers assessed. Some key issues to assess are as follows:

▶ Incident, problem, and change request workflows

▶ Self-Service Portal usage

▶ Impact of connectors on Active Directory, OpsMgr, and ConfigMgr

▶ Performance of SvcMgr servers

▶ Database growth

Evaluating these and other metrics ensures that the Service Manager infrastructure is performing as expected during the design and planning sessions.

The major tasks for the Pilot phase include the following:

▶ Deploy production Service Manager infrastructure

▶ Configure Service Manager infrastructure

▶ Configure and tune workflows

▶ Configure the administrative model

▶ Configure the notification model

▶ Deploy the pilot console

▶ Deploy pilot users, analysts, and help desk

▶ Conduct cross-training

▶ Adjust workflows

Users, analysts, help desk personnel, and sites scheduled for deployment in this phase should be a representative sample that includes extremes. They would be migrated to the Service Manager systems and would be submitting incidents and change requests through the system. The number of individuals to deploy in the Pilot phase can vary, but a good rule of thumb is to target 5%–10% of the total number of users in production.

The deliverables for the Pilot phase include the following:

▶ Working production Service Manager infrastructure

▶ Users deployed (5%–10%)

▶ Functionality (100%)

▶ Tuned workflows (80%)

▶ Updated documents

▶ Cross-training

▶ Issues database (90%)

All the functionality of the Service Manager 2012 infrastructure should have been deployed by the end of the Pilot phase.

Production Phase

With successful Proof of Concept and Pilot phases, the Production phase should be well understood and offer few surprises. The main purpose of the Production phase is to integrate the system into all aspects of service management, which at this stage in the project should have relatively low risk. Any major issues or concerns will have been uncovered in the Proof of Concept and Pilot phases.

The major tasks for the Production phase include the following:

▶ Deploy users

▶ Conduct cross-training

▶ Tune workflows

In this final phase, the various tasks that were in progress from previous phases (such as the workflow tuning, user deployment, and the issues database) will be finalized. The deliverables for the production phase include the following:

▶ Users deployed (100%)

▶ Tuned workflows (100%)

▶ Cross-training

▶ Issues database (100%)

▶ Transition to support

By the conclusion of the Production phase, the Service Manager infrastructure should be completely tuned and ready to hand over to support. The transition to support is a critical point in the project, as the staff assuming the support and maintenance of the Service Manager infrastructure should be cross-trained on the procedure to ensure that the infrastructure continues to operate at 100%.

Time Estimates

The time needed per phase on any given project will vary according to the size of the organization, the organization culture, the scope of the project, and the complexity of the Service Manager project.

Table 14.13 provides some estimates of the time needed to execute the phase for small, medium, and large organizations.

TABLE 14.13   Sample Project Time Estimates

Phase	Small	Medium	Large
Design Principles Training phase	1 hr	4 hrs	1 day
Design and Planning phase	1 day	2 days	1 week
Proof of Concept phase	N/A	N/A	2 weeks
Pilot phase	N/A	1 week	1 month
Production phase	1 week	2 weeks	1 month

For some of the organization sizes, certain phases are not normally done. For example, a small organization will likely move from the Design and Planning phase directly into a Production phase. There would be no need for a Proof of Concept nor a Pilot phase with a small organization. This is reflected in the table.

Deploying Service Manager

To demonstrate a sample installation deployment of the Service Manager, a three-server architecture is used. Deploying the Service Manager is done in five steps:

- ▶ Deploy the Service Manager server
- ▶ Deploy the Service Manager data warehouse
- ▶ Register the Service Manager management group
- ▶ Enable the ETL job
- ▶ Deploy the Self-Service Portal

The servers need to meet the prerequisites defined earlier in the chapter.

Deploying SvcMgr Components

The first server (SM1) in the Service Manager two-server deployment will host the following Service Manager components:

- ▶ Service Manager management server
- ▶ Service Manager database
- ▶ Service Manager console

> **NOTE**
>
> The SM servers cannot have any OpsMgr agents or other components installed on them. The products cannot coexist. The OpsMgr agent should be removed prior to installing the Service Manager components.

To install the Server, Database, and Console components for Service Manager, complete the following steps:

1. On the Service Manager server, navigate to the installation media for Service Manager.

2. Double-click `Setup.exe` to launch the Setup Wizard.

3. Under the Install heading, click Service Manager Management Server.

4. Enter the product registration information, enter a product key, accept the license agreement, and click Next.

5. Select the installation location and click Next.

6. The prerequisites will be checked. If any prerequisite checks are failed, the Next button will be grayed out until the failure is corrected. Once you have addressed any failed prerequisites, you can click the Check Prerequisites Again button to have Setup reevaluate the server. When all prerequisites are passed with a green check mark or yellow warning symbol, you can click Next to continue the installation.

7. Select the Database Server, SQL Server Instance, and the file locations. Click Next to continue.

> **NOTE**
>
> The Service Manager installation will check the SQL Server collation at this point. If it is not one of the supported collations, then the install will present a warning. This can be ignored if the Service Manager will not be multilingual. If Service Manager will need to support multiple languages, then the installation should be canceled and the SQL server reinstalled with a supported collation.

8. Enter the Service Manager Management Group Name, in this example **Company ABC SM**.

9. Click Browse and select the Management Group Administrators.

> **NOTE**
>
> The built-in Domain\Administrators group is not allowed by the wizard, although the COMPUTER\Administrators and DOMAIN\Domain Admins are allowed. It is recommended to use a domain group.

10. Click Next.

11. To configure the account for the Service Manager services, click the Domain Account option button and enter a domain account and password.

NOTE

The Service Manager service account must be a local administrator on the management server and the same as the account used for the data warehouse service account.

12. Click Test Credentials and wait for the "The credentials were accepted." message.

NOTE

The domain credentials that are entered on this screen must be tested successfully to enable the Next button.

13. Click Next to continue.

14. To configure the account for the Service Manager workflows, click the Domain Account option button and enter a domain account and password.

NOTE

The Service Manager workflow account needs to be mail enabled for email notifications to be sent.

15. Click Test Credentials and wait for the "The credentials were accepted." message.

NOTE

As on the previous screen, the domain credentials that are entered must be tested successfully to enable the Next button.

16. Click Next.

17. Select the appropriate options for the Improvement Programs and for Error Reporting, and then click Next.

18. Review the Installation Summary and then click Install.

19. After the install completes successfully (shown in Figure 14.5), click Close.

20. The Encryption Key Backup or Restore Wizard will launch. Click Next.

21. Select Backup the Encryption Key and click Next.

22. Enter a path and filename and then click Next.

23. Enter a password and confirm the password, and then click Next.

24. Click Finish to close the wizard.

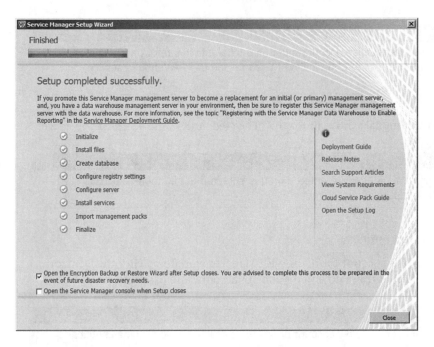

FIGURE 14.5   Service Manager server install complete.

The Service Manager server installation is complete. The next step is to install the data warehouse component.

Deploying SvcMgr Data Warehouse

The second server (SM2) in the three-server deployment will host the following Service Manager components:

- ▶ Data warehouse management server
- ▶ Data warehouse databases

To install the data warehouse management server and data warehouse database components for Service Manager, complete the following steps:

1. On the Service Manager data warehouse server, navigate to the installation media for Service Manager.

2. Double-click Setup.exe to launch the Setup Wizard.

3. Under the Install heading, click Service Manager Data Warehouse **Management Server**.

4. Enter the product registration information, accept the license agreement, and click Next.

5. Select the installation location and click Next.

6. The prerequisites will be checked. If any prerequisite checks are failed, the Next button will be grayed out until the failure is corrected. Once you have addressed any failed prerequisites, you can click the Check Prerequisites Again button to have Setup reevaluate the server. When all prerequisites are passed with a green check mark or yellow warning symbol, you can click Next to continue the installation.

NOTE

The Service Manager installation will check the SQL Server collation at this point. If it is not one of the supported collations, then the install will present a warning. This can be ignored if the Service Manager installation will not be multilingual. If the install will support multiple languages, then the installation should be canceled and the SQL server reinstalled with a supported collation.

14

7. Select the Database Server, SQL Server Instance, and the file locations. Click Next to continue.

NOTE

The database options for the databases (Staging and Configuration, Repository, and Data Mart) can be individually changed by clicking on the database name and then changing the default options.

8. Enter the Data Warehouse Management Group Name, in this example **DW_Company ABC DW**.

NOTE

The "DW_" will be prepended automatically to the management group name to ensure that the name is unique.

9. Click Browse and select the Management Group Administrators.

10. Click Next.

11. The wizard automatically validates the SQL Reporting Services website, as shown in Figure 14.6. After getting the message "The SSRS Web server URL is valid," click Next.

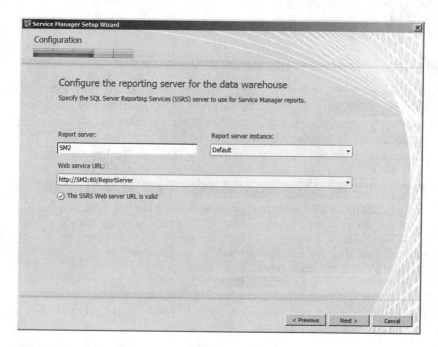

FIGURE 14.6   Data warehouse SSRS validation.

12. To configure the account for the Service Manager services, click the Domain Account option button, and enter a domain account and password.

> **NOTE**
>
> The Service Manager service account must be a local administrator on the data warehouse server and the same as the account used for the Service Manager server installation.

13. Click Test Credentials and wait for the "The credentials were accepted." message.

> **NOTE**
>
> The domain credentials that are entered on this screen must be tested successfully to enable the Next button.

14. Click Next to continue.

15. Enter the Reporting Account credentials.

16. Click Test Credentials and wait for the "The credentials were accepted." message.

17. Click Next to continue.

18. On the Configure Analysis Services for OLAP Cubes screen, review the selections for database server, SQL Server instance, and database name (DWSADataBase by default) and adjust these settings to reflect your environment. You also have the option to change the database storage directory by checking the box and entering an alternate path. When done, click Next to continue.

19. Enter the Analysis Services credentials.

20. Click Test Credentials and wait for the "The credentials were accepted." message.

21. Click Next to continue.

22. Select the appropriate options for the Improvement Programs and for Error Reporting, and then click Next.

23. Review the Installation Summary and then click Install.

24. After the install completes successfully (shown in Figure 14.7), click Close.

25. The Encryption Key Backup or Restore Wizard will launch. Click Next.

26. Select the Backup the Encryption Key and click Next.

27. Enter a path and filename, and then click Next.

28. Enter a password and confirm the password, and then click Next.

29. Click Finish to close the wizard.

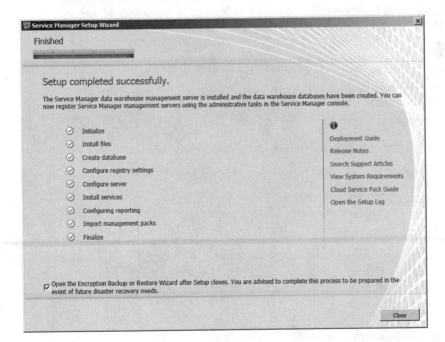

FIGURE 14.7   Service Manager data warehouse server install complete.

Registering the SvcMgr Management Group

After the Service Manager management server and the Service Manager data warehouse have been deployed, the Service Manager management server must be registered with the data warehouse to enable their integration and allow data to be transferred to the data warehouse.

To register the Service Manager management group "Company ABC SM" with the data warehouse "DW_Company ABC DW," execute the following steps:

1. Launch the Service Manager console.

2. Select the Administration node (should already be selected).

3. In the Administration Overview workspace, click the Register with Service Manager Data Warehouse link.

4. Click Next at the wizard introduction page.

5. Enter the data warehouse management server name in the Server Name field. In this case, the name is **SM2**.

6. Click the Test Connection button. The message "Your connection to the data warehouse management server was successful" should appear, as shown in Figure 14.8.

> **NOTE**
>
> Port 5724 needs to be open for inbound communications to the server. The port is used by the Service Manager console and should be opened on all Service Manager server systems.

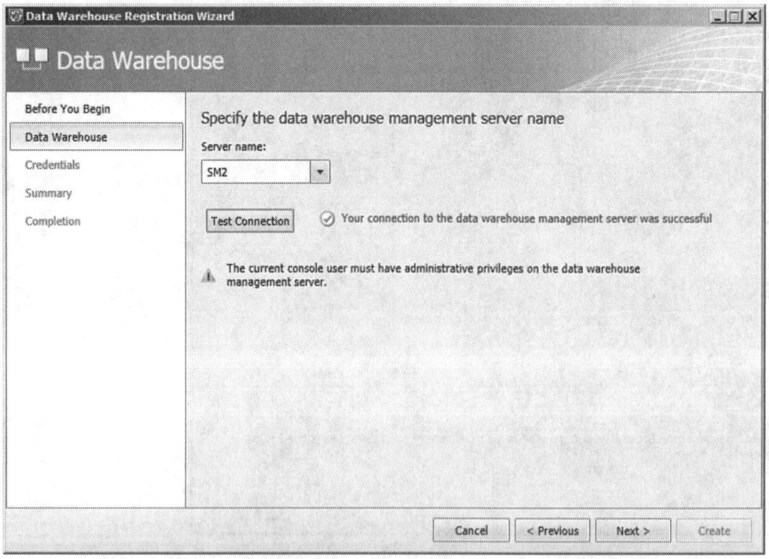

FIGURE 14.8   Service Manager data warehouse server connection test.

7. Click Next.

8. Leave the default RunAs account, which is the DW management group name with "SecureReference" appended. Click Next.

9. Enter the credentials to be used and click OK.

10. Click Create to complete the registration.

11. After the registration is completed, the screen shows the message "The data warehouse registration succeeded."

12. After a brief time, an informational pop-up message appears indicating that the report deployment process has not completed. This is normal, as the report deployment process takes some time. Click OK to close the pop-up message.

13. Click Close to exit the Data Warehouse Registration Wizard.

> **NOTE**
>
> The MPSyncJob might take as long as two hours to complete. You can view the status of the Data Warehouse Management Pack deployment process by clicking on the Data Warehouse node and selecting Management Packs. For any management packs that have a Failed deployment status, you can right-click on the management pack and select Restart Deployment.

After the jobs complete, the data warehouse reports will be available.

Viewing Data Warehouse Job Schedules

The Service Manager Data Warehouse jobs are enabled by default. These are the jobs that move data from the Service Manager database into the data warehouse. You can view the status of these jobs using the Service Manager PowerShell commands. They can also be disabled or enabled using the PowerShell commands.

> **NOTE**
>
> The scheduled jobs are visible in the Service Manager console in the Data Warehouse space under the Data Warehouse Jobs folder. However, they cannot be enabled or disabled in the user interface, only paused and resumed. If you do need to disable or enable these jobs, you must use the `Disable-SCDWJobSchedule` or `Enable-SCDWJobSchedule` PowerShell commands as described below.

In this example, the steps are shown to view the job schedules. To view the ETL job schedules, execute the following steps:

1. On the data warehouse management server, launch PowerShell with the Run As Administrator option.

2. Enter the command **cd "C:\Program Files\Microsoft System Center 2012\Service Manager"** to change to the directory c:\Program Files\Microsoft System Center 2012\Service Manager.

3. Enter the command **import-module .\Microsoft.EnterpriseManagement.Warehouse.Cmdlets.psd1**. This imports the Service Manager Data Warehouse cmdlets module, which makes the PowerShell commands available.

4. To list the current data warehouse jobs and their status, enter the command **Get-SCDWJobSchedule -computer <ServerName>**. In this example, the command would be **Get-SCDWJobSchedule -computer SM2** (because SM2 is the data warehouse server). Note that if you are logged on to the data warehouse server, you can simply run the Get-SCDWJobSchedule command with no parameters.

5. The data warehouse jobs will be listed as shown in Figure 14.9. Note that by default, the *LastRun* column is not included in this report due to display space limitations. To output all of the information for the data warehouse jobs in a list format, run the command Get-SCDWJobSchedule -computer <ServerName> | fl. This formats the command output in a list format, which includes all available data fields.

FIGURE 14.9   Viewing the status of the data warehouse jobs.

If you need to disable one or more jobs, simply run the command Disable-SCDWJobSchedule -JobName <name of job to be disabled>. If the job name has spaces, you will need to enclose the entire name of the job in quotes, as shown in Figure 14.10. To enable a job, simply run the command Enable-SCDWJobSchedule -JobName <name of job to be disabled>.

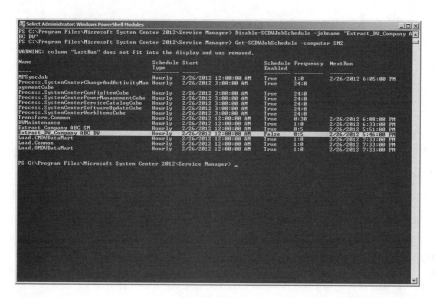

FIGURE 14.10   Data warehouse job status after disabling a job schedule.

Deploying the Service Manager 2012 Self-Service Portal

The Service Manager Self-Service Portal component allows users to access service offerings that are published by IT management. Some of the tasks that users can perform using the portal include submitting new incidents, viewing announcements, obtaining self-help through the IT knowledge base, and resetting their passwords.

The Service Manager Self-Service Portal is deployed after the Service Manager component is installed.

> **NOTE**
>
> The Service Manager Web Portal web server must be installed with SharePoint Foundation 2010 with SP1, ASP.NET, Windows Authentications, and IIS 6 Metabase Compatibility role services and must have an SSL certificate. For lab testing, the portal can be deployed without an SSL certificate by selecting an alternate port (such as 8082), but this configuration is insecure and is not recommended for production environments.

To install the Self-Service Web Portal, complete the following steps:

1. On the server that will host the Self-Service Portal, download SharePoint Foundation 2010 and the SharePoint Foundation 2010 SP1 and run the installation files for the products.

2. On the SharePoint Foundation 2010 installation screen, click the Install software prerequisites link.

3. Click Next to launch the prerequisite checker.

4. Accept the license terms for the SharePoint 2010 Products Preparation Tool and click Next.

5. Confirm that all required prerequisites are installed or enabled, and then click Finish to close the preparation tool.

6. On the SharePoint Foundation 2010 installation screen, click the Install SharePoint Foundation link.

7. Accept the license terms for SharePoint Foundation 2010 and click Continue.

8. Click the Standalone button to select a standalone SharePoint installation.

9. Click Close to exit the installation wizard and launch the SharePoint Products Configuration Wizard.

10. On the SharePoint Products Configuration Wizard screen, click Next.

11. Click Yes to confirm restarting services during the configuration process.

12. The wizard will perform a series of 10 SharePoint product configuration tasks, which might take several minutes to complete.

13. Once the configuration tasks complete, click Finish to close the wizard. The default SharePoint Web Application home page will open after the wizard is closed.

14. Verify that the default SharePoint Web Application home page launches correctly, and then close the browser.

15. Once the SharePoint Foundation 2010 installation is complete, double-click on the executable for Service Pack 1 that was downloaded in step 1 above.

16. Review the license agreement when it appears, then select the check box to accept the Microsoft Software License Terms and click Continue.

17. The installer will identify any SharePoint application components that need to be closed before continuing with the install. Select the option to automatically close these applications and click OK to continue.

18. When the installation completion screen appears, click OK to complete the Service Pack 1 installation.

19. Once the SharePoint Foundation 2010 Service Pack 1 installation is complete, navigate to the installation media for Service Manager.

20. Double-click Setup.exe to launch the Setup Wizard.

21. Under the Install (Optional) heading, click the Service Manager Web Portal link.

22. On the Portal Parts screen, check both boxes to install the Web Content Server and SharePoint Web Parts on the local server, and then click Next.

23. Enter the product registration information, accept the license agreement, and click Next.

24. Select the installation location and click Next.

25. The prerequisites will be checked. Remediate any issues; otherwise, click Next.

26. Accept the default website name of SCSMWebContentServerl, port 443, and select an SSL certificate. Click Next.

> **NOTE**
>
> If there is no certificate installed yet, then the certificate selection can be skipped. The SSL certificate will not be bound to the SCSMPortal site and will need to be done manually later in the process. It is important to note that if the SSL certificate that is installed on the portal server is not trusted by the client machine accessing the web portal, none of the Silverlight content will be displayed and the portal page will appear blank.

27. Select the Database Server, SQL instance, and then select the ServiceManager database from the Database drop-down menu. In this scenario, the ServiceManager database is hosted on the SM1 server. Click Next.

> **NOTE**
>
> The Service Manager installation will check the SQL Server collation at this point. If it is not one of the supported collations, then the install will present a warning. This can be ignored if the Service Manager installation will not be multilingual. If the install will support multiple languages, then the installation should be canceled and the SQL server reinstalled with a supported collation.

28. To configure the account for the Service Manager portal, click the Domain Account option button and enter a domain account and password.

> **NOTE**
>
> The Service Manager service account must be the same as the account used for the Service Manager server installation.

29. Click Test Credentials and wait for the "The credentials were accepted." message.

> **NOTE**
>
> The domain credentials that are entered on this screen must be tested successfully to enable the Next button.

30. Click Next to continue.

14

31. On the next screen, accept the default website name of Service Manager Portal, port 443, and select an SSL certificate. For the SharePoint database, identify the local server as the SharePoint server, select the SHAREPOINT SQL instance, and accept the default database name of Sharepoint_SMPortalContent. When finished, click Next to continue.

32. Enter the credentials that will be used by the Service Manage SharePoint application pool, and then click Test Credentials to validate the credentials. When done, click Next to continue.

33. Select the appropriate options for the Improvement Programs and for Error Reporting, and then click Next.

34. Select the preferred update methodology and click Next.

35. Review the Installation Summary and then click Install.

36. After the install completes successfully (shown in Figure 14.11), click Close.

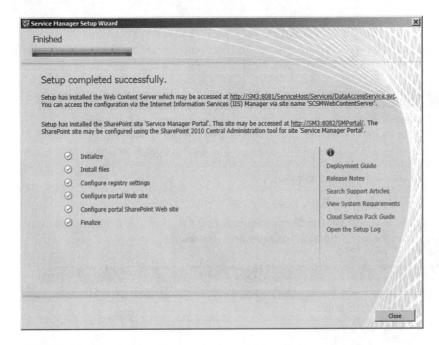

FIGURE 14.11   Service Manager web portal installation complete.

If the SSL certificate was not available at the time of installation, then the certificate will need to be bound to the site once the certificate is obtained and installed on the server. To bind the certificate to the site manually, run the following steps:

1. Launch Server Manager.

2. Expand the Roles node.

3. Expand the Web Server (IIS) node.

4. Select the Internet Information Services (IIS) Manager node.

5. In the Connections pane, expand the server name, expand the Sites node, and select the Service Manager Portal site.

6. In the Actions pane, click the Binding link.

7. Select the https type and click Edit.

8. In the SSL Certificate pull-down menu, select the appropriate certificate and click OK.

9. Click Close to close the Site Bindings window.

10. Exit Service Manager.

The Self-Service Portal will be available for use immediately at the URL https://server-name/SMPortal after the installation. A full discussion of the use of the Service Manager portal in conjunction with service offerings can be found in Chapter 16, "Using Service Manager 2012 for Service Offerings and Change Control Management."

Deploying Service Manager Connectors

The Service Manager connectors provide crucial integration between the Service Manager CMDB and Active Directory, Operations Manager, and Configuration Manager. This allows the CMDB to be the central touch point for the organization IT knowledge base, with the synthesized directory, configuration, and operational data.

Active Directory Connector Deployment

The Active Directory connector imports Active Directory users, groups, printers, and computers into the Service Manager database. This is the base of the CMDB, as it provides a record of every object in the organization. This information will be enriched later with configuration and operational data, but must be populated first from Active Directory.

The tasks needed to create an Active Directory connector are as follows:

▶ Install an Active Directory connector and import data from Active Directory.

▶ Synchronize an Active Directory connector to reflect changes.

To install the Active Directory connector, complete the following steps:

1. Launch the Service Manager console.

2. Select the Administration space and then the Connectors folder.

3. Right-click the Connectors folder, select Create Connector, and then select Active Directory Connector.

4. Click Next at the introduction screen.

5. Enter the name of the connector, something like `<DOMAINNAME>` **Active Directory Connector**, and then click Next.

6. Select the domain to use by selecting the Let Me Choose the Domain or OU option button. Click the Browse button to select a domain and optionally an OU.

7. In the Credentials section, click the New button to create a RunAs account to access Active Directory.

8. Enter a Display Name for the account, something like `<DOMAINNAME>` **Account**, and then enter the credentials. Click OK to save the RunAs account.

9. Click the Test Connection button to test. There should be a "The connection to the server was successful" pop-up message. Click OK to clear the pop-up message.

10. Click Next.

11. Leave the default All Computers, Printers, Users, and Groups selected and click Next.

12. Click Create to create the connector.

13. Click Close to close the wizard.

The new Active Directory connector will be listed in the console. However, the status will show as Never Run.

To run the connector manually, do the following:

1. Select the Active Directory connector.

2. Click Synchronize Now in the Tasks pane.

3. A pop-up message appears stating "The synchronization request has been submitted." Click OK to close the message.

4. Select the Active Directory connector and click Refresh in the Tasks pane. The status should show as Running.

5. After some time, the status should show as Finished Success. Click Refresh to update the status.

Now the Active Directory objects will have been imported into the CMDB. Each object will have a corresponding Configuration Item (CI) in the database.

Operations Manager Connector Deployment

The Operations Manager connector is really a two-part connector, one for the configuration information that OpsMgr collects and the other for the alerts that OpsMgr generates. The OpsMgr configuration information enriches the CMDB object store and the OpsMgr alerts can automatically generate incident processes.

The tasks needed to create an Operations Manager connector are as follows:

▶ Import the Service Manager management packs necessary for the configuration item connector.

▶ Create an Operations Manager 2012 connector and import configuration items and alerts from Operations Manager 2012.

▶ Synchronize an Operations Manager 2012 connector to reflect changes made in Operations Manager.

The Service Manager management pack import task is a manual process and requires using PowerShell. To import the Service Manager management packs, execute the following steps:

1. Launch PowerShell with the Run As Administrator option.

2. Change the Execution Policy to Unrestricted by running the command Set-ExecutionPolicy unrestricted. At the confirmation question, press Y and Enter.

3. To change the directory to the location of the management pack files, enter **cd \"Program Files\Microsoft System Center 2012\Service Manager\Operations Manager Management Packs"** and press Enter.

4. Run the import script by entering the command **.\installOMMPs.ps1** and pressing Enter. The script imports 13 management packs. The results are shown in Figure 14.12.

5. Type **Exit** and press Enter to close PowerShell.

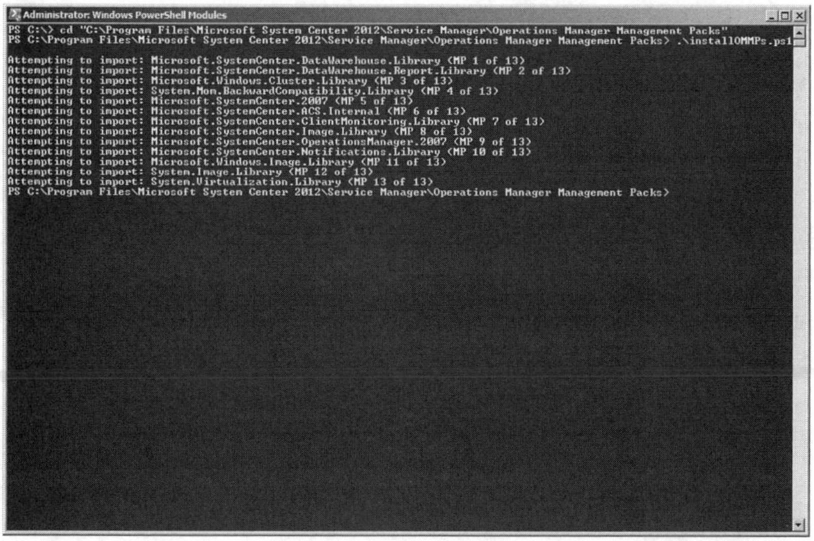

FIGURE 14.12   Operations Manager connector management pack import.

The next task is to create the Operations Manager connector. There are two connectors to create, an Alert connector and a Configuration Item (CI) connector.

Before creating the Operations Manager Alert connector, an affected user needs to be created. This will allow a user to be assigned by default to any automatically generated incidents. To create the affected user, execute the following steps:

1. Launch the Service Manager console.

2. Select the Configuration Items space.

3. Select the Users view.

4. In the Tasks pane under Users, click the Create User link.

5. In the First Name field, enter **OpsMgr** and in the Last Name field, enter **Alert**.

6. Click OK to create the user.

There is now a new user with the username OpsMgr.Alert and the domain SMInternal. This will be used with the Operations Manager connector.

To create the Operations Manager Alert connector, complete the following steps:

1. Launch the Service Manager console.

2. Select the Administration space.

3. Select the Connectors node.

4. In the Tasks pane, click Create Connector and select Operations Manager Alert Connector from the list.

5. Click Next at the introduction screen.

6. Enter a name for the connector, such as **Company ABC Alerts Connector**, and click Next.

7. In the Server Name field, type the name of the Operations Manager Root Management Server.

8. In the Credentials section, click the New button to create a RunAs account to access the Operations Manager management group.

9. Enter a Display Name for the account, something like **OpsMgr Account**, and then enter the credentials. Click OK to save the RunAs account.

10. Click the Test Credentials button to test. There should be a "The connection to the server was successful" pop-up message. Click OK to clear the pop-up message.

11. Click Next.

12. Click Add to add a routing rule.

13. In the Rule Name field, enter **All Critical Severity High Priority Alerts**.

14. Select the Operations Manager Incident Template.

15. Check the Priority box and select High.

16. Check the Severity box and select Critical. The result should look like Figure 14.13.

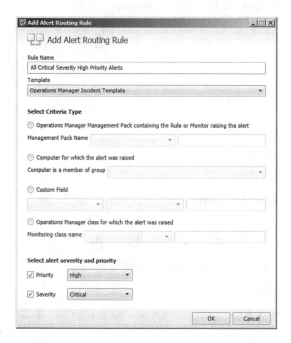

FIGURE 14.13   Operations Manager Alert Routing rule.

17. Click OK.

18. Click Next.

19. Check the Resolve Incidents Automatically When the Alerts in Operations Manager Are Closed check box and click Next.

20. Click Create to create the Operations Manager Alert connector.

21. Click Close to close the wizard.

The connector has been created in Service Manager and a corresponding Operations Manager Internal connector has been created as well, but a subscription needs to be created in the Operations Manager console to forward the appropriate alerts to the Service Manager management group.

The Operations Manager product connectors allow administrators to set up subscription rules to synchronize alerts with Service Manager. In this example, all alerts will be synchronized. To create the Operations Manager connector subscriptions, execute the following steps:

1. Launch the Operations Manager console.

2. Select the Administration space.

3. Select the Product Connectors, Internal Connector node.

4. Select the Alert Sync connector.

5. Select Properties of the Alert Sync connector.

6. Click Add in the Subscriptions section.

7. Enter **All Critical Severity High Priority Alerts** in the Subscription Name field and click Next.

8. Leave all groups approved on the Approve Groups page and click Next.

9. Leave the all targets selected on the Approve Targets page and click Next.

10. Uncheck the Medium Priority box on the Criteria page and click Create.

11. Click OK to close the connector properties.

Now all critical-severity high-priority alerts in Operations Manager will be synchronized with Service Manager. Each alert will create an incident in Service Manager, which will be automatically closed if the alert is resolved in Operations Manager.

The next task is to create the second type of Operations Manager connector, the Configuration Item connector (or CI connector). This connector will synchronize discoveries from Operations Manager.

To create the Operations Manager CI connector, execute the following steps:

1. Launch the Service Manager console.

2. Select the Administration space.

3. Select the Connectors node.

4. In the Tasks pane, click Create Connector and select Operations Manager CI Connector from the list.

5. Click Next at the introduction screen.

6. Enter a name for the connector, such as **Company ABC CI Connector** and click Next.

7. In the Server Name field, type the name of the Operations Manager Root Management Server.

8. In the Credentials section, select the RunAs account used for the Alert connector.

9. Click the Test Credentials button to test. The system prompts for a password, essentially verifying access to the RunAs account. Enter the password for the RunAs account and click OK.

10. There should be a "The connection to the server was successful" pop-up message. Click OK to clear the pop-up message.

11. Click Next.

12. Check the Select All box to select all available management packs for synchronization and click Next.

13. For the schedule, leave the default of Every Day, select 1:00 AM for the time, and click Next.

> **NOTE**
>
> Many of the Operations Manager discoveries run daily at 12:00 a.m., so setting the CI connector synchronization to 1:00 a.m. will give those discoveries time to complete before being imported into the CMDB.

14. Click Create to create the Operations Manager CI connector.

15. Click Close to close the wizard.

The Operations Manager CI connector will run a first-time synchronization right after being created and will then synchronize according to the schedule thereafter. The Operations Manager CI data will be merged with the Active Directory data, creating a more comprehensive view of the assets.

Configuration Manager Connector Deployment

The Configuration Manager connector both extends the object data imported from Active Directory and updates the data where needed. In addition, Configuration Baseline information can automatically generate incidents due to noncompliance from the Desired Configuration Management feature of ConfigMgr.

The tasks needed to create a Configuration Manager connector are as follows:

▶ Create the Configuration Manager 2012 connector to import inventory hardware and software data.

▶ Synchronize the Configuration Manager 2012 connector to reflect changes made in Configuration Manager.

To create the Configuration Manager connector, execute the following steps:

1. Launch the Service Manager console.

2. Select the Administration space.

3. Select the Connectors node.

4. In the Tasks pane, click Create Connector and select Configuration Manager Connector from the list.

5. Click Next at the introduction screen.

6. Enter a name for the connector, such as **Company ABC Configuration Manager Connector**, and click Next.

7. Make sure the System Center Configuration Manager Connector Configuration is selected in the Management Pack pull-down and then click Next.

8. Enter the name of the Configuration Manager Database Server and the Database Name.

9. In the Credentials section, click the New button to create a RunAs account to access the Operations Manager management group.

10. Enter a Display Name for the account, something like **ConfigMgr Account**, and then enter the credentials. Click OK to save the RunAs account.

11. Click the Test Credentials button to test. There should be a "The connection to the server was successful" pop-up message. Click OK to clear the pop-up message.

12. Click Next.

13. Check the All Systems Collection for Synchronization check box, and click Next.

14. For the schedule, select Every Day, 1:00 AM and click Next.

15. Click Create to create the Configuration Manager connector.

16. Click Close to close the wizard.

The Configuration Manager connector will appear in the Connectors window. The initial synchronization should start automatically in a few minutes. To trigger a manual synchronization, select the connector and click the Synchronize Now link in the Tasks pane.

Orchestrator Connector Deployment

The Orchestrator connector allows predefined procedures known as runbooks to be imported into the CMDB. This allows the Orchestrator runbooks to be incorporated into service offerings within Service Manager, which greatly enhances the automation capabilities of Service Manager. The tasks needed to create an Orchestrator connector are as follows:

▶ Create the Orchestrator connector to allow runbook data to be imported into the CMDB.

▶ Synchronize the Orchestrator connector to reflect changes made in Orchestrator.

To create the Orchestrator connector, execute the following steps:

1. Launch the Service Manager console.

2. Select the Administration space.

3. Select the Connectors node.

4. In the Tasks pane, click Create Connector and select Orchestrator Connector from the list.

5. Click Next at the introduction screen.

6. Enter a name for the connector, such as `Company ABC Orchestrator Connector`, and click Next.

7. Enter the Orchestrator Web Service URL in the field. This will be similar to `https://ORCH1:443/Orchestrator2012/Orchestrator.svc`. You should be able to enter the URL in a browser and have it bring up an XML formatted page containing information on Orchestrator.

8. In the Credentials section, click the New button to create a RunAs account to access the Orchestrator environment.

9. Enter a Display Name for the account, something like `Orchestrator Account`, and then enter the credentials. Click OK to save the RunAs account.

10. Click the Test Credentials button to test. There should be a "The connection to the server was successful" pop-up message. Click OK to clear the pop-up message.

11. Click Next.

12. Accept the default Sync Folder setting and click Next.

13. For the Orchestrator Web Console URL, enter the Web console URL of your Orchestrator server (such as `http://ORCH1:82`) and click Next.

14. Click Create to create the Orchestrator connector.

15. Click Close to close the wizard.

The Orchestrator connector will appear in the Connectors window. The initial synchronization should start automatically in a few minutes. To trigger a manual synchronization, select the connector and click the Synchronize Now link in the Tasks pane.

Backing Up Service Manager 2012

In the event of a disaster, it is important to have backups of the components needed to restore the Service Manager 2012 infrastructure. The components needed for disaster recovery include the following:

▶ ServiceManager database

▶ Service Manager encryption key

▶ DWStagingAndConfig database

▶ DWRepository database

▶ DWDataMart database

These components need to be backed up on different schedules. Table 14.14 lists the recommended schedule for the backups.

TABLE 14.14   SvcMgr Component Backup Schedules

Component	Full Backup	Differential Backup
Service Manager database (ServiceManager)	Weekly	Daily
Root Management Server encryption key		At IInstallation
Service Manager data warehouse databases (DWStagingAndConfig, DWRepository, DWDataMart)	Weekly	Daily

These backups are above and beyond the standard backups needed for servers, such as file-level backups, System State, and SQL Server backups.

ServiceManager Database Backup

The ServiceManager database contains most of the Service Manager environment configuration settings, workflow information, templates, management packs with customizations, configuration information, and other data required for Service Manager to operate properly.

The loss of the ServiceManager database requires a complete rebuild of the Service Manager 2012 infrastructure.

The ServiceManager database should be backed up on a daily basis. The recommendation is to do a full backup weekly and a differential backup daily to reduce disk space requirements.

To set up the full and differential backups for the ServiceManager database, execute the following steps:

1. Launch SQL Server Management Studio on the Service Manager operations database server.

2. Click the Connect button.

3. Expand the Databases folder.

4. Right-click the ServiceManager database, select Tasks, and click Back Up.

5. In the Back Up Database dialog box, type the name of the backup set in the Name box.

6. In the Destination section, click Add.

7. In the Select Backup Destination dialog box, type a path and a filename in the Destination on Disk box, and then click OK.

NOTE

The destination location selected must have enough disk space to hold the backups.

8. In the Script pull-down menu at the top of the window, select Script Action to Job.

9. In the Name field, enter a name for the job such as `Back Up Database - ServiceManager Full`.

10. In the New Job window, select the Schedules page and click New.

11. In the New Job Schedule dialog box, type `ServiceManager Weekly Full Backup` as the job name in the Name box, specify the job schedule as weekly, and then click OK.

12. Click OK.

13. At this point, click OK to execute a manual full backup or click Cancel to skip it.

14. Right-click the ServiceManager database, select Tasks, and click Back Up.

15. Select Differential in the Backup Type pull-down menu.

16. In the Back Up Database dialog box, type the name of the backup set in the Name box.

17. In the Destination section, click Add.

18. In the Select Backup Destination dialog box, type a path and a filename in the Destination on Disk box, and then click OK.

NOTE

The destination location selected must have enough disk space to hold the backups.

19. In the Script pull-down menu at the top of the window, select Script Action to Job.

20. In the Name field, enter a name for the job such as `Back Up Database - ServiceManager Differential`.

21. In the New Job window, select the Schedules page and click New.

22. In the New Job Schedule dialog box, type **ServiceManager Daily Differential Backup** as the job name in the Name box, specify the job schedule as daily, and then click OK.

23. Click OK.

24. Click OK to execute a manual differential backup right away or click Cancel to skip it.

> **NOTE**
>
> The full backup will have had to run before running the differential backup; otherwise, it will fail.

The ServiceManager database backup will now execute automatically according to the recommended schedule.

Repeat this procedure for each of the following Service Manager data warehouse databases:

▶ DWStagingAndConfig database

▶ DWRepository database

▶ DWDataMart database

Make sure to change the job names to reflect each of the databases.

Service Manager Encryption Key Backup

The Service Manager encryption key encrypts the data going between the Service Manager management server and the ServiceManager database in the management group. The encryption key is needed to bring the Service Manager back online after a disaster recovery.

The SecureStorageBackup tool is used to back up the RMS (Root Management Server) encryption key. To back up the RMS encryption key, complete the following steps:

1. Log on to the Service Management server with a Service Manager administrator account.

2. Launch Explorer.

3. Navigate to \Tools\SecureStorageBackup\ on the Service Manager installation media.

4. Double-click SecureStorageBackup.exe.

5. Click Next.

6. Select Backup the Encryption Key and click Next.

7. Enter a path and file for the backup, such as **c:\backup\SMEncryptionKey.bin**, and click Next.

8. Enter a password to protect the backup and confirm the password, and then click Next.

9. Click Finish to complete the backup.

The key is now backed up and password protected.

> **NOTE**
>
> The encryption key does not change over time, so it only needs to be backed up once and stored securely.

Summary

System Center Service Manager 2012 is key to managing IT service management processes. This is a critical solution to efficiently integrating people, processes, and technologies, as mandated by IT frameworks, such as MOF and ITIL.

In addition, Service Manager leverages the data in its sister System Center products, Operations Manager and Configuration Manager. It integrates and synthesizes the operational and configuration data from those products to automatically spawn service management processes.

Finally, Service Manager extends the IT department's reach by providing Self-Service Portals to end users and analysts that provide rapid solutions to problems while reducing the level of effort of IT staff.

Designing and implementing Service Manager 2012 into the organization will improve the operational efficiency, leverage the existing IT investments, and improve the service levels of the IT department.

Best Practices

The following are best practices from this chapter:

▶ Always create a design and planning document when deploying Service Manager, even if it is a simple one.

▶ Take future expansion and relevance of hardware into account when sizing servers for SvcMgr deployment.

▶ Keep the installation of SvcMgr components on a separate server or set of separate dedicated member servers that do not run any other separate applications.

▶ Use SQL Server Enterprise Edition when combining components on the same server.

▶ Use SQL Server Enterprise Edition when scaling up Service Manager.

▶ Allocate adequate space for the databases depending on the length of time needed to store work items and the number of computers in the organization.

▶ Size the disk subsystems to provide sufficient IOps to support the anticipated data flows.

▶ Use SANs where possible for the improved throughput.

▶ Connect Service Manager to Active Directory, Operations Manager, Configuration Manager, and Orchestrator for maximum benefit.

CHAPTER 15

Using Service Manager 2012 for Incident Tracking and Help Desk Support

IN THIS CHAPTER

▶ Incidents and Problems

▶ Configuring Incident Settings

▶ Service Manager Notifications

▶ Creating New Incidents

▶ Working with Incidents

▶ Configuring Problem Settings

▶ Working with Problems

▶ Incident and Problem Reports

▶ Best Practices

Unfortunately, information technology (IT) systems fail. This can occur when a system directly breaks down—as in a server hardware failure, a misguided configuration change, or an application glitch—or when a system does not function properly from a user's perspective by not behaving as expected or being difficult to understand. These failures result in incidents. Service Manager creates and tracks incidents to help resolve those failures.

Service Manager tracks incidents and problems, which are fundamentally different. ITIL defines incident management and problem management as different but interrelated processes.

Incidents and Problems

In the ITIL Service Support discipline, incidents are events where the standard operation of IT services is disrupted or the quality is impacted. Incidents are resolved when operations of IT services are returned to a predefined standard. Incident management attempts to resolve incidents as quickly as possible while minimizing the impact to the organization.

Problems, on the other hand, might actually reflect standard operations. Problems might have unknown causes or be the result of a known error. The resolution of a problem is normally a workaround or a solution in the form of a change to standard operations.

The ITIL definition of problem management attempts to reduce the number of problems and the severity of those problems.

Service Manager is designed to automate and facilitate both incident and problem management.

Understanding Service Manager Incidents

Incident records are Service Manager entries of incidents and are the core of the incident management process. The goal of the Service Manager incident management process is to restore normal operations as quickly as possible.

Incidents are equivalent to trouble tickets. These are created in response to a variety of events.

The Service Manager incident process covers all the steps in the ITIL incident management process. These steps are as follows:

- ▶ Incident detection and recording
- ▶ Classification and support
- ▶ Investigation and diagnosis
- ▶ Resolution and recovery
- ▶ Incident closure
- ▶ Incident reporting

The outcome of incident resolution is the resumption of service, meaning a return to normal service operations. An additional outcome might be the initiation of a problem to identify and address the root cause of the incident.

Understanding Service Manager Problems

Service Manager problems are records that group incidents with a common root cause, allowing the underlying problem to be addressed and the associated incidents to be resolved when the problem is resolved.

Typically, a problem record will not be created until multiple incidents have occurred.

The Service Manager problem process covers the steps in the ITIL problem management process. These steps are as follows:

- ▶ Problem identification and recording
- ▶ Problem classification
- ▶ Problem investigation and diagnosis

The outcome of problem resolution is likely to be a change and, thus, leads to the change of management processes. This is covered in Chapter 16, "Using Service Manager 2012 for Service Offerings and Change Control Management."

Configuring Incident Settings

Before working with incidents, a number of settings should be configured. These settings are as follows:

- ▶ Incident prefix

- ▶ File attachment limits

- ▶ Priority calculation

- ▶ Resolution time

- ▶ Operations Manager Web console

- ▶ Inbound email

In some cases, such as the OpsMgr Web console setting, there is no default and a setting must be configured to get it operational. For other cases, such as the default resolution times, the default is not acceptable for most organizations and needs to be set for effectiveness.

Incident Prefix

By default, each incident is prefixed with the letters IR, for incident record. This can be adjusted to something different, such as TT for trouble ticket or TICKET. The maximum number of characters is 15.

To change the incident prefix, complete the following steps:

1. Launch the Service Manager console.

2. Select the Administration space.

3. Select the Administration/Settings folder.

4. In the right pane, select the Properties of the Incident Setting object.

5. In the General section, change the Prefix field to the desired setting.

6. Click OK to save the change.

The change takes effect for all new incidents. This value should only be changed if needed.

NOTE

The new prefix is not applied to the existing incident records, only to new records.

File Attachment Limits

File attachments to incidents have built-in limiters. This ensures that huge files or large numbers of files don't get attached to incidents and bloat the database unnecessarily. This can be a real issue if help desk personnel or end users attempt to attach 100MB log files or gigabyte PST files to incidents.

File attachments are limited by the number of attachments and the size of the attachments. The permitted ranges and the default settings are given in Table 15.1.

TABLE 15.1   File Attachment Settings

File Attachment Limits	Range	Default Setting
Maximum number of attachments	0–10	10
Maximum size (KB)	0–10240	2048

To adjust the default file attachment settings, complete the following steps:

1. Launch the Service Manager console.

2. Select the Administration space.

3. Select the Administration/Settings folder.

4. In the right pane, select the Properties of the Incident Setting object.

5. In the General section, change the Maximum Number of Attached Files and the Maximum Size (KB) fields to the desired settings.

6. Click OK to save the changes.

The changes take effect immediately in the console and web interfaces.

> **NOTE**
>
> The new file attachment settings are not applied to the existing incident records; the new settings only apply to new records or when changes are made to existing records.

Priority Calculation

Incidents are rated by priority, which is a combination of the impact and urgency of the incident. The priority rating is used to determine the appropriate resolution time for the incident, which drives sending notifications, escalating, and service-level metrics. Impact and urgency are generally defined by ITIL, but the specifics are left to the organizations.

Impact is rated as low, medium, or high. It is a subjective measure of how much the incident is affecting the organization. This is frequently measured in terms of the number of users impacted or the level of impact to the organization. For example, an incident for a single end user not being able to access email would have a lower impact than an incident for all users not being able to access email.

Urgency is also rated as low, medium, or high. It is a subjective measure of how quickly the incident must be addressed. For example, an incident for a mission-critical system like email being unavailable would have a higher urgency than an incident for a non-mission-critical system like the company event web page. Even though those two systems might impact the same number of users—that is, the entire company—they are assigned different urgencies.

The default Service Manager priority gives weighting to the urgency over impact, and incident priorities are assigned as shown in Table 15.2. The highest priority is assigned 1 and the lowest priority is assigned 9. In Service Manager 2012, these values are not set by default and need to be configured by the administrator.

TABLE 15.2   Priority Table

	Impact Low	Impact Medium	Impact High
Urgency Low	9	8	7
Urgency Medium	6	5	4
Urgency High	3	2	1

These priority assignments can be changed, if needed, for consistency with other systems in the organization or to adjust the behavior of Service Manager.

To configure the priority assignments, complete the following steps:

1. Launch the Service Manager console.

2. Select the Administration space.

3. Select the Administration/Settings folder.

4. In the right pane, select the Properties of the Incident Setting object.

5. In the Priority Calculation section, use the drop-down menu to change the priorities, as shown in Figure 15.1.

NOTE

Be sure that the chosen priorities match all possible priorities in your Service Manager configuration.

6. Click OK to save the changes.

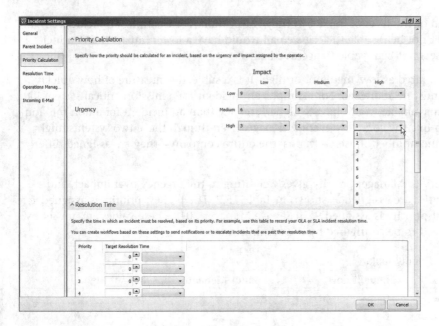

FIGURE 15.1   Priority calculation adjustment.

These new settings are used by Service Manager immediately.

> **NOTE**
>
> These priority calculation times should only be adjusted for specific and well-
> understood reasons. In addition, the resolution times need to be adjusted in response
> to changes in the priority calculations.

Resolution Times

The resolution time incident settings define the service levels for the time it is expected to take to resolve an incident based on the priority.

Incidents that fall outside of their resolution times can be viewed in the Overdue Incidents folder in the Work Items space under the Incident Management tree. These can also trigger workflows for notification and escalation.

The incident resolution times can be set in terms of the following intervals:

- ▶ Minutes
- ▶ Hours
- ▶ Days
- ▶ Weeks

The numeric value can be set from 0 to 2,147,483,647, which should cover the most granular requirements. If set to 0, the resolution time for that priority is ignored. The default resolution time for all priorities is 0, so by default all resolution times are disabled.

To set resolution times for the priorities, complete the following steps:

1. Launch the Service Manager console.

2. Select the Administration space.

3. Select the Administration/Settings folder.

4. In the right pane, select the Properties of the Incident Setting object.

5. In the Resolution Time section, use the pull-down menu to change the target resolution time for the specific priorities. For example, set the resolution times for the Priority 1 incidents (high impact and high urgency) to 2 hours, as shown in Figure 15.2.

6. Click OK to save the changes.

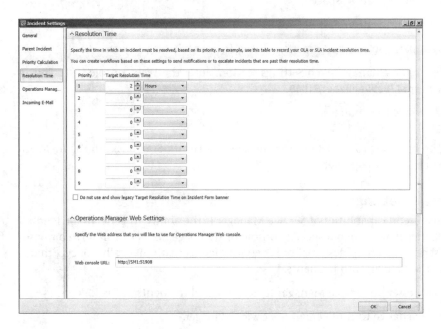

FIGURE 15.2   Setting resolution times.

These new settings are used by Service Manager immediately. However, the console might need to be closed and launched again to see the changes reflected in the views.

Operations Manager Web Console Setting

The incidents created by the Operations Manager connector include links back into the Operations Manager Web console. These links launch the Operations Manager Web console to show the following:

- ▶ **View Alert Details**—This is the detailed view of the Operations Manager alert that created the incident.

- ▶ **View CI Health State**—This is the Operations Manager Health Explorer view of the object that generated the alert.

These help drill down into the details of the alert, leveraging the Operations Manager wealth of data and showing the level of integration of the System Center products.

To set the Operations Manager Web console address, complete the following steps:

1. Launch the Service Manager console.
2. Select the Administration space.
3. Select the Administration/Settings folder.
4. In the right pane, select the Properties of the Incident Setting object.
5. In the Operations Manager Web Settings section, enter the Web console URL. This is typically `http://servername:51908`.
6. Click OK to save the changes.

Now, clicking on the View Alert Details and the View CI Health State tasks in the incident shows the Operations Manager details.

Inbound Email Settings

One of the most useful capabilities of Service Manager is the ability to generate incidents from emails. Rather than launch a special console or web page, users can simply compose an email and send it to a help desk mailbox. Service Manager automatically collects that mail and converts the mail into incidents.

The tasks needed to set up Service Manager to accept email incidents are as follows:

- ▶ Configure Exchange to route email to Service Manager.
- ▶ Configure Service Manager to accept Simple Mail Transfer Protocol (SMTP) mail.
- ▶ Configure Service Manager to monitor the mail folders.

The first task is to configure Exchange 2010 to route email to Service Manager. This requires configuring an accepted domain and a send connector to route the mail to Service Manager.

To configure Exchange 2010 to route email to Service Manager, complete the following steps:

1. On the Exchange 2010 Hub Transport server, launch the Exchange Management Console.

2. Select the Organization Configuration, Hub Transport folder.

3. In the Actions pane, click the New Accepted Domain link.

4. Enter a name, such as **Service Manager Helpdesk Domain**, and the domain, such as **helpdesk.companyabc.com**.

5. Select the Internal Relay Domain option button (shown in Figure 15.3) and then click New.

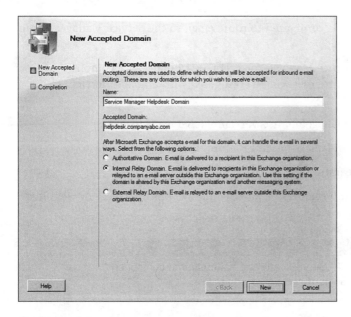

FIGURE 15.3   Exchange 2010 accepted domain settings.

6. After the wizard completes, click Finish to close the wizard.

7. In the Actions pane, click the New Send Connector link.

8. Enter a name for the send connector, such as **Service Manager Helpdesk Send Connector**.

9. In the Select the Intended Use for This Connector pull-down menu, select Internal and then click Next.

10. Click Add to add an SMTP address space to route.

11. In the SMTP Address Space window, enter the domain used earlier, such as **helpdesk.companyabc.com**.

12. Check the Include All Subdomains check box and then click OK.

13. Click Next.

14. Click Add to add a smart host to route mail to.

15. Select the FQDN option button, enter the Service Manager SMTP server name (in this case, `sm1.companyabc.com`), and click OK.

16. Click Next.

17. Leave the Smart Host Authentication at None and click Next.

18. Select additional hub transport source servers if appropriate and then click Next.

19. Click New to create the connector and then click Finish when you are done.

Now the Exchange 2010 system is configured to route email to the Service Manager infrastructure.

The next task is to configure Service Manager to accept SMTP mail. To accomplish this, the Service Manager management server will be configured with an SMTP service. To do this, complete the following steps:

1. On the Service Manager management server, launch Server Manager.

2. Select the Features node and click the Add Features link.

3. Select the SMTP Server feature.

4. If the Add Role Services and Features Required window pops up, click Add Required Role Services.

> **NOTE**
>
> The Windows Server 2008 SMTP Server feature is an integrated component of the Web Server (IIS), so the Web Server (IIS) role is required.

5. Click Next.

6. Click Next at the Web Server (IIS) screen.

7. Click Next to accept the role services.

8. Click Install to install the SMTP Server feature.

9. Click Close to close the Add Features wizard.

10. Select Start, Administrative Tools, and then Internet Information Services (IIS) Manager 6.0.

11. Expand the Server node, expand the SMTP Virtual Server #1 node, and then select the Domains folder.

12. Right-click the Domains folder and select New, Domain.

13. Select the Alias option button and click Next.

14. Enter the help desk domain name used earlier, such as **helpdesk.companyabc.com** and click Finish.

The Service Manager management server is now configured to accept mail. The default configuration will only accept mail for the configured domains and will not relay mail to other domains.

NOTE

Make sure that the Simple Mail Transfer Protocol (SMTP) Windows service is set to Automatic in the Services startup type so that the service will start at boot.

Finally, the last task is to configure Service Manager to monitor the mail folders. There will be two, one for email (the Drop folder) and one for bad mail (the Badmail folder). The default location for these folders is c:\inetpub\mailroot\.

To configure Service Manager to accept emails, complete the following steps:

1. Launch the Service Manager console.

2. Select the Administration space.

3. Select the Administration/Settings folder.

4. In the right pane, select the Properties of the Incident Setting object.

5. Click the Incoming E-Mail link to go to that section.

6. In the SMTP Service Drop Folder Location field, enter **c:\inetpub\mailroot\Drop**.

7. In the SMTP Service Bad Folder Location field, enter **c:\inetpub\mailroot\Badmail**.

8. Enter the maximum number of messages that Service Manager will process at a time, for example **100**.

NOTE

Service Manager will convert incoming emails to incidents. Service Manager should not generate too many incidents from emails, so this number does not have to be all that high. A high volume of inbound emails is probably a spam issue rather than real incidents.

---

9. Enable incoming email by checking the Turn On Incoming E-Mail Processing check box, as shown in Figure 15.4.

10. Click OK to save the changes.

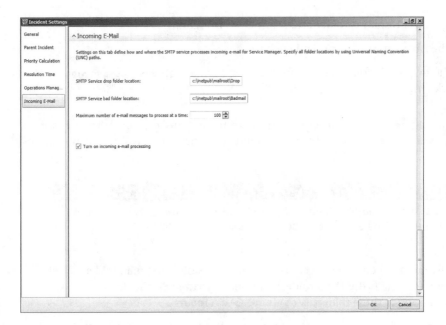

FIGURE 15.4   Enabling incoming email.

Service Manager now accepts incoming emails to the target domain and creates incidents
for them. The sender becomes the affected user, the incident title becomes the subject
line of the message, the body of the message becomes the incident description, and the
original message is attached to the incident as a file.

Service Manager Notifications

Service Manager notifications allow emails to be delivered to help desk personnel,
analysts, administrators, and end users notifying them of additions, changes, and deletions of the records that matter to them. The notification architecture is very deep and
granular, allowing notification on any Service Manager object and on almost any condition.

In addition to configuring the notification infrastructure, this section creates a sample
notification. For this example, the network engineer for the company needs to get a high-
priority email message when a network incident is created.

Service Manager Notification Architecture

Service Manager can notify via SMTP email of changes to objects. Notifications can be
made for any class of object defined in the schema, which is extensive. The frequently
used classes of objects are as follows:

▶ Announcement

▶ Change Request

- ▶ DCM Incident

- ▶ Domain User

- ▶ Incident

- ▶ Knowledge Article

- ▶ Manual Activity

- ▶ Problem

- ▶ Review Activity

- ▶ Windows Computer

Changes to the object of the classes are what trigger notification emails to be sent. Notifications can be triggered for the following events:

- ▶ Creations

- ▶ Updates

- ▶ Deletions

Finally, notifications can be filtered by additional criteria based on attributes from the targeted object class. For example, if the Incident object class is chosen, attributes such as Assigned to User, Source, Priority, and all the other Incident fields can be used as criteria. The field can be filtered using the following operators:

- ▶ Contains

- ▶ Does Not Contain

- ▶ Starts With

- ▶ Ends With

- ▶ Equals

- ▶ Does Not Equal

- ▶ Is Empty

- ▶ Is Not Empty

This gives the notification a fine-grained specification for targeting notification emails. The additional criterion allows the notification to be precisely targeted by exactly the right conditions needed to meet even the most demanding business requirements.

The Service Manager notification architecture is composed of three elements:

- ▶ **Channels**—The channel is the path by which the notifications are sent. Service Manager 2012 currently only supports SMTP email as a notification channel. Multiple SMTP server destinations can be configured to provide failover capabilities.

▶ **Templates**—Templates are used by subscriptions to correctly format the notification emails. The notification templates use variables to insert information into the form. The templates use the $Context object to get the current object.

▶ **Subscriptions**—Subscriptions specify the objects, trigger events, criteria, templates, and, finally, a recipient of the email notification.

There is no limit to the number of subscriptions that can be created, so a sophisticated notification model can be developed that delivers precise notifications where they are needed.

> **NOTE**
>
> The Service Manager 2012 notification architecture benefits from the issues that the Operations Manager notification architecture had during the evolution of the product. The early revisions of MOM 2000, MOM 2005, and even OpsMgr 2007 made delivering the proper notifications difficult. Microsoft finally delivered a top-notch notification architecture in OpsMgr 2007 R2, and the Service Manager 2012 architecture benefits from that evolution.

Configuring the SMTP Notification Channel

The notification email channel is disabled by default. The channel needs to be configured with a destination SMTP server and enabled to be able to send notifications.

To configure the notification channel, execute the following steps:

1. Launch the Service Manager console.

2. Select the Administration space.

3. Select the Administration/Notifications/Channels folder.

> **NOTE**
>
> The folder is named Channels, but there is only a single channel predefined in the folder and no way of creating a new one in the UI. In the future, Service Manager will incorporate the ability to create different SMTP channels as well as other types of channels.

4. In the Tasks pane, select the Properties link.

5. Check the Enable E-Mail Notifications check box.

6. Click Add to add an SMTP server.

7. Enter the SMTP Server Name and click OK.

8. Enter the Return E-Mail Address for the notification emails.

9. Click OK to save the settings.

The channel is ready to send notification emails to the SMTP server. If needed, additional SMTP servers can be configured to provide failover in the event of the outage of a given SMTP server.

Creating Notification Templates

Notification templates can be generic or they can be specific depending on the requirements. There is no limit to the number of templates that can be created, so creating additional templates to customize notification messages is highly recommended.

As an example, the network engineer notification of network incidents requires the message be sent with high priority. To format the message properly, a new template needs to be created.

To create an incident notification template, complete the following steps:

1. Launch the Service Manager console.

2. Select the Administration space.

3. Select the Administration/Notifications/Templates folder.

4. In the Tasks pane, click the Create E-mail Template link.

5. Enter the name **Network Incident Notification Template**.

6. In the Targeted Class section, click the Browse button.

7. Select the incident class and click OK.

8. Select the Service Manager Incident Management Configuration Library in the Management Pack section. It should be listed under the Recommended Management Packs in the pull-down menu.

9. Click Next.

10. In the Message Subject field, enter **New Network Incident Created:**.

11. With the cursor still in the Message Subject field, click the Insert button to select a database variable.

12. Select the Work Item ID property from the list and click Add. The string `$Context/Property[Type='WorkItem!System.WorkItem']/Id$` will be inserted at the cursor point.

> **NOTE**
>
> The long string `$Context/Property[Type='WorkItem!System.WorkItem']/Id$` is called a substitution string and will be replaced when the email is generated with the value from the object record. Any field from the target class can be chosen, in this case, with the record ID.

13. In the Message Body field, enter **A network incident was created**.

14. Change the Urgency field from Medium to High.

15. Click Next to display the Summary page.

16. Click Create to create the template and then click Close to close the wizard.

The template is now ready, but needs to be paired with a subscription to actually send messages.

Creating Notification Subscriptions

To bring it all together, subscriptions are used. These use the templates, channels, and the objects to deliver email messages.

In the example of the notification of network incidents, the requirement is for the message to be sent to the network engineer when a network incident is created. To target the notification, a new subscription needs to be created.

To create a notification subscription, execute the following steps:

1. Launch the Service Manager console.

2. Select the Administration space.

3. Select the Administration/Notifications/Subscriptions folder.

4. In the Tasks pane, click the Create Subscription link.

5. Click Next at the introduction screen.

6. In the Notification Subscription Name field, enter the name **Network Incident Notification Subscription**.

7. In the Targeted Class section, click the Browse button.

8. Select the incident class and click OK.

9. In the When to Notify pull-down menu, select When an Object of the Selected Class Is Created.

10. Select the Service Manager Incident Management Configuration Library in the Management Pack section. It should be listed under the Recommended Management Packs in the pull-down menu.

11. Click Next.

12. On the Additional Criteria page, check the Classification Category check box in the Available Properties section and then click Add.

> **NOTE**
>
> The check mark clears from the Available Properties after adding the property to the criteria. This allows the property to be added again for multiple OR clauses such as Networking Problems or Printing Problems classifications.

13. From the pull-down menu, select the Networking Problems classification category, as shown in Figure 15.5.

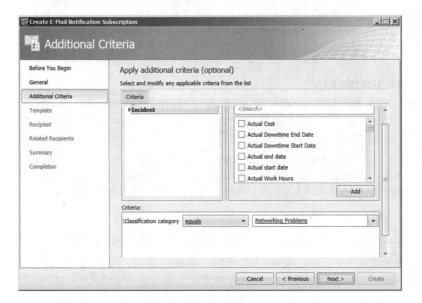

FIGURE 15.5   Notification Subscription Additional Criteria.

14. Click Next.

15. In the E-mail Template section, click the Select button, select the previously created Network Incident Notification Template, and click OK.

16. Click Next.

17. In the Recipients section, click Add.

18. In the Select Objects window, select the appropriate user or group to target the notifications to (in this case, the network engineer), and click Add. Click OK to save the recipients.

NOTE

This list of users and groups comes from the configuration management database (CMDB), which is synchronized via the Active Directory connector.

19. In the Specify Related Recipients for This Subscription window, click Next.

20. Review the settings on the Summary screen, click Create to create the notification subscription, and then click Close to exit the wizard.

Now any new incident with the classification of Networking Problems generates a high-priority email to the network engineer.

Creating New Incidents

Incidents can be created from a variety of sources, including manually, from OpsMgr alerts, from emails, and even from Configuration Manager. Each of these sources of incidents has different features, requiring different levels of work to evaluate, complete, and assign the incident to an analyst.

Manually Created Incidents

Manually created incidents are those created by analysts in response to a service event. They could be creating the incident in response to a help desk call, an email from an end user, or an observed service outage.

For example, suppose a help desk analyst receives a report from an end user named Kim who is unable to access a server named WEBSERVER. The analyst wants to create a new incident to resolve the issue. To create a new incident, complete the following steps:

1. Launch the Service Manager console.

2. In the Search field in the upper-right corner of the console, enter **WEBSERVER**.

3. From the Search pull-down menu, select Windows Computer (as shown in Figure 15.6).

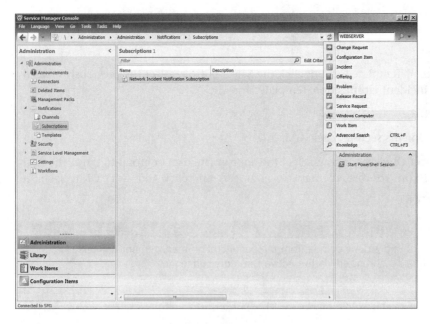

FIGURE 15.6   Searching for a computer.

4. A Search Result window pops up with a list of matching objects from the CMDB. Select the WEBSERVER record and click the Create Related Incident report.

NOTE

Searching is a fast way to track down any object in the CMDB. This allows analysts to quickly locate users, computers, incidents, problems, and any other record. The CMDB records can be reviewed and tasks launched directly from the search results.

---

5. The Incident form loads with the required fields highlighted in red. Enter a Title for the incident, such as `User Unable to Access WEBSERVER`.

6. To fill in the Affected User field, click the ellipses (...) button next to the field. Enter the affected user's name in the Search By Name field, in this example `Kim`, and click the Search icon. Select the user from the resulting list and click OK.

7. In the Classification Category, use the pull-down menu to select the appropriate category.

8. In the Impact and Urgency pull-down menus, select the appropriate impact and urgency. The priority is calculated automatically.

NOTE

The Assigned To and Primary Owner fields are automatically populated with the help desk analyst who is entering the incident. The analyst needs to change these to the application administrator for the object.

---

9. To locate the appropriate application owner to assign the incident to, scroll down to the Affected Items section of the form, select the affected item WEBSERVER, and click the Open button, as shown in Figure 15.7.

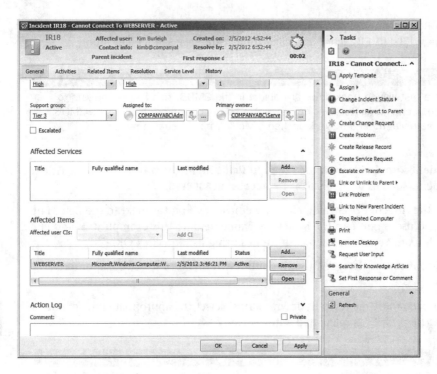

FIGURE 15.7   Opening the affected item.

10. On the Computer form, scroll down to the CI Information section and note the CI Custodian, in this example "Tyson." Click Cancel to close the form.

11. Back on the Incident form, to fill in the Assigned To field, click the ellipses (...) button next to the field. Enter the CI Custodian name in the Search By Name, in this example "**Tyson**," and click the Search icon. Select the user from the resulting list and click OK.

12. To fill in the Primary Owner field, click the ellipses (...) button next to the field. Enter the CI Custodian name in the Search By Name, in this example "**Tyson**," and click the Search icon. Select the user from the resulting list and click OK.

13. Click OK to save the incident.

The incident is now created and assigned to the application owner.

OpsMgr Alert Created Incidents

Incidents that are created by Operations Manager alerts via the connector are not complete and usually need to be classified, the affected user(s) specified, and assigned to an analyst. Optionally, the impact and urgency might need to be adjusted as all the incidents from the Operations Manager source have the same impact and urgency.

To complete an Operations Manager–generated incident, complete the following steps:

1. Launch the Service Manager console.

2. Select the Work Items space.

3. Expand the Incident Management folder.

4. Select the All Open OM Incidents folder.

5. The middle pane shows a list of all open Operations Manager–generated incidents. Double-click an incident to open the incident form.

> **NOTE**
>
> The OK button to save the incident is disabled. This is because the incident form is not complete and the key fields need to be entered to be able to save the incident.

6. Select the Affected User from the CMDB. This can be a user or a group.

7. Select the Classification Category from the pull-down menu.

8. In the Tasks pane, click the Assign to Analyst link.

9. Select the appropriate analyst and click OK.

10. Click OK to save the updated incident.

The alert-generated incident is now complete and ready for an analyst to work with the incident.

Operations Manager alert incidents are generated with a template, the Operations Manager incident template. This template can be re-created to prepopulate and make it easier to complete the Operations Manager–generated incidents. For example, the template can specify the affected user, adjust the urgency and impact, and classify the incident automatically. Then, the only thing that needs to be done to complete Operations Manager incidents is to assign the incident to an analyst.

To create a new template and assign it to the Operations Manager connector, complete the following steps:

1. Launch the Service Manager console.

2. Select the Library space.

3. Select the Templates folder and click Create Template in the Tasks pane.

4. Enter a name, such as `Company ABC Operations Manager Incident Template`.

5. In the Class section, click the Browse button.

6. Change the View to All Basic Classes and select the Operations Manager–Generated Incident class and click OK.

15

7. Make sure the Service Manager Incident Management Configuration Library is selected in the Management Pack section and click OK.

8. When the template form appears, select an Affected User for the template. The OpsMgr.Alert user created in Chapter 14, "Service Manager 2012 Design, Planning, and Implementation," is a good candidate user.

> **NOTE**
>
> Unfortunately, the Operations Manager connector will not be able to determine the actual affected users for the incidents. This is done by the analyst when evaluating the specific incidents.

9. Select the Classification Category as Other Problems.

10. Select the Source as Operations Manager.

11. Adjust the Impact and Urgency to Medium.

12. Click OK to save the new template.

13. Select the Administration space.

14. Select the Connectors folder.

15. Select the previously created Operations Manager Alerts connector, for example the Company ABC Alerts Connector.

16. Open the Properties of the connector.

17. Select the Alert Routing Rules page.

18. Change the default template from the default Operations Manager Incident Template to the new template, in this example Company ABC Operations Manager Incident Template. Note that notifications that match a user-defined routing rule use the defined template rather than the default template.

19. Also change the template for any routing rules by selecting the routing rule, and then clicking the Edit button.

20. Click OK to save the changes.

> **NOTE**
>
> Changes made to the template are applied to all future incidents generated by the Operations Manager connector. The changes do not affect existing incidents.

Now, when the incident is generated, it already contains all the required information. Rather than having to open an incident to complete and then assign it to an analyst, the incident can be assigned simply by selecting it in the console and clicking the Assign to Analyst link in the Tasks pane (as shown in Figure 15.8).

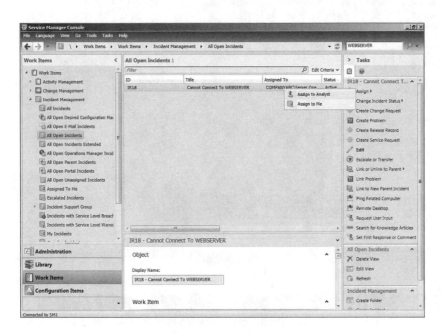

FIGURE 15.8   Assigning an incident to an analyst.

Creating Incidents Using the Self-Service Portal

In Service Manager 2012, administrators can configure the Self-Service Web Portal to allow users to create and submit incidents using only a web browser. Although Service Manager 2010 also included a self-service web portal component, the Service Manager web portal functionality has changed significantly in Service Manager 2012, so this chapter will provide an overview of the updated Self-Service Web Portal.

The Self-Service Web Portal in Service Manager 2012 consists of a SharePoint website, a web content server, and a number of Silverlight applications. The Silverlight applications and the web content server work together to create a conduit for displaying data from the Service Manager server in a browser interface. The initial view of the Self-Service Web Portal is shown in Figure 15.9. Many elements of the default site (such as portal title, background image, and site theme) can easily be changed through SharePoint administration tools. Microsoft provides step-by-step instructions to perform some basic portal customization steps at http://technet.microsoft.com/en-us/library/hh770170.aspx.

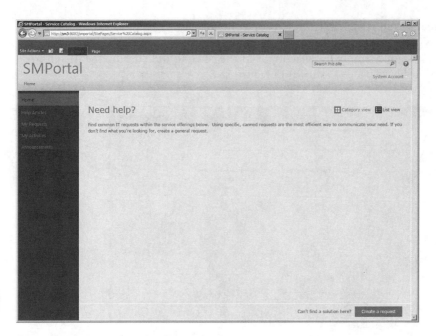

FIGURE 15.9   The Self-Service Portal in initial configuration.

> **NOTE**
>
> To access the content on the Self-Service Portal, client machines must have Microsoft
> Silverlight installed. In addition, the certificate that is used for SSL on the portal
> website must be trusted by the client; otherwise, the Silverlight content will not be
> displayed.

As you can see, the initial view of the portal does not contain much content. In this
initial configuration, users can submit requests by clicking the Create Request button in
the lower-right corner. This submits a request using the Generic Incident Request offering.
However, this generic offering does not provide the ability to attach a file to an incident,
so many organizations will choose to create a custom request offering to address specific
business requirements. Chapter 16 covers the configuration of service offerings in detail
(including the service offering described below), but for this example we walk through the
steps of a user creating an incident through the portal using a customized service offering.

In this scenario, you'll play the role of a user having issues with a laptop cellular modem.
You want to include the log file (modem_diagnostics.txt) that is generated with the
request for help. You want to create a request to have this fixed, that is, create an incident. To create the incident using the web portal, complete the following steps:

1. Launch the Internet Explorer web browser.

2. Enter the URL of the Self-Service Portal, typically **https://<servername>/SMPortal**. In the case of this example, the URL is **http://sm3:8082/SMPortal**.

3. When the portal page loads, click on the End User Hardware Support service offering, as shown in Figure 15.10.

4. Clicking on the End User Hardware Support service offering takes you to the page for the selected service offering. On this page, select a request named End User Hardware Support. After clicking on this link, select the Go To Request... button, which begins the process of entering information for the request.

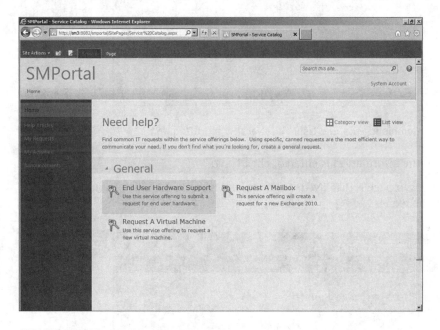

FIGURE 15.10   Self-Service Portal with customized service offerings.

5. After clicking the Go To Request... button, the screen shown in Figure 15.11 appears. This screen contains two free text fields in which to enter information about the incident, a drop-down list to select the incident severity, a field for alternate contact information, and a button to attach the modem diagnostic file.

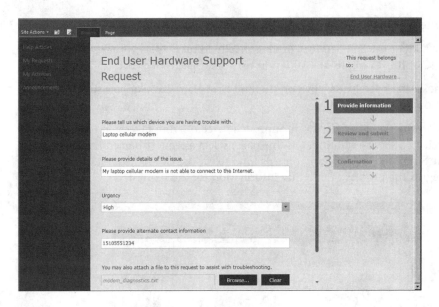

FIGURE 15.11   Completing the End User Hardware Support Request.

6. Once all of the information is entered, click Next.

7. A summary web page is displayed, as shown in Figure 15.12. Click Submit to complete the request.

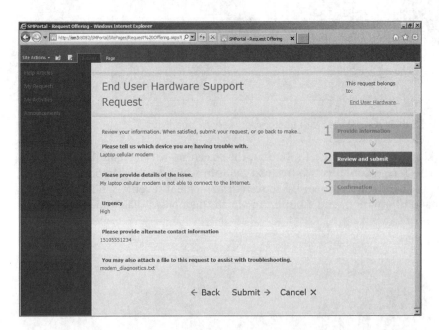

FIGURE 15.12   Submitting the End User Hardware Support Request.

You are presented with a page indicating the request was submitted and showing the Request ID. You can see your recent requests by clicking the View All link in the Recent Requests box.

The resulting incident is complete and can easily be assigned to an analyst from the Service Manager console.

Email-Created Incidents

Incidents can also be created from emails. This provides a low-effort method of creating an incident. This method is useful for the following sources:

- ▶ Users

- ▶ Analysts

- ▶ Automated systems

The ability to have an automated system generate an incident is particularly useful. Many applications and systems generate alerts, but it is difficult to create a connector for each of these disparate systems—as was done for Operations Manager or Configuration Manager. However, many applications and systems generate an email for an alert. This can be targeted at the Service Manager email and have incidents generated automatically for those systems.

Earlier in the chapter, the capability to accept emailed incident requests was configured and enabled.

To create an incident from an email, complete the following steps:

1. Launch Microsoft Office Outlook.

2. Click New to create a new email message.

3. In the To field, enter the Service Manager email address. For the one created earlier in this chapter, enter **service@helpdesk.companyabc.com**.

4. In the Subject field, enter **Problem Synchronizing Files**.

5. In the Body, enter a description of the issue.

6. Click Send to submit the incident.

The incident is submitted. The Affected User is the sender, the Title of the incident is the email subject, the incident Description is the body of the email, and the Source of the incident is E-Mail. However, the incident is not complete, as the Classification Category is not entered.

Working with Incidents

Once incidents are created, analysts need to work with those incidents. The incidents
need to be

- ▶ Evaluated

- ▶ Analyzed

- ▶ Resolved

The steps move the incident along the process toward resolving the service outage.

Evaluating and Assigning Incidents

The first step in working with incidents is for an analyst to evaluate the new incident and
route it to the proper analyst for analysis and resolution. Depending on the nature of the
specific incident, different expertise, authority, or availability is required to process the
incident effectively and efficiently.

In addition, many new incidents are not complete, such as those created from Operations
Manager alerts or email incidents. Operations Manager incidents need to be assigned
based on the source of the Operations Manager alert. Email alerts will typically need to be
classified and assigned.

An analyst must evaluate the new incidents and correctly do the following:

- ▶ **Complete the incident**—This means filling out any required fields, such as the
  Affected User, Title, Classification Category, Source, Impact, and Urgency.

- ▶ **Evaluate the incident**—This entails reviewing affected items and services, the
  nature of the issue, the priority of the incident, and making a determination about
  the best way to assign the incident.

- ▶ **Assign the incident**—Finally, the incident needs to be assigned.

These steps might vary by organization and by incident. It is important to develop procedures and train analysts to perform these tasks.

To evaluate and assign an incident, complete the following steps:

1. Launch the Service Manager console.

2. Select the Work Items space.

3. Expand the Incident Management folder.

4. Select the All Open Unassigned Incidents folder.

5. Select an incident to evaluate from the list pane and click the Edit task in the Tasks
   pane.

6. Complete any of the fields highlighted in red (required fields). These fields should generally be completed, but might not be depending on the source of the incident.

7. In the Affected Items section, select the item and click the Open button.

8. In the CI Information section of the item form, note the CI Custodian. (This is the individual to assign the incident to by default.)

9. Click OK to exit the affected item form.

10. Back on the incident form, click the Assign to Analyst link in the Tasks pane.

11. Locate the CI Custodian name noted before and click OK.

12. The Assigned To field in the incident form now contains the CI Custodian name.

13. Click OK to save the changes and exit.

The incident is now gone from the All Open Unassigned Incidents view and is assigned to the custodian of the affected item.

In the evaluation, the analyst can also easily add affected services or affected items to the incident.

Analyzing Incidents

This is where the real work of fixing the issue and bringing the incident to resolution occurs. The assigned analyst reviews the incident and performs the following activities:

▶ Analyze

▶ Troubleshoot

▶ Update

▶ Escalate

▶ Link

The analyst reviews the incident to better understand the nature of the problem, investigates related configuration and work items, links these related items where appropriate, and leverages the CMDB to perform these activities quickly and efficiently.

As an example of an analysis, suppose you, as the analyst, are coming in to work first thing in the morning and will review incidents that have been assigned to you. This would be completed using the following steps:

1. Launch the Service Manager console.

2. Select the Work Items space.

3. Expand the Incident Management folder.

4. Select the My Incidents folder.

NOTE

The My Incidents folder is filtered to only show incidents that have been assigned to
the current analyst. This is very helpful for rapidly drilling into the incident the analyst
is responsible for.

---

5. To quickly prioritize which incidents to process first, click the Priority column to
   sort by priority. The analyst has four total incidents assigned, with one active priority 1 incident (the highest level), as shown in Figure 15.13. There is also a priority 6
   incident that is resolved.

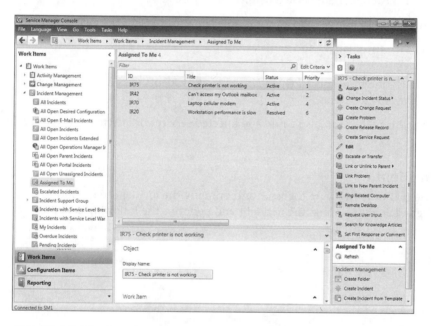

FIGURE 15.13   My Incidents sorted by Priority.

6. Select the active priority 1 incident, which is the IR75 incident, and click Edit in the
   Tasks pane.

7. Review the description of the incident to get a better understanding of the issue.
   The affected item, ACCTPTR01, is not able to connect to its print queue on the
   PRINTSERVER server.

8. To record that relation, select the Related Items tab in the incident form.

9. In the Configuration Items: Computers, Services, and People section of the Related
   Items, click Add.

10. From the CMDB, select the PRINTSERVER server, click Add to add the related item,
    and then click OK to save.

11. To review the status of the related PRINTSERVER server, click the Open button. This opens the Computer form for the PRINTSERVER server.

12. To determine if there were any issues with the PRINTSERVER server that correlate with the incident, select the Related Items tab in the Computer form.

13. In the Work Items Affecting This Configuration Item section, note that incident IR81 Print Spooler Service Stopped was resolved and was the root cause of the printing failure in incident IR75.

14. With the root cause identified, close the Computer form by clicking OK.

15. In the Work Items section of the Related Items form of incident IR75, click Add.

16. Locate the root cause incident IR81, select the incident, click Add, and click OK to add the related incident to the current incident. The resulting changes to the incident are shown in Figure 15.14.

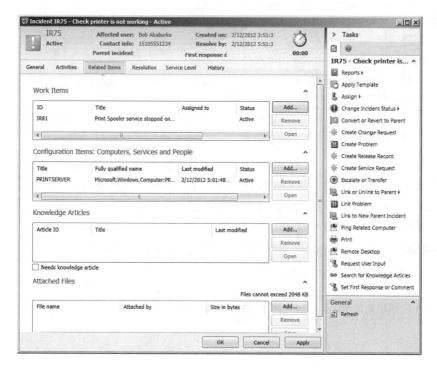

FIGURE 15.14   Related configuration and work items recorded.

17. Click OK to save the changes to the incident.

The incident has now been analyzed, troubleshot, and updated to reflect the findings. Service Manager's CMDB and related items features allow for rapid troubleshooting and root cause analysis and, more important, clear documentation of the relationships between not only objects, but also work items such as incidents.

Publishing Announcements

Sometimes an incident will result in a protracted service outage. Rather than leave the end users in the dark, it is best to get the information out that there are service-level problems.

Service Manager announcements accomplish this goal. To create an announcement on the Self-Service Portal, complete the following steps:

1. Start a browser, and connect to the Self-Service Portal home page, for example, http://<WebServerName>:8082/SMPortal.

2. In the upper-left corner, click Site Actions, and then click Site Settings.

3. On the Site Settings page, in the Look and Feel area, click Quick Launch.

4. On the Quick Launch page, click New Navigation link.

5. In the Type the Web Address field, type `/SMPortal/Lists/Announcements/AllItems.aspx`, and then in the Description box, type **Announcements**.

6. Click OK, and then navigate to the home page.

To create an announcement, do the following:

1. Start a browser, and connect to the Self-Service Portal home page, for example, http://<WebServerName>:8082/SMPortal.

2. Click Announcements.

3. On the Announcements – All items page, click Add New Announcement.

4. In the Title box, type a name for the announcement. For example, type **Active Directory Performance Slow**.

5. In the Body field, you can type additional information for the announcement.

6. Click Save to close the announcement.

The announcement will be immediately visible in the Self-Service Web Portal, as shown in Figure 15.15.

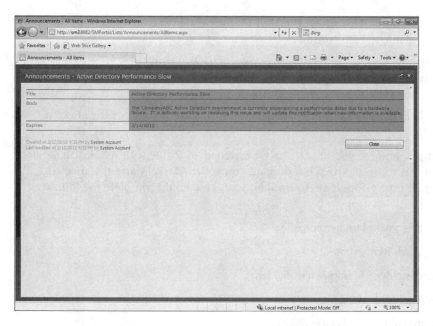

FIGURE 15.15   Service outage announcement.

NOTE

The Announcement functionality in Service Manager 2012 has changed from the previous version of Service Manager. In Service Manager 2010, it was possible to configure an announcement and expiration date from within the Service Manager console and have the announcement displayed on the Service Manager web portal. This functionality is not currently present in Service Manager 2012, but may be implemented in a future release.

Running Troubleshooting Tasks

In addition to the CMDB, Service Manager has a number of built-in tasks to help analyze incidents directly. A number of troubleshooting tasks are available to assist the analyst in analyzing and troubleshooting incidents.

The troubleshooting tasks include the following:

▶ **Ping Related Computer**—This runs a ping against affected items or related items. The task allows the analyst to select which item to ping. The results are recorded in the activity log of the incident.

▶ **Remote Desktop**—This launches an RDP session to an affected or related item.

▶ **Request User Input**—This requests user input and places the incident in a pending status.

▶ **View Alert Details**—This shows the alert that generated the incident in the
  Operations Manager Web console.

▶ **View CI Health State**—This shows the affected item's health state in the Operations
  Manager Web console.

These tasks can help the analyst quickly understand the current status of the affected
items.

By way of example, suppose you are an analyst assigned an incident IR312 Health Service
Heartbeat Failure. The affected item is a domain controller ATHENA and the affected
service is Active Directory Topology. To troubleshoot, you would complete the following
steps:

1. Launch the Service Manager console.

2. Select the Work Items space.

3. Expand the Incident Management folder.

4. Select the My Incidents folder.

5. Open the incident, in this case IR312.

6. The incident shows that the Affected Service is Active Directory Topology and the
    Affected Item is ATHENA.

7. Click the Remote Desktop link in the Tasks pane to establish an RDP session to be
    able to interact directly with the affected computer. The task prompts for which
    computer to connect to, as there might be more than one affected computer or
    related computer.

8. Then click the Ping Related Computer link in the Tasks pane to ping the affected
    item. Select the computer and click OK to ping.

> **NOTE**
>
> The ping does not show any results directly, which can be confusing. The results of the
> ping are recorded in the action log.

9. To see the results of the Ping task, go to the Action Log section of the incident. The
    action log shows that the record was assigned and that the Remote Desktop task was
    run before the Ping task.

10. Because the computer is responding to pings, click the View Alert Details link in the
    Tasks pane to show the Operations Manager alert in the Web console. After review-
    ing the alert description, close the Operations Manager Web console.

11. Then click the View CI Health State task in the Tasks pane to view the configuration item's health state in the Operations Manager Web console. Select the appropriate object, in this case ATHENA. After reviewing the health state, close the Operations Manager Web console.

12. Based on the analysis, the problem is that the Operations Manager agent is stopped. Start the agent on ATHENA to resolve the issue. The incident closes automatically when the Operations Manager alert closes.

Tasks help analysts quickly execute diagnostic and repair tasks from the Service Manager console without having to launch another tool. They also have the advantage of documenting the tasks that were executed in the action log, allowing fellow analysts to review and understand what transpired on a given incident.

> **NOTE**
>
> Custom tasks can be created in the Library space in the Tasks folder. This allows administrators to extend the task mechanism to include custom diagnostic and resolution commands.

Resolving Incidents

Resolving the incident is really resolving the incident record in Service Manager. The results of the incident analysis should be a resolved issue, which then allows the analyst to resolve the incident. Incidents can be resolved in the following ways:

- ▶ Manually by the analyst
- ▶ Automatically by the system
- ▶ By end users

The most common method of resolving incidents is done manually by an analyst. To resolve an incident manually, complete the following steps:

1. Launch the Service Manager console.

2. Select the Work Items space.

3. Expand the Incident Management folder.

4. Select the My Incidents folder.

5. Select an active incident.

6. Click the Resolve link in the Tasks pane to resolve the selected incident.

7. At the Resolve pop-up window, select a Resolution Category and document the results of the analysis in the Comments field.

> **NOTE**
>
> The Comments field automatically checks the spelling of the text, which is extremely
> helpful to ensure quality documentation of incident resolutions.

8. The incident status now shows a status of Resolved. Click OK to save the incident.

Manually resolved incidents are controlled by the analyst, so the resolution details can be
updated when the incident is resolved.

However, auto-resolved incidents present a bit of a challenge, as they do not prompt for
resolution details. An alert might auto-resolve in response to actions by the analyst, such
as when starting the Print Spooler for incident IR75 in a previous example.

To properly document the incident or update the resolution details of the incident,
complete the following steps:

1. Launch the Service Manager console.

2. Select the Work Items space.

3. Expand the Incident Management folder.

4. Select the My Incidents folder.

5. Select and edit the resolved incident that needs to have the resolution details
   updated.

6. Select the Resolution tab.

7. The Resolution Description field on the Resolution tab of the incident should be
   updated with a description of the fix, as shown in Figure 15.16.

8. Click OK to save the incident update.

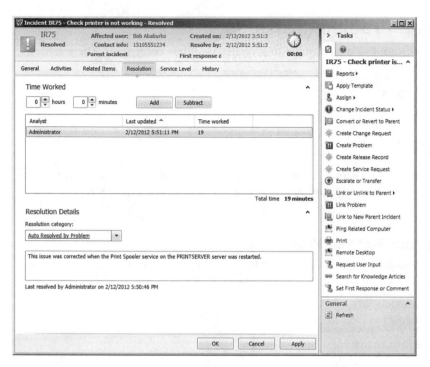

FIGURE 15.16   Resolution Details update.

Another way that incidents can be resolved is by the end users themselves. When an end user creates an incident in the Self-Service Web Portal, Service Manager tracks the user's incidents and displays them in the web portal. The end user can close his or her own incidents if the problem goes away.

To close their own incidents, end users would complete the following steps:

1. Launch the Service Manager Self-Service Web Portal.

2. In the My Recent Request section, click the View All link.

3. Select an active incident and click the Close Request button.

4. At the confirmation pop-up, click OK. The status of the incident now shows as Closed.

This gives end users the capability to close their own incidents and reduces the burden on the IT department to close unneeded incidents.

15

Configuring Problem Settings

Before working with problems, a number of settings should be configured. These settings are as follows:

- ▶ Problem ID prefix
- ▶ File attachment limits
- ▶ Priority calculation

The problem prefix and attachment limits are optional configurations. The priority calculation must be set for the proper computation of priority from the urgency and impact values.

Customizing the Problem Prefix String

By default, each problem is prefixed with the letters PR, for problem record. This can be adjusted to something different, such as PT for problem ticket or PROBLEM. The maximum number of characters is 15.

To change the problem prefix, complete the following steps:

1. Launch the Service Manager console.

2. Select the Administration space.

3. Select the Administration/Settings folder.

4. In the right pane, select the Properties of the Problem Setting object.

5. In the General section, change the Prefix field to the desired setting.

6. Click OK to save the change.

The change takes effect for all new problems. This value should only be changed if needed.

> **NOTE**
>
> The new prefix is not applied to the existing problem records, only to new records.

File Attachment Limits

File attachments to problems have built-in limiters. This is supposed to ensure that huge files or large numbers of files don't get attached to change requests and bloat the database unnecessarily. This can be a real issue if help desk personnel or end users attempt to attach 100MB data files or gigabyte installation files to change requests.

File attachments are limited by the number of attachments and the size of the attachments. The permitted ranges and the default settings are given in Table 15.3.

TABLE 15.3   Change Request File Attachment Settings

File Attachment Limits	Range	Default Setting
Maximum number of attachments	0 to 2,147,483,647	10
Maximum size (KB)	0 to 2,147,483,647	64

NOTE

The number 2,147,483,647 seems like an odd upper boundary at first. Interestingly, it is 2^31-1 and is the eighth Mersenne prime number. More important, it is the maximum value of a 32-bit signed integer, that is, the maximum value of a variable of type int. Hence, the seemingly arbitrary limit is actually a programmatic limit.

The limit on both the number of files and the size is over 2 billion. This seems excessive, especially for the maximum number of attachments, and likely isn't supportable. It future revisions, these are likely to be set to more reasonable limits.

To adjust the default file attachment settings, complete the following steps:

1. Launch the Service Manager console.

2. Select the Administration space.

3. Select the Administration/Settings folder.

4. In the right pane, select the Properties of the Problem Setting object.

5. In the General section, change the Maximum Number of Attached Files and the Maximum Size (KB) fields to the desired settings.

6. Click OK to save the changes.

The changes take effect immediately in the console and web interfaces.

NOTE

The new file attachment settings are not applied to the existing problem records; the new settings are applied only to new records or during changes to existing records.

Customizing Values for Priority Calculation

Problems are rated by priority, which is a combination of the impact and urgency of the problem. Impact and urgency are generally defined by ITIL, but the specifics are left to the organizations.

Impact is rated as low, medium, or high. It is a subjective measure of how much the problem is impacting the organization. This is frequently measured in terms of the number of users impacted or the level of impact to the organization. For example, a problem for a single end user not being able to access email would have a lower impact than a problem for all users not being able to access email.

Urgency is also rated as low, medium, or high. It is a subjective measure of how quickly the problem must be addressed. For example, a problem for a mission-critical system like email being unavailable would have a higher urgency than a problem for a non-mission-critical system like the company event web page. Even though those two systems might impact the same number of users—that is, the entire company—they are assigned different urgencies.

The default Service Manager priority gives weighting to the urgency over impact, and problem priorities are assigned, as shown in Table 15.4. The highest priority is assigned 1 and the lowest priority is assigned 9.

TABLE 15.4   Priority Assignments Table

	Impact Low	Impact Medium	Impact High
Urgency Low	9	8	7
Urgency Medium	6	5	4
Urgency High	3	2	1

These priority assignments can be changed, if needed, for consistency with other systems in the organization or to adjust the behavior of Service Manager.

To configure the priority assignments, complete the following steps:

1. Launch the Service Manager console.

2. Select the Administration space.

3. Select the Administration/Settings folder.

4. In the right pane, select the Properties of the Problem Setting object.

5. In the Priority section, use the pull-down menu to change the priorities.

NOTE

Be sure that the chosen priorities match all possible priorities in your Service Manager configuration.

6. Click OK to save the changes.

These new settings are used by Service Manager immediately.

Working with Problems

Problem records are typically created in response to several incidents. These incidents could be a group of incidents that is congruent in time or a group of incidents that is spaced out over time. Sometimes a cluster of dissimilar incidents is due to a common root cause, such as the loss of an SMTP routing server resulting in an incident about mail routing, an incident about reports not being delivered, and a Windows service failure. Sometimes there is an incident that occurs, is resolved, occurs again, and so on, which is due to the same root cause.

Problems give analysts a way to manage groups of incidents, updating and resolving them as a group. This reduces the administrative overhead and allows the easy documentation of root causes of incidents.

Creating a Problem Record

Problems can be created from scratch, but more often they are created directly from incidents. This is a natural outcome of the purpose of problems, which is to group incidents.

For example, an analyst might review the assigned incidents and find a group of two User Account Locked Out incidents (shown in Figure 15.17) related to a hacking attempt. The hacking attempt is from the same attack vector, which was a particular client machine that was infected with malware and reimaged to resolve the issue. Rather than resolve each incident separately, the analyst would rather resolve them all at once and have a problem record identifying the root cause.

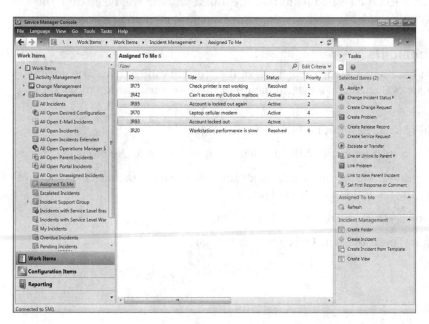

FIGURE 15.17   Cluster of incidents.

To create a problem record from the incident, complete the following steps:

1. Launch the Service Manager console.

2. Select the Work Items space.

3. Expand the Incident Management node and select the My Incidents folder.

4. Ctrl-click to select the incidents to link the problem, and then click the Create
Problem link in the Tasks pane.

5. In the Title field, enter a title for the problem such as **Hacking Attempt**.

6. Enter a Description for the problem.

7. Select the Assigned To analyst.

8. Select a Category, Impact, and Urgency.

9. Note that the Affected Items will be populated automatically from the incidents that
were selected when the problem was created.

10. Click the Related Items tab to see the linked incidents.

11. Click OK to create the problem.

The problem, PR85 in this example, is now created and the affected items and related
incidents are automatically linked. To see that the problem has been linked, open one of
the incidents and select the Related Items tab. The linked problem will be listed in the
Work Items section.

Analyzing Problems

Once a problem has been created, the analysis of the problem can be done. The underlying incidents are evaluated and a determination of the appropriate action to take is
made.

Problems can have detailed status notes, in several categories:

▶ **Error**—This is the root cause of the incidents that are linked to the problem.

▶ **Workarounds**—These are the workarounds to allow resolving the incidents, but not
necessarily the resolution of the problem.

▶ **Review Notes**—These are notes on the problem.

▶ **Resolution**—This is the actual resolution of the problem.

This provides overarching documentation of the root cause, known errors, known workarounds, and the long-term resolution to the problem.

In reality, most of the analysis is done at the incident level. Based on that analysis, the problem root cause and solution are developed. The problem serves as mainly an organizing element.

For the problem created in the sample Hacking Attempt, the following steps to analyze the problem would be followed:

1. Launch the Service Manager console.

2. Select the Work Items space.

3. Expand the Problem Management node and select the My Problems folder.

4. Select the PR85 Hacking Attempt problem and click the Edit link in the Tasks pane.

5. The user's workstation was a related item, so select the Related Items tab and click Add in the Configuration Items: Computers, Services, and People section.

6. Select the WIN7-1 computer, click Add, and then click OK to add the workstation to the related items.

7. To update the status, select the Resolution tab.

8. In the Error Description field, enter a description of the hacking attempt.

9. In the Workarounds field, enter a description of any workarounds. In this case, instructing users not to open email attachments from unknown senders is the main workaround.

10. In the Review Notes field, enter any notes, as shown in Figure 15.18.

11. Click OK to save the problem updates.

The problem is now documented, so when future incidents of the same type are linked, the analysts can review the notes.

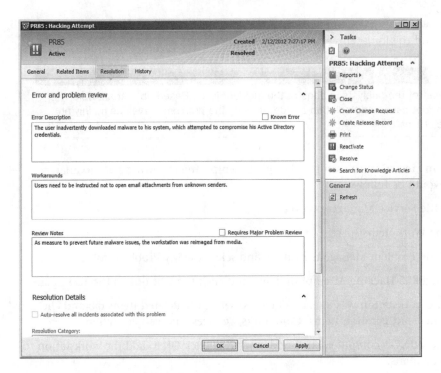

FIGURE 15.18   Problem analysis and documentation.

Resolving Problems

Once the underlying root cause of the problem has been identified and addressed, the
problem needs to be resolved.

To resolve a problem, complete the following steps:

1. Launch the Service Manager console.

2. Select the Work Items space.

3. Expand the Problem Management node and select the My Problems folder.

4. Select the PR85 Hacking Attempt problem and click the Edit link in the Tasks pane.

5. Click the Resolve link in the Tasks pane.

6. Select the Resolution tab.

7. In the Resolution Details section, check the Auto-resolve All Incidents with This
   Problem check box.

8. Select a Resolution Category.

9. Enter a Resolution Description, in this case, `Malware Issue - Workstation Reimaged`.

10. Click OK to save the edits to the problem.

After saving the problem, the incidents are automatically resolved as well. This saves the analyst the effort of having to update each incident individually.

Incident and Problem Reports

Reports help analysts, administrators, and management view and understand what is happening with incident and problem work items. This is useful to track the ebb and flow of issues, as well as understand how well the IT department is handling the workload.

The default reports are included in the report library management packs, specifically:

▸ Incident Management Report Library

▸ Problem Management Report Library

The reports pull data from the data warehouse. The data warehouse must be installed, the Service Manager management group must be registered, and the Extraction, Transformation, and Loading (ETL) jobs must be run for data to be available for reports.

Service Manager Report Controls

The Service Manager reports are very sophisticated, although not many reports are included in the management packs. The reports are very flexible and each report has the following options:

▸ **Parameter Control Header**—Allows the report parameters to be adjusted.

▸ **Print**—Allows the report to be printed.

▸ **Print Layout**—Shows the report onscreen as it will print. This addresses a really annoying problem where the report looks one way onscreen and another way when printed.

▸ **Page Setup**—This allows the page size to be adjusted to change how the report paginates when printed.

▸ **Export**—Allows the report to be exported to a file. This supports a variety of formats such as XML, CSV, PDF, MHTML, Excel, TIFF, and Word.

The tasks allow reports to be generated and reports to be saved. Report tasks include the following:

▸ **Run Report**—This generates the report onscreen with the current parameters.

▸ **Save as Favorite Report**—This allows a report with specific parameters to be saved to the Favorite Reports folder.

▶ **Save as Linked Report**—This allows a report with the specific parameters to be
saved in a management pack for exporting.

The reports all include the parameter control header to filter the results as needed. The
options in the parameter control header vary depending on the report requirements.
When the parameters for a particular report are adjusted, the report can be saved in the
Favorite Reports folder to generate it quickly in the future with all the adjusted parameters.

NOTE

At present, there is no ability to schedule the Service Manager reports. This will likely
be included in future releases.

Exploring Incident Reports

Five different incident reports are included with the Incident Management Report Library.
These incident reports allow analysts to view incidents in aggregate and allow management to evaluate analyst performance and service management performance.

The incident management reports are as follows:

▶ **Incident Analyst report**—This report shows a summary of the analyst performance
in working on and resolving incidents.

▶ **Incident Detail report**—This report shows the details of a single incident.

▶ **Incident KPI Trend report**—This report shows the incident key performance indicator (KPI) trends.

▶ **Incident Resolution report**—This report shows a graphical analysis of incidents not
meeting the target resolution times.

▶ **List of Incidents report**—This report shows a list of incidents in tabular form. Each
incident includes a link to the Incident Detail report.

To generate the List of Incidents report, complete the following steps:

1. Launch the Service Manager console.

2. Select the Reporting space.

3. Expand the Reports node.

4. Select the Incident Management folder.

5. In the Incident Management folder, select the List of Incidents report and click the
Run Report task in the Tasks pane.

6. The report opens with a default set of parameters, which include all incidents in the past month. The parameters can be modified if needed and the report can be generated using the Run Report task, as shown in Figure 15.19.

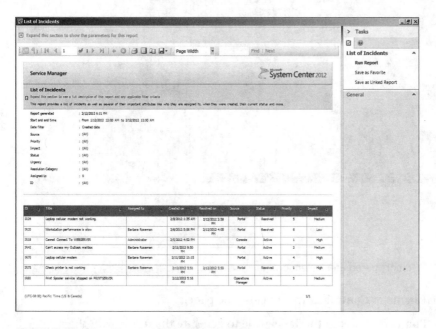

FIGURE 15.19   The List of Incidents report.

7. Any of the parameters are available for filtering the report. Click the Source pull-down menu to show the different options. Click the Source pull-down menu again to close it.

NOTE

Each of the parameters with defined values allow the (All) option or selection from a prepopulated drop-down menu. This allows multiple values to be selected without having to guess what the possible values are.

8. Select Add in the Assigned To section and pick an analyst. This filters the report by the selected analyst, in this case "Barbara."

9. Select the Status pull-down menu, uncheck the (All) selection, and check the Active selection. This filters the report to show only Active incidents. The results should look similar to Figure 15.20.

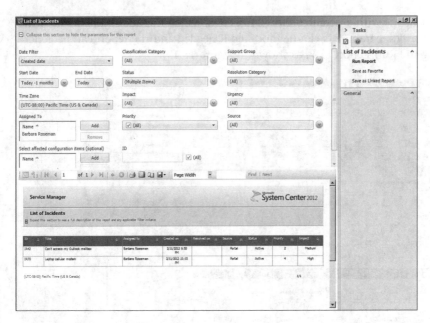

FIGURE 15.20   Report parameter selection.

10. Click the Parameter Control Header to close the panel.

11. Click the Run Report task in the Tasks pane to generate the report with the new parameters. The report shows those incidents that meet the parameters, specifically those active incidents assigned to the selected analyst.

The report is generated onscreen, but might be needed in the future. Rather than duplicate the parameter selections each time the report is needed, the report can be saved to the Favorite Reports to save time in the future.

To save the report, complete the following steps:

1. With the desired report onscreen, click the Save As Favorite Report task in the Tasks pane.

2. Enter a name for the favorite report, in this example **Active Incidents for Barbara**.

3. Click OK to save the report.

4. Close the current report.

5. In the Service Manager console, select the Reporting space.

6. Select the Favorite Reports folder.

7. Select the previously created favorite, in this example, "Active Incidents for Barbara."

8. Click the Run Report task in the Tasks pane.

9. Verify that the report generated with the correct parameters.

Saving to the Favorite Reports folder can save a lot of time when customizing reports. Individual incidents can be drilled into by clicking on the incident ID in the list. This launches the Incident Detail report for that incident record. This is helpful for investigating individual incidents without having to go back to the console.

In addition to the list and detail incident reports, two analysis reports provide insight on how analysts are performing and on how the organization is performing.

To evaluate analyst performance, generate the Incident Analyst report. To generate this report, complete the following steps:

1. Launch the Service Manager console.

2. Select the Reporting space.

3. Expand the Reports node.

4. Select the Incident Management folder.

5. In the Incident Management folder, select the Incident Analyst report and click the Run Report task in the Tasks pane.

6. The report opens with a default set of parameters, which include data from the past month. The parameters can be modified if needed and the report can be generated using the Run Report task, as shown in Figure 15.21.

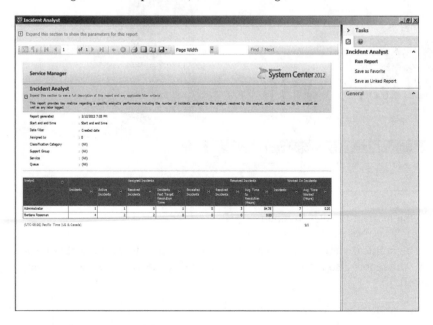

FIGURE 15.21   Incident Analyst report.

The report includes a detailed table of stats for each analyst. The report shows an uptick in resolution times that should probably be investigated.

To instigate analyst resolution performance, generate the Incident Resolution report. To generate this report, complete the following steps:

1. Launch the Service Manager console.

2. Select the Reporting space.

3. Expand the Reports node.

4. Select the Incident Management folder.

5. In the Incident Management folder, select the Incident Resolution report and click the Run Report task in the Tasks pane.

6. The report opens with a default set of parameters, which include data from the past month. The parameters can be modified if needed and the report can be generated using the Run Report task, as shown in Figure 15.22.

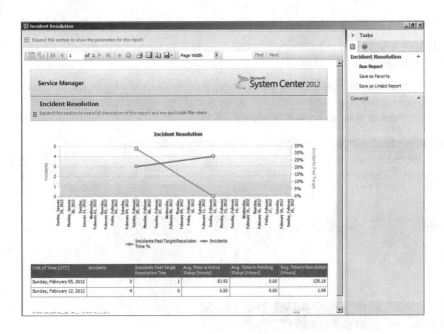

FIGURE 15.22   The Incident Resolution report.

The report shows a graphical view of the organization performance toward meeting resolution time goals. The report also includes a table with detailed statistics by week during the reporting period.

Exploring Problem Reports

Three problem reports are included with the Problem Management Report Library. The reports basically allow analysts to get lists and details of problems.

The problem management reports are as follows:

▶ **List of Problems**—This report shows a list of problems in tabular form. Each problem includes a link to the Problem Details report.

▶ **Configuration Items (CIs) with Most Incidents**—This report shows a list of the CI with the most incidents associated with them. This is useful for tracking down problem hardware or users.

▶ **Problem Details**—This report shows the details of a single problem.

To generate the List of Problems report, complete the following steps:

1. Launch the Service Manager console.

2. Select the Reporting space.

3. Expand the Reports node.

4. Select the Problem Management folder.

5. In the Problem Management folder, select the List of Problems report and click the Run Report task in the Tasks pane.

6. The report opens with a default set of parameters, which include data from the past month. The parameters can be modified if needed and the report can be generated using the Run Report task.

Individual problems can be drilled into by clicking on the problem ID in the list. This launches the Problem Detail report for that problem record. This is helpful for investigating individual problems without having to go back to the console.

Summary

System Center Service Manager 2012 is a valuable tool for managing and resolving IT systems failures. The Service Manager service management process allows incidents to be generated from a wide variety of sources, then provides tools for the analysts to rapidly analyze and resolve the issues.

The Service Manager platform also provides key information that allows analysts to spot incident trends, group those into problems to track and resolve the root causes, and ensure that the information is recorded in the organization's CMDB for future reference.

Finally, Service Manager allows management to set target goals, and then provides reports that evaluate the performance of individual analysts and the service desk as a whole against those targets to ensure that the IT department is meeting service levels.

Best Practices

The following are best practices from this chapter:

▶ Develop policies and procedures for processing incidents and problems. These policies and procedures should leverage Service Manager capabilities as much as possible.

▶ Deploy the Self-Service Web Portal to allow end users to create their own incident requests and close those requests to reduce the help desk workload.

▶ Deploy the Self-Service Web Portal to allow end users to view announcements.

▶ Configure resolution times to allow incident resolution times to be measured against target goals.

▶ Create a custom Operations Manager incident template to complete incidents generated from alerts.

▶ Configure the Operations Manager Web console setting to allow analysts to use the tasks to get Operations Manager health state and alert details from the Service Manager console.

▶ Don't adjust the Priority Calculation setting unless required for interoperability with other systems.

▶ Configure the Inbound Email setting to allow incidents to be easily generated from emails to the help desk.

▶ Link clusters of incidents to a single problem to ease the administrative burden of managing incidents.

▶ Save reports with adjusted parameters to the Favorite Reports folder to easily generate custom reports.

▶ Generate the Incident Analyst report to analyze how analysts are performing.

▶ Generate the Incident Resolution report to analyze how the service management is performing.

Using Service Manager 2012 for Service Offerings and Change Control Management

IN THIS CHAPTER

▶ Service Manager 2012 and the Infrastructure Optimization Model

▶ Service Offerings and Request Offerings in SM 2012

▶ Release Management in SM 2012

▶ Change Requests and Activities

▶ Configuring Change Settings

▶ Change Management Templates and Workflows

▶ Initiating Change Requests

▶ Working with and Approving Change Requests

▶ Implementing Change Requests

▶ Managing Configuration Items

▶ Working with Change, Activity, and Configuration Management

Information technology (IT) systems change.

As Winston Churchill put it, "To improve is to change; to be perfect is to change often."

Because change is unavoidable, it is important to have a process for managing those changes to minimize the drawbacks and discomforts. ITIL defines the change management process to accomplish this. Service Manager 2012 implements and automates the change management process.

Service Manager 2012 and the Infrastructure Optimization Model

One of the key concepts that Microsoft uses to frame the discussion around IT process management is infrastructure optimization. Microsoft's concept of infrastructure optimization for information technology is built around four levels of optimization: basic, standardized, rationalized, and dynamic. Each of these optimization levels has different characteristics, as described in Table 16.1.

TABLE 16.1   Infrastructure Optimization (IO) Levels

Infrastructure Optimization Level	Description
Basic	Manual, localized processes; minimal central control; reactive incident management; and unenforced IT policies and standards
Standardized	Unified directory service; policies for desktop and server management; standard desktop images and applications; defined support services; limited security tools; and policy compliance automation
Rationalized	Policy-based identity management; automated OS and application deployment; defined service levels and release management; established security compliance levels; and automated audit tools
Dynamic	Automated account provisioning; virtual workstation infrastructure with dynamic workload shifting; automated threat management and mitigation across clients and servers; improvement of service levels, business continuity and availability; and automated security policy verification

Infrastructure optimization leverages concepts from Microsoft Operations Framework (MOF), ITIL, and Control Objectives for Information and Related Technology (COBIT) to develop and maintain a business-centered approach to IT, which focuses on efficiency, responsiveness, and results. Service Manager 2012 supports these and other business goals through the use of automation interfaces (such as .NET and PowerShell), centralized data storage in the configuration management database and IT data warehouse, and integration with other System Center products such as Virtual Machine Manager (VMM) and Orchestrator to provide end-to-end process management. This chapter focuses on demonstrating the capabilities of Service Manager 2012 to support business goals by delivering **service offerings** and performing **change-control management**.

Service Offerings and Request Offerings in SM 2012

In Service Manager 2012, service offerings define the high-level services that the IT organization will deliver to its users. Examples of service offerings may include access services, desktop services, or cloud services. Because each organization has different requirements, service offerings are fully customizable and can be modified to address individual business needs. Each service offering can include one or more request offerings. A request offering is a specific type of request that IT wants to offer to the business. For example, a request

CHAPTER 17

System Center Orchestrator 2012 Design, Planning, and Implementation

IN THIS CHAPTER

▶ Overview of System Center Orchestrator

▶ History of System Center Orchestrator

▶ System Center Orchestrator 2012 Installation Prerequisites

▶ Orchestrator Security Planning

▶ Installing System Center Orchestrator 2012 on a Single Server

▶ Installing System Center Orchestrator 2012 on Separate Systems

▶ Additional Tasks Following Orchestrator Installation

▶ Getting Familiar with the Orchestrator 2012 Management Consoles

▶ Installing Integration Packs

▶ Designing and Using Runbooks

▶ Runbook Permissions

▶ Best Practices

The daily workload of systems administrators is typically filled with routine tasks and procedures that are required to maintain the health of the computing environment they are responsible for. These daily activities commonly require administrative controls that are spread across a variety of systems. Although there may be individual tasks or subtasks that are automated, the entire series of tasks required to complete a job, such as setting up a new employee with network access, is typically not automated. This results in a significant amount of administrative overhead for IT operations, and is a challenge that increases exponentially with the size of the network. It is this very situation that System Center Orchestrator 2012 was designed for. Orchestrator 2012 can be used to tie disparate tasks and procedures together and automate processes across multiple platforms, greatly reducing administration and increasing efficiency of IT operations.

Overview of System Center Orchestrator

System Center Orchestrator is a workflow management solution that allows you to automate the creation, monitoring, and deployment of resources in a data center. Although the level of automation provided by Orchestrator can be addressed by building complex scripts, Orchestrator offers a graphical interface to greatly simplify the process of automating even complex systems administration tasks

without requiring scripting knowledge. A simple example of the power of Orchestrator is
the common requirement to notify personnel and then take some action to remediate an
issue based on an alert that appears in the Windows event log. With Orchestrator, it is
possible to simply drag and drop an event monitoring item onto the Orchestration
console, configure that event to send an email notification to the appropriate personnel,
and then connect the item to another item that takes a specific action, such as restarting
a service. This automated sequence can be configured in minutes, without requiring any
scripting knowledge.

Business Needs Addressed by System Center Orchestrator

The automation provided by System Center Orchestrator has the power to greatly increase
the efficiency of data center operations. Instead of spending a large portion of time
performing routine but time-consuming operations across multiple platforms on a daily
basis, Orchestrator allows IT personnel to consolidate repetitive manual tasks in an efficient, reliable, and timely manner, and allows more time to be spent proactively planning
the network to meet changing business requirements. Just as manufacturing companies
use assembly lines to automate common and repeatable tasks, Orchestrator allows IT to
adopt this same efficiency in the data center.

Some of the main business needs addressed by System Center Orchestrator 2012 include
the following:

▶ **Custom automation**—Orchestrator provides tools to build, test, debug, deploy, and
  manage automation of systems administration tasks. These automated procedures,
  called runbooks, can function independently or can spawn other runbooks. Each
  orchestrator deployment provides a variety of standard monitors, tasks, and
  runbook controls that can be used to integrate a wide range of system processes. In
  addition, a wide variety of actions can be triggered based on defined criteria, including the creation of emails, alerts, log files, accounts, and more.

▶ **Cross-platform integration**—Most data center networks today are heterogeneous,
  involving a variety of hardware, operating systems, and other platforms. Managing
  these disparate systems on a daily basis can, therefore, be both challenging and time
  consuming for the systems administrator. Orchestrator not only integrates with the
  other System Center products, but also many other Microsoft and non-Microsoft
  products to enable interoperability across multiple platforms. The capabilities of
  Orchestrator are extended through the use of Integration Packs, which provide additional functionality and allow cross-platform automation.

▶ **End-to-end orchestration**—System Center Orchestrator 2012 provides tools for
  orchestration that allow software, hardware, and manual processes to be combined
  to form a seamless solution. Orchestrator also integrates seamlessly with other
  System Center products to integrate administrative tasks from start to finish.

Orchestrator Components

The following are the components that are included in all basic deployments of System Center Orchestrator:

- ▶ **Runbook Designer**—The tool used to build, edit, and manage Orchestrator runbooks.

- ▶ **Orchestration database**—A Microsoft SQL Server database that contains all of the deployed runbooks, log files, and configuration data for Orchestrator.

- ▶ **Management server**—The system that acts as a communication layer between the Runbook Designer and the orchestration database.

- ▶ **Runbook server**—The system where an instance of a runbook is run. For larger deployments, it is possible to deploy multiple runbook servers to increase capacity and redundancy.

- ▶ **Runbook tester**—A runtime tool used to test runbooks developed in the Runbook Designer.

- ▶ **Orchestration console**—A web-based management console used to start or stop runbooks and view real-time status.

- ▶ **Orchestrator web service**—A Representational State Transfer (REST)–based service that enables custom applications to connect to Orchestrator to start and stop runbooks and retrieve information about operations using custom applications or scripts. The Orchestration console uses the Orchestrator web service to interact with Orchestrator.

- ▶ **Deployment Manager**—A tool used to deploy Integration Packs to systems where the runbook server or Runbook Designer is installed.

Several methods can be used to extend the basic functionality of Orchestrator. The following are the components that are available to extend the functionality provided by a standard Orchestrator installation:

- ▶ **Integration Packs (IPs)**—A collection of custom activities specific to a product or technology. In addition to the Integration Packs provided by Microsoft, a number of third-party companies provide Integration Packs that enable interaction with their product from an Orchestrator runbook.

- ▶ **Orchestration Integration Toolkit**—A collection of tools that extends the libraries of activities beyond the standard activities and Integration Packs. The Integration Toolkit contains wizard-based tools that can be used to create new Orchestrator activities and Integration Packs and can be used by developers to create Integration Packs from custom activities built using the Orchestrator software development kit (SDK).

History of System Center Orchestrator

System Center Orchestrator was originally a third-party product named Opalis, which Microsoft bought in 2009. The previous version of the product was named System Center Opalis Integration Server 6.3. With the 2012 version of the product, it is being rebranded as System Center Orchestrator for the first time. Although the product has a different look and feel than the previous version, the underlying engine is the same, such that policies built using Opalis Integration Server can be imported into Orchestrator.

Prior to Microsoft acquiring Opalis, the product already featured integration with prior versions of Operations Manager, Configuration Manager, and Virtual Machine Manager. With the release of the 6.3 version, Microsoft expanded that list to also include current versions of Data Protection Manager and Service Manager. With the 2012 release, Microsoft is again providing Integration Packs for the entire System Center product suite, including the 2012 versions of the products as well as prior versions.

Among the changes that prior users of the Opalis product can expect to see are the following:

▶ The management console, formerly based on Java, has been rewritten using Microsoft Silverlight.

▶ The web service, formerly based on Java, has been replaced by an OData web service.

▶ Standard activities (formerly known as foundation objects) have been updated, along with the icons for these objects.

▶ The security model has been updated to allow centralized security management.

▶ Windows Server 2008 R2 is now the only supported OS, and SQL Server 2008 R2 is the only supported database engine (support for Oracle database engine has been removed).

▶ The installation no longer requires the download of over a dozen separate, specific versions of Java packages from separate websites.

System Center Orchestrator 2012 Installation Prerequisites

The following sections detail the hardware and software prerequisites that must be in place to prepare for the installation of System Center Orchestrator 2012.

Supported Operating Systems

The only operating system supported for System Center Orchestrator 2012 is Windows Server 2008 R2. The only exception to this is the Runbook Designer, which can be installed on a Windows 7 system if installed as an individual feature. Windows Server 2008 R2 is 64-bit only; therefore, Orchestrator 2012 is only available as a 64-bit product.

Although not required, it is recommended that the Orchestrator 2012 server be joined to an Active Directory (AD) domain. However, Orchestrator is not supported for installation on a domain controller system.

Beyond the base operating system, additional components are required to be installed on the server that will be running Orchestrator 2012. The additional components required include the following:

▶ Internet Information Services (IIS)

▶ Microsoft .NET Framework v3.5 SP1

▶ Microsoft .NET Framework v4

▶ Microsoft Silverlight v4

> **NOTE**
>
> The Orchestrator 2012 installation process checks to see if the additional components are present on the target server, and will automatically install most of the required components if necessary. The only component that must be installed manually prior to installing Orchestrator is Microsoft .NET Framework v4. The Silverlight component will be installed when the Orchestration console is started for the first time if it is not already installed.

Supported Versions of SQL Server

System Center Orchestrator 2012 requires a SQL server to host runbooks, log files, and configuration data. Orchestrator 2012 supports only the 2008 R2 version of Microsoft SQL Server. Only the basic features of the Database Engine Service are required. The installation wizard automatically selects SQL_Latin1_General_CP1_CI_AS as the default collation to create the Orchestration database when the database is installed using the Orchestrator installation wizard. If the database is installed ahead of Orchestrator installation, this is the collation that should be used. Also, the installing user requires at least dbcreator rights on the SQL Server instance.

Hardware Requirements for a Single-Server Configuration

A System Center Orchestrator 2012 server running all four of the required components (management server, Orchestrator web service, Runbook Designer, and runbook server) should have the following minimum hardware: 2GB of RAM, a dual-core Intel 2.1Ghz or faster processor, and at least 200MB of available disk space.

Hardware and Software Requirements for a Multiserver Configuration

If the Orchestrator 2012 server components will be split across multiple systems, then each system has the same hardware requirements as the single-server configuration detailed above. Specifically, each system should have the following minimum hardware:

17

2GB of RAM, a dual-core Intel 2.1Ghz or faster processor, and at least 200MB of available disk space.

The management server, runbook server, and Orchestrator web services components must be installed on a Windows Server 2008 R2 system. If the Runbook Designer will be installed on a separate system, the following operating systems are supported: Windows Server 2008 R2 or Windows 7 (32-bit or 64-bit).

High-Availability Considerations

Several options are available to meet high-availability requirements for the various components of an Orchestrator installation. For example, the following high-availability configurations are supported:

▶ The Orchestration database can be deployed on a SQL Server cluster with a minimum of two nodes.

▶ The Orchestrator web service can be installed on multiple IIS web servers and configured for load balancing to meet both availability and capacity requirements.

▶ To configure high availability for the runbook server, a minimum of two runbook servers should be deployed.

NOTE

The runbook server is not designed to run on a cluster node, and this is not required. Rather, if one runbook server is unavailable, a particular runbook can simply be run on another server. For the management server, only one instance is supported per Orchestrator deployment. However, the management server does not need to be available for runbook servers or runbooks to function. If the management server is unavailable, the Runbook Designer cannot be used to publish, start, monitor, or stop runbooks. However, in this situation, the Orchestration console can be used to start, monitor, and stop runbooks.

Orchestrator Security Planning

Several areas of security must be considered prior to a System Center Orchestrator 2012 installation, as detailed in the following sections.

Service Accounts

One service account is required to meet Orchestrator security requirements, and is used to run the following Orchestrator services: Orchestrator Management Service, Orchestrator Runbook Service, and Orchestrator Runbook Server Monitor Service. The service account is specified during the installation of Orchestrator, and, therefore, needs to be created prior to installation. Although it is possible to use a local account on the management server if the Orchestration database is installed locally, this configuration is not recommended, as it may not allow access to other network resources. For example, if the Orchestration database is installed separately from the management server, the service account must be a domain account to access the database server.

The service account does not require administrative access within the domain, but must be a member of the local administrators group on the server hosting the management server and runbook server components. The service account must also have the rights to log on to the management server as a service, and must be a member of the Microsoft.System.Center.Orchestrator.Admins role in the Orchestration database (the account is automatically granted this database role during installation).

There is an instance of the Runbook Service that runs on each runbook server installed in the environment. On the management server, the same service account is used by default for both the Orchestrator Management Service and the Orchestrator Runbook Service. If additional runbook servers are installed, different service accounts can be used for each of these; however, this is not a requirement. If separate service accounts are used, these should be domain accounts so that they can be granted access to resources on other systems. By default, all activities in a runbook run under the service account of the runbook server on which they are running.

Security Groups

Full administrative access to Orchestrator is granted through a security group, which is referred to as the Orchestrator Users group within Orchestrator; however, it actually consists of either a local security group or an Active Directory security group that has been chosen for this purpose. User accounts that are added to the group are granted permission to use the Runbook Designer and Deployment Manager tools. The security group used for this purpose is specified during the Orchestrator installation process and can either be an AD security group or a local group on the system where Orchestrator is installed. If the Orchestration console is not installed on the same system as the management server, then an Active Directory security group must be used for this. If the components are installed on the same server, then a local security group may be specified. With a single-server Orchestrator deployment, the decision of whether to use a local or domain group is dependent on the preference of where the group should be managed, either locally on the system or centralized using Active Directory.

If an Active Directory security group will be used, the group must be created prior to the Orchestrator installation. If a local security group is to be used, the group can be created prior to the Orchestrator installation; however, if an existing group is not specified, then the installer will automatically create a local security group named OrchestratorUsersGroup. Regardless of the choice of security group, the Orchestrator installer process will add the account of the user installing the software as the first member of the group.

17

> **NOTE**
>
> It is not necessary to add a user to the Orchestrator Users group to grant access to
> view and execute runbooks from the Orchestration console. For example, a member of
> the Orchestrator Users group can grant access to another user to view and run, but
> not create, runbooks. Users that only use the Orchestration console in this limited
> capacity are referred to as operators.

Firewall Requirements

An additional security consideration is the firewall port requirements to allow communication between the various Orchestrator components. This is important not only when Orchestrator is installed on multiple servers in an environment, but also for communication between client components (Runbook Designer or a client browser) and the corresponding back-end server components (management server and Orchestrator web service). Following are the default firewall ports that must be opened to allow communication between Orchestrator components (note that several of these ports can also be configured to alternate values during the installation of the various components, if desired):

▶ For Runbook Designer installations on a management station, TCP ports 135 and 1024-65535 must be open between the Runbook Designer (source) and the management server (target) to allow management via Distributed Component Object Model (DCOM).

▶ When the Orchestration database is installed as a separate SQL instance, TCP port 1433 must be open between systems running management server, runbook server, and Orchestrator web service features (sources) and the SQL system hosting the Orchestration database (target).

▶ For client web browser connections to the Orchestration console, TCP ports 81 and 82 must be open between the web browser (source) and the Orchestrator web service (target).

▶ Additional ports may need to be opened to allow full functionality of the activities included in the various Integration Packs that are available. This information is typically documented within the corresponding Integration Pack guide.

Installing System Center Orchestrator 2012 on a Single Server

Although the System Center Orchestrator 2012 components can be installed on multiple servers, the product is commonly installed using a single server, including the management server, Orchestrator web service, Runbook Designer, and runbook server. The following sections detail the procedures required to install Orchestrator 2012 on a single server.

Preparing the System Center Orchestrator 2012 Server

Before the installation of Orchestrator can be performed, the base Windows Server 2008 R2 operating system needs to be installed.

> **NOTE**
>
> Although System Center Orchestrator 2012 must be installed on a Windows Server 2008 R2 server, the Active Directory version can be 2003 or 2008. The Windows Server 2008 R2 server running Orchestrator is simply a member server in Active Directory, so earlier releases of Active Directory are supported.

When installing the base Windows operating system, an administrator is not required to install the various subcomponents needed for Orchestrator 2012 that are included with the operating system, such as .NET Framework 3.5 SP1 and IIS. These will be enabled and/or installed automatically during the installation of Orchestrator. However, .NET Framework 4 is not included in the operating system, and must be installed prior to installing Orchestrator. Once the Windows operating system is installed, configure the server with a name and IP address, and join the Active Directory domain. Also make sure to download the latest OS patches and updates.

Preparing the SQL Database Instance

Prior to installing Orchestrator, Microsoft SQL Server 2008 R2 must first be installed on the system to serve as host for the Orchestration database. The full version of SQL Server 2008 R2 is the only supported version, although either Standard or Enterprise Editions can be used. The only SQL Server component required to support Orchestrator is the SQL Server Database Engine Services. It is not required to install the Orchestration database before Orchestrator installation, as the Orchestrator installation wizard can install the database and assign the required permissions.

> **NOTE**
>
> Microsoft .NET Framework 3.5 SP1 is also a prerequisite for SQL Server 2008 R2. Therefore, on a single-system Orchestrator deployment, this Orchestrator prerequisite will actually be installed automatically as part of the SQL 2008 R2 installation process, if it is not installed already. Microsoft .NET Framework 4 must still be installed manually prior to the installation of Orchestrator.

Running the System Center Orchestrator Installation

After meeting all of the hardware, operating system, and software requirements, the next step in your deployment is to execute the Orchestrator Setup Wizard to perform a basic Orchestrator installation on a single system. To start the installation, log on to the Orchestrator server using an account that is a member of the local administrators group. Then initiate the Orchestrator Setup Wizard by executing the startup file (SetupOrchestrator.exe) from the installation media or an ISO file, or use a copy of the setup files from a shared network location.

Once the wizard has started, use the following steps to perform the installation:

1. From the System Center Orchestrator 2012 Setup screen, shown in Figure 17.1, click on Install.

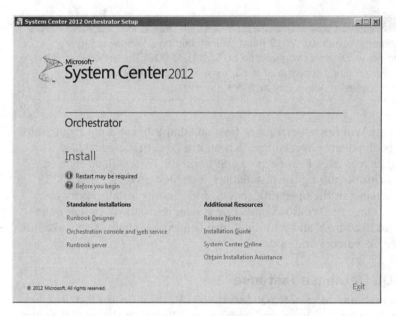

FIGURE 17.1   Main setup screen for Orchestrator 2012.

2. For product registration, enter in your Name, Organization Name, and a Product Key, and click Next.

3. Read the terms of the licensing agreement, and if you agree to the terms, select the I Accept the License Terms option, and click Next.

4. At the Select Features to Install screen, select the components you want to install. At a minimum, the Management Server option will always be installed and is, therefore, automatically selected. The other options are selected by default, but you could choose to *not* install the Runbook Server, Orchestration Console and Web Service, and the Runbook Designer components on this same system by unchecking any of these options. For a single-server configuration, keep all the options selected and click Next.

5. The system begins a process of checking for additional requirements and prerequisites. If your system does not meet the basic requirements for the installation of Orchestrator 2012 (such as not enough memory, not enough disk space, or missing software prerequisites), you are prompted to fix the problem.

6. If your system passes the basic requirements but IIS is not installed, you are prompted to enable the IIS role, as shown in Figure 17.2. Select the Enable IIS Role option button to install IIS on the system and click Next.

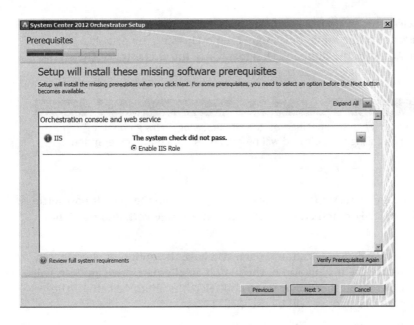

FIGURE 17.2   Choosing to install required components of Orchestrator on the system.

If IIS was missing and was installed, click Next to continue.

7. At the Configure the Service Account screen, enter the username and password of the service account previously created, and use the drop-down menu to select the Active Directory domain of the service account. Once the credentials have been entered, click Test to validate the credentials. Once the credentials have been accepted, click Next to continue.

8. At the Configure the Database Server screen, enter the name of the SQL server that will be used to host the Orchestration database in the Server field. If the SQL instance is a named instance as opposed to the default instance, this can also be specified using the format server\instance. Because this is a single-server Orchestrator installation, simply enter the hostname of the local server, keeping the default Port setting of 1433 and the default Authentication Credentials option of Windows Authentication. Once the server name has been entered, click Next to continue.

9. At the Configure the Database screen, keep the default Database option of New Database. If desired, the database name can be changed from the default name of Orchestrator. Once the database name has been specified, click Next.

10. At the Configure Orchestrator Users Group screen, a local security group named OrchestratorUsersGroup is specified by default. If a local or Active Directory security group has been created in advance to be used as the Orchestrator Users group, click

Browse and select this group instead. If the members of this group will be connecting to this instance of the Runbook Designer remotely, keep the default selection of Grant Remote Access to the Runbook Designer. Once the Orchestrator Users group has been configured, click Next to continue.

> **NOTE**
>
> Regardless of the security group specified as the Orchestrator Users group, the account of the user installing the software will be added as the first member of the group.

11. At the Configure the Ports for the Web Services screen, keep the default port settings of 81 for Web Service Port and 82 for Orchestration Console Port, and then click Next.

12. At the Select the Installation Location screen, you have the option of choosing an alternate location for the installation of the files. If an alternate drive location will be used, click Browse, and then navigate to and select the alternate path. If the default location on the C: drive will be used, click Next.

13. At the Microsoft Update screen, select the On option to use Microsoft Update to automatically check for updates to the OS as well as Orchestrator software, or select the Off option to prevent automatic updates. Once the desired Microsoft Update option has been selected, click Next to continue.

14. At the Help Improve Microsoft System Center Orchestrator screen, options are presented for participation in the Customer Experience Improvement Program, as well as Error Reporting, which is used to automatically send program error reports to Microsoft. For Error Reporting, it is also possible to queue the reports such that these can be sent manually on a periodic basis by the administrator. After choosing the desired level of participation, click Next to continue.

15. At the Installation Summary screen, review the summary of the choices made for installation, and click Install to begin the installation of Orchestrator 2012.

16. Once the installation of the software has been completed, a summary of the components installed is shown, similar to what is shown in Figure 17.3. Review the list to confirm everything was successfully installed, and then click Close.

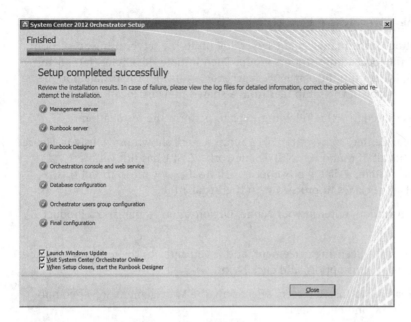

FIGURE 17.3   Summary of the installation status of Orchestrator.

Installing System Center Orchestrator 2012 on Separate Systems

In larger environments, it might be necessary to install individual Orchestrator features onto separate systems. For example, to meet performance requirements, the management server, the runbook server, and the Orchestrator web service can be installed individually. Also, installing the Runbook Designer onto multiple systems can be helpful for management of Orchestrator when several administrators are managing the Orchestrator environment. The procedures in the following sections can be used to install these individual Orchestrator features onto separate systems.

Preparing a Server for Installation of an Orchestrator Feature

The tasks required to prepare a server for the installation of the management server, the runbook server, and the Orchestrator web service are similar to the tasks required to prepare a server for installation of all of the components onto a single server, as described previously. The Windows Server 2008 R2 operating system must first be installed, along with the applicable patches. Prior to installing the management server, a SQL Server 2008 R2 system must be prepared to serve as host for the Orchestration database, and the Orchestrator service account must be created. For the Orchestrator web service, Microsoft .NET Framework 4 must be installed prior to the Orchestrator installation. Once these requirements are met and the system has been prepared for installation, the procedures in the following sections can be used to install these individual Orchestrator features onto separate systems.

17

Installing the Management Server

To start the installation of the management server, log on to the server using an account that is a member of the local administrators group. Then initiate the Orchestrator Setup Wizard by executing the startup file (SetupOrchestrator.exe) from the installation media or an ISO file, or use a copy of the setup files from a shared network location.

Once the wizard has started, use the following steps to perform the installation:

1. From the System Center Orchestrator 2012 Setup screen, shown previously in Figure 17.1, click on Install. If Microsoft .NET Framework 3.5 SP1 has not yet been installed on the system, a dialog box appears asking if you want to install this prerequisite. If so, click Yes to proceed with the installation.

2. For product registration, enter in your Name, Organization Name, and a Product Key, and click Next.

3. Read the terms of the licensing agreement, and if you agree to the terms, select the I Accept the License Terms option, and click Next.

4. At the Select Features to Install screen, select only the Management Server component for installation, and click Next.

5. The system begins a process of checking for additional requirements and prerequisites. If your system does not meet the basic requirements for the installation of Orchestrator 2012 (such as not enough memory, not enough disk space, or missing software prerequisites), you are prompted to fix the problem.

6. Once all of the prerequisites have installed, click Next to continue.

7. At the Configure the Service Account screen, enter the username and password of the service account previously created, and use the drop-down menu to select the Active Directory domain of the service account. Once the credentials have been entered, click Test to validate the credentials. Once the credentials have been accepted, click Next to continue.

8. At the Configure the Database Server screen, enter the name of the SQL server that will be used to host the Orchestration database in the Server field. If the SQL instance is a named instance as opposed to the default instance, this can also be specified using the format server\instance. For most SQL installations, the default Port setting of 1433 and the default Authentication Credentials option of Windows Authentication should also be used. Once the server name has been entered, click Next to continue.

9. At the Configure the Database screen, keep the default Database option of New Database. If desired, the database name can be changed from the default name of Orchestrator. Once the database name has been specified, click Next.

10. At the Configure Orchestrator Users Group screen, a local security group named OrchestratorUsersGroup is specified by default. If a local or Active Directory security group has been created in advance to be used as the Orchestrator Users group, click

Browse and select this group instead. If the members of this group will be connecting to this instance of the Runbook Designer remotely, keep the default selection of Grant Remote Access to the Runbook Designer. Once the Orchestrator Users group has been configured, click Next to continue.

NOTE

Regardless of the security group specified as the Orchestrator Users group, the account of the user installing the software will be added as the first member of the group.

---

11. At the Select the Installation Location screen, you have the option of choosing an alternate location for the installation of the files. If an alternate drive location will be used, click Browse, and then navigate to and select the alternate path. If the default location on the C: drive will be used, click Next.

12. At the Microsoft Update screen, select the On option to use Microsoft Update to automatically check for updates to the OS as well as Orchestrator software, or select the Off option to prevent automatic updates. Once the desired Microsoft Update option has been selected, click Next to continue.

13. At the Help Improve Microsoft System Center Orchestrator screen, options are presented for participation in the Customer Experience Improvement Program, as well as Error Reporting, which is used to automatically send program error reports to Microsoft. For Error Reporting, it is also possible to queue the reports such that these can be sent manually on a periodic basis by the administrator. After choosing the desired level of participation, click Next to continue.

14. At the Installation Summary screen, review the summary of the choices made for installation, and click Install to begin the installation of the management server.

15. Once the installation of the software has been completed, a summary of the components installed is shown. Review the list to confirm everything was successfully installed, and then click Close.

Installing the Runbook Server

To start the installation of the runbook server, log on to the server using an account that is a member of the local administrators group. Then initiate the Orchestrator Setup Wizard by executing the startup file (SetupOrchestrator.exe) from the installation media or an ISO file, or use a copy of the setup files from a shared network location.

Once the wizard has started, use the following steps to perform the installation:

1. From the System Center Orchestrator 2012 Setup screen, shown previously in Figure 17.1, under Standalone Installations, click on Runbook Server. If Microsoft .NET Framework 3.5 SP1 has not yet been installed on the system, a dialog box appears asking if you want to install this prerequisite. If so, click Yes to proceed with the installation.

2. For product registration, enter in your Name, Organization Name, and a Product Key, and click Next.

3. Read the terms of the licensing agreement, and if you agree to the terms, select the I Accept the License Terms option, and click Next.

4. The system begins a process of checking for additional requirements and prerequisites. If your system does not meet the basic requirements for the installation of Orchestrator 2012 (such as not enough memory, not enough disk space, or missing software prerequisites), you are prompted to fix the problem.

5. Once all of the prerequisites have installed, click Next to continue.

6. At the Configure the Service Account screen, enter the username and password of the service account previously created, and use the drop-down menu to select the Active Directory domain of the service account. Once the credentials have been entered, click Test to validate the credentials. Once the credentials have been accepted, click Next to continue.

7. At the Configure the Database Server screen, enter the name of the SQL server that was specified during the installation of the management server. If the SQL instance is a named instance as opposed to the default instance, this can also be specified using the format server\instance. For most SQL installations, the default Port setting of 1433 and the default Authentication Credentials option of Windows Authentication should also be used. Once the server name has been entered, click Next to continue.

8. At the Configure the Database screen, use the drop-down menu to select the existing Orchestration database, and then click Next.

9. At the Select the Installation Location screen, you have the option of choosing an alternate location for the installation of the files. If an alternate drive location will be used, click Browse, and then navigate to and select the alternate path. If the default location on the C: drive will be used, click Next.

10. At the Microsoft Update screen, select the On option to use Microsoft Update to automatically check for updates to the OS as well as Orchestrator software, or select the Off option to prevent automatic updates. Once the desired Microsoft Update option has been selected, click Next to continue.

11. At the Help Improve Microsoft System Center Orchestrator screen, options are presented for participation in the Customer Experience Improvement Program, as well as Error Reporting, which is used to automatically send program error reports to Microsoft. For Error Reporting, it is also possible to queue the reports such that these can be sent manually on a periodic basis by the administrator. After choosing the desired level of participation, click Next to continue.

12. At the Installation Summary screen, review the summary of the choices made for installation, and click Install to begin the installation of the runbook server.

13. Once the installation of the software has been completed, a summary of the components installed is shown. Review the list to confirm everything was successfully installed, and then click Close.

Installing the Orchestrator Web Service

To start the installation of the Orchestrator web service, log on to the server using an account that is a member of the local administrators group. Then initiate the Orchestrator Setup Wizard by executing the startup file (`SetupOrchestrator.exe`) from the installation media or an ISO file, or use a copy of the setup files from a shared network location.

Once the wizard has started, use the following steps to perform the installation:

1. From the System Center Orchestrator 2012 Setup screen, shown previously in Figure 17.1, under Standalone Installations, click on Orchestration Console and Web Service. If Microsoft .NET Framework 3.5 SP1 has not yet been installed on the system, a dialog box appears asking if you want to install this prerequisite. If so, click Yes to proceed with the installation.

2. For product registration, enter in your Name, Organization Name, and a Product Key, and click Next.

3. Read the terms of the licensing agreement, and if you agree to the terms, select the I Accept the License Terms option, and click Next.

4. The system begins a process of checking for additional requirements and prerequisites. If your system does not meet the basic requirements for the installation of Orchestrator 2012 (such as not enough memory, not enough disk space, or missing software prerequisites), you are prompted to fix the problem. If your system passes the basic requirements but IIS is not installed, you are prompted to enable the IIS role, as shown previously in Figure 17.2. Select the Enable IIS Role option button to install IIS on the system and click Next.

5. If IIS was missing and was installed, click Next to continue.

6. At the Configure the Service Account screen, enter the username and password of the service account previously created, and use the drop-down menu to select the Active Directory domain of the service account. Once the credentials have been entered, click Test to validate the credentials. Once the credentials have been accepted, click Next to continue.

7. At the Configure the Database Server screen, enter the name of the SQL server that was specified during the installation of the management server. If the SQL instance is a named instance as opposed to the default instance, this can also be specified using the format server\instance. For most SQL installations, the default Port setting of 1433 and the default Authentication Credentials option of Windows Authentication should also be used. Once the server name has been entered, click Next to continue.

17

8. At the Configure the Database screen, use the drop-down menu to select the existing Orchestration database, and then click Next.

9. At the Configure the Ports for the Web Services screen, keep the default port settings of 81 for Web Service Port and 82 for Orchestration Console Port, and then click Next.

10. At the Select the Installation Location screen, you have the option of choosing an alternate location for the installation of the files. If an alternate drive location will be used, click Browse, and then navigate to and select the alternate path. If the default location on the C: drive will be used, click Next.

11. At the Microsoft Update screen, select the On option to use Microsoft Update to automatically check for updates to the OS as well as Orchestrator software, or select the Off option to prevent automatic updates. Once the desired Microsoft Update option has been selected, click Next to continue.

12. At the Help Improve Microsoft System Center Orchestrator screen, options are presented for participation in the Customer Experience Improvement Program, as well as Error Reporting, which is used to automatically send program error reports to Microsoft. For Error Reporting, it is also possible to queue the reports such that these can be sent manually on a periodic basis by the administrator. After choosing the desired level of participation, click Next to continue.

13. At the Installation Summary screen, review the summary of the choices made for installation, and click Install to begin the installation of the Orchestrator web service.

14. Once the installation of the software has been completed, a summary of the components installed is shown. Review the list to confirm everything was successfully installed, and then click Close.

Installing the Runbook Designer

Unlike the other Orchestrator features, Runbook Designer can be installed on a Windows 7 workstation in addition to a Windows Server 2008 R2 server. To start the installation of the Runbook Designer, log on to the server using an account that is a member of the local administrators group. Then initiate the Orchestrator Setup Wizard by executing the startup file (SetupOrchestrator.exe) from the installation media or an ISO file, or use a copy of the setup files from a shared network location.

Once the wizard has started, use the following steps to perform the installation:

1. From the System Center Orchestrator 2012 Setup screen, shown previously in Figure 17.1, under Standalone Installations, click on Runbook Designer. If Microsoft .NET Framework 3.5 SP1 has not yet been installed on the system, a dialog box appears asking if you want to install this prerequisite. If so, click Yes to proceed with the installation.

2. For product registration, enter in your Name, Organization Name, and a Product Key, and click Next.

3. Read the terms of the licensing agreement, and if you agree to the terms, select the I Accept the License Terms option, and click Next.

4. The system begins a process of checking for additional requirements and prerequisites. If your system does not meet the basic requirements for the installation of Orchestrator 2012 (such as not enough memory, not enough disk space, or missing software prerequisites), you are prompted to fix the problem.

5. Once all of the prerequisites have installed, click Next to continue.

6. At the Select the Installation Location screen, you have the option of choosing an alternate location for the installation of the files. If an alternate drive location will be used, click Browse, and then navigate to and select the alternate path. If the default location on the C: drive will be used, click Next.

7. At the Microsoft Update screen, select the On option to use Microsoft Update to automatically check for updates to the OS as well as Orchestrator software, or select the Off option to prevent automatic updates. Once the desired Microsoft Update option has been selected, click Next to continue.

8. At the Help Improve Microsoft System Center Orchestrator screen, options are presented for participation in the Customer Experience Improvement Program, as well as Error Reporting, which is used to automatically send program error reports to Microsoft. For Error Reporting, it is also possible to queue the reports such that these can be sent manually on a periodic basis by the administrator. After choosing the desired level of participation, click Next to continue.

9. At the Installation Summary screen, review the summary of the choices made for installation, and click Install to begin the installation of the Runbook Designer.

10. Once the installation of the software has been completed, a summary of the components installed is shown. Review the list to confirm everything was successfully installed, and then click Close.

Additional Tasks Following Orchestrator Installation

Once Orchestrator has been installed, several basic tasks can be performed to increase the functionality of the product. The following sections describe the postinstallation tasks that are recommended for all installations of Orchestrator 2012.

Enabling Network Discovery for the Runbook Designer

Network discovery is a network setting built in to all Windows operating systems; it controls whether or not the system can find other systems on the local network using built-in network services. The Runbook Designer in particular requires visibility to other

systems on the network, yet the Network Discovery setting might or might not be
enabled on a Windows system where Runbook Designer is installed.

To enable network discovery on a system where Runbook Designer has been installed, do
the following:

1. Log on to the system where Runbook Designer is installed using an account that is a
   member of the local administrators group.

2. From the desktop, click Start, Control Panel. Then select Network and Internet,
   Network and Sharing Center, Change Advanced Sharing Settings.

3. At the Advanced Sharing Settings screen, click the down arrow next to the Domain
   profile if needed to expose the domain profile options.

4. In the Network Discovery section, select Turn On Network Discovery, as shown in
   Figure 17.4, and then click Save Changes.

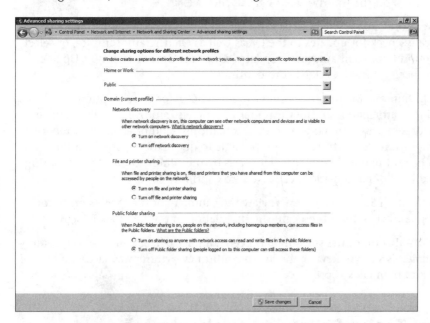

FIGURE 17.4   Enabling network discovery for the Runbook Designer.

Connecting Runbook Designer to a Management Server

If the Runbook Designer is installed individually on a system, for example to manage
Orchestrator runbooks using a Windows 7 workstation, the Runbook Designer will need
to be connected to a management server when run for the first time.

To connect Runbook Designer to a management server, do the following:

1. Log on to the system where Runbook Designer is installed using an account that is a member of the Orchestrator Users group.

2. Open the Runbook Designer, and then in the navigation pane on the left side, click the Connect to a Server icon.

> **NOTE**
>
> If the Runbook Designer is already connected to a management server, the Connect to a Server icon will be disabled. To connect to a different management server, click the DiOrchestratornnect from a Server icon first.

3. In the System Center Orchestrator 2012 dialog box, enter the name of the server hosting the management server, and then click OK.

Enabling GNU Privacy Guard for the Runbook Designer

GNU Privacy Guard (GnuPG) is an open source program based on the OpenPGP standard defined by RFC4880, and allows encryption and decryption of data. Within Runbook Designer, GnuPG is used by the PGP Encrypt File and PGP Decrypt File standard activities to encrypt and decrypt files. The GnuPG executable and associated DLL file must be downloaded to each system where Runbook Designer is installed in order to enable these activities.

GnuPG and is freely distributed under the terms of the GNU General Public License, and can be downloaded from the GNU Project website at http://www.gnupg.org.

To download and install GnuPG on a system where Runbook Designer is installed, perform the following steps:

1. Log on to the system where Runbook Designer is installed, and connect to the GNU Project website at http://www.gnupg.org.

2. Locate and download GnuPG version 1.4.10 or later for Windows.

3. From the downloaded set of files, locate the `gpg.exe` and `iconv.dll` files, and copy these to the following subdirectory: `<System drive>:\Program Files (x86)\Common Files\Microsoft System Center 2012\Orchestrator\Extensions\Support\ Encryption`.

> **NOTE**
>
> It might be necessary to download a full package from the GNU Project website, and then extract the files needed for Orchestrator from the download, depending on the GnuPG version and format.

17

Getting Familiar with the Orchestrator 2012 Management Consoles

Orchestrator 2012 includes two management consoles: the Runbook Designer and the Orchestration console. The Runbook Designer is used to create, manage, and run runbooks and is, therefore, intended for the highest-level Orchestrator administrators. The Orchestration console, on the other hand, contains a subset of the Runbook Designer functionality and is used to run runbooks and view their status. The Orchestration console is, therefore, intended for users who are required to manage runbook operations, but do not need to modify runbooks. Because the Orchestration console is a web-based tool, it can be accessed from any web browser without requiring installation of a separate tool and is, therefore, more widely available than the Runbook Designer.

In the following sections, each of these Orchestrator management consoles is described in detail to gain familiarity with their use.

Runbook Designer

The main screen of the Runbook Designer is organized into four panes, as shown in Figure 17.5.

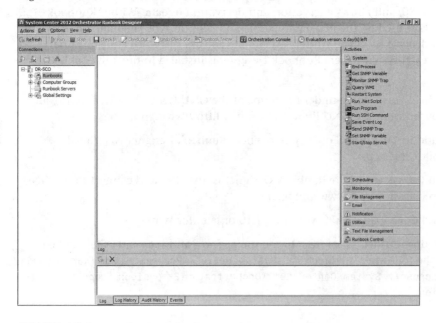

FIGURE 17.5   The Runbook Designer main screen.

The four main areas of the Runbook Designer console are the Connections pane along the left side, the Runbook Designer workspace in the center, the Activities pane on the right side, and the Log pane at the bottom. The following sections provide a description of the purpose and available functions for each section of the Runbook Designer console.

Connections Pane

The Connections pane allows a folder structure to be created and used to organize workflows within Orchestrator. The Connections pane is also used to edit permissions on the folder structure and provides access to Computer Groups, Runbook Servers, and Global Settings.

Figure 17.6 shows how the Orchestrator folder structure can be designed to meet the specified needs of an organization. Once created, individual runbooks can be moved into the appropriate folder, and then permissions can be configured on each folder in the hierarchy to grant the required permissions at each level.

FIGURE 17.6   Folder structure within Runbook Designer.

The Connections pane also allows management of computer groups, which are used to target specific activities against a collection of similar systems. This greatly increases the flexibility of runbook operations, as it is possible to target new systems dynamically simply by adding them to the computer group. Computer groups can also be created using Active Directory queries, and can be managed outside of Orchestrator. For example, it is possible to create an Active Directory query that finds all instances of SQL Server in the environment, and then each new instance of SQL Server will automatically be retrieved and included in the computer group.

The Runbook Servers section of the Connections pane allows management of the individual runbook servers in the environment. Here, it is possible to change the roles of multiple runbook servers between primary and secondary by promoting or demoting servers as needed.

The Global Settings section of the Connections pane provides access to the following three items:

▶ **Counters**—Global counters are used to create values, which can be incremented in order to track important statistics. Only one runbook activity should be used to modify a global counter; however, several runbooks can read the value of a global counter while running simultaneously.

▶ **Variables**—Global variables are used to specify a specific value or setting globally, and then use that value within multiple Orchestrator runbook activities. When the value is updated, it automatically becomes updated in each of the activities in which it has been used.

▶ **Schedules**—Global schedules are used to define specific times when a runbook can run. Once created, schedules can then be assigned to multiple runbooks as needed to optimize resource usage or to meet other business requirements.

Runbook Designer Workspace

The Runbook Designer workspace is used to build and edit Orchestrator runbooks. Once a folder is selected with the Connections pane, the runbooks that are contained within that folder are displayed as tabs across the top of the Runbook Designer workspace. Selecting the tab then displays the individual runbook for viewing or editing, as shown in Figure 17.7.

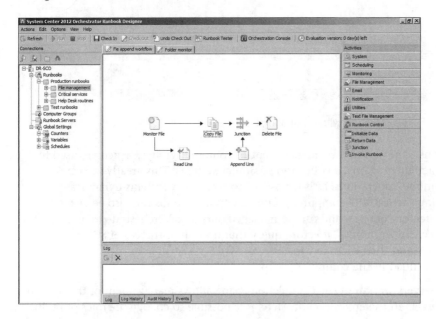

FIGURE 17.7   The Runbook Designer workspace.

Once a runbook tab has been selected in the Runbook Designer workspace, all of the tools in the Activities pane are available for editing the runbook. The runbook creation procedure is described in the "Designing and Using Runbooks" section of this chapter.

Activities Pane

The Activities pane contains all of the activities that are used to build runbooks, including standard activities that ship with the product as well as activities that are made available from the installation of Integration Packs. Activities are dragged from the Activities pane into the Runbook Designer workspace and then linked together to form runbooks. The standard activities are organized into nine categories, as shown in Figure 17.8. The nine categories of standard activities are System, Scheduling, Monitoring, File Management, Email, Notification, Utilities, Text File Management, and Runbook Control. Adding Integration Packs adds more categories. Use and configuration of the activities will be covered in the "Designing and Using Runbooks" section of this chapter.

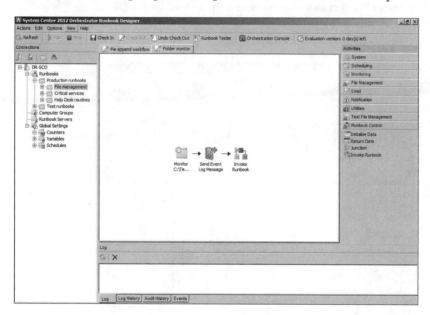

FIGURE 17.8   Standard activity categories in the Activities pane.

Log Pane

The Log pane is used to show the activity and history for the runbook that is currently selected in the Runbook Designer console. There are four tabs that appear in the Log pane. The Log tab displays a real-time log of information about a running runbook instance. The Log History tab displays historical displays about instances of a runbook. The Audit History tab displays audit information about changes to a runbook. The Events tab shows status information about the Orchestrator management server, runbook servers, and database.

Orchestration Console

The Orchestration console can be accessed from any web browser that supports Microsoft Silverlight 4. You can use several methods to access the Orchestration console. In addition to Start menu access on the system where the Orchestrator web service is installed, the console can be reached from any supported web browser by connecting to http://<computer name>:<port#>, where *computer name* is the hostname of the server where the Orchestrator web service is installed, and *port#* is the port selected during the configuration of the web service (by default, the port used is 82). The Orchestration console can also be accessed from the Runbook Designer by clicking on the Orchestration Console button on the toolbar. The main screen of the Orchestration console is organized into three panes, as shown in Figure 17.9.

> **NOTE**
>
> Upon first connection to the Orchestration console from a client browser, it will be necessary to install Silverlight if this component has not already been installed.

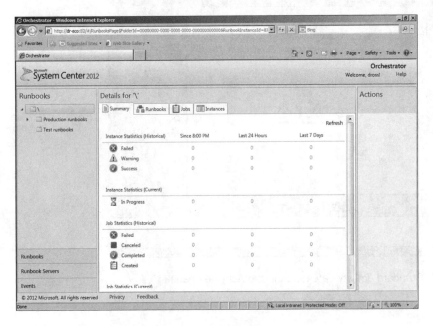

FIGURE 17.9   The Orchestration console main screen.

The three main areas of the Orchestration console are the navigation pane along the left side, the details pane in the center, and the Actions pane on the right side. The navigation pane provides access to three workspace areas, including the Runbooks workspace, the Runbook Servers workspace, and the Events workspace. Depending on the workspace selected, various tabs appear within the details pane and activities appear within the Actions pane that are relevant to the workspace chosen. The following sections provide a description of the purpose and available functions for each of the three available workspaces in the Orchestration console.

Runbooks Workspace

The Runbooks workspace allows an administrator to start and stop runbooks and also view information about the runbooks, such as the jobs and instances created for each. Four tabs appear in the details pane when the Runbooks workspace is selected, as shown previously in Figure 17.9. The following is a description of the purpose of each of these tabs:

- ▶ **Summary**—The Summary tab displays summary information for the jobs and instances of the selected runbook or for all of the runbooks in a selected folder. Each column displays the number of jobs that finished with a status of Succeeded, Warning, or Failed within the last hour, the last day, and the last week. Jobs or instances that are in progress, or jobs that have been queued, are also displayed. The statistics are automatically updated every 10 minutes, but can also be refreshed manually using the link at the top of the page.

- ▶ **Runbooks**—The Runbooks tab is displayed when a folder is selected in the Runbooks workspace, and lists the runbooks in that folder along with the status of any running jobs and instances for each. Selecting one of the listed runbooks allows access to control runbook operation using the Actions pane, as shown in Figure 17.10. A filter is also available above the list of runbooks, and can be used to refine the list of runbooks viewed if there is a large list.

- ▶ **Jobs**—The Jobs tab is displayed when a folder or runbook is selected in the Runbooks workspace, and lists the jobs created for a runbook along with completion status. When a folder is selected, the list includes jobs for all runbooks in that folder. When a runbook is selected, only the jobs for that runbook are displayed.

- ▶ **Instances**—The Instances tab is displayed when a folder or runbook is selected in the Runbooks workspace, and lists the instances created for a runbook along with completion status. When a folder is selected, the list includes instances for all runbooks in that folder. When a runbook is selected, only the instances for that runbook are displayed.

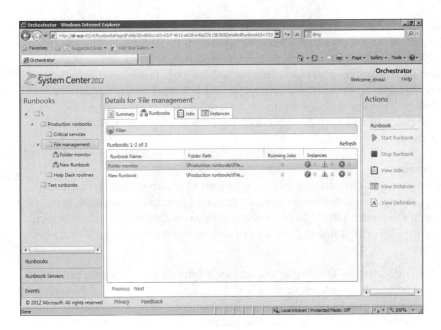

FIGURE 17.10   Runbooks pane within the Orchestration console.

Runbook Servers Workspace

The Runbook Servers workspace allows an administrator to view the status of current and completed jobs and instances for each runbook server. There are two tabs that appear in the details pane when the Runbook Servers workspace is selected. The following is a description of the purpose of each of these tabs:

▶ **Jobs**—The Jobs tab lists the jobs that have been run on the selected runbook server along with completion status. A job is a request for a runbook server to run a runbook.

▶ **Instances**—The Instances tab lists the instances created on the selected runbook server along with completion status. An instance is a running copy of a runbook.

Events Workspace

The Events workspace displays log events, including all events for the management server and all runbook servers. A filter is also available above the list of events and can be used to refine the list of events according to specific criteria entered into the filter. If an event is specific to a particular runbook server, the name of the runbook server is displayed in the Source Name column, as shown in Figure 17.11. In this case, after selecting the event, the View Runbook Server link in the Actions pane can be selected, which opens the Jobs tab in the Runbook Servers workspace for that runbook server.

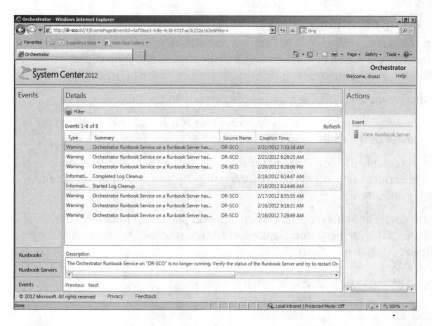

FIGURE 17.11   Events pane within the Orchestration console.

Installing Integration Packs

System Center 2012 ships with a set of standard activities that are useful for creating workflows involving the most common operations. To expand on this default functionality and allow integration with other Microsoft software as well as third-party platforms and products, Integration Packs are available from the Microsoft Download Center. For example, Microsoft provides Integration Packs for all of the System Center products, as well as Active Directory, VMware vSphere, IBM Tivoli, and a number of other third-party products and technologies. Each Integration Pack has a guide that provides installation instructions, known issues, and reference information for the activities that are included in the Integration Pack.

> **NOTE**
>
> Microsoft supports Integration Packs that are specifically designed for System Center Orchestrator 2012. Integration Packs that were designed for previous versions of the product are not supported with the 2012 version.

To use an Integration Pack, it must first be registered with the management server, and then deployed to runbook servers as well as systems where Runbook Designer is installed. The following sections provide general instructions for registering and then installing an Integration Pack.

Registering an Integration Pack

The first step in registering an Integration Pack is to download it from the Microsoft Download Center. Once downloaded, the executable file should either be copied to a local directory on the management server or made available on the network.

To register the Integration Pack on the management server, do the following:

1. Log on to the system where the management server is installed using an account that is a member of the Orchestrator Users group.

2. Locate the executable file downloaded for the Integration Pack, and then double-click on it to extract the contents of the Integration Pack to a local subdirectory on the management server.

3. Start the Deployment Manager utility by clicking on Start, All Programs, Microsoft System Center 2012, Orchestrator, Deployment Manager. The Deployment Manager console opens, as shown in Figure 17.12.

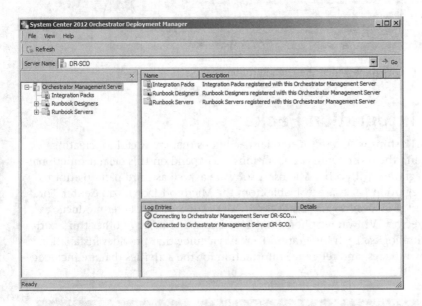

FIGURE 17.12   The Deployment Manager console.

4. In the navigation pane of the Deployment Manager, expand Orchestrator Management Server, and then right-click on Integration Packs and select Register IP with the Management Server. This starts the Integration Pack Registration Wizard.

5. At the Welcome to the Integration Pack Registration Wizard screen, click Next.

6. At the Select Integration Packs or Hotfixes dialog box, click Add.

7. Navigate to the local subdirectory where the Integration Pack files were extracted in step 2, select the `.OIP` file, click Open, and then click Next.

8. At the Completing the Integration Pack Wizard screen, click Finish.

9. At the End-User License Agreement dialog box, read the license terms and then click Accept.

10. View the Log Entries pane in the Deployment Manager to confirm that the Integration Pack registration was successful.

Deploying an Integration Pack

Once an Integration Pack has been registered, it can be deployed to a runbook server or a system where Runbook Designer is installed.

To deploy an Integration Pack to a runbook server or a system where Runbook Designer is installed, perform the following steps:

1. Log on to the system where the management server is installed using an account that is a member of the Orchestrator Users group.

2. Start the Deployment Manager utility by clicking on Start, All Programs, Microsoft System Center 2012, Orchestrator, Deployment Manager.

3. In the navigation pane of the Deployment Manager, expand Orchestrator Management Server, and then right-click on Integration Packs and select Deploy IP to Runbook Server or Runbook Designer. This starts the Integration Pack Deployment Wizard.

4. On the Integration Pack or Hotfix Deployment page, select the Integration Pack to be deployed from the list, and then click Next.

5. On the Computer Selection page, enter the name of the first system where the Integration Pack is to be deployed, and click Add. Repeat this procedure to deploy the Integration Pack to any additional runbook servers or systems where Runbook Designer is installed. After all systems to which the Integration Pack will be deployed have been added, click Next to continue.

6. On the Installation Configuration page, to schedule the deployment for a later time, click the Schedule Installation option, and then use the drop-down menus to choose a time and date for the deployment. Under the Advanced Options section, choose whether or not all running runbooks should be stopped before the Integration Pack is deployed. Once the desired installation options have been selected, click Next.

7. On the Completing the Integration Pack Deployment Wizard page, click Finish.

8. View the Log Entries pane in the Deployment Manager to confirm that the Integration Pack registration was successful.

17

Connecting Runbook Designer to Active Directory

If Orchestrator will be used to create workflows involving Active Directory using the AD Integration Pack, a connection must first be configured between Orchestrator and an Active Directory domain controller.

Once the AD Integration Pack is installed, use the following procedure to connect an instance of Runbook Designer with an Active Directory domain controller:

1. Log on to the system where Runbook Designer is installed using an account that is a member of the Orchestrator Users group.

2. Open the Runbook Designer, and then click the Options drop-down menu and select Active Directory.

3. On the Configurations tab, click Add.

4. At the Add Configuration dialog box, enter a descriptive name for the connection, such as **Active Directory Connection**, or the name of the target domain controller.

5. Click the ellipsis (...) button next to the Type field, and then from the Item Selection list, select Microsoft Active Directory Domain Configuration and click OK.

6. In the Configuration User Name and Configuration Password fields, enter the credentials for the user account that Orchestrator will use to connect to Active Directory.

> **NOTE**
>
> The user account specified for the Active Directory connection must have permissions to perform the AD-related actions configured in any runbook where this connection is used.

7. In the Configuration Domain Controller Name (FQDN) field, enter the fully qualified name of either the Active Directory domain or a specific domain controller in that domain, and then click OK.

8. Click Finish to complete the configuration of the Active Directory connection.

Designing and Using Runbooks

The operational efficiencies that are gained from using System Center Orchestrator 2012 are directly tied to the design and use of runbooks. A runbook is a set of instructions that are combined to create a workflow, or an automated series of tasks. The individual steps within a runbook are called activities. Within each runbook, additional controls and properties are used to dictate the sequence of activities within the runbook, resulting in a highly flexible, completely automated sequence of tasks.

Standard Activities

To design runbooks effectively using Orchestrator 2012, it is essential to understand the activities that are used to make up a runbook. Each installation of Orchestrator 2012 includes a set of standard activities. The standard activities are organized into categories within the Runbook Designer to assist in locating the appropriate activity for a given task. The following are the categories for the standard activities that ship with Orchestrator 2012, along with a description of the types of tasks that can be performed within each category:

▶ **System**—Runs system commands, such as executing a program, ending a process, or restarting a system

▶ **Scheduling**—Performs schedule-based activities, such as monitoring the date and time or checking a predefined schedule

▶ **Monitoring**—Allows actions to be taken based on system-level events, such as the status of a process or the generation of a particular event log entry

▶ **File Management**—Allows interaction with files and folders, such as file or folder copy, deletion, or encryption

▶ **Email**—Allows email notifications to be sent

▶ **Notification**—Provides support for non-email notification mechanisms, such as Syslog log entry, or pop-up notifications

▶ **Utilities**—Provides a number of options for manipulating data or performing subtasks within a workflow, such as querying a database, modifying a counter, or mapping a network path

▶ **Text File Management**—Allows manipulation of text files

▶ **Runbook Control**—Allows for the control of runbook logic, such as a junction, which dictates that no further activities run until several other activities are completed

Building a Runbook

The number of combinations of activities that can be configured within Orchestrator is tremendous, allowing for a wide variety of workflow possibilities. Perhaps the best way to gain an understanding of how to organize and configure activities into an effective runbook is to consider some examples. With that in mind, within this section two sample runbook builds will be described, providing details on the runbook build process. The first runbook example will make use of only standard activities, while the second example will combine activities from an Integration Pack along with standard activities.

Sample Runbook Using Standard Activities—Copy File and Log Event

The first example is a simple runbook that can be used to manipulate files and generate notifications based on a particular event, in this case the creation of a text file in a folder that is being monitored. Once a new text file is detected, it is copied to a different target folder. After the file copy is completed, the name of the original file is inserted as the first line of the new copy of the file, and then an event log entry is generated describing the event. Finally, the original file is deleted.

This runbook uses a number of the standard Orchestrator activities to coordinate this workflow. From the File Management category, the Monitor File activity is used to detect the presence of a file, and the Copy File and Delete File activities are used as well. From the Text File Management category, the Insert Line activity is used to insert the original filename at the top of the copied file. From the Notification category, the Send Event Log Message activity is used to generate the event. Finally, a Junction activity is also used from the Runbook Control category to ensure that all activities are complete before the original file is deleted.

To create the sample runbook, complete the following steps:

1. Log on to a system where Runbook Designer is installed using an account that is a member of the Orchestrator Users group.

2. Open Runbook Designer by clicking on Start, All Programs, Microsoft System Center 2012, Orchestrator, Runbook Designer.

3. In the Connections pane on the left side, right-click on Runbooks, select New, and then click Runbook.

4. A tab labeled New Runbook appears at the top of the Designer workspace, as shown in Figure 17.13. Right-click on the tab and select Rename.

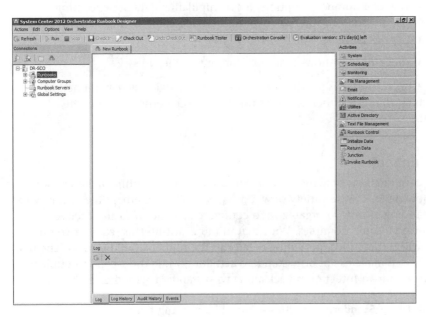

FIGURE 17.13   The New Runbook tab in the Designer workspace.

5. At the Confirm Check Out prompt, click Yes to confirm check out of the new runbook.

6. With the New Runbook label on the tab now selected, enter `Copy File and Log Event` as the new name for the runbook.

7. In the Activities pane, expand the File Management category and then click and drag the Monitor File activity to the Designer workspace.

8. Double-click on the Monitor File activity to open the Monitor File Properties dialog box.

9. In the Files to Monitor section, enter the folder location that will be monitored for text files into the text box. For this example, enter a local subdirectory, such as `C:\Monitored`.

10. In the Filters section, click Add.

11. At the Filter Settings dialog box, from the Name drop-down menu, select File Name. From the Relation drop-down menu, select Matches pattern. In the Value field, enter `*.txt`, and then click OK.

12. Click the Triggers tab.

13. In the Trigger If One of the Files Was section, select Created, and then click Finish to complete the configuration of the File Monitor activity.

14. In the Activities pane, in the File Management category, click and drag the Copy File activity to the right of the Monitor File activity in the Designer workspace.

15. Create a link between the Monitor File activity and the Copy File activity by clicking the right arrow next to the Monitor File activity and dragging it to the Copy File activity, as shown in Figure 17.14.

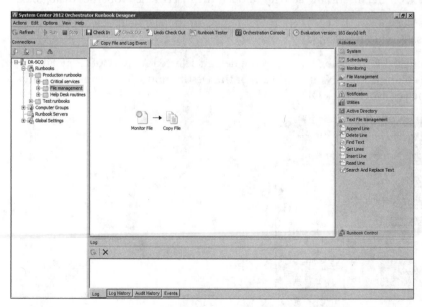

FIGURE 17.14   Linking two activities in the Designer workspace.

16. Double-click on the Copy File activity to open the Copy File Properties dialog box.

17. At the Details tab, right-click on the File box in the Source section, select Subscribe, and then select Published Data.

18. At the Published Data dialog box, keep the default selected Activity of Monitor File. In the Name column, select Name and Path of the File, and click OK.

> **NOTE**
>
> The Monitor File activity is automatically selected in the Published Data dialog box because Monitor File is the activity that is immediately prior to the selected activity in the Designer workspace.

19. In the folder box under Destination, enter the path for the folder that will be used as the target for the file copy. For this example, enter a local subdirectory, such as **C:\CopyTarget**.

20. Click Finish to complete the configuration of the File Copy activity.

21. In the Activities pane, expand the Text File Management category and then click and drag the Insert Line activity underneath the Copy File activity in the Designer workspace.

22. Create a link between the Copy File activity and the Insert Line activity by clicking the right arrow next to the Copy File activity and dragging it to the Insert Line activity.

23. Double-click on the Insert Line activity to open the Insert Line Properties dialog box.

24. On the Details tab, in the File section, right-click on the File field, select Subscribe, and then select Published Data.

25. At the Published Data dialog box, keep the default selected Activity of Copy File. In the Name column, select Name and Path of the Destination File, as shown in Figure 17.15. When finished, click OK.

FIGURE 17.15   Subscribing to published data within an activity.

26. Click the ellipsis (...) button next to the File Encoding field.

27. At the File Encoding dialog box, use the drop-down menu to select ASCII, and click OK.

28. In the Insert section, right-click on the Text field, select Subscribe, and then select Published Data.

29. At the Published Data dialog box, keep the default selected Activity of Copy File. In the Name column, select Name and Path of the Origin File, and click OK.

30. In the Line Number field, enter the number 1, and then click Finish to complete the configuration of the Insert Line activity.

31. In the Activities pane, expand the Notification category and then click and drag the Send Event Log Message activity to the right of the Insert Line activity in the Designer workspace.

32. Create a link between the Insert Line activity and the Send Event Log Message activity by clicking the right arrow next to the Insert Line activity and dragging it to the Send Event Log Message activity.

33. Double-click on the Send Event Log Message activity to open the Send Event Log Message Properties dialog box.

34. On the Details tab, enter the name of the computer that contains the Windows event log where the message will be written to. For this example, enter the name of the local system.

35. In the Message text box, start by entering the following text: `Sample runbook now in progress—the following text file has been copied to the target folder:`.

36. Type one blank space at the end of the text box, then right-click in the text box, select Subscribe, and then select Published Data.

37. At the Published Data dialog box, use the drop-down menu to select Copy File. In the Name column, select File Name, and click OK.

38. In the Severity section, select the appropriate severity for the event. For this example, keep the default setting of Information, and then click Finish to complete the configuration of the Send Event Log Message activity.

39. In the Activities pane, expand the Runbook Control category and then click and drag the Junction activity to the right of the Copy File activity and above the Send Event Log Message activity in the Designer workspace.

40. Create a link between the Copy File activity and the Junction activity by clicking the right arrow next to the Copy File activity and dragging it to the Junction activity.

41. Create a link between the Send Event Log Message activity and the Junction activity by clicking the right arrow next to the Send Event Log Message activity and dragging it to the Junction activity. This creates separate branches within the runbook, as shown in Figure 17.16.

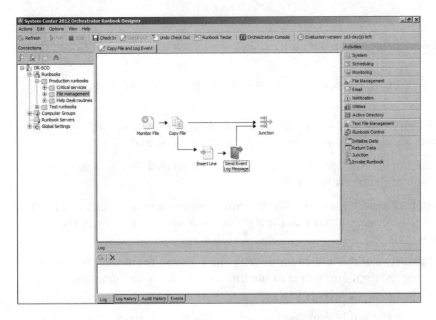

FIGURE 17.16   Separate branches of activities within a runbook.

42. Double-click on the Junction activity to open the Junction Properties dialog box.

43. On the Details tab, click the ellipsis (...) button to the right of the Return Data From box.

44. At the Select an Activity dialog box, select the Copy File activity from the list, click OK, and then click Finish to complete the configuration of the Junction activity.

NOTE

The purpose of the Junction activity is to allow the activities from multiple branches in the runbook to complete before continuing past the junction. In this example, the Copy File, Insert Line, and Send Event Log Message activities will complete before continuing with the remainder of the workflow. Republishing data from one of the branches allows the activities that are downstream past the junction to consume the same data published prior to the junction. In this example, the data from the Copy File activity is republished at the junction to allow this data (the name and path of the file from the Monitor File activity) to be consumed by the Delete File activity after the junction.

---

45. In the Activities pane, expand the File Management category and then click and drag the Delete File activity to the right of the Junction activity in the Designer workspace.

46. Create a link between the Junction activity and the Delete File activity by clicking the right arrow next to the Junction activity and dragging it to the Delete File activity.

47. Double-click on the Delete File activity to open the Delete File Properties dialog box.

48. At the Details tab, right-click on the Path box, select Subscribe, and then select Published Data.

49. At the Published Data dialog box, use the Activity drop-down menu to select Copy File.

50. From the Name column, select Name and Path of the Origin File, and then click OK.

51. Click Finish to complete the configuration of the Delete File activity. The Copy File and Log Event runbook is now complete, and should appear in the Designer workspace, as shown in Figure 17.17.

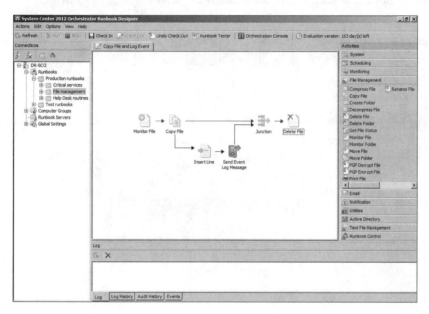

FIGURE 17.17   Completed Copy File and Log Event sample runbook.

Testing the Copy File and Log Event Runbook

Once a runbook has been built, it can be tested using the built-in Runbook Tester utility. This tool runs the entire runbook and allows the completion status of each activity to be inspected. To test the Copy File and Log Event runbook created previously, the folders that are referenced in the runbook activities must first be created.

To test the runbook, complete the following steps:

1. Log on to a system where Runbook Designer is installed using an account that is a member of the Orchestrator Users group.

2. Create two directories: C:\Monitored and C:\CopyTarget.

3. Open Runbook Designer by clicking on Start, All Programs, Microsoft System Center 2012, Orchestrator, Runbook Designer.

4. In the Connections pane, either click on the Runbooks node (if the target runbook is not in a folder), or expand the Runbooks node and navigate through the folder structure, and click on the folder hosting the target runbook.

5. In the Designer workspace, select the Copy File and Log Event Runbook tab.

6. Click the Runbook Tester icon on the toolbar.

7. If the runbook is not already checked out, the Confirm Check Out prompt appears. If so, click Yes to check out the runbook.

8. The System Center Orchestrator 2012 Runbook Tester screen opens, as shown in Figure 17.18.

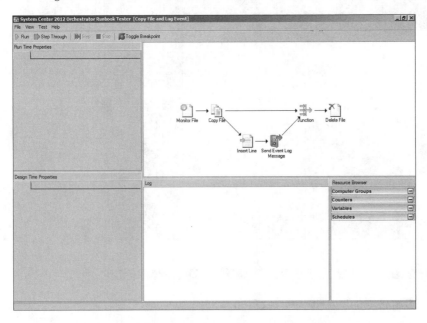

FIGURE 17.18   The Runbook Tester screen.

9. Click the Run icon on the toolbar. This loads the first activity in the workflow (Monitor File) and waits for a text file to be created in the monitored folder.

10. Use Notepad to create a text file, and save the file to the directory being monitored in the Monitor File activity.

11. Wait a few moments to allow all activities in the runbook to run. Once all activities have run, each activity will be listed in succession in the log section of the Runbook Tester, as shown in Figure 17.19. To verify the results for each activity, click the Show Details link, then scroll down to review the results; the result listed in the Activity Status column will be Success if the activity has run successfully.

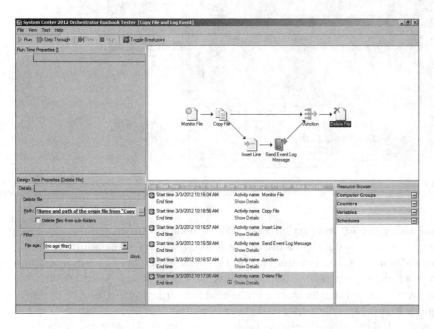

FIGURE 17.19   Viewing the runbook tester results in the Log pane.

12. After viewing the status of each activity, look for other indications that the entire workflow has run successfully. For example, the text file should be copied to the target folder specified in the Copy File activity, with the original file name inserted as the first line in the file, and the original file should be removed from the folder specified in the Monitor File activity. Also, the log entry specified in the Send Event Log Message activity should appear in the event log, as shown in Figure 17.20.

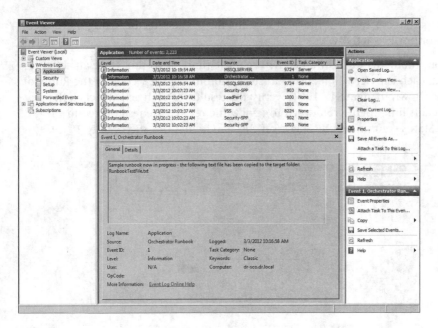

FIGURE 17.20   Log entry generated using the Send Event Log Message activity.

Sample Runbook Using the AD Integration Pack—Move Disabled Users

The second sample runbook involves the use of the Active Directory Integration Pack along with standard activities, and is a simple workflow that represents a common maintenance routine that might be performed by help desk personnel. Every organization experiences turnover of personnel; as an employee leaves an organization, one of the first maintenance items that is typically performed is the disabling of the user's Active Directory user account. Over time, there may be an accumulation of many such disabled user accounts, and these are often located in different areas of the directory structure. For some organizations, it is desirable to periodically consolidate all disabled user accounts into a single organizational unit that has been created specifically for this purpose. The sample runbook described in the next set of steps can be used to quickly perform this maintenance routine by running the runbook on a periodic or scheduled basis.

This runbook uses two of the activities from the Active Directory Integration Pack to coordinate this workflow, followed by one standard activity to notify the IT team that the maintenance routine has been completed. From the AD Integration Pack, the Get User activity is used to retrieve all user accounts that have been disabled, and the Move User activity is used to move the user account to the target OU. The Send Email standard activity is then used to provide notification.

The following procedure can be used to create this sample runbook:

1. Log on to a system where Runbook Designer is installed using an account that is a member of the Orchestrator Users group.

2. Open Runbook Designer by clicking on Start, All Programs, Microsoft System Center 2012, Orchestrator, Runbook Designer.

3. In the Connections pane on the left side, right-click on Runbooks, select New, and then click Runbook.

4. A tab labeled New Runbook appears at the top of the Designer workspace. Right-click on the tab and select Rename.

5. At the Confirm Check Out prompt, click Yes to confirm check out of the new runbook.

6. With the New Runbook label on the tab now selected, enter `Move Disabled Users` as the new name for the runbook.

7. In the Activities pane, expand the Active Directory category and then click and drag the Get User activity to the Designer workspace.

8. Double-click on the Get User activity to open the Get User Properties dialog box.

9. At the Properties tab, click the ellipsis (...) button next to the Name field.

10. At the Item Selection dialog box, select Active Directory Connection, and then click OK.

11. Click the Filters tab, and then click Add.

12. At the Filter Settings dialog box, use the Name drop-down menu to select Disabled, use the Relation drop-down menu to select Equals, type `True` into the Value field, and then click OK.

13. Click Finish to complete the configuration of the Get User activity.

14. In the Activities pane, from the Active Directory category, click and drag the Move User activity to the right of the Get User activity in the Designer workspace.

15. Create a link between the Get User activity and the Move User activity by clicking the right arrow next to the Get User activity and dragging it to the Move User activity.

16. Double-click on the Move User activity to open the Move User Properties dialog box.

17. At the Properties tab, click the ellipsis (...) button next to the Name field.

18. At the Item Selection dialog box, select Active Directory Connection, and then click OK.

19. At the Properties tab, click on Optional Properties.

20. At the Add/Remove Property dialog box, double-click on New Container Distinguished Name, then click OK.

17

21. In the New Container Distinguished Name field, enter the distinguished name of
the target Active Directory OU that will host the disabled user accounts, using the
canonical name format, as shown in Figure 17.21. For example, `OU=Disabled`
`Users,DC=Mydomain,DC=local` could be used to specify the Disabled Users OU in the
Mydomain.local AD domain. Once the distinguished name is entered, click Finish
to complete the configuration of the Move User activity.

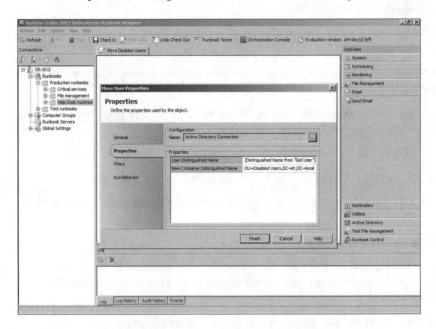

FIGURE 17.21   Adding properties to the Move User activity.

22. In the Activities pane, expand the Email category and then click and drag the Send
Email activity to the right of the Move User activity in the Designer workspace.

23. Create a link between the Move User activity and the Send Email activity by clicking
the right arrow next to the Send Event Log Message activity and dragging it to the
Send Email activity.

24. Double-click on the Send Email activity to open the Send Email Properties dialog
box.

25. On the Details tab, enter a descriptive subject for the email, such as `Disabled user`
`accounts move notification`.

26. Next to the Recipients field, click Add.

27. At the Recipient Properties dialog box, enter the email address of the recipient, then
select a recipient type of either primary recipient, copy recipient, or blind copy
recipient. When finished, click OK.

28. In the Message section, keep the default message type of Text, and then enter a descriptive message for the body of the email into the Message field, such as **All disabled AD user accounts have now been consolidated into the Disabled Users OU.**

29. Select the Connect tab, and then in the Mail account section, enter the email address that will be used as the sender of the email.

30. In the SMTP Connection section, enter the name of the SMTP server where the message will be sent. If the default SMTP port of 25 is not used, select the Port check box and enter the number of the SMTP port in use. If SSL is required, select the Enable SSL check box. Once the connection information is entered, click Finish to complete the configuration of the Send Email activity.

31. The Move Disabled Users runbook is now complete, and should appear in the Designer Workspace, as shown in Figure 17.22.

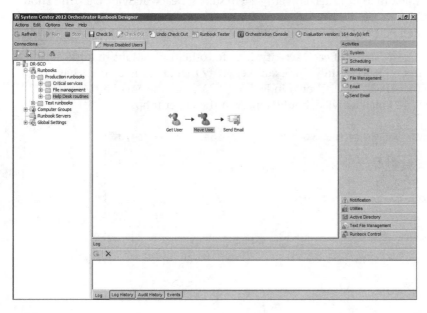

FIGURE 17.22   Completed Move Disabled Users sample runbook.

Testing the Move Disabled Users Runbook

To test the Move Disabled Users runbook, first disable a sampling of test Active Directory user accounts throughout the target AD domain.

The following steps can then be used to test the runbook:

1. Log on to a system where Runbook Designer is installed using an account that is a member of the Orchestrator Users group.

2. Open Runbook Designer by clicking on Start, All Programs, Microsoft System Center 2012, Orchestrator, Runbook Designer.

3. In the Connections pane, either click on the Runbooks node (if the target runbook is not in a folder), or expand the Runbooks node and navigate through the folder structure, then click on the folder hosting the target runbook.

4. In the Designer workspace, select the Move Disabled Users runbook tab.

5. Click the Runbook Tester icon on the toolbar.

6. If the runbook is not already checked out, the Confirm Check Out prompt appears. If so, click Yes to check out the runbook.

7. The System Center Orchestrator 2012 Runbook Tester screen opens.

8. Click the Run icon on the toolbar. This runs each activity in succession until the workflow is complete.

9. Once all activities have run, each activity will be listed in succession in the log section of the Runbook Tester. To verify the results for each activity, click the Show Details link, then scroll down to review the results; the result listed in the Activity Status column will be Success if the activity has run successfully.

10. After viewing the status of each activity, look for other indications that the entire workflow has run successfully. For example, verify that all disabled users have been moved to the target OU, as shown in Figure 17.23. Also, the email message sent using the Send Email activity should appear in the target Inbox.

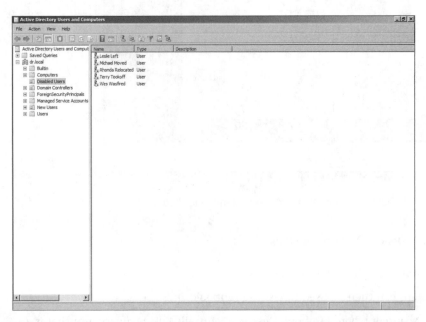

FIGURE 17.23   Disabled user accounts consolidated into the target OU using the Move Disabled Users runbook.

Runbook Permissions

By default, only the members of the Orchestrator Users group have access to the runbooks that are created using Runbook Designer. To grant additional users the ability to manage runbook operations, including the ability to run, start, stop, change, or view runbooks, it is necessary to grant permissions at either the folder or runbook level within Runbook Designer.

To grant permissions to runbooks using Runbook Designer, complete the following steps:

1. Log on to a system where Runbook Designer is installed using an account that is a member of the Orchestrator Users group.

2. Open Runbook Designer by clicking on Start, All Programs, Microsoft System Center 2012, Orchestrator, Runbook Designer.

3. If permissions will be granted to an individual runbook, then in the Connections pane, click on the Runbooks node (if the target runbook is not in a folder), or expand the Runbooks node, navigate through the folder structure, and click on the folder hosting the target runbook. Once the folder is selected, right-click on the tab for the target runbook at the top of the Designer workspace, and select Permissions.

4. If permissions will be granted to folder, then in the Connections pane, expand the Runbooks node, navigate through the folder structure, right-click on the folder hosting the target runbook, and select Permissions.

5. At the Permissions dialog box, click Add, then select the target user or security group from either the domain or the local system, and click OK.

6. To grant permissions to view and run the runbook, select the Allow check box next to Read. To grant permissions to change the runbook, select the Allow check box next to Write. To grant the ability to change permissions for the runbook, select the Allow check box next to Full Control.

7. Once the permissions have been set, click OK to save the changes.

Summary

This chapter provided a primer on System Center Orchestrator 2012, allowing anyone unfamiliar with the technology to gain an understanding of what this product is and how it can be used to increase the efficiency of IT operations. System Center Orchestrator is an extremely powerful tool that allows the automation of workflows involving multiple systems, without requiring scripting knowledge. Although it should be evident that Orchestrator offers significant benefits to larger enterprises with many systems being managed, even smaller organizations can improve the efficiency of their daily IT operations by consolidating repetitive tasks into automated workflows using Orchestrator.

Best Practices

The following are best practices from this chapter:

▶ Although not required, the Orchestrator 2012 server should be joined to an Active Directory domain to gain the maximum benefit from the product in an AD environment.

▶ Other than Microsoft .NET v4, the remaining software prerequisites for Orchestrator are automatically installed as part of the Orchestrator installation.

▶ Install the 2008 R2 version of Microsoft SQL Server ahead of the Orchestrator installation to host the Orchestration database. Only the basic features of the Database Engine Service are required.

▶ Create an Orchestrator service account prior to Orchestrator installation, using a domain account to allow maximum flexibility.

▶ Create an Active Directory security group prior to Orchestrator installation, to be assigned as the Orchestrator Users group during the install. Using an AD security group for this will allow maximum flexibility and allow Orchestrator administration to be managed centrally.

▶ Small- to medium-sized organizations should plan to install all Orchestrator features on a single server for simplicity and ease of management. In larger network environments, or where high availability is a requirement, the individual Orchestrator features can be installed on separate systems as needed.

▶ Install Runbook Designer on Windows 7 management workstations in addition to the Orchestrator server to allow multiple administrators to design and manage runbooks.

▶ Connect each instance of Runbook Designer to Active Directory to allow the configuration of workflows involving AD using the AD Integration Pack.

▶ Administrators who will design and manage runbooks should be granted full access to Orchestrator using the Orchestrator Users group, and should manage runbooks using Runbook Designer. Users who only need to run runbooks and view their status should be granted access to specific runbooks or folders using Runbook Designer, and should use a web browser to connect to the Orchestration console.

▶ Create a folder structure within Runbook Designer to organize the types of runbooks that will be used, and also to manage permissions to collections of runbooks.

Index

Numbers

64-bit agents, 59

A

Access Violation reports (ACS), 542
accessing Client Agents node, 248
Account Management reports (ACS), 542-543
accounts. *See names of specific accounts*
ACS (Audit Collection Services)
    hardware/software requirements, 311
    installing, 368-373
    overview, 310-311
    reports
        Access Violation reports, 542
        Account Management reports, 542-543
        custom reports, 545-548
        explained, 541-542
        Forensic reports, 543
        generating, 544-545
        Planning reports, 543
        Policy reports, 543
        System Integrity reports, 543
        Usage reports, 544
Action accounts, 315-316
Active Alerts, 436
Active Directory
    connectors, deploying, 805-806
    Runbook Designer, connecting to, 952
    schema, extending, 64-66, 118-119
    site detection, 60
Active Directory Client Monitoring, 453-454
Active Directory Domain Controller Performance
   Collection, 458-460
Active Directory forest discovery, 139
Active Directory Group Discovery, 95, 144

Active Directory Management Pack, 451
  configuring, 451-460
  reports, 465-466
  tasks, 464
  views, 460-463
Active Directory Management Pack Helper Object installation files, 452
Active Directory Replication Monitoring, 454-458
Active Directory Server Client object discovery, 453
Active Directory System Discovery, 143-144
Active Directory User Discovery, 144
activities
  dependent activities, 886
  manual activities, 886, 898
    adding to change requests, 897
    completing and failing, 905-907
  parallel activities, 886
  review activities, 886
  runbook activities, 952-953
  runbook automation activities, 886
  Service Manager 2012, 886
Activities pane (Runbook Designer), 945
Activity Distribution report, 917
activity management reports, 917-918
activity prefixes, 888-889
Add Configuration dialog box, 952
Add Disks to Storage Pool dialog box, 592
Add Properties page (Convert Physical Server Wizard), 723
Add Resource Wizard, VMM Agent installation, 695-697
Additional Properties page (Convert Virtual Machine Wizard), 728
administration
  DPM (Data Protection Manager)
    custom volumes, 613-614
    data recovery, 614-616
    DPM Administrator Console, 607-608
    DPM Central Console, 610-613
    DPM Management Shell, 608-610
  guest sessions, delegating, 37
  Operations Manager
    dip stick health checks, 403-404
    file exclusions for antivirus and defrag-mentation applications, 409-410
    management pack updates, 404-405

  notifications and alert tuning, 405-409
  Web console Performance view time frame, 410-411
  VMM (Virtual Machine Manager), 707-708
    VMM Administrator Console, 707-715
    VMM command shell, 715-716
Administration Console (DPM)
  overview, 607-608
  protection agent deployment, 594-596
Administrator Console (VMM), 679-680, 707-709
  configuring VMM library, 710-711
  creating host groups, 708-709
  creating private clouds, 711-714
  deploying VMs with, 742-744
  explained, 668
  General settings, 715
  hardware requirements, 679
  installing, 692-693
  managing host clusters, 710
  managing hosts, 709
  managing VMs, 714
  monitoring and reporting, 714
  Security settings, 715
  software requirements, 680
  supported operating systems, 680
  System Center settings, 715
Administrator Properties dialog box, 731
Administrator role (Operations Manager), 312
Administrator role (VMM), 672, 729-731
Advanced Operator role (Operations Manager), 312
advantages of Microsoft System Center, 6-7
Agent (VMM), installing, 695-700
Agent Action accounts, 316
Agent Compliance report, 284
Agent Health State, 437
Agent Performance dashboard, 435-436
Agent Proxy configuration, 396-398
Agent State Dashboard view, 437
agents, 99
  64-bit agents, 59
  automatic upgrades, 59
  Operations Manager agents, 373
    audit forwarders, configuring, 376-379
    configuring to use certificates, 392
    installing on DMZ servers, 391-392
    security, 313

UNIX/Linux agents, installing, 379-385

Windows agents, installing, 373-376

overview, 298-299

protection agents, deploying

  with certificates, 599-601

  with DPM Administration Console, 594-596

  manual installation process, 596-599

  with PowerShell, 601

proxy agents, configuring, 396-398

pushing, 59

Restart Health Service Recovery, enabling, 398-399

Server App-V Agent

  definition of, 753

  installing, 754-755

supported operating systems, 298

VMM Agent

  explained, 668

  installing, 695-700

AI (Asset Intelligence), 72-73, 269

importing software license data, 275-277

reporting, 277

reporting classes, 270-274

synchronizing, 269-270

Alert Logging Latency report, 534-536

alert widgets

  adding to dashboards, 558

  explained, 556

alerts

  generating, 294

  overview, 292

  state-based alerting, 59

  tuning, 405-409

Alerts reports (Operations Manager), 525-527

All Application Deployments (Basic) report, 253

All Audit Messages for a Specific User report, 254

All Management Servers Resource Pool, 318

All Software Updates container, 68

All Task Sequence Deployments report, 254

analyzing

  incidents, 847-849

  problems, 860-861

announcements, publishing, 850

antivirus applications, file exclusions for, 409-410

Application Catalog Web Services Points, 58

Application Catalog Website Points, 58

Application Compliance report, 253

application deployment, reports, 253

application management (Configuration Manager), 59, 66-68, 189. See also deployment management

  application model, 67-68, 189-190

  complex application configuration, 196

  complex application creation, 198-202

  complex application installation automation, 197-198

  distributing content to Distribution Points, 202-203

  EXE application configuration, 192-196

  MSI application configuration, 191-192

  package model, 67, 190-191

  targeting deployments to primary systems, 200-202

application model (application management), 67-68, 189-190

applications, 67-68

  monitoring, 21, 290

  preparing for OS deployment, 227

  virtual application packages

    creating, 755-758

    definition of, 753

    importing into VMM, 758

approving RAs (review activities), 903-905

architecture

  Configuration Manager, 75-76

  multisite Configuration Manager hierarchy, 95-96

  Operations Manager, 296-298, 317

  Service Manager, 766-767, 830-832

asset data, 246

  IDMIF files, 247

  inventory collection, 246-247

  NOIDMIF files, 247

Asset Intelligence. See AI (Asset Intelligence)

Asset Intelligence Synchronization Point role, 269-270

  installing, 153-154

  overview, 81-82

asset management (Configuration Manager), 70

  Asset Intelligence. See AI (Asset Intelligence)

  Compliance Management, 73-74

  hardware and software inventory, 71

  software metering, 73

asset tracking, 12
assigning incidents, 846-847
audit collection database, 309-310
Audit Collection Services. *See* ACS
audit collectors, 309
audit forwarders, 308, 376-379
auditing reports (Configuration Manager), 254
auditing review, 48
Author role (Operations Manager), 312
Authoring Console, 503
automatic agent upgrades, 59
automatic deployment rules, 69, 222-224
automatic deployments, 211-213
automatic load balancing, 58
Automatic Placement (VMM), 741
automatic user notification, change requests, 908-910
automating complex application installation, 197-198
Availability reports (Operations Manager), 527-531
Availability Tracker report, 528

B

Back Up Database dialog box, 412-416, 815
Background Intelligent Transfer Service. *See* BITS
Backup Destination dialog box, 414
backups
    cloud backups, 31
    database backups, 30
    Hyper-V server backups, 31
    Microsoft server backups, 28
    Operations Manager backups, 321-322
        component backup schedules, 411-412
        IIS 7.x configuration backup, 417-418
        OperationsManager database, 412-414
        OperationsManagerAC database, 416-417
        OperationsManagerDW database, 414-415
    server backups, 29
    Service Manager backups, 814
        backup schedules, 814
        database backups, 814-816
        encryption key, 816-817

SharePoint data backups, 30
Site Server database backups, 81
SQL backups, 30
tape backups, 31
    limitations of, 569-570
bandwidth
    Operations Manager requirements, 325-326
    site deployment and, 96
baselines, 283
benefits of Microsoft System Center, 6-7
best practices
    Configuration Manager, 112-114, 178-179
    deployment management, 243-244
    DPM (Data Protection Manager), 617-618, 661-662
    Operations Manager, 354, 418-419, 566
    Service Manager, 817-818, 870
    System Center Orchestrator, 968
    VMM (Virtual Machine Manager), 701-702, 759-760
BITS (Background Intelligent Transfer Service)
    client settings, 100, 156
    troubleshooting, 138
BITS-enabled Distribution Points, 83-84
boot images
    managing, 231
    MDT boot images, creating, 240
boundaries
    configuring, 139-143
    establishing, 97-99
    explained, 61
boundary groups, configuring, 139-143
Branch Distribution points, 59
BranchCache, 84
building runbooks
    Copy File and Log Event runbook, 953-959
    Move Disabled Users runbook, 962-965
business solutions, addressing
    Configuration Manager, 10
    DPM (Data Protection Manager), 28
    Operations Manager, 19-20
    Orchestrator, 46-47, 922
    Service Manager, 41
    VMM (Virtual Machine Manager), 35-36, 664-665

C

calculating storage requirements for DPM (Data Protection Manager) deployment, 585

cancelling change requests, 900-901, 903

Capacity Planner, 9

captured data, storing, 329

capturing existing user state, 231

CDP (continuous data protection), 571-572

CEC (Common Engineering Criteria), 421

Central Administration Site, 15, 57, 124
  database, 246
  installing, 124-126
  validating installation, 127-129

Central Administration Site Servers, 77-78

Central Console (DPM), 610-613

Certificate Auto-Enrollment GPO, configuring, 166-168

certificate requirements (IBCM), 108-109

Certificate Services website, configuring for SSL, 174-175

certificates
  deploying, 165
  Enterprise Root CA, 163-165
  monitoring DMZ servers with, 385-386
    agent configuration, 392
    agent installation, 391-392
    certificate templates, creating, 386-387
    root CA server certificates, requesting, 387-390
  OS Deployment certificate requests, 176
  protection agents, deploying with, 599-601
  root CA server certificates, requesting, 387-390
  security DMZ servers with, 316
  templates, 109-110
    creating, 168-172, 386-387
    publishing, 172-173

CFS (Clustered File System), 676

change control, 42

Change Management KPI Trend report, 916

Change Management Pack, 764

change management reports, 915-917

change management templates, 889-891

change management workflows, 891-892

Change Request Details report, 916

Change Request Prefix, 887

change request templates, 889-891

change request workflows, 891-892

change requests, 896
  adding
    manual activities, 897
    planning details, 898
    reviewers, 898-899
  automatic user notification, 908-910
  cancelling, 900-903
  closing, 907-908
  creating
    from configuration items, 893-894
    from incidents or problems, 895
    from scratch, 893
  holding, 900-901, 903
  implementing, 903
    approving and rejecting review activities, 903-905
    automatic user notification, 908-910
    closing, 907-908
    completing and failing manual activities, 905-907
  initiating, 892-893
  investigating, 896-898
  resuming, 900-901, 903
  Return to Activity, 902
  Service Manager 2012, 885

change settings, configuring, 887
  activity prefixes, 888-889
  Change Request Prefix, 887
  file attachment limits, 887-888

changing. See modifying

charts, displaying with Operations Manager reports, 531-532

choosing. See selecting

CI (configuration items), 885, 911
  creating change requests, 893-894
  defining items to monitor, 278-282
  deleting, 913-914
  restoring, 914
  searching, 911-912

Citrix XenServer, VMM support for, 670

client agents
  Configuration Management client agents, 278
  configuring software metering, 278

Client Agents node, accessing, 248

Client Authentication certificate template, creating, 168-169

client certificates, 109

client configuration settings, 156

Background Intelligent Transfer settings, 100, 156

client installation settings, 162-163

client policy settings, 156

Compliance settings, 100, 156

Computer Agent settings, 100, 157

Computer Restart settings, 100, 157

Endpoint Protection settings, 100, 157-158

Hardware Inventory settings, 100, 158

Remote Tools settings, 100, 158-159

Software Deployment settings, 101, 159

Software Inventory settings, 101, 159-160

Software Metering settings, 101, 160

Software Update settings, 160-161

State Messaging settings, 161

User and Device Affinity settings, 161-162

client installation settings, 162-163

Client Performance report, 477

Client Policy section (client settings), 100

client policy settings, 156

Client Push Installation account, 91

Client Push Installation Status Details report, 254

Client Push Installation Status Summary report, 254

client roaming, 65-66, 182-183

client schedules, 105-106

client settings (Configuration Manager)

adding hardware class, 266

configuring for inventory collection, 248-249

planning, 99-101

Client Status History report, 254

Client Status Summary report, 254

client-side monitoring scripts, 452

clients (Configuration Manager)

configuring. See client configuration settings

discovering and deploying, 94-95

explained, 62

HTTP and HTTPS client connections, 12

IBCM (Internet-based client management), 106-107, 163

Certificate Auto-Enrollment GPO configuration, 166-168

certificate deployment, 165

Certificate Services website, configuring for SSL, 174-175

certificate requirements, 108-109

certificate templates, 109-110, 168-173

client site assignment, 108

content distribution, 184

enabling, 176-177

Enterprise Root CA, 163-165

limitations of, 107

OS Deployment certificate requests, 176

PKI creation, 163

planning PKI, 109

planning site system placement, 107-108

WSUS website, configuring for SSL, 175-176

monitoring, 20-21

overview, 76-77

Registry keys, creating, 261-262

Clients That Have Not Reported Recently (in a Specified Number of Days) report, 254

closing change requests, 907-908

cloud computing

backing up to cloud, 31

VMM private clouds

creating, 711-714

explained, 704

fabric resources, 704

networks, 706

servers, 705

storage, 706-707

Clustered File System (CFS), 676

clusters

database, 319-320

file server clusters, protecting data on, 622

host clusters, managing, 710

VMM (Virtual Machine Manager) support for, 671

CMDB (configuration management database), 765, 911

cmdlets, 716

cmtrace.exe log viewing utility, 128, 133

collections, 89

creating, 204

defining, 185-188

designing, 94

maintenance windows, 187

update schedules, 187

command line, sealing management packs, 507

command shell, 422
    Operations Manager, 306-307
    VMM, 715-716
Common Engineering Criteria (CEC), 421
compiling configuration.mof files on test
    clients, 265
completing manual activities, 905-907
complex applications
    automating installation, 197-198
    configuring, 196
    creating, 198-202
compliance
    monitoring, 283
    service offerings, 874
Compliance 1 - Overall Compliance report, 253
Compliance 2 - Update Group report, 253
compliance management, 12, 73-74
Compliance Settings (Configuration Manager
    clients), 60, 100, 156, 278
    applying baselines to collections, 283
    client agents, 278
    configuration baselines, defining, 282-283
    configuration items to monitor, defining,
        278-282
Computer Agent section (client settings),
    100, 157
Computer Details report, 918
Computer Inventory report, 918-919
Computer Management, 438
Computer Restart section (client settings),
    100, 157
computer$ account, 95
Computers That Have a Metered Program
    Installed but Have Not Run the Program Since
    a Specified Date report, 278
Computers with a Specific File report, 253
Concurrent Usage for All Metered Software
    Programs report, 254
ConfigMgr. See Configuration Manager
configuration baselines, defining, 282-283
Configuration Changes report, 528
configuration items. See CI (configuration items)
configuration management database (CMDB),
    765, 911
configuration management reports, 918-919
Configuration Manager, 8, 14, 245
    Active Directory schema extensions, 64-66
    administration best practices, 178-179

application management, 189
    application model, 189-190
    complex application configuration, 196
    complex application creation, 198-202
    complex application installation
        automation, 197-198
    distributing content to Distribution
        Points, 202-203
    EXE application configuration, 192-196
    MSI application configuration, 191-192
    package model, 190-191
architecture, 75-76
AI (Asset Intelligence), 72-73, 269
    importing software license data, 275-277
    reporting, 277
    reporting classes, 270-274
    synchronizing, 269-270
Asset Intelligence Synchronization Points,
    81-82
asset data, 246-247
asset management, 70. See also AI (Asset
    Intelligence)
    Compliance Management, 73-74
    hardware and software inventory, 71
    software metering, 73
best practices, 112-114
boundaries, establishing, 97-99
business solutions addressed by, 10
Central Administration Site, 124
    installing, 124-126
    validating installation, 127-129
Central Administration Site Servers, 77-78
client configuration, 156
    Background Intelligent Transfer settings,
        100, 156
    client installation settings, 162-163
    client policy settings, 156
    Compliance settings, 100, 156
    Computer Agent settings, 100, 157
    Computer Restart settings, 100, 157
    Endpoint Protection settings, 100,
        157-158
    Hardware Inventory settings, 100, 158
    Remote Tools settings, 100, 158-159
    Software Deployment settings, 101, 159
    Software Inventory settings, 101,
        159-160

Software Metering settings, 101, 160
Software Update settings, 160-161
State Messaging settings, 161
User and Device Affinity settings, 161-162
client schedules, 105-106
client settings
configuring for inventory collection, 248-249
planning, 99-101
clients
discovering and deploying, 94-95
overview, 76-77
collections
defining, 185-188
designing, 94
Compliance Settings, 278
applying baselines to collections, 283
client agents, 278
defining configuration baselines, 282-283
defining configuration items to monitor, 278-282
connectors, deploying, 811-812
content distribution, 181
application management, 66-68
client roaming, 182-183
Distribution Point selection, 184-185
for Internet-based clients, 184
operating system deployment, 69-70
software update distribution, 68-69
customizing hardware Inventory, 261
adding hardware class in client settings, 266
creating Registry keys on the client, 261-262
editing configuration.mof files, 263-265
manually compiling configuration.mof on test clients, 265
validating custom inventory data, 267-268
viewing custom inventory data, 268
data flow, 101-102
database sizing, 93
deployment management
automatic deployments, 211-213
best practices, 243-244

monitoring deployments, 213-215
self-service deployments, 207-211
targeting users, 203-207
design scenarios
large enterprises, 111-112
small and medium enterprises, 110-111
disk subsystem performance, 102
SAN versus DAS, 102-104
SQL versions, 104-105
Distribution Points
BITS-enabled Distribution Points, 83-84
BranchCache features, 84
overview, 82-83
protected Distribution Points, 84
SMB-based Distribution Points, 83
Fallback Status Point (FSP), 84
hardware requirements, 92-93
health reports, 254
Health Validator Point, 85
hierarchy configuration, 62-63, 138
boundaries and boundary groups, 139-143
discovery methods, 143-144
Exchange connectors, 147-148
hierarchy and geographic views, 145-147
how it works, 60-62
IBCM (Internet-based client management), 106-107, 163
Certificate Auto-Enrollment GPO configuration, 166-168
certificate deployment, 165
certificate requirements, 108-109
Certificate Services website, configuring for SSL, 174-175
certificate template creation, 168-172
certificate template publication, 172-173
certificate templates, 109-110
client site assignment, 108
enabling, 176-177
Enterprise Root CA, 163-165
limitations of, 107
OS Deployment certificate requests, 176
PKI creation, 163
planning PKI, 109
planning site system placement, 107-108
WSUS website, configuring for SSL, 175-176

installation prerequisites, 118
  adding Windows roles on Site Servers, 121-124
  configuring System Management container, 120-121
  extending Active Directory schema, 118-119
major features of, 11-12
Management Points, 85-86
MDT (Microsoft Deployment Toolkit), 238
  creating task sequences, 240-242
  installing, 238
  integrating together, 239-240
Mobile Device Management, 87-88
MOF files, editing, 261
monitoring baselines and compliance, 283
multisite hierarchy, 95-96
new features, 15-17, 56
  administration changes, 60
  console redesign, 56
  hierarchy changes, 56-57
  operations changes, 59-60
  Site System role changes, 58-59
OS deployment, 225-227
  application and deployment type preparation, 227
  boot image management, 231
  creating operating system install task sequences, 231-234
  creating task sequence deployment, 235-236
  creating User State Migration package, 227-228
  driver management, 230-231
  importing unknown computers, 234-235
  monitoring, 236-238
  operating system image management, 229-230
  operating system installer management, 228-229
  scenarios for, 226-227
  technologies for, 225-226
Out-of-Band Service Points, 86
Primary Site Servers
  installing, 129-131
  overview, 78
  validating installation, 131-133

PXE-enabled Distribution Points, placement of, 97
reporting, 249
Reporting Service Point (RSP), 87
reports, 74-75
  editing, 256-261
  generating, 250-252
  lists of, 252-255
  scheduling, 255-256
revisions and product history, 13-15
sample organization in illustrations, 115-117
secondary sites, 64
  installing, 134-136
  validating installation, 136-138
security, 88
  port requirements, 89-90
  role-based administration, 89
  for server communication, 88-89
  service accounts, 91
site configuration, 148
  Asset Intelligence Synchronization Point role installation, 153-154
  Endpoint Protection Point role installation, 152-153
  FSP (Fallback Status Point) installation, 149
  OS deployment preparation, 154-155
  RSP (Reporting Service Point) installation, 149-150
  Software Update Point role installation, 150-152
Site Server database, 79-81
SMS Providers, 78-79
software metering, 277-278
software requirements, 93
Software Update Point (SUP), 87
State Migration Point (SMP)
  overview, 86-87
  placement of, 97
update deployment, 219
  automatic deployment rules, creating, 222-224
  deployment packages, creating, 219-220
  monitoring, 224-225
  Software Update deployments, creating, 220-222

update management, 215
  creating software update groups, 216-219
  viewing Update Repository, 215-216
  Wake On LAN functionality, 81
configuration.mof file, 263-265
Configure Orchestrator Users Group screen (Orchestrator Setup Wizard), 931
Configure the Database screen (Orchestrator Setup Wizard), 931
Configure the Ports for the Web Services screen (Orchestrator Setup Wizard), 932
Configure the Service Account screen (Orchestrator Setup Wizard), 931
ConfigureSharePoint.exe utility, 645
configuring. See also deploying
  Active Directory Client Monitoring, 453-454
  Active Directory Domain Controller Performance Collection, 458-460
  Active Directory Forest Discovery, 139
  Active Directory Management Pack, 451-460
  Active Directory Replication Monitoring, 454-458
  agents for certificates, 392
  audit forwarders, 376-379
  Certificate Auto-Enrollment GPO, 166-168
  Certificate Services website for SSL, 174-175
  change settings, 887
    activity prefixes, 888-889
    Change Request Prefix, 887
    file attachment limits, 887-888
  client settings for inventory collection, 248-249
  clients (Configuration Manager), 156
    Background Intelligent Transfer settings, 100, 156
    client installation settings, 162-163
    client policy settings, 156
    Compliance settings, 100, 156
    Computer Agent settings, 100, 157
    Computer Restart settings, 100, 157
    Endpoint Protection settings, 100, 157-158
    Hardware Inventory settings, 100, 158
    Remote Tools settings, 100, 158-159
    Software Deployment settings, 101, 159
    Software Inventory settings, 101, 159-160
    Software Metering settings, 101, 160
    Software Update settings, 160-161
    State Messaging settings, 161
    User and Device Affinity settings, 161-162
  complex applications, 196
  Configuration Manager hierarchy, 138
    boundaries and boundary groups, 139-143
    discovery methods, 143-144
    Exchange connectors, 147-148
    hierarchy and geographic views, 145-147
  Cross Platform Management Packs, 487-488
  DPM (Data Protection Manager)
    protection agents. See protection agents
    storage pool, 591-593
    tape libraries, 593
  email subscriptions for reports, 255
  EXE applications, 192-196
  incident settings
    file attachment limits, 822
    inbound email settings, 826-830
    incident prefix, 821
    Operations Manager Web console settings, 826
    priority calculation, 822-824
    resolution times, 824-825
  MSI applications, 191-192
  Network Access Account, 227
  notifications and subscriptions, 399-402
    notification subscriptions, 834-835
    notification templates, 833-834
    SMTP notification channels, 832-833
  Operations Manager
    global management group settings, 393-396
    notifications and subscriptions, 399-402
    proxy agent configuration, 396-398
    Restart Health Service Recovery, 398-399
  Operations Manager Dashboard Viewer web part, 562
  Operations Manager Management Pack, 433-434

problem settings
    file attachment limits, 856-857
    priority calculation, 857-858
    problem prefix string, 856
proxy agents, 396-398
release management workflows, 883-884
Restart Health Service Recovery, 398-399
sites (Configuration Manager), 148
    Asset Intelligence Synchronization Point
        role installation, 153-154
    Endpoint Protection Point role
        installation, 152-153
    FSP (Fallback Status Point)
        installation, 149
    OS deployment preparation, 154-155
    RSP (Reporting Service Point)
        installation, 149-150
    Software Update Point role installation,
        150-152
software metering client agents, 278
SQL Server Management Pack, 479
SSL for VMM Self-Service Portal, 695
System Management container, 120-121
VMM library, 710-711
Windows Authentication for VMM
    Self-Service Portal, 695
Windows Management Pack, 440-441
WSUS website for SSL, 175-176
Connections pane (Runbook Designer), 943-944
Connector Framework, 765
connectors, 768
    Active Directory, 805-806
    Configuration Manager, 811-812
    Operations Manager, 806-811
    Orchestrator, 812-813
consoles. See names of specific consoles
consolidated reporting, 43
containers (System Management), configuring,
    120-121
content databases, recovering, 649
content distribution (Configuration Manager), 181
    application management, 66-68
    client roaming, 182-183
    Distribution Point selection, 184-185
    for Internet-based clients, 184
    operating system deployment, 69-70
    software update distribution, 68-69

content library, 57
continuous data protection (CDP), 571-572
Control+Alt+Delete (remote control), 59
Conversion Information page (Convert Physical
    Server Wizard), 723
Convert Physical Server Wizard, 718-724
    Add Properties page, 723
    Conversion Information page, 723
    Select Host page, 721
    Select Networks page, 723
    Select Path page, 723
    Specify Virtual Machine Identity page, 720
    Summary page, 723-724
    System Information page, 720
    Volume Configuration page, 721
Convert Virtual Machine Wizard, 726-729
    Additional Properties page, 728
    Select Host page, 727
    Select networks page, 728
    Specify Virtual Machine Identity page, 727
    Summary page, 728
    Virtual Machine Configuration page, 727
converting VMs (virtual machines)
    P2V (physical-to-virtual) conversions,
        717-724
    V2V (virtual-to-virtual) conversions, 725-729
Copy File and Log Event runbook
    building, 953-959
    testing, 959-961
Copy File Properties dialog box, 955
core client access licenses, 50
Correlation Engine service, 467-468
cost of SQL licensing, 105
Count Operating Systems and Service Packs
    report, 252
counters (Runbook Designer), 944
Create Cloud Wizard, 711-714
Create New Protection Group Wizard, 601-606
    Exchange database protection, 625-628
    Hyper-V virtual machine protection, 654, 656
    SharePoint farm protection, 645-647
    SQL database protection, 636-638
Create User Role Wizard, 732-737
CRL, publishing, 165
Cross Platform Management Packs, 487
    configuring, 487-488
    reports, 489-490
    views, 488-489

Cross Platform Performance History report, 491
Cross Premises Mailflow Monitoring report, 477
custom ACS (Audit Collection Services) reports, 545-548
custom management packs, 503
  Authoring Console, 503
  creating, 504-506
  for service offerings, 875
  modifying existing XML management pack, 506
  sealing via command line, 507
custom schedules, 106
custom volumes, assigning to protection group members, 613-614
customizing
  hardware inventory (Configuration Manager), 261
    adding hardware class in client settings, 266
    creating Registry keys on the client, 261-262
    editing configuration.mof files, 263-265
    manually compiling configuration.mof files on test clients, 265
    validating custom inventory data, 267-268
    viewing custom inventory data, 268
  host ratings, 741-742
  problem prefix strings, 856

D

D2D (disk-to-disk) storage, 570
D2D2C (disk-to-disk-to-cloud) storage, 571
D2T (disk-to-tape) storage, 570
Daily Alerts report, 538-540
DAS (direct attached storage), 331-333, 773
  SAN (storage area network) versus, 102-104
Dashboard views, 290, 424, 444
dashboards
  Operations Manager
    creating, 557-559
    explained, 554-555
    publishing, 561-565
    viewing, 559-560
    widgets, 556-559
  Service Level Dashboards, 293

data. See asset data
data flow in Configuration Manager, 101-102
Data Protection Manager. See DPM (Data Protection Manager)
data recovery. See recovery
Data Warehouse Reader accounts, 316
Data Warehouse Write Action accounts, 316
data warehouses
  deploying, 794-797
  explained, 762, 765
  job schedules, viewing, 799-800
Database State view, 482
databases
  audit collection database, 309-310
  backups, 30
  Central Administration Site database, 246
  clusters, 319-320
  CMDB (configuration management database), 765
  design, 686
  Exchange databases
    protecting with DPM (Data Protection Manager), 625-628
    restoring, 628-631
  growth estimates, 93, 326-327
  integrated solutions databases, 22
  Operations Manager database
    backing up, 412-414
    hardware/software requirements, 302
    overview, 301-302
  OperationsManagerAC database, backing up, 416-417
  OperationsManagerDW database, backing up, 414-415
  Orchestration database, 923
  Primary Site Server databases, 246
  replication, 57
  SharePoint content databases, recovering, 649
  Site Database, 246
  Site Server database, 79-81
  SQL databases
    choosing versions, 104-105
    preparing for System Center Orchestrator installation, 929
    protecting with DPM, 636-638
    restoring with DPM Recovery Wizard, 638-640
    self-service restores, 640-642

DC Active Alerts, 460

DC events, 460

DC performance data, 460

DC Replication Bandwidth report, 465

DC State, 461

DCM (Desired Configuration Management). *See* Compliance Settings

Default Management Pack, 456

defining

    collections, 185-188

    management groups, 328-329

defragmentation applications, file exclusions for, 409-410

Delegated Administrator role (VMM), 672, 729, 731-734

delegating guest session administration, 37

deleting

    CI (configuration items), 913-914

    user roles, 740

dependent activities, 886

Deploy Virtual Machine Wizard, 743-744

deploying, 67-68. *See also* configuring; deployment management; installing

    applications, reports on, 253

    certificates, 165

    Configuration Manager clients, 94-95

    DPM (Data Protection Manager)

        DPM server, 587

        DPM Setup Wizard, 588-591

        planning for, 580-587

        remote SQL instances, 588

    geographic-based management groups, 335

    IPs (Integration Packs), 951

    operating systems, 11

    Operations Manager, 345-346

        design and planning phase, 346-348

        design principles training, 346

        pilot phase, 351-352

        production phase, 352-353

        proof of concept (POC) phase, 348-350

    Operations Manager agents, 373

        audit forwarders, 376-379

        UNIX/Linux agents, 379-385

        Windows agents, 373-376

    Operations Manager Dashboard Viewer web part, 561-562

    political or security-based management groups, 335

protection agents

    with certificates, 599-601

    with DPM Administration Console, 594-596

    manual installation process, 596-599

    with PowerShell, 601

Service Manager

    Active Directory connectors, 805-806

    components, 791-794

    Configuration Manager connectors, 811-812

    data warehouse job schedules, viewing, 799-800

    data warehouses, 794-797

    management group registration, 798-799

    Self-Service Portal, 801-805

    Operations Manager connectors, 806-811

    Orchestrator connectors, 812-813

software, 12

VMM (Virtual Machine Manager)

    multiple-server deployment, 688

    planning for, 682-687

    single-server deployment, 688

    VMM Administrator Console installation, 692-693

    VMM Agent installation, 695-700

    VMM Self-Service Portal installation, 694

    VMM Self-Service Portal security, 695

    VMM server installation, 688-691

VMs (virtual machines) with VMM Administrator Console, 742-744

deployment configuration files, 753

deployment management. *See also* **application management**

    automatic deployments, 211-213

    best practices, 243-244

    MDT (Microsoft Deployment Toolkit), 238

        creating task sequences, 240-242

        installing, 238

        integrating with Configuration Manager, 239-240

    monitoring deployments, 213-215

    OS deployment. *See* OS deployment

    self-service deployments, 207-211

    targeting users, 203-207

update deployment, 219
    automatic deployment rules, creating,
        222-224
    deployment packages, creating, 219-220
    monitoring, 224-225
    Software Update deployments, creating,
        220-222
Deployment Manager utility, 923, 950-951
deployment packages, creating, 219-220
**Deployment Status of All Task Sequence
    Deployments report, 254**
deployment templates, 221
deployment types, 68
    preparing for OS deployment, 227
design and planning phase
    Operations Manager deployment, 346-348
    Service Manager deployment, 784-786
**design principles training (Operations
    Manager), 346**
**Design Principles Training phase (Service
    Manager deployment), 784**
design requirements (Service Manager)
    disk subsystem performance, 773
    hardware requirements, 769-771
    large enterprise design, 780-783
    medium enterprise design, 778-780
    SAN versus DAS, 773
    small enterprise design, 776-778
    software requirements, 771-772
    SQL versions, 773-774
design scenarios (Configuration Manager)
    large enterprises, 111-112
    small and medium enterprises, 110-111
designing
    collections, 94
    Configuration Manager configuration for
        sample organization, 117
    database servers, 686
    databases, 686
    DPM servers, 586-587
    infrastructure fabric, 686-687
    library servers, 687
    Operations Manager
        large enterprise design, 341-345
        medium enterprise design, 338-341
        small enterprise design, 336-338
    protection groups, 582-585

    Self-Service Portal web server, 686
    VMM Library, 687
    VMM servers, 686
**Desired Configuration Management (DCM). *See*
    Compliance Settings**
DFS namespaces, protecting data in, 621
Diagram view (Operations console), 424
**dialog boxes. *See names of specific dialog
    boxes***
**dip stick health checks (Operations Manager),
    403-404**
direct attached storage (DAS), 331-333, 773
Disable Audit Collection, 438
**disaster recovery (Operations Manager),
    320-323**
    component backup schedules, 411-412
    IIS 7.x configuration backup, 417-418
    OperationsManager database, 412-414
    OperationsManagerAC database, 416-417
    OperationsManagerDW database, 414-415
discovering
    Configuration Manager clients, 94-95
    sites and subnets, 98-99
discovery methods, configuring, 143-144
Discovery Wizard, 373, 375
Disk Performance Analysis report, 449
Disk Performance Dashboard view, 445
disk subsystem performance, 329-330
    Configuration Manager, 102
        SAN versus DAS, 102-104
        SQL versions, 104-105
    Service Manager, 773
disk-to-disk (D2D) storage, 570
disk-to-disk-to-cloud (D2D2C) storage, 571
disk-to-tape (D2T) storage, 570
disks, adding to storage pool, 591-593
distribution. *See* content distribution
Distribution Points, 58, 61
    BITS-enabled Distribution Points, 83-84
    BranchCache features, 84
    distributing content to, 202-203
    overview, 82-83
    protected Distribution Points, 84
    PXE-enabled Distribution Points, 97
    selecting, 184-185
    SMB-based Distribution Points, 83

DMZ servers

  certificates, 316

  monitoring with certificates, 385-386

    agent configuration, 392

    agent installation, 391-392

    certificate templates, creating, 386-387

    root CA server certificates, requesting, 387-390

domain controller discovery, 453

domain controller monitoring scripts, 452

Domain Join account, 91

downloading management packs from Internet, 427-428

Downtime report, 528

DPM (Data Protection Manager), 8

  advantages over tape-based backup, 569-570

  best practices, 617-618, 661-662

  business solutions addressed by, 28

  CDP (continuous data protection), 571-572

  custom volumes, 613-614

  D2D (disk-to-disk) storage, 570

  D2D2C (disk-to-disk-to cloud) storage, 571

  D2T (disk-to-tape) storage, 570

  data recovery, 614-616

  DPM Administration Console

    overview, 607-608

    protection agent deployment, 594-596

  DPM Central Console, 610-613

  DPM Management Shell, 608-610

  DPM servers

    deploying, 587

    designing, 586-587

    preparing for deployment, 587

  DPM Setup Wizard, 588-591

  Exchange Server, protecting, 624

    additional considerations, 635

    Exchange databases, 625-631

    high-availability considerations, 633-634

    mailboxes, 631-633

  file servers, protecting data, 620-621

    on DFS namespace, 621

    on file server clusters, 622

    on mount points, 622

  hardware requirements, 578

  Hyper-V, 654

    item-level recovery, 659-660

    protecting Hyper-V virtual machines, 654-656

    protecting nondomain joined Hyper-V hosts, 656

    recovering Hyper-V virtual machines, 658-659

    targeting Hyper-V hosts across firewalls, 656-657

  major features of, 28-31

  new features, 32-34

  overview, 8, 26-27, 567-568

  planning for, 580

    DPM servers, 586-587

    environment, 580-581

    project scope, 581-582

    protection groups, 582-585

    storage requirements, 585

  ports used by, 657

  protection agents, deploying

    with certificates, 599-601

    with DPM Administration Console, 594-596

    manual installation process, 596-599

    with PowerShell, 601

  protection groups

    creating, 601-606

    custom volumes, 613-614

  remote SQL instances

    deploying, 588

    requirements, 579

  revisions and product history, 31-32

    Data Protection Manager 2006, 572

    Data Protection Manager 2006 SP1, 573

    Data Protection Manager 2007, 573-574

    Data Protection Manager 2007 SP1, 574-575

    Data Protection Manager 2010, 575-577

    Data Protection Manager 2010 SP 1, 575-577

    Data Protection Manager 2012, 577-578

  Self Service Recovery Tool, 640-642

  SharePoint farms

    content databases, recovering, 649

    item-level recovery, 650-653

    preparing for protection, 644-645

    protecting, 645-647

    recovering, 647-649

    SharePoint data sources and recoverable data, 643-644

How can we make this index more useful? Email us at indexes@samspublishing.com software requirements, 579

SQL Server, 635

   protecting SQL databases, 636-638

   restoring SQL databases with Recovery Wizard, 638-640

   self-service restores, 640-642

storage pool, adding disks to, 591-593

supported operating systems, 579

System State, protecting, 622-624

tape libraries, configuring, 593

dragging and dropping VMs (virtual machines)

   onto host groups, 752

   onto host servers, 751-752

driver packages, 70

drivers

   managing, 230-231

   operating system deployment, 70

E

early virtualization management techniques, 673

Edge role, 474

editing

   configuration.mof files, 263-265

   reports (Configuration Manager), 256-261

   SCCM MOF file, 261

email

   email-created incidents, 845

   inbound email settings (Service Manager), 826-830

Email activity (Orchestrator), 953

email subscriptions for reports, configuring, 255

email-created incidents, 845

Enable Audit Collection, 438

enabling. *See also* **configuring**

   Internet-based client management, 176-177

   network discovery for Runbook Designer, 939-940

   PXE support, 154-155

   unknown computer support, 234-235

encryption key, backing up, 816-817

Encryption Key Backup or Restore Wizard, 793, 797

end-to-end service monitoring, 292

Endpoint Protection Point section (client settings), 100, 157-158

Endpoint Protection Points, 57-58, 152-153

Enrollment Points, 58

Enterprise Root CA, 109

   deployment, 163-165

   validation, 165

environment

   DPM deployment, 580-581

   VMM deployment, 682-683

   virtualized environments. *See* Hyper-V

estimating time requirements for Service Manager projects, 791

ETL (Extraction, Transformation, and Loading) process, 767

evaluating incidents, 846-847

event correlation, 20

event logs, 20

Events workspace (Orchestration console), 948

Exchange 2010 ActiveSync Connectivity view, 473

Exchange 2010 Client Performance report, 478

Exchange 2010 Management Pack, 466

   Correlation Engine service, 467-468

   installing, 468-469

   preparing to install, 466-467

   reports, 477-478

   synthetic transaction event collection, 470-471

   test mailbox configuration, 469-470

   views, 471-477

Exchange 2010 Service State view, 472

Exchange connectors, configuring, 147-148

Exchange databases

   protecting with DPM, 625-628

   restoring, 628-631

Exchange Server

   mailboxes, restoring, 631-633

   protecting with DPM, 624

      additional considerations, 635

      Exchange databases, 625-631

      high-availability considerations, 633-634

      mailboxes, 631-633

Exchange Server connectors, 57

EXE applications, configuring, 192-196

existing user state, capturing, 231

exporting management packs, 429-430

extending Active Directory schema, 118-119

extraction, 767

Extraction, Transformation, and Loading (ETL) process, 767

F

fabric management (VMM), 677, 686
fabric resources, 704
   networks, 706
   servers, 705
   storage, 706-707
failing manual activities, 905-907
fallback sites (Configuration Manager), 57
Fallback Status Point (FSP), 164
   installing, 149
   overview, 84
farms (SharePoint)
   content databases, recovering, 649
   item-level recovery, 650-653
   preparing for protection, 644-645
   protecting with DPM, 645-647
   recovering, 647-649
   SharePoint data sources and recoverable
      data, 643-644
fault tolerance (Operations Manager)
   architecture, 317
   database clusters, 319-320
   management group redundancy, 318
   resource pools, 318-319
file attachment limits, 887-888
   for incidents, 822
   for problems, 856-857
File Encoding dialog box, 957
File Management activity (Orchestrator), 953
file server clusters, protecting data on, 622
file servers, protecting data with DPM, 620-621
   in DFS namespace, 621
   on file server clusters, 622
   on mount points, 622
files
   deployment configuration files, 753
   exclusions for antivirus and defragmenta-
      tion applications, 409-410
Filter Settings dialog box, 955, 963
firewalls
   Operations Manager requirements, 314
   System Center Orchestrator, 928
   targeting Hyper-V hosts across, 656-657
Flush Health Service State and Cache, 438
folders, creating for service catalog
  knowledge-base articles, 876

Forensic reports (ACS), 543
forest discovery, configuring, 139
FSP (Fallback Status Point), 164
   installing, 149
   overview, 84

G

Gateway server, 307-308
General License Reconciliation report, 276
General settings (VMM Administrator
  Console), 715
generating
   Activity Distribution report, 917
   Computer Inventory reports, 919
   Configuration Manager reports, 250-252
generating reports. See schedules, report
  schedules
geographic views, configuring, 145-147
geographic-based management groups, 335
Get the Agent Processor Utilization, 438
Get the Pool Member Monitoring a Top-Level
  Instance, 439
Get Top-Level Instances Monitored by a Pool
  Member, 439
Get User Properties dialog box, 963
Get-Help cmdlet, 716
global management group settings (Operations
  Manager), 393-396
global roaming, 65, 182
GnuPG (GNU Privacy Guard), 941
group discovery, 95
groups
   host groups
      creating, 708-709
      definition of, 705
   management groups
      defining, 328-329
      geographic-based management
         group, 335
      global management group settings
         (Operations Manager), 393-396
      multiple management group, 334
      political or security-based management
         group, 335
      registering, 798-799

protection groups
creating, 601-606
custom volumes, 613-614
designing, 582-585
security groups (Orchestrator), 927
software update groups, creating, 216-219
guest sessions, 37-38

H

Hardware 01A - Summary of Computers in a Specific Collection, 270
Hardware 02A - Estimated Computer Age by Ranges Within a Collection, 270
Hardware 02B - Computers Within an Age Range Within a Collection, 270
Hardware 03A - Primary Computer Users, 270
Hardware 03B - Computers for a Specific Primary Console User, 270
Hardware 04A - Shared (Multi-User) Computers, 271
Hardware 05A - Console Users on a Specific Computer, 271
Hardware 06A - Computers for Which Console Users Could Not Be Determined, 271
Hardware 07A - USB Devices by Manufacturer, 271
Hardware 07B - USB Devices by Manufacturer and Description, 271
Hardware 07C - Computers with a Specific USB Device, 271
Hardware 07D - USB Devices on a Specific Computer, 271
Hardware 08A - Hardware That Is Not Ready for a Software Upgrade, 271
Hardware 09A - Search for Computers, 271
hardware class, adding in client settings, 266
Hardware History node, 269
hardware inventory (Configuration Manager), 59, 71, 261
adding hardware class in client settings, 266
creating Registry keys on the client, 261-262
editing configuration.mof files, 263-265
manually compiling configuraiton.mof files on test clients, 265
validating custom inventory data, 267-268
viewing custom inventory data, 268

Hardware Inventory Client Agent, 248-249
Hardware Inventory section (client settings), 100, 158
hardware requirements
ACS (Audit Collection Services), 311
Configuration Manager, 92-93
DPM (Data Protection Manager), 578
Gateway server, 307-308
Operations Manager, 323-324
agents, 301
audit collection database, 310
audit collector, 309
command shell, 307
database, 302
Operations Console, 305
Web console, 306
Reporting data warehouse, 303
Reporting Server, 304
Service Manager, 769-771
System Center Orchestrator, 925-926
VMM Administrator Console, 679
VMM Self-Service Portal, 680
VMM server, 678
hash values, 82
Health Service Heartbeat Failure, 433
Health Service Watcher monitors, 433
Health Validator Point, 85
heterogeneous VM management, 670
hierarchy configuration (Configuration Manager), 62-63, 138
boundaries and boundary groups, 139-143
changes in, 56-57
discovery methods, 143-144
Exchange connectors, 147-148
hierarchy and geographic views, 145-147
hierarchy views, configuring, 145-147
high-availability considerations
DPM (Data Protection Manager), 633-634
System Center Orchestrator, 926
holding change requests, 900-903
host clusters, managing, 710
host groups
creating, 708-709
definition of, 705
dragging and dropping VMs onto, 752
host ratings, customizing, 741-742
host servers, dragging and dropping VMs onto, 751-752

hosts
  Hyper-V hosts
    protecting, 656
    targeting across firewalls, 656-657
  managing, 709
  virtual machine hosts, system
    requirements, 682
HTTP client connections, 12
HTTPS
  client connections, 12
  selecting by roles, 57
Hub Transport role, 474
Hyper-V, 654. *See also* **VMM (Virtual Machine Manager)**
  item-level recovery, 659-660
  protecting with DPM
    protecting Hyper-V virtual machines, 654-656
    protecting nondomain joined Hyper-V hosts, 656
    targeting Hyper-V hosts across firewalls, 656-657
  recovering Hyper-V virtual machines, 658-659
  server backups, 31
  VMM support for, 670

I

I/O Latency, 331
I/Os Per Second (IOps), 331
IBCM (Internet-based client management), 106-107, 163
  Certificate Auto-Enrollment GPO configuration, 166-168
  certificate deployment, 165
  certificate requirements, 108-109
  Certificate Services website, configuring for SSL, 174-175
  certificate templates, 109-110
    creating, 168-172
    publishing, 172-173
  client site assignment, 108
  content distribution, 184
  enabling, 176-177
  Enterprise Root CA, 163-165
  limitations of, 107

  OS Deployment certificate requests, 176
  PKI creation, 163
  planning PKI, 109
  planning site system placement, 107-108
  task sequence deployment, 59
  WSUS website, configuring for SSL, 175-176
IBM AIX 5.3 dependencies, 379
IBM AIX 6.1 dependencies, 380
IDMIF files, asset data, 247
IIS
  configuration backup, 417-418
  implementing on Site Servers, 121-124
ILR (item-level recovery)
  on Hyper-V virtual machines, 659-660
  of SharePoint items, 650-653
implementing change requests, 903
  approving and rejecting review activities, 903-905
  automatic user notification, 908-910
  closing, 907-908
  completing and failing manual activities, 905-907
importing
  application packages into VMM, 758
  management packs, 365-368, 426-427
  software license data, 275-277
  unknown computers, 234-235
inbound email settings (Service Manager), 826-830
incident management, 42
incidents
  analyzing, 847-849
  announcements, publishing, 850
  assigning, 846-847
  email-created incidents, 845
  evaluating, 846-847
  explained, 819-820
  incident reports, 864-868
  incident settings
    file attachment limits, 822
    inbound email settings, 826-830
    incident prefix, 821
    Operations Manager Web console settings, 826
    priority calculation, 822-824
    resolution times, 824-825

manually created incidents, 836-838

Operations Manager alert–generated incidents, 838-841

resolving, 853-855

Self-Service Portal–generated incidents, 841-845

troubleshooting tasks, running, 851-853

infrastructure fabric design, 686-687

infrastructure optimization model (Service Manager 2012), 871-872

initiating change requests, 892-893

installation prerequisites (Configuration Manager), 118

adding Windows roles on Site Servers, 121-124

configuring System Management container, 120-121

extending Active Directory schema, 118-119

Installation Summary screen (Orchestrator Setup Wizard), 932

installing. *See also* **deploying**

agents on DMZ servers, 391-392

Asset Intelligence Synchronization Point role, 153-154

Central Administration Site, 124-129

clients (Configuration Manager), installation settings, 162-163

complex applications, automating installation, 197-198

Endpoint Protection Point role, 152-153

Exchange 2010 Management Pack, 468-469

FSP (Fallback Status Point), 149

IPs (Integration Packs), 949, 951

management packs from downloads, 429

MDT (Microsoft Deployment Toolkit), 238

Operations Manager, 356

ACS (Audit Collection Services), 368-373

management packs, importing, 365-368

multiserver installs, 359-365

single-server installs, 356-359

Primary Site Servers, 129-133

RSP (Reporting Service Point), 149-150

secondary sites, 134-138

Server App-V Agent, 754-755

Server App-V Sequencer, 754

Service Manager

Active Directory connectors, 805-806

components, 791-794

Configuration Manager connectors, 811-812

data warehouse job schedules, viewing, 799-800

data warehouses, 794-797

management group registration, 798-799

Self-Service Portal, 801-805

Operations Manager connectors, 806-811

Orchestrator connectors, 812-813

Software Update Point role, 150-152

State Migration Point, 155

System Center Orchestrator

multiserver installation, 933-939

single-server installation, 928-932

UNIX/Linux agents, 379-385

VMM Administrator Console, 692-693

VMM Agent, 695-700

VMM Self-Service Portal, 694

VMM servers, 688-691

Windows agents, 373-376

instances (VMM), number of, 685

Instances tab

Runbook Servers workspace, 948

Runbooks workspace, 947

integrated solutions databases, 22

integrating MDT 2012 with Configuration Manager 2012, 239-240

Integration Pack Deployment Wizard, 951

Integration Packs. *See* **IPs (Integration Packs)**

Integration Toolkit (Orchestrator), 923

Internet-based client management. *See* **IBCM**

Internet-based Management Points, 58

inventory collection, 71

asset data, 246-247

configuring client settings, 248-249

inventory data

validating, 267-268

viewing, 268

inventory reports, 252

investigating change requests, 896-898

IOps (I/Os Per Second), 331

IPs (Integration Packs)

deploying, 951

explained, 923

installing, 949, 951

registering, 950-951

ISO 20000 international standard, 885
IT Process Automation (ITPA), 765
Item Selection dialog box, 963
item-level recovery (ILR)
    on Hyper-V virtual machines, 659-660
    of SharePoint items, 650-653
items (SharePoint), recovering, 650-653
ITIL Change Management, 885
ITIL Service Management, 885
ITPA (IT Process Automation), 765

J–K

job schedules, viewing, 799-800
Jobs dialog box, 714
Jobs tab
    Runbook Servers workspace, 948
    Runbooks workspace, 947
Junction Properties dialog box, 958

Kerberos tickets, refreshing, 91, 120, 171
keys, backing up encryption key, 816-817
knowledge base (KB), 765, 768
    creating folders for articles, 876

L

large enterprise design
    Configuration Manager, 111-112
    Operations Manager, 341-345
    Service Manager, 780-783
latency, 331
libraries
    tape libraries, configuring, 593
    VMM Library
        configuring, 710-711
        designing, 687
        explained, 668-669
library servers, 687, 705
License 01A - Microsoft License Ledger for Microsoft License Statements, 271
License 01B - Microsoft License Ledger Item by Sales Channel, 272
License 01C - Computers with a Specific Microsoft License Ledger Item and Sales Channel, 272

License 01D - Microsoft License Ledger Products on a Specific Computer, 272
License 02A - Count of Licenses Nearing Expiration by Time Ranges, 272
License 02B - Computers with Licenses Nearing Expiration, 272
License 02C - License Information on a Specific Computer, 272
License 03A - Count of Licenses by License Status, 272
License 03B - Computers with a Specific License Status, 272
License 04A - Count of Products Managed by Software Licensing, 272
License 04B - Computers with a Specific Product Managed by Software Licensing Service, 273
License 05A - Computers Providing Key Management Service, 273
license data, importing, 275, 277
licensing, 6, 50
    core client access licenses, 50
    costs, SQL, 105
    server management suite volume licensing, 50-51
    tracking, 72
limits on file attachments, 887-888
Linux agents, installing, 379-385
List of Activities report, 917
List of Change Requests report, 916
List of Manual Activities report, 917
List of Review Activities report, 917
listings
    Customizing the configuration.mof File, 264
    PowerShell Script to Check the Hardware Warranty Status, 279
    Query for Count Operating Systems and Service Packs Report, 259
    Query for Listing Systems with Operating Systems and Service Packs, 259
    VBScript to Check the Hardware Warranty Status, 280
lists
    Configuration Manager reports, 252-255
    SharePoint lists, recovering, 650-653
load balancers, 706
loading, 767
Local Administrator accounts, 316

Local Agent Compliance report, 285
Local Service account, 91
Local System account, 91
Log pane (Runbook Designer), 945
Logical Disk Free Space monitor, 441
logical networks, 706
logs, event, 20

M

MAC address pools, 706
Machine Level Capacity Trending report, 477
Mailbox role, 475
mailboxes, restoring, 631-633
Maintenance mode (VMM 2008 R2), 675-676
maintenance reports (Operations Manager), 532
    Alert Logging Latency report, 534-536
    Daily Alerts report, 538-540
    Most Common Alerts report, 533-534
    Send Queue % Used Top 10 report,
        536-537
    SQL Database Space report, 540-541
maintenance windows for collections, 187
managed systems, 62
Management 2 - Updates Required but Not
    Deployed report, 253
management console (Configuration Manager),
    role-based administration, 89
management groups
    defining, 328-329
    geographic-based management groups, 335
    global management group settings
        (Operations Manager), 393-396
    multiple management groups, 334
    political or security-based management
        groups, 335
    redundancy, 318
    registering, 798-799
Management Pack Import Wizard, 367-368
Management Pack Templates, 491-492
    OLEDB Data Source Template, 497-499
    Process Monitoring Template, 499-500
    TCP Port Template, 501-502
    UNIX/Linux Log File Template, 502
    UNIX/Linux Service Template, 503
    Web Application Template, 492-494
    Windows Service Template, 494-497

management packs, 291. See also names of
    specific management packs
    importing, 365-368, 426-427
    updating, 404-405
Management Point (MP), 58, 61, 246
    overview, 85-86
    secondary sites and, 64
    server locator functionality, 58
management server (Orchestrator), 923
    connecting to Runbook Designer, 940-941
    installing, 934-935
Management Server Action accounts, 315
Management Server State Dashboard view, 437
Management Server to Management Group
    Availability Health Rollup, 433
management servers, 300-301
Management Servers State, 436
Management Shell (DPM), 608-610
managing. See also administration
    Administrator user role, 730-731
    host clusters, 710
    hosts, 709
    Hyper-V with VMM. See VMM (Virtual
        Machine Manager)
    VMs (virtual machines), 714
manual activities, 886, 898
    adding to change requests, 897
    completing, 905-907
    failing, 905-907
Manual Activity Details report, 917
manually created incidents, 836-838
MBps (Megabytes Per Second), 331
MDT (Microsoft Deployment Toolkit), 70, 238
    creating task sequences, 240-242
    installing, 238
    integrating with Configuration Manager,
        239-240
medium enterprise design
    Configuration Manager, 110-111
    Operations Manager, 338-341
    Service Manager, 778-780
Megabytes Per Second (MBps), 331
Message Properties dialog box, 957
Microsoft Deployment Toolkit. See MDT
    (Microsoft Deployment Toolkit)
Microsoft Installer, 189
Microsoft Operations Manager (MOM) 23

Microsoft Software License Terms dialog box, 589
Microsoft Solution Accelerators, 9
Microsoft System Center Enterprise Suite Unleashed, 9
Migrate action (VMM), 748-750
Migrate Storage action (VMM), 750-751
Migrate Virtual Machine Wizard
    Migrate action, 748-750
    Migrate Storage action, 750-751
migrating VMs (virtual machines)
    dragging and dropping onto host group, 752
    dragging and dropping onto host server, 751-752
    with Migrate action, 748-750
    with Migrate Storage action, 750-751
    supported storage migration technologies, 748
    supported VM migration technologies, 747-748
Mobile Device Management, 9, 87-88
Mobile Device section (client settings), 100
Modify Disk Allocation dialog box, 614
modifying
    existing XML management pack, 506
    stored procedures, 450
    user roles, 739-740
mofcomp.exe utility, 263
MOF files (Configuration Manager), editing, 261
MOM (Microsoft Operations Manager), 23
Monitor Availability report, 528
Monitor File Properties dialog box, 955
monitoring
    applications, 21, 290
    baselines and compliance, 283
    clients, 20-21
    deployments, 213-215
    DMZ servers, 385-386
        agent configuration, 392
        agent installation, 391-392
        certificate templates, creating, 386-387
        root CA server certificates, requesting, 387-390
    networks, 290, 385
    non-domain member considerations, 327-328
    OS deployment, 236-238

rules, 294
servers, 20
system monitoring, 21
update deployment, 224-225
VMs (virtual machines), 714
Monitoring activity (Orchestrator), 953
monitors, 292
Most Common Alerts report, 533-534
mount points, protecting data on, 622
Move Disabled Users runbook
    building, 962-965
    testing, 965-966
Move User Properties dialog box, 963
MSI applications, configuring, 191-192
MSI extension, 189
multiple Internet-based Management Points, 58
multiple management groups, 334
multiple-server deployment (VMM), 688
multiserver installations
    Operations Manager, 359-365
    Orchestrator, 933
        hardware requirements, 925-926
        management server installation, 934-935
        Orchestrator web service installation, 937-938
        Runbook Designer installation, 938-939
        runbook server installation, 935-937
        server preparation, 933
multisite hierarchy in Configuration Manager, 95-96

N

namespaces, protecting data in, 621
Native mode, 57
NetIQ Enterprise Event Manager, 23
Network Access account, 91, 95, 227
Network Access Protection section (client settings), 100
Network Discovery, 95, 939-940
networks
    logical networks, 706
    monitoring, 290, 385
    Operations Manager requirements, 325-326
    SANs (storage area networks), 331-333
    VMM private cloud, 706

new features
  Configuration Manager, 15-17, 56-60
  DPM (Data Protection Manager), 32-34
  Operations Manager, 24-25, 290-291
  Service Manager, 44-45, 762-763
  System Center 2012 Orchestrator, 48-49
  VMM (Virtual Machine Manager), 39,
    677-678
**New Job Schedule dialog box, 413-417,
815-816**
NOIDMIF files, 247
**nondomain joined Hyper-V hosts,
protecting, 656**
Notification activity (Orchestrator), 953
notifications
  alert tuning, 405-409
  configuring, 399-402
  definition of, 293
  Notifications Resource Pool, 319
  Service Manager notifications, 830
    architecture, 830-832
    notification subscriptions, 834-835
    notification templates, 833-834
    SMTP notification channels, 832-833
Notifications Resource Pool, 319

O

Office Customization Wizard, 197-198
OLAP cubes, 768-769
OLEDB Data Source Template, 497-499
Opalis, 48
operating system deployment. *See*
  OS deployment
Operating System Health Dashboard view, 444
operating system images, managing, 229-230
operating system install package, 70
**operating system install task sequences,
creating, 231-234**
operating system installers, managing, 228-229
Operating System Performance view, 444
operating system source files, 69
operating systems, support for
  in DPM (Data Protection Manager), 579
  in Operations Manager, 298
  in System Center Orchestrator, 924-925
  in VMM (Virtual Machine Manager),
    679-681

Operations console, 304-305, 422-424
Operations Manager, 18, 421
  ACS (Audit Collection Services)
    hardware/software requirements, 311
    installing, 368-373
    overview, 310-311
  agents, 373
    audit forwarders, configuring, 376-379
    configuring to use certificates, 392
    installing on DMZ servers, 391-392
    overview, 298-299
    proxy agent configuration, 396-398
    Restart Health Service Recovery,
      398-399
    security, 313
    supported operating systems, 298
    UNIX/Linux agents, installing, 379-385
    Windows agents, installing, 373-376
  alerts
    generating, 294
    overview, 292
    tuning, 405-409
  architecture, 296-298
  audit collection database, 309-310
  audit collector, 309
  audit forwarder
    configuring, 376-379
    overview, 308
  backups
    component backup schedules, 411-412
    IIS 7.x configuration backup, 417-418
    OperationsManager database, 412-414
    OperationsManagerAC database,
      416-417
    OperationsManagerDW database,
      414-415
  best practices, 354, 418-419, 566
  business solutions addressed by, 19-20
  command shell, 306-307
  connectors, deploying, 806-811
  dashboards
    creating, 557-559
    explained, 554-555
    publishing, 561-565
    viewing, 559-560
    widgets, 556-559
  data storage, 329

database sizing, 326-327
deploying, 345-346
    design and planning phase, 346-348
    design principles training, 346
    pilot phase, 351-352
    production phase, 352-353
    proof of concept (POC) phase, 348-350
    time estimates, 353
design
    large enterprise design, 341-345
    medium enterprise design, 338-341
    small enterprise design, 336-338
dip stick health checks, 403-404
disaster recovery, 320-323
disk subsystem performance, 329-330
DMZ servers, monitoring with certificates,
    385-386
    agent configuration, 392
    agent installation, 391-392
    certificate templates, creating, 386-387
    root CA server certificates, requesting,
        387-390
fault tolerance
    architecture, 317
    database clusters, 319-320
    management group redundancy, 318
    resource pools, 318-319
file exclusions for antivirus and
    defragmentation applications, 409-410
Gateway server, 307-308
global management group settings,
    393-396
hardware requirements, 323-324
how it works, 291, 293
installing, 356
    ACS (Audit Collection Services), 368-373
    management packs, importing, 365-368
    multiserver installs, 359-365
    single-server installs, 356-359
integrating with VMM deployment, 684
major features, 20-23
management groups
    defining, 328-329
    geographic-based management
        group, 335
    multiple management group, 334
    political or security-based management
        group, 335

management packs, 291, 425-426
    downloading from Internet, 427-428
    exporting, 429-430
    importing from Internet, 426-427
    manually installing from downloads, 429
    overrides, 430-432
    updating, 404-405
management servers, 300-301
monitoring rules, 294
monitors, 292
network bandwidth requirements, 325-326
network monitoring, 385
new features, 24-25, 290-291
non-domain member considerations,
    327-328
notifications
    alert tuning, 405-409
    configuring, 399-402
Operations console, 304-305, 422-424
Operations Manager database, 301-302
overview, 8, 19
Reporting data warehouse, 302-303
Reporting Server, 304
reports, 295-296
    Alert Logging Latency report, 534-536
    Alerts reports, 525-527
    Availability reports, 527-531
    charts, displaying, 531-532
    explained, 512-513
    Most Common Alerts report, 533-534
    Performance By System reports,
        523-524
    Performance By Utilization reports,
        523-524
    Performance reports, 514-520
    Performance Top Instances reports,
        520-522
    Performance Top Objects reports,
        520-522
    Send Queue % Used Top 10 report,
        536-537
    Service Level Tracking reports, 551-554
    SLAs (service-level agreements),
        548-549
    SLOs (Service Level Objectives),
        549-551
responses, generating, 294
revisions and product history, 23-24

rules, 292

SAN versus DAS, 331-333

security

  Action accounts, 315-316

  agents, 313

  certificates, 316

  firewalls, 314

  role-based security model, 311-313

  RunAs accounts, 316

SLT (Service Level Tracking), 293

software requirements, 324

SQL Server versions, 333-334

subscriptions, configuring, 399-402

Web console, 424-425

  hardware/software requirements, 306

  overview, 305-306

  Performance view time frame, 410-411

Operations Manager alert–generated incidents, 838-841

Operations Manager Dashboard Viewer web part

  adding to SharePoint page, 562-565

  configuring, 562

  deploying, 561-562

Operations Manager Management Pack, 421, 432-433

  configuring, 433-434

  tasks, 438-439

  views, 434-437

Operations Manager Web console settings (Service Manager), 826

OperationsManager database, backing up, 412-414

OperationsManagerAC database, backing up, 416-417

OperationsManagerDW database, backing up, 414-415

Operator role (Operations Manager), 312

OpsMgr. See Operations Manager

OpsMgrLatencyMonitors container, 457

Orchestration console, 923, 946-948

Orchestration database, 923

Orchestration Integration Toolkit, 923

Orchestrator

  best practices, 968

  business solutions addressed by, 46-47, 922

  connectors, deploying, 812-813

Deployment Manager, 923

hardware requirements, 925-926

high-availability considerations, 926

IPs (Integration Packs)

  deploying, 951

  explained, 923

  installing, 949, 951

  registering, 950-951

major features of, 47-48

management server, 923

  connecting to Runbook Designer, 940-941

  installing, 934-935

multiserver installation, 933

  management server installation, 934-935

  Orchestrator web service installation, 937-938

  Runbook Designer installation, 938-939

  runbook server installation, 935-937

  server preparation, 933

new features, 48-49

Orchestration console, 923, 946-948

Orchestration database, 923

Orchestration Integration Toolkit, 923

Orchestrator web service, 923

  installing, 937-938

overview, 9, 45, 921-922

postinstallation tasks

  connecting Runbook Designer to management server, 940-941

  enabling GNU Privacy Guard, 941

  enabling network discovery for Runbook Designer, 939-940

product history, 48

revisions and product history, 924

Runbook Designer, 923

  Activities pane, 945

  connecting to Active Directory, 952

  connecting to management server, 940-941

  Connections pane, 943-944

  enabling network discovery for, 939-940

  GNU Privacy Guard, 941

  installing, 938-939

  Log pane, 945

  main screen, 942

  workspace, 944-945

runbook server, 923
    installing, 935-937
runbook tester, 923
runbooks
    Copy File and Log Event runbook,
        953-961
    Move Disabled Users runbook, 962-966
    permissions, 967
    standard activities, 952-953
    security
        firewall requirements, 928
        security groups, 927
        service accounts, 926-927
    single-server installation, 928
        Orchestrator Setup Wizard, 929-932
        server preparation, 929
        SQL database preparation, 929
    supported operating systems, 924-925
Orchestrator Setup Wizard, 929-932
    management server installation, 934-935
    Orchestrator web service installation,
        937-938
    Runbook Designer installation, 938-939
    runbook server installation, 935-937
Orchestrator web service, 923
    installing, 937-938
OS deployment, 11, 69-70, 225-227
    application and deployment type
        preparation, 227
    boot image management, 231
    driver management, 230-231
    importing unknown computers, 234-235
    monitoring, 236-238
    operating system image management,
        229-230
    operating system install task sequences,
        creating, 231-234
    operating system installer management,
        228-229
    preparing for, 154-155
    scenarios for, 226-227
    task sequence deployment, creating,
        235-236
    technologies for, 225-226
    User State Migration package, creating,
        227-228
OS Deployment certificate requests, 176

**OS Deployment certificate template,
    creating, 170**
OSCapture Account, 91
Out-of-Band Service Points, 86
overlapping boundaries, 98
Override Properties dialog box, 432, 613
overrides, management packs, 430-432
Overrides nodes, 432

P

**P2V (physical-to-virtual) conversions, 36,
    717-724**
**package model (application management),
    190-191**
packages, 67
    User State Migration package, creating,
        227-228
    virtual application packages
        creating, 755-758
        definition of, 753
        importing into VMM, 758
parallel activities, 886
patch management. *See* **software update
    distribution; update management**
patches, 11
Performance by System report, 449, 523-524
**Performance by Utilization report, 449-450,
    523-524**
Performance Counter View Raw report, 477
Performance Counter View report, 477
Performance Data view, 436
performance in Configuration Manager, 102
    SAN versus DAS, 102-104
    SQL versions, 104-105
Performance Nutrition report, 477
**Performance reports (Operations Manager),
    514-520**
**Performance Top Instances reports (Operations
    Manager), 520-522**
**Performance Top Objects reports (Operations
    Manager), 520-522**
Performance view (Web console), 410-411
performance widgets
    adding to dashboards, 558-559
    explained, 556

permissions
Operations console, 424
runbook permissions, 967
Permissions dialog box, 967
**physical-to-virtual (P2V) conversions, 36,
717-724**
Pilot phase
Operations Manager deployment, 351-352
Service Manager deployment, 789-790
Ping Computer (with Route), 439
Ping Computer Continuously (ping —t), 439
PKI (Public Key Infrastructure)
creating, 163
planning, 109
placement of VMs (virtual machines), 740-741
planning
Configuration Manager client settings,
99-101
DPM (Data Protection Manager)
deployment, 580
DPM servers, 586-587
environment, 580-581
project scope, 581-582
protection groups, 582-585
storage requirements, 585
Operations Manager deployment, 345-346
design and planning phase, 346-348
design principles training, 346
pilot phase, 351-352
production phase, 352-353
POC (Proof of Concept) phase, 348-350
time estimates, 353
Service Manager deployment, 783-784
Design and Planning phase, 784-786
Design Principles Training phase, 784
Pilot phase, 789-790
POC (Proof of Concept) phase, 786-788
Production phase, 790
time estimates, 791
VMM (Virtual Machine Manager)
deployment, 682
database server and database
design, 686
environment, 682-683
infrastructure fabric, 686-687
library server and library design, 687
Operations Manager integration, 684
project scope, 683-684

Self-Service Portal web server
design, 686
VMM instances, 685
VMM server design, 686
**planning details, adding to change
requests, 898**
Planning reports (ACS), 543
POC (Proof of Concept) phase
Operations Manager deployment, 348-350
Service Manager deployment, 786-788
policies, explained, 62
Policy reports (ACS), 543
political-based management groups, 335
pool tasks, 439
port groups for virtual switches, 676
**port requirements in Configuration Manager,
89-90**
portals, support for, 44
ports, DPM (Data Protection Manager), 657
postinstallation tasks (Orchestrator)
connecting Runbook Designer to
management server, 940-941
enabling GNU Privacy Guard, 941
enabling network discovery for Runbook
Designer, 939-940
PowerShell. See Windows PowerShell
Preboot Execution Environment. See PXE
prefixes
for incidents, 821
problem prefixes, 856
preparing
applications and deployment types for
OS deployment, 227
SharePoint for protection, 644-645
Prerequisite Checker tool, 60, 125
**prerequisites, Configuration Manager
installation, 118**
adding Windows roles on Site Servers,
121-124
configuring System Management container,
120-121
extending Active Directory schema, 118-119
primary computers, designating, 205-207
Primary Site Server databases, 246
Primary Site Servers
Central Administration Site, 124
installing, 124-126
validating installation, 127-129

installing, 129-133

overview, 78

primary sites (Configuration Manager), 57

primary systems, targeting deployments to, 200-202

priority

of incidents, 822-824

of problems, 857-858

private clouds

creating, 711-714

explained, 704

fabric resources, 704

networks, 706

servers, 705

storage, 706-707

problem prefix strings, customizing, 856

problems. *See also* **troubleshooting**

analyzing, 860-861

creating change requests, 895

explained, 819-821

problem records, creating, 859-860

problem reports, 869

resolving, 862-863

settings

file attachment limits, 856-857

priority calculation, 857-858

problem prefix string, 856

Process Management Packs, 764

Process Monitoring Template, 499-500

process validation, 48

processes, service management, 764-765

Production phase

Operations Manager deployment, 352-353

Service Manager deployment, 790

profiles. *See* **roles**

programs, 67

Progress of All Task Sequences report, 254

project scope. *See* **scope**

Proof of Concept (POC) phase

Operations Manager deployment, 348-350

Service Manager deployment, 786-788

protected Distribution Points, 84

protecting data. *See* **DPM (Data Protection Manager)**

Protection Agent Installation Wizard, 595-596

protection agents, deploying

with certificates, 599-601

with DPM Administration Console, 594-596

manual installation process, 596-599

with PowerShell, 601

protection groups

creating, 601-606

custom volumes, 613-614

designing, 582-585

Protocol Downtime Details report, 477

proxy agents, configuring, 396-398

Public Key Infrastructure (PKI)

creating, 163

planning, 109

Published Data dialog box, 956-957, 959

publishing

announcements, 850

certificate templates, 172-173

CRL, 165

Operations Manager dashboards, 561

adding web part to SharePoint page, 562-565

configuring web part, 562

deploying web part, 561-562

pushing agents, 59

PXE servers, 705

PXE support, enabling, 154-155

PXE Server Points, 58

PXE-enabled Distribution Points, 58, 83, 97

Q–R

RAID, 103, 332-333

RAs (review activities), 886, 903-905

Read-Only Administrator role (VMM)

creating, 734-735

explained, 730

Read-Only Operator role (Operations Manager), 312

reboots, suppressing, 227

Recipient Properties dialog box, 964

records, creating problem records, 859-860

recovery

Configuration Manager options, 60

content databases, 649

with DPM (Data Protection Manager), 614-616

Hyper-V item-level recovery, 659-660

Hyper-V virtual machines, 658-659

modern data recovery needs, 568-569

Operations Manager, 320-323

Restart Health Service Recovery, enabling, 398-399

SharePoint farms, 647-649

SharePoint sites, lists, and items, 650-653

tape-based solutions, limitations of, 569-570

Recovery Wizard, 638-640

Exchange databases, 629-631

Exchange mailboxes, 632-633

Hyper-V virtual machines, 659

SharePoint farms, 648

SQL databases, 639-640

refreshing Kerberos tickets, 91, 120, 171

regional roaming, 65, 182

registering

IPs (Integration Packs), 950-951

Service Manager management groups, 798-799

Registry keys, creating on clients, 261-262

rejecting RAs (review activities), 903-905

release management (Service Manager), 882-884

Reload Configuration, 439

Remote Control - All Computers Remote Controlled by a Specific User report, 255

remote control (Control+Alt+Delete), 59

remote control (Configuration Manager), 12

Remote Data Access Service Check monitor, 434

Remote Desktop, 439

Remote Desktop (Admin), 439

Remote Desktop (Console), 439

Remote PowerShell Service report, 477

remote SQL instances, DPM deployment, 588

Remote Tools section (client settings), 100, 158-159

removing. See deleting

replication latency, 120

Report Builder report, 258

Report Operator role (Operations Manager), 312

Report Security Administrator role (Operations Manager), 312

reporting, 249

AI (Asset Intelligence), 277

software metering data, 278

VMs (virtual machines), 714

reporting classes, AI (Asset Intelligence), 270-274

Reporting data warehouse, 302-303

Reporting Points, 58

Reporting Server, 304

Reporting Service Point (RSP)

installing, 149-150

overview, 87

Reporting Services, 255

reports, 12, 23, 914

ACS (Audit Collection Services) reports

Access Violation reports, 542

Account Management reports, 542-543

custom reports, 545-548

explained, 541-542

Forensic reports, 543

generating, 544-545

overview, 310-311

Planning reports, 543

Policy reports, 543

System Integrity reports, 543

Usage reports, 544

Active Directory Management Pack, 465-466

activity management reports, 917-918

change management reports, 915-917

configuration management reports, 918-919

Configuration Manager reports, 74-75

editing, 256-261

generating, 250-252

lists of, 252-255

scheduling, 255-256

configuring email subscriptions for, 255

consolidated reporting, 43

Cross Platform Management Packs, 489-490

Exchange 2010 Management Pack, 477-478

Operations Manager reports, 295-296

Alert Logging Latency report, 534-536

Alerts reports, 525-527

Availability reports, 527-531

charts, displaying, 531-532

Daily Alerts report, 538-540

explained, 512-513

Most Common Alerts report, 533-534

Performance By System reports, 523-524

Performance By Utilization reports, 523-524

Performance reports, 514-520

Performance Top Instances reports, 520-522

Performance Top Objects reports, 520-522

Send Queue % Used Top 10 report, 536-537

Service Level Tracking reports, 551-554

SQL Database Space report, 540-541

Report Builder report, 258

Service Manager reports, 863

incident reports, 864-868

problem reports, 869

report controls, 863-864, 915

SLA (service-level agreement) reporting, 23

SQL Server Management Pack, 486-487

Windows Management Pack, 448-451

request offerings (Service Manager 2012), 873

creating, 877-879

submitting with Self-Service Web Portal, 880-881

requesting

OS Deployment certificates, 176

root CA server certificates, 387-390

requirements. See hardware requirements; prerequisites; software requirements; system requirements

resetting status summarizer, 128, 133

resolution times for incidents, 824-825

resolving

incidents, 853-855

problems, 862-863

resource pools, 290, 318-319

responses, generating, 294

Restart Health Service Recovery, enabling, 398-399

restoring

CI (configuration items), 914

Exchange databases, 628-631

mailboxes, 631-633

SQL Server databases

with DPM Recovery Wizard, 638-640

self-service restores, 640-642

Resume Health Service recovery, 433

resuming change requests, 900-903

Return to Activity change requests, 902

review activities (RAs), 886, 903-905

Review Activity Details report, 917

reviewers, adding to change requests, 898-899

roaming, 62

client roaming, 65-66, 182-183

global versus regional roaming, 65, 182

role Level Capacity Trending, 477

role-based administration (Configuration Manager), 60

role-based security, 89, 311-313

roles

explained, 61

selecting HTTPS by, 57

VMM user roles, 672-673, 729

Administrator, 729-731

Delegated Administrator, 729, 732-734

modifying, 739-740

Read-Only Administrator, 730, 734-735

removing, 740

Self-Service User, 730, 735-739

root CA server certificates, requesting, 387-390

RSP (Reporting Service Point)

installing, 149-150

overview, 87

Rule node, 442

rules, 292-294

RunAs accounts, 316

runbook automation, 765, 886

Runbook Control activity (Orchestrator), 953

Runbook Designer, 923

Activities pane, 945

connecting to Active Directory, 952

connecting to management server, 940-941

Connections pane, 943-944

enabling network discovery for, 939-940

GNU Privacy Guard, 941

installing, 938-939

Log pane, 945

main screen, 942

workspace, 944-945

runbook server (Orchestrator), 923

installing, 935-937

Runbook Servers workspace (Orchestration console), 948

runbook tester (Orchestrator), 923

runbooks
Copy File and Log Event runbook
building, 953-959
testing, 959-961
creating, 47
definition of, 764
Move Disabled Users runbook
building, 962-965
testing, 965-966
permissions, 967
runbook automation, 765
standard activities, 952-953
testing, 47
Runbooks tab (Runbooks workspace), 947
Runbooks workspace (Orchestration console), 947
running troubleshooting tasks, 851-853

S

Sanbolic Clustered File System (CFS), 676
SANs (storage area networks), 331-333, 773
DAS (direct attached storage) versus, 102-104
VMM support for transfers, 676
Scan 1 - Last Scan States by Collection report, 253
SCCM (System Center Configuration Manager). See Configuration Manager
schedules
client schedules, 105-106
report schedules
ACS (Audit Collection Services) reports, 541-548
Alert Logging Latency report, 534-536
Alerts reports, 525-527
Availability reports, 527-531
Configuration Manager, 255-256
Daily Alerts report, 538-540
Most Common Alerts report, 533-534
Performance By System reports, 523-524
Performance By Utilization reports, 523-524
Performance reports, 514-520
Performance Top Instances reports, 520-522

Performance Top Objects reports, 520-522
Send Queue % Used Top 10 report, 536-537
Service Level Tracking reports, 551-554
SQL Database Space report, 540-541
Runbook Designer schedules, 944
Scheduling activity (Orchestrator), 953
schema (AD) extensions, 64-66
SCOM (System Center Operations Manager). See Operations Manager
scope
DPM deployment, 581-582
VMM deployment, 683-684
SCSM (System Center Service Manager). See Service Manager
SDK and Configuration service accounts, 315
sealing management packs via command line, 507
searching CI, 911-912
secondary sites (Configuration Manager), 57
installing, 134-138
Management Points and, 64
security. See also DPM (Data Protection Manager)
certificates. See certificates
Configuration Manager, 88
port requirements, 89-90
role-based administration, 89
server communication, 88-89
service accounts, 91
Distribution Points, 82
Exchange Server, 624
additional considerations, 635
Exchange databases, 625-631
high-availability considerations, 633-634
mailboxes, 631-633
file servers, protecting with DPM (Data Protection Manager), 620-621
data in DFS namespace, 621
on file server clusters, 622
on mount points, 622
Hyper-V, 654
item-level recovery, 659-660
protecting Hyper-V virtual machines, 654-656
protecting nondomain joined Hyper-V hosts, 656
recovering Hyper-V virtual machines, 658-659

targeting Hyper-V hosts across firewalls, 656-657

Operations Manager
Action accounts, 315-316
agents, 313
certificates, 316
firewalls, 314
role-based security model, 311-313
RunAs accounts, 316

runbook permissions, 967

SharePoint farms
content databases, recovering, 649
item-level recovery, 650-653
preparing for protection, 644-645
protecting with DPM, 645-647
recovering, 647-649
SharePoint data sources and recoverable data, 643-644

SQL Server, 635
protecting with DPM, 636-638
restoring with DPM Recovery Wizard, 638-640
self-service restores, 640-642

System Center Orchestrator
firewall requirements, 928
security groups, 927
service accounts, 926-927

System State, protecting, 622-624

VMM Self-Service Portal, 695

security groups (Orchestrator), 927

security roles, 89

security scopes, 89

Security settings (VMM Administrator Console), 715

security-based management groups, 335

Select Backup Destination dialog box, 412-417, 815

Select Features to Install screen (Orchestrator Setup Wizard), 930

Select Host page
Convert Physical Server Wizard, 721
Convert Virtual Machine Wizard, 727

Select Networks page
Convert Physical Server Wizard, 723
Convert Virtual Machine Wizard, 728

Select Path page
Convert Physical Server Wizard, 723
Convert Virtual Machine Wizard, 727

Select Source page (Convert Physical Server Wizard), 719

Select the Installation Location screen (Orchestrator Setup Wizard), 932

Select Virtual Machine Source dialog box, 726

selecting
Distribution Points, 184-185
SQL versions, 773-774

Self Service Recovery Tool (DPM), 640-642

self-service creation of guest sessions, 37

self-service deployments, 207-211

Self-Service Portal (VMM)
creating VMs with, 745-747
deploying, 801-805
explained, 668, 763, 765
hardware requirements, 680
installing, 694
security, 695
software requirements, 681
supported operating systems, 681

self-service restores of SQL databases, 640-642

Self-Service User role (VMM), 673
creating, 735-739
explained, 730
modifying, 739-740
removing, 740

Self-Service Web Portal
creating incidents with, 841-845
publishing service offerings, 874
submitting requests, 880-881

Send Email Properties dialog box, 964

Send Queue % Used, 435

Send Queue % Used Top 10 report, 536-537

Sequencer (Server App-V), 753-754

Server App-V, 753
deployment configuration files, 753
Sequencer, 753-754
Server App-V Agent
definition of, 753
installing, 754-755
virtual environment, 753
virtual application packages
creating, 755-758
definition of, 753
importing into VMM, 758

Server Authentication certificate template, creating, 170-172

server certificates, 109

server communication, securing in Configuration Manager, 88-89

server locator functionality in Management Points, 58

Server Locator Point (SLP), 58, 85

server management suite volume licensing, 50-51

server OS deployment, 226

servers

  backups, 28-29

  database server design, 686

  DMZ servers, monitoring with certificates, 316, 385-386

    agent configuration, 392

    agent installation, 391-392

    certificate templates, creating, 386-387

    root CA server certificates, requesting, 387-390

  DPM servers

    designing, 586-587

    preparing for deployment, 587

  file servers, protecting with DPM (Data Protection Manager), 620-622

  Gateway server, 307-308

  host groups, dragging and dropping VMs onto, 752

  host servers, dragging and dropping VMs onto, 751-752

  Hyper-V servers

    backups, 31

    VMM support for, 670

  library servers, 705

  management servers

    connecting to Runbook Designer, 940-941

    hardware/software requirements, 301

    installing, 934-935

    overview, 300

  monitoring, 20

  PXE (Preboot Execution Environment) servers, 705

  Reporting Server, 304

  runbook server (Orchestrator), installing, 935-937

  Self-Service Portal web server design, 686

  SQL Server versions, 333-334

  System Center Orchestrator, 923

  update servers, 705

  vCenter servers, 705

  VMM private cloud, 705

  VMM servers, 705

    design, 686

    explained, 667

    hardware requirements, 678

    installing, 688-689, 691

    multiple-server deployment, 688

    preparing for VMM deployment, 688

    remote SQL instance requirements, 679

    single-server deployment, 688

    supported operating systems, 679

  Web console, hardware/software requirements, 306

service account security (Configuration Manager), 91

service accounts (Orchestrator), 926-927

service catalog, 44

Service Level Dashboards, 293

Service Level Tracking (SLT), 293

  reports, 551-554

  SLAs (service-level agreements), 23, 548-549

  SLOs (Service Level Objectives), 549-551

Service Manager, 8, 40

  activities, 886

  announcements, publishing, 850

  architecture, 766-767

  backing up, 814

    backup schedules, 814

    database backups, 814-816

    encryption key, 816-817

  best practices, 817-818, 870

  business solutions addressed by, 41

  Change Management Pack, 764

  change requests, 885, 892-893

    creating from configuration items, 893-894

    creating from incidents or problems, 895

    creating from scratch, 893

  CMDB (configuration management database), 765

  components, 768-769

    deploying, 791-794

    explained, 765-768

Connector Framework, 765

connectors, 768

    Active Directory, 805-806

    Configuration Manager, 811-812

    Operations Manager, 806-811

    Orchestrator, 812-813

data warehouses

    deploying, 794-797

    explained, 765

    job schedules, viewing, 799-800

deployment

    components, 791-794

    connectors. See connectors

    data warehouse job schedules, viewing, 799-800

    data warehouses, 794-797

    management group registration, 798-799

    Self-Service Portal, 801-805

disk subsystem performance, 773

Extraction, Transformation, and Loading (ETL) process, 767

hardware requirements, 769-771

incident settings

    file attachment limits, 822

    inbound email settings, 826-830

    incident prefix, 821

    Operations Manager Web console settings, 826

    priority calculation, 822-824

    resolution times, 824-825

incidents

    analyzing, 847-849

    announcements, 850

    assigning, 846-847

    email-created incidents, 845

    evaluating, 846-847

    explained, 819-820

    incident reports, 864-868

    manually created incidents, 836-838

    Operations Manager alert–generated incidents, 838-841

    resolving, 853-855

    Self-Service Portal–generated incidents, 841-845

    troubleshooting tasks, 851-853

infrastructure optimization model, 871-872

KB (knowledge base), 765, 768, 876

large enterprise design, 780-783

major features of, 42-43

management groups, registering, 798-799

medium enterprise design, 778-780

new features, 44-45, 762-763

notifications, 830

    architecture, 830-832

    notification subscriptions, 834-835

    notification templates, 833-834

    SMTP notification channels, 832-833

OLAP cubes, 768-769

planning, 783-784

    Design and Planning phase, 784-786

    Design Principles Training phase, 784

    Pilot phase, 789-790

    POC (Proof of Concept) phase, 786-788

    Production phase, 790

    time estimates, 791

problem settings

    file attachment limits, 856-857

    priority calculation, 857-858

    problem prefix string, 856

problems

    analyzing, 860-861

    explained, 819-821

    problem records, creating, 859-860

    problem reports, 869

    resolving, 862-863

processes, 764-765

release management, 882-884

reports, 863

    incident reports, 864-868

    problem reports, 869

    report controls, 863-864, 915

request offerings, 873

    creating, 877-879

    submitting with Self-Service Web Portal, 880-881

revisions and product history, 43

SAN versus DAS, 773

Self-Service Portal

    deploying, 801-805

    explained, 763-765

Self-Service Web Portal, creating incidents with, 841-845

service offerings, 872, 874
   creating, 879-880
   custom management packs, 875
   publishing through self-service web
      portals, 874
   small enterprise design, 776-778
   software requirements, 771-772
   SQL versions, 773-774
   technologies, 765
   templates, 767
   troubleshooting tasks, running, 851-853
   workflow engine, 765
   workflows, 767
service monitoring, 292
service offerings (Service Manager), 872, 874
   creating, 879-880
   custom management packs, 875
   publishing through self-service web
      portals, 874
service requests, 44
service-level agreements (SLAs), 23, 548-549
service-level management, 44
Setup Wizard (Service Manager)
   component installation, 792-794
   data warehouse installation, 794-797
   Self-Service Portal installation, 802-804
SharePoint data backups, 30
SharePoint farms
   content databases, recovering, 649
   item-level recovery, 650-653
   preparing for protection, 644-645
   protecting with DPM, 645-647
   recovering, 647-649
   SharePoint data sources and recoverable
      data, 643-644
SharePoint pages, adding web parts to,
   562-565
SharePoint Products and Technologies
   Configuration Wizard, 649
SharePoint web part, 290
Show Enabled Rules and Monitors for This
   Health Service, 439
Show Failed Rules and Monitors for This Health
   Service, 439
simple schedules, 106
single-server deployment (VMM), 688

single-server installations
   Operations Manager, 356-359
   Orchestrator, 928
      hardware requirements, 925
      Orchestrator Setup Wizard, 929-932
      server preparation, 929
      SQL database preparation, 929
Site Addresses, 63
site boundaries, establishing, 97-99
site codes, 63
site configuration (Configuration Manager), 148
   Asset Intelligence Synchronization Point role
      installation, 153-154
   Endpoint Protection Point role installation,
      152-153
   FSP (Fallback Status Point) installation, 149
   OS deployment preparation, 154-155
   RSP (Reporting Service Point) installation,
      149-150
   Software Update Point role installation,
      150-152
Site Database, 246
Site Senders, 63
Site Servers, 62
   adding Windows roles to, 121-124
   database, 79-81
   overview, 78
Site System role changes (Configuration
   Manager), 58-59
sites
   discovering, 98-99
   explained, 61
   SharePoint sites, recovering, 650-653
sizing databases
   Configuration Manager, 93
   Operations Manager, 326-327
SLA report, 477
SLAs (service-level agreements), 23, 548-549
SLOs (Service Level Objectives), 549-551
slow boundaries, 97
SLP (Server Locator Point), 58, 85
SLT. See Service Level Tracking (SLT)
small enterprise design
   Configuration Manager, 110-111
   Operations Manager, 336-338
   Service Manager, 776-778

SMB-based Distribution Points, 83

SMI-S (Storage Management Initiative – Specification), 706

SMP (State Migration Point)
  installing, 155
  overview, 86-87
  placement of, 97

SMS (Systems Management Server), 13-14

SMS Providers, 78-79

sms_def.mof editing, 59

SMTP (Simple Mail Transfer Protocol), 255

SMTP Availability report, 477

SMTP notification channels, configuring, 832-833

Software 01A - Summary of Installed Software in a Specific Collection, 273

Software 02A - Software Families, 273

Software 02B - Software Categories with a Family, 273

Software 02C - Software by Category and Family, 273

Software 02D - Computers with a Specific Software Product, 273

Software 02E - Installed Software on a Specific Computer, 273

Software 03A - Uncategorized Software, 273

Software 04A - Auto-Start Software, 273

Software 04B - Computers with a Specific Auto-Start Software, 252, 273

Software 04C - Auto-Start Software on a Specific Computer, 274

Software 05A - Browser Helper Objects, 274

Software 05B - Computers with a Specific Browser Helper Object, 274

Software 05C - Browser Helper Objects on a Specific Computer, 274

Software 06A - Search for Installed Software, 252, 274

software deployment, 12

Software Deployment section (client settings), 101, 159

software distribution. See content distribution system

software inventory, 71

Software Inventory Client Agent, 248-249

Software Inventory section (client settings), 101, 159-160

software licensing, 6, 50
  core client access licenses, 50
  importing license data, 275-277
  server management suite volume licensing, 50-51

software metering, 73
  Configuration Manager, 277-278
  reports, 254

Software Metering section (client settings), 101, 160

Software Registered in Add Remove Programs on a Specific Computer report, 253

software requirements
  ACS (Audit Collection Services), 311
  Configuration Manager, 93
  DPM (Data Protection Manager) support, 579
  Gateway server, 307-308
  Operations Manager, 324
    agents, 301
    audit collection database, 310
    audit collector, 309
    command shell, 307
    database, 302
    Operations Console, 305
    Web console, 306
  Reporting data warehouse, 303
  Reporting Server, 304
  Service Manager, 771-772
  VMM Administrator Console, 680
  VMM Self-Service Portal, 681
  VMM server, 679

Software Update Client Agent section (client settings), 101

Software Update deployments, creating, 220-222

software update distribution (Configuration Manager), 68-69. See also update deployment

software update groups, 68
  creating, 216-219

software update management, 215
  creating software update groups, 216-219
  viewing Update Repository, 215-216

Software Update Point (SUP)
  installing, 150-152
  overview, 87

software update reports, 253
Software Update section (client settings), 160-161
Specify Virtual Machine Identity page
    Convert Physical Server Wizard, 720
    Convert Virtual Machine Wizard, 727
SQL
    backups, 30
    choosing SQL versions, 773-774
    DPM deployment, 588
    preparing databases for System Center Orchestrator installation, 929
    versions, choosing, 104-105
    VMM support for, 679
SQL Cluster configuration (SQL Server Management Pack), 479-480
SQL Database Space report, 540-541
SQL MPDatabase State view, 483
SQL Server
    databases
        protecting with DPM, 636-638
        restoring with DPM Recovery Wizard, 638-640
        self-service restores, 640-642
    DPM support for, 579
    versions, 333-334
SQL Server Database Engine Counters report, 486
SQL Server Management Pack, 478
    configuring, 479
    reports, 486-487
    SQL Cluster configuration, 479-480
    tasks, 484-485
    tuning, 480-482
    views, 482-484
SSL, configuring
    Certificate Services website for, 174-175
    for VMM (Virtual Machine Manager) Self-Service Portal, 695
    WSUS website for, 175-176
standard activities (runbooks), 952-953
standardization, service offerings, 874
Start Audit Collection, 439
Start Online Store Maintenance, 439
Start WMI Service, 439
State Messaging section (client settings), 161

State Migration Point (SMP)
    installing, 155
    overview, 86-87
    placement of, 97
state widgets, 556-557
state-based alerting, 59
States 1 - Enforcement States for a Deployment report, 253
States 2 - Evaluation States for a Deployment report, 253
status summarizer, resetting, 128, 133
Status Summary of a Specific Task Sequence Deployment report, 254
storage
    calculating for DPM deployment, 585
    VMM private cloud, 706-707
storage area networks. See SANs (storage area networks)
Storage Management Initiative – Specification (SMI-S), 706
storage pool, adding disks to, 591-593
stored procedures, modifying, 450
submitting requests (Self-Service Web Portal), 880-881
subnets, discovering, 98-99
subscriptions
    configuring, 399-402
    notification subscriptions, 834-835
Summary page
    Convert Physical Server Wizard, 723
    Convert Virtual Machine Wizard, 728
Summary tab (Runbooks workspace), 947
SUP (Software Update Point)
    installing, 150-152
    overview, 87
suppressing reboots, 227
switches (virtual), VMware port groups for, 676
synchronizing AI (Asset Intelligence), 269-270
synthetic transaction event collection (Exchange 2010 Management Pack), 470-471
System activity (Orchestrator), 953
System Center Capacity Planner, 9
System Center Configuration Manager (SCCM). See Configuration Manager
System Center Data Protection Manager. See DPM (Data Protection Manager)
System Center Essentials, 9
System Center Mobile Device Manager, 9

System Center Online Services, 82

System Center Operations Manager (SCOM).
See Operations Manager

System Center Orchestrator. *See* Orchestrator

System Center Service Manager (SCSM). *See*
Service Manager

System Center settings (VMM Administrator
Console), 715

System Center Virtual Machine Manager. *See*
VMM (Virtual Machine Manager)

System Information page (Convert Physical
Server Wizard), 720

System Integrity reports (ACS), 543

System Management container, configuring,
120-121

system monitoring, 21

system requirements

  ACS (Audit Collection Services), 311

  command shell, 307

  Configuration Manager, 92-93

  DPM (Data Protection Manager), 578-579

  Gateway server, 307-308

  Operations Manager, 323-324

    agents, 301

    audit collection database, 310

    audit collector, 309

    database, 302

    Operations Console, 305

  Reporting data warehouse, 303

  Reporting Server, 304

  virtual machine hosts, 682

  VMM Administrator Console, 679-680

  VMM Self-Service portal, 680-681

  VMM server, 678-679

  Web console, 306

System State, protecting, 622-624

systems management challenges, 6-7

Systems Management Server (SMS), 13-14

T

tape backups, 31

  limitations of, 569-570

tape libraries, configuring, 593

targeting

  Hyper-V hosts across firewalls, 656-657

  users, 203-207

task sequences

  deployment, 59

    creating, 235-236

    reports, 254

  for MDT (Microsoft Deployment Toolkit),
creating, 240-242

  for operating system deployment, 70

    creating, 231-234

tasks

  Active Directory Management Pack, 464

  Operations Manager Management Pack,
438-439

  SQL Server Management Pack, 484-485

  Windows Management Pack, 446-448

TCP Port Template, 501-502

technical problems addressed by VMM (Virtual
Machine Manager), 665-667

templates, 889

  certificate templates, 109-110

    creating, 168-172, 386-387

    publishing, 172-173

  change request templates, 889-891

  definition of, 767

  deployment templates, 221

  Management Pack Templates, 491-492

    OLEDB Data Source Template, 497-499

    Process Monitoring Template, 499-500

    TCP Port Template, 501-502

    UNIX/Linux Log File Template, 502

    UNIX/Linux Service Template, 503

    Web Application Template, 492-494

    Windows Service Template, 494-497

  notification subscriptions, creating, 834-835

  notification templates, creating, 833-834

Terminal Services Management Pack, 425

test clients, manually compiling
configuration.mof files, 265

test mailbox configuration (Exchange 2010
Management Pack), 469-470

testing runbooks, 47

  Copy File and Log Event runbook, 959-961

  Move Disabled Users runbook, 965-966

Text File Management activity (Orchestrator), 953

time estimates

  Operations Manager deployment, 353

  Service Manager projects, 791

Top X Performance reports (Operations
Manager), 520-522

Total Usage for All Metered Software Programs report, 254
tracking
    assets, 12
    licensing, 72
    SLA (service-level agreement) tracking, 23
transact SQL (TSQL), 257
transformation, 767
Transport Platform Distribution Group Usage report, 478
Transport Platform Hourly Server Statistics report, 478
Transport Platform Server Statistics report, 478
Transport Platform Top Users report, 478
troubleshooting. See also problems
    BITS (Background Intelligent Transfer Service), 138
    extending Active Directory schema, 120
    Service Manager troubleshooting tasks, running, 851-853
Troubleshooting 1 - Scan Errors report, 253
TSQL (transact SQL), 257
tuning
    alerts, 405-409
    SQL Server Management Pack, 480-482
    Windows Management Pack, 441-443

U

UMLocal Service report, 478
Unified Messaging role, 476
UNIX agents, installing, 379-385
UNIX/Linux Log File Template, 502
UNIX/Linux Service Template, 503
unknown computers, importing, 234-235
update deployment, 11, 219
    automatic deployment rules, creating, 222-224
    deployment packages, creating, 219-220
    monitoring, 224-225
    Software Update deployments, creating, 220-222
update lists. See software update groups
update management. See software update management
Update Repository, viewing, 215-216
update schedules for collections, 187

update servers, 705
updating management packs, 404-405
Usage reports (ACS), 544
User and Device Affinity section (client settings), 161-162
User Device Affinity Associations per Collection report, 252
user notification change requests, 908-910
user roles (VMM), 672-673, 729
    Administrator, 729-731
    Delegated Administrator, 729, 732-734
    Read-Only Administrator, 730, 734-735
    Self-Service User
        creating, 735-739
        explained, 730
        modifying, 739-740
        removing, 740
user self-service (service offerings), 874
user state, capturing, 231
User State Migration Tool, creating package for, 227-228
users, targeting, 203-207
Utilities activity (Orchestrator), 953

V

V2V (virtual-to-virtual) conversions, 36, 725-729
validating
    Central Administration Site installation, 127-129
    custom inventory data, 267-268
    Enterprise Root CA, 165
    Primary Site Server installation, 131-133
    processes, 48
    secondary site installation, 136-138
vCenter servers, 705
VDS (Virtual Disk Service), 707
Veritas Storage Foundation 5.1 for Windows, 676
viewing
    custom inventory data, 268
    data warehouse job schedules, 799-800
    Operations Manager dashboards, 559-560
    Update Repository, 215-216
views
    Active Directory Management Pack, 460-463
    Cross Platform Management Packs, 488-489
    Dashboard views, 290

Exchange 2010 Management Pack, 471-477
Operations Manager Management Pack,
   434-437
SQL Server Management Pack, 482-484
Windows Management Pack, 443-445
VIP (virtual IP) templates, 706
virtual application packages
   creating, 755-758
   definition of, 753
   importing into VMM, 758
Virtual Disk Service (VDS), 707
virtual IP (VIP) templates, 706
Virtual Machine Configuration page
   Convert Physical Server Wizard, 721
   Convert Virtual Machine Wizard, 727
virtual machine hosts, system requirements, 682
Virtual Machine Manager. See **VMM (Virtual**
   Machine Manager)
virtual machines. See **Hyper-V virtual machines;**
   VMs (virtual machines)
virtual switches, VMware port groups for, 676
virtual-to-virtual (V2V) conversions, 36, 725-729
VMM (Virtual Machine Manager), 8
   Administrator Console, 679-680
   best practices, 701-702, 759-760
   business solutions addressed by, 35-36,
      664-665
   cluster support, 671
   components, 667
   deploying
      multiple-server deployment, 688
      single-server deployment, 688
      VMM Administrator Console installation,
         692-693
      VMM Agent installation, 695-700
      VMM Self-Service Portal installation, 694
      VMM Self-Service Portal security, 695
      VMM server installation, 688-691
      VMM server preparation, 688
   fabric management, 677, 686
   heterogeneous VM management, 670
   hosts
      host clusters, 710
      host groups, 705, 708-709
      managing, 709
   major features of, 36-38
   new features, 39, 677-678

overview, 8, 34-35, 663-664
planning for, 682
   database server and database
      design, 686
   environment, 682-683
   infrastructure fabric, 686-687
   library server and library design, 687
   Operations Manager integration, 684
   project scope, 683-684
   Self-Service Portal web server
      design, 686
   VMM instances, 685
   VMM server design, 686
PowerShell support, 669-670
private clouds
   creating, 711-714
   explained, 704
   fabric resources, 704
   networks, 706
   servers, 705
   storage, 706-707
revisions and product history, 38, 673-677
   early virtualization management
      techniques, 673
   Virtual Machine Manager 2007, 673-674
   Virtual Machine Manager 2008, 674
   Virtual Machine Manager 2008 R2,
      674-677
role-based access control, 672-673
Self-Service Portal
   creating VMs with, 745-747
   hardware requirements, 680
   software requirements, 681
   supported operating systems, 681
   web server design, 686
Self-Service User role, 673
Server App-V, 753
   deployment configuration files, 753
   Sequencer, 753-754
   Server App-V Agent, 753-755
   virtual application packages, 753-758
   virtual environment, 753
technical problems addressed by, 665-667
user roles, 729
   Administrator, 729-731
   Delegated Administrator, 729, 732-734
   modifying, 739-740

Read-Only Administrator, 730, 734-735
removing, 740
Self-Service User, 730, 735-739
virtual machine hosts, system requirements, 682
VMM Administrator Console, 707-708
configuring VMM library, 710-711
creating host groups, 708-709
creating private clouds, 711-714
deploying VMs, 742-744
explained, 668
General settings, 715
managing host clusters, 710
managing hosts, 709
managing VMs, 714
monitoring and reporting, 714
Security settings, 715
System Center settings, 715
VMM Administrator role, 672, 729-731
VMM Agent
explained, 668
installing, 695-700
VMM command shell, 715-716
VMM Delegated Administrator role, 672, 729,
731-734
VMM library
configuring, 710-711
designing, 687
explained, 668-669
VMM Self-Service Portal
explained, 668
installing, 694
security, 695
VMM servers, 705
designing, 686
explained, 667
hardware requirements, 678
installing, 688-693
remote SQL instance requirements, 679
software requirements, 679
supported operating systems, 679
VMM Setup Wizard
VMM Administrator Console installation,
692-693
VMM Self-Service Portal installation, 694
VMM server installation, 689-691

VMs (virtual machines)
creating with Self-Service Portal, 745-747
customizing host ratings for, 741-742
deploying with Administrator Console,
742-744
managing, 714
migrating
by dragging and dropping onto host
group, 752
by dragging and dropping onto host
server, 751-752
with Migrate action, 748-750
with Migrate Storage action, 750-751
supported storage migration
technologies, 748
supported VM migration technologies,
747-748
monitoring and reporting, 714
P2V (physical-to-virtual) conversions,
717-724
placement, 740-741
V2V (virtual-to-virtual) conversions, 725-729
VMware
port groups for virtual switches, 676
VMM support for, 670
Volume Configuration page (Convert Physical
Server Wizard), 721

W–Z

Wake On LAN functionality, 81
Web Access Confirmation dialog box, 388-389
Web Application Template, 492-494
Web console, 422-425
hardware/software requirements, 306
overview, 305-306
Performance view time frame, 410-411
Web Page view (Operations console), 424
web parts
Operations Manager Dashboard Viewer
web part
adding to SharePoint page, 562-565
configuring, 562
deploying, 561-562
SharePoint web part, 290
web services (Orchestrator), installing, 937-938

widgets
  adding to dashboards, 557-559
  explained, 556
Windows agents, installing, 373-376
Windows Authentication, configuring for VMM Self-Service Portal, 695
Windows Core OS monitoring, management packs, 440
Windows Installer, 189
  configuring MSI applications, 191-192
Windows Management Instrumentation (WMI), 245
Windows Management Pack, 440
  configuring, 440-441
  reports, 448-451
  tasks, 446-448
  tuning, 441-443
  views, 443-445
Windows PowerShell
  attaching protection agents with, 601
  cmdlets, 290
  VMM support for, 669-670, 677
Windows roles, adding on Site Servers, 121-124
Windows Server 2008 Core Operating System object, 442
Windows Server 2008 Logical Disk object, 442
Windows Server 2008 Network Adapter object, 443
Windows Server performance reports, 523-524
Windows Server Update Services (WSUS), 11, 150
Windows Service Template, 494-497
WinPE environment, 69
wizards. *See names of specific wizards*
WMI (Windows Management Instrumentation), 245
WOL (Wake On LAN) functionality, 81
workflow engine, 765
workflows, 767, 889-892
workspaces
  Orchestration console, 947-948
  Runbook Designer, 944-945
WSSCmdletsWrapper, 645
WSUS (Windows Server Update Services), 11, 150
WSUS website, configuring for SSL, 175-176

XML management pack, modifying, 506

UNLEASHED

Unleashed takes you beyond the basics, providing an exhaustive, technically sophisticated reference for professionals who need to exploit a technology to its fullest potential. It's the best resource for practical advice from the experts, and the most in-depth coverage of the latest technologies.

informit.com/unleashed

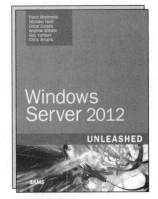

Windows Server 2012 Unleashed
ISBN-13: 9780672336225

OTHER UNLEASHED TITLES

Microsoft SharePoint 2010 PerformancePoint Services Unleashed
ISBN-13: 9780672330940

Microsoft SharePoint 2010 Unleashed
ISBN-13: 9780672333255

Windows Server 2008 R2 Unleashed
ISBN-13: 9780672330926

Microsoft Dynamics CRM 4 Integration Unleashed
ISBN-13: 9780672330544

Microsoft Exchange Server 2010 Unleashed
ISBN-13: 9780672330469

Microsoft SQL Server 2008 Reporting Services Unleashed
ISBN-13: 9780672330261

Microsoft SQL Server 2008 Integration Services Unleashed
ISBN-13: 9780672330322

Microsoft SQL Server 2008 Analysis Services Unleashed
ISBN-13: 9780672330018

C# 4.0 Unleashed
ISBN-13: 9780672330797

Silverlight 4 Unleashed
ISBN-13: 9780672333361

ASP.NET 4 Unleashed
ISBN-13: 9780672331121

Microsoft Visual Studio 2010 Unleashed
ISBN-13: 9780672330810

WPF 4 Unleashed
ISBN-13: 9780672331190

Visual Basic 2010 Unleashed
ISBN-13: 9780672331008

WPF Control Development Unleashed
ISBN-13: 9780672330339

Exchange Server 2010 Unleashed
ISBN-13: 9780672330469

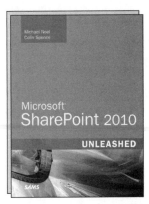

Microsoft SharePoint 2010 Unleashed
ISBN-13: 9780672333255

SAMS

informit.com/sams

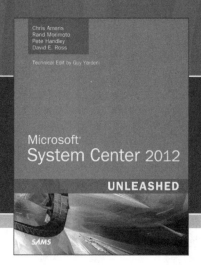

FREE
Online Edition

Your purchase of *Microsoft® System Center 2012 Unleashed* includes access to a free online edition for 45 days through the **Safari Books Online** subscription service. Nearly every Sams book is available online through **Safari Books Online**, along with thousands of books and videos from publishers such as Addison-Wesley Professional, Cisco Press, Exam Cram, IBM Press, O'Reilly Media, Prentice Hall, Que, and VMware Press.

Safari Books Online is a digital library providing searchable, on-demand access to thousands of technology, digital media, and professional development books and videos from leading publishers. With one monthly or yearly subscription price, you get unlimited access to learning tools and information on topics including mobile app and software development, tips and tricks on using your favorite gadgets, networking, project management, graphic design, and much more.

Activate your FREE Online Edition at
informit.com/safarifree

STEP 1:   Enter the coupon code: RVXFXBI.

STEP 2:   New Safari users, complete the brief registration form.
                 Safari subscribers, just log in.

If you have difficulty registering on Safari or accessing the online edition,
please e-mail customer-service@safaribooksonline.com